W0328344

Business Proficiency

Wirtschaftsenglisch für Hochschule und Beruf

mit interaktiver Medien-DVD

Ernst Klett Verlag Stuttgart

Business Proficiency

Wirtschaftsenglisch für Hochschule und Beruf

Autoren:
Stephanie Ashford, MSc, Business English Programme Coordinator,
Baden-Wuerttemberg Cooperative State University Villingen-Schwenningen

Dr. Tom Smith, Co-Director of Executive English, Brigachtal

Berater:
Sabine Kärcher, BA, LCCI CertTEB
Freelance English Business English Trainer, Löffingen

Anthony R. Lee
EUROPEAN BUSINESS SCHOOL International University
Applied Language Centre, Oestrich-Winkel

Prof. Dr. Richard G. Wilcox
Prof. of International Management, Dir. of International Programs
Nuertingen-Geislingen University

Prof. Dr. Sharon Zaharka
Professor of Business English and Intercultural Communication,
University of Applied Sciences Konstanz

1. Auflage

1 5 4 3 2 1 | 14 13 12 11 10

Alle Drucke dieser Auflage sind unverändert und können im Unterricht nebeneinander verwendet werden.
Die letzte Zahl bezeichnet das Jahr des Druckes.
Das Werk und seine Teile sind urheberrechtlich geschützt. Jede Nutzung in anderen als den gesetzlich zugelassenen Fällen bedarf der vorherigen schriftlichen Einwilligung des Verlages.
Hinweis § 52 a UrhG: Weder das Werk noch seine Teile dürfen ohne eine solche Einwilligung eingescannt und in ein Netzwerk eingestellt werden. Dies gilt auch für Intranets von Schulen und sonstigen Bildungseinrichtungen. Fotomechanische oder andere Wiedergabeverfahren nur mit Genehmigung des Verlages.
Auf verschiedenen Seiten dieses Heftes befinden sich Verweise (Links) auf Internet-Adressen. Haftungshinweis: Trotz sorgfältiger inhaltlicher Kontrolle wird die Haftung für die Inhalte der externen Seiten ausgeschlossen. Für den Inhalt dieser externen Seiten sind ausschließlich die Betreiber verantwortlich. Sollten Sie daher auf kostenpflichtige, illegale oder anstößige Inhalte treffen, so bedauern wir dies ausdrücklich und bitten Sie, uns umgehend per E-Mail davon in Kenntnis zu setzen, damit beim Nachdruck der Verweis gelöscht wird.

© Ernst Klett Verlag GmbH, Stuttgart 2009. Alle Rechte vorbehalten.
www.klett.de

Redaktion: Volker Wendland
Herstellung: Angelika Lindner

Gestaltung: Marion Köster, Stuttgart
Umschlaggestaltung: Marion Köster, Stuttgart
Illustrationen: Jeongsook Lee, Köln
Satz: Marion Köster, Stuttgart; Satzkiste, Stuttgart
Reproduktion: Meyle + Müller Medien-Management
Druck: Mediahaus Biering GmbH, München

Printed in Germany
ISBN 978-3-12-800021-3

Interaktive Medien-DVD (Multisession)

DVD-ROM
Diesem Lehrwerk liegt eine Medien-DVD mit Software, Audios und Dokumenten bei. Die Urheber und Mitwirkenden sind den entsprechenden Verzeichnissen auf der DVD-ROM zu entnehmen. Sollten Sie Probleme mit dem vorliegenden Programm haben, finden Sie in der Datei „Hotline.txt“, die sich auf der obersten Ebene der DVD-ROM befindet, unsere Kontaktdaten und weitere Hilfestellungen.

Audio-Aufnahmen
Aufnahmeleitung: Ernst Klett Verlag GmbH, Stuttgart

BBC Video-Aufnahmen: Alle Videos sind von der BBC Motion Gallery bereitgestellt.

Tontechnik: Bauer Studios, Ludwigsburg;
Presswerk: OK Medien Service, Boizenburg / Elbe

Das Werk und seine Teile sind urheberrechtlich geschützt. Das Gleiche gilt für die Software sowie das Begleitmaterial. Jede Nutzung in anderen als den gesetzlich zugelassenen oder in den Lizenzbestimmungen (DVD) genannten Fällen bedarf der vorherigen schriftlichen Einwilligung des Verlages. Hinweis zu § 52 a UrhG: Weder das Werk noch seine Teile dürfen ohne eine solche Einwilligung eingescannt und in ein Netzwerk eingestellt werden. Dies gilt auch für Intranets von Schulen und sonstigen Bildungseinrichtungen. Fotomechanische oder andere Wiedergabeverfahren nur mit Genehmigung des Verlages.
© und ℗ Ernst Klett Verlag GmbH, Stuttgart 2010.
Alle Rechte vorbehalten.
www.klett.de

9 783128 000213

To the student

Welcome to **Business Proficiency**, a comprehensive Business English course for German-speaking students who need English to be able to operate effectively in an international business environment.

This course will help you to raise your level of spoken and written English to C1 ('effective operational proficiency') on the Common European Framework (CEF). On reaching this level, you will be able to express yourself fluently and spontaneously, use your English effectively and flexibly in a wide range of business and social contexts, understand a variety of English speakers, understand business texts and correspondence, and write clear, well-structured texts that express your ideas in a professional manner. These are ambitious goals, so we recommend that you familiarise yourself with this book and the DVD before you get started.

The course consists of 16 units, covering a range of business topics and communication skills. The units are structured as follows:

- **A – Introduction:**
  realistic business situations that familiarise you with the topic
- **B – Business briefing:**
  background, views and concepts, with key vocabulary presented in context
- **C – Language:**
  focus on vocabulary and grammar relating to the topic
- **D – Business leaders:**
  profiles of people who have had an impact on the world of business
- **E – Business communication:**
  step-by-step approach to developing the skills you need in business
- **F – Consulting:**
  case studies and projects involving in-depth research, reflection and analysis

In each section, you will find tips to guide you through the tasks and activities.

- **SKILLS**
  tips on study and communication skills
- **LANGUAGE TIP**
  aspects of language that often present problems for German-speaking learners
- **PHRASES**
  useful phrases for speaking and writing in a business context
- **WORD BANK**
  business terms grouped by topic, including British and American variations (BE / AE)
- **INFO**
  background information on business concepts and issues

Certain types of tasks are identified by symbols.

(Internet symbol)	Internet research tasks to help you explore issues in more depth, and keep up-to-date
Online Link	Online links that provide number-coded access to additional online resources
A	Listening practice with audio files and transcripts on the DVD
V	BBC Motion Gallery Videos supplied by BBC Motion Gallery

To help you monitor your progress, there are three **revision sections** and a **practice exam**. The format of the practice exam is modelled on typical Business English exams that are used in Bachelor degree courses in German-speaking countries. It will also prepare you for other types of Business English exam.

The **appendix** contains role cards, transcripts, a topic-based and an alphabetical vocabulary list, acronyms and abbreviations used in business, and false friends.

Business Proficiency is designed to be used both as a classroom course, with a wide range of group and pair-work activities, and for studying on your own. The Consulting assignments (Part F of each unit) lend themselves particularly well to self-study. On the **interactive media DVD** you will find BBC video clips, audio files and transcripts for listening practice, grammar files, vocabulary learning lists, and interactive e-learning software that will enable you to practise grammar and vocabulary on your own and at your own pace.

We wish you all the best as you work towards your career goals, and hope that you find **Business Proficiency** both interesting and rewarding.

Stephanie Ashford and Tom Smith

Business Proficiency – Contents

Content of the interactive media DVD:

› Video-Pool: original BBC videos
› Audio-Pool: Student book's audios
› Document-Pool:
  - Transcripts of audios and videos
  - Business letter templates
  - Grammar files
  - Vocabulary learning lists
› Software: Self paced learning with interactive elearning

Unit 1
Communication

Online Link
800021-0001

A Introduction | In the office

Tanja, a German business student, is doing an internship at the Stuttgart subsidiary of a German firm that has been taken over by an American multinational, Synysys Inc. The new policy of 'English-only' for all internal correspondence is just one of several changes resulting from the takeover.

1 Listening

A 1.1 **a.** It is 8 o'clock on Monday morning. Listen and take notes about the relationship between Tanja and David, what Tanja notices is different in the office, and changes that have taken place in the company.

b. What would you prefer – to have your own office or to share one? Discuss the pros and cons.

2 Listening and reading

A 1.2–4 **a.** Listen to the phone messages and read the post-it note, email and schedule, and do the tasks that follow.

Dear Ms Fischer,
Thanks for agreeing to co-ordinate the visit of our new CEO, Mr Jeremy Spicer. He'd like to meet the management and staff, and have a tour of our factory in Böblingen. Since this is his first visit to Germany, we need to give a good impression.
I am attaching a draft schedule so that you can start making arrangements. Some details still need to be finalised, so please email me your suggestions together with an updated version of the schedule asap.
Many thanks once again, and I hope you have an enjoyable weekend.
Kind regards,
Martin Ebner

Friday, 24 Oct.
Hi Tanja and David
Great news! I've won the Trainee of the Year award! We're having a knees-up in Room 1.12 on Monday at 10am with bubbly and nibbles. Hope you can make it!
Best, Marion

bubbly (informal) Champagner, Sekt, **knees-up** (informal) Party, **nibbles** Knabberzeug

Schedule:
Visit of Jeremy Spicer, Gregory Miller and Kazuo Nagata, Synysys Inc.

Wednesday, 5th November

10.00 Arrival Stuttgart airport, Flight AA17 from NY (JFK). Transfer by company car to headquarters in Stuttgart. *Herrn Koll bitten, Gäste vom Flughafen abzuholen.*

11.00 Official welcome to Synysys Germany by Dr Martin Ebner. *Konferenzraum reservieren und Getränke organisieren – Sekt, Orangensaft und Kaffee/Tee.*

12.30 Transfer to hotel. Lunch at hotel. Hire car (Hertz) with SatNav delivered to hotel as requested *

19.00 Dinner with Dr Martin Ebner and all heads of department. *Tische reservieren – Restaurant?????*

** Zimmer für die 3 Gäste und Mittagessen für 8 Leute reservieren. Hotel Adler wenn möglich!*

Thursday, 6th November

9.00 Meet staff at Synysys Germany. *Kaffee usw. organisieren.*

9.30 Presentation by CEO Jeremy Spicer "Synysys: Light Years Ahead".

10.30 Drive to Böblingen factory. *Fragen, ob Synysys Minibus frei ist. Wenn nicht, Taxi bestellen.*

11.00 Tour of factory by Frau Schneider of Production Dept. *Schon erledigt – Sie müssen nichts machen.*

13.00 Lunch in company canteen. *Kaltes Buffet bestellen? Oder warmes Essen?*

14.00 Meeting with R & D and Product Manager. *Raum organisieren u. die Herren entsprechend informieren.*

19.00 Evening entertainment at Stuttgart venue to be confirmed.
Herr Spicer will etwas 'typisch Deutsches'. Bitte etwas Passendes aussuchen und Tisch für zehn Personen reservieren.

Friday, 7th November

9.00 Check out of hotel, drive to Synysys Germany HQ. *Firmenwagen? Synysys Minibus? Mietwagen?*

9.30 Presentation by CFO Gregory Miller: group financial report.

10.30 Presentation by Kazuo Nagata: "The Global Marketplace" *Ist Kazuo oder Nagata der Familienname?*

12.00 Lunch *Kaltes Buffett usw. Bitte auch geeignete Gastgeschenke kaufen – max. €20 pro Person.*

13.00 Drive to Stuttgart airport (Leave hire car at Hertz depot), Departure Flight AA18 to NY (JFK) at 14.45.

b. Write a 'To do' list for Tanja. Organise the tasks in order of priority according to Stephen Covey's time management matrix. Then compare your list with other pairs.

c. Decide on gifts (or one gift) for the visitors and a suitable venue for the Thursday evening entertainment.

d. Which boxes in Covey's matrix should effective managers concentrate on? Which should they avoid?

e. Write your own 'To do' list for the coming week. Explain your list to another student, and discuss how to manage your time more effectively.

Time management matrix

Urgent and important	Not urgent but important
Urgent but not important	Not urgent, not important

3 Listening and writing

A 1.4 **a.** Listen to the third phone message again. Tanja is too busy to deal with the request by Nicola Stahl of EazyPrinz, so she decides to pass it on to her colleague David. What should Tanja tell David?

b. Write Tanja's reply to Dr Ebner in which she summarises what she has done, makes suggestions for the schedule and attaches the new version. Use the phrases below, including any further relevant points.

> Dear Dr Ebner,
> Thank you for sending ... As requested, I have ... I have also ... Unfortunately it was not possible to ... because ... Therefore I suggest that ... As far as ... is concerned, I would recommend ... I am attaching ... Regards, Tanja Fisher

B Business briefing | Soft skills

1 Reading

a. Read the article and explain how it relates to the title 'From nerd to networker'.

From nerd to networker

Being a boffin is not going to get graduates the well-paid jobs they want – the stakes have been raised. As well as academic success, employers want people who are able to communicate properly, work as part of a team, are culturally aware and can lead others, says Carl Gilleard, chief executive of the Association of Graduate Recruiters (AGR) – skills gained outside of the lecture theatre.
"Traditionally the boffin or nerd was hired for their brains and put in a backroom job and didn't have to communicate much. But those jobs are now few and far between. Employees have to communicate all the time with colleagues and clients so companies want people who can do that effectively. They have higher expectations now."
So, for those who spend more time with computers than with fellow humans, here's a quick guide to brushing up on the social skills required to get ahead in business.

Communicating

Mumbling, avoiding eye contact, talking to their shoes – the boffin's biggest challenge can often be talking to another human being. They can decipher the most complicated equation but trying to work out the social etiquette required to converse with someone else leaves them baffled – and making small talk can be plain scary.
But the only way to improve communication skills is to get out of the house and actually talk to someone, says celebrity life coach, Gladeana McMahon. As the basis for conversation, she recommends a formula called OPEN, which stands for occupation, personal, environment and non-work activities.
"It's all aimed at encouraging small talk," says Ms McMahon. "Some people find it hard to know where to start, but stick to these four areas and you shouldn't be lost for words."

Team working

Some students are so focused on one thing – getting their degree – it can come as no surprise when they are no good at team activities after leaving university, says Ms McMahon. "They need to get involved in different social groups and mix. At first they will be awful but they will eventually learn the skills they need to be a good team player."
Those skills include being a good listener and being assertive, but in a way that is respectful to other people. Using "link" words is the key.
"A good team worker would say 'I see your point, however why don't we look at it from this perspective'. The all-important link word here is however. It gets your views across in a confident but respectful way."

Leadership

Talk of "taking a lead" in an office environment usually means picking up a computer cable for most geeks. But the ability to lead and inspire a team of people is essential in a lot of jobs. To improve this skill, seek out a role model, says Ms McMahon. "Look for someone who has good leadership skills in your own office and watch what they do and what they say. It's called modelling and involves taking their successful skills and making them your own. It's not about mimicking, it's about adapting good skills for yourself. It's using your initiative, a quality that is always admired in the world of work.

Cultural awareness

The day-to-day life of a boffin involves a lot of isolation. Largely based in their bedroom, visitors are few and far between, let alone someone from another country or a member of the opposite sex. But in today's global community, graduates will have to work with people or deal with clients from many different backgrounds. Ignorance can result in an embarrassing faux pas.
Learning about other cultures does not automatically mean spending time and money on travel. People learn about differences in things like personal space and eye contact by using books and the internet (a chance to put those computer skills to good use).
Also, just ask. "Treat it as an exploration," says McMahon. "Use your newly acquired chitchat skills and ask questions. It's the best way to learn and get to know people."

BBC NEWS

nerd intelligente, aber kontaktarme Person, **boffin** Eierkopf, Fachidiot, **to raise the stakes** den Einsatz erhöhen, **few and far between** ganz vereinzelt, to **brush up on** wieder auffrischen, **to mumble** nuscheln, **to decipher an equation** eine Gleichung enträtseln, **baffled** vor ein Rätsel gestellt, **plain** schlichtweg, **geek** Computer-Versessener, **let alone** geschweige denn, **chitchat** Geplauder

b. List the advice about improving communication skills as 'Do's and Don'ts. Compare your lists and discuss the merits of each tip. Suggest further tips to add to the lists.

DO	DON'T
Brush up on your social skills. ...	Mumble. ...

c. Complete the grid and match the questions to the topics they refer to. Suggest further questions for each topic and discuss topics you would avoid with people you don't know well.

O	Occupation
P	
E	
N	

[ ] Where are you from?
[ ] What do you do?
[ ] Isn't this weather awful?
[ ] Do you have a girlfriend?
[ ] Do you enjoy your job?
[ ] What do you do at the weekends?
[ ] How old are your kids?
[ ] That's a cool mobile you've got. Where did you get it?
[ ] What's like to live in Berlin?

d. Read these responses to the BBC article. Continue the discussion in class or online.

1 I'm an Engineering graduate and in my third and fourth years at university we focused on developing skills for the work place, applying our technical knowledge, producing documentation, working in teams, etc. I also spent a summer working as a door-to-door salesman in Australia, which really improved my communication skills! Even though I don't have a degree in business, I am able to apply for almost any graduate position in business or finance. *Shane, Winchester*

2 I also studied Engineering. We were forced to take soft skills courses to make us more balanced, whereas the arts and business students didn't have to do extra science courses. I now work in global finance, and I'm shocked at how little basic science or technology skills the average non-science graduate has. They should be forced to learn some 'hard skills' to make them more balanced! *Brian, London*

3 What is this world of 'boffins' and 'geeks' you're talking about? Why is it such a terrible thing for people to be focused and good at something? Some people may not be social climbers but they're brilliant at their job, precisely because they're so single-minded and less prone to chit-chat. *Louise, Nottingham*

e. Check that you understand the vocabulary in the word bank. Suggest further examples for each category.

WORD BANK

Information and communications technology (ICT): internet | email | fax | landline phone | mobile phone (AE: cell phone) | text message | video conference | teleconference | scanner | PowerPoint | digital projector
Written communication: letter | memo | report | email | fax | schedule | itinerary | agenda | minutes | sales literature | catalogue | brochure | leaflet | enquiry | offer | order
Face-to-face communication (F2F): conference | sales meeting | annual general meeting (AGM) | team briefing | debriefing | negotiation | rumour | grapevine | gossip 'around the water cooler'
Non-verbal communication (NVC): body language | posture | facial expression | eye contact | gesture | to shake hands | to give a 'high five' | to kiss | to embrace | to give a bear hug | appearance | dress | silence

2 Discussion

a. Compare how you communicate professionally with how you communicate with friends and family. Consider the choice of methods as well as aspects of style and formality.

b. Which are the appropriate forms of communication in the following situations?

1. inviting guests to a college graduation ceremony
2. congratulating a colleague on her birthday
3. informing staff about topics to be discussed in a meeting
4. showing appreciation after a lecture
5. excusing yourself from next week's English lesson
6. request for new passport (enclosing old one)
7. discussing an issue with colleagues abroad

c. A 1975 Business Week article about communication technology predicted that the office of the future would be paperless. Has this prediction come true? If not, why not?

C Language | Business correspondence

1 Letter-writing conventions

a. Put the numbers in the letter next to the tip it refers to. (The first one has been done for you.)

- [ ] It is usual to separate the paragraphs with a line space.
- [ ] Short for 'reference'. The German equivalent is *Unser Zeichen*.
- [ ] If documents are sent with the letter, write *Encl.* or *Enc.* (= *enclosure(s), enclosed*) at the bottom.
- [ ] The date can go on the left or the right.
- [1] The sender's address usually goes below the letterhead or on the right.
- [ ] If you start with a named person, it is usual to end with *Yours sincerely.* If you start *Dear Sir or Madam*, use *Yours faithfully.* (AE: *Sincerely* or *Sincerely yours*, in both situations).
- [ ] The subject line can also go below the salutation in BrE.
- [ ] If you do not know the name of the person you are writing to, start with *Dear Sir or Madam* (BrE), or *To whom it may concern* (AmE).
- [ ] If you leave out the comma after the salutation, leave it out after the *"Yours ..."* ending, too.
- [ ] Always start with a capital letter after the salutation.

SYNYSYS International Inc

Ms Marion Hengstler
Erikaweg 7
78086 Brigachtal

Synysys International Inc
Siemensstr. 12–14 ❶
D-70174 Stuttgart
Tel: 0711/6788-0
www.synysys.com

24 October 20... ❷
Our ref: ZD/HR ❸

❹ **Announcement of Trainee of the Year Award**

Dear Ms Hengstler, ❺
❻ We are delighted to announce that you have been selected as overall winner in the Synysys Trainee of the Year Award. The selection committee praised your professional integrity, enthusiasm and diligence, as well as your team spirit and courteous manner.

The award ceremony will be held on Monday, 27 October at 11am in Room 1.21 in Block C. We will be celebrating the occasion with champagne and canapés, and you are welcome to take this opportunity to invite colleagues in the Marketing department. A list of all the award winners is enclosed. Should you be unable to attend the ceremony for any reason, I would appreciate it if you could inform me at your earliest convenience.

❼ On behalf of the management, I would like to congratulate you on your outstanding achievement and your commitment to Synysys International Inc., and I very much look forward to presenting you with the certificate and a book voucher for 100.

❽
Yours sincerely, ❾

Zafer Dogan
Zafer Dogan
Director of Human Resources

Encl. ❿

b. Most organisations have their own house-style for business letters. Compare the features of the letter above with those of a typical German business letter.

c. Match the dates with the usage.

1. 12.08.11	a. standard AE
2. August 12, 2011	b. traditional BE
3. 12 August, 2011	c. modern BE
4. 12th August 2011	d. could be December or August
5. 12. August 2011	e. standard continental (e.g. German)

d. Why is it sometimes safer to write the month as a word?

e. Use the international date settings on a computer to compare usage in Canada, New Zealand, Singapore and the Philippines. What explanation can you suggest for the differences?

LANGUAGE TIP

Conventions in correspondence
There are no rules for starting and finishing business letters and emails, just conventions. These conventions change over time so keep an eye open for current examples of business correspondence written by native English speakers and compare the language and layout.

f. Complete the summary below based on the letter and the following email. Be careful with the verb forms.

From: fischer.t@synysys.com
Subject: Re: Bubbly
Date: Monday, October 27th, 08:36:05 AM CET
To: hengstler.m@synysys.com

Hi Marion
Thanks for the invitation, and congrats on winning the TOY Award. You really deserve it! I'm afraid I can't make it at 11am, much as I'd love to. I'm up to my eyes in work (... my fault for leaving early on Friday). David will be there – he never misses a chance to party, especially if you're there! ;o)
Btw, while I was making some photocopies I saw Fabian in his latest outfit. Today he's wearing Lederhosen, a bolero jacket and roller blades, but I guess in Marketing anything goes.
So ... have fun!!!!!!

Cheers, Tanja

PS: If you find some keys with a fluffy pig mascot, they're Penny's. She's going crazy with worry!
PPS: Don't tell Dr Ebner that I left early. (Anyway, I'm going to do overtime tonight to make up for it!)

Summary

In Zafer Dogan's letter to Marion Hengstler he i.. n.......... her that she has w.......... the Trainee of the Year Award and i.. n.......... her to a ceremony where she will be p.. r.......... with a certificate and book voucher. Tanja r.. e.......... to Marion's email to t.......... her for the invitation and to c.. o.......... her on w.. i.......... the award. She e.. x.. c.......... s.. herself from a.. t.. t.......... the celebration, e.. x.. p.......... that she has too much work, but a.......... s.. that David will be there. She also m.. e.. n.......... Fabian, whom she saw wearing an unusual outfit, and she r.. e.. f.......... to the key that Penny has l.......... . Finally, she ....k...... Marion not to tell Dr Ebner about her .... early on Friday.

g. **Match the phrases. Underline the one in each pair that is more formal.**

1. Well done on winning the award.
2. champagne and canapés
3. I'm up to my eyes with work.
4. Please let me know asap.
5. Should you be unable to attend, …
6. I'm afraid I can't come …
7. Feel free to …
8. Please also note that …

a. If you can't come
b. I regret that I will be unable to attend …
c. I have a lot of deadlines to meet.
d. I would like to congratulate you on your achievement.
e. bubbly and nibbles
f. Btw (by the way)
g. You are welcome to take this opportunity to …
h. I would appreciate it if you could inform me at your earliest convenience.

h. **Are the phrases below formal (F) or informal (I)? Find their equivalents in the correspondence on pages 8 and 12. Identify further examples of formal / informal style.**

1. You will be pleased to hear …
2. We're having a knees-up.
3. I would be delighted if you could attend.
4. Here's …
5. He wants to …
6. Some things haven't been sorted out yet.
7. Have a great weekend!

i. **In a letter you might write 'I am enclosing'. What is the equivalent expression used for emails?**

LANGUAGE TIP

Written style

Correspondence between people who know each other well tends to be informal and conversational, and punctuation can be fairly free. A written style with too many of these features can be seen as rushed or unprofessional.

Formal / courteous	Conversational / time-saving
Cannot / I am / they have	can't / I'm / they've
for your information	fyi
I have a lot of deadlines to meet.	I'm up to my eyes in work.
I hope you enjoy your stay.	Have fun!!! ;o)
Could you please inform me …	Let me know …
My train arrives at 17.32.	My train gets in at about 5.30.

2 Greetings and introductions

a. **Which of these phrases would you use with someone you meet for the first time? Which one would you use when you are saying goodbye?**

1. You must be Robert Sachs.
2. Nice to meet you.
3. Fancy meeting you here!
4. Nice meeting you.
5. What brings you here?
6. How do you do?
7. I'm the Marketing Director.
8. It's been a long time.

b. **Delete the wrong option and write the visitor's part of the dialogue.**

1. Good (~~day~~ / morning), can I help you?
   Yes, please. I'm looking for Mr Manconi's office.
2. Do you have (an appointment / a date)?
   ……………………………………
3. Could you tell me what (is your name / your name is), please?
   ……………………………………
4. Just a moment, Mrs Lorenzo. I'll call Mr Manconi's office and (look / see) if he's there.
   ……………………………………
5. Mr Manconi is (expecting / attending) you, but I'm afraid he's still in a meeting.
   ……………………………………
6. Don't worry, he'll be down to meet you (briefly / shortly). He's sorry to (hold / keep) you waiting.
   ……………………………………
7. May I (take / have) your coat?
   ……………………………………
8. Did you manage (finding / to find) us alright?
   ……………………………………
9. Can I offer you something to drink (during / while) you wait?
   ……………………………………

c. **Practise short dialogues, where one of you is a visitor. Use phrases from each group.**

Do come in.	That suits me.	So you found us OK?
Have a seat.	Thanks.	How was your trip?
Can I take your coat?	Good idea.	Is this your first visit to …?
Make yourself comfortable.	Me too.	Have you ever been to …?
Would you like a coffee?	That would be nice.	Have you come far?

3 Spot check: Tenses

a. **Go through the letter (p. 12) and email (p. 13) again and identify examples of the following verb forms:**

simple present | present progressive | simple past | past progressive | present perfect | will + infinitive | future progressive | going-to future

b. **Choose the most suitable verb form.**

A WINNING PROFILE

Marion Hengstler (*joined / has joined*) Synysys two years ago and since then she (*does not only work / has not only worked*) in three different departments but she (*travels also / has also travelled*) all over Germany.

"I (*go / am going*) on business trips on a regular basis, but before I (*started / have started*) at the company I (*haven't / hadn't*) travelled anywhere on my own", says Marion, who (*turned / has turned*) 22 last year. She (*currently learns / is currently learning*) Chinese because she (*goes / will be going*) to Shanghai to attend a trade fair next July.

"Business with China (*booms / is booming*) right now, so it's a great opportunity for Synysys, and for me. My Chinese (*improves / is improving*) but I expect I (*will speak / am speaking*) English most of the time."

So what are her plans for the future? "Well, first of all I (*am buying / am going to buy*) myself a good financial dictionary," she says. "Next month (*I work / I'll be working*) in the Accounts Department."

D Business leaders | Steve Jobs

1 Reading

Read the article and make notes about Steve Jobs under the following headings:

Communication style | Personal image | Presentation techniques | Personality

2 Discussion

a. Discuss whether Steve Job's 'bad' side makes him less effective as a communicator. What might be the downside of trying to be 'everybody's darling'?

b. Weigh up the risks and benefits of having a CEO whose personality is closely associated with the success of a company.

c. Find out about the products Apple have launched recently, and discuss what innovations or gadgetry might be in the pipeline.

d. Find words in the text that mean the same.

1. advantage
2. relaxed and informal (two examples)
3. event where company presents a new product
4. to be less successful at work than expected

e. Explain these expressions in your own words.

1. … when he is showing off brand-new features

....

....

....

2. … Jobs leaves nothing to chance

....

....

....

3. … up-and-down relationship with the media

....

....

....

passion Leidenschaft, **infectious** ansteckend, **plain,** schlicht, **spotlight** Scheinwerfer, to **incorporate** einbauen, **wizard** Zauberer, **frenzy** Ekstase, **ferocious temper** Gereiztheit, Zorn, **disloyal** abtrünnig

In the late 1970s Steve Jobs and Apple co-founder Steve Wozniak created one of the first commercially successful personal computers. Apple products have the reputation of being pioneers in technology, yet they also appeal to non-technical people who like the user-friendly software and the simple but stylish designs. Jobs resigned from Apple Inc in 1985 after disagreements with the board, but later returned to the company to serve as its CEO.

Steve Jobs is known for communicating his ideas with passion and energy. His enthusiasm for Apple products can be highly infectious, especially when he is showing off brand-new features and innovations. He uses plain, simple language to emphasise the benefits of the latest devices: "It has a gorgeous screen", "The colour is fantastic", and "The video quality is amazing".

However, despite his relaxed and informal performances in front of large audiences, Jobs leaves nothing to chance. He is known to practise for hours, even days, in advance of his 'stage shows' in order to ensure a perfect result every time. These shows are strongly visual, with Jobs performing under a spotlight in front of a giant screen displaying the latest Apple gadgetry. He usually includes his famous catchphrase "And one more thing!", signalling that he is about to reveal yet another brilliant invention.

But what is the man behind the Apple phenomenon really like? Alan Deutschmann, author of the biography *The Second Coming of Steve Jobs*, has described him as having two personalities – Good Steve and Bad Steve. The Good Steve character is the popular image we all know, the easy-going California college kid who became a technical wizard. He still dresses casually, in a black polo-neck and jeans, even at top-level meetings. With his pop star persona and a large following of loyal Apple fans, he has the ability to create a frenzy at product launches, where the audience is left believing that anything is possible.

In contrast, there is Bad Steve – the one seldom seen in public. A perfectionist who has always driven himself hard, he is rumoured to have a ferocious temper with members of his staff that he thinks have underperformed or been disloyal. He has an up-and-down relationship with the media, too. While Good Steve enjoys networking with celebrities, Bad Steve dislikes the intrusive attention of the press and has a reputation for being 'difficult' in interviews.

E Business communication | Telephoning

1 Usage

a. Discuss the questions below.

1. You are in your office when your desk phone rings. How long do you wait before you pick up the receiver?
2. You are having a meeting with a colleague in your office when the phone rings. What do you do?
3. "Calling a cell phone just a phone seems a little silly these days" (Charlie Sorrel, Wired Magazine). Do you agree? What additional functions do cell phones offer? How useful are they to business people?

b. In what situations might you use the following phrases?

1. I'll just put you through.
2. I didn't catch your name.
3. Have you got a pen handy?
4. I'm afraid it's a very bad line.
5. Can I get her to call you back?
6. If you could just bear with me.
7. Who shall I say is calling?
8. He hung up.
9. Hope I'm not disturbing you.

2 Dealing with callers

A 1.5–6 **a.** Anita Schmelz, Sales Manager of Bahu Interiors, is on a business trip and Markus Burger is standing in for her. Listen to the calls and complete the table. If there is no information, write 'NI'.

	Call 1	Call 2
Who the caller wants to speak to		
Caller's contact details		
Reason for the call		
Action Markus needs to take		

A 1.5–6 **b.** Listen again and complete the phrases. Then translate them into German.

Call 1

1. Good morning, ... Bob Holder.
2. Yes, ... How can I help you?
3. Just a moment, I'll .... my diary.
4. Where .... we meet?

Call 2

1. Oh, he's .... a different ....
2. If you ...., I'll just .... you.
3. Can I .... him to .... you ....?
4. I'll make sure he .... your call.

c. What phrase does Markus use to express "Er geht nicht ans Telefon"?

d. Compare the calls. In what ways are they different?

e. What do you hate about phones or phone behaviour? Complete the statements and then discuss them in class. Feel free to let off steam!

1. I really get annoyed by ....
....
2. What really irritates me is ....
....
3. I can't stand it when ....
....

LANGUAGE TIP

Improving your fluency
There are many fixed expressions in telephone language. By learning them as if they were single words you can improve your fluency and confidence.

False friends
irritate ≠ irritieren
Das hat mich irritiert. = I was confused.
Das ärgert mich. = It irritates me.

3 Making arrangements

A 1.7 **Complete the dialogue using the words below. Then listen and check.**

by | suit | check | tricky | free | about | until | should | confirm | of the office | on | make | busy | schedule | prefer | go for | sounds

Fabian: So, when .... we meet?
Jim: How .... Friday morning?
Fabian: I'm afraid I'll be .... then. The afternoon would .... me better.
Jim: Hmm, that might be .... What's your .... like for next week?
Fabian: Well, I can't .... Monday or Tuesday, and I'll be out .... all morning on Wednesday. But I'd be .... any time in the afternoon.
Jim: That .... fine. I haven't got anything .... then either. So what time would you ....?
Fabian: Oh, any time would suit. Shall we .... 3pm, and have the meeting in your office?
Jim: I just need to .... with Anita, since we share the office. Can I call you back to .... it?
Fabian: I'll be in my office .... lunchtime. If I don't hear from you .... then, I'll assume it's OK.

4 Dictating words and numbers

A 1.8 **You will hear ten dialogues in which words and numbers are dictated. Listen and do the tasks.**

1. Note down what the second speaker says in each exchange.
2. Can you remember what the first speaker said? Listen again to check.
3. Read out the following facts and figures, as if you were dictating them over the phone:

Example: 30 June 2009 = "The thirtieth of June, two thousand and nine, that's three-oh, not one-three."

1. $5,353.59
2. Tel: 0710 – 33002 (Ext. 14)
3. Account no: 59796404
4. 13 Sept 1996
5. www.worldwidewines.co.uk
6. The plane leaves at 15.50 and arrives at 18.35.
7. albert_marketing@t-online.de
8. 1500 sq. metres
9. It weighs exactly 6.04 grams.

PHRASES

Exchanging information on the phone
Dictating: Have you got something to write with? | Are you ready? | Have you got that? | Could you read that back to me?

Checking and clarifying: Sorry, I didn't catch / get that last number. | Was that a 'P' or a 'B'? | Could you spell that, please? | Did you say 'word' or 'world'?

5 Exchanging information

Practise exchanging information in pairs, based on the instructions below.

1. Use the information on page 216 (cards ❶ – ❹). Dictate the information on your card to your partner. Then check whether your partner noted it correctly.
2. Make short phone calls using the role cards on page 216 (Student A and Student B), where A is the caller. Record the calls and play them back after each call. Remember to keep them short and snappy.
3. List some scenarios for telephone calls and improvise them. If possible, record them and then check.

LANGUAGE TIP

Numbers and amounts
› Use points (not commas) with decimals.
→ 0.09 (nought) point oh nine (*BE*), point zero nine (*AE*)
› Say 'dot', not 'point' with internet addresses
→ synysys.com = dot com
› Translating *Milliarde*
→ 1,000,000,000 = one billion (*BE / AE*)
→ Some people in Britain say 'one thousand million'. If necessary, ask "How many zeros does your billion have?"
› Abbreviations
→ 58 m (Mio) = 58 million

INFO

Preparing for phone calls
› Note down key phrases before opening the call.
› Speak slowly and clearly, especially when you say the name of the company and your own name.
› Check and clarify the important points as you go along.
› Always have paper and pen near the phone.
› Keep calls short and simple

F Consulting | In the suggestions box

1 Reading

You work for Synysys Inc. Read the documents on these two pages and do the tasks that follow.

From: spicer.j@synysys.com
Subject: Improving communication
To: dogan.z@synysys.de
cc: ebner.m@synysys.de

Hi Zafir

It was great meeting you last week, and I was impressed by how well you guys in Stuttgart are adapting to the Synysys way of doing things. Still, I realize it isn't easy for you, and I've been thinking a lot about the issues raised at our meeting on Friday. I must admit that I was surprised at the controversy created by some of our policies (ban on alcohol, enforcement of dress code, monitoring of internet usage). Maybe this controversy is due to cultural differences – I don't know. It seems to me that if we're going to merge our corporate cultures and integrate the international project teams, the first step is to improve communication.

Zafir, have you considered using a Suggestions Box to find out what people really think? It's something we do here at HQ, and it's an effective way of empowering people at grassroots level. If you don't already have one, you should definitely give it a try.

Let me know how it goes.
Jim

Some people here dress too casually in my opinion, so I recommend introducing a dress code. When I worked in the States, we had to wear formal business attire (dark suit and tie for men, matching jacket and pants/skirt for women). It looked more professional. Fridays was 'dress-down day', when we could wear what we like, eg. jeans, T-shirt, sneakers, etc.

I'm worried about this new policy of monitoring of our emails and internet usage. I've got nothing to hide, but on the other hand I don't like the idea of 'Big Brother' management spying on me! I do a lot of networking on Facebook, which can be useful to Synysys. My suggestion is to allow people to use the internet for private purposes for a maximum of 30 minutes a day.

I'm TOTALLY against this new ban on alcohol. What's wrong with a couple of beers at lunchtime? Also, it's a tradition here to celebrate birthdays with a glass of Sekt. We don't have a problem with alcoholism in this company, so what's the problem?

I notice that a lot of people in this company keep their doors closed, so I never know whether they're in their offices or not. What about introducing an 'open-door policy'? Or - even better - open-plan offices. (My office feels like a prison cell!)

This company is like Fort Knox. We need so many different keys for all the locked doors. My bunch of keys is so big now that I feel like a jailer. Also, if I lose my keys, all the locks will have to be changed, which could be really expensive. A convenient and cheap solution might be a 'transponder' key that we can use to open any door.

2 Writing

a Write a one-line summary in English of each suggestion.

Example:
Dress-code: Formal business attire Monday – Thursday, with casual clothes allowed on Friday.

b. Evaluate each suggestion in terms of whether it is reasonable and feasible.

c. Consider how Zafir Dogan and his colleagues might respond to each of the suggestions and write his reply to Jim Spicer.

TIPS
- Bear in mind that there may be differences in business culture as well as national labour law.
- Use the internet to research some of the issues (dress code at work, corporate gifts, legislation regarding the monitoring of internet usage, …)

Ich habe gehört, dass die Firmenleitung uns alle mit Handys ausstatten will, damit wir rund um die Uhr erreichbar sind. Eine echte Zumutung! Man kann doch nicht erwarten, dass wir während unserer (inzwischen gekürzten!) Pausen telefonisch erreichbar sind. Ich habe auch gehört, dass wir unsere E-Mails zu Hause lesen sollen. Ist das wahr?

I think it's OK to give gifts to customers and suppliers, but we should place a limit on the value. Expensive gifts could give the wrong impression, and make people feel uncomfortable.

Although we're supposed to be a global company, the way some people address each other is very stiff and formal (Mr X, Frau Dr. Y, etc.). I suggest switching to first name terms. In my opinion, this is much friendlier and it would help to break down barriers and hierarchies.

In order to create a cosier and more intimate working environment, everyone should be allowed to bring their own furniture (e.g. a nice rug, a comfortable chair).

I notice a lot of eating goes on in the offices here. Is this normal? It's one thing to have a bowl of candy on the desk or in reception, but I think bringing all those bags of bread and cakes into the office is a bit gross. And do people REALLY need all those plates of cookies in meetings? I mean, we're not kids.

attire Kleidung, **pants** (AE) Hose, **sneakers** (AE) Turnschuhe, **spying** Bespitzelung, **to switch** wechseln auf, **rug** kleiner Teppich, **jailer** Gefängniswärter, **No way!** Auf keinen Fall, **gross** unappetitlich, ekelig

Unit 2
Company organisation

Online Link
800021-0002

A Introduction | Organisations and sectors

1 Discussion

a. Complete the statements as they apply to you. Then discuss what you have in common.

- I have worked for an organisation that …
- I am currently working for a company that …
- I am studying at an institution that …

LANGUAGE TIP

British / American?
BE: organisation
BE / AE: organization

b. Match the parts of the statements. Underline the ones that you agree with.

1. I'd never work for a company
2. I'd rather work in a team
3. Face-to-face contact is
4. I'd prefer to be offered a higher salary

a. than to be given a fancier job title.
b. if I didn't approve of their products.
c. than on my own.
d. always preferable to phone calls or emails.

c. Weigh up the pros and cons of each statement.
Then suggest other ways of completing the first half of each one.

2 Business sectors

a. Check that you understand the terms on the right, using a dictionary. Then copy the grid below and complete it.

Economic sector	Activity	Business sectors
Primary	extraction and production of raw materials	mining, …
Secondary	manufacturing or processing	textiles, …
Tertiary	provision of services to consumers or businesses	tourism, …

b. Check the latest headlines on a business website. Which sectors are doing well, and which are not? Try to explain why.

WORD BANK

Business sectors
aerospace | agriculture | automotive | biotechnology | chemicals | clothing | construction | consumer electronics | cosmetics | engineering | energy | food & beverages | finance | furniture and furnishings | healthcare | household goods | insurance | IT | media & publishing | mining | pharmaceuticals | restaurant & catering | retail | telecommunications | tourism | transport & logistics | tobacco | utilities | waste & recycling | wholesale

3 Reading

a. Read the profiles below and write the names of the companies that fit the discriptions.

1. selling food and drink ....
2. providing services ....
3. manufacturing ....
4. selling via the internet ....
5. distributors or retailers ....
6. selling mainly in the UK ....

b. Discuss which of the companies you would most like to work for. Consider their size, sector and location, and any other aspects you think are relevant.

Zeus

Zeus plc is one of the largest food and non-food retailers in the world. We currently operate more than 2,300 supermarkets and convenience stores and employ 326,000 people. Our core business is in Great Britain, where we also have an online grocery shopping and delivery service, and over the last decade we have expanded into mainland Europe, Asia and the United States.

Selaware

We are number one for household appliances. Our products are designed to make kitchens not only more functional but more beautiful. With our headquarters in Chicago, USA, we are leading producers of refrigerators, freezers, dishwashers, washing machines and tumblers. All appliances are ENERGY STAR qualified, incorporating innovative technology that uses 10 – 50 % less energy and water than standard models.

Pobjoy, Heath & Partners

With over ten years of experience in accountancy and consulting services, we have developed an impressive portfolio of clients that ranges from freelancers and small businesses to multinational companies. We run our partnership from a penthouse office in Canary Wharf, which boasts breathtaking views of the Thames and the city's most famous landmarks.

Offaly Fine Crystal

Offaly Fine Crystal Ltd. has long been one of the world's best-known and best-loved brands of traditionally crafted Irish crystal glassware. Wine goblets, champagne flutes, whiskey tumblers, all made by skilled craftsmen in Ireland and Indonesia. Holidays, weddings, anniversaries - why not enhance a special occasion with Offaly's elegant crystal engraved with your very own initials, or a personal monogram of that special person in your life.

TEXAN HOUSE PARTY

It's the American Dream going global! **Texan House Party™** is actively seeking franchisees in all regions. THP has always been a franchising company and has relied on its franchisees to play a major role in its success. Approximately 70 % of our worldwide Tex-Mex restaurant businesses are owned and operated by independent franchisees. If owning a Texan House Party™ outlet is your dream, wake up and smell the coffee!

Footloose Fandango

A Leeds businesswoman who started her own dance shoe mail-order business has been described as an outstanding entrepreneur after increasing her turnover to £ 250,000 in three years. Madhur Vikram, 37, a former IT sales director, launched the upmarket **Footloose Fandango** footwear firm in Bradford in 2006. More than 85 % of her sales are through its website, supplying customers with leading brands of dance shoes at discount prices.

to boast aufweisen, bieten **breathtaking** atemberaubend, **goblet** Kelch, **champagne flute** Champagnerkelch, **tumbler** 1. Wäschetrockner, 2. Becher, **to engrave** (ein)gravieren

Street stall to superstore: the rise and rise of a retail giant

In 1919, young Jack Cohen invested his £30 war pension in stock for his street fruit and vegetable stall in the East End of London, and so began his career as a retailer. He had a talent for selling, and soon became so successful that, in 1929, he decided to expand his activities as a sole trader by opening a small grocery store. Searching for a name for his new business, he combined the initials from a name he saw on a packet of tea in his shop – T.E.Stockwell – with the first two letters of his own surname, to form Tes-co.

The business flourished, and Cohen invested his profits in building new premises in Burnt Oak, North London. In 1932, Tesco became a private limited company, and over the next eight years more than 100 small stores were opened, mainly in the London area. In 1935, Cohen visited the United States and was impressed by the food retailing system there. His vision of establishing the American self-service supermarket concept in Britain became a reality in 1947 when he opened the first self-service store in St Albans. In the same year, it was decided to raise capital by offering shares on the Stock Exchange, making Tesco Stores (Holdings) Limited a public limited company.

Over the next two decades, Tesco expanded rapidly across the UK by buying up numerous smaller grocery chains. In 1968, the company opened its first 40,000 sq. ft. superstore in Crawley, Sussex. The term superstore referred not only to the store's size but to the vast selection of inexpensive food and non-food items. By 1976, Tesco was operating nearly 900 stores on the 'pile 'em high, sell 'em cheap' formula that Cohen had imported from America. However, around this time shopping habits began to change, and people began to value quality goods rather than rock-bottom prices. It was time to take Tesco in a new direction.

Tesco embarked on a massive modernisation programme, closing 500 unprofitable outlets and upgrading its image. In the early eighties, the company (now known simply as Tesco plc) pursued its superstore concept even more aggressively, sparking price wars with its main competitor J. Sainsbury plc, and developing new stores in out-of-town areas close to major cities. By the end of the decade, Tesco had 370 stores in the UK and was one of the country's top three food retailers, with other lucrative business activities such as petrol stations and financial services.

The next decision was to make Tesco into a multinational company, and look for new takeover targets abroad. After first testing the highly volatile French market, Tesco turned its attention to the central European market, where it rapidly acquired retail chains in Poland, Hungary and the Czech Republic. In 1997, shareholders appointed a new CEO, Sir Terry Leahy, who brought in a new management style and further extended Tesco's operations into the emerging markets of Asia. Now Tesco was not only a successful retail giant in the home market, but had grown into a truly global company.

In 2006, in a bold move aimed at capturing a share of the world's biggest grocery market, Tesco set up a subsidiary in the United States and began to open stores in the western states of California and Arizona with the brand name Fresh and Easy. The concept was very different – small, friendly stores designed to create a 'neighbourhood' feel and promote a green image. In the 21st century, Jack Cohen's vision of developing an American-style supermarket empire out of a chain of small neighbourhood stores had come full circle.

to embark on etw. beginnen, **to upgrade** (here) aufwerten, **to pursue** verfolgen, **to spark** auslösen, **to capture** sich sichern

B Business briefing | Forms of organisation

1 Reading

a. What are the three biggest supermarket chains in your country? Discuss reasons for their success.

b. Read the article and summarise how it relates to the title 'the rise and rise of a retail giant'.

c. Place the events in the order in which they happened. Add dates where relevant.

A Buying up of retail chains in Eastern Europe
B Opening of first self-service store in St. Albans
C Acquisition of many UK grocery chains
D Establishment of subsidiary in USA
E Start of business selling fruit and vegetables
F Creation of private limited company
G Appointment of new CEO; penetration of Asian markets
H Relocation to new premises in Burnt Oak North London
I Opening of small grocery store in East End of London
J Listing of shares on the stock exchange
K Modernisation strategy with closure of unprofitable stores
L Launch of first superstore selling both food and non-food items

E

1919 2006

d. Explain these idioms in your own words. Then discuss possible German equivalents.

1. **'pile 'em high and sell 'em cheap'** (l. 45)
2. in a **bold move** (l. 85)
3. **rock-bottom prices** (l. 50)
4. Jack's vision **had come full circle** (l. 95 – 99)

e. List the types of retail outlets (e.g. superstore) and the forms of business organisation (e.g. sole trader) mentioned in the text. Add further examples of your own.

f. Discuss the following questions.

1. How did Tesco's get its name? Give examples of how other companies created their name.
2. What were the turning points in Tesco's history, and why? Speculate as to what might happen next.
3. Not everyone loves Tesco. Why might people oppose the growth of superstores such as Tesco?

g. Check the websites of Tesco and Sainsbury. Compare the companies in terms of size (turnover, number of employees, number of stores) and the range of goods and services they offer today.

2 Companies as legal entities

a. Complete the grid with words from the article.

Legal structure	Features
Sole .... (UK) Sole proprietorship (US)	› Easy to set up. › The business is owned by one self-employed person. › The owner is personally liable for any debts.
Partnership	› Run by two or more self-employed people, who share the .... as well as the costs, risks and responsibilities. › Each partner is personally liable for any debts.
Limited partnership	› Similar to an ordinary partnership, except that the liability is limited to the amount of money the partners have .... in the business. The company name is followed by LLP (UK). › At least one partner must have unlimited liability (the 'sleeping partner').
Limited liability company	› The company's finances are separate from the personal finances of their owners, who have limited liability. › The people who run the business can be different from the owners (i.e. the ....). › There are several official procedures to follow, e.g. publishing accounts.
Also known as: Joint-stock company (UK) Stock corporation (US)	**Two types:** › 1. .... limited company, which cannot offer its shares for sale to the public. The company name is followed by .... (UK). › 2. .... limited company, whose shares are offered to the public and .... on the .... exchange. The company name is followed by .... (UK) or Inc / Corp (US). When a company goes public, this is known as a flotation or an Initial Public Offering (IPO).
.... company	› Has .... in several countries that are owned and controlled by the parent or holding company, and who refer to each other as affiliates.
Cooperative	› Owned and run by the people involved, who share the profits.

b. Discuss the pros and cons of each legal structure. Which would you recommend for Footloose Fandango (p. 21)?

c. Conduct research into the types of company that exist in another country (not the UK or US). Produce a grid modelled on the one above and present your results in class. Be prepared to answer questions.

LANGUAGE TIP

Translating legal terms
Do not try to translate terms that are specific to a particular legal system. Instead, use the original term and explain it, or say what it is equivalent to.

C Language | Jobs and responsibilities

1 Describing tasks

a. Copy the diagram below and add as many examples as you can *in three minutes* of the tasks and responsibilities of managers.

LANGUAGE TIP

Collocations
Collocations are combinations of words that commonly go together, e.g.

- He changed his mind. (NOT ~~changed his thoughts~~)
- You're absolutely right. (NOT ~~totally right~~)
- I do the bookkeeping. (NOT ~~make the bookkeeping~~)

Using the right combinations will make your English sound more natural. Learn them as if they were one word.

b. Compare your results with other pairs / groups. Develop your mind map further, and highlight examples of useful verb-noun collocations.

c. Match the parts to create logical statements about jobs and responsibilities. Write on a separate sheet.

1. I work in the Purchasing	we invent new products	the buildings and machinery.
2. I'm in charge of organising	to identify what kind of	running the company.
3. In Market Research we try	I'm in charge of	components from suppliers.
4. As a maintenance officer	organise distribution	with all kinds of people problems.
5. Here in Logistics we	courses for employees	products and brands.
6. In the Marketing Dept.	Resources Dept., dealing	everything to do with computers.
7. I'm the CEO, which	Department where we order	and transportation.
8. In Research & Development	my job is to look after	products customers want.
9. I'm an IT specialist, so	we promote the company's	in the Training Department.
10. I work in the Human	means I'm responsible for	and improve current ones.

d. Choose four of the departments listed on the right and write statements that employees who work in those departments might make about their jobs. Then read out the statements, leaving out the name of the department or job. Can other students guess which one you are referring to?

WORD BANK

Customer Relations | Sales | Shipping | Advertising | Quality Assurance | Legal Department | Finance | Production | Public Relations

2 Company structure

a. The operations of Selaware PLC are split into four divisions. The board of directors oversees the management board and represents the interests of the shareholders. Decide which of the departments and jobs listed above belong to which part of Selaware PLC, and produce a more detailed version of the organisation chart below.

INFO

Management structure
There is no direct equivalent in the US or UK of the two-tier management structure characteristic of German companies, where there is a supervisory board (*Aufsichtsrat*) and an executive board (*Vorstand*) with worker representation. Also, there is no legal obligation to provide for worker participation (*Mitbestimmung*).

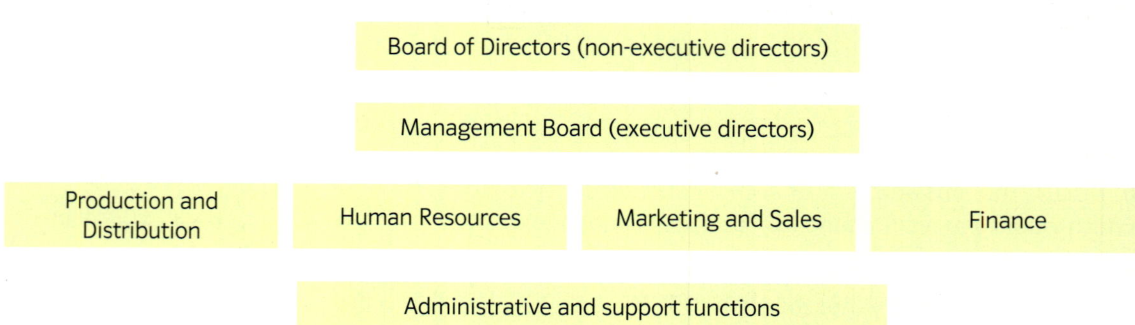

b. Describe the company structure of Selaware PLC on the basis of your organisation chart.

3 Listening: Organisational structure

a. You are going to hear a short lecture on company structure. Before you listen, match the terms with the definitions on the right.

1. subordinate
2. delegation
3. span of control
4. delayering
5. line managers
6. chain of command

a. the practice of removing managers from an organisation to make it more flexible
b. someone who is accountable to someone more senior in the organisation
c. those who have objectives set, have specific authority and are part of an organisational structure
d. the number of subordinates a manager has authority over
e. how instructions are passed down the organisation and feedback is passed up
f. the power to give a certain amount of authority or responsibility to someone else in the organisation.

A 1.9 **b.** Now listen to Part 1 of the lecture and take notes in the grid below.

Two types of business mentioned:

....

Three factors affecting the structure of organisations:

....

Why small businesses have less formal structures:

....

What the formal structures of large organisations can show:

....

A 1.10 **c.** Listen to Part 2. Number the diagrams in the order in which they are mentioned.

flat pyramid structure

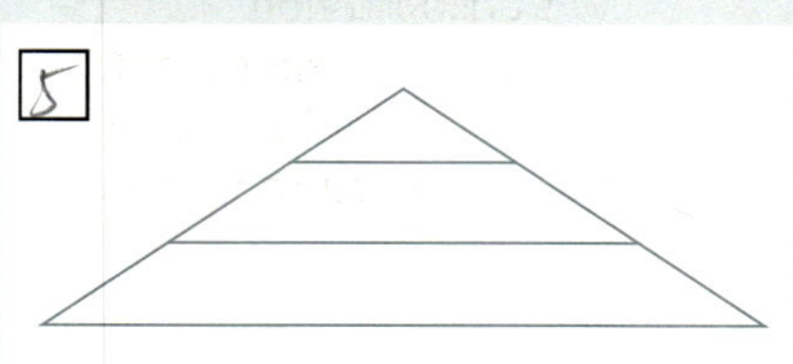

cat's cradle structure

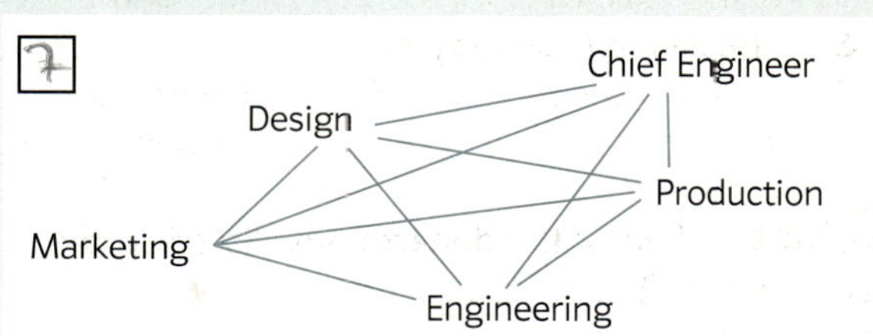

pyramid structure

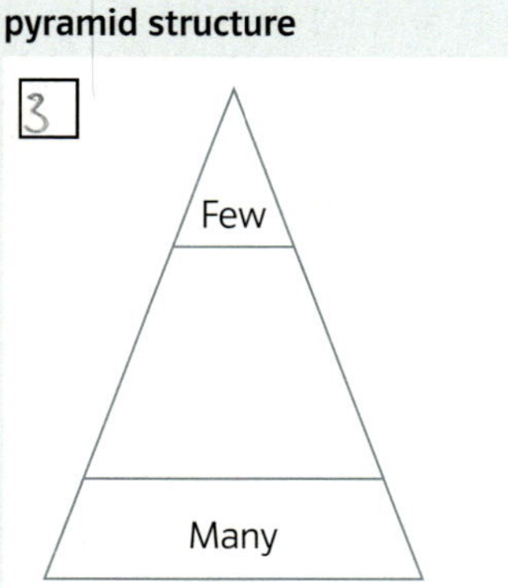

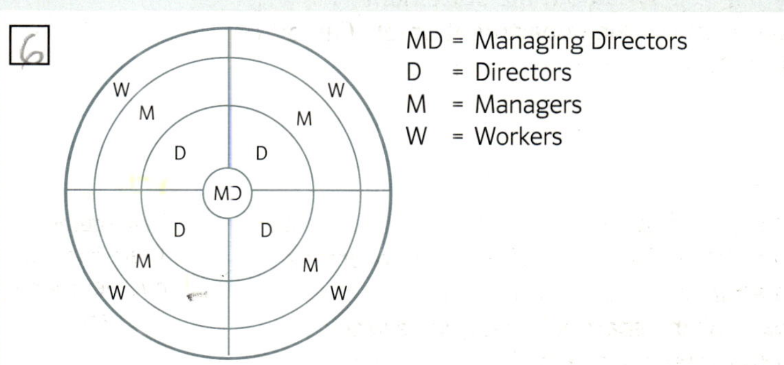

hierarchical pyramid

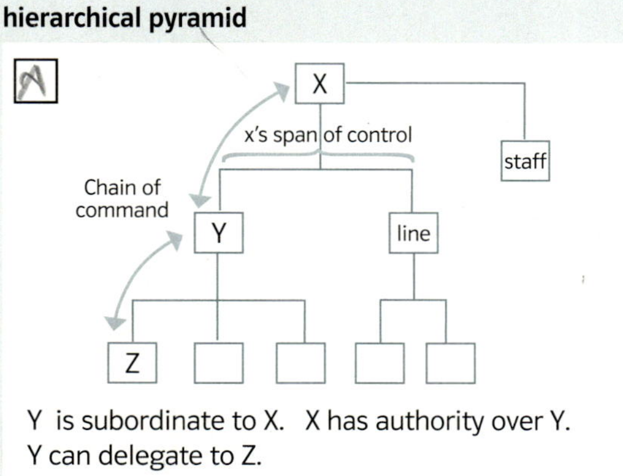

tall pyramid structure

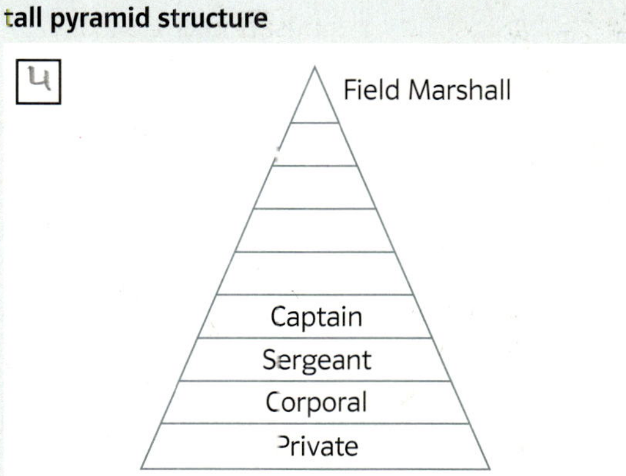

d. Choose one of the following tasks:

Task A
Prepare and deliver a short presentation describing the structure of an organisation you know, e.g. your college or the company you work for. If there is no existing organisation chart, you can design one. Suggest any improvements to the existing structure.

Task B
Work in teams to devise an organigram of a fictitious company in which you are managers. Decide on the company's main activity, the legal form, the departments, and how they are structured. Decide who does what and who reports to whom.

PHRASES

Describing company structure
- The company is organised according to region / product / process / function.
- The supervisory board oversees the executive board.
- The company is split into four main divisions / areas.
- Each division / area is sub-divided into several departments.
- The Human Resources Manager / Director is in charge of … / is responsible for …
- There are two clerks in the Payroll Department, who report to … / work for … / assist …
- The Head of Training liaises with … / works closely with …
- This job entails … / involves …

4 Intonation

A 1.11 **Circle or underline the syllable that is stressed. Then listen and check.**

1. **SU**-PER-VISE
2. SU-PER-**VI**-SOR-Y
3. EX-E-CU-TIVE
4. EX-E-CUTE
5. AD-MIN-IS-TRA-TIVE
6. AD-MIN-IS-TRA-TION
7. REP-RE-SENT-A-TION
8. REP-RE-SENT-A-TIVE
9. OB-LI-GA-TION
10. OB-LI-GA-TOR-Y
11. PAR-TI-CI-PATE
12. PAR-TI-CI-PA-TION

LANGUAGE TIP

Intonation
With some words, there are regional variations in intonation (the rise and fall of the voice and the rhythm of speech) as well as pronunciation.

AD-VER-TISE-MENT (BE)
[əd'vɜ:tismənt]

AD-VER-TISE-MENT (AE)
[ˌædvə'taɪzmənt]

False friends
chef ≠ *Chef*
boss = *Chef*
chef = *Koch*
chief (n). = *Häuptling*
chief (adj.) = *Haupt-*

5 False friends and idioms

a. **Give the correct alternative to the false friends.**

1. One day you might become a successful ~~undertaker~~.
2. My ~~chef~~ told me not to work so hard.
3. The ~~Personal~~ Department deals with employing and training people.
4. There's an organisation chart on the ~~blackboard~~ outside my office.
5. They closed the department because it wasn't ~~rentable~~ enough.

b. **Explain these idioms and how they might be used when talking about organisations.**

1. Too many chiefs and not enough Indians.
2. Too many chefs spoil the broth.

6 Discussion

a. 'Chief' can be used as an adjective for top management titles such as chief executive officer, chief financial officer and chief operating officer ('C-Level' jobs). However, it can make some jobs sound more important than they really are. Discuss the titles below. What do they refer to? Do you see them as important or 'inflated'?

1. chief ethics officer (Hewlett Packard)
2. chief diversity officer (Siemens)
3. chief privacy officer (IBM)
4. chief cultural officer (Google)
5. chief reputation officer (vMoksha Technologies)

b. The Senior Manager of Proactive Customer Communications of an international airline has been dubbed 'Chief Apology Officer'. Why might an airline need someone to do this job?

c. A Wharton Business School professor, Betsey Stevenson, claims that people who push for higher titles are "The same ones who, as students, pushed for 'A's and caused grade inflation. Now they are making it into the corporate world and they want big titles". Do you agree with her? And is grade inflation a problem? If so, suggest what can be done to limit the problem.

D Business leaders | Charles Handy

1 Reading

Charles Handy described organisations in terms of four distinct cultures, each represented by a Greek god. As you read, match the cultures to the gods listed below. Which culture do you think you would fit into best, and why? Do you find these models helpful?

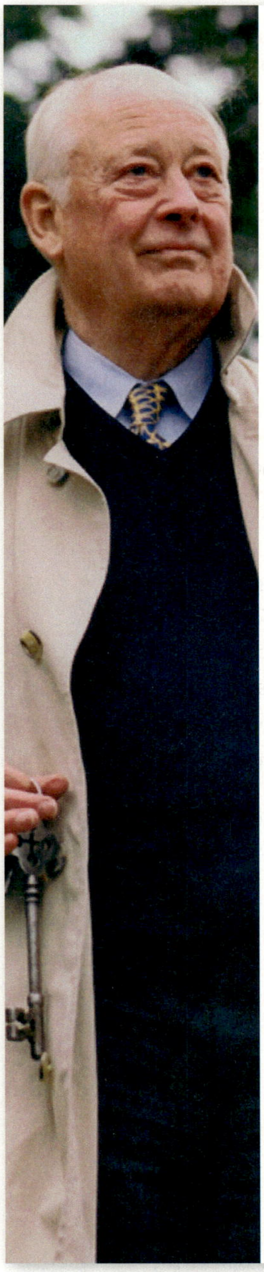

Charles Handy (born 1932) is one of the most influential management thinkers in the world. He graduated from Oxford University and worked for Shell International before becoming a professor at the London Business School. He is best known for his books on the purpose of work, business and organisations.

POWER CULTURE – This culture is like a spider's web, with the boss at the centre. Like a web, there are ever-widening circles of influence spreading outwards, affecting the other people in the organisation. The closer to the centre you are, the more power you have, because power radiates out from the boss. The personal relationship with the boss matters more than formal titles or positions. The idea of a power culture is that the organisation is a club that exists to promote the persona of the boss. If you are part of the club, it can be an exciting place to work. If you want to succeed and grow closer to the centre of influence, you have to share the views and beliefs of the boss.

ROLE CULTURE – Often referred to as a bureaucracy, the picture of this organisation is a pyramid made of boxes, with a job title in each box. Even if the individual leaves the box, the structure will continue because the boxes do not change. The boxes are joined together in a logical structure that allows the work of the organisation to be done effectively. Individuals are 'role occupiers' with precise job descriptions and responsibilities. Communication passes from one job title to another job title, rather than from one individual to another. Such cultures thrive on routine.
Difficulties occur if they are confronted with change or exceptions to the norm. Role cultures are managed, not led.

TASK CULTURE – The emphasis here is on the task itself, which involves teamwork and problem solving. The organisational idea is of a team of talents or resources that can deal with a specific task or project in a less individualistic way than a Power Culture, and quicker than a Role Culture. The process dislikes the routine of administration and sees the reward of solving one problem as being given another one. Warm, friendly and meritocratic, the culture is built around supportive groups of colleagues. It can be expensive, because it requires professional, competent people to spend a lot of time talking to each other. Usually a task culture will have team leaders rather than managers.

PERSON CULTURE – Here, individual talent is all-important, and professionals who possess the special talent and have tenure and high status. The organisation exists so that individuals can achieve their purposes. If there is a structure it exists only to serve those individuals, and administrative staff have lower status. They tend to have strong values about how they will work, and are often difficult for the organisation to manage. Professionals in such cultures can be persuaded, not commanded; influenced or bargained with , but not managed.

to radiate austrahlen, **role occupier** Rollenbesitzer, **to thrive** gedeihen, blühen, **meritocratic** leistungsorientiert

The Gods	Typical areas of business
Apollo: God of order and rules	The civil service, life insurance
Athena: Goddess of knowledge	Advertising agencies, consultancies, study groups, working parties
Dionysus: God of wine and song	Universities, doctors or lawyers in a practice with 'no boss'
Zeus: The strong leader	Small entrepreneurial firms, political groups, investment banks

2 Discussion

Charles Handy also advanced the idea of the Shamrock organisation, a structure consisting of three distinct parts: (1) a core staff of highly trained professionals who form the senior management, (2) freelance specialists or contractual workers, (3) flexible force of part-time, temporary workers or seasonal workers. To what extent is this true of where you work or study? Give examples.

E Business communication | Presentations

1 Discussion

a. Compare the types of presentation in the box. In what ways are they different? Which ones are you likely to give in future, either in your studies or your career?

INFO

Types of presentation
talk | demonstration | sales pitch | speech | lecture | group presentation | multimedia | training

b. Comment on these presentation tips. Are there any that you disagree with? Explain why.

1. Tell people what you're going to say. Then say it. Then tell them what you've said.
2. Presentations should never last more than 20 minutes.
3. Keep it short and simple (KISS principle). No one ever complains about a presentation being too short.
4. Avoid 'death by PowerPoint'. It's difficult for people to listen and look at the same time.
5. Don't overload people with information. Nobody can remember more than three points.
6. For every minute of presentation time, spend one hour of preparation time.
7. Wear something unusual or eye-catching.
8. Allow the audience to ask questions during your presentation.
9. Start with an ice-breaker, for example an interesting anecdote, a rhetorical question or a joke.
10. Don't read from notes. Use prompt cards if necessary.
11. Be well prepared for questions.

c. Suggest further tips.

2 Listening: Company presentation

A 1.12 **a.** You are going to hear a short presentation by Peter Haas of the Weindler-Haas Design Consultancy. As you listen, number the slides in the right order. Then listen again and complete the missing information.

COMPANY OF THE YEAR AWARD ☐
Innovative packaging that is:
....
Now expanding into:
....

WELCOME TO W&H DESIGN CONSULTANCY ☐
Part One: ....
Part Two: ....
Part Three: Company of the Year Award – why us?

W&H DESIGN CONSULTANCY ☐
2003: Founded .... with office in Munich
2005: Set up Weindler-Haas Interactive Studio
2007: Offices in ....

TWO SUCCESSFUL PROJECTS ☐
Green Genie: packaging that can
....
Jet Pak: aerosol spray that is
....

A 1.12 **b.** Complete the phrases. Then listen again to check.

1. Good morning, everyone. Are we .... to begin?
2. I'd like to .... myself. My name is Peter Haas.
3. Today, I'm .... a success story.
4. I've .... my presentation .... three parts.
5. If you have ...., I'd be .... to .... them at the end of my presentation.
6. Thank you for your .... And now, if you have any ...., I'd be .... to answer them.

c. Note down any questions that you might ask if you were in the audience.

A 1.13 **d.** Now listen to Part 2. What were the questions, and how did the presenter deal with them?

e. Look at these responses to questions from the audience. Which show that the question was unclear (UC), and which show that the presenter is 'playing for time' (PT)?

1. That's a good question, thank you.
2. I'm glad you asked that question.
3. Could you repeat your question, please?
4. I'm sorry, but I don't know the answer to that one.
5. Sorry, I didn't catch your question.
6. Just a moment, let's go back to the first slide.

3 Simulation

a. You are going to attend the annual event 'Company of the Year Award', where some of you will be representing the companies and presenting a 'pitch' to the jury. This prize is worth €10,000 to the winner, so competition is tough. Before you start, decide which part you will play:

- Member of the jury
- Presenter in a group presentation (max. four)
- Presenter in an individual presentation.

b. Depending on the part you have chosen, follow the instructions below. The tips will also help you.

Jury Discuss what you will look for in a company that deserves the award "Company of the Year", and how you will come to your decision. Create two lists:
1. Criteria for 'Company of the Year Award'.
2. Checklist to compare and evaluate the companies.
Distribute the criteria for 'Company of the Year Award' to the presenters to help them prepare.

Group presenters Choose one of the companies on page 21 (Part A of this unit), and make sure that no other group has chosen the same company. Brainstorm how you will structure the presentation and decide who will present which part. Prepare a presentation that meets the criteria given to you by the judges. You will need to invent details, so here is an opportunity to be creative!

Individual presenters Decide on any company that you think deserves the title and carry out research. Prepare a presentation that meets the criteria given to you by the judges, and also create any handouts that they might find useful. Make sure you get your facts right, because they will probably ask you questions about details.

Tips for presenters

Follow these five steps.
1. Introduction: Summarise what the presentation is about. Give clear information in the form of 'signposts' to the audience.
2. Facts and figures: Present three key pieces of information about the company.
3. Key strengths and successes: Give three points that will impress the judges.
4. Make your pitch: Explain why your company should win the award.
5. Summarise the main points.

Use OHP or PowerPoint slides if you think they will help you, and refer to the phrases in the fold-out cover.

Tips for the judges

As you listen, take notes and be prepared to 'grill' the candidates on aspects such as the following:
1. What does the company do? Is it clear?
2. What is the company's value to society?
3. Can the presenter support claims that the company is so successful?
4. Why is it better than other candidates?
5. What will it do with the prize money?
6. Is anything unclear or unconvincing? Think of 'probing' questions that you can ask.
7. Later discuss how skilled the presenters were at dealing with your questions.

c. Take turns giving your presentations. While others are presenting, make notes so that you can ask them questions about their company.

d. When everyone in the group has given their presentation, hold a vote to find the winner of the Company of the Year Award.

F Consulting | Planning an internship/semester abroad

1 Choosing a company

In this task, you will be working in pairs to help each other find an internship or work placement. You will interview each other and carry out research in order to find three suitable companies to recommend to your partner.

LANGUAGE TIP
British / American?
BE: work placement
AE: internship

a. Do the questionnaire on your own first. Add any further points about your preferences.

Questionnaire Finding the right internship

1 Motivation: Why do you want to do an internship? Tick the statements that apply to you.

[ ] It's part of my studies. I have to do an internship.
[ ] I'd like to improve my foreign language skills.
[ ] I'd like to experience working in another culture.
[ ] I'd like to gain work experience in general.
[ ] It will look good on my CV.

2 Location: Is there any particular region or country that interests you? If so, give examples and reasons.

[ ] I don't mind where I do my internship.
[ ] I would prefer to work in ____________________
____

3 Sector: What type of sector or area would you prefer to work in?

[ ] I have no preference. Any sector or area would be fine.
[ ] I would prefer to work in ____________________

4 Other aspects: Is there a sector or company that you would not work for, e.g. for ethical reasons?

[ ] I don't mind which sector or type of business I work in.
[ ] I would not want to work for a company that
____

5 Company size: What size of company would you prefer to work in?

[ ] I'd prefer to work in a large company because ____________________
[ ] I'd prefer to work in a small company because ____________________
[ ] I don't mind how big the company is, as long as I have interesting tasks to do.

6 Departments (variety): How important is it for you to work in different departments?

[ ] I'd like to work in one area or department in order to specialise.
[ ] I'd like to work in several areas or departments, but not too many.
[ ] I'd like to work in as many different departments as possible.

7 Departments (type): List up to three departments you would like to work in, in order of preference.

1. ____________________
2. ____________________
3. ____________________

8 Tasks: What tasks or skills would you like to develop? Give three examples, in order of preference.

1. ____________________
2. ____________________
3. ____________________

9 Your skills: What can you offer? In one sentence, explain how a company could benefit from you.

____
____
____

10 Further preferences: List any further points that are important in your choice of internship.

____
____
____
____
____
____

b. Use the same questionnaire to interview your partner. Note the answers on a separate sheet.

c. From your notes, produce a profile of your partner's requirements and what he or she can offer a company during the internship or work placement.

d. Carry out research into companies that your partner might be interested in applying to. Draw up a shortlist of three companies. Note down information about each company, including the URL and any useful contact details.

e. Write the results of your research in the form of a short report giving recommendations to your partner. You can use the template below as the basis for your report.

To: **(your partner's name)**
From: **(your name)**
Re: Internship opportunities – some recommendations
Date: **(today's date)**

Dear **(your partner's name)**

Thank you for asking me for advice about internship opportunities, and for agreeing to answer my questions in the interview. I have since analysed your responses, and on the basis of my research I would like to recommend the following three companies.

1. **(first choice)**
2. **(second choice)**
3. **(third choice)**

I chose these companies for the following reasons:
(List the reasons, weighing up the pros and cons.)

If you have any questions about my recommendations or would like help with your application, please do not hesitate to contact me again.
In the meantime, I look forward to hearing which company you have chosen and wish you a successful and enjoyable internship.

Regards

(Your name)

f. Ask your partner to comment on your report. Was it helpful? What would you do differently next time?

2 Choosing a university

Find someone who needs advice on choosing a university or business school for a study semester abroad. Prepare a questionnaire similar to the one on the left. Adapt the questions to the situation, considering aspects such as the following:

- Type of institution
- Type of course
- Size of institution
- Reputation
- Country
- Location
- Culture
- Cost of course

PHRASES

Evaluating options
- X has the advantage of being …
- Y, on the other hand, is …
- As you can see, Z is …, whereas Y is …
- You mentioned that you would like to … In this respect, Z would be a good option.
- However, if you prefer to …, then X would probably be the best choice.

Unit 3
Money and payment

Online Link 800021-0003

A Introduction | Methods of payment

1 Quick response

How might these people like to be paid, and why?

taxi drivers | landlords | employees | online retailers | plumbers

WORD BANK

Methods of payment
barter | cash | cheque (AE check) | coins | credit transfer | credit card | debit card | direct debit | note (AE bill) | prepaid card | standing order | traveller's cheque (AE traveler's check)

2 Reading

Relative importance of the main payment instruments in the EU: Percentages of total volume of transactions (2007)

	Credit transfers	Direct debits	Cards	Cheques
Germany	36.0	48.3	14.5	0.6
UK	21.0	19.9	48.4	10.7
Poland	68.4	1.2	30.4	0.0
Denmark	20.6	13.7	64.8	0.9

Source: ECB

a. Comment on the statistics in the table, dealing with the points listed below.

- Comparisons between and within countries
- Possible reasons for the differences
- Companies who might find these statistics useful
- Future trends: forms of payment that are likely to decrease / increase in relative importance

b. Find the latest statistics from the European Central Bank (ECB) and information about payment methods preferred in the US. Comment on factors that you find interesting or surprising.

PHRASES

Discussing statistics
- Hardly anyone …
- Relatively few people …
- The vast majority of people …
- … account(s) for almost … % of …
- The percentage of people who … is negligible.
- The use of … is significantly higher in … than in …
- The use of … is slightly lower in … than in …
- The most / least popular … is …
- This could be because …

3 Reading and discussion

a. Match the views expressed by the people below to the questions that prompted them.

1. Does talking about money embarrass you?
2. What do you hate about dealing with money?
3. How do you prefer to pay?
4. How do you tip?
5. Do you bank online?
6. Have you ever learned any difficult lessons about money?

b. Discuss what individuals and cultures have in common in their dealings with money, and how they differ.

Ken Hom, Chinese American chef

"I like the American system where you don't have to tip someone who doesn't perform – it infuriates me in France that I get shoddy service and there's a 15 % service charge anyway."

"It's not an indiscretion to talk about money in Chinese culture. In China you are commonly asked how many pieces of real estate you own by people who have only just met you."

"I hate what it does to families. It makes them greedy and they start plotting."

"I like cash, but I used credit cards for convenience. I am one of these people credit card companies hate – I always pay off my balance in full."

Katie Melua, singer/songwriter from Georgia

"When relatives in Georgia want to borrow from me I usually end up giving it to them and not asking for it back. My relatives don't have a realistic sense of the money I have. They don't understand mortgages, for example, because lending money in Georgia has only just begun."

"I have dual nationality and I was advised early on that I could take advantage of that to put some earnings offshore to avoid tax. (...) I pay nearly half of what comes to me in taxes."

"If it's just standard service, I'll only give a standard 15 %."

Vic Reeves, British comedian

"I don't like talking to my bank or looking at statements. It's a mutual hatred."

"By debit card – I've got only one. I also use a prepaid card. This helps me manage my money because you can only use what's loaded on to it, which is great for spenders like me. It also helps me to support charity as all the profits from transaction fees are donated back to the cause... and the card is free."

"No, I don't like doing much online. I don't even really like going into a bank. When I first started working, I used to keep my wages under my mattress. I like having my money physically close to me."

Maureen Lipmann, British actress

"I was defrauded 12 years ago – someone stole my chequebook. This was before the rise of modern credit card fraud. In the end the money was refunded, but it was pretty scary that the bank cleared it without checking properly."

"I'm quite fond of cheques, but I also use plastic and pay the balance off at the end of the month. I worry about credit cards in garages. I've read about unscrupulous people behind the counter skimming your cards."

"Yes, but only because if you are British you are conditioned into believing talking about money is bad."

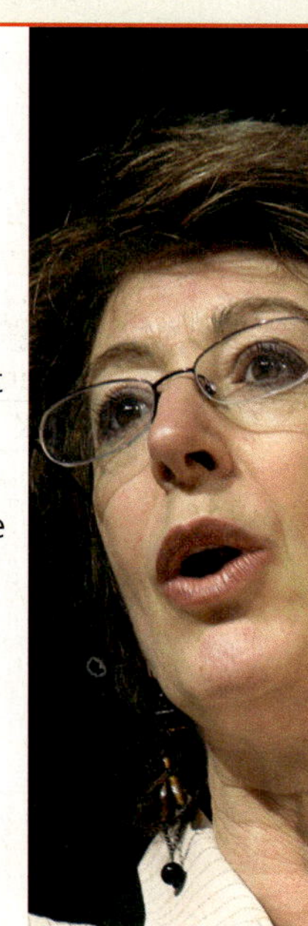

From: The Daily Telegraph, Fame and Fortune, Nov–Dec. 2008

to infuriate wütend machen, **shoddy** schäbig, **greedy** habgierig, **mutual** gegenseitig, **unscrupulous** skrupellos, **garage** (hier) Tankstelle, **(good) cause** (guter) Zweck

B Business briefing | Cash flow

1 Reading

a. Before you read, list examples of financial problems that students typically have. Then read the article and the comments on the next page and do the tasks below.

b. Make notes under the following headings. Then compare notes. Add further examples to each category.

- Sources of income: loan, …
- Expenditure: rent, …
- Tips for saving: share costs with friends, …

c. Explain the following expressions.

1. to make a dent in the lump sum
2. a nine-to-five lifestyle

SKILLS

Working without a dictionary

If there are a lot of 'new' words in a text, don't panic.

- You should still be able to understand the main points.
- When you try to guess from the context, you're probably guessing right.
- Even native speakers don't understand everything they read.

d. Discuss whether full-time students should concentrate on their studies instead of earning money.

2 Listening: Managing cash flow

a. Before you listen, discuss how each of the measures listed below could be used to improve a business's cash flow.

ask for a bigger overdraft | threaten customers with legal action | lease rather than buy | ask for payment in stages | improve stock control | negotiate with suppliers | charge interest for late payment | assess credit risk | offer discounts | send reminders if payment is overdue | sell assets | issue prompt invoices

INFO

Cash flow

This is the balance between money received and paid by a business in a particular period, especially as it affects liquidity.

A 1.14 **b.** You will hear an interview in which a financial expert describes ways of improving cash flow. Identify items in the list above that he refers to, and list other measures that he recommends.

c. Complete the sentences in your own words.

1. Cash is like oxygen because …
2. Companies can run into cash flow problems when …

Video lounge Can't Pay, Won't Pay

BBC Motion Gallery

V 1 **a.** Before watching, discuss the questions below.

1. What are the most reliable sources of credit available to borrowers?
2. Are there any that you think should be avoided? Why?
3. Should lenders treat debtors who can't pay differently to those who won't pay?
4. What reasonable steps can lenders take to recover 'bad debt'?

b. Watch the video 'Can't Pay, Won't Pay' and compare the two cases, noting:

- Their attitudes to money
- Their attitudes to being in debt
- The difference in the situations they face
- The way they deal with the situation

STUDENT FINANCE: a balanced equation

Most students get into debt, but a few simple budgeting sums can ensure things don't get out of hand

Budgeting: The key is to get on top of things right from the beginning. Work out exactly what you've got coming in – student loan, any grants and bursaries, parental contribution – and then tot up your outgoings. As a rough guide you should budget between £6,500 and £7,500 per academic year to cover living costs such as rent, energy, food, clothes, books, transport and socialising. Most universities have online budget planners to get you started.

Remember the hidden costs of living: Do you know how much a load of laundry costs to wash and dry? What about a TV licence? Make sure your budget includes insurance too: Student digs can be targeted by opportunistic criminals.

Think long term: Don't get carried away when your student loan hits your bank account. The first few weeks of term will quickly make a dent in the lump sum as rent gets paid, book lists arrive and a round of giddy socialising begins. "It looks like a lot of money when you get it in September but it has to last until January," warns Barbara Wooden, senior welfare adviser at Northumbria University.

Spend wisely: Shop with friends to share the costs of common items such as cooking oil, salt and loo roll and steer clear of expensive brands: go for supermarket value ranges. Learn to cook, too: frequent takeaways add to your waistline and quickly subtract from your bank account. Make good use of college and public libraries rather than buying books; if you have to make purchases, go down the second-hand route.

Stay informed: Make sure you know what's going in and out of your bank account to avoid nasty surprises. "Students don't live a nine-to-five lifestyle so register for internet and telephone banking so you can get access to your accounts at times that suit you," says Catherine McGrath, director of current accounts at Lloyds TSB.

Ditch the car: From petrol to insurance, it's a crippling expense. Most student accommodation is within walking or cycling distance of the main campus and even those further afield can take advantage of discounted student travel on buses and trains.

Make a little extra: Most students end up working part-time to supplement their income. Most jobs are minimum wage but look out for better paying opportunities: some universities pay £10 an hour for students willing to take on admin or ambassadorial roles, while private tuition can pay even more. The recommended maximum is 16 hours a week.

Don't struggle in silence: If your debts are getting out of control, speak to your university student-finance advisers. They will be able to help with budgeting.

Amy McLellan, *The Independent*, 17 September 2008

"I'm a bit of a geek, so I used an Excel spreadsheet to keep track of my money. I knew what I had to pay for and I'd put that money to one side so I couldn't touch it. You have to learn how to be strict with yourself and work out your own system."

Victoria McBride, 23, graduate of Lancaster University

"Keep an eye out for money-saving incentives. Many retailers offer discounts on student essentials such as books, music and computer equipment."

Lucy Payne, youth manager, HSBC

"If you live in private accommodation, pay utility bills monthly rather than quarterly: it's easier to manage that way. Also, make sure all the tenants' names are on the bill, not just yours."

Barbara Wooden, welfare adviser, Northumbria University

"Get advice on all your entitlements, such as bursaries, welfare benefits, childcare grants and disability allowances."

Meg Vickers, Manchester Metropolitan University student union

"Keep track of your money by signing up for free text alerts that tell you what your balance is and let you know when you are about to go into unplanned overdraft. When you're having a fantastic time, it can be easy to lose track of how much you are spending."

Catherine McGrath, director, Lloyds TSB

"Don't go to the cashpoint every day. Try to allocate a certain amount of cash to last all week and then stick to it. When you use cashpoints, make sure they don't charge a handling fee."

Tricia Joyce, student financial support officer, Manchester Metropolitan University

to get out of hand aus dem Ruder laufen, **to tot up** zusammenrechnen, **digs (sl.)** Wohnung, Bude, **giddy socialising** ausgelassenes Feiern, **loo roll** Klopapier, **to steer clear of** vermeiden, **crippling expense** großer finanzieller Aufwand, **tuition** (hier) Nachhilfe, **to struggle**, sich abrackern, sich abmühen

C Language | Money

1 Automated Teller Machine (ATM)

a. Match the customer requirements with the ATM screen instructions.

1. read everything in English
2. find out how much money you have in your account
3. take money out of your account
4. move money from one account to another
5. pay money into your own account
6. buy US dollars
7. find out how many dollars you'll get for 50 euros
8. get a list of changes to the money in your account

a. withdraw cash
b. print statement
c. deposit cash
d. choose language
e. transfer funds
f. choose currency
g. do a balance enquiry
h. check exchange rate

b. Put the instructions into a logical order.

Please remove your card. | Please enter your personal identification number (PIN). | Please take your receipt. | Please select a service. | Your cash is being counted. | Welcome. Please insert your card. | Please take your cash and wait for the receipt. | Please key in the amount you require.

c. Discuss these questions.

1. What other services do ATMs offer? Do ATMs in Germany charge for these services?
2. What problems sometimes happen at ATMs? Suggest what people can do to avoid these problems.

2 Money idioms

a. Match the idioms with the German equivalents.

1. Money's **tight** at the moment.
2. She made **a small fortune**.
3. All our cash is **tied up** in the business.
4. You need to **tighten** your **belts**.
5. We're **in the black** at last.
6. I have to **cough up** again.
7. She's been on a **spending binge** again.
8. I picked up some great **bargains** in the sales.
9. They're running the business **on a shoestring**.
10. Now they're **raking it in**.

a. schwarze Zahlen schreiben
b. tüchtig absahnen
c. den Gürtel enger schnallen
d. das Geld locker machen
e. fest angelegt
f. knapp
g. Kauforgie
h. mit wenig Geld
i. ein kleines Vermögen
j. Schnäppchen

b. Explain an idiom in plain English. Can your partner guess which one you are referring to?

3 Prepositions

a. Put in the prepositions. (In some cases they can be left out.)

When I go out in the evenings, I usually pay .... cash, but I pay .... big purchases .... credit card. I always pay .... my balance .... full. I don't like being .... debt. I used to pay .... cheque, but hardly any supermarkets accept cheques nowadays. My salary is paid .... my current account. I spend most of it .... groceries, clothes and household bills, so there isn't much left .... my account .... the end of the month. I pay fixed amounts such as rent and insurance .... standing order and I put €100 .... every month because I'm saving ...., I don't waste money .... expensive haircuts. My sister runs her own hair salon and cuts my hair .... free.

b. 'Pay' or 'pay for'?

1. the goods
2. a high rate of interest
3. a haircut
4. the invoice
5. a low amount
6. my monthly rent
7. tax
8. a pair of shoes
9. tuition fees
10. Chinese lessons

LANGUAGE TIP

Pay or pay for?
pay + money word (I'll pay the tip.)
pay + request for payment (I'll pay the bill.)
pay for + what is bought (I'll pay for the meal.)

c. Practise using prepositions and the finance vocabulary by writing a summary of how you budget.

4 Fine-tuning

a. Choose from the words below to complete the sentences.

fine | expenditure | penalty | fee | charge | lend | borrow | expenses | fare

1. People who don't pay their tax on time have to pay a .... for late payment.
2. I had to pay a speeding .... for driving 34 km/h in a 30 km/h zone.
3. It's cheaper to .... books from the library than to buy them.
4. British Airways is offering a special one-way .... of €70 for students flying to London.
5. Always ask lawyers about their ....s before taking legal action.
6. Many restaurants add on a 10 % service ....
7. Would you be prepared to cover my travel ....?
8. The budget provides for a total .... of $26 billion.

b. Write an example sentence with the ninth word.

c. Replace the false friend in the sentences below.

Example: Our agent gets a ~~provision~~ of 10 % on sales. → commission

1. Many old people find it difficult to live on their state ~~rent~~.
2. I'll have to ask my bank for a bigger ~~credit~~.
3. Ask for a ~~recipe~~ as proof of purchase.
4. Please complete and return the enclosed ~~formula~~.
5. Please go to the ~~cash~~ with your purchases.
6. We can offer you a 5 % ~~rebate~~ for early payment.
7. It is important to ~~control~~ your bank statements carefully.
8. Online shopping may be ~~comfortable~~ but it isn't always safe.

5 Explaining an invoice

a. The invoice below also serves as a receipt. Study the invoice and identify the following (1. – 14.):

1. Name und Anschrift des Verkäufers
2. Name und Anschrift des Käufers
3. Umsatzsteuernummer
4. Ausstellungsdatum
5. Rechnungsnummer
6. Menge und Art der gelieferten Artikel
7. Zeitpunkt der Lieferung
8. Nettobetrag
9. Bruttobetrag
10. Steuersatz
11. Steuerbetrag
12. Lieferkosten
13. Zahlungsart
14. aktueller Wechselkurs

b. Check the current conversion rate. What would the order total be in euros today?

c. Find an example of an invoice issued in your country. Explain the details in English and say which items are legally required on an invoice.

book-world.biz

Invoice for: DTRckrncR

14 June, 2009

Invoice / Receipt for:
Your order of 14 June 2009
Order ID: 026-3319407-8481161
Invoice number: DTRcdrncR
Invoice date / Date of supply:
14 June, 2009

Paid by:
Craig McNeil
Hardtstrasse 46
78054 Schwenningen

Delivered to:
Craig McNeil
Hardtstrasse 46
78054 Schwenningen

Qty	Item	Our price (excl. VAT)	VAT Rate	Total Price (excl. VAT)	Total Price (excl. VAT)
1	Writing Short Stories Cox, Alisa 0415303877, Paperback	£10.99	7.00 %	£10.99	EUR 13.84
	Shipping Subtotal (excl. VAT)			£4.98	EUR 6,27
	Subtotal (excl. VAT) (7.00 %)			£15.97	EUR 20,12
	VAT at (7.00 %)			£1.12	EUR 1,41
	Order total			£17.09	EUR 21,53
	Sale order paid by VISA			£17.09	EUR 21,53
	Balance due			£0.00	EUR 0,00

Conversion rate £1.00 (EUR 1,26)

This shipment completes your order. You can always check the status of your order or change your account details from the "Your Account" link at the top of each page on our site.
Book-world EU S.àr.l; 5, Rue Plaetis. L-2338 Luxembourg Tax ID number: 040190837
VAT number: DE814584193 Thank you for shopping at book-world.biz!

6 Pointing out mistakes

a. For each pair, decide which way of pointing out mistakes is more tactful. Explain why.

1. a. I don't normally have to pay VAT.
   b. You shouldn't have charged me VAT.
2. a. You promised me a 3% discount.
   b. Didn't we agree on a 3% discount?
3. a. Your Accounts Department has made a mistake.
   b. It looks as if a mistake has been made.
4. a. There appears to be an error in the calculation.
   b. You've miscalculated the total amount.
5. a. It seems there's been a misunderstanding.
   b. You've failed to comply with the terms.
6. a. You obviously didn't understand a word I said.
   b. Maybe I didn't express myself clearly enough.
7. a. I think we've been invoiced the wrong amount.
   b. You've overcharged us.
8. a. You didn't check the bill carefully enough.
   b. There seems to be a discrepancy in the bill.
9. a. We need a corrected invoice, please.
   b. Could you please issue a new invoice?
10. a. We have not had any response to our reminders.
    b. You have repeatedly ignored our reminders.

b. Suggest how to make the following statements more polite.

1. Send us the receipts, please.
2. You've forgotten to send the attachment.
3. We must have payment by 30 July.
4. The total amount is incorrect because you have omitted delivery charges.
5. You have neglected to follow the correct procedure.
6. I've spotted tons of mistakes in your report.
7. You haven't paid the invoice yet.
8. An exchange rate of $1 to €54 is impossible!

c. What problems can arise if you are too tactful?

LANGUAGE TIP

Pointing out mistakes
Telling someone that they have made a mistake is not easy, but tact can help. Here are some tips on using tact in English.

Use the passive to make it less personal.
- – You have made a mistake. (It's your fault.)
- + A mistake has been made. (It doesn't matter who made it.)

Allow for the possibility that it is not a mistake.
- – There is a mistake. (There's no question about it.)
- + It looks as if a mistake may have been made. (Maybe it hasn't.)

Use questions where possible.
- – You agreed to meet me at 3.30. (You forgot our appointment.)
- + Didn't we agree to meet at 3.30? (Maybe the time wasn't clear.)

Use positive words.
- – It's wrong. You forgot the VAT. (You're incompetent.)
- + The correct amount would include VAT. (Here's the solution.)

Use soft and gentle language.
- – You've made a lot of mistakes in your report.
- + A few errors have found their way into (or: crept into) your report.
- – What a cock-up!
- + It was an oversight. We all make mistakes.

Be supportive.
- – You'll have to go through it again for mistakes. (It's your problem.)
- + Would you like me to double-check for you? (I can help.)

to creep into sich einschleichen, **to double-check** nachprüfen, **cock-up** (BE) Schlamassel

7 Error-spotting

Identify and correct the mistakes.
Refer to the code below.

1. You will receive a refund of 1.345 EUR in the next days. (Punct, WM)
2. We have received your letter two days ago. (T)
3. I look forward to receive your payment. (G)
4. I've already payed the bill. (Sp)
5. I think we should discuss about the discounts. (NN)
6. I buy all my books in the internet. (Prep)
7. We offer also the option of paying by direct debit. (WO)
8. The interests on this credit are too high. (UC, FF)

Marking code

Punct	punctuation	**WW**	wrong word	**SYN**	syntax
Prep	preposition	**T**	tense	**FF**	false friend
WM	word missing	**G**	grammar	**WF**	word form
NN	word not necessary	**WO**	word order	**VF**	verb form
UC	uncountable	**St.**	style / register	**C**	convention

SKILLS

Proofreading
Marking codes can help you to identify the type of mistakes you make most often. Find out the marking code your teacher uses. How is it different from the one on the left?

D Business leaders | Philanthropists

1 Reading and discussion

Read the profiles and answer the questions below.

"I resolved to stop accumulating and begin the infinitely more serious and difficult task of wise distribution."

Andrew Carnegie (1835 – 1919)
The Andrew Carnegie story is in the true 'rags to riches' tradition. Born to a poor Scottish family that emigrated to the United States, Carnegie worked hard from childhood. He gradually built a vast steel empire and became enormously wealthy at a time of peak industrial prosperity. As a 'self-made man' from humble beginnings, he believed that the rich had an obligation to give back to society, so he gave much of his wealth away to educational foundations and other worthy causes.

Anita Roddick (1942 – 2007)
In 1976 Anita Roddick opened the first Body Shop in England, selling a range of 'ethical' cosmetics. Although she had no previous business experience, the company became highly successful. When she died in 2007, she fulfilled her promise to leave her two daughters nothing. She had told them "they would not inherit one penny". Instead, she gave away her entire £51m fortune to the Body Shop Foundation, which donates the money to charities.

"Money does not mean anything to me. The worst thing is greed. The accumulation of money."

"My advice to young people? Stay away from credit cards and bank loans and invest in yourself."

Warren Buffet (1930 –)
Warren Buffet's first business enterprise was selling newspapers as a boy. Later he took over the local textile firm Berkshire Hathaway in his hometown of Omaha, and is still the CEO today. He also made huge sums of money from investments in some of America's biggest corporations, becoming one of the world's richest men. In 2006 he gave $31 billion of his personal fortune to the Bill & Melinda Gates Foundation, and has also given billions of dollars to foundations run by his three children.

1. Compare the three philanthropists. What do they have in common, and how do they differ? Consider their background, how they became rich and what they did with their money.
2. Explain the quotes in your own words. Do you disagree with any of them?
3. Some people criticise philanthropists who give large donations to the poor or needy. Why?
4. Should parents leave money to their children? Discuss the pros and cons.

2 Vocabulary

a. Find words in the text to match the definitions.

1. a rapid rise from poverty to wealth
2. very big (two examples)
3. sb. who has become wealthy by his own efforts
4. duty
5. something deserving of support, e.g. a charity

b. Find translations for the following:

1. erben
2. Vermögen
3. für einen guten Zweck spenden
4. Stiftung, Gründung
5. Anlagen, Investitionen

c. Sort the adjectives into two groups: 'Haves' and 'have-nots'.

underclass | prosperous | well-heeled | needy | loaded | penniless | wealthy | deprived | well-off | destitute | high-income | unfortunate | starving | well-to-do | deserving | affluent | hard-up

3 Simulation

You work for an organisation that helps wealthy philanthropists donate their money wisely. A client has asked you to help her manage a $31 million donation. Decide which charities should receive the money, the amounts to be given to each, and the best way to distribute it. Present your recommendations in class.

E Business communication | Negotiating

1 Analysis

A recent study has revealed that almost half of British adults are prepared to haggle over prices. More than a third claimed to have negotiated a lower price for a new car, and 60 % said they would bargain over the price of TVs and consumer electronics. Give further examples of situations in which haggling, bargaining and negotiating often take place.

2 Listening: Haggling around town

A 1.15–18 **a.** A man is trying to haggle in London. He visits two dry-cleaners, a hairdressers and a theatre box office. Listen to his attempts and explain how successful he was in each case.

A 1.15–18 **b.** Listen again and complete the phrases below. Suggest further phrases to add to each category.

LANGUAGE TIP

Ways of doing deals
to haggle: to argue in order to get a better deal
to bargain: to discuss prices, pay or conditions in order to reach an agreement that suits everyone
to negotiate: to try to reach agreement or to arrange something by formal discussion

Negotiating prices

Requesting a service / product
- I w.................. if you m.................. be a.................. to iron this for me?
- Do you have two .... for the evening's p..................?

Asking for a price reduction:
- And w.................. you have any f.................. with that price?
- Can you k.................. 10 % ....?
- Can you r.................. them at ....?
- Can you .... it any .... than that?

Offering a price
- How .... two quid?
- How does £25 s..................?

Suggesting a compromise
- Come ....!
- If it's a b.................. order, then maybe we could .... something out.
- If you .... back b.................. the performance, then maybe.
- Can't we find some m.................. g.................. here?
- If you're .... to get it done right now, our top s.................. is free.
- You can't even m.................. on that f.................. by, say, 5 %?

Refusing an offer
- Well, I can't really .... you anything .... the one shirt.
- That's .... too much for me.
- S.................. too much, I'm ....

Making a last attempt at a deal
- Is that your f.................. o..................?

3 Discussion

a. "Germans do not haggle" (W.R. Smyser, How Germans Negotiate). Do you agree with Smyser?

b. Do you enjoy haggling? Why, or why not?

4 Negotiating a deal

a. You are going to practise four key stages of a negotiation, using the dialogue below as a model. Read the dialogue and do the tasks for each stage, taking turns as buyers and sellers of antiques.

Stage 1: Signalling interest

A: Good morning, can I help you?
B: Yes, I'm interested in this necklace. Is it genuine silver?
A: It is. It's Mexican ... antique, a very rare piece.
B: And what are the stones in it?
A: Turquoise, coral and blue quartz. It's from the Yucatan region.

SALES TIP Initiate the negotiation with a friendly greeting. When answering the buyer's questions, talk up the product by referring to further benefits.

b. Improvise the opening stage of a negotiation, where one of you is selling an antique clock. The seller should try to talk up the item.

Stage 2: Stating terms and expectations

B: It is a lovely necklace, but there's no price tag. How much are you asking for it?
A: The price is ... €300.
B: Three hundred! That's too much for me, I'm afraid.
A: Well, that's what you have to pay for the real thing. But if you want to try it on, go ahead. Look at it in the mirror over there.

SALES TIP The buyer will try to beat down your price, so be prepared. Quote a starting price that is at least 30% higher than your lowest price. Encourage the buyer to touch or try the product to 'feel' the benefit.

c. Now practise the first two stages of the negotiation, as modelled on the right. This time, one of you is selling an antique carpet.

Stage 3: Getting a deal

B: OK, thanks. Hmm ... yes, I like it, I must say. But it is rather expensive. If I paid in cash, would you give me a discount?
A: I might. What figure did you have in mind?
B: I could go to €250. That's absolutely my last offer.
A: Sorry, I can't drop the price by €50. There's been a lot of interest in this necklace. I could knock €30 off for cash, that's a 10% reduction.
B: You drive a hard bargain. OK then, but if you want cash, I'll have to go to the ATM across the street.

SALES TIP When the buyer tries to knock down the price, this can be a sticking point or even result in deadlock. In order to close the deal, the seller will have to make a concession or offer something in return.

d. Identify the two 'if clauses' used in Stage 3. How are they different, and why?

e. Suggest alternative ways of expressing the words and phrases marked in bold.

1. But it is **rather** expensive.
2. What **figure did you have in mind**?
3. That's **absolutely** my **last** offer.
4. **Sorry,** I can't **drop** the price by €50.
5. I could **knock** €30 **off**.
6. You **drive a hard bargain**.
7. I'll have to go to the **ATM** across the street.
8. This can be a **sticking point.**
9. ... or even **result in a deadlock.**
10. The seller will have to **make a concession.**

Stage 4: Closing the deal

A: No problem. If you want to reserve the necklace, you can leave a deposit of €25 and I'll take it off the display.
B: OK, I'll do that then.
A: That's great! So come with me over to the cash desk, and I'll write you a receipt for the €25 deposit. And would you like me to wrap the necklace for you?
B: That's very good of you. Thanks!

SALES TIP
....
....
....
....
....
....

f. Write up the sales tip for Stage 4.

g. Practise the whole negotiation where one of you is selling a classic car. Switch roles and try again from memory.

5 Talking about negotiating

Explain the meaning of these idioms in plain English and suggest equivalent expressions in German.

1. I can offer you a discount if you pay the first 50% **up front**.
2. I'm sure that we will be able to reach **a win-win situation**.
3. A well-prepared negotiator will always **keep an ace up his sleeve**.
4. I've presented you with my final offer – now **the ball is in your court**.
5. It was a long and difficult negotiation, but he finally **signed on the dotted line**.
6. We achieved an important **breakthrough** when we offered to pay the delivery costs.
7. I decided to lower my asking price at the start in order **to get the ball rolling**.
8. After a lot of **give-and-take** we finally reached an agreement on the price.
9. Good luck in the negotiation – she's got a reputation as a **hard-nosed** businesswoman.
10. I offered her several concessions but she refused **to give ground**.

6 Simulation 1: Negotiating a second-hand laptop

a. Decide who is going to be the buyer and who is going to be the seller. Read the advert and the instructions for your role and note down points to use in the negotiation.

Laptop for sale

- ✔ 15" screen
- ✔ Bluetooth wireless mouse
- ✔ plug-in stereo speakers
- ✔ brand-new lithium battery
- ✔ lots of software installed
- ✔ only 2 years old.

Price: €500 o.n.o

Role card: Seller

You are trying to sell a laptop. You have just advertised it on your university bulletin board, hoping for a quick sale since you need the money urgently. The laptop is in relatively good condition and comes with a lot of useful software and accessories. You hope to get more than the asking price of €500, but may have to accept a lower price. Note down points that you can use in the negotiation for talking up the laptop, and anything else you can offer to get a good deal. Decide on the minimum price you would be prepared to accept.

Role card: Buyer

You are looking for a cheap laptop that you can use for your studies. You have seen one advertised on the university bulletin board for €500. That's considerably more than you wanted to pay, but it looks like a good one. Besides, you need one as soon as possible, so you can't afford to be too picky. Note down some points that you might use in the negotiation for getting a better deal, i.e. a lower price, added benefits such as extra software, a 60-day credit period. Decide what is the maximum you would be prepared to pay.

PHRASES

Talking up a product
It comes with …
It's top of the range.
The features include …
It's still state-of-the-art.
It has the latest …
I hate to part with it, because it's …
Something I really love about it is …
One of the best things about it is …

Knocking down the price
It looks a bit scratched.
Is that the original … ?
It looks well-used.
How old is it, exactly?
It sounds a bit noisy.
It's not quite what I was expecting.
Since it's so scratched, how much would you be prepared to knock off the price?
If I paid cash, would you include …?

b. Conduct the negotiation and make a note of the deal you achieved.

c. Compare your deal with other pairs and discuss why one result was better than another.

7 Simulation 2: Negotiating a bank loan

Student A is trying to get a bank loan. Student B is a bank manager. Use the role cards on page 217 to negotiate the loan.

F Consulting | Online payments

1 Analysis and research

Upstart is a consultancy that advises start-ups. Use the search terms below and carry out the internet research needed to answer Ruby's questions in the following email. Write it up in the form of an email from Jochen to Ruby.

From: blingalong@hotmail.com
Subject: **Online payments – advice please!**
Date: Tuesday, December 30th, 04:36:05 PM CET
To: jochen.ritzmann@upstart.de
Attachment

Dear Jochen,
Sorry I didn't have time to talk when you returned my call this morning – I had to dash off for a meeting.
The reason I called was to ask about a payment system for my new business, BLING-A-LONG. As you know, I design and sell musical jewellery together with my partner Oliver. Sales have been fantastic and we've even started to get enquiries from outside Germany! As you suggested, we're going to revamp our website and create an online shop. However, we're not sure what payment system to use. Until now, customers have paid in cash or by bank transfer, but we'd consider accepting credit/debit cards for online payments. We need an option that is cost-effective, convenient and secure, both for us and for our customers. Therefore we'd appreciate your advice on the following:

- What are the advantages and disadvantages of accepting debit/credit cards?
- What types of plastic should we accept?
- Is a payment service provider (e.g. PayPal) better than an internet merchant account? Or are there any other options for online payments that you would recommend?
- Which payment terms should we accept when selling outside Germany/the EU? We don't want to give them too much credit because we can't wait long to get paid.

I look forward to your reply, and wish you a Happy New Year.
Best,
Ruby Lawson

to dash off forthetzen, **payment service provider** Zahlungsanbieter, **to revamp** umgestalten

Search terms:
e-commerce | doing business online | accepting credit cards | accepting online payments | foreign currency and exchange risks | payment terms

2 Writing

a. Write Ruby's application for an internet merchant account. Use this checklist but also be inventive.

b. Follow-up: Use the application as the basis for a negotiation between Ruby and her bank manager. Decide on the amount of the loan, the repayment period, the interest rate, security, and any other points you think are important.

Checklist: Applying for an internet merchant account

- set out your business plan, with details of cash flow and how you promote your online activities
- describe your product or service in detail
- explain how you will deliver the product or service
- list your terms and conditions for online trading
- supply your website address
- give details of your suppliers
- include details of the secure server you'll use
- supply your bank details and authority to carry out a check with credit reference agencies
- provide details of the directors or partners in the business – including full contact details

Unit 4
Products and brands

Online Link
800021-0004

A Introduction | Brands

1 Quick response

Describe your spontaneous responses to the brands you can see in the picture above. What associations spring to mind?

2 Analysis

a. Pool your knowledge of the brands listed on the right and the sectors in which they operate, and discuss the points below.

- Why the top brands were so successful
- Why the rankings of the brand consultancies differ
- Why the winners were winning and the losers were losing

b. If you were a brand researcher and could ask people in the street three questions, what would they be? Put your questions to each other.

c. Find out the current top five brands and any important or interesting trends.

TOP 5 Global Brands 2008	
1. Coca Cola	1. Google
2. IBM	2. General Electric
3. Microsoft	3. Microsoft
4. General Electric	4. Coca Cola
5. Nokia	5. China Mobile
Interbrand	BrandZ

The Big Winners	
1. Google	+43 %
2. Apple	+24 %
3. Amazon	+16 %
4. Zara	+15 %
5. Nintendo	+13 %
BrandZ	

The Big Losers	
1. Merrill Lynch	-21 %
2. Gap	-21 %
3. Morgan Stanley	-16 %
4. Citi	-14 %
5. Ford	-12 %
BrandZ	

3 Discussion

a. How brand conscious are you? For each of the items below, discuss the brands you prefer / avoid, and factors that influence your buying decisions other than the brand itself.

trainers | shampoo | bread | jeans | chocolate | mobile phone | car

b. Is there a brand name that you find simply magic? Explain why.

4 Business terms

Check that you understand the expressions on the right using a dictionary or glossary. Then give examples of the following:

1. a car accessory you would like to buy
2. a fast-moving consumer good
3. a way of encouraging brand loyalty
4. a supermarket chain that sells own brand products
5. why a company might decide to reposition a brand
6. brand extension unrelated to the original product
7. designer label from your country
8. merchandise sold in connection with the World Cup

WORD BANK

Products and brands
brand image | brand loyalty | brand awareness | brand conscious | brand stretching | brand extension | to switch brands | label | own brand / private label | manufacturer's brand | repositioning | consumer durables | fast-moving consumer goods (FMCGs) | industrial goods | merchandise | commodity | trademark | packaging | to diversify | to differentiate | feature | benefit | accessory

5 Listening: A new product range

a. Sarah Fisher is Marketing Director of Glam AG, a German cosmetics firm. She is discussing the Smoothie® range with her colleague, Pedro Fernandez, the head of R&D at the firm's subsidiary in Lisbon. Before you listen, do the following tasks:

1. Check that you understand the words below. Which would you not use to describe a customer, and why?

   recycled | upmarket | glossy | choosy | demanding | shiny | discerning | sophisticated | mature | obsolete

2. Suggest why the aims of Marketing and R&D departments may sometimes conflict with one another.

A 1.19 **b.** Listen and make notes in the grid. Compare notes, then listen again to check.

	Target market	Product & packaging	Brand image	Marketing strategy
Existing product				
Proposed brand extension				

c. Why do you think Smoothie® was chosen as a brand name? Is it a good choice? Explain your view.

d. Draft the email that Sarah sends to the Product Manager.

6 Problem-solving

Household products tend to be very similar, so product managers need to find ways of distinguishing them from the competition. Work in teams, where each team chooses a different product. Suggest ways of adapting the product in order to justify the claim "NEW AND IMPROVED". Present your ideas in class.

Examples:
› "Something could be added to Alpinland butter to make it spread more easily."
› "The packaging could be improved by replacing (X) with (Y). In this way …"
› "(X) could be used instead of (Y) to make it more …"

B Business briefing | Brand extension

1 Reading

a. Read the article quickly for the gist. Explain the reference to 'ego trip' in the context of the article.

Brand extension or ego trip?

Success in a new market will be out of reach unless your brand offers something new and relevant while avoiding stepping on the competition's toes.

Extending your brand beyond its original market remains a hot topic for many marketing teams. The most famous example of stretching a brand has to be Virgin, which sells everything from bridal gowns to business-class travel. Or maybe Apple computers. Its iPod and iPhone extensions have helped quadruple the share price in the last two years.

But diversifying successfully is a tricky business. More than half of all brand extensions fail, joining the likes of Cosmopolitan yoghurts, Bic perfume and Levi's suits in the over-crowded diversification graveyard. So what can we do to avoid betting on a dud?

First and foremost we need to focus on bringing something new, different and relevant to the market we're attempting to enter. This sounds obvious, but many companies get too big for their brand boots. They hope that simply slapping a popular name on an average product or service will guarantee success. This kind of brand ego trip can be expensive.

When we look more closely at Virgin, we find that for every successful extension such as Virgin Atlantic, there were also several flops. Virgin Vodka and Virgin Jeans both lacked the style credentials and differentiation to compete.

Low price in an already flooded market was not enough to make it in those lifestyle categories. In contrast, Dove brought something new to the deodorant market when it successfully moved beyond soap bars to moisturising anti-perspirant. It also spent several years before the deodorant launch ensuring that the product offered effective enough protection to match the best on the market.

Of course, the Dove brand was already famous for the skin-friendly properties it was bringing to this new niche. Apple's iPod and iPhone both built on the brand's reputation for beautifully designed and intuitive interfaces. Transferring brand benefits to new products and markets improves the chances that people will trust your new offer. It also means that the extension will further reinforce your brand.

Many unsuccessful Easyjet extensions, such as men's cosmetics and pizzas, have had little connection with the original airline brand values of a no-frills service with cheaper prices for booking early.

Remember to be careful who you take on in a new market. Smart companies respect the competition because they will fight the new kid on the block with vigour. Procter & Gamble had the product technology and trusted brand, Pampers, to launch a successful baby shampoo. But the company still held back because the response from market leader Johnson & Johnson would have led to a costly battle that just wouldn't have paid off. So our watchword for new market ventures should not be "what can the market do for our brand?" but rather "what can our brand do for the market"?

From: *The Marketer* (Chartered Institute of Marketing)

bridal gown Brautkleid, **to quadruple** vervierfachen, **graveyard** Friedhof, **to bet** wetten, **dud** Niete, **first and foremost** in erster Linie, **get too big for one's boots** größenwahnsinnig werden, **credentials** Legitimation, **moisturising** befeuchtend, **anti-perspirant** schweißhemmendes Mittel, Deo, **properties** Eigenschaften, **with vigour** energisch, **trusted** vertraut, **watchword** Parole

b. Copy the grid, adding information about the brands mentioned in the article. Where there is no information, write NI.

Brand	Original product	Image / value	Extension	Success / flop	Reason
Apple	*computers*	*beautiful design, intuitive interfaces*	*iPhone*	*success*	*built on brand image / reputation*

c. Which company decided not to extend its brand, and why?

d. For each of the brand extensions that flopped, suggest alternative products that meet the criteria listed in the first paragraph. Then compare your ideas.

2 Product strategy and risk

a. Label the Ansoff Matrix on the right with the strategies marked in bold, and discuss them in terms of risk.

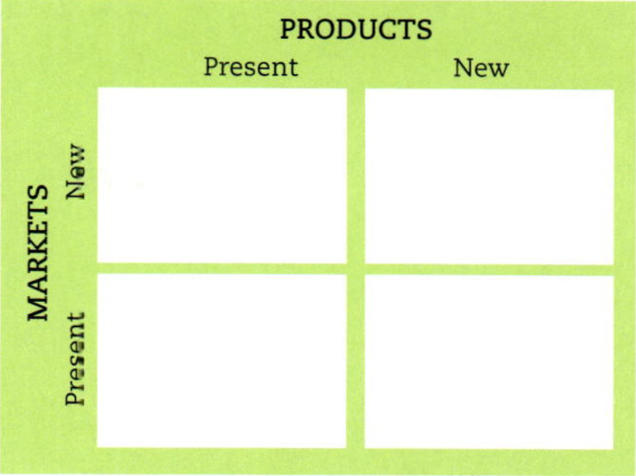

- **Diversification** (developing new products for new markets)
- **Market development** (selling existing products in new markets, e.g. by exporting or repositioning)
- **Market penetration** (increasing sales of existing products in existing markets)
- **Product development** (creating new products for existing markets)

b. Below are two further strategies. In which quadrant would you put them, and why?

- **Product imitation** (copying successful brands to win market share)
- **Product revision** (adapting products for existing markets)

3 Mistakes in brand strategy

a. Read the examples and identify mistakes that were made and their consequences. Discuss how the mistakes could have been avoided.

1 Coca-Cola sued Sainsbury's for producing packaging for an own brand cola that copied the shape, style and colouring of the lettering which Coca-Cola uses. Not only the brand, but also the brand image, was under threat.

2 Procter and Gamble had to adapt Cheer washing powder because Japanese consumers wash their clothes in cold tapwater, use leftover bath water and like to add fabric softeners.

3 The C5, a battery-assisted three-wheel cycle launched in 1985, was promoted by its inventor Sir Clive Sinclair as a revolution in personal transport. However, it was seen by many people as ridiculous and even dangerous. After sales of only 17,000, it was withdrawn from the market, leaving Sir Clive with losses of over £8 million.

4 A drinks company tried to introduce a two-litre drinks bottle into Spain, but found it hard to enter the market. They soon discovered this was because few Spaniards had fridge doors big enough to accommodate the larger size of the bottle.

5 Strawberry shampoo failed in China where consumers shun non-edible items that smell like food.

6 In April 1985 the management of Coca-Cola annnounced its decision to change the flavour of the company's flagship brand, based on the fact that research had discovered that the majority of consumers preferred the taste of Pepsi to that of Coke. However, the decision proved disastrous, and the company had to re-introduce its original product.

to be under threat gefährdet werden, **ridiculous** lächerlich, **to shun** meiden, **edible** essbar, **fabric softener** Weichspüler

b. Find out more about the 'disastrous' decision by Coca-Cola in 1985. How did customers respond, and why?

4 Product adaptation

Carry out research into how and why products are adapted for different markets. Choose a product where culture plays a key role in the need for adaptation, and present your results in class.

INFO

Cultural factors affecting brands
The greater the cultural differences between target markets, the greater the need for adaptation. Cultural considerations may influence product design, branding, labelling, packaging and service arrangements.

C Language | Describing products

1 Product attributes

Suggest further expressions for each group. Tip: You can sometimes make opposites by adding prefixes.

Positive attributes

Design and construction		Usage	Performance	Cost
well-designed	stylish	practical	efficient	inexpensive
state-of-the-art	sophisticated	handy	reliable	value-for-money
innovative	classic	convenient	low-maintenance	competitively-priced
sturdy	contemporary	versatile	powerful	affordable
robust	attractive	easy-to-use	effective	economical
....	....	....	....	....
....	....	....	....	....
....	....	....	....	

Negative attributes

Design and construction		Usage	Performance	Cost
badly-designed	ugly	impractical	inefficient	expensive
....	....	....	....	....
....	....	....	....	....
....	....	....	....	....

2 Describing features and benefits

a. Describe the products below in terms of the following:

› what they are made of / made from / consist of
› what they are used for
› the qualities expected of them

WORD BANK

Materials
Raw materials: crude oil | timber / wood | cotton | iron ore | grain | cow hide | tobacco | sap / resin | salt | sugar beet
Semi-finished / finished products: vinegar | silk | steel | flour | plastic | leather | gelatine | glue | car tyres
(Some materials, e.g. rubber, can be synthetic or natural.)

LANGUAGE TIP

Features and benefits
A **feature** describes what a product is like, whereas a **benefit** describes what it does for the customer.

b. Match the features of an industrial machine with its benefits, using the phrases below.

Feature		Benefit
"It's reliable, "It's low-maintenance, "It's fast, "It's easy to use, "It's versatile, "It's economical,	which means that in other words the advantage being that	… it's very cheap to operate." … it requires minimal training for operatives." … it can perform a wide range of operations." … it requires very little attention or repair." … it's available for more hours of the working day." … it produces 10 % more widgets than comparable machines."

c. Explain how each of the services offered by Optima Opticians might benefit customers.

Example:
"They offer 40 minute eye tests, which means that customers can expect a detailed and thorough eye examination."

d. Decide which features are standard (i.e. offered by most opticians) and which are different. Mark them with an 'S' or a 'D'.

e. Create a one-minute radio spot that focuses on what makes Optima Opticians special.

3 Comparing features and benefits

a. Compare the cars below in terms of their specifications.

b. Find out which of the two cars your teacher prefers. Make a sales pitch in which you persuade your teacher to buy the other one. Describe the benefits (be creative), and explain why it offers better value-for-money.

LANGUAGE TIP

Making comparisons
Car B is **much longer** than Car A, but **on the other hand**, it is **not as high**.
Car A is **slightly narrower** than Car B.
Car B is **significantly more expensive**.
Which of the cars **has the bigger** engine?
Neither Car A **nor** Car B has a …
Car A is a coupe, **whereas** Car B is …

Car comparisons

	CAR A	CAR B

Length	8.9 feet	14.4 feet
Height	5.2 feet	5.0 feet
Width	5.4 feet	5.6 feet
Top speed	95mph	98 mph
Fuel consumption	40 mpg	58 mpg
Engine capacity	1000 cc	1500 cc
Engine type	3 cylinder petrol	4 cylinder petrol/electric
Power output	75 hp	115hp
Body type	2-door coupe	4-door hatchback
CD player	Not included	standard
Sat-Nav	Not included	optional
Basic price (Euro)	**13,690**	**23,400**

mph = miles per hour, mpg = miles per gallon, ft = foot/feet, HP = horsepower

INFO

Converting measurements
- 1 mile (m) ≈ 1.6 km
- 1 foot (ft) ≈ 30 cm
- 1 inch (in) ≈ 2.5 cm
- 1 pound (lb) ≈ 500 g
- The British gallon (≈ 4.5 litres) is one-fifth bigger than the American gallon (≈ 3.8 litres)

D Business leaders | Sir James Dyson

1 Reading

a. Read the interview and make notes under the following headings:

Sources of inspiration | Marketing strategy | Way of working | Attitude to failure

The British inventor and entrepreneur Sir James Dyson developed the innovative G-Force vacuum cleaner. He was unable to persuade European companies to manufacture it, so he worked with a Japanese company that launched it in 1986. His design soon attracted attention, and in 1993 he opened a research centre and factory in Malmesbury, UK, producing what became the best-selling vacuum cleaner on the market – the DC01.

I often get irritated with things that I use in my life, and that's where I find inspiration. The vacuum struck me as being a particularly bad frustration. Vacuums clog very quickly with dust, and lose suction. I saw a possible solution to it, but it was another four years or so before I had it working – another 5,127 prototypes later. I look for things that don't work properly, things that could be done better, things that are cumbersome or disappointing in performance. Something fails, something is difficult to use – that's the starting point.

I believe if you bring out something better, people will want it. And so I'm not afraid of being naive. In making vacuum cleaners, I was going into an area which is very densely populated with very big companies that have been making these things for years. I thought if I was frustrated by a vacuum cleaner, then other people would be too. I wasn't particularly frightened by all these big companies, because I felt they weren't doing anything about it. They were making the same old thing year after year and not really changing the technology.

My office is a bit like my kitchen. I want a relaxed atmosphere of creativity. I try to avoid the phone and e-mail. If I read three e-mails a day, that's a lot. I would rather go and speak to somebody. I have a BlackBerry that I don't think is brilliantly designed visually, but the software is very good. A pencil is the tool of my trade. I've got a very nice drafting pencil that I've used since I was at university.

An engineer's life is 99 percent failure. So failure clearly doesn't depress me. I think it has the reverse effect on me. You don't learn from success, and your successes are few and far between. Failure is like a drug, actually. You go to work each day excited, because you know there are hundreds of problems there that you haven't solved. It's living on the edge, because you might come up with the solution or you might not. The future of the company depends on it."

From: Fortune Magazine, January 16 2007

vacuum cleaner Staubsauger, **to strike** (here) auffallen, **to clog** verstopfen, **suction** Saugkraft, **cumbersome** unhandlich, **dense** dicht, **drafting pencil** Bleistift für Entwürfe, **few and far between** ganz vereinzelt, **to live on the edge** gefährlich leben

b. Are mistakes and failure good or bad for business? Give examples from different professions.

2 Vocabulary

a. Match the terms on the left with their everyday equivalents and translate them into German.

1. kleenex	a. waterproof coat
2. biro	b. paper tissue
3. to google	c. transparent sticky tape (for office use)
4. mackintosh	d. ballpoint pen
5. band-aid	e. to photocopy
6. sellotape*	f. business with coin-operated washing machines
7. laundrette*	g. sticking plaster for small injuries
8. to xerox	h. to look sth. up on the internet

*AE: scotch-tape, laundromat

LANGUAGE TIP

Brand names in everyday use
In the UK, a vacuum cleaner is sometimes referred to as a 'hoover', a trademark that has become an everyday word through constant use. It is even used as a verb ("I hoover with a Dyson.").

b. Are there any other brand names that have become everday words in your own language?

→ Video Lounge Interview with James Dyson, page 55

E Business communication | Meetings

1 Effective meetings

Comment on the statistics on the right. How do they compare with your own experience of meetings?

Meetings – a waste of time?

According to a survey of employees in the USA,

27% described the meetings they attended as 'disorganised and rambling'.

17% had taken part in meetings where aggressive individuals constantly interrupted their colleagues and tried to dominate the discussion.

16% of employees were interrupted by mobile phones during meetings.

9% of employees fell asleep during meetings.

6% of meetings were very long and offered no coffee or refreshments.

5% of meetings were interrupted by people arriving late, and the same percentage of meetings had people leaving early.

4% of meetings started late

4% of employees said that they received no written minutes of the meeting.

© Opinion Research Corporation, 2007

2 The process

a. Match the expressions on the left with the definitions on the right.

1. decide on a venue
2. chair the meeting
3. take the minutes
4. draw up an agenda
5. write (up) the minutes
6. delegate action
7. adjourn the meeting
8. postpone the meeting
9. circulate handouts

a. make notes during the meeting of what is said or decided
b. give tasks to other people to do
c. choose where the meeting will take place
d. re-schedule the meeting to a later date
e. give or send documents to participants
f. control the process of the meeting
g. create a list of items to be discussed
h. write a report of what was said or agreed in the meeting
i. stop for a break, or to continue the meeting at a later date

b. Which of the activities listed above normally take place during a meeting, rather than before or after?

c. Complete the quote below. Then compare your ideas:

"Expecting a meeting to produce results without an agenda is like ..." Steve Kaye

3 Listening: Starting a meeting

A 1.20 You will hear the first part of a meeting in which the chairman goes through a sequence of steps. As you listen, number the steps in the right order. Then listen again and note down the phrases he uses. (The first one has been done for you.)

INFO

Chairing meetings

In order to be effective, someone should chair the meeting. This person (called the chairman / chairperson) should:

- open the meeting and state the purpose
- follow the agenda, dealing with each item in turn
- control time, knowing when to move the discussion on
- check and clarify points that are not clear
- deal with any disagreements or conflicts that arise
- make sure everyone has a chance to contribute
- summarise and close the meeting

Steps

[ ] Asking someone to take the minutes ....
[ ] Checking that everyone has the agenda ....
[ ] Going through the agenda ....
[ ] Introducing the first item for discussion ....
[ ] Checking that everyone is present ....
[ ] Stating the purpose of the meeting ....
[1] Welcoming the participants to the meeting *Good morning, everyone.*
[ ] Asking if everyone is ready to start ....

4 Keeping time

Describe situations in which the chairperson might use the following expressions.

1. "Let's turn to item two." ....
2. "I'll go over the main points again." ....
3. "Is there any other business?" ....
4. "We have half an hour." ....
5. "That's all we have time for." ....

5 Solving problems

Describe a problem you are experiencing at work or in college. Ask your partner for suggestions, then respond appropriately.

PHRASES

Making suggestions	Responding to suggestions
How about …?	That's a good idea.
Why don't you …?	Sounds great!
If I were you, I'd …	That might be a solution.
What do you think of …?	I'm not convinced.
I think you'd better …*	That would never work!

* you'd better = you had better

6 Decision-making

Sarah Fisher needs a catchy slogan for the Smoothie® ad campaign. She is unsure about her ideas and needs your input. Hold a meeting to come to a decision. Consider her ideas and follow the steps below.

Smoothie – problem salved!

Smoothie – for that New Age feeling!

It's smooth, naturally.

1. Chairperson
   Open the meeting, stating the purpose and inviting comments from participants. Make sure everyone contributes.

↓

2. Participants
   Comment on Sarah's slogans. Suggest alternatives and respond to other suggestions. Make sure you get your ideas across.

↓

3. Chairperson
   Call for a vote. Ask people to raise their hands in favour or against. Count the votes and the abstentions.

↓

4. Chairperson
   Summarise the results and close the meeting.

PHRASES

Making a point
In my view …
If you ask me, …
As far as I'm concerned, …
Speaking from experience, …
I'm sure you'd agree that …
It's obvious that …

Responding and turn-taking
Sorry to interrupt, but …
Can I just come in here …?
Just let me finish, please.
But don't you think that …?
Absolutely! And what's more …
I'm afraid I don't follow you.

Voting and summarising
I suggest we take vote on this.
Shall we have a show of hands?
Hands up all those in favour. Hands up all those against. Any abstentions?
Right, that's … in favour and … against, with … abstentions.
That means the consensus is …

7 Effective meetings

Use your experience of meetings to complete the tips below. Add a further tip of your own.

Top tips for effective meetings

1. In a meeting room there should always be ....
2. Before starting a meeting, everyone should ....
3. For meetings to be successful, the chairperson should ....
4. During a meeting, it is not polite to ....
5. For meetings to be successful, participants should..........
6. At the end of a meeting, everyone should ....
7. ....

8 Simulation

Scenario

› You are product managers of a company that manufactures goods in a highly competitive business environment.
› You have called a 'concept meeting' today to come up with an idea for a completely new product to add to your existing range. You will need to agree on the basic concept and also discuss issues affecting other departments such as R&D and Marketing. The overall objective is to develop a concept and a strategy that will appeal to the CEO and secure a more generous budget for your department than you have had in the past.

a. Prepare for the meeting by carrying out the tasks below.

› Decide what type of products you already have in your range. Typically, these might include consumer durables, for example household appliances, bathroom fittings, consumer electronics, cars, sports equipment, or non-durables such as food and beverages, toiletries or stationery.
› Allocate tasks. Who is going to chair the meeting? Who will take the minutes?
› Decide whether you want to invite participants from other departments, e.g. R&D. If so, allocate roles.
› Agree on a time limit.
› Draw up an agenda that reflects the objectives of the meeting. This could include items such as:
  - Target market: who will buy the product
  - Product features
  - Marketing
  - Budgeting
› Design an agenda that will help you to record the decisions (action / summary minutes), as in the example on the right. Remember to include the item AOB (any other business) at the bottom of the agenda.

Action Minutes – Product Development Meeting

Date:
Time:
Venue:
Participants:
Product idea:

Topic	Decision / Action	Person responsible
1. Target market: Who will buy the product?		
2. …		

b. Hold the meeting, following the agenda and noting down what was discussed, the decisions that were taken, the action that was agreed, and who is responsible for what.

c. Follow up the meeting by choosing one of the options below:

› Writing: After the meeting, write an email to your colleagues in other departments summarising what was decided. Base this on the notes you made during the meeting.
› Speaking: Present your ideas in class, as if you were addressing the CEO.

F Consulting | Developing a pet food brand

1 Preparation

a. You work for Ad-Wise Consulting. Read the documents to prepare for the tasks that follow.

To: The 'A' Team
From: c.goetz@ad.wise.de
Subject: PetPride

Dear team members
As you know, PetPride have asked us to develop a product strategy for them, possibly including the German market. This is an exciting project, and it promises to be VERY lucrative for us! I've already conducted some preliminary research into the company and the dogfood market, and am attaching the findings.
Please analyse them carefully and send me your recommendations in the form of a short report by next Tuesday. They'll give us a good basis for discussion in our meeting next Wednesday.
Unfortunately, I have to dash off to Paris at short notice, so won't be back in my office until Tuesday.
However, I'm sure you'll manage without me. I look forward to reading your reports when I return!

Regards
Clarissa Götz

Attachments: Research_findings.doc

Ad-Wise Consulting – "Wise advice at the right price"
Re: Product strategy for PetPride – Initial briefing

Background

PetPride is a leading UK manufacturer of pet food. Their R&D department has recently patented an innovative process in extrusion technology. Here, the ingredients can be moulded into any shape or size, then sprayed with a coating of fat, oil, vitamins and other additives.
The 'snacks, treats and chews' category account for a significant part of their revenue. An area that seems underdeveloped is the market for large dogs and their owners. According to PetPride, owners are more likely to give treats to small dogs than large dogs, even though large dogs have higher calorie requirements. Apparently, owners of large dogs prefer to give real 'butcher's bones', despite the uncleanliness and inconvenience.
We have conducted a study into European dog owners of large dogs to find out why they don't feed their dogs with treats and prefer to give them 'butcher's bones' instead. The findings are listed below.

Findings

- Most owners give butcher's bones to their dogs on a regular basis.
- They would like to give snacks, treats and chews, but see manufactured products as insufficient for a large dog, and often, therefore, inappropriate or poor value for money. A butcher's bone is seen by owners as the ultimate dog treat, satisfying the basic instincts of their dog.
- However, real bones have major drawbacks including availability, hygiene and concern over BSE.
- Private label petfood products are competing with manufacturer brands, a trend that pet superstores could exploit.
- Customers are increasingly concerned about the origin of ingredients.
- 'Green' or environmentally-friendly products seem to have an especially bright future.
- Dog ownership is falling. Cat ownership is stable and pet fish ownership is increasing.
- Despite the decline in households which keep pets, the value of the pet food and pet care market is rising. This is due to owners' willingness to spend more on premium food.
- Over the last five years, petfood sales have grown by 7.6 % in Western Europe compared to 200 % in Eastern Europe. France, Germany and the UK represent 60 % of the total market in Europe

Points to consider in your recommendations:

- Current and future consumer trends
- Development of a new brand to provide an alternative to butcher's bones (features / benefits / risks)
- Target market (only large dogs? expansion into German market?)
- Alternatives to product / brand development
- Areas where further research is needed

b. Identify the most significant findings and mark them in the text.

c. Decide what action is required.

2 Research

Decide what further information you need for your report, and how you will find it. (It might be enough to do some informal research with colleagues, friends and family.)

LANGUAGE TIP

Recommend

I recommend ~~them to launch~~ a new brand.
› I recommend that they launch a new brand.
› I recommend launching a new brand.
(Same applies to 'suggest')

3 Reporting back

Choose one of the following options:

› Oral report: Discuss your results in class and try to come up with a strategy that everyone agrees with.
› Written report: Write a short report for Frau Götz recommending a product strategy for PetPride.

INFO

Short reports

Short reports present an overview of a situation and sometimes offer recommendations. Use this checklist to remind you of key elements.

The structure is …
› clear (organised into sections, paragraphs and bullet points)
› logical (title, introduction, discussion, summary and conclusions, recommendations, sources, appendices)
› coherent (ideas connected with 'linking' words)

The language is …
› concise (short and simple sentences)
› plain (understandable words, no slang or jargon)
› direct (active verbs where possible)

The content is …
› relevant (task fulfilled)
› complete (no more / less than needed)
› accurate (carefully checked)

SKILLS

Writing clearly

Avoid the passive where the active is clearer.
– Research was conducted. (unclear)
– Research was conducted by me. (unnatural)
+ We conducted research. (clear and direct)

Avoid words your reader might not understand.
– We googled it. (slang)
– We subjected it to critical scrutiny. (meaning?)
+ We did research. (everyday verb)

Avoid short forms, unless you want to sound as if you are speaking.
–/+ We've done research. (conversational tone)

Avoid noun combinations where verbs are clearer.
– The report made reference to the budget.
+ The report referred to the budget.

4 Package design

Design the packaging for the new product. Include information about the product, benefits and ingredients.

Video lounge Interview with James Dyson

BBC Motion Gallery

V 2 Watch the video 'Interview with James Dyson' and answer the questions.

1. What type of products does Dyson compare to his vacuum cleaners? Why?
2. What was the secret of Dyson products that made them so successful?
3. How would you describe Dyson's 'obsession'?

Revision 1
Units 1 – 4

Online Link
800021-0017

1 Complete the grid to show the meaning of common short forms.

	Clue / Definition	Long form	German
1. IPO	stock market listing	Initial Public Offering	Börsengang
2. CEO	top manager		Vorstandsvorsitzende(r)
3. AGM	company event	Annual General Meeting	
4. cc		carbon copy	
5. AOB			
6.			Mehrwertsteuer
7.	cash point/dispenser		Geldautomat
8. HQ			
9. FMCG			

2 Fill in the missing letters in this text about company types.

The smallest type of company is known as a s........ t........ in the UK and a s........ p........ in the US.
When professionals (e.g. architects or lawyers) get together to form a company, this is known as a p......... Larger companies that are 'incorporated' as a legal entity are known as j........-s........ companies in the UK. There are two types: Firstly, the p........ l........ company (Ltd.), whose share ownership is limited (comparable to a GmbH in Germany), and secondly the p........ l........ company (PLC), which issues shares to the public and is comparable to the German AG. Both types have l........ l......... In the USA, the equivalent of a PLC is a s........ corporation (........). Companies usually decide to g........ p........ in order to r........ capital.

3 Rearrange the letters to find names of company departments.

1. DRIVING SEAT A........
2. BLUE PLASTIC IRON P........
3. NORDIC POUT P........
4. II BRIT DONUTS D........
5. MEN LOVE SHARP DENTED CARS R........
6. ACQUIRE ANY TUSSEL Q........
7. CAN TUG COIN A........
8. TRUST ME OR I CAN LOSE C........
9. GREEN GINNIE D........

4 Choose the right option between these commonly confused words.

1. Please (insure / ensure) that the windows are closed before you leave the room.
2. Have you chosen a (venue / location) for this year's office party?
3. I took back the pullover and asked for a (refund / rebate).
4. Could you please (write / take) the minutes during the meeting?
5. The (economic / economical) situation has started to improve again.
6. It isn't the final version. It's just a (concept / draft).
7. Attractive (packing / packaging) can help to sell products.

5 Translate these expressions into English.

1. wie gewünscht ....
2. eine engere Auswahl treffen ....
3. etwas als Gegenleistung anbieten ....
4. die Vor- und Nachteile abwägen ....
5. ich stelle Sie durch ....
6. bitte beachten Sie, dass ....

6 Translate these expressions into German.

1. to hear something through the grapevine ....
2. to have a pen handy ....
3. budget airline ....
4. no-frills product ....
5. to donate to a good cause ....
6. to tighten one's belt ....

7 Fill in the gaps with the missing prepositions.

1. She's speaking .... the other line.
2. I've applied .... another job.
3. It depends .... what you mean.
4. We need to weigh .... the pros and cons.
5. Did you agree .... the request?
6. I've got nothing .... my account.
7. How much did you spend .... raw materials?
8. They're selling them .... rock-bottom prices.

8 a. Give the noun forms.

1. to acquire ....
2. to withdraw ....
3. to consume ....

b. Give the verb forms.

1. maintenance ....
2. allocation ....
3. expansion ....

c. Give the adjective forms.

1. impression ....
2. competition ....
3. contract ....

9 Write the verb that makes a common collocation with the noun.

1. to *c*.................... fraud
2. to *m*.................... a concession
3. to *c*.................... a deal
4. to *c*.................... VAT
5. to *c*.................... research
6. to *d*.................... a hard bargain
7. to *r*.................... deadlock
8. to *c*.................... a meeting (= lead)

10 Underline the word where the marked letters are pronounced differently.

1. b**ea**r – h**ea**r – f**ea**r – d**ea**r
2. a**g**enda - tar**g**et – le**g**islation – re**g**ister
3. mea**su**re – lei**su**re – ca**su**al – per**su**ade
4. **ch**emicals – **ch**aracter – **ch**est - **Ch**ristmas
5. c**ei**ling – h**ei**ght – rec**ei**pt – hyg**ie**ne
6. barg**ain** – cont**ain** – maint**ain** – reg**ain**

11 Underline the word that does not fit in the group, and note down why.

1. cheque – cash – debit card – mail order – barter
2. picky – anxious – discerning – selective – choosy
3. well-off – prosperous – rich – penniless – wealthy
4. hard-up – needy – loaded - underclass – destitute
5. polite – tactful – rude – courteous – diplomatic
6. iron ore – coal– grain – crude oil – brand

12 Match words from each group to create a compound noun.

self | profit | sticking | direct | ~~limited~~ | parent | exchange | unit | final

company | offer | debit | price | margin | ~~liability~~ | rate | point | employed

limited liability, ...

....

13 Rephrase the sentence using the word in brackets.

1. He's totally unreliable. (*depend*) You can't depend on him at all.
2. Smoking is not allowed. (*ban*) ....
3. What price are you thinking of? (*mind*) ....
4. I'll make sure he gets back to you. (*return*) ....
5. I didn't catch your name. (*repeat*) ....

14 Add a prefix to create the opposite. (Example: **dis**agreement)

1. ....loyal
2. ....expensive
3. ....reasonable
4. ....comfortable
5. ....practical
6. ....sufficient
7. ....experienced
8. ....appropriate

15 Complete the sentences with words meaning the opposite of the ones in bold.

1. I asked for the photos to be printed on **matt** paper, not g.......... paper.
2. You told me that this bag was **genuine** leather, but it's actually sy.......... .
3. I haven't come to the bank to **withdraw** cash. I've come to d.......... €10,000!
4. Last month the market was **stable**, but at the moment it's highly v.......... .
5. This computer isn't **primitive** at all. In fact, it's extremely s.......... .
6. We need a **sturdy** box because the contents are f.......... .
7. The situation hasn't improved **significantly**, but it has got sl.......... better.

16 Identify and correct the mistakes. Refer to the marking code on p.38.

1. Keep your receipts for stationary and other office supplies. (Sp)
2. I hope my boss will rise my salary. (WW)
3. She has an own office. (G)
4. We deliver customers all over the world. (WW)
5. He gave me a good advice. (UC)
6. They have paid the invoice two days ago. (T)
7. Dear Madams and Sirs (C)
8. Tanja speaks English quite good. (G)
9. I'll pay the meal if you give the tip. (WM)
10. They said that the delivery already had arrived. (WO)
11. I work in the mail-order business, which means I have to deal with a lot of reclamations. (FF)
12. The company I work for is selling medical instruments. (T)
13. I would like to suggest you to change your marketing strategy. (G)
14. We discussed about the pros and cons of investing in Germany. (NN)
15. As you know the Internet becomes more and more important. (Punct + T + St.)
16. They said, that they would come to a decision in the next months. (Punct + WM)
17. I work for the company Mayer AG since three years. (T + NN + Prep.)

17 Write the missing letters of the compound nouns.

1. event at which companies show and sell their products tr........ fa........
2. getting back money that is owed to you de........ re........
3. fixed, one-off amount of money lu........ su........
4. invoice for electricity, gas or water, for example ut........ bi........
5. adjective for products that are only partly made se........ - fi........

18 Complete the sentences with compounds starting with 'over'. (Be careful with the word form.)

overdue | oversee | overview | overspend | oversight | overcharge | overheads | overtime

1. I'm not willing to work .... without pay.
2. This organisation chart gives you an .... of the company.
3. No wonder you're in debt. You always .... at Christmas.
4. The delay was due to an .... in the dispatch department.
5. Selling online helps us to keep our .... low.
6. Some of the payments are more than 90 days ....
7. Check the bill to make sure you haven't been ....
8. The supervisory board .... the executive board.

19 Listening

A 3.1 **a.** Listen to a presentation in which a product is being demonstrated and correct the mistakes (9 in total).

THE BABY BEAM PROJECTOR

Dimensions 10 cm x 8 cm x ~~3 cm~~ 5 cm
(small enough to put in your handbag)
Weight slightly more than 1 kg
Casing polished aluminium and black, robust technology;
LED lamp reaches full power after just a few minutes –
no risk of bulb damage, quiet fan
Guarantee two-years on all the parts
Wholesale price 150 Euros

b. List six accessories that come with the Baby Beam.

....
....

c. Complete the grid with words used by the presenter.

"This (1.) and (2.) projector makes real sense to users who want (3.) technology that is (4.) and (5.)."

Words in last sentence	Expressions with related meanings
1. s........	t........
2. e........	s........
3. a........	s........-........-........-........, s........
4. a........	c........ p........, excellent v........
5. c........	p........, e........ ...., r........

Unit 5
Marketing

Online Link
800021-0005

A Introduction | The marketing mix

1 Quick response

Describe the kind of people who work in marketing. What do you think attracts them to this field?

2 Reading

a. This advert was annotated by a business student looking for an internship in marketing. Add your own annotations. Then discuss what you would want to know about QuAD or the internship before applying.

QuAD Consulting: Internship Opportunities in Marketing and Public Relations
We are currently seeking talented students for our internship program in Bonn. As a QuAD intern you will learn from marketing experts and have a unique opportunity to join an ad agency whose clients include politicians, athletes and entertainers. The internship can be combined with a Bachelor/Master thesis. ☺

Your tasks: Supporting account managers in the coordination of client projects; carrying out market research; identifying market trends; conducting competitor analysis; working closely with designers, artists and copywriters to conceptualise and create advertisements; helping to ensure that ads are produced within budget and on schedule, drafting press releases; assisting in corporate events, business pitches and product launches. ☺

Very low!

We offer: €6 an hour plus great perks free access to on-site fitness facilities; a buzzy, supportive working environment; opportunities to attend press screenings of movies and receive promotional items. ☺

You offer: an undergraduate degree (current/completed) in a relevant subject; an understanding of the marketing mix and measures related to marketing campaigns; excellent German and English in speaking and writing; a sound knowledge of PowerPoint, Excel, Word and other applications; superb analytical and organisational skills; good team skills; a creative outlook; willingness to travel when required, e.g. to visit outside TV and production companies; an ability to handle multiple assignments independently and to tight deadlines.

Interested? Then apply by email to quad@t-online.de, attaching your CV/résumé. English or German? (both!!)

b. Which of the tasks most appeal to you, and why?

c. Which of the requirements are specific to marketing? Which might apply to jobs in other areas?

3 The marketing mix

List brands that are popular with students in your country. Choose one and discuss the reasons for its success with reference to the '7 Ps' of the marketing mix.

According to a survey carried out by Anderson Analytics, the favourite brands of US college students in 2008 were Nike, Apple, American Eagle, Sony and GAP. The survey also looked at brands by product category, e.g. soft drinks, books, TV shows and fast-food restaurants.

Generation X2Z College Brand Study 2009, Anderson Analytics

The 7 Ps

- **Product:** the features and benefits of the product or service, the target market, demand, packaging, etc.
- **Price:** how it compares with competition, and the likely effects of lowering / raising the price
- **Place:** where you can buy it, or the distribution channels
- **Promotion:** the methods used to communicate benefits and encourage sales
- **People:** the extent to which sales or service personnel seem skilled and knowledgeable
- **Processes:** the systems or procedures that make the product easier to buy, e.g. fast delivery, efficient after-sales service
- **Physical evidence:** the visible or tangible aspects that suggest the product is from a good company, e.g. well-dressed staff, attractive premises, modern facilities

tangible materiell, konkret

INFO

The marketing mix
The **marketing mix** is the combination of factors that need to be considered when marketing a product or service. Sometimes it is referred to as the **4 Ps**: Product, Price, Place and Promotion, or even the **7 Ps**, the additions being People, Processes and Physical evidence. The product's **USP** (**Unique Selling Proposition**) is the feature or benefit that makes it stand out from the competition. Where products have no unique features, marketers may instead focus on the brand's **ESP** (**Emotional Selling Proposition**), i.e. emotions or ideas associated with it such as 'freedom' or 'happiness', or its **value proposition** (what it is worth to the customer)

4 Listening

a. You are going to listen to an interview with Jackie Parsons, the founder of ***Gifted in Design***, an online store that sells personalised gifts. Before you listen, discuss what might be interesting about Jackie and her business, and note down questions you would ask her.

A 1.21 **b.** Listen to Part One. Note down the interviewer's questions as well as Jackie's answers. Compare the interviewer's questions with your own, and discuss Jackie's answers.

A 1.22 **c.** Now listen to Part Two. Note down the advice she gives for web-based marketing.

d. Use your notes to write an article about Jackie's business.

5 Definitions of marketing

a. Suggest your own definition of marketing.

b. Translate the DMV definition and compare it with the ones below. Comment on any differences.

"Marketing im Sinne einer marktorientierten Unternehmensführung kennzeichnet die Ausrichtung aller relevanten Unternehmensaktivitäten auf die Wünsche und Bedürfnisse der Anspruchsgruppen."

Deutscher Marketing-Verband (DMV)

"Marketing is the management process responsible for identifying, anticipating and satisfying customer requirements profitably."

Chartered Institute of Marketing (CIM)

"Marketing is the activity, set of institutions, and processes for creating, communicating, delivering and exchanging offerings that have value for customers, partners, and society at large."

American Marketing Association (AMA)

SKILLS

Defining terms
Many business terms mean different things to different people. Before you use them in a discussion, presentation or report, define what *you* understand by them.

B Business briefing | Segmentation

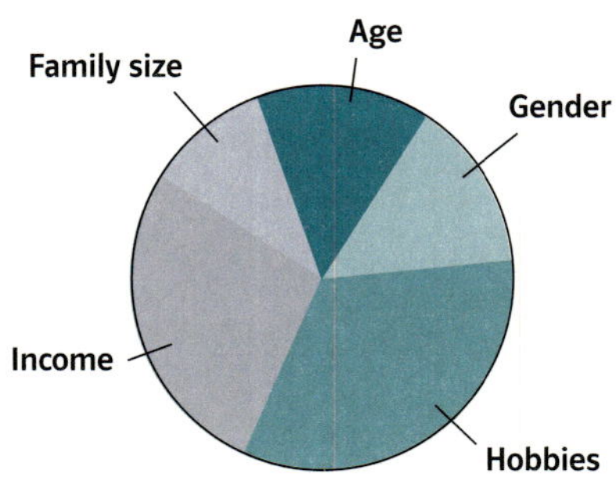

1 Students as consumers

Discuss why college students might be an attractive target market. What do they have in common as consumers?

2 Reading

a. Read the article, highlighting the main points and useful vocabulary relating to marketing.

Segmentation

Segmentation is the process of slicing a market for a particular product or service into a number of different segments. The segments are usually based on factors such as demographics, beliefs or the occasion of use of the product. One segment of the market for video cameras, for instance, might be the group of people who have new-born babies. Another could be the group of people visiting relatives living abroad. (...)

The idea of segmentation has spread beyond its consumer origins. Human-resources departments now talk about segmenting their "customers" – that is, the different groups of employees within their own organisation. In a bank, for example, three such segments might be retail bank tellers, investment bank advisers and money-market traders.

Once different segments of a market have been identified, suppliers to that market can target their advertising and promotional efforts more profitably. Different segments can be reached through the most appropriate channel: parents of new-borns through antenatal clinics, for instance, and foreign travellers through airlines' websites.

Each market segment represents a group of potential customers with common characteristics. In consumer markets, segmentation is usually based on the following:

- Demographic factors: Gender, age, family size, and so on.
- Geography: In most countries there are marked differences in the consumer preferences of different regions. The consumption of wine in the north of England, for example, is very different from that in the south.
- Social factors: One classic segmentation is by income and occupation, but this is proving to be less and less useful. There are a lot of extremely wealthy people who do not spend much and vice versa. So the focus is shifting to lifestyle. In recent years, marketers have become more interested in categorising consumers as "generation Xers" or "the millennial generation" rather than by the size of their bank accounts. Consumers are thought to have more in common with the same generation than with any other grouping.

Industrial markets have been notoriously more difficult to segment than consumer markets. Firms find it hard to decide which factors are most useful in categorising their corporate clients. Should it be size, industry sector, or geography? Computer-maker Hewlett-Packard segmented its big industrial customers into five categories based on the value of their purchases and the complexity of their IT systems.

Segmentation was in part a reaction to the mass-marketing tactics sparked off by Henry Ford when he said that customers could buy his Model T car "in any colour as long as it's black". Many of its classifications, however, have proved to be of little use. Baby boomers have been found to have little more in common than their defining characteristic: a birth date in the years following the Second World War. (...)

The internet promises to provide new opportunities for segmentation. It offers continuous opportunities to capture information about customer behaviour. Consumers identify themselves and their characteristics by their electronic participation in particular interest groups, and by their general online behaviour.

Tim Hindle, *Guide to Management Ideas and Gurus*, 2008

to slice schneiden, **ante-natal clinic** Klinik für Schwangerschaftsfürsorge, **gender** Geschlecht, **marked** deutlich, **notorious** notorisch, **to spark off** auslösen, **baby boomer** nach dem 2. Weltkrieg Geborene(r), to **capture** erfassen

b. Complete the missing information in the diagram, based on the information in the article.

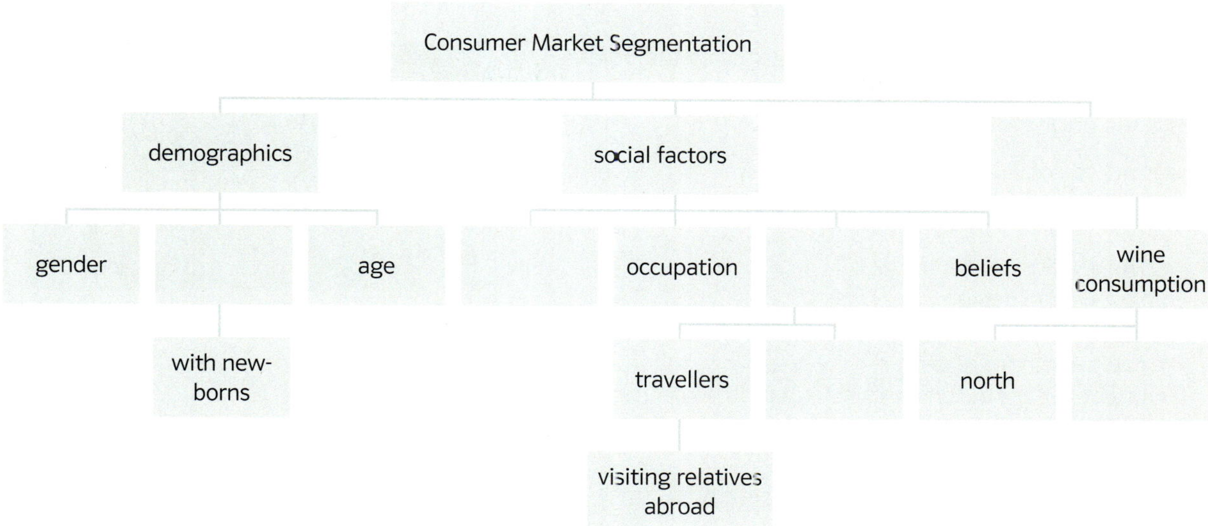

c. Discuss further categories and add them to the diagram.

d. Answer the questions below.

1. How can the market for video cameras be segmented and targeted?
2. What examples are given of non-market segmentation?
3. Why is it becoming difficult to segment according to income? What category is preferred, and why?
4. Which type of market is known to be difficult to segment, and why?
5. What points are illustrated by the following examples in the text?
   - Henry Ford – baby boomers – the internet
6. How can industrial markets be segmented? Refer to the text, and suggest further examples.

3 Discussion

Nowadays automobiles are available in almost any colour, not only black. Discuss how the market has changed since the Model T Ford. How is this reflected in the range of colours and designs?

4 Lifestyle acronyms

a. Which of the acronyms in the box below best describes you?

b. Are there similar acronyms in your language? Invent some that might be useful for marketing purposes.

c. Read the profile of a DINKY written by a travel company. Choose another acronym and write a similar text describing the person and recommending a holiday.

DINKY - Double Income No Kids Yet
With a high disposable income but perhaps not a great deal of free time due to heavy work commitments, the DINKY's holiday of choice is definitely the European city break. Heading straight to the airport after work to locations such as Paris, Vienna or Barcelona is particularly appealing to a group who are looking to fit as much into a 2–3 day break as possible.

www.amazines.com

INFO

Demographic and lifestyle acronyms
The acronym 'YUPPY' (Young Urban Professional. Or Young Upwardly Mobile Professional) was invented in the 1980s. Since then, demographic and lifestyle acronyms have become part of everyday speech. People in marketing and the media are always creating new ones, often just for fun.

- FLY – Fun Loving Youth
- LIPS – Low Income, Parents Supporting
- SINBAD – Single Income, No Boyfriend, Absolutely Desperate
- DINKY – Double Income No Kids Yet
- ORCHID – One Recent Child, Heavily In Debt
- SITCOM – Single Income, Two Children, Oppressive Mortgage
- GLAM – Greying, Leisured, Affluent, Married
- SKI – Spending Kids' Inheritance

C Focus on language | Advertising

1 Analysing an advertisement

a. Describe the ad on the right, referring to the points below, the examples of advertising strategies, and the useful phrases.

Points to consider:
› The advertiser
› The product being advertised
› The implied target market
› Layout and design
› The claim or message
› The use of language
› Effectiveness in terms of AIDA and other strategies

Timeless ◉ Values ◉ Trust ◉ Mulholland.

In these uncertain times it is reassuring to know that some things never change.
The Mulholland Trust was founded in 1796 and has remained true to its core principles, offering a range of specialist financial services to an impressive portfolio of private and corporate clients. We continue to build on our bedrock values of growth, security, and yield. Now is the time to take the decisions that will pave your way to a prosperous future.
There is no time like the present. Call us today on 0800 50000 for advice on all your banking and investment needs. Trust Mulholland.

INFO

Advertising strategies
PPPP: Include a **P**ICTURE, a **P**ROMISE, some **P**ROOF and a **P**USH to act.
AIDA: Attract **A**TTENTION, create **I**NTEREST, arouse **D**ESIRE, and prompt **A**CTION.
WIFM: Answer the customer's question: "**W**HAT'S **I**N IT **F**OR **M**E?"

PHRASES

Describing printed advertisements

Design
The advertisement is divided into … / consists of …
In the foreground / background … / On the left / right …
It features a … / It shows an image of …
The product is presented / depicted as a …

Impact
The design is colourful / busy / simple / bold / …
It grabs / catches the reader's attention by …
The eye is drawn towards …
The arrangement of text and images has the effect of …
The most striking feature is ….
The use of … conveys an impression of …
It evokes a sense of … / arouses the desire for …
The choice of font creates a retro / modern look.

Product and target market
The product / service being advertised is a …
It might appeal to people who …
The advert seems to be directed / aimed at …
It appeals to the desire for status / prestige / security / …

Claim and message
The slogan / strapline promises the customer …
It claims to … / It makes the claim that …
The claim is supported with statistics / endorsements / …
The hidden / underlying message seems to be that …
It makes fun of … / It plays with the idea of …
The language is flowery / plain / straightforward / …
It makes use of alliteration / pun / wordplay / irony …
It prompts / urges the reader to …

b. Read the news item below and look up the words 'gobbledygook', 'spin' and 'fluff'. Explain how they relate to the advertising campaign, which was aimed at middle-aged men.

Volkswagen launch plain English advertising campaign

The car manufacturer Volkswagen has launched a new marketing campaign that attacks the use of gobbledygook and 'spin' in modern advertising. The campaign, which promotes the firm's Passat model, features simple descriptions of everyday items such as a cup of coffee, alongside longer versions such as 'double-choc cinnamon mochaccino with cream'. The car is then 'positioned as a simple concept in a world of fluff' according to Proximity London, the agency behind the campaign. Volkswagen is keen to be seen as a company that 'thinks like its audience'.

c. Follow-up: Volkswagen is famous for its advertisements. Find an example of a printed ad or a TV commercial that you think works well. Write a short report analysing its features.

2 Advertising language

a. Several studies have tried to identify the most persuasive words used in advertising. For each category, add words you could use to sell a new brand of detergent. Examples are given below.

Verbs choose, select, enjoy, indulge, compare, hurry, save, guarantee
....

Nouns miracle, magic, offer, improvement, challenge, bargain, results, health, safety, discovery, love, ...

Adjectives and adverbs now, quick, easy, amazing, sensational, natural, revolutionary, proven, new, improved, best, fresh, full, sure, clean, wonderful, special, ...

b. Advertisers often try to appeal to our senses and emotions, for example our sensory perceptions or need for security. Match the verbs and the adjective pairs, and use them to complete the sentences.

taste | smell | look | ~~keep~~ | sound | feel

big + bright | spicy + delicious | soft + gentle | crisp + clear | ~~safe + warm~~ | clean + fresh

1. A SNUGGLE™ baby-carrier will ....keep.... your baby ....safe.... and ....warm.... .
2. This angel fleece dressing gown .... and .... against your skin.
3. You'll love how .... and .... these loudspeakers ....
4. VITACURRY not only .... and ...., but it's also full of vitamin C!
5. Spray your garbage can with AIRCLEAN®, and it'll .... and .... again.
6. This mascara will make your eyes .... and ....

c. Work in pairs or groups. Decide on a product and write a 100-word advertisement for a poster, or the dialogue for a TV commercial which you direct and act out yourselves.

3 Slogans

a. Read the statements below. What points do they illustrate? Do you know any similar examples?

» Clairol's hair-curling iron "Mist Stick" and the drink "Irish Mist" were both marketing flops in Germany.
» Electrical appliance retailer Currys was banned from using its "unbeatable prices" slogan after it emerged that the chain was frequently more expensive than its rivals.
» The BBC got its fingers burnt after using CNN's internationally trademarked slogan "Be the first to know" for its Arabic newsletter.
» L'Oreal decided to change the long-standing "because I'm worth it" tag to "because you're worth it" in an effort to give the brand a friendlier face.
» Furniture shop Sofa King had its poster banned for carrying the slogan "sofakinggood". The Advertising Standards Authority stated it "was likely to cause widespread offence".
» Germany has banned its government agencies from using untranslated English slogans such as "all you can eat" because the German public doesn't understand them.

Adapted from *The Marketer*, September 2008, p. 7

curling iron Lockenstab, **to get one's finger's burnt** in Schwierigkeiten geraten, **offence** Beleidigung, Anstoß

b. Suggest a suitable German brand name for Clairol's curling iron.

c. A creative director says a slogan should never be more than six words. Do you agree with him?

LANGUAGE TIP

Advertising **copy** is the written material used in an advertisement. The person who writes it is known as a **copywriter**.
The words **strapline**, **tag** and **catchphrase** have similar meanings.

d. Pepsi's 1972 advertising campaign coined a term that became a slogan and a jingle. Discuss how many words it contains, and whether the number is at all relevant.

"Lipsmackinthirstquenchinacetastinmotivatingoodbuzzincooltalkinhighwalkinfastlivinevergivincoolfizzinpepsi"

4 Listening: Problems with slogans

A 1.23 You will hear a marketing expert describing problems that councils and government departments have experienced with their slogans. Listen and match the parts.

City / Country:	Slogan:	Problem:
1. City of Leeds	a. "My council clears up my mess."	w. contradictory
2. Nottingham	b. "Big country"	x. controversial
3. Wales	c. "Live it, love it"	y. uninspiring
4. Local Government Association	d. "N"	z. unoriginal

5 Translation

a. Match the English slogans with their German equivalents.

1. Just do it	a. Köstlich – erfrischend (Coca Cola)
2. The pause that refreshes	b. Globale Mobilität erfahren (Avis)
3. Make a house a home	c. Wohnst du noch oder lebst du schon? (Ikea)
4. The future of the automobile	d. Alles für diesen Moment (Lufthansa)
5. There's no better way to fly	e. Ich liebe es (McDonald's)
6. We try harder	f. Fortschritt beginnt mit einem Mercedes (Mercedes Benz)
7. I'm loving it.	g. Die Geheimwaffe der Athleten (Nike)

b. The verb 'to love' is not normally used in the progressive form. Do you know any slogans in German that use 'wrong' grammar? Discuss possible reasons for this.

c. The Cologne agency Endmark asked over 1000 German consumers whether they understood the meaning of well-known English slogans. What conclusions do you draw from the findings below?

Marke	Spruch	Diese Botschaft steht hinter dem Spruch	Spruch verstanden?	Einige ungewöhnliche Übersetzungen
Douglas	**"Come in and find out"**	*Komm herein und finde das Richtige (Bei Douglas finden Sie Ihr wahres 'Ich')*	34 %	*- Komm herein und finde wieder heraus. - Erst In sein, dann Out.*
Vodafone	**"Make the most of now"**	*Mach das Beste aus dem Augenblick*	33 %	*- Mach meist nicht alles - Mach keinen Most daraus*
Esso	**"We are drivers too"**	*Wir sind auch Autofahrer (Esso-Mitarbeiter sprechen die Sprachen der Kunden)*	31 %	*- Wir fahren nach … - Wir sind zwei Fahrer*
Audi TT	**"Driven by instinct"**	*Gefahren vom Instinkt (Ein Audi TT weckt einen neuen Instinkt beim Fahrer – den puren Fahrspaß)*	22 %	*- Abdriften der Instinkte - Triefen vor Gestank*
Mitsubishi	**"Drive alive"**	*Fahre lebend (Wer einen Mitsubishi fährt, entdeckt ein völlig neues Lebensgefühl)*	18 %	*- Leblos-Fahrer - Die Fahrt überleben*
Siemens	**"Be inspired"**	*Sei angesporn̈t (Siemens-Mobiltelefone inspirieren den Benutzer)*	15 %	*- Inspiziert sein - Bienen-Inspektion*
Centerparcs	**"A state of happiness"**	*Ein Platz / Zustand der Glückseligkeit*	13 %	*- Ein Staat der Glücklichkeit - Statt happy zu sein*

www.rp-online.de

d. Choose three slogans. Create a German slogan that expresses the message behind it. Then compare.

e. Follow-up: Suggest English equivalents for other slogans in German that you know.

D Business leaders | Shelly Lazarus

1 Reading

a. Read the article and note down the changes Shelly Lazarus has seen during her career in advertising.

b. Choose the correct option.

1. Shelly Lazarus is (enthusiastic / cautious / dismissive) about Facebook as an advertising platform.
2. She is (sceptical / positive / optimistic) about the role of banner ads and display ads as a way of advertising.
3. Her clients are (keen / reluctant / unprepared) to embrace new advertising media.
4. She is (gloomy / anxious / excited) about the rapid changes taking place in advertising.

c. What is Shelly Lazarus's view on product placement and 'branded content'? Give examples of other TV shows where these techniques are used.

2 Idioms

Explain the meanings of the expressions in bold.

1. … advertising campaigns for **blue-chip clients** …
2. They want to know how to deal with the **blogosphere**.
3. People shouldn't **wring their hands** …

3 Discussion

What methods of internet advertising do you think are effective? Which do you find annoying?

INFO

Product placement
Product placement is a form of advertising in which a company pays to have its product appear in a film or on television.

Madison Avenue
Madison Avenue is the street in New York City where the advertising industry originated. The name is still used to describe the New York advertising business generally and the larger agencies in particular.

'If you can think it, you can do it'

… "When I started in this business, if you had two television commercials, three print ads, some radio and a little bit of outdoor (billboards), that was something in those days. (…) The number of women is far higher. And everything in this business has a global perspective now. We run global accounts out of Beijing and Bangalore, we never used to do that." Today, says Lazarus, clients expect 'big ideas' expressed across an array of media platforms. "There's not just an openness, but a hunger to see what's possible. There's almost disappointment when you bring a client a media plan that looks like something they would have seen two years ago. They want new ideas. They want to know how to deal with the blogosphere."

What does she make of the advertising potential of the social networking phenomenon, particularly Facebook?

"The issue there is, 'Yes, it's a big, big thing, but how do you advertise on it? I'm not convinced banner ads and display ads do all that much. There are guys in the business who will show you those great charts, which say that people spend 20 % of their time online and those dumb advertisers only spend 4 % of their budgets there. Well … not so fast. How many times do you click on a display ad when you're online? And if you're not doing it and your friends aren't doing it, then you have to ask, who is? I think what the next few years are all about is figuring out how you advertise on the internet beyond display ads."

But if she thinks Facebook's moment as an effective advertising platform has yet to arrive, she's convinced that 'branded content' – a term that refers to brands playing an active role in TV drama or made-for-web video, rather than old-style product placement – is an increasingly important part of what advertising agencies do. "We've had the experience with Pond's (skin cream) in this TV show called The Starter Wife. You don't realise it, but there's always a moment in the show when, just as the lead character, who's taking life on again after her husband has left her for another woman, goes out into the world, she actually puts Pond's on her face. Now, that is a really cool thing for a brand. It says, 'I'm all set, I'm ready to go and take on the world.'"

"These days if you can think it, you can do it," she explains. "People shouldn't wring their hands and worry about how fast everything's changing. I always think that it's so much more interesting when we do things that have never been done before." She laughs. "That can be pretty wild, actually."

From: *The Guardian*, 6 October 2008

Shelly Lazarus (born 1947) is one of the most prominent figures in US advertising. Known as the Queen of Madison Avenue, she joined the advertising agency Ogilvy and Mather in 1971 when advertising was still a man's world. She rose to become chairman and CEO of the company, and created hugely successful advertising campaigns for blue-chip companies such as IBM, American Express and Unilever.

E Business communication | Conducting a survey

1 Listening: Market research

◎ A 1.24 **a.** You are going to hear an interview with Julia Hobday, an expert on market research. Which of the expressions in the word bank does she use? How does she explain them?

WORD BANK

Market research
to do research | to conduct a study | to carry out a survey | to gather data | to administer a questionnaire | qualitative / quantitative research | desk research | field research | primary / secondary research | benchmarking | to observe behaviour | cold call | response rate | (blind) tasting | to run a focus group | to conduct an interview | to evaluate the findings | to identify a trend | to avoid bias | to draw conclusions | to make recommendations

b. Decide whether these statements are true or false.

1. Personal interviews are less effective than online surveys, because people don't like human contact.
2. Many people don't like phone interviews because the caller is intruding into their private lives.
3. Focus groups are a good way of observing customer behaviour, by watching how shoppers respond.
4. Customers in supermarkets don't like tasting new things, because they think they'll have to pay for them.
5. A personal interview can be an opportunity to influence the customer to answer in a particular way.

c. Create a mind map to show the ways in which information is gathered through market research.

2 Questionnaires

a. The type of questions asked in a survey depend on what information is required. Match the following question types with those in the questionnaire.

1. Graded (a scale is given, 1 – 3 or 1 – 5).
2. Either / Or (only one box can be ticked).
3. Open (people can say anything).
4. Closed (specific information required).
5. Multiple choice (more than one answer).

b. Which questions are designed to obtain quantitative rather than qualitative information?

c. Can you guess what type of product the questionnaire is about? What other questions could you add to the list to get further information about the product?

LANGUAGE TIP

"What is your occupation?" is a more open question than "What is your profession?". It allows answers such as "I'm a student", "I'm a housewife, or "I'm looking for work".

Questionnaire

Please tick the boxes that apply to you, adding information as requested.

a. Which of the following age ranges are you in?
▪ below 18 ▪ 18 – 25 ▪ 25 – 40 ▪ 40 – 50 ▪ over 50

b. What is your occupation?
▪ office worker ▪ shop worker ▪ factory worker
▪ student ▪ other

c. Where does your annual income fit on the following scale?
▪ below € 30 k ▪ € 30 – 40 k ▪ € 40 – 50 k ▪ over € 50 k

d. What is your family status? (You may tick more than one item.)
▪ single ▪ couple ▪ one child ▪ more than one child

e. How often do you go food shopping?
▪ once or twice a month ▪ about once a week
▪ several times a week

f. Have you ever been to an Asian country? ▪ Yes ▪ No

g. If yes, which one(s)? ____________________

h. Do you like Asian food? ▪ Yes ▪ No

i. Do you know the names of any Asian desserts? ▪ Yes ▪ No

j. If yes, give examples ____________________

k. What flavours of dessert are popular at the moment?
____

l. Would you ever try a savoury ice-cream?
▪ Yes ▪ No ▪ Maybe

m. How do you rate the following aspects in a dessert?
(1 = very important, 2 = quite important, 3 = less important)
▪ creamy ▪ sweet ▪ exotic ▪ spicy ▪ colourful

n. How important are the following aspects when you buy a dessert?
▪ ingredients ▪ brand ▪ packaging ▪ price ▪ flavour

k = 1,000, **savoury** pikant, salzig, **spicy** scharf, würzig

3 Business writing

Write an email to respondents that could accompany the questionnaire. Bear in mind that you want to maximise the response rate in order to get reliable information.

4 Conducting a survey

a. You are a team of market researchers. Read the following brief from a client in Scotland who would like to launch a product on the German market.

Market research brief: MacDougall's Little Chieftain

The traditional haggis producers MacDougall's of Troon have been successful in repositioning their product on the UK market as an up-market specialty food, eaten at celebrations such as Burns Night and weddings. Now they are keen to break into the German-speaking regions of Europe, where sausages and other meat products are said to be very popular. The proposed strategy is to appeal to the mass market with new type of haggis sold under the brand name 'The Little Chieftain'. This is a revolutionary concept: a highly nutritious, bite-sized snack food that may be eaten cold or micro-waved and enjoyed in the Scottish way with 'mashed tatties and neeps'. This concept has not been tested in other markets, so it carries some risk. Research should aim to assess potential demand in Germany, Switzerland and Austria with a view to recommending a suitable marketing mix. Please carry out background research as well as a vox pop survey. An English version of your questionnaire should be submitted with the findings. Where possible, conduct the interviews in English.

nutritious nahrhaft, gesund, **bite-sized** mundgerecht, **mashed tatties and neeps** Kartoffelpüree und Steckrüben

b. Find out about the history of haggis, the ingredients, why 'Little Chieftain' was chosen as the brand name, and any interesting myths surrounding the product.

c. Before administering the vox pop survey, consider the following points.

- What type of people do you want to interview?
- Where will you conduct the interviews?
- How big should your sample be? How many responses are needed for reliable data?
- How long should your questionnaire be?
- What kind of questions do you need to ask to get the right information?
- Should you try the questionnaire out on a test person before taking it out to the public?
- Will you film or record the interviews? If so, for what purpose?
- How will you allocate tasks? Who should do what?

PHRASES

Conducting a survey

Asking for permission
- Excuse me. Have you got a moment?
- Could you spare a few moments of your time?
- Do you mind if I ask you a few questions?
- May I just ask you a few questions?
- Good morning. I'm interviewing people about … and I was wondering whether I could ask you a few questions.

Explaining the survey
- It will only take about five minutes.
- We're doing a survey on … in order to find out …

Closing the interview
- That was the last question.
- Well, I think that's everything.
- This has been really useful.
- You've been really helpful.
- Thanks once again for your time.

d. There are some things to avoid when interviewing. Explain the meaning of the words in bold.

1. When conducting a survey it is important that you remain **impartial**.
2. Don't ask questions that might result in **ambiguous** answers.
3. Make sure you don't **reveal** any personal bias during the interview.
4. Don't be **overbearing** when approaching a member of the public.
5. Resist the temptation to **anticipate** the answer in advance.
6. Interviewees will be **put off** by long or confusing questions.

e. Before conducting the survey, discuss how to optimise your response rate. Can you think of any special gimmick or event that might appeal to people, so that they are more prepared to give their time?

LANGUAGE TIP

The term vox pop comes from the Latin (*vox populi*), meaning interviews with the general public to find out opinions.

5 Debriefing

a. After conducting the interviews, get together to discuss what was difficult and what seemed to work. Consider the following questions to help you decide how to present your findings.

- What kind of information is best presented visually?
- How will you present the visual information?
- Do the findings correspond to what you expected?
- What responses do you find particularly surprising?
- Where are majority opinions clearly shown?
- Were any questions not satisfactorily answered?
- How do you interpret the more subjective responses?
- What findings are difficult to evaluate?
- Where is further research needed?

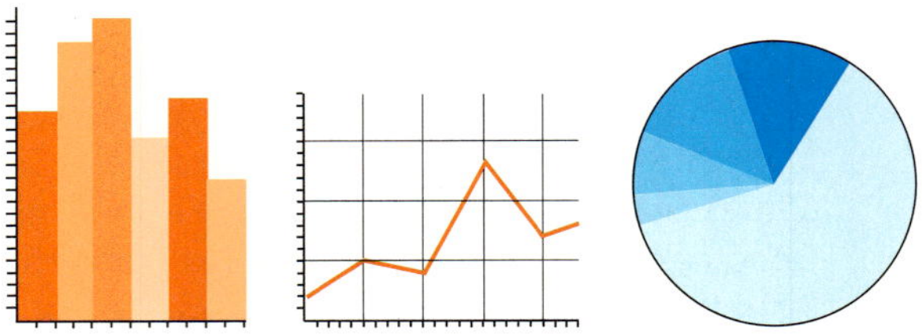

b. Prepare a summary of your findings to present in class. The tips and phrases below will help you.

Tips for the presenters
Deal with the quantitative data first, as this is more objective and can be supported with diagrams. Then deal with opinions and interpretations. Draw on both the quantitative and qualitative data in your conclusions.

Tips for the audience
Prepare a table for noting the results of the other groups as you listen to their presentations. In this way you can easily check their findings against your own. Also note down questions that you would like to ask afterwards.

PHRASES

Presenting results
- We were interested in people who were …
- Data was collected by means of …
- We devised a questionnaire that would help us to find out …
- We decided that the ideal number of interviews should be …
- The findings show that …
- As you can see from this graph, …
- A clear majority of those interviewed preferred …
- More than half of the respondents said that …
- Of all the people we spoke to, only …
- One of the most surprising findings was …
- One of the difficulties was …
- The important conclusion from these results is …

6 Presenting the findings

Present and discuss your findings and conclusions. Suggest possible reasons for any differences.

7 Writing

Write a report for MacDougall's in which you describe your research and present your findings. A possible structure is shown below.

- Title of report
- Introduction: Background | Rationale
- Scope and procedures: Lines of inquiry | Research methods
- Findings: Response rate | Problems of interpretation | Analysis
- Evaluation: Conclusions and recommendations

Video Lounge Advertising campaign

BBC Motion Gallery

V 3 **a.** Hanna is a business student working as an intern at an advertising agency. You will see excerpts from a campaign that she helped with. As you watch, take notes on the following:

1. The customer's brief and the aims of the campaign
2. Hannah's ideas for the advertising campaign
3. The things that she learns during her time working at the agency
4. The director's response and comments when she presents her ideas

b. After viewing: What do you think could be the next step in the campaign?

F Case study | Advertising standards

Reading

a. Read the following ASA cases. Decide whether the complaints are justified according to the following criteria.

- Is the marketing communication socially irresponsible?
- Is it likely to offend its audience, or cause fear or distress without good reason?
- Does it show unsafe or anti-social behaviour?
- Does it encourage people to break the law?

INFO

The Advertising Standards Authority
The Advertising Standards Authority (ASA) regulates the content of advertisements, sales promotions and direct marketing in the UK. It makes sure standards are kept high by applying codes, monitoring ads to spot problems, and it investigates complaints. The outcomes of the complaints process are published on its website: http://www.asa.org.uk/asa/

They're not so grrr-eat!
A member of the public had gone to the cinema expecting to enjoy a film and a box of popcorn. Upon leaving the cinema they contacted the Advertising Standards Authority (ASA) to complain about a commercial they had seen for the breakfast cereal Frosties.
The cinema commercial in question featured young boys playing football and practising their skills in the streets of Rio. Tony the Tiger, the cartoon character used to promote Kellogg's Frosties, appeared and encouraged the boys with the line, 'Not bad ... but we can do better than that'. As the boys continued to practice a voiceover stated, 'Train hard, eat right and earn your stripes.' before finishing with a shot of a bowl of cereal and a packet of Frosties.

Why do you think the complaint was made? ....
Do you think the ASA agreed with the complaint? Yes [ ] No [ ]

Is it clear that this is an advertisement?
A typed letter drops through the letterbox. 'Everyone has their weakness', it says. 'So, what might drive you wild? Could it be the touch of skin on your fingertips? A long, honed body? Firm sensuous curves? A deep, responsive purr? Or, do you simply like the feeling of raw power? If so, I think I have the perfect match for you. I'll send you a photograph next week'. The letter is signed by 'Elizabeth Jones' if the recipient is male; 'Ian Major' if female. What would you think if the letter was sent to you?
Clarification came when a follow-up mailing arrived a week later. A large envelope arrived, stating 'Prepare to be seduced', and contained promotional information on the new Jaguar XK. 37 people wrote to the ASA to complain.

Why do you think the complaint was made? ....
Do you think the ASA agreed with the complaint? Yes [ ] No [ ]

The stuff of nightmares?
Six parents contacted the ASA to complain about two advertisements for Marmite. The ad began in a supermarket where a woman ran screaming in terror into the street. A large amorphous brown blob then appeared, squeezing through the entrance to the supermarket, whilst a young couple were seen running away from it and trying to hide. Suddenly, the young woman realised that the blob was made of Marmite, a smile spread over her face, she began running towards the blob and dived into it. As the woman appeared half submerged in the blob, eating Marmite and smiling, onscreen text stated, 'YOU EITHER LOVE IT OR HATE IT.'
The six viewers who complained were upset because their children, aged between two and three years, had been distressed by the ad. It was broadcast on a children's TV channel.

Why do you think the complaint was made? ....
Do you think the ASA agreed with the complaint? Yes [ ] No [ ]

b. Look on page 218 to see how the ASA responded in each case. Give your opinion of their decisions.

c. Follow up: Compare the ASA standards in the UK with those of another country, such as Germany, France or the USA. What are the main differences?

Unit 6
Sales and distribution

Online Link
800021-0006

A Introduction | Music distribution

1 Quick response

a. Do you know any professional musicians? Discuss how you think they make most of their money.

b. How do you listen to music and how do you access it? Take turns asking and answering questions.

Example:
"When did you last buy a CD from a record store?" - "I don't remember. I always buy them online!"

c. Which of the formats on the right can be easily be copied? Discuss how this affects the music industry.

WORD BANK

Music distribution
Sources of revenue CD sales | sales of concert tickets | sponsorship deals | merchandising | media interviews | …
Formats audio cassette | mini-disc | vinyl | CD | music video | MP3 file | live music | …
Sources of supply record stores | street traders | vendors at gigs | P2P file-sharing | websites | download stores | …

gig Auftritt, Engagement, **vinyl** Schallplatte

2 Music sales and distribution

a. Work in pairs. Design PowerPoint slides to present this information in diagrammatic form.

For a CD that retails at $15.99, only $1.60 (10%) goes to the artist and $1.76 (11%) to the record company. The major costs are $3.84 (24%) for retail overheads, $2.88 (18%) for record label overheads, and $2.40 (15%) for marketing and promotion. The remainder is accounted for by distribution $0.96 (6%), retailers' profit of 80 cents (5%), and 80 cents (5%) in publishing royalties. Finally, $0.80 (5%) goes to manufacturing, $0.16 (1%) to the musician's unions.
In 1991 consumers spent $11.8bn on recorded music, more than half of that on CDs. By 1994 the figure was $16.7bn, with CDs accounting for three quarters of sales. Vinyl was on the way out. In 2000, music sales peaked at $17bn, nearly 100% from CDs. By 2006, however, sales had fallen to $10.6bn and 10% of this total was in the form of digital music. It is predicted that by 2012 as much as half of all music purchases will be in digital form.

b. How do you expect the trend in digital recordings to continue?

c. Suggest a form of distribution that would reduce the markups on the $15.99 CD.

3 Distribution models

a. Read the descriptions of two distribution models at either ends of a spectrum. Which one would you recommend for artists who have limited resources but want to make their own decisions?

The 360-deal
One company handles every aspect of the artist's career. The artist receives a lump sum, usually up front. The company makes money from concert revenue, music and video sales, and merchandising. The artist has limited creative control. The singer Madonna signed a 360-deal with LiveNation in return for around $250m.

The DIY-model
The artist writes, produces, plays, markets and distributes the music. CDs are sold at gigs and through a website. Promotion is done through the internet, e.g. on MySpace. The artist has complete creative control. The band Radiohead, for example, even allowed fans to name their own price for downloading their music.

b. What kind of companies are LiveNation and MySpace? Suggest ways in which they can help artists.

c. Describe the kind of deals that might exist between these two extremes.

4 Listening

A 1.25 You are going to hear an interview with a concert promoter, Greg Harris, in which he talks about distributing music online. Take notes on the following points:

methods of selling online | benefits | taking payments | profits | merchandising

5 Your advice

a. Read the quotes, then note down some survival strategies for musicians and the record business.

"What is called the music business today is not the business of producing music. At some point it became the business of selling CDs in plastic cases, and that business will soon be over. But that's not bad news for music, and it's certainly not bad news for musicians. Indeed, with all the ways to reach an audience, there have never been more opportunities for artists."

David Byrne, singer/songwriter of Talking Heads

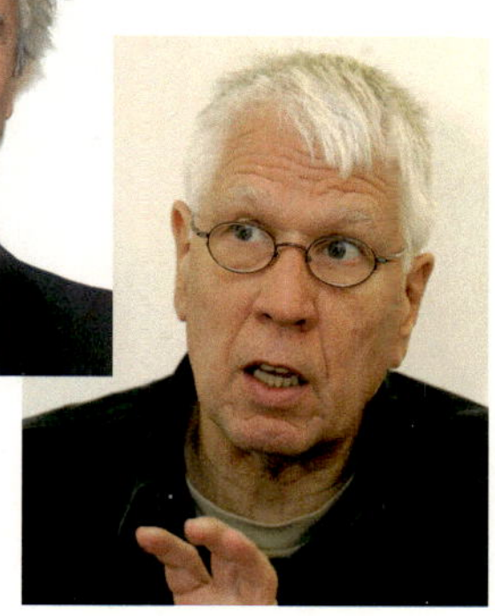

"Let's face up to it. We're in a crisis, which is not getting better. The last ten years have got consistently worse. The reality is that people are downloading for free. We've got to compete with free. I can't see that anything that's going on at the moment with the record business is going to solve what's happening."

Peter Jenner, former manager of Pink Floyd and Marc Bolan

Opportunities for musicians include …

› ....

› ....

› ....

The record business could survive by …

› ....

› ....

› ....

b. Discuss your ideas. What advice would you give to a new band starting out in your country today?

6 Business terms

The term 'merchandise' is often used in connection with marketing. Suggest merchandise that could be used to promote or exploit the following products and events:

- a celebrity chef
- a Harry Potter film
- the Olympic Games

B Business briefing | Distribution channels

1 Listening

A 1.26 **a.** You are going to hear a lecture on distribution channels, in which students were given handouts of six PowerPoint slides. The first four are shown below. Listen to the first part of the lecture and take notes.

❶ DISTRIBUTION CHANNELS

Definition:

How ______________ get goods and services
to ______________ at the right ___________
and at the right ___________

❷ DIRECT SALES

Producer → Outlet → Customer

- Producer: • Example:
- Outlet: • Example:

❸ AGENTS

Producer → Agent → Final customer

❹ REPRESENTATIVES

Producer → Representative → Final customer

b. Compare your notes with a partner and make any necessary changes.

A 1.26 **c.** Listen to the lecture again and decide what the remaining slides show. Create a handout of the two slides and swap it with a partner. Complete your partner's handout and then compare notes.

SKILLS

5–7 rule
When you make slides in PowerPoint, the 5–7 rule can be useful:
- No more than 5–7 slides in a 10-minute presentation
- No more than 5–7 bullet points per slide.
- No more than 5–7 words per bullet point.

d. The lecturer asks students for examples of franchises. Note their answers and add your own examples.

Students' examples: ....

Further examples: ....

e. What was the lecturer's final question? Write his exact words.

....

f. Discuss the lecturer's question above as well as the two below.

- What are the advantages / disadvantages in shortening the distribution chain?
- How can small retailers respond in the face of competition from out-of-town superstores?

LANGUAGE TIP

Tante Emma Laden
= corner shop / village shop (BE)
= mom n' pop store (AE)

2 Business issue: the grey market

a. Read the article and summarise the main points. The following headings may help you.

brand owner | official distributor | unofficial supplier | retailer | the dispute | precedents | aspects to consider

Grey market

A row between high-street chemist Boots and premium haircare brand Paul Mitchell has cast the spotlight back on the murky world of so-called 'grey market' goods.

Boots has begun to sell Paul Mitchell products in its flagship stores, to the annoyance of the brand's distributor, Salon Success, which wants them stocked in select hairdressers only. Boots obtained the goods from an unnamed supplier, without permission from Salon Success, and the spat now appears to have reached deadlock.

At the heart of this and other grey-market rows is the struggle between the retailer and the brand over which calls the shots in terms of distribution. Brand owners believe that a product's channel to market is intrinsically linked to its brand equity. It may be that they have also signed an exclusivity deal with a certain chain, as is common with FMCG brands. Whatever the reasons, retailers often show little sympathy with the brand owner's strategy.

The grey market is, indeed, opaque. Verdict Research consulting director Neil Saunders defines it as 'not illegal, but an unofficial channel through which goods are sold'. He says the concept covers anything from intermediaries to official buyers who find themselves with excess stock and offload it to another retailer.

'Buyers are very well-connected, and know where they can get certain goods while others are approached directly by people. It's all very ad hoc,' he adds.

To some people, the idea of wanting to limit a brand's distribution seems absurd. A few eyebrows were raised last year when it was revealed that SABMiller was considering restricting sales of beer brand Peroni to maintain its integrity. John Littleton, Miller Brands UK corporate services director, says: 'It's very important that a brand like Peroni is presented in the best way in the right outlets'.

The grey market, inevitably, also occupies a grey area of the law. Predicting the outcome of a dispute based on past examples is therefore impossible, as each has to be taken on a case-by-case basis, argues Peter Lidgey, managing director of shopper marketing specialist OgilvyAction.

Tesco and Levi's, for example, had a 'grey' row, from which the jeans brand emerged triumphant in 2002. Lidgey says it was the fact that Tesco was buying its stock from outside Europe that swung the case in Levi's favour.

However, he sounds a note of caution with regards to the reaction of Paul Mitchell. Lidgey claims to have seen research indicating that 40 % of consumers are visiting hairdressing salons less frequently. 'With this in mind, perhaps Paul Mitchell should revisit its channel strategy, reconsider Boots and move to a position where it is in control.'

Brands wanting to retain exclusivity could face a dilemma in a recession. As consumers' spending power diminishes, the prospect of wider distribution through grey-market channels may be an opportunity, rather than a threat, for brands. ◆

Marketing Magazine, 24 February 2009

row Streit, **murky** dunkel, finster **spat** Streit, **to call the shots** das Sagen haben, **opaque** (here) unklar, **excess** überschüssig, **to raise a few eyebrows** für etwas Stirnrunzeln sorgen, **to sound a note of caution** als Warnung hinzufügen

b. Conduct a simulation in which you discuss the case from the viewpoints of those involved.

Scenario
Paul Mitchell, Salon Success and Boots all want to avoid a legal battle. In order to find a solution, an emergency meeting has been arranged with managers representing each company.

Step 1 Preparation
Divide into three groups, each group representing one of the companies. Discuss the options available to you and agree on a strategy. If your strategy involves 'secret' communication with one of the other companies, do this in writing.

Step 2 Meeting
Regroup, so that in the meeting you have at least one representative from each company. Agree on a time limit and choose someone to chair the meeting.

Step 3 Outcome
Draft a press release in which you summarise the outcome of the meeting.

c. Find out whether and how the dispute has been resolved.

LANGUAGE TIP

Types of market
Grey market: legal but secret trade in goods and services through unofficial or unauthorised channels. Also called the parallel market.
Black market: illegal trade in goods and services that are themselves illegal or are traded through illegal channels, e.g. unregistered guns, stolen cars, counterfeit goods

SKILLS

Simulations
When you analyse an issue, doing a simulation can help you to identify the main issues and viewpoints and offer an insight into the 'human element', or the subjective factors that affect the issue.

C Language | Delivery and payment

1 Types of transport

a. Draw lines linking the types of transport to the modes, nodes and examples.

Type	Mode	Node	Examples
vehicles	by sea, canal or inland waterway	airport	barge, boat, container ship, ferry, hovercraft, yacht, tanker
aircraft	by air, through space	port, harbour	cargo plane, jumbo jet, helicopter, zeppelin, rocket, hot-air balloon, parachute
vessels	by road	station	bicycle, car, van, motorbike, lorry, truck, road train
	by rail	depot	freight train, tram, monorail, rack (or cog) rail, cable car, funicular, locomotive

b. Give examples of the following:

Goods that can be sent by pipeline: ....

Goods that can be sent by cable: ....

c. Compare types and modes of transport in terms of the following:

- Cost over long distances
- Speed over long distances
- Safety and security
- Flexibility and convenience

LANGUAGE TIP

Safety vs. security
Safety: protection against physical damage or harm
Security: protection against crime, terrorism, loss or theft

d. Compare the forms of transport shown below. Where might they be useful, and why?

e. Discuss the best way to transport these items.

1. urgent medical supplies from Basel to Colombia
2. fresh coriander from Thailand to Frankfurt
3. a painting from Munich to London
4. cuckoo clocks from Triberg to Beijing
5. toxic waste from Naples to Stuttgart
6. a racehorse from Dubai to Vienna
7. steel from Cologne to Palermo
8. a kidney (for transplant) from Delhi to Liechtenstein
9. cut glass bowls from Prague to Chicago

WORD BANK

Transporting goods
bulky | can be delivered in bulk | fragile | perishable | urgently required | valuable | dangerous | hazardous | toxic | inflammable

LANGUAGE TIP

Place names

Bayern – Bavaria	Köln – Cologne
Wien – Vienna	München – Munich
Hannover – Hanover	Luzern – Lucerne

2 Transport logistics

Complete the text with these words.

packages | forwarding | destination | weight | paperwork | transportation | quantities | consider | meets | uneconomical | perishable | deciding | account | consolidated | lease | bulk | deliveries | warehousing | premises | container | depending | ship | haulage | delivered

When .... on a type of transport that .... the distribution needs of your business, there are several factors to ....
First of all, it is important to take into .... the nature of the goods to be .... In the case of .... goods, for example, it makes sense to use refrigerated transport. Secondly, you need to decide whether to buy your business vehicles, ... them, or use a carrier. If you prefer to use a carrier, there are several options to choose from, ... on whether you plan to .... goods on a regular basis and in ...., or infrequently and in small ....:

- **Couriers** specialise in the fast and secure delivery of important papers and small .... They only deliver goods up to a certain ...., but most operate internationally as well as nationally.
- **Hauliers**, also known as .... firms, transport goods by road. They will collect goods from your .... and deliver them to your chosen .... However, if your consignment does not completely fill up the van or truck, this option may be ....
- **Freight forwarders**, also known as .... agencies, specialise in .... shipments. This means that they combine your goods with other .... in a single vehicle or ...., which reduces the costs. They usually offer support services, such as organising the .... for export.
- **Logistics service providers** manage the complete .... process, as well as tracking goods and arranging the shipping documents. They can also provide .... and local distribution centres.

LANGUAGE TIP

liefern / Lieferung
liefern – to deliver, to ship, to send, to transport
beliefern – to supply
Lieferung (als Handlung) – delivery, shipping
Lieferung (als Warensendung) – delivery, consignment, shipment

3 Terms of payment

a. Match the English terms with their German equivalents.

1. payment in instalments	a. Zahlung gegen Nachnahme
2. one third with order	b. Zahlung bei Auftragserteilung
3. within 30 days of receipt of goods	c. ein Drittel bei Auftragserteilung
4. on open account	d. innerhalb von 30 Tagen nach Erhalt der Waren
5. 10 days 3 %, 30 days net	e. Ratenzahlungen, Teilzahlungen
6. cash on delivery (COD)	f. auf offene Rechnung, mit offenem Zahlungsziel
7. cash with order (CWO)	g. 3 % Skonto bei Zahlung innerhalb von 10 Tagen

b. Complete the sentences giving a payment term and a reason.

1. .... carries a high risk for the customer because
....
....

2. .... carries a high risk for the supplier because
....
....

c. What could a customer say to persuade a supplier to offer more favourable terms? Write sentences with 'if'. Then compare your sentences.

Example:
If I place a larger order, would you be willing to reduce the price?

4 Business idioms

The same verb is missing in each sentence. Decide what it is and complete the sentences by putting the verb in the right form. Then match the sentences with the meaning in which the verb is used.

1. We've .... short of supplies.
2. We .... out of fuel.
3. When does your visa .... out?
4. Our costs .... into seven figures last year.
5. They are .... into difficulties.
6. I've .... up a lot of debts.
7. Would you mind .... off some copies for me?
8. Let's .... through the presentation again.

a. expire
b. have not enough left
c. rehearse or practise
d. produce on a machine
e. amount to
f. incur
g. exhaust the supply of sth.
h. unexpectedly encounter sth.

5 Commonly confused words

a. Explain the difference in meaning. Use a dictionary if necessary.

1. a. It will be **delivered** on Monday.
   b. It will be **dispatched** on Monday.
2. a. We can deliver **until** Christmas.
   b. We can deliver **by** Christmas.
3. a. We can't deliver **until** Christmas.
   b. We can't deliver **by** Christmas.
4. a. We can **assure** you that you …
   b. We can **ensure** that you …
5. a. It's impossible to **control**.
   b. It's impossible to **check**.
6. a. They can't **deliver** us.
   b. They can't **supply** us.
7. a. Didn't you **notify** XYZ?
   b. Didn't you **notice** XYZ?
   c. Didn't you **note** XYZ?
8. a. He **requested** an invoice.
   b. He **required** an invoice.
9. a. The bar code is on the **packing**.
   b. The bar code is on the **packaging**.
   c. The bar code is on the **package**.

b. Complete the sentences, choosing from the words above.

1. To .... the smooth delivery of your order, we must draw your attention to the following points.
2. You order will not be .... from our warehouse .... payment has been received in full.
3. Please .... us in advance of any access problems, such as narrow doors or difficult stairs.
4. If a later delivery date is ...., you must .... it as soon as possible, and no later than 48 hours before the confirmed delivery date.
5. On delivery you will be asked to .... whether the correct number of .... have been delivered.
6. If you have not received your delivery .... the agreed date or within the given timescale, please leave seven days before contacting our customer service team.
7. Please .... that we do not .... customers outside mainland England and Wales. Contact us for more information about where we can and cannot ....

c. Match the illustrations with 7 corresponding words from the list on the left. Which are packing and which are packaging?

[ ] bubble wrap
[ ] carton
[ ] shrink wrap
[ ] polystyrene peanuts
[ ] polystyrene blocks
[ ] crate
[ ] cardboard box
[ ] blister pack
[ ] aerosol can
[ ] drum
[ ] barrel
[ ] bottle
[ ] pallet

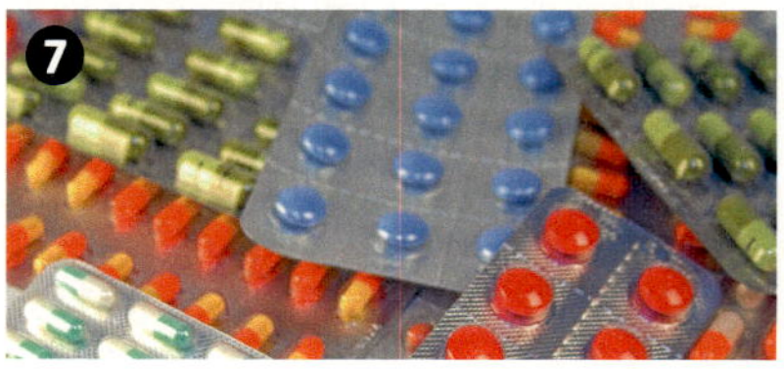

D Business leaders | Gary Corner (Lands' End)

1 Quick response

Have you ever bought clothes by mail order? Why, or why not?

2 Speed reading

Scan the paragraphs and put in the following headings:

The apostrophe | Snapshot | Direct merchants | Inlets and outlets | Landsend.com | Lifetime guarantee

LANDS'END DIRECT MERCHANTS

....

Lands' End Inc is an international mail order company based in Dodgeville, Wisconsin, that sells everyday clothing and accessories. It has a reputation for offering good quality at affordable prices, and for its customer service.

....

The company refers to itself as direct merchant rather than a retailer or marketer because it buys directly from mills and manufacturers and sells directly to customers. It claims that this method reduces prices by "eliminating the markups of middlemen", and also makes shopping "simpler, faster and more convenient".

....

Most of Lands' End's business is conducted through catalogues and the internet, but it also runs its own 'brick and mortar' retail operations. In 2009, it was operating 16 stores in the US, three in the UK and one in Germany. The company distinguishes between its so-called Inlet® stores that sell full price catalogue items and 'outlet' stores that sell overstocks and NQP™ (not quite perfect) items at a discount.

....

Lands' End is seen as one of the 'early adopters' of the internet with the launch of its website in 1995. It has separate websites for the UK, Japan and Germany, as well as a Business Outfitters website selling corporate gifts and clothing. It was also the website that enabled customers to see what clothes would look like on their body types. Using a tool called My Virtual Model™, they can create a 3-D model of themselves and 'try on' clothes from the catalogue.

....

The business started out in 1963 as Lands' End Yacht Stores, selling sailing equipment by mail order. It was named after the headland in Cornwall, Land's End. The founder, Gary Corner, admitted that the apostrophe in the company name is in the wrong place. He wrote: "There have been some silly explanations along the way, but the truth is, it was a mistake. It was a typo in our first printed piece, and we couldn't afford to reprint and correct it."

....

As well as its apostrophe, Lands' End is also known for its 'Guaranteed.Period' policy. This refers not to a guarantee period, but an unconditional guarantee: "If any purchase fails to meet your expectations in any way, you can return it at any time for an exchange, or refund, whether you've worn it, washed it or simply don't like the colour. No questions, no quibble, no problem." When Lands' End entered Germany, the courts banned it from using the guarantee in its advertising on the grounds that it violated competition rules. Lands' End filed a complaint with the European Commission, and in August 2001 the rules were abolished. Since then, not only Lands' End but also other companies have been able to promote their products in Germany with similar guarantees.

quibble Herumrederei, **to violate a rule** eine Regel missachten

3 Analysis

1. Where does Lands' End operate? Why do you think it chose these particular countries and types of outlet?
2. Summarise the benefits that Lands' End offers its customers.
3. Explain the mistake in the name and suggest why it has not been corrected. (Tip: Check the website for the official reason.)
4. What problem did Lands' End have with its guarantee? How was it resolved, and how did this affect other suppliers?
5. Is this guarantee good business practice? Discuss your views.

LANGUAGE TIP

We say "dot com" for internet addresses, but the **dot** at the end of a sentence is known as a **period** (AE) or a **full stop** (BE). When a statement is ended with the word 'period', as in "You're not going to the movies, period", the speaker means that there is no **point** in arguing. An equivalent expression is "No ifs or buts".

4 Planning and presenting

Develop a concept for a mail order company that would be able to beat Lands' End at its own game in your country. List the factors that give it a competitive advantage and present your concept in class.

E Business communication | Solving delivery problems

1 Writing for business

a. Read the email and mark the phrases that call for action, directly or indirectly.

From: kress_f@brammertz.bit
Subject: Dispatch of fleece jackets, Order no. 277/09AU
Date: August 18, 03:32:44 PM CET
To: A.Khmel@bigshot.com

Dear Mr Khmel,
I am writing to confirm that your order for 500 fleece jackets (277/09AU) has been dispatched from our depot today. The goods should reach you by the end of August, delivered to your premises DDP as agreed.
The consignment is packed in five batches of 100, in sizes S-M-L-XL-XXX as requested. Each batch contains the logos of the five top German Bundesliga football teams applied to 20 jackets each. The batches are individually labelled and bar-coded as per the consignment note. You will also find enclosed a certificate of origin, packing list and commercial invoice.
We can confirm receipt of the €2,000 part-payment of our invoice and would ask you to transfer the remaining sum of €8,500 within 14 days of receipt of the goods. Please also notify us once the goods have arrived.
We are sure you will be delighted with our products, and we look forward to receiving further orders from you.
Yours sincerely,
Florian Kress
Sales Department
Brammerts SportsLife GmbH

b. The vowels in the marked words are missing. Write the words in full.

Brammert SportsLife GmbH
Attn.: Florian Kress
Sls Dprtmnt
Waldenburger Str. 20-25
89231 Neu-Ulm
Germany

BIGSHOT BOUTIQUES
Levstikov trg 7
1000 Ljubljana
Slovenia

28 August 20...

Dlvry of Brammerts Sportslife jackets 227/09AU

Dear Mr Kress,

Frthr to your email of 18 August, I can **cnfrm rcpt** of the **bv**-mentioned **cnsgnmnt**. However, on unpacking it, our Goods Inward **dprtmnt** discovered that the wrong **tms** have been sent. The address and the **br cd** on the boxes appear to be **crrct**, but the items **cntnd** in the boxes are children's football **bts**, not the Bundesliga jackets we **rdrd**. The **pckng** list indicates that they are intended for a **rtlr** in Ljublana that **spclss** in school **clthng** and children's **sprtswr**.

An **rrr** has **clrly** been made in the processing of the **dlvry**. With the new **Erpn** football **ssn** only a few **wks** away, a **hgh dmnd** is **xpctd** for **ths** jackets, so you will **pprct** that this is an **rgnt** matter. We **wld** therefore be **grtfl** if you could **cntct** us at your earliest **pprtnty** to let us **knw** how you **pln** to **rctfy** the **mttr**.

We look **frwrd** to your **prmpt rspns**.

Bst rgds,

Alexander Khmel

Prchsng Mngr

Note: It is usual to abbreviate 'attention' as 'attn' in addresses, so it is not a mistake here.

c. Discuss what options are open to Florian when he receives Alexander's fax. What could he suggest to Alexander?

d. Florian decides to put his suggestions in writing. Write his email reply to Alexander.

e. Swap emails. Choose one of the emails to use as a basis for a role-play in which Alexander phones Florian in order to decide on a solution.

2 Listening

A 1.27–29 **a.** You are an intern at the Glasgow-based transport firm McKellar European Logistix. Listen to three recorded messages that were left on your phone and note down any important details.

MESSAGE 1
Caller: ____
Tel. No of caller: ____
Message: ____
Action: ____

MESSAGE 2
Caller: ____
Tel. No of caller: ____
Message: ____
Action: ____

MESSAGE 3
Caller: ____
Tel. No of caller: ____
Message: ____
Action: ____

b. Compare your notes. Decide what to do and the order in which to do it.

- How will you explain the delay in delivery to Kränzle in Troisdorf?
- What action do you need to take before contacting Stella McKeenan?
- Who should you contact about the delivery of spoiled milk powder?
- What else do you need to do?

c. Role-play the phone calls you need to make.

PHRASES

Dealing with urgent problems

Presenting the problem

Getting attention
- Do you have a moment / a few minutes?
- May I (just) have a quick word with you?
- I hate to bother you right now, but …

Describing the problem
- We're having a bit of a problem here.
- There's been (another) hitch with …
- I'm afraid it looks as if …

Asking for help
- I wonder if you could possibly …
- I was wondering whether you could …
- I'd really appreciate it if you could …
- Would you mind helping me out here?

Expressing urgency
- I'm afraid it's urgent.
- I'm sorry, but it really can't wait.
- Look, we've got a meltdown situation here.

Thanking for help
- Thanks, you've been such a help.
- Thanks, you've saved my skin / my neck.
- That's really kind of you.
- You're a star!

Responding to the problem

Asking for details
- So what's the problem exactly?
- What seems to be the matter?
- And what do you think has caused / is causing it?

Expressing surprise / sympathy
- Oh dear! I'm very sorry to hear that.
- How awful / terrible / strange / embarrassing!
- Yes, that is a bit unfortunate / awkward, isn't it?

Reassuring
- Don't worry! We'll sort it out in no time.
- Never mind. We'll manage.
- I'm sure we can come to some arrangement.

Agreeing to help / Refusing to help
- Yes, by all means. / Yes, of course.
- Sure, no problem. I'll get on to it right now.
- I'll look into the matter straight away.
- The best thing to do in this situation is …
- Well, all right. But it won't be easy.
- I'm afraid there's absolutely nothing I can do.
- No, I'm afraid I can't because …
- This isn't really my department.
- I'm sorry I can't be more helpful.

F Consulting | In-store design

Supermarket retailing has become increasingly competitive, and issues such as store layout and consumer behaviour present a huge challenge in retail management.

1 Analysis and preparation

a. You work for the consultancy 1-Handel. Read the emails and the attachment and draw up a list of the tasks assigned to you by your boss, Marco Heidinger.

b. Decide which tasks involve field research and which desk research. If you are working in a team, make sure everyone knows who is going to do what, and by when.

Von: hei@1-handel.de
Betreff: Wtrlt: FW: Hi-Lo
Datum: Montag, 30.März, 10:26:34 AM CET
An: intern.i-handel
Anhang: Anhang, 148bytes

Guten Morgen,
unten finden Sie eine E-Mail von Clive Parker, dem Leiter der amerikanischen Lebensmittelkette Hi-Lo. Er hat vor, in unserer Region eine Filiale aufzumachen (die erste in Europa!) und hat unsere Firma als Berater beauftragt. Wir sollen unter anderem einen Grundriss erstellen, der zeigt, wo die verschiedenen Regale und Waren platziert werden sollen. Ich möchte Ihnen dieses Projekt übergeben.
Bitte lesen Sie seine E-Mail und die angehängten Hinweise durch, die auf der Basis neuester wissenschaftlicher Erkenntnisse erstellt worden sind. Es wäre auch sinnvoll, ein oder zwei Supermärkte in der Region zu besuchen, um die Stärken und Schwächen des regionalen Einzelhandels festzustellen.
Bitte schicken Sie mir Grundrissentwurf und Empfehlungen sobald wie möglich zu.
Viele Grüße,
Marco Heidinger

>>

From: c.parker@hi-lo.com
To: hei@1-handel.de
Date: Monday, March 29, 04:36:05 PM GMT
Subject: Re: Hi-Lo

Hi Marco
Thanks for the quick response! As you say, we should focus on quality and service, and not try to compete with the discount stores on price. So now we'd like some concrete suggestions from you on how to optimize in-store traffic and maximize purchases and profits.
In particular, we need a 'plan-a-gram' of the store layout, plus any ideas you have about brands, promotions, buyer behavior, and of course the 'human dimension'. For example, at our stores here in Chicago, we hire greeters to welcome shoppers as they enter. Do you have those, too? And will German speakers understand the reference to 'high quality, low prices' in Hi-Lo? If not, please give alternatives!

I look forward to discussing your ideas when we meet next month.
Clive

in-store traffic Anzahl von Kunden, die durch den Laden gehen **buyer behavior** Kundenverhalten

In-store planning checklist

Decompression zone:
Design an entrance area that forces people to slow down when they enter the store. This helps them get into shopping mode and is a good place for promotions. Consider whether to hire 'greeters', as this is said to cut shoplifting.

Dwell time:
The longer customers dwell in the store, the more they spend. Place everyday items and perishables such as milk at the back of the store to force people to explore. In this way, they can be tempted into buying more products.

Fruit and vegetables:
Place these near the entrance because selecting healthy, fresh food is an uplifting way to start shopping. It might be more practical to have fruit and vegetables near the tills so that they don't get squashed in the trolley. But here psychological factors are more important.

Aromas:
The smell of freshly baked bread makes people feel hungry. If there's an in-store bakery, place it near the entrance. The smell will encourage people to buy not just bread but other food as well. If there is no in-store bakery, the smell should be created artificially.

Shelf positioning:
Arrange branded products at eye-level (or slightly higher), and cheaper ones lower down, along with the supermarket's own-label products. The most profitable goods should be on the right of eye-level goods, since most people are right-handed and their eyes drift rightwards.

End caps:
Place potential treats and impulse buys at the end caps (the ends of each aisle), because this is where shoppers have to slow down to turn their trolleys.

Pester-power:
Place sweets at the eye-level of children. This is particularly effective at the tills, where it is difficult for parents to resist their children's pester-power.

Complaints:
Suggest ways to avoid queues, goods out of stock, poor levels of service, lack of price tags.

Music:
Suggest music that will encourage purchases. For example, French accordion music is said to boost sales of wine, whereas Bavarian oompah tunes sell more lager.

Radio Frequency Identification (RFID) tags:
These contain more information than bar codes and are revolutionising the distribution process. They can be used to track 'movable assets' (goods and customers) and have the potential to deter shoplifting, reduce queues, and even make tills redundant. However, there are issues of privacy that should be considered.

Further statistics to bear in mind:
* 71 % of shoppers look right when they enter a store.
* 89 % of Americans are compulsive shoppers.
* Only 22 % of consumers throw away food that has passed its sell-by date.
* Women tend to browse in shops, while men adopt a 'grab-and-exit' strategy.

Adapted from: *BBC Focus Magazine*, Issue 198, January 2009; *The Economist*, 18 December 2008

decompression zone hier: Entspannungszone (um Kunden in Einkaufsstimmung zu bringen), **dwell time** Verweilzeit, **to tempt** verlocken, ködern, **treat** Leckerei, Süßigkeit, **to pester** plagen, bedrängen, **oompah music** Volksfestmusik, **to deter** abschrecken, **compulsive** zwanghaft, **to browse** stöbern, durchsuchen

2 Presenting the results

Present the results in the form of a written report and / or an oral presentation. Describe your methods, findings and conclusions.

LANGUAGE TIP

BE	AE
shopping trolley	shopping cart
till / checkout	checkout
queue	line
sweets	candy
behaviour	behavior
optimise	optimize

Unit 7
Manufacturing

Online Link
800021-0007

A Introduction | Inside a factory

1 Discussion

a. Have you ever done any of these things? Describe what you learned from the experience.

- taken part in a factory tour
- entered a clean-room
- driven a forklift
- operated machinery
- worked on a production line
- attended a lecture on a manufacturing topic

b. Suggest different ways of completing the sentences below.

1. Companies organise factory tours because …
2. The kind of people they typically invite include …
3. Visitors often want to know …
4. The organiser of the tour has to make sure that …

2 A factory tour

a. In groups, plan how to organise a factory tour. Read the scenario and follow the steps below.

Scenario: You are management trainees at Alustahl AG, a Swiss producer of steel and aluminium parts for the automotive industry. The CEO has decided that the company should offer factory tours, even though the production area is a harsh and noisy environment for visitors. Your task is to organise the tours. You have just learned that the first group consists of 30 teenagers from an American high school.

Step 1: Decide how visitors should tour the factory. Weigh up the options listed, adding your own suggestions or combining ideas from the ones given. Summarise your decision below.

1. Record a tour of the factory for visitors to listen to on headphones as they walk from one point of interest to the next.
2. Organise factory tours for small groups of people with production supervisors acting as 'tour guides' for each group.
3. Show a short film about the company and the production process before the visitors walk around, and then invite them to a Q&A session afterwards.
4. Give visitors worksheets when they arrive, which they can fill in during the tour. Then invite them to a Q&A session afterwards.

Decision: ....

Step 2: Discuss where to take them. Choose from the places listed on the right and note them below.

Decision: ....

Step 3: You intend to give everyone a Visitors' Kit when they arrive. Choose from the list of clothing and equipment, and note the items below.

Decision: ....

LANGUAGE TIP

Automobiles are produced on the **shop floor**, painted in the **paint shop** and repaired in the **body shop**.

Step 4: You would like the visitors to interview three people involved in manufacturing, especially skilled workers. Discuss who the visitors might want to interview and note down the jobs.

1. ....
2. ....
3. ....

WORD BANK

Places in factories
reception | locker room / changing room | assembly line / production line | shop floor | workshop | body shop | paint shop | clean-room | mill | stockroom | warehouse | …

Clothing and equipment
hard hat | goggles | fire extinguisher | hard boots | life jacket | overalls | ear defenders | waterproof suit | factory map | company brochure | gloves | fluorescent jacket | torch (AE flashlight) | mask | ID badge (AE button) | …

Jobs in manufacturing
assembly line worker | supervisor | health and safety officer | canteen staff | trainer | IT support | production manager | forklift driver | packer | quality manager | R&D engineer | welder | maintenance engineer | welder | procurement / purchasing manager | machine operator | foreman | …

b. Compare your decisions with those of other groups. Discuss how a tour organised for a group of Welsh pensioners or Japanese quality assurance managers might be different.

3 Listening

A 1.30–32 **a.** Listen to three interviews and take notes. Compare what three interviewees say about their jobs and discuss which jobs in manufacturing you would most / least like to do.

Interview	Name	Job	Tasks	Impressions of the job
1	....	....	....	....
2	....	....	....	....
3	....	....	....	....

b. How important is it for management trainees in industry to gain experience by 'getting their hands dirty' on the factory floor? Discuss the pros and cons of this policy.

4 Manufacturing methods

a. Match the terms with the definitions.

1. Kanban
2. just-in-time production
3. mass production
4. Industrial Revolution
5. cottage industry
6. agile manufacturing
7. lean production
8. nanotechnology
9. craft production

a. system where things are made only when they are needed
b. emergence of the factory system of production, starting in England
c. producing goods in large quantities using machinery
d. small business in which the work is done by people in their homes
e. making things by hand using traditional skills
f. system aiming to cut costs by minimising waste and optimising efficiency
g. making very small items using molecular processes
h. operations that can be rapidly configured to satisfy changes in the market
i. a visual tool that signals the movement of parts around a factory

b. Discuss where to place a – h as milestones on the timeline below.

Early manufacturing → Today

B Business briefing | Manufacturing processes

1 Discussion

In the film *Modern Times* (1936), the factory worker played by Charlie Chaplin has a mental breakdown after frantically screwing nuts at an ever-increasing rate onto pieces of machinery. What does the image on the right suggest about the 'human factor' in manufacturing processes?

2 Reading

a. Read the article and decide which of the three statements gives the most accurate summary.

- Agile manufacturing is just another name for lean manufacturing.
- Agile manufacturing is a natural development from lean manufacturing.
- Agile manufacturing is going to replace lean manufacturing.

From lean ...

Ever since the invention of the assembly line, industrial innovators have constantly focused on improvement through a variety of different manufacturing strategies. Lean manufacturing, or lean production, is a recent development that seeks to maximise throughput with a minimum of inventory. The term is used to describe the production system originally developed by Toyota along with the Just-In-Time (JIT) system. The idea of lean, the opposite of fat, comes from the ability to achieve more with fewer resources, through the continuous elimination of waste.

The system centres on placing small stockpiles of inventory – such as raw materials and components – in strategic locations around the assembly line, instead of in centralised warehouses. This not only reduces waste but also enhances productivity on the shop floor.

In addition to eliminating waste, lean manufacturing seeks to ensure quality by building in a method whereby each part is examined immediately after manufacture. If there is a defect, the production line stops so that the problem can be detected and put right. Both strategies give workers on the assembly line a much greater role in the process, in the belief that those closest to production have the greatest knowledge of how the production system should work.

Lean manufacturing can save millions in costs and produce excellent results. Advantages include lower lead times, reduced set-up times, lower equipment costs, and of course, increased profits. It gives manufacturers a competitive edge by reducing costs and increasing quality, and by allowing them to react more quickly to customer requirements.

... to agile?

But now, according to many experts, manufacturing industry may be moving beyond lean manufacturing and into a world of agile manufacturing. Agile manufacturing is being described as the next logical step in the evolutionary chain of manufacturing technologies. The term is applied to an organisation that has created the processes, tools, and training to enable it to respond rapidly to specific customer requirements while still controlling costs and quality. The development of manufacturing and information technology allows the developers, the marketers and the people in production to share a common database of parts and products, and to share data on production capacities and problems. This also means that quality problems can be detected at the earliest possible point in the process.

Agile simply means 'able to move quickly and easily'. The key difference between lean and agile can be described as the difference between a thin person and an athlete. If customers place orders but are not willing to wait – in other words, if the order processing cycle is short – then lean manufacturing offers speed. But in a complex and fast changing market, flexibility is also important. Using new technology, agile manufacturers can quickly and easily move from the assembly of one product to the assembly of another with a minimum of retooling and software. This agility makes it possible to take advantage of vitally important windows of opportunity that, from time to time, appear in the market place. Of course, in an ideal world, it is desirable to be both lean and agile!

agile agil, gewandt, **responsive** empfänglich, **beneficial** vorteilhaft

b. Make notes on the following points. You may need to read between the lines, but if there is no information write 'NI'. Then compare and comment on your notes.

	Lean manufacturing	Agile manufacturing
Origin		
Concept		
Technology / IT important?		
Effects on manufacturers		
Effects on workers		
Effects on customers		

c. Some workers are critical of the idea that lean manufacturing gives them 'a greater role in the process'. What might they dislike about the system?

d. Explain these idioms in your own words, and suggest German equivalents.

1. it gives manufacturers **a competitive edge**
2. the next logical step in **the evolutionary chain** of manufacturing technologies
3. to take advantage of vitally important **windows of opportunity**

3 Discussion

Read the explanation of the term stakeholders and the descriptions of recent technological developments below. For each of the developments, discuss which stakeholders might be affected, and explain how.

Technological developments

1. **Intelligent manufacturing:** The use of production process technology that can programme robots to work with minimal supervision and assistance from operators. This includes the development of artificial intelligence in manufacturing.
2. **Micro-manufacturing:** The use of 'nanotechnology' to manufacture tiny finished products, using new materials and special tools such as laser technology. The major concepts and principles of micro-manufacturing are laser technology, micro-machining and micro-finishing.
3. **Green manufacturing:** Processes are designed to reduce the 'carbon footprint' in order to become more environmentally friendly. This will focus on becoming more energy efficient, using new fuels and renewable resources, and recycling.
4. **Space manufacturing:** The production of manufactured goods in outer space, using the advantages of zero gravity and a vacuum atmosphere. The unique environment can allow for industrial processes that cannot be easily carried out on Earth.

tiny winzig, **zero gravity** Schwerelosigkeit

INFO

Stakeholders
Stakeholders are people or groups who are involved in and can be affected by a particular organisation, project, system, etc. They are called stakeholders because they have a stake or a vested interest in it, i.e. they benefit if it succeeds, but risk losing something if it fails. Examples of stakeholders include producers, shareholders, employees, consumers, society and governments.

4 Location

a. It is important for manufacturing companies to choose the best possible location for their operations. Create a mind map of the key factors for a successful manufacturing location. Among other things, consider factors such as costs, people, communication, and services.

b. Choose a region that you know well. Give examples of manufacturing companies and say where they are based. Discuss why you think these particular locations were chosen.

c. Discuss whether manufacturing in your chosen region is changing. If so, what are the reasons?

C Language | Manufacturing processes

1 Collocations

a. Put in 'make' or 'do'. Underline expressions where 'do' is used in English, and 'machen' in German.

1.	this task	7.	a pizza
2.	a big purchase	8.	arrangements
3.	the purchasing	9.	the organisation
4.	the stocktaking	10.	a phone call
5.	an internship	11.	quality checks
6.	the cooking	12.	progress

b. Explain the difference in meaning.

1. You've made a lot of work for me.
2. You've done a lot of work for me.

c. Underline items where the verb 'produce' is more appropriate than 'manufacture':

butter | mobile phones | wheat | bottles | aircraft | jeans | honey | ballpoint pens | leather | wine | great ideas | lawnmowers | a letter | a home-made quilt

LANGUAGE TIP

Make and do
We've **done** a lot of planning.
(do + activity / process)
We've **made** a lot of plans.
(make + outcome / result)

Manufacture, produce and process
Manufacturing is a form of production that requires many materials, processes and machines and results in finished goods. Things that are made or grown, especially connected to farming, are known as produce *(Erzeugnisse)*. Raw materials are often processed or refined to make them pure, or more easily used.

2 Expressions with 'lean'

Decide whether the following expressions convey a positive or negative meaning. Explain why.

1. She came back from her holiday **looking lean and fit**.
2. These are **lean times** for the financial services sector.
3. The Ferrari California is a **lean and mean machine**.
4. With no rain for many months, farmers are expecting a **lean harvest**.
5. Bayern's new Brazilian striker has a **lean and hungry look**.

3 Expressions with 'time'

a. Check the expressions with time in a dictionary or glossary. Then use them to complete the sentences.

time-and-motion study | time clock | lead time | overtime | time server | set-up time | time and a half | downtime | time-to-market

1. "I don't mind working .... at the weekends because they pay me ...., which is 50% more than what I normally get!"
2. "For big customer orders we've brought the .... down from two weeks to one week."
3. "It used to take up to half an hour to prepare the machinery and equipment, but we've managed to reduce .... to just a few minutes."
4. "There's been a major software failure, so we've got .... until the problem's been fixed."
5. "When you put your card into the ...., it records when you arrive or leave."
6. ".................................... is vitally important in the software industry."
7. "He isn't ambitious at all. He's just a ...., looking forward to when he retires."
8. "The .... showed that many of our operations are not efficient enough."

b. Collect further expressions with 'time' that might be used in a business context.

4 Pronunciation and intonation

A 1.33 **a.** Some words have the same form as verbs or nouns, but are pronounced differently. Read out the following sentences. Then listen and check. What do you notice about the words where the stress falls on the second syllable?

1. a. We only sell fresh **produce**.
   b. Bees **produce** honey.
2. a. Did you **record** it?
   b. I don't have a **record** of it.
3. a. We **convert** raw materials into useful items.
   b. He's a recent **convert** to the church.
4. a. I'll have to **reject** it.
   b. It's a **reject**.
5. a. How are you going to **transport** it?
   b. What form of **transport** are you going to use?
6. a. There has been an **increase** in productivity
   b. We need to **increase** productivity.
7. a. Can you **present** us with a better offer?
   b. It was given to me as a **present**.
8. a. We only hire **graduates**.
   b. She **graduates** in September.

A 1.34 **b.** Some words have the same form but a different meaning and pronunciation. Read the sentences aloud, then listen and check. How would you translate the words into German?

1. a. Only add a **minute** amount of chilli.
   b. Could you hold on a **minute**?
2. a. Your passport is **invalid**.
   b. He quit his job because he became an **invalid**.
3. a. I've had some awful **rows** with my boss.
   b. Seats are arranged in **rows** in lecture halls.
4. a. It was located in the **desert**.
   b. Please don't **desert** me.
5. a. I need to put a bandage on my **wound**.
   b. The company had to be **wound** up.
6. a. Petrol that contains **lead** is dangerous to health.
   b. He has no idea of how to **lead** a team.

A 1.35 **c.** Some sounds can be tricky for German speakers. Listen and underline the sentence you hear.

1. a. You need a hard head.
   b. You need a hard hat.
2. a. I'd like a white desk.
   b. I'd like a wide desk.
3. a. It's the wrong batch.
   b. It's the wrong badge.
4. a. Four tickets.
   b. Forty kids.
5. a. No access
   b. No excess
6. a. It's a vast machine.
   b. It's a fast machine.
7. a. I always walk there.
   b. I always work there.
8. a. the gross rate
   b. the growth rate
9. a. a tiny fairy
   b. a tiny ferry

d. Write a list of any ten words below. Dictate the words to your partner, and then compare.

very / vary | patch / batch | think / sink | bed / bad | west / vest | chip / cheap | shoes / choose | pepper / paper | beer / bear | still / steel | breathe / breeze | chess / jazz | think / sink | letter / later

5 Describing a sequence

a. Decide on a logical sequence for the steps in manufacturing ice cream.

[ ] The various flavoured mixes are frozen to become ice cream.
[ ] The raw materials are mixed with other ingredients, such as cocoa powder and stabilisers.
[ ] They are packed on pallets in batches of 60 tubs, ready for distribution.
[ ] The mix, now either white or chocolate, is pasteurized and homogenized.
[ ] The tubs are then further frozen to the 'soft scoop' temperature of −23°C.
[ ] A final quality check is carried out before they leave the factory.
[ ] Raw materials – cream, milk, egg yolks – arrive at the factory.
[ ] The ice cream is put into tubs in the automated filling machine.
[ ] The liquid mix flows to flavouring and colouring vats.

b. Use the expressions in the box to describe the sequence.

c. Mark the passive forms that are used.
Explain why this form is chosen rather than the active.

PHRASES

Sequencing
- First of all, …
- Then, …
- After that, …
- The next step is to …
- When that has been done, …
- And finally, …

6 Health and safety

a. Categorise the following words, as shown below. Some words fit into more than one category.

filter | filtered | filtering | repeat | repeated | repeatedly | repetitively | repetition | special | specialised | specialising | specialisation | sensitised | sensitive | sensitivity | contamination | contaminating | contaminated | contaminable | regulate | regulated | regulation

nouns: *filter,* ....
gerunds: *specialising,* ....
adverbs: ....
adjectives: *filtered* ....
past participles: *filtered* ....
present participles: ....
verbs: ....

b. Choose words from the list above to complete the definition of a clean-room.

A clean-room is a highly s.................... work area in which air quality, temperature and humidity are r.................... in order to protect s.................... equipment and components from c..................... The air in a clean-room is r.................... f.................... to remove dust particles and other impurities.

c. List examples of products that might be manufactured in a clean-room.

A 2.1 **d.** Listen and answer the questions below.

1. What is being manufactured in the clean-room?
2. Why is it important to keep the environment dust-free?
3. Why might a job in a clean-room be attractive to workers?

A 2.1 **e.** Listen again and make notes about the following:

› What people have to do
› What people don't have to do
› What people mustn't do

LANGUAGE TIP

Modals of obligation
You **must** do it. (I decide because I have the authority.)
You **have to** do this. (It's the rule.)
You **mustn't** do this. (It's forbidden, or not a good idea.)
You **don't have to** do this. (It's not necessary.)

f. Rewrite the sentences using the verbs in brackets, so that the sentence keeps the same meaning.

1. All staff must obey the clean-room regulations. (*comply*)
2. There is a ban on eating and drinking in the clean-room. (*allow*)
3. Visitors must also observe these regulations. (*apply*)
4. Everyone in the clean-room has to wear an ID badge. (*require*)

g. Discuss why hazard warning signs are important in companies with an international workforce.

h. The following symbols are EU hazard warnings used in industrial workplaces. Explain what they mean, and give further examples of hazard warnings from industry or daily life.

i. You have been asked to produce a notice that can be put up on the entrance to a clean-room. Write eight short 'do's and don'ts', and design a hazard warning symbol that indicates 'Warning: Clean-Room Area'. Then compare your notices and discuss which is the most effective.

D Business leaders | Henry Ford

Reading

a. Read and make notes under the following headings. Then compare your notes.

Ford's key innovations | Ford's influence on society | Ford's famous lawsuit | Ford's legacy today

Model T

In October 1908, the Model T Ford was offered for sale at a price of $950. In the Model T's nineteen years of production, its price dropped as low as $280. Nearly 15,500,000 were sold in the United States alone. The Model T heralds the beginning of the Motor Age; the automobile evolved from being a luxury item for the well-to-do, to essential transportation for the man in the street.

Ford revolutionized manufacturing. By 1914, his Michigan plant, using innovative production techniques, could turn out a complete vehicle every 93 minutes. Using a constantly-moving assembly line, subdivision of labour, and careful coordination of operations, Ford rapidly increased productivity; his mass-production techniques would eventually allow for the manufacture of a Model T every 24 seconds. He began paying his employees five dollars a day, nearly doubling the wages offered by other manufacturers. He cut the workday from nine to eight hours in order to convert the factory to a three-shift workday. His innovations made him an international celebrity.

Ford's affordable Model T also completely changed American society. As more Americans owned cars, urbanization patterns changed. The United States saw the growth of suburbia, the creation of national highways, and a population entranced with the possibility of going anywhere, anytime. Ford witnessed many of these changes during his lifetime, although he personally longed for the simple farming lifestyle of his youth.

Henry Ford also fought a long legal battle with George B. Selden, a patent attorney who had never built a motor vehicle but had taken out a patent on a 'road engine' in 1895. Selden had set up a company for the purpose of collecting royalties from all American car manufacturers. In 1904, the judge in the 'Selden *versus* Ford' court case ordered an automobile built according to the George Selden patent. The Selden car was a failure and the Selden patent was overturned in 1911. This stopped Selden from collecting any more royalties and, thanks to Henry Ford, American car manufacturers were free to build cars at a much lower cost.

Ford's legacy reaches into every aspect of modern day manufacturing. Apart from the assembly line and mass-production, he was the first to describe the Just-In-Time philosophy that would later be taken up by other producers, fifty years later. He also patented the first plastic-bodied automobile, and designed the first V8 engine. He was constantly innovative and always ready to accept change; in spite of his insistence that all his automobiles should be black, by 1925 the Ford Motor Company was offering vehicles in a range of colours.

Henry Ford

Henry Ford was born in 1863, on the family farm in Dearborn, Michigan. As a young boy, he enjoyed tinkering with machines, and farm work gave him plenty of opportunities to experiment. Ford set up the Ford Motor Company in 1903, proclaiming "I will build a car for the great multitude".

to tinker herumbasteln, **to herald** ankündigen, **the well-to-do** die wohlhabenden Leute, **man in the street** Normalbürger, **suburbia** Vorstadt, **entranced** hingerissen, **to witness** miterleben, **to long for** sich sehnen nach, **court battle** Rechtsstreit, **to overturn a law** ein Gesetz aufheben, **insistence** Beharrlichkeit

b. As well as being a great innovator, Henry Ford was a powerful personality and his opinions are often quoted. Read the following quotations and explain what you think Ford meant in your own words.

1. "Don't find a fault. Find a remedy."
2. "Thinking is the hardest work there is, which is probably the reason so few engage in it."
3. "Failure is only the opportunity to begin again more intelligently."
4. "A business that makes nothing but money is a poor kind of business."

c. Are there any statements you disagree with? Explain why.

d. Research: Find out where the Ford Motor Company is today in the ranking of world automobile makers. Which is the current Number One? What is it that makes that company so successful?

E Business communication | Demonstrating processes

1 Listening

A 2.2 **a.** A supervisor in a computer factory is demonstrating a manufacturing process to a worker who will be using it for the first time. Listen and take notes on the following points. Then compare notes.

the task | the equipment | the procedure | checking and reporting | safety and protection | questions and answers

A 2.2 **b.** Study the phrases on the right. Then listen again and mark the phrases that are used. Suggest other ways of saying the same thing.

PHRASES

Giving instructions

Responsibilities
- You'll be in charge of …
- It's up to you to ensure that …
- You're responsible for …
- It will be your job to …

Procedures
- The first thing you have to do is …
- You must always check that …
- The finished work is then …
- Everyone has to fill in a job card.

How to operate equipment
- Make sure the machine is set up for work.
- Do not operate the machine if …
- Check that it is safe to …
- Do not switch on the machine until …

Communicating
- Any defects must be reported.
- If you have any questions, ask.
- It is important to tell colleagues if …
- Don't hesitate to ask for help or advice.

Linking
- Now let's look at …
- Let's move on …
- The second step is …
- Now, are you ready to …?

Checking understanding
- Is everything clear?
- Are you following this?
- Have I explained that clearly?
- Is there anything you didn't catch?

c. From the notes you took earlier, write key words in the boxes to show the steps in the process.

task	equipment	procedure	checking	or
Bonding two components				*Reworking*

2 Giving instructions

a. Make a paper plane, for example using the method shown in the diagram. Then explain to another student exactly how you did it.

Example:
"You take a piece of paper and fold it in half lengthwise. Then you …"

b. How do you make a paper boat, or a paper hat? Give each other instructions.

c. Choose one of the following and explain how to do it.

- Boiling an egg
- Ironing a shirt
- Repairing a flat tyre (bike or car)
- Withdrawing cash from an ATM

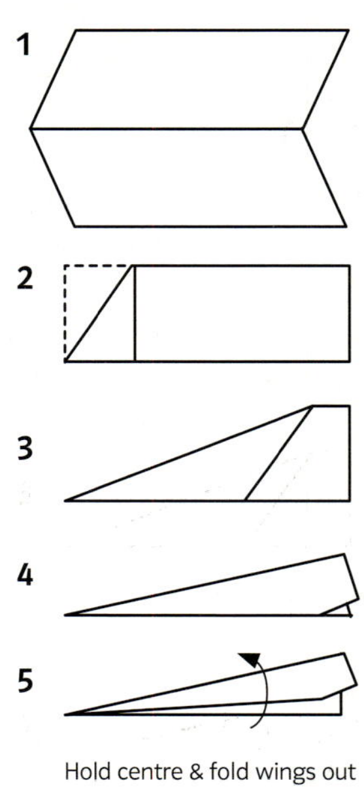

Hold centre & fold wings out

3 Translating

Translate the instructions into English.

AUF EINEN BLICK

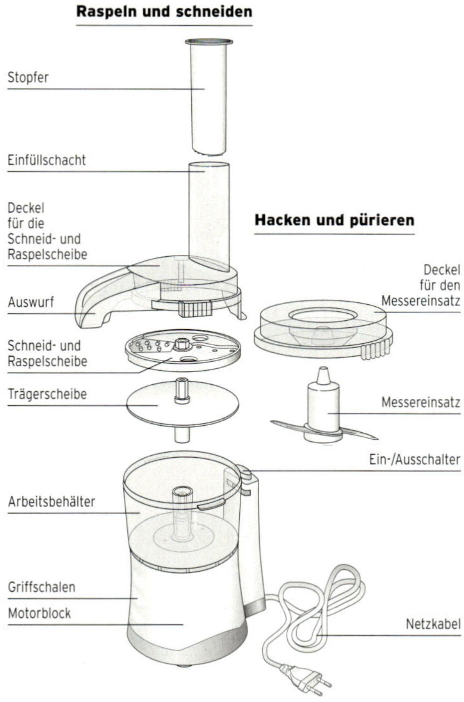

4

SICHERHEITSHINWEISE

Deutsch

Einsatzbereich

- Das Gerät ist ausschließlich für den privaten Gebrauch konzipiert und darf nicht gewerblich genutzt werden.
- Das Gerät ist nicht für die Verarbeitung von harten Lebensmitteln wie z.B. harte Backschokolade geeignet.
- Das Gerät soll ausschließlich gemäß dieser Anleitung benutzt werden. Für Schäden oder Unfälle, die durch Nichtbeachten dieser Anleitung entstehen, übernehmen wir keine Haftung.

Kinder

- Verpackungsmaterial gehört nicht in Kinderhände.
- Halten Sie Kinder von dem Zerkleinerer fern! Kinder können die Gefahren, die von dem Zerkleinerer ausgehen, nicht richtig einschätzen. Kinder dürfen den Zerkleinerer keinesfalls bedienen.

Allgemeine Sicherheitshinweise

- Bevor Sie den Zerkleinerer in Betrieb nehmen, lesen Sie bitte diese Anleitung, damit Sie sich mit dem Gerät vertraut machen. Heben Sie diese Anleitung an einem festen Platz auf, damit Sie immer nachlesen können.
- Das Gerät darf nur unter Aufsicht betrieben werden.
- Nehmen Sie das Gerät nicht in Betrieb, wenn das Gerät oder die Anschlussleitung sichtbare Schäden aufweist oder wenn das Gerät zuvor fallengelassen wurde.
- Nehmen Sie das Gerät nicht auseinander. Um eine Gefährdung zu vermeiden, lassen Sie Reparaturen am Gerät oder dessen Anschlusskabel nur in einer Fachwerkstatt bzw. in unserem Service-Center durchführen.
- Bei Weitergabe des Gerätes an andere Personen ist auch die Bedienungsanleitung mit zu übergeben.

5

LANGUAGE TIP

Translating

- Scan the whole text before you start.
- Watch out for words that can be translated in different ways: *Gerät* → device? equipment? tool? utensil?
- Compounds are often written as separate words: *Anschlusskabel* → power supply cord
- Don't translate word for word: *Halten Sie Kinder von dem Gerät fern* → Keep the device out of children's reach.

Stopfer tamper, **Einfüllschacht** fill shaft, **Deckel** lid, **Trägerscheibe** carrier disk, **Messereinsatz** blade insert, **Arbeitsbehälter** container, **Griffschalen** handle recess, **Motorblock** motor unit, **Netzkabel** mains lead, **hacken und pürieren**, chopping and pureeing

Video Lounge Real bread

BBC Motion Gallery

V 4 **a. Before watching, discuss the questions below.**

1. What qualities do you look for in really good bread?
2. How is homemade bread baked in a kitchen different from manufactured bread?
3. Compare breads from different countries or regions that you know, e.g. French, American, Indian, Russian bread
4. What can the typical bread of a region tell you about its culture?

b. Watch the video 'Real bread' and make notes on the following:

- Changes that are taking place in the bread industry
- Traditional processes used in preparing the raw materials used in bread
- Advantages and disadvantages of mass-produced bread
- Personal qualities needed to become a successful independent baker

F Consulting | STEP analysis

1 Preparation

a. Read the article to find out whether it presents an optimistic or a pessimistic view of German manufacturing.

SKILLS

When you read an article without a dictionary, don't give up too soon if there are many unknown words. Use 'intelligent guessing': You can usually guess the meaning from the context, the form of the word, or because the word is similar to one you know in another language.

Manufacturing in Germany

As worldwide demand for goods continues to melt away there are fears that Germany's exporting economy could grind to a halt. Until recently, it was hard to imagine that Germany's ferociously efficient manufacturing industry would be beset by the global downturn. There was a time when Germany's unit labour costs were the highest in Europe, but as a result of a determined policy of wage restraint and labour market reforms they are now some 13 % below the euro-zone average. Perhaps because of their cost-cutting success, German firms were not having as much trouble raising finance as their European counterparts.

Now, following a rash of recent reports showing evidence of a decrease in export orders, any feelings of satisfaction or complacency have disappeared. Germany's industrial production output is falling sharply. The number of employees being encouraged to work shorter hours, in return for government wage subsidies, has surged to 250,000. Meanwhile demand for energy from its biggest industrial customers is also hitting Germany's major utilities hard.

This is not to say that Germany is alone in facing the biggest manufacturing slump in decades. All across Europe the effect of the slowdown is being felt, and it is the same story in Japan, where industrial production has sunk to unprecedented levels. However, the sense that Germany will fare worse than its competitors in the slump is based on the fear that much of the distress will fall on the *Mittelstand*, the family-owned small and medium-sized enterprises (SMEs) that make up an important part of the German economy.

It is Germany's position as the world's largest exporter of manufactured goods that makes it so vulnerable to the downturn. A quarter of all employment, as well as a fifth of the country's economic output, is based on exports and led to Germany's reputation as the 'workshop of the world'. And of these exports, the *Mittelstand* firms account for more than 40 % of the total.

Many of these small companies produce highly-specialised products for other manufacturing industries, such as machine-tools and textile-spinning machinery. Their reputation for quality and expertise has given them a dominant position in their niche markets. However orders for these products has slumped, as the economic slowdown has forced regular customers to trim back their budgets.

Not all is doom and gloom, however. There is a stimulus programme in place, and the benefits are beginning to show. A scheme offering cash for used cars is encouraging people to purchase new ones, to the delight of dealers faced with stocks of unsold cars. In turn, carmakers are getting production moving again and hope to avoid laying off more workers. Having already been through so much industrial reform, Germany is still in a good position to benefit from any upturn in the global economy.

economy [ɪ'kɒnəmɪ] Wirtschaft, **downturn** ['daʊntɜ:n] Abschwung, **unit labour costs** [ˌju:nɪt 'leɪbə ˌkɒsts] Lohnstückkosten, **average** ['ævrɪdʒ] Durchschnitt, **economic output** [ˌi:kənɒmɪk 'aʊtpʊt] wirtschaftliche Ausbeute, **subsidy** ['sʌbsədɪz] Subvention, Zuschuss, **to surge** [sɜ:dʒ] (stark) ansteigen, **slump** [slʌmp] (starker) Rückgang, Einbruch, **to account for** [ə'kaʊnt fɔ:] ausmachen, betragen, ergeben

b. Decide on the closest meaning in context.

1. ferociously	[ ] extremely	[ ] fairly	[ ] hardly
2. to grind to a halt	[ ] to recover	[ ] to get faster	[ ] to slow down and stop
3. be beset by	[ ] be helped by	[ ] be badly affected by	[ ] be stimulated by
4. melts away	[ ] falls	[ ] rises	[ ] grows
5. wage restraint	[ ] keeping wages low	[ ] reducing wages	[ ] increasing wages
6. some 13 %	[ ] exactly 13 %	[ ] nearly 13 %	[ ] approximately 13 %
7. a rash	[ ] a sudden loss	[ ] a surprising lack	[ ] an unexpected appearance
8. surged	[ ] risen rapidly	[ ] fallen quickly	[ ] grown slowly
9. slump	[ ] sudden fall in orders	[ ] economic boom	[ ] business cycle
10. vulnerable to	[ ] resistant to	[ ] easily affected by	[ ] immune to
11. to trim	[ ] to reduce	[ ] to increase	[ ] to abolish

c. Draw a line on the graph to indicate your view as to whether things have got better or worse since the article was written, and how you think the trend is likely to continue.

2 Assignment

Check your own assumptions and those expressed in the article by carrying out research into the current state of German manufacturing. Follow the guidelines below and collect evidence to show whether or not the optimism expressed in the final paragraph of the text was justified.

Guidelines for research

- Carry out a STEP analysis of manufacturing in Germany and collect statistics to back your statements.
- Give examples of *Mittelstand* companies that have suffered, survived or succeeded.
- Interview bank managers in the UK and your own country about current trends in manufacturing. Find out who they think is the 'sick man of Europe' and get some interesting quotes to put in your article.

3 Presentation

a. Write an article in which you present your findings and paint either a rosy or a gloomy picture of the current state of German manufacturing.

b. Present your findings in class. Suggest what manufacturers can do to ensure their survival.

INFO

STEP analysis

A STEP (or PEST) analysis is a tool for understanding a situation by examining the external factors affecting it. They are listed under four headings:
Social: lifestyle trends, demographics, cultural attitudes, language, ethical issues, education, industrial relations, consumer habits, …
Political: government policies, legislation, lobby groups, environmental issues, wars and conflict, EU regulations, international relations, …
Economic: domestic economic situation, international economies and trends, taxation, inflation, unemployment rate, interest rates, exchange rates, …
Technological: computerisation, internet, infrastructure, competing technological developments, legislation, intellectual property rights, innovation potential, …

PHRASES

Expressing optimism and pessimism

Optimistic

- The picture looks rosy.
- Prospects are excellent.
- Things are looking up.
- It's a bright future.
- Every cloud has a silver lining.
- There's hope on the horizon.
- The benefits of the measures are already being felt.

Pessimistic

- The picture looks gloomy.
- Prospects are dire.
- Things are going from bad to worse.
- It's a bleak future.
- Clouds are looming.
- There's no sign of recovery.
- Consumers will have to tighten their belts.

LANGUAGE TIP

Tense

Use the **present progressive** to express current trends and developments.

- The economy **is grinding** to a halt.
- Production **is falling** steeply.

Use the **present perfect** to express the current impact of past events or situations.

- New data **has pointed** to a sharp downturn in orders.
- For years Germany **has been** the world's largest exporter.

Use **will / won't + infinitive** to express hopes and warnings.

- There **won't be** any talk of us being the sick man of Europe.
- Germany **will fare** worse than most in the slump.

Unit 8
Business travel

Online Link
800021-0008

A Introduction | Why travel?

1 Discussion

a. Suggest different ways of completing these sentences:

1. I'd like a job that involves regular business travel if …
2. Business trips can be a nightmare, for example when …

b. Study the chart on the right and discuss the following questions:

1. Which is the least common reason for business travel?
2. Suggest further reasons for travel that are not included in the chart.
3. What kind of business trips are most likely to be cancelled when a company needs to cut costs?

Reasons for business travel

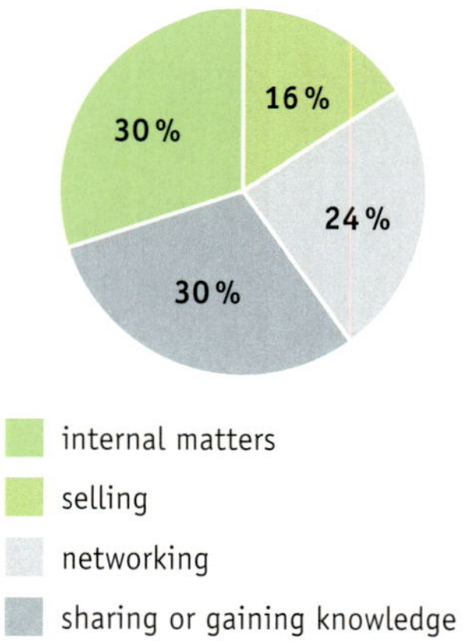

From: Asian and Pacific Migration Journal, 2005

c. The expressions on the right represent the tag cloud of a business travel website.
Match them with the topics below.

1. cheap flights
2. impact of financial crisis on travel business
3. rise in female business travellers
4. surviving a plane crash
5. delays due to tighter baggage checks
6. winner of Best In-flight Entertainment Award
7. who to call in an emergency abroad
8. solar-powered luggage
9. doing business in Dubai

airlines, airports, air-traffic control, British Airways, budget airlines, credit crunch, convention centres, etiquette, expenses, gadgets, green issues, health, Heathrow, Hotels, immigration, living abroad, luggage, passengers, rankings, resorts, restaurants, safety, security, technology, terrorism, tipping, tourism, travel clothing, travel trends, video conferencing, visas, upgrades, weather, working habits

d. What are the current 'hot topics' in business travel and tourism?

INFO

Tag cloud
A tag cloud displays the most popular topics in a blog or website. The bigger the font, the more popular the topic.

2 Planning a business trip

a. Emma is doing an internship in the Sales Department of SydneySider, an Australian boatbuilding company. Read the emails and summarise the situation facing the company and the people involved.

Hi Kenny,
Yes!!!!!!!!!!!!!!!!!!!!!!!!!!!!!! Emma
>>>
Hi Emma,
I'm afraid I can't make lunch today because I'm meeting Bruce to discuss preparations for the International Boat Show in London. It's the most important trade fair for us and we'll need an extra pair of hands this year, so I thought maybe you'd like to join me and the other sales reps. It's hard work but a fantastic experience: 5-star hotel, slap-up meals, loads of freebies, great networking opportunities, all expenses paid! It would also look good on your CV. Interested? Let me know asap and I'll put in a word.
Cheers, Kenny

To: Bruce Wallace, Sales Director
From: Pauline Reed, CEO
CC: Fraser Nelson, Accounts Manager
Subject: Business travel

As you know, a 50 % reduction in the travel budget has been planned for this year, which is not only due to the current economic crisis. It has come to my attention that the company's money is being frittered away on lavish events and frivolous junkets, and some employees have been fiddling their expenses.
You will understand that we need to be more disciplined about travel management. This means clamping down on unnecessary travel, reducing the number of travellers per trip, and downgrading the comfort of those who have to travel. Please also note that all planned business trips require prior authorisation by the Accounts Department.

to fritter away verplempern, **lavish** üppig, **junket** als Geschäftsreise getarnte Vergnügungsreise, **to fiddle expenses** Reisekosten(abrechnung) manipulieren, **to clamp down on** hart durchgreifen gegen

Dear Emma,
Thanks for agreeing to help with preparations for the Boat Show. Now that we know exactly who's going (me, Kenny, Jason, Livvie, Greg and you), you can start looking into transport and accommodation.
We've got a very tight travel budget this year, so please go for the cheapest possible deals and suggest how we could minimise expenses. Don't make any bookings until I've checked your draft itinerary, and remember to cc to the Accounts Department. ;o)
Best,
Bruce Wallace

b. Discuss how Emma can save money for the company while still making the trip worthwhile for the company and for herself.

c. Write Emma's email to Bruce Wallace in which she outlines her suggestions for saving money and defends any expenditure that might possibly be considered frivolous. Use the structure below.

Dear Mr Wallace,
Please find attached my draft travel itinerary for the Boat Show. According to my calculations, the total cost will be approximately 50 % of what was spent last year, due to savings made in the following areas:
...
However, cutting too much expenditure on travel and accommodation would be a 'false economy' in my view. This is because ...

B Business briefing | Trends in business travel

1 Quick response

What does the image below indicate about changes in the airline industry?

2 Reading

a. Read the article and identify trends that could be good news for business travellers.

LANGUAGE TIP

British / American English
BE: economy class, luggage trolley
AE: coach class, baggage cart

The changing face of business travel

First it was the rise in oil prices, pushing up travel costs and causing business travellers to tighten their belts and reconsider their travel plans. Now, as the global recession begins to bite, travel prices are falling again, and hotels, airlines and car hire firms are responding with new strategies in order to survive. So what are these strategies, and how will they affect business travellers?

1. Discounts on air travel: With passenger numbers plunging, airlines are desperately trying to fill seats. Since the beginning of 2009, airlines have been reducing fares in order to attract customers. In the US, many ticket prices are as low as they were before 2007. For anyone with funds in their travel budget, this is a good time to fly.

2. Cuts in travel spending: A recent survey of top companies showed that many of them are trimming their travel budgets by downgrading travellers from business class to economy class on all flights, lowering the class of hotel used for business travel. As a result, anyone who can still afford business class flights and luxury hotels will find it easier to find both flights and rooms.

3. Priority for business travellers: During times of economic hardship, travel companies try harder to attract their most profitable customers. Many airlines are upgrading their first class and business class services, especially on long-haul flights, for example by offering in-flight Wi-Fi, 'priority boarding' and free cocktails for its business class passengers who pay the full fare. Economy class passengers, whether business travellers or families with small children, are pushed to the back of the boarding queues, while the more lucrative business class passengers benefit.

4. Fewer meetings: The global economic meltdown has also led to a decline in meetings and conferences, with an increasing number of companies deciding to run online video conferences rather than invest in face-to-face meetings. Cancelled meetings and dwindling numbers of participants are adversely affecting the hotel and hospitality industry. For anyone planning to hold such a meeting or conference, now could be a very good time to negotiate a deal.

5. Added-on fees. As the price of basic airfares continues to tumble, many airlines are boosting their revenues with added-on fees such as charging for check-in, luggage trolleys, in-flight snacks, entertainment and even the use of the toilet in the aircraft. Now hotels are beginning to follow suit, adding charges for services that were previously free – toiletries and newspapers in the rooms, bowls of sweets and fruit in lobby areas – as well as for 'value add' services such as gift chocolates, turn-down service and broadband internet access.

6. The return of web bookings: Travel websites have grown rapidly in response to people searching for cheap deals and last-minute bargains. After the 9/11 attacks, when demand for travel plummeted, third-party websites such as Expedia and Travelocity did particularly good business selling on unwanted tickets at rock-bottom prices. When people started travelling again, fewer deals were offered on the internet. But now travellers are once again returning to online booking, and rediscovering juicy bargains at the click of a mouse.

desperately verzweifelt, **long-haul flight** Langstreckenflug, **power outlet** Steckdose, Stromanschluss, **turn-down service** Verwöhnservice am Abend / zur Nacht, **to turn down the covers** die Bettdecke zurückschlagen

b. Explain the expressions marked in bold.

1. causing business travellers to **tighten their belts** ....
2. as the global recession **begins to bite** ....
3. hotels are beginning to **follow suit** ....
4. at **rock-bottom prices** ....
5. rediscovering **juicy bargains** ....

c. Put in arrows (↗ or ↘) to indicate the impact of the global recession on the following:

[↘] oil prices
[ ] passenger numbers
[ ] airline fares
[ ] spending on travel
[ ] seat capacity in business class
[ ] room capacity in luxury hotels
[ ] standard of services in first and business class on long-haul flights
[ ] standard of services in economy class on long-haul flights
[ ] number of meetings and conferences held
[ ] video conferencing
[ ] hotel capacity for meetings and conferences
[ ] airline revenue from extra charges
[ ] hotel revenue from extra charges
[ ] online demand for cheap air fares

d. Identify language in the text that relates to trends and measures that affect quality (↗ or ↘), and list them below. Note whether they are verbs (v.) or nouns (n.) Add corresponding forms where possible.

↗	rise (n.), rise (v.), …
↘	fall (v.), fall (n.), …

e. Without looking back at the article, try to remember as much of the content as possible using the language in the tasks on this page as prompts.

3 Discussion

a. Discuss the questions below.

1. Should airline passengers be charged for 'add-on fees' such as those mentioned in the text? Consider the pros and cons from the passengers' point of view.
2. What kind of guests might be prepared to pay for a 'turn-down service' at a hotel? Would you value a service such as this?
3. How might car rental firms be affected by a downturn in the economy? Suggest strategies that would help them to survive or even prosper in a recession.

INFO

Turn-down service
If you ask for a turn-down service at a hotel, your room will be tidied in the evening and the sheets on your bed will be pulled back. You might find a mint or chocolate on your pillow, with your pyjamas laid out neatly on the bed, and fresh towels or soap in the bathroom.

b. Follow-up: The article describes trends at the beginning of 2009. Find out whether the situation has changed, and whether there are any new trends. Before you start, discuss where you can find useful information for your research, and people who you could interview.

C Language | Travelling on business

1 Services and amenities

a. Sort the services and amenities listed below into what makes a hotel comfortable and what makes it convenient. Add further items to each group.

close to the station | soft mattress | online booking possible | central location | king-size bed | free parking | thermostat (adjustable) | spacious room | regular airport shuttle service | TV pay-per-view | fluffy carpets | high-speed internet access | safety deposit box | within easy reach of shops | currency exchange | luxury bath products | ironing board | auto wake up service | complimentary champagne on arrival

LANGUAGE TIP

Convenient vs. comfortable
convenient – making things easier or more efficient
comfortable – creating a sense of physical well-being

For your comfort	For your convenience

b. The text below contains ten mistakes. Identify and correct them. (The first has been done for you.)

GUEST QUESTIONNAIRE

Dear guest,
We are delighted to have you ~~by~~ *with* us and hope you are satisfying with our facilities and services. It is our aim to guarantee costumer satisfaction by providing the highest possible standarts. We always welcome guest feedback and would appreciate if you could take a few minutes to complete this questionnaire. I can insure you, that your comments will receive my personal attention.
Please be so kind to leave your completed questionnaire at the reception desk.
We look forward to welcome you again at our hotel.

Samuel Barker
general manager

FORBES HOTEL
★★★★
ZÜRICH

(A 2.3) **c.** Listen to two guests talking about their stay at Forbes hotel and complete the form.

Please take a moment to rate our services. Thank you for giving us the opportunity to serve you.

	Excellent	Good	Average	Poor	N/A
Service on arrival and check-in					
Staff hospitality (courtesy, friendliness, responsiveness)					
In-house services (laundry, concierge, babysitting, etc.)					
Décor of room					
Cleanliness of room					
Facilities in room (TV, mini-bar, internet access)					
Temperature in room					
Bathroom amenities package (shampoos, soaps, etc)					
Promptness of room service delivery					

Are you likely to stay at our hotel again? Yes ☐ No ☐

Comments

d. Discuss what Samuel Barker needs to do to improve customer satisfaction in future.

2 English for dining out

A 2.4 **a.** Stefan Damer is a German software engineer who is on a secondment in Shanghai. During his first week, Mark Cole, a British colleague who has been living in China for more than 10 years, invites him out to dinner at a local restaurant. Listen to their conversation and answer the questions.

1. What are Stefan's impressions of the restaurant?
2. Why is it easy to get German beer in Shanghai?
3. What problems does Stefan have with the menu?
4. What local dishes does Mark suggest?
5. What dishes does Stefan choose?

b. Explain in your own words how the Shanghai dish of Steamed-and-Fried Duck is prepared.

c. Describe how the following foods can be prepared and / or cooked.

chicken | potatoes | salmon | eggs | apples

d. In pairs, read the examples of textures and tastes on the right. Which ones do you both like?

e. If you were a restaurant reviewer, what words would you use to describe these experiences?

1. Your steak was cooked for too long.
2. Your salad was made with very fresh ingredients.
3. Your curry was as you like it, with plenty of chillies.
4. Your chocolate pudding was much too sweet.

f. Have you ever eaten a strange or unusual dish? Describe where you ate it and what it was like.

WORD BANK

How food is prepared: peeled | chopped | sliced | diced | grated | mixed | shredded | stuffed | wrapped | blended | beaten | whipped | ground (from 'grind') | pickled | marinated
How food is cooked: boiled | steamed | fried | braised | baked | roasted | grilled | stewed | barbecued | poached
Textures: crispy | chewy | crunchy | runny | oily | rubbery | gritty | crusty | sloppy | juicy | greasy | creamy | flaky | fatty
Tastes: sweet | salty | fizzy | nutty | smoky | spicy | sour | savoury | bland | strong | sugary | sickly | bitter | watery | fruity | tasteless
Wine: sweet | medium | dry | fruity | light | full-bodied
Complaints: underdone / overdone | gone off | burnt | mouldy | frozen | wrong order | stale | small portion

g. You are entertaining Chinese visitors at a traditional German restaurant. They are keen to try out some national and regional dishes, but need your advice before ordering. Choose items from the menu and explain what they are by completing the sentences below.

1. The main ingredient of this dish is ……………………
2. If you like ……………………, then I would recommend ……………………
3. If you prefer a vegetarian dish ……………………
4. The sauce is made of ……………………
5. This dish comes from the …………………… region.
6. With this dish you might like to drink …………………… ……, or maybe even ……………………

SPEISEKARTE

Ungarische Gulaschsuppe

Gemischter Salat

Schweineschnitzel mit Pommes Frites
Kalbsmedaillons in Weißweinsoße
Paniertes Hähnchenschnitzel mit Paprikagemüse
Spargel mit Sauce Hollandaise
Matjesfilet Hausfrauen-Art

Pflaumenkuchen mit Sahne

h. What advice would you give about giving tips to waiters in your country? What other types of services do people give tips for?

i. You have been asked by the organisers of an international conference to come up with a menu that will be acceptable to all the participants. It should be a three-course menu and include drinks. Brainstorm factors that need to be taken into consideration when catering for such a diverse group. Then compare your menu with others, and decide which one is the most likely to be accepted.

3 English for travel

a. Complete the sentences below with the right words: travel, tour, trip or journey.

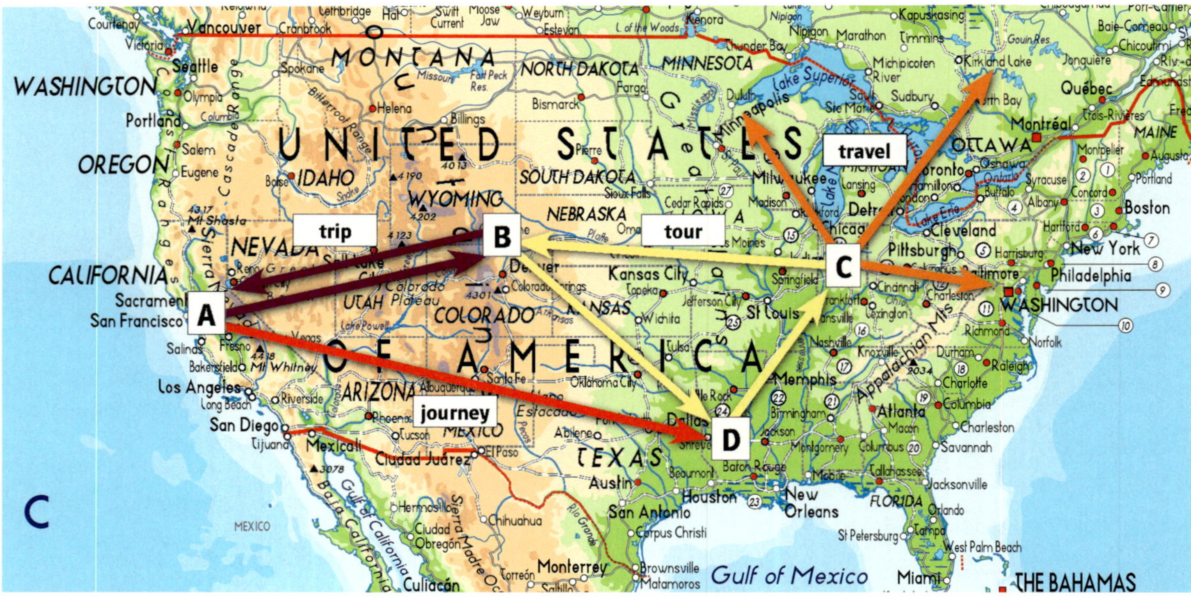

1. I hope there'll be time for a sightseeing .... while we're in St Petersburg.
2. Who usually makes the .... arrangements in your company?
3. The longest train .... I've ever been on was from London to Naples.
4. I'm usually exhausted when I come back from a business ....
5. Would you like me to give you a .... of the factory?
6. The German ICE train can .... up to 240 kilometres an hour.
7. I'm going on a three-day business .... to Vietnam.

b. Where would you be if you heard the statements and questions below?

A **Immigration**

B **On the plane**

C **Check-in desk**

D **Security control**

E **Customs**

F **Departure Lounge**

1. ....A.... How long are you planning to stay?
2. .... How many pieces of luggage do you have?
3. .... Would you prefer an aisle seat or a window seat?
4. .... Please fasten your seatbelts.
5. .... Place your coat on the tray. Make sure you've taken any keys or coins out of the pockets.
6. .... Have you got anything to declare?
7. .... Did you pack your bags yourself? Could anyone have interfered with your bags?
8. .... Stow away your hand luggage in the overhead compartment and prepare for takeoff.
9. .... Good morning, ladies and gentlemen. Flight BA912 to Gatwick is now ready for boarding.
10. .... What is the purpose of your visit: business or pleasure?
11. .... Is this your bag? Would you mind opening it, please?

c. Have you ever had problems in any of the above situations? Describe what happened.

d. Answer the following questions:

1. What will happen if you try to take on cabin bags that exceed the size restrictions?
2. What might happen if you don't have a valid passport when you travel internationally?
3. Even though most places accept credit and debit cards, why is it a good idea to carry cash with you?
4. If you need to pack insect repellent, suntan lotion and adaptors, where might you be flying to?
5. How can nervous travellers overcome their fear of flying?
6. Have you ever checked in for a flight online? What are the advantages?

D Business leaders | Michael O'Leary

Reading

a. Before you read: Have you ever flown on a budget airline such as Ryanair? Describe the experience.

b. Read and summarise O'Leary's formula for success and criticisms made of his concept.

Michael O'Leary and Ryanair

Michael O'Leary is rarely out of the media spotlight for long, and when he makes headlines there is bound to be controversy – whether he is announcing new lower fare offers to customers, or criticising government policy on airlines legislation, or engaging in heated debate with journalists and critics on issues such as the environment or unfair competition. There are many who say that his public performances are carefully planned to be part of Ryanair's advertising campaigns. The more attention the company receives, the more people will want to fly with the airline. So far, the idea of 'any publicity is good publicity' seems to be working.

Away from the public attention, however, O'Leary is a serious business player. He is determined to ride out the current downturn in the airline industry, and he is aware of the fact that rising fuel costs forced 30 carriers out of business in 2008. The global recession will mean that travellers decide to put off unnecessary flights, and many of Ryanair's passengers – 49 million last year – are what are known in the airline business as 'discretionary travellers' who fly because they choose to, rather than because they have to.

In this increasingly competitive sector, O'Leary is confident that Ryanair can not only survive, but prosper. He believes that he can continue to undercut his main competitors – Aer Lingus, easyJet and British Airways – and he intends to stick to this strategy. In fact, he recently announced that he is aiming to double traffic and profits by 2012. The recipe for success has been a simple one. Ryanair keeps its 195 planes (all the same type, the fuel-efficient Boeing 737 – 800) in the air for as long as possible, with tight scheduling and fast turnaround times. The planes are packed with passengers who pay a very low price for their ticket but boost profits by paying for add-ons such as baggage check-in, food, and hotels. These passengers may also find themselves arriving in lesser-known airports (with cheaper landing fees) a long way from the major cities they want to get to.

There is no denying that the Ryanair concept is highly successful, but Michael O'Leary has plenty of critics. There are those who point to the idea of the '€1 flight' as a cheap gimmick, given the costs and charges added to any ticket purchased. There are also people who object to the queues, the undignified scramble for seats, and the fact that rock-bottom fares can only be obtained if you fly mid-week at very awkward hours. On the other hand, Michael O'Leary is stripping the expense and mystique out of air travel and creating what is increasingly seen as a flying bus service. This is surely an accusation that he will be quite satisfied to live with

www.independent.co.uk

Michael O'Leary

(born 1961) is the controversial and outspoken boss of the Irish low-cost airline, Ryanair. He began his career as a tax consultant, became financial adviser to Ryanair in 1987 and was appointed CEO in 1994. He helped to make Ryanair one of the most profitable airlines in the world through new ways of cutting costs and increasing revenue. As well as being a leading force in the airline business, O'Leary has enjoyed success as a breeder of racehorses.

bound to be vorprogrammiert sein, **determined** entschlossen, **to ride out** überstehen, **discretionary travellers** Freizeitreisende, **to overturn a law** ein Gesetz aufheben, **insistence** Beharrlichkeit, **undignified scramble** würdeloses Gedrängel, **mystique** geheimnisvoller Nimbus

c. What impression do you get of O'Leary's character? Work in groups. Write a list of five questions you would ask O'Leary if you had the chance to interview him.

d. Use your questions to interview someone from another group. When it is your turn to be interviewed, give answers that are in keeping with O'Leary's character and the Ryanair concept.

e. Is it true that "any publicity is good publicity"? Discuss this view with reference to recent news items about budget airlines.

E Business communication | Networking

1 Why network?

Discuss ways of completing these statements.

1. Business people need to network in order to …
2. Typical opportunities for business networking include …
3. The key to good networking is …
4. If you're going to be mingling, don't forget to take …
5. Online social networking sites offer the advantage of …
6. There will always be a need for F2F networking because …

INFO

Business networking
Business networking is the informal process of making contacts and exchanging information with people who may be useful to you in your work. Networking events usually involve **mingling**, where participants try to meet as many different people as possible.

2 Listening

A 2.5 **a.** A regular conference-goer is talking about his experience of networking. Listen to Part One and take notes on the following points. Then use your notes to reconstruct what was said.

places | people | information | facilities | events

A 2.6 **b.** Now listen to Part Two and take notes. Discuss whether the advice would be useful to you.

3 Conversation skills

a. Match the opening lines with the tips on the right for striking up a conversation.

1. I really enjoyed your presentation yesterday.
2. Hey, I'm glad I'm not the only one in jeans.
3. Hello, I don't think we've met. I'm Mel Roberts.
4. So, how did you find this morning's workshop?
5. May I have a quick look at your programme?
6. Ah, I see you're from Tula. You've come a long way!
7. Phew, it's hot in here, isn't it?
8. Here, try one of these canapés. They're delicious.
9. Excuse me, I've heard you design bikes. Is that right?

a. Introduce yourself in a friendly way.
b. Refer to information on the person's ID badge.
c. Pay a compliment.
d. Point out something you have in common.
e. Invite the person to talk about their job.
f. Offer the person something to eat or drink.
g. Find out what he / she thinks of the last event.
h. Ask about something the person is holding.
i. Comment on the surroundings.

b. What other opening lines could you use? Suggest further examples.

c. Work in pairs to improvise conversations.

SKILLS

Building a conversation
- Show interest in the other person and their business. *(Hey, I've always wanted to meet a NASA engineer!)*
- Show what you have in common. *(You've been to Puna? Hey, so have I!)*
- Use open questions. *(What do you think of Apple's latest notebook?)*
- Refer to future contacts. *(Will you be at the fair in Dresden next month?)*
- Exchange comments on business cards. *(I see you have an MBA. So where did you do it?)*

d. The sentences below include some phrases for ending conversations. Underline the right word.

1. Well, it's been really nice (talking / to talk) to you. I hope we'll be able to (meet / meet us) again soon.
2. Is it time we (go back / were getting back) to the conference?
3. If you don't (care / mind), I'll just go and get (me / myself) another drink.
4. How about (joining / that you join) me for breakfast tomorrow?
5. Could you (apologise / excuse) me for a moment? I just need a (fast / quick) word with the organiser.
6. Anyway, do (keep / stick) in touch, now you've got my card.
7. I'm sorry to (cut / break) you short here, but I've just (noticed / remarked) that someone is waving to me.
8. (Do / Would) you like me to introduce you (my boss / to my boss)?

SKILLS

Ending a conversation
When the aim is to talk to as many people as possible in a short time, signal that you want to move on. If you find yourself stuck with a rude or boring person, remain polite but use 'restless' body language. Agree in advance for a colleague to rescue you if needed, or introduce the person to someone else. Prepare a few 'convincing excuses' (migraine attack?) for emergencies!

4 Simulation: Mingling in the break

Scenario: You are delegates at an international watch and jewellery conference in Basel, Switzerland. The buffet lunch from 12.00 to 13.00 will be an excellent opportunity to make some key contacts.

Preparation: Decide whether you will be a delegate or a conference organiser. The delegates work in pairs (customers or suppliers). Make sure that there are as many pairs of suppliers as customers, and then carry out the tasks as described below.

Delegates: Customer / Supplier

Work as a pair of customers or a pair of suppliers. Create business cards with your name, job title, company (+ logo), address and website. Decide on a target for your networking efforts, e.g. as many contacts or possible (quantity) or contacts that are valuable to you or your company (quality). You may also want to network with other customers. Complete and return the registration form that the conference organisers give you.

Conference organisers

Produce a registration form for delegates that will give you the details you need to plan the event, for example the delegates' names and titles, the companies they represent, their position in the company, whether they are suppliers or customers, and any special extra information such as dietary choices. From these details, design an ID badge for each delegate that is colour-coded according to whether they are suppliers or customers.

The event: Before the event starts, the delegates should collect their ID badges from the conference organisers and check that any special dietary requirements have been met.

Delegates: Customer / Supplier

Find customers and suppliers to network with, making as many contacts as you can and building rapport. If you think that they will be useful contacts for future business, note down their contact details. Liaise with your partner at regular intervals to keep each other informed about your progress and minimise the risk of 'double booking'. Watch out for competitors who try to 'eavesdrop' on your conversations.

Conference organisers

Circulate during the buffet lunch and check that everyone has got a drink or ordered one. Make sure that nobody is left standing alone. Get people together and try to maintain a good level of mingling. You can also join in, of course, for example to find out whether people are enjoying the conference. You are already thinking about next year's conference, so you want to get some feedback from delegates as to a good venue and possible topics for presentations.

to eavesdrop lauschen, abhören

After the event: When the lunch break is over, get back together in your groups / pairs and carry out the following tasks.

Delegates: Customer / Supplier

Compare the contacts and appointments you have made. Discuss the best way to cultivate the business relationships further and produce a 'to do' list.

Then write an email to your boss summarising how you think the conference went and listing the contacts you made. Explain what you intend to do next in order to follow up your leads.

Conference organisers

Share information that you managed to pick up during the break and produce a feedback form that will give you some ideas for making next year's conference even more successful.

Then write an email to the delegates thanking them for attending the conference and encouraging them to complete the feedback form that you have attached to the email.

Doing business in London

London is not a difficult place to do business. Forget the stereotypes you might have heard elsewhere: in general terms, the transport systems work, the weather is okay and the British are a tolerant bunch. These tips below should help you to stride into meetings with that extra bit of confidence. Stiff upper lips and old-school ties are much rarer than they used to be, but Londoners are still relatively shy. Buy a round of drinks in the pub later in the day, though, and you'll find the reserve starts to crumble.

Meeting and greeting

London is a multicultural city. It is worth finding out where your contact is from. You are quite as likely to be dealing with an Indian or an Australian as you are with a born-and-bred Londoner.

Business cards are typically exchanged at the end of a meeting. But it is not unusual for a Brit to forget about them entirely. If your contact fumbles around for his card, or fails to produce one, don't take it personally.

The British tend to be punctual, and meetings generally follow the Anglo-Saxon norm, with brief chit-chat swiftly followed by a focused, action-oriented discussion.

Working habits

E-mails perfectly suit the famous British reserve. In general, they are promptly responded to and are often the preferred method of communication, at least at the outset. As a relationship strengthens, and certainly if complex negotiations are involved, expect face-to-face meetings and telephone conversations.

The strongest relationships are forged after work—be that in a pub or at an informal evening meal. The line between work and private life is not as clearly delineated as in America, and the British tend to socialise with colleagues quite regularly. Drunken behaviour on a Friday evening will be laughed off the following Monday, and in some cases is quite the norm.

The woes of public transport are a sure-fire way of reviving flagging conversation. London's motorists have to pay a congestion charge to drive into the city. Your contacts will be sure to have an opinion on whether the experiment is working.

Eating and drinking

A business lunch can just as easily mean a quick sandwich and coffee as a slap-up meal in a smart restaurant. Breakfast meetings are rare. Most Brits subscribe to Oscar Wilde's claim that "only dull people are interesting at breakfast."

Midday drinking has declined, but it is still normal to have a glass of wine or a beer, with food or without.

Likewise, smoking has fallen off dramatically. Smoking was banned in all public spaces (including restaurants and bars) from July 2007 and the smoky haze that used to be a feature of many pubs is but a memory. If you want to smoke, you have to be outside. When in a pub, do not expect table service, unless you are seated in the restaurant area. And don't tip the bar staff unless they bring the drinks and bill over to you.

Table manners are keenly observed as a subtle sign of good breeding. Never talk with your mouth full; never reach across the table; do not wave cutlery around or yell "I'm done" to the waiter. London's top restaurants are expensive (£100 a head is not unheard of). Furthermore, an increasing number insist on taking credit card details before accepting a booking.

The British are less politically correct than their American counterparts. Wittiness can still mean an agility with sexual innuendo, with a pint in one hand and a cigarette in the other.

The Economist, November 15th 2009

bunch (hier) Völkchen, **to stride** große Schritte machen, **stiff upper lip** kontrollierte Emotionen, **old school tie** alte Seilschaft aus der gleichen Schule, **reserve** Scheu, Förmlichkeit, **to crumble** zerfallen, sich auflösen, **born-and-bred** einheimisch, to **fumble around** herumfummeln, **chit-chat** Geplauder, **at the outset** am Anfang, **delineated** abgegrenzt, **woes** Leiden, Probleme, **sure-fire** todsicher, **to revive a flagging conversation** ein erschlaffendes Gespräch beleben, **congestion charge** Staugebühr, **to subscribe to a claim** sich einer Behauptung anschließen, **dull** langweilig, **smoky haze** Rauchqualm, **good breeding** gute Erziehung, **wittiness** Witzigkeit, **agility** Gewandtheit, **innuendo** Anspielung, **counterpart** Gegenstück, Pendant

a. Answer the questions with information from the text. If there is no information, write 'NI'.

Questions	Answers
How cosmopolitan is the business environment? How likely am I to meet people from different cultures?	
What's the practice with regard to the exchange of business cards?	
What are the preferred methods of communication at work?	
How do colleagues address each other? Do they use first name terms? Are titles important?	
How important is punctuality?	
Is there a dress code? If so, should I adopt this dress code myself?	
How do firms usually entertain visitors from other countries?	
If a colleague invites me home for dinner, should I take a gift? If so, what gifts might be suitable?	
What is considered to be 'bad manners' during a meal?	
Do colleagues socialise after work? If so, what do they do and where do they go?	
What are the 'safe' conversation topics?	
Are there any conversation topics I should avoid?	
What about body language? For example, is it normal for colleagues to hug, kiss, shake hands, etc.?	
Are there any gender issues I should be aware of? Are men and women treated equally at work?	
Are there any rules and regulations I should be aware of?	
Are there any superstitions I should be aware of?	
Do you have any practical tips with regard to transport, weather, tipping, etc.?	

b. Carry out research in order to answer the questions where you put 'NI'.

c. Consider the answers you would give if the questions referred to your own culture, and make notes. Compare your views with other students.

d. Write an article giving advice on business etiquette in the capital city of your country, using a similar structure to the article on the left. Follow these tips:

- Avoid simple stereotypes. Check your assumptions through research and support your statements with examples.
- Use hedging language when you make generalisations. (See language tip on the right.)
- The heading should refer to a place rather than its inhabitants, for example: 'Doing business in Switzerland' (NOT: ~~Doing business with the Swiss~~). This is because inhabitants may not necessarily share the same culture. Also, you can include practical tips on weather, transport, rules and regulations, etc.
- If possible, interview business people with relevant experience and include any interesting quotes.

LANGUAGE TIP

Hedging

Use 'hedging' language to show you are making a generalisation or being careful about your claims.

- **Most** Britons subscribe to this view.
- Londoners are **relatively** shy.
- Business cards are **typically** exchanged at the end of a meeting.
- It is **not unusual** for a Brit to forget about them entirely.
- The British **tend to** be punctual.
- Meetings **generally** follow the Anglo-Saxon norm.

In this way, you show that you do not claim to have the last word on the subject. At the same time, however, you reduce the risk of being contradicted.

Revision 2
Units 5–8

Online Link
800021-0018

1 Complete the grid to show the meaning of some common short forms.

	Clue / Definition	Long form	**German**
1. COD	pay when goods arrive	....	*Zahlung per Nachnahme*
2. CWO	advance payment	....	....
3. DDP	....	....	*frei Haus, verzollt geliefert*
4. DIY	self-assembly	....	....
5. JIT	....	just-in-time	....

2 Complete the words and give the acronym on the right. (The first has been done for you.)

An ad should…
answer the customer's question: "What's In It for Me?" *WIFM*
feature the product's .... que .... ling .... position. ....
include a .... ture, ... mise, some .... of and a .... h to act. ....
attract .... ention, create .... erest, arouse .... ire, and .... mpt action. ....

3 Choose from the words to complete the sentences. (Note that there are more words than gaps.)

wholesale | retail | factory | advertising | advertisements | vending | vendor | brand-stretching | product placement | diversify | launch | copywriter | copyright | strapline | jingle | supplier

1. Levis Inc. tried to .... into men's suits, but this attempt at .... failed.
2. A .... is a person who writes the text of ....
3. A .... is a short, catchy tune or song, whereas a .... is a type of slogan.
4. A .... is a company or person who sells something, or a .... of goods to manufacturers.
5. A .... machine is type of .... outlet, a way of making goods available to customers.

4 How are the following people paid?

1. Artists, writers and musicians receive *r*........ .
2. Taxi drivers charge *f*........, and their passengers may give them *t*........ as well.
3. Agents get a *c*........ . Distributors make a *p*........ or a loss.
4. Sales reps receive a *s*........, but they may also be paid a basic *r*........ .
   If they reach their targets, they may also get a *b*........ .
5. Lawyers and tax consultants charge *f*........ .

5 Choose the right option between these commonly confused words.

1. Please let us know if you (require / request) assistance.
2. We will (notify / notice) you as soon as the goods are ready for dispatch.
3. The Health and (Security / Safety) Officer is responsible for protecting employees in the workplace.
4. Retailers usually offer big (rebates / discounts) after Christmas.
5. German farmers receive generous (subsidies / subsidiaries) from the state.
6. Guests are given (complementary / complimentary) champagne on arrival.
7. The central location makes the hotel very (comfortable / convenient).
8. Would you be willing to refund my (travel / journey) expenses?

6 Complete the sentences.

1. Would you prefer an a.................... seat or a window seat?
2. For takeoff and landing, please ensure that all electronic d.................... are switched off.
3. All hand luggage should be safely s.................... away in the overhead lockers.
4. Please .... your seatbelts and put your trays upright.
5. Airlines rarely offer hot meals on s....................-h.................... flights.

7 Translate the expressions into English.

1. *Zahlung bei Auftragserteilung* ....
2. *Ratenzahlung* ....
3. *wie vereinbart* ....
4. *Ursprungszeugnis* ....
5. *Ladendiebstahl* ....
6. *Binnenmarkt* ....
7. *Lohnstückkosten* ....

8 Translate the expressions into German.

1. sell-by-date ....
2. to sell on your own account ....
3. to break bulk ....
4. to take a cut of the profits ....
5. intellectual property rights ....
6. a false economy ....
7. rock-bottom prices ....
8. carbon footprint ....

9 Give the English spellings.

1. Köln ....
2. Wien ....
3. München ....
4. Bayern ....
5. Luzern ....
6. Hannover ....

10 What labels would you put on goods that …

1. are easily broken? f....................
2. have a high worth? v....................
3. burn easily? i....................
4. are poisonous? t....................
5. lose freshness quickly? p....................
6. are dangerous? h....................

11 Put in the missing prepositions.

1. This product might appeal .... young people.
2. We're targeting this product .... the over-50s.
3. We'd like to break .... new markets.
4. They want us to pay .... front.
5. People associate the colour green .... nature.
6. Does this product stand .... from the competition?
7. We always buy .... bulk.
8. Do you have the goods .... stock?

12 Write the verb that commonly goes with these nouns.

1. to p.................... orders
2. to a.................... demand
3. to l.................... with suppliers
4. to i.................... costs
5. to s.................... bias
6. to e.................... findings
7. to r.................... deadlock
8. to d.................... conclusions

13 Underline the word that does not fit in the group. Note down why.

1. barge – ferry – yacht – cable car – hovercraft ....
2. helicopter – car – hot-air balloon – parachute – plane ....
3. bicycle – van – lorry – zeppelin – road train ....
4. freight train – tram – monorail – tanker – funicular ....

14 Group the adjectives according to the categories. Add a further example to each group.

medium | crispy | burnt | beaten | salty | full-bodied | mouldy | boiled | rubbery | steamed | sour | chopped | crunchy | diced | gone off | poached | savoury | light

1. How food is prepared: ....
2. Cooking food: ....
3. Textures: ....
4. Tastes: ....
5. Wine: ....
6. Complaints: ....

15 Match words from each group to create a compound noun.

public | press | market | spending | ~~business~~ | supply | trade | air-traffic | urnaround

relations | times | release | control | fair | chain | research | power | ~~pitch~~

....

....

16 Put in arrows to indicate a rising (↗) or falling (↘) trend. Underline the word that is not used as a verb.

1. downturn
2. surge
3. slump
4. recover
5. plunge
6. decline
7. dwindle
8. tumble
9. boost

17 Complete the sentences with words that mean the opposite of the ones in bold.

1. Those goods aren't **genuine**, they're c.................... .
2. We've **added** VAT, but we've d.................... 10% from the sale price.

18 Choose the right option.

1. I (am not / was not / have not been) paid since I (start / started / have started) this job.
2. While I (made / was making / was doing) my internship, I (also designed / designed also / had also designed) a new website.
3. If we (would have done / had done / will do) (a market research / some market research / some market researches), we might have designed the product differently.
4. Would you mind (wait / to wait / waiting) a moment? I've just seen a colleague of (me / mine) over there.

19 Underline the word stress.

1. We discovered a **defect** in the item.
2. I can't **convert** the files Windows format.
3. Bill Gates didn't **graduate** with an MBA.
4. Your passport is **invalid**.
5. She's on a **secondment** in Shanghai.
6. We only sell fresh **produce**.

20 Identify and correct the mistakes. Refer to the marking code on p. 38.

1. Our headquarter is in Singen. (WF + VF)
2. All the ingredients are listed on the etiquette. (FF)
3. A dutch customer called to say that his consignment has not arrived. (Punct. + VF)
4. The responsible driver left the goods without telling anyone. (WO)
5. I really enjoy doing researches. (UC)
6. Please send us your actual price list. (FF)
7. I learned a lot about working independent. (G)
8. I've worked in the Production Department in my last internship. (T)
9. Would it be more rentable to outsource production? (FF)

21 Complete the definitions with the missing letters.

1. legal but secret trade in goods and services	g..........	m..........
2. ordering goods through a catalogue or online	m..........	o..........
3. a purchase made spontaneously	i..........	b..........
4. any place from where goods are sold	r..........	o..........
5. symbol used in front of items in a list	b..........	p..........
6. giving an advantage over rival firms	c..........	e..........
7. the price of borrowing money	i..........	r..........
8. relations between employers and employees / unions	i..........	r..........
9. where the parts of a product are fitted in a fixed order	a..........	l..........
10. production area of a company	s..........	f..........

22 Note where you are more likely to hear these sentences (US / UK) and give an equivalent expression.

1. Our local **mom-and-pop store** sells great donuts. (...US...) corner shop (UK)..........
2. Please **wait in the queue**. (..........) ....
3. A lot of heavy **lorries** pass through our town. (..........) ....
4. Do we need a coin for the **baggage cart**? (..........) ....
5. I've sent them my **résumé** and grade certificates. (..........) ....
6. I always fly **economy**. I can't afford first class. (..........) ....

23 Listening

A 3.2 **a.** Listen to an interview about British manufacturing. Note what the following statistics refer to.

1. 6.5%
2. 50%
3. 4 million
4. 31% to 13%
5. 75%
6. 3 million
7. more than half
8. one and a half times
9. 6th

b. Complete the text, based on Professor Champion's comments.

A disadvantage of being export-oriented is that a country is more .... in a recession. However, a recession can make firms .... and more ...., destroying weak manufacturers and stimulating .... The problem is ...., so manufacturers would like the government to set up a ....

c. Which question could Professor champion not answer? Write a paragraph explaining your own view.

25 The expressions below are chapter headings from the book 'Deutsche Unsitten' by Martin Hecht. Choose five examples and explain why you think they were chosen. Use the hedging language on p. 107.

Weiße Socken in Sandalen | Alptraum-Kunde | Abzocke | Duzen in der Arbeitswelt | Werbeschleim | Mahlzeit | Aldi, Lidl etc. | Schrebergärtnerei | Mittelstandskultur | Schnäppchenjagd

Unit 9
Human resources

Online Link
800021-0009

A Introduction | Training

1 Investing in training

a. Describe the system of vocational training in your country. Explain how it is structured, and the role that the state plays in encouraging companies to invest in training.

b. The directors of Synysys AG have decided to slash the company's training budget by 50%. Assuming that each of the courses below costs the same amount, what cuts would you recommend?

- Coaching and mentoring for managers
- Teambuilding weekends
- English language training
- Occupational accident prevention
- Empowering women in the workplace
- Effective PowerPoint presentations
- Managing cultural diversity
- Video conferencing
- Time management skills
- Giving performance appraisals

c. Give examples of training courses that you have attended. Were they useful, or a waste of time? Explain why.

- I recommend cutting the …
- We can certainly drop …, because …
- I think we should keep …. After all, …

LANGUAGE TIP

Education, training and apprenticeships
Education refers to formal schooling. You get an education at school or university and by studying on your own.
Training puts the emphasis on skills. You do vocational training to prepare for a job, and develop your skills further by training on the job. The person being trained is referred to as **trainee**, e.g. trainee nurse, trainee accountant. An **apprenticeship** is a traditional form of work-based training in a certain trade, such as the carpentry trade or car mechanics. The **apprentice** is usually supervised by a 'master' of the trade.
A **work placement** is another way to get work experience. It may be paid or unpaid. In the US this is called an **internship**, and the person who does it is called an **intern** (NOT ~~internee~~). Some companies send employees on **secondments** to give them experience of working abroad or in other areas of the business.

- to do training (NOT ~~make a training~~)
- to attend training courses (NOT ~~visit trainings~~)

2 Invitation to a job interview

a. Hans-Jürgen Elstermann, HR manager at Synysys AG, has advertised in the UK for a bilingual secretary. One of the applicants is Paula Redman from Chelmsford in Essex. As Herr Elstermann's assistant, you have been asked to draft a letter inviting her to an interview based on the notes on the right.

- Bedanken Sie sich für die Bewerbung.
- Laden Sie die Bewerberin zu einem Vorstellungsgespräch am … um … in unserem Haus ein.
- Weisen Sie auf die beigelegte Anfahrtsskizze und auf den Besucherparkplatz hin.
- Das Vorstellungsgespräch wird etwa 20 Minuten dauern. Die Bewerberin muss zusätzlich einen Eignungstest (10 Minuten) machen.
- Die Namen und Berufstitel der Anwesenden: Karin Kohl (Vertriebsleiterin), Jochen Nägele (Mitglied des Betriebsrats), und ich (Leiter Personalabteilung).
- Die Bewerberin sollte die folgenden Unterlagen mitbringen: Zeugnisse, Zertifikate (z.B. Fremdsprachenzertifikat), Arbeitsgenehmigung, Führerschein
- Reisekosten (Fahrt und Übernachtung im Hotel) werden von uns erstattet (bei Vorlage von Belegen).
- Bitten Sie die Bewerberin um eine kurze Bestätigung, dass sie den genannten Termin wahrnehmen kann.
- Bei Fragen soll sich die Bewerberin entweder an mich oder an Sie wenden.

Eignungstest aptitude test, **Arbeitsgenehmigung** work permit, **erstatten** to reimburse, to refund, **Anfahrtsskizze** map with directions to the company, **Besucherparkplatz** visitor parking, **Zeugnisse** grade reports, references, **Betriebsrat** works council

LANGUAGE TIP

False friends: "house"
The word 'house' only refers to where people live.
Er ist nicht im Haus = He isn't in the building.
in unserem Haus = in our company / on our premises

b. Exchange letters with another student. Write Paula's reply in which she confirms her willingness to attend the interview and asks about organisational matters (e.g. hotel booking).

3 Listening

Cheryl Kellermann has just started an internship in a company in London. Her friend Nick calls her to find out how she is getting on. A few days later she calls him back to ask for advice.

a. Before you listen, match the expressions on the left with the German equivalents on the right.

1. a stepping-stone (in one's career)	a. jemanden von oben herab behandeln
2. to be a tall order	b. die Grundlagen lernen
3. to start off on the wrong foot	c. ein bisschen viel verlangt sein
4. to think on one's feet	d. am Ball bleiben
5. to get into someone's good books	e. einen schlechten Start haben
6. a golden opportunity	f. Sprungbrett
7. to learn the ropes	g. eine einmalige Chance
8. to dump on somebody	h. einen Stein im Brett haben

A 2.7 **b.** Listen to Part One and take notes on the following points:

› The type of work Cheryl would like to do
› The type of work she wants to avoid
› The first job she was given
› Why she was asked to do it
› Her initial reaction to being asked
› What the job involved
› What she feels she has learned from the experience

A 2.8 **c.** Listen to Part Two, where Cheryl asks Nick for advice. Take notes about the problem that has arisen and how it came about. Then summarise the situation that Cheryl faces.

d. Nick decides to send Cheryl an email rather than call her back. Discuss Cheryl's problem with another student. Then work together to write Nick's email in which he gives Cheryl his advice.

B Business briefing | Working in Human Resources

1 Reading

a. Complete the interview by putting in the questions. (The first one has been done for you.)

Is my age a problem? | What's the money like? | Is there any training available? | What is your motto as a human resources officer? | Give me a quick summary of the job. | What qualifications would I need? | What skills are desirable? | Sounds simple. But what exactly does it involve?

Human Resources Officer

■ *What is your motto as a human resources officer?*

■ People are a company's best asset.

■ Give me a quick summary of the job

■ Human resources officers are responsible for getting the best from people working for an organisation. You help to recruit the right staff, provide the right training, and ensure that good employees stay with the company. You also make sure the organisation deals with its employees fairly and legally.

■ Sounds simple. But what exactly does it involve?

■ Depending upon the size and type of organisation, your duties could include helping to draw up plans for the organisation's future personnel needs; recruiting people with suitable skills and qualifications; providing staff training and development; running pay and benefits policies which keep within the law and the organisation's resources; overseeing employee services such as health and safety, and sports and social facilities; counselling staff about problems, both work and personal; advising management on matters such as pay negotiations, disciplinary and grievance procedures, redundancy programmes, equal opportunities policy and employment law.

■ What qualifications would I need

■ There are no minimum entry requirements, but most human resources/personnel officers enter with degrees or higher national diplomas. Some people enter routine administrative or clerical jobs in personnel departments and work towards promotion. There are some postgraduate personnel management courses.

■ Is there any training available

■ Most human resources officers are trained on the job, and many employers expect staff to work towards Chartered Institute of Personnel and Development (CIPD) qualifications. Certain business studies degrees will give students exemption from the CIPD professional qualification scheme.

■ What skills are desirable

■ Patience, tact, diplomacy, approachability and the ability to deal with people who are stressed or upset. You need to be able to see things from the employer's point of view, have good commercial awareness and be able to stay calm in difficult situations. Good spoken and written communication skills are indispensable. You'll need confidence in gathering facts and statistics and making financial calculations for planning, and it's essential that you can keep confidences in dealing with employees' personal details. Apart from that, you'll need good organising skills for drawing up plans and policies, problem-solving skills for disputes and staffing problems, and the ability to work as part of a team. Accuracy and attention to detail are also paramount.

■ What's the money like ?

■ Graduate entrants start at around £14,000 to £16,500. An experienced personnel manager earns between £25,000 and £40,000. A human resources/personnel director earns in the region of £55,000.

■ Is my age a problem?

■ Mature entrants are usually valued, especially if their previous work experience has been relevant. There's generally no upper age limit.

The Guardian, 7 October 2003

approachability Ansprechbarkeit, **upset** aufgeregt, verletzt, **indispensable** unverzichtbar, **exemption** Freistellung, **to keep confidence** als vertraulich behandeln, **paramount** vorrangig, **mature entrants** (hier) ältere Einsteiger in dem Beruf

b. Try to find the average salaries today for comparable jobs in your country. Compare the figures and explain where you found them.

LANGUAGE TIP

False friends
personal (adj.) - ['pɜ:snel] *persönlich*
personnel (n.) - [ˌpɜ:s'nel] *Personal*

c. Find expressions in the article that correspond to the definitions.

1. a thing of value that a person or company owns .... assit
2. advantages that you get from your company in addition to wages or salary .... benefits
3. giving professional advice to somebody about a problem .... councelling
4. a cause for complaint, e.g. about unfair treatment .... grievance
5. a situation where a person loses a job because there is no work for them .... redundancy
6. treating employees and others without discrimination .... opportunities
7. a move to a more important job, usually with more money .... promotion

d. Suggest German translations of the expressions.

e. Discuss the relationship between the skills and the tasks mentioned in the article.

Example:
Tact and diplomacy are needed when counselling staff about personal problems.

f. Choose a different profession and make notes using the same headings. Describe the profession to another student without actually naming it. Can he or she guess which one you are referring to?

2 Discussion

According to statistics from the US Department of Labor (2007), women outnumber men as human resources managers. Do you think this is true of your own country? Discuss possible reasons why women predominate in some professions and men in others.

3 Research

a. EU law has a significant impact on the employment laws in its member states. Choose one of the issues listed below and carry out research in order to compare EU legislation with that of your own country. Find out what the EU policy or law is on the issue, and whether it has been implemented.

b. Report your findings in class and discuss the impact of the law on business in your country.

"It was a compromise. We got to keep our jobs, but our lunch break was outsourced to Romania."

INFO

EU employment policy
The EU has a long-standing commitment to improved working conditions and employee rights in its member states. There are EU-directives and policies on issues such as:

- Collective redundancies
- Data protection
- Anti-discrimination (gender, racial and ethnic origin, disability, age, religion / belief and sexual orientation)
- Equal treatment of men and women in the workplace
- Information and consultation of employees
- Protection of 'atypical' workers (for example part-time, fixed-term and teleworkers)
- Protection of pregnant workers
- Maternity rights
- Parental leave
- Social security and pension rights
- Rights of workers transferred within the EU and to the EU from third countries ('posting of workers directive')
- Working time

posting of workers directive Arbeitnehmerentsenderichtlinie

C Language | Recruitment

1 The recruitment process

a. Number the steps in the recruitment process in a logical order.

[ ] The candidate confirms acceptance of the job offer.
[ ] HR draw up a job description and person specification.
[ ] The employment contract is signed.
[ ] The job interviews are conducted.
[ ] HR evaluate the applications received.
[ ] A job offer is made to the chosen candidate.
[ ] The employer identifies a need to create a vacancy or find someone new to fill a post.
[ ] Candidates are shortlisted for interview.
[ ] HR create a job advertisement.
[ ] Letters are sent to the rejected candidates.
[ ] The candidate is inducted into the job.
[ ] Shortlisted candidates are invited to a job interview.
[ ] The best candidate is selected.
[ ] The vacancy is advertised.

b. Draw a flow chart that depicts the sequence, using keywords only.
Show your flowchart to another student and explain the process in your own words.

c. Describe the different ways in which companies can advertise for jobs.

2 Hiring and firing

Match the statements on the left with ones on the right that have a similar meaning.

1. She handed in her notice.
2. She gave me my notice.
3. She was laid off.
4. She was hired.
5. He was sacked.
6. He stood in for me.
7. He was dismissed without notice.

a. He was fired.
b. She was given the job.
c. He was told to leave immediately.
d. She told her employer she was going to leave.
e. She told me I had to leave the company.
f. She was made redundant.
g. He did my job while I was away.

3 Words in context

Complete the text with the missing words.

headhunters | prospective | candidates | social networking | applications | flexible | freelancers | cash-strapped | recruitment costs | employee benefits | hiring freeze | bonuses | advancement

According to a survey, three quarters of all American companies have implemented a .... However, other companies have started to hire in new ways. The hiring of .... and consultants has become more common, allowing companies to avoid spending on .... and delay hiring decisions until the economy picks up. Firms are also marketing themselves differently to job .... Lucrative .... and international travel were once the main attractions for .... employees, but the new selling points are sandwiches with the boss, opportunities for ...., ... working hours and more holiday time.
As companies cut their budgets for hiring, tricks to cut .... are gaining popularity. A consultant firm called MBA Scouting Report, which identifies promising MBA students for companies but charges less than ...., has seen business increase by 40% since the recession began. Sales are also strong at TalentDrive, a firm that makes CV-screening software which helps companies sort through thousands of .... Some .... firms are making connections with potential hires in an even cheaper way: through .... sites like LinkedIn and Facebook.

The Economist, 30 April 2009

Agapanthus Exteriors

Vacancy for a PA to the CEO

We are a Bristol-based company specialising in patio and garden furniture, with retail and wholesale operations in six European countries. We are seeking a **Personal Assistant** to our CEO, Mr. Javed Patel.

The successful applicant will be a highly motivated individual with proven business skills and the ability to organise busy schedules and work under pressure. This position would suit an energetic and ambitious business graduate (MBA preferred) with excellent communication skills and the necessary drive to succeed in a competitive market. In return, we offer a competitive salary, generous benefits and opportunities fast-track promotion.

Apply with CV and covering letter in English to:
Karen Carter, Agapanthus Exteriors
Mellor House, 25 Park St , Bristol BS1 5HX
Closing date for applications: June 30th.

We are an equal opportunities employer.

1

Job category: Human Resources
Job type: Assistant Manager
Location: Cork, Rep. of Ireland
Ref. No: HR / 900809

Description: We are one of the UK's leading producers of organic cosmetics and beauty products, supplying wholesale and retail customers in the UK and abroad. The company has recently expanded into Ireland, where we are preparing to launch a major sales campaign. We are therefore seeking an experienced manager who will report directly to the HR director and be responsible for the recruitment of sales staff.

Requirements: A good knowledge of all aspects of human resources management is essential and experience of product promotion would also be an advantage. We are looking for an effective communicator with a proven track record in recruitment interviews and staff selection. If you are a motivated and adaptable person, with a first degree, proficiency in English and a willingness to take on new challenges, we would welcome your application.

Salary: negotiable

2

proven track record nachweisbare Erfolge, nachgewiesene Erfolgsbilanz

4 Job advertisements

a. Tick off (✓) the items in the checklist that are mentioned in the job advertisements above. (You may find it helpful to copy the checklist and complete it with the relevant details.) Which advertisement has the most ticks?

b. Which of the two jobs appeals to you most, and why?

c. Choose one of the advertisements and translate it into German.

d. Start your own word bank of expressions useful for describing personal qualities and abilities. Use the headings below and look for further examples in the texts and tasks of this unit.

WORD BANK

Describing qualities and abilities
Approach to work: reliable, hard-working, …
Motivation: competitive, enthusiastic, …
Qualifications / experience: to have experience in …
Talent and ability: innovative, imaginative, …
Manner with customers / colleagues: caring, tactful, …

Job advertisement checklist	Ad 1	Ad 2
The organisation		
Name		
Location		
Sector / branch		
Reason for vacancy		
The position		
Job title		
Tasks and responsibilities		
Reporting to / Working for		
The candidate		
Qualifications		
Experience		
Skills		
Personal qualities		
The offer		
Remuneration		
Benefits / perks		
How to apply		
Contact address		
Documents required		
Deadline for application		

e. Work in teams of three to four. Write a job advertisement for a 'dream job' that would appeal to other students in your class. This advertisement will be needed in further tasks in this unit.

5 The application

a. An application letter (or cover / covering letter) accompanies your CV or résumé when you apply for a job. The sample letters on pages 219 and 220 are addressed to the same person but the objective is different. Discuss the similarities and differences between them.

b. Choose a job advertisement created by another team in ***Task 4e***. Write an application letter explaining why you think you are the right person for the job. Refer to the CV that you enclose with the letter.

6 The curriculum vitae

a. Discuss the following questions from the perspective of a recruiter who regularly receives CVs from all over the world for different types of job.

1. In your view, which is more important – the CV or the letter of application? Explain why.
2. What information should all CVs contain? What headings do you recommend?
3. Should information be presented chronologically? If not, should it be organised differently?
4. How would you expect CV conventions to differ from country to country?
5. Some applicants choose not to include the following details in their CVs. What is your own view?

age | religion | photo | marital status | nationality | gender | health | details about family

b. Analyse the structure, layout and content of Jan-Peter Ulrich's CV on page 221. How does it differ from a traditional German-style CV? What type of internship do you think he would be suited to?

c. Action verbs combine with nouns to create collocations for describing tasks and responsibilities, e.g. ***to plan a budget***, ***to lead a team.*** Identify the action verbs in Jan-Peter's CV, and suggest further examples to add to the following:

Action verbs			
Initiating	Realising	Performing	Managing
devise | spearhead | introduce | found | set up | …	conduct | liaise with | execute carry out | coordinate | …	analyse | promote | deliver | audit | present | …	lead | supervise | oversee | organise | run | …

d. Write a CV tailored to your dream job / internship. Include details that will help the recruiter know the kind of tasks that you are capable of.

LANGUAGE TIP

British or American?

German	**British**	**American**
Lebenslauf	curriculum vitae (CV)	curriculum vitae / résumé
Praktikum	work placement	internship
Grundschule	primary school	elementary school
Gesamtschule	comprehensive school	school / high school
Realschule	≈ secondary modern	≈ high school
Gymnasium	≈ grammar school / academic high school	≈ high school / junior college
Mittlere Reife	≈ GCSEs	≈ high school diploma
Abitur	≈ 'A' Levels	≈ high school diploma
Hochschule	university, college	university, college

≈ equivalent to, but not a translation

SKILLS

Translating

Do not attempt to translate qualifications and names of institutions if there is no official translation. Give the original name followed by a brief explanation in brackets. The *Abitur* can be explained as 'advanced school-leaving certificate', or 'general qualification for university entrance'.

Be careful with false friends (*Gymnasium* ≠ gymnasium, *Hochschule* ≠ high school) and words that mean one thing in British English and another in American English. For example, a grammar school (the UK equivalent of *Gymnasium*) refers in the US to a type of elementary school (*Grundschule*).

The verb 'graduate' has a more restricted meaning in British English, referring to the completion of university studies. In American English, the verb can also be used to refer to completing high school.

D Business leaders | Industrial management gurus

1 Reading

a. Scan the profiles for contrasting views on how productivity and performance can be improved. Summarise what each 'guru' contributed to ideas on the subject of industrial management.

F.W. Taylor (1856 – 1915) was an American mechanical engineer who tried to improve industrial efficiency. He is regarded as the father of scientific management, and he was the first to consider work to be a subject worthy of scientific study. Taylor was critical of the industrial management of his day, and believed that the best way to achieve results was a partnership between a highly trained and efficient management, and a willing and cooperative workforce.

The principles that became known as 'Taylorism' involved using scientific methods to maximise efficiency, for example in the way workers were selected, trained and supervised, and the division of labour between those who planned the work (the managers), and those who carried it out (the workers). In this model, there would be no need for trade unions, because they would block efficiency of production.

Taylor's scientific approaches to increasing human output were not popular with workers and often provoked strike action, something that he had hoped to avoid. He also made enemies by criticising the owners of factories where scientific management was not in use. His vision of progress was a genuine one, but it placed efficiency before anything else, including human motives and aspirations.

Elton Mayo (1880 – 1949) was an Australian psychologist whose early research was the study of 'shell-shock' in soldiers returning from the battlefield. He went on to become a pioneer in the study of human behaviour in the workplace, and carried out experiments demonstrating the relationship between working conditions and productivity. He moved to the USA, where he conducted research into motivation in the workplace, and in particular the effects of improved working conditions on staff turnover and absenteeism. He went on to supervise the so-called Hawthorne experiments, which were perhaps the most groundbreaking in industrial history. In one experiment, the quality of the lighting was improved, and productivity rose as a result. However, when the lighting was dimmed again, productivity unexpectedly continued to rise. Mayo and his team concluded that the workers were responding not to the changes themselves, but to the fact that they were being consulted about the changes. Although considered controversial at the time, and criticised by some who felt that workers should not be used as guinea pigs, Mayo's experiments highlighted conflicting attitudes between managers and workers that have still not been fully resolved today.

Douglas McGregor (1906 – 1964) was a social psychologist and lecturer at Harvard University and MIT. His speciality was industrial relations, and he went on to write 'the Human Side of Enterprise' which became highly influential in shaping modern management thinking. In contrast to the ideas put forward by scientific management theory, he suggested two very different management styles – Theory X and Theory Y.

According to Theory X, people are opposed to work and try to avoid it as much as possible. It is the job of management to supervise these workers continually, and use pressure to make them perform. Theory Y, on the other hand, assumes that people enjoy work and like to have responsibility. Managers should support them, giving them opportunities to succeed and acknowledging their achievements.

McGregor himself urged companies to adopt the Theory Y approach, but insisted that the wider aim of his XY idea was designed to encourage managers to think about a whole range of management issues. At the time of his early death, aged 58, he was said to be working on Theory Z.

shell-shock Kriegsneurose, **guinea pig** Versuchskaninchen, **to dim** abdunkeln, **to urge** dringend nahelegen, drängen

b. Explain the connections between the ideas, for example how McGregor's ideas evolved from Mayo's, and Mayo's from Taylor's.

c. Which management approach did McGregor believe would produce better results – Theory X or Theory Y? Construct an argument in favour of the opposite view.

d. With a partner, discuss where to place yourselves on the *Theory X – Theory Y* spectrum.

2 Discussion

a. Is the term 'guru' appropriate in the business world? If so, who are your favourite gurus?

b. Undergraduate business degrees can be classified as BSc (Bachelor of Science) or BA (Bachelor of Arts). Is the study of business a science, or is it an art?

E Business communication | Interviewing

1 Why interview?

Discuss ways of completing the following statements.

1. For the candidate, the interview is an opportunity to …
2. For the organisation, the interview is an opportunity to …
3. A poorly conducted interview could result in …

INFO

Interviews
According to a 2008 survey of recruitment practices by the Chartered Institute of Personnel and Development (CIPD), interviews based on the contents of a CV or application form were the most commonly used selection method (72 %).

SKILLS

Interview checklists
A checklist with items that can be circled or underlined is an efficient way to make notes in an interview. If you are not the only interviewer, using the same version of the checklist makes it easier to compare impressions. Bear in mind that candidates who later make a complaint to an employment tribunal have the right to ask for copies of notes made during the interview.

2 Preparing to hold an interview

a. Develop a checklist for assessing interview candidates, modelled on the one below. Add further items to each category.

VACANCY: ____________ NAME OF CANDIDATE: ____________________ DATE OF INTERVIEW: __________

Appearance	☐ well-groomed	☐ appropriately dressed	☐ scruffy
Manner	☐ confident	☐ professional	☐ reserved
Motivation	☐ enthusiastic	☐ competitive	☐ shows little interest in job
Communication skills	☐ easy to understand	☐ struggles to express himself / herself	
Abilities	☐ creative	☐ good head for figures	☐ versatile
Experience	☐ fits requirements	☐ adequate	☐ inexperienced
Skills / Qualifications	☐ over-qualified	☐ adequate	☐ under-qualified
Interests	☐ wide-ranging	☐ narrow	☐ unusual
Recommendation	☐ suitable / accept	☐ unsuitable / reject	

Comments: ____

b. Discuss the impression you would get of candidates who …

1. tremble
2. smile a lot
3. don't look you straight in the eye
4. lean backwards, with their legs outstretched
5. lean forwards, with their elbows on the table
6. frown and scratch their head a lot

Example: "If a candidate is trembling, they are probably feeling very nervous".

c. How important is body language, in your view? Give further examples of behavioural cues that 'give away' thoughts and feelings.

d. Match the parts to make questions.

1. How would you deal with
2. Tell me about the time when
3. How much experience have you had
4. Would you be prepared to
5. Could you tell us about
6. What are your
7. What would you do
8. Give us some examples of

a. relocate if the job required it?
b. the distribution network for sportswear in Germany?
c. the creativity you referred to in your CV.
d. a customer who is complaining loudly about sloppy service?
e. you had to make a particularly difficult decision.
f. long-term career goals?
g. using PowerPoint?
h. if a member of your team wasn't reaching the sales targets?

e. Match each one with the types of interview question below.

job knowledge | hypothetical / situational | personal experience | work-willingness | open question

f. Some interviewers deliberately ask 'stress questions' such as 'Don't you think you're overqualified for the job?', 'How do you feel after a failure?', 'What is it you don't like about me?'. Discuss the value of such questions and the impression they might give the candidate of the organisation.

3 Preparing to be interviewed

Discuss the list below and complete it with two more 'top tips'.

Ten top tips for interviewees

- Collect information about the company.
- Create a sales pitch for yourself.
- Predict common interview questions.
- Write down answers to those questions.
- Practise your answers out loud and time them.
- Prepare a few 'positive anecdotes'.
- Dress for the occasion; formal dress is safer.
- Take pen and paper, plus CV and references.
- …
- …

PHRASES

Gaining thinking time

- That's a very interesting question.
- Ah, yes, that's a very important point.
- When you ask …, do you mean …?
- It depends on what you mean by …

Emphasising your qualities

- As you can see on my CV, …
- What really excites me about the job is …
- That's something that really interests me …
- My work experience mainly involves …

4 Simulation

Continue the recruitment process you started in Section C, Task 4, using your job advertisements and letters of application. Follow the steps below:

1. Ask your teacher to pass your letter of application on to the company of your choice.
2. Regroup with your company. Read the applications that you receive and shortlist **two candidates** for interview. (If you do not receive any applications, consider how you can make the vacancy more attractive and identify a suitable candidate to headhunt.)
3. Invite the shortlisted candidates to an interview. Decide whether to do this by email, formal letter or phone. Send short and polite rejection letters to the rest.
4. If you have been shortlisted, attend the interview and then rejoin your company's interview panel afterwards. If you are not shortlisted, you are an interviewer. Follow the guidelines in the role cards below.

Role card: Interviewees

Think 'positive'. Don't be fazed by unexpected questions, and find ways to gain 'thinking time' during the interview. Look out for opportunities to sell yourself, and have some questions of your own about the job and the company.

Role card: Interviewers

Remember that your objective is to find the best person for the job. Decide on an interview strategy, e.g. different questioning styles. Keep notes that will help you to make comparisons of candidates' strengths and weaknesses.

5. After the interviews, decide who gets the job. Write to the successful candidate congratulating them and making a job offer. Write to the unsuccessful candidate(s) telling them of your decision.
6. Hold a 'debriefing session'. Give each other feedback on your experience.

Video lounge The interview

BBC Motion Gallery

V 5 **Watch the video 'The interview' and take notes on:**

- the qualities that the HR Director is looking for in the candidates
- the strengths and weaknesses of each candidate
- Carluccio's decision

Discuss whether you agree with Carluccio's decision. What advice would you give the candidates?

F Consulting | Assessment centre

1 Career advice

a. Lucy Kellaway's 'agony aunt' column in the *Financial Times* gives advice about office life and allows readers to add their own thoughts. Read this excerpt and complete the summary of the problem below.

No one wants to hire my clever daughter

My daughter is an Oxford graduate with a 2:1 in English. She has a business degree and is bilingual in French. She is working in marketing for a small company but is looking for something better. She has applied for twenty jobs and has had many interviews but keeps getting rejected. She has asked for feedback but has had nothing useful. An internet search engine said, 'We are not obliged to give feedback'. A PR company replied, 'We thought you were very bright but not convinced you were truly committed to a career in PR'. Is there any point in asking for reasons? And what can be done to get her a job?'

Magistrate, female 52

No, there is no point asking for feedback. Most interviewers can't or won't explain their decisions, and why should they? They are not running a careers advice service and giving reasons simply invites future lawsuits. (...)
Before her next interview she should find out as much as she can about the job and the company. This will put her far ahead of most candidates – who can't even be bothered to check the website. She would also do well to get a trusted friend to give her a dummy interview and tell her some home truths about how she came across. *Lucy Kellaway*

First, forget about the French – it has not been a serious business advantage since the nineteenth century. Second, twenty applications is nothing. What sort of hit rate do you expect? Third, the fact that you are writing on your daughter's behalf suggests that she lacks the extrovert personality required for PR. *Fund manager, male, 40s*

Why doesn't she want to stay in her current job? Why is she looking for something better? Could it be parental pressure? *Central banker, male, 36*

As an employer, I get a lot of these candidates. They are bright but give me the feeling that they'll leave when something better comes along. I never offer a job to anyone who implicitly assumes our jobs are generic enough to be done by anyone with a 2:1 from a top university. *Entrepreneur, male, 37*

This sounds familiar. I am bilingual in Russian and English, an accountant and a graduate of Oxford's Said Business School. I have an MSc and an MBA. I have spent three years applying to every investment bank in London, Moscow and New York. Still nothing. *Clerk, female, 29*

Source: *The Answers*, Lucy Kellaway, Profile Books, London, pp. 169–172

agony aunt Kummerkastentante, **magistrate** Richter(in), **can't be bothered to do sth.** zu faul sein, etwas zu tun, **dummy** (hier) probeweise, als Testlauf, **home truths** unbequeme Wahrheiten, **hit rate** Erfolgsquote, Trefferquote, **generic** allgemein

- The daughter already has a job in ...., but ....
- Her mother can't understand why... .
- She wonders whether ....
- She also wants to know what ....

b. Kellaway's response had the heading 'THE ANSWER'. Match the headings below with the other responses.

IN THE SAME BOAT | OUBLIEZ FRANÇAIS | PUSHY MOTHER | OXBRIDGE ARROGANCE

c. Consider the role of assessment centres as an alternative to the 'interview-only' method of selecting candidates. How might they have helped the magistrate's daughter? Does the cost to the employer justify the benefit? Continue this discussion online with other students.

INFO

Assessment centres
In an assessment centre, job applicants are given a number of tests and interviews to find out their strengths and weaknesses. A range of methods is valuable when there are many good candidates and the potential cost of a recruitment error is high. In a survey published by the Chartered Institute of Personnel and Development in 2008, 34% of employers had used assessment centres. The term refers to the event or the place where it is carried out.

2 Project

Carry out this project in teams of three or four, following the descriptions in the role cards and the instructions below.

Role card: Assessors

One assessor should introduce the tasks, distribute the handouts and make sure the process runs smoothly. The others monitor the tasks. Some can be actively involved in the tasks.

Role card: Candidates

Carry out the tasks assigned to you, bearing in mind the criteria that will be used to assess you. Note down any feedback you would like to give the assessors.

INFO

Assessment centre tasks

- Questionnaire (e.g. self-assessment)
- In-tray task (prioritising real-life tasks)
- Individual presentation on job-related topic
- Test (e.g. of knowledge, intelligence, concentration)
- Traditional job interview
- Checking or drafting pieces of writing
- Group discussion (with / without moderator)
- Negotiation
- Small talk or 'over dinner' conversation
- Problem-solving task (e.g. building bridge with Lego)
- Disaster scenario (e.g. sinking ship)
- Simulation (replicating real-life job tasks)
- Case study (analysis of job-related issue)
- Role-play (e.g. employment tribunal)

Scenario

You work for a large company that has its own assessment centre. There is a vacancy for a Human Resources Officer and eight candidates have been shortlisted from over 600 applicants. The candidates look good on paper, but further evidence is needed of their commitment and ability to do the job. They have agreed to attend the assessment centre, and your team has been commissioned to design the tasks.

Preparation

1. Each person in your team is responsible for designing a different task. Choose four assessment tasks from the list on the right and decide who is responsible for creating which one. Set a deadline for your first drafts.
2. Read each other's drafts and suggest corrections and improvements.
3. Redraft your tasks based on feedback from other team members. Present them in the form of handouts to give the candidates.
4. Compare your tasks with those of other teams. Decide which tasks will be used at the assessment centre, and the order in which they should be done.
5. Decide on assessment criteria. Produce a checklist for the assessors.
6. Decide whether or not candidates should be given feedback. (Only if asked? What aspects?)

SKILLS

Designing assessment centre tasks

- Be clear about what you want to test or observe, e.g. competitiveness, co-operation, creativity, etc.
- Match the exercise to the job requirements, e.g. only include a presentation if it is relevant to the job.
- Make sure the task can be assessed objectively. List criteria and make notes.

The event

Regroup as candidates (there should be at least eight) and assessors and follow your role cards.

Debriefing

The assessors give the candidates feedback on their performance. The candidates give feedback on their experience of the event. What is useful? What could be done better?

3 Research

Complete the classifications for Bachelor degrees in Germany (Bologna system).

Bachelor degree classifications United Kingdom	United States	Germany
First class honours (First or 1st)	Summa cum laude (with highest honours)	....
Upper second class honours (2:1)	Maxima cum laude (with maximum honours)	....
Lower second class honours (2:2)	Magna cum laude (with great honours)	....
Third class honours (Third or 3rd)	Cum laude (with honours)	....
Ordinary (pass / without honours)	Fail (no degree awarded)	....
Fail (no degree awarded)		....

Unit 10
Project management

Online Link
800021-0010

A Introduction | Teams

1 Planning

a. Give examples of the following:

› projects you do in your studies
› professions that are project-based

b. What skills are essential for project managers, in your view?

c. With a partner, start planning a project from scratch. Cover as many of the points below as you can in ten minutes. Then compare your results.

purpose | time schedule | tasks | labour required | resources required | costs involved

INFO

Project management
Projects come in all shapes and sizes, but have certain features in common: defined objectives, a time limit, specified resources (staff, budget, equipment, etc), and a sponsor. Also, the team members have defined roles and responsibilities. The role of the project leader is to plan and manage the tasks, costs and resources of the project so that the objectives are reached in the most efficient way.

2 Teams

a. Draw a diagram that represents a team you have worked in before, showing the relationship between your role and that of other team members.

b. Work with a partner. Compare your diagrams with reference to the points below.

› Differences between the diagrams
› The purpose of the team (e.g. was it a project? a competition?)
› Feelings about your role and that of the other members
› Problems that arose, and how they were dealt with
› How a team differs from a group

c. Which of these sayings best reflects your experience of working in a team? Give examples.

Together **E**veryone **A**chieves **M**ore. | **TEAM** | **T**oll! **E**in **A**nderer **M**acht's.

3 Listening

a. Project Manager Sharon Watson created a checklist to plan her first large-scale project. The kickoff meeting has just taken place and members of the team, Ruth and Leo, are discussing how it went. Listen to their conversation and tick the tasks / goals that Sharon has accomplished.

b. Leo quotes something Sharon said about teams. What did she say, and what point was she making?

c. What metaphor does Leo use for working on a project?

d. Compare Ruth's and Leo's feelings about the project and their approach to working in teams. Which of the two would you prefer to work with, and why?

PLANNING CHECKLIST: Project X

Planning goals
- ensure the project fits in with the firm's overall strategy
- conduct a feasibility study
- secure the necessary resources
- create a work breakdown structure (WBS) so people know who does what / when
- draw up a realistic schedule
- make contingency plans for unforeseen events
- build time buffers into the planning
- pick the perfect team (with the right expertise, mindset, etc.)
- develop a communication plan

Kick-off meeting
- motivate team members
- develop their commitment to the project
- give everyone an opportunity for relationship-building, networking, etc.
- explain the purpose / objective of the project
- make sure everyone understands their roles and tasks
- build the team members' confidence in me!!!

4 Project life cycle

a. Match the five phases of the project life cycle with the tasks of a project manager.

1. Initiation	a. Implement the plan by managing, motivating and informing the team.
2. Planning	b. Agree with stakeholders on the aims, scope, timescale and resources of the project.
3. Execution	c. Complete the project, review and report on performance, thank the project team.
4. Controlling	d. Create a work breakdown structure (WBS) so people know who does what and when.
5. Closure	e. Monitor progress, adjust plans if necessary, keep members of the team informed.

b. Some project managers participate very little in direct activities that lead to the end result. Others are more 'hands on'. What activities might a project manager prefer to delegate to a team leader?

WORD BANK

Project planning

Types of project: construction project | development project | aerospace project | academic project / assignment | large-scale project | long-term project | pilot project | research project | viable project | sub-project | turnkey project

Phases and events: to tender / to bid for a project | in the pipeline | project approval / acceptance | to back a project | initiation | planning | kickoff meeting | execution | controlling | monitoring | closure | to pull the plug on / abandon a project | to scrap / reject a project | to shelve a project | to put a project on ice

Planning: sponsors / backers | objectives / goals / aims / targets | outcomes | risk analysis | feasibility study | feasible | to forecast | to estimate | resource planning | procurement plan | scope | budgeting | timescale | deadline | work breakdown structure (WBS) | deliverables | overlap | fast-tracking | to build in time buffers | contingency plan | to take precautions | constraints | contractual requirements

B Business briefing | Managing large-scale projects

1 Reading

a. Before you read, discuss why a project might fall behind schedule or overrun its budget.

b. Read the article and make notes on the following points:

- Projects that failed to meet their targets
  - Problems that arose
  - Reasons for the problems
- Attitudes to project management
  - Evidence that project managers have not learned from experience
  - Evidence of investment in project managements
- An example of successful management and the key to success

c. Write a 30-word abstract of the article. Focus on the main points, and omit reference to the examples.

d. Find out about 'Stuttgart 21'. What are the aims, and what stage is it at now? Discuss the chances of it being completed on time and within budget.

INFO

Project management tools
A **critical path** is a series of events or tasks that depend on each other, and whose durations affect the length of the whole project. The tasks must be finished on time in order for the project to be completed on time.
A **Gantt chart** shows when each stage in a project should start and end, and compares the amount of work done with the amount planned. (An example is given on page 128.)

© Mike Baldwin / Cornered

"The project is a little behind schedule. It was proactive, now it's retroactive."

Overdue and over budget

When George Stephenson built a railway from Liverpool to Manchester in the 1820s, it cost 45% more than budget and was subject to many delays. In the intervening 180 years the management of large-scale projects seems to have improved little. The reconstruction of Wembley Stadium, the home of English soccer, was threatened when the developers admitted that they faced mounting losses on the £750m project. A rise in the cost of steel and the extra labour required to ensure the building was ready on time were said to have thrown the management's calculations out of the window.

Even projects deemed a success these days sometimes fail to meet their targets. The 1,770km oil pipeline from Azerbaijan to the Turkish port of Ceyhan was opened with much fanfare (...) but the $4 billion project, led by BP, became several months overdue and 10% over budget. Although oil finally entered the pipeline at Baku, it was another six months before it was delivered to tankers in the Mediterranean.

It is not as if project management is a new science. It has its origins in critical paths and Gantt charts – planning tools first widely used in the early 20th century – and its own well-established international association, the Project Management Institute (PMI), based in Pennsylvania, USA. The PMI sets standards and professional exams that are taken by thousands every year. It boasts 150,000 members in 150 countries, all of them specialists in managing projects. So why do so many still go so wrong?

Projects, says the PMI, have five distinct phases: initiation, planning, execution, control and closure. Problems arise most frequently when initiation gets separated from execution. To secure a project, bidders often make overly optimistic assumptions about costs and revenues. This may be particularly so with prestige projects (such as Wembley Stadium) where bidders are chasing glory almost as much as commercial gain.

A study published in the Journal of the American Planning Association examined 210 big rail and road projects in 14 different countries, and found their forecasts of future passengers to be wildly optimistic: for the rail projects, they were, on average, an astounding 106% higher than eventually turned out to be the case, with one in eight out by over 400%; the road projects' miscalculations were more modest, by over 20% in more than half the cases. The article's authors claim that

intervening dazwischenkommend, **with much fanfare** mit großem Trara, **to boast** aufweisen, **overly** allzu (sehr),

the forecasts on such projects are no more accurate now than they were 30 years ago.

Greg Balestrero, the head of PMI, says that for years project management was largely ignored. But that is now changing. A recent PMI survey found that three out of four European companies employ project managers. When Compaq, a computer maker, was taken over by Hewlett-Packard in 2002, it had some 1,400 on its payroll.

Three years ago the board of Siemens launched a worldwide initiative to improve its project management. The company had worked out that half its turnover came from project-like work, and it calculated that if it could complete all of these projects on time and to budget, it would add 3 billion ($3.7 billion) to its bottom line over three years. A key element of the scheme was the introduction of project managers to the company's sales teams.

Good project management can certainly make a difference. BP's fortunes were transformed when it converted its exploration division, BPX, into a portfolio of projects, each of them more or less free from head-office control (...). Project managers can no longer rely on head office for support. They are required to build their own self-sufficient teams.

Moreover, there are still difficult individual projects that get completed with time and money to spare. The winner of last year's PMI Project of the Year award was the Saudi-Aramco Haradh gas pipeline, whose original contracting document was lauded for the way it 'defined the mix of contracts best suited to accomplish the project's objectives'. The three-year project to build a $2 billion gas terminal deep in the desert, 10km from the nearest road, was completed six months ahead of schedule and 27% under budget.

The Economist, June 9th, 2005

to chase glory Ruhm suchen, **fortunes** Schicksal, **to convert** umwandeln, **lauded** gelobt

2 Describing a process: method

a. Read the definition of 'critical path' on page 126 and study the example below. Decide what cooking equipment, crockery, utensils and condiments you need, and how much time it will take. Then explain the process in detail.

Critical path: Making a fried breakfast

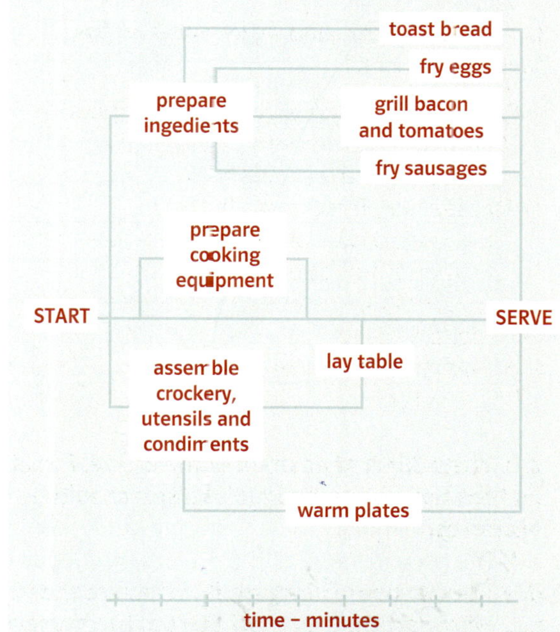

Source: www.businessballs.com/project.htm

PHRASES

Describing a process
- **First of all,** you ... / **The first step is to ...**
- **Then**, prepare the ... using the ...
- **While** you are doing that, you can also ...
- You **can't** ... **until** ...
- **As soon as** ... is ready, you should ...
- **After** you have ..., then you can ...
- **When / Once** you have ..., you can ...
- **Finally**, you ... / **The last step is to** ...

Describing a process: method
- The liquid should be heated **gradually**.
- **Gently** stir the mixture until ...
- This operation has to be done **manually**.
- It must be checked **carefully** for mistakes.
- These steps are carried out **simultaneously** so that ...

b. Work in a team. Present a group project such as a student party, study trip or class magazine in the form of a critical path diagram.

c. Show your diagram to another team and explain the process.

C Language | Time and targets

1 Listening

a. Before you listen: Study the project schedule and the statements below, five of which are false. Identify and correct the mistakes.

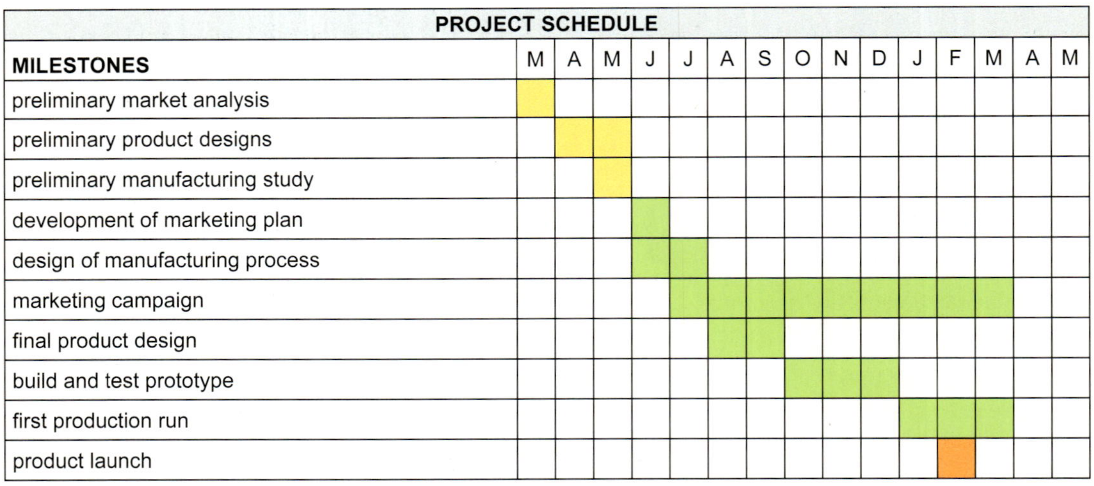

1. The preliminary market analysis is due to start in March and will take four weeks.
2. The preliminary product designs should be completed by the end of March.
3. The preliminary manufacturing study won't get under way until May.
4. The second stage of the project is scheduled to begin in June.
5. The marketing campaign won't start until the final product design is complete.
6. The final product design has to be completed before work on the prototype can begin.
7. The first production run is supposed to start at the end of January, once the prototype is ready.
8. If everything runs to plan, the product will be launched in January.
9. The marketing campaign will go on until the end of March.
10. The scheduled lifetime of the project is twelve months.

b. Explain what will / won't happen if there is a delay in the final product design.

A 2.10 **c.** Listening: A project manager is asking two members of his team, Jens and Carola, to update him on progress. As you listen, make any necessary adjustments to the schedule.

d. Complete this summary of the situation.

The preliminary product designs were finished .... s.................. but the team is now being h.................. .... by problems with the manufacturing process. Their supplier had guaranteed to deliver some parts .... July .... the l.................., but some of the parts had to be sent back because they didn't c.................. to s.................. . The de.................. for launching the product is February. The launch date was originally s.................. .... January, but since it had already been p.................. o.................. once, the project manager doesn't want to p.................. it yet again. He doesn't want to risk another d.................. because if the product is l.................. to m.................., the competitors will get in a.................. of them. It's important to deliver the product .... t.................., and not f.................. b.................. s.................. even more. Carola has not only m.................. her d.................., but is already two months o.................. . One of the main problems is that there are no t.................. b.................. . Fortunately, the marketing campaign is well u.................. w.................. . The project manager decides to r.................. the plan in order to m.................. up t.................. and get the project back on t.................. .

WORD BANK

Timescales

Events and periods: start date | finish date | phase | stage | duration | milestone | time buffer | slippage

Verbs: to catch up | to make up time | to meet / observe / stick to / miss / extend a deadline | to fall behind (schedule) | to hold sth. up | to put sth. off | to postpone sth. | to be delayed |

Punctuality: (right) on schedule | ahead of schedule | behind schedule | in time (for) | on time | on the dot | delayed | a delay in | overdue | on track | by … at the latest | late to market

2 Managing time

a. Do the quiz in pairs. Discuss whether you agree with the diagnosis and discuss possible remedies.

QUIZ Do you suffer from student syndrome?

'Student syndrome' refers to the phenomenon in which people only fully apply themselves to a task at the last possible moment before a deadline. This form of procrastination is said to be typical of students and was noted by the project management expert Eliyahu M. Goldratt in his book *Critical Chain*. Try this quiz to find out whether you suffer from student syndrome.

1. Tomorrow is the deadline for your term paper. You've done all the research but you haven't actually written anything yet. It's now midnight. What will you do?
   a work flat out through the night to finish it
   b go to bed and worry about the problem tomorrow

2. The following morning you ask your professor for an extension. How do you defend your request?
   a by pointing out how much better your term paper will be given more time
   b by claiming extenuating circumstances, e.g. a family crisis or illness

3. You had planned to devote the whole of Sunday to some last-minute exam revision. However, you've been offered free tickets to an open-air concert and the weather couldn't be better. What will you do?
   a stay at home and knuckle down to revision
   b go to the concert and cross your fingers you'll have time to revise when you come home

4. Some tasks take people longer than expected. What is the most likely reason in your case?
   a you allow yourself to get distracted too easily
   b you want to do the best you can, so you drop everything else

Diagnosis: If you answered mostly 'b', you are displaying the classic symptoms of student syndrome. Remember that procrastination is the thief of time.You need to get help now.

b. Find English expressions in the text that correspond to the following words and phrases:

1. sich einer Aufgabe widmen (3 examples) ....
2. Aufschub oder Verschleppung ....
3. auf Hochtouren arbeiten ....
4. Härtefall ....
5. die Daumen drücken ....
6. abgelenkt werden ....
7. alles stehen und liegen lassen ....

c. Suggest a German translation of the expression 'Procrastination is the thief of time'.

....

3 Defining objectives

SMART is an acrostic that is sometimes used as a way of evaluating the objectives or goals of a project. There are different variations of the SMART acrostic, for example using 'achievable' instead of 'agreed'. Suggest further possible adjectives to add to those listed below.

› **SMART** objectives are …
› **S**pecific, …
› **M**easurable, …
› **A**greed, …
› **R**ealistic, …
› **T**imely, …

4 Gerunds and infinitives

a. Complete the sentences using the gerund or infinitive form of the verbs. Add 'to' where necessary.

1. Are you used .... projects? (do)
2. What kind of project have you agreed .... and why? (take part in)
3. Are you looking forward .... on it? (work)
4. Do you think it's worth .... a kick-off meeting? (hold)
5. Would you recommend .... large time buffers? (build in)
6. Do you think you'll manage .... your targets? (meet)
7. Do you intend .... funding? (apply for)
8. Has anyone got round .... a Gantt chart? (prepare)
9. How can people avoid .... deadlines? (miss)
10. Have you considered .... a communication plan? (draw up)

b. Use the questions to interview someone about one of their future projects.

5 Tenses for reporting

a. A project manager is reporting on an automotive project to the CEO. Choose the right option.

1. In May we (tested / have tested) the engines over a three-day period.
2. Up to now we (are having / have had) no serious technical problems.
3. We (didn't finish / haven't finished) the body design yet.
4. By July we (have built / will have built) a full-size test track.
5. So far, we (have only created / only created) two prototypes.
6. At the moment we (work / are working) on the third prototype.
7. Our R&D people (gave / were giving) a presentation at the Geneva Motor show.
8. We (have / will have) the pre-production model ready by the end of March 2011.
9. We (run / have been running) the training workshops since the beginning of the year.
10. Just yesterday we (have received / received) the computer simulation from the IT department.
11. We (still look / are still looking) for a partner for the Chinese joint venture.
12. It (gets / is getting) increasingly difficult to negotiate with suppliers.

b. Discuss whether the sentences refer to work-in-progress or work completed.

6 Checking, controlling and monitoring

Complete the sentences with the right word.

supervise | control | examine | monitor | verify | check | inspect

1. The software allows companies to .... employees' internet use.
2. Before you hand in your term paper, ... that you haven't made any spelling mistakes.
3. His conclusions were .... by later experiments.
4. The trainees complained because they were not .... properly.
5. The negative feedback from our clients forced us to .... every aspect of our business.
6. People shouldn't have dogs if they can't .... them.
7. The maintenance engineer .... the machine to make sure there was no damage.

LANGUAGE TIP

Translating *kontrollieren*

In English the noun 'control' has the same meaning as *Kontrolle*, but the verb 'control' is a false friend. In English, it generally means 'direct', 'manage' or 'keep in order'. When translating *kontrollieren*, consider the sense in which it is used:

überwachen – supervise
laufend überwachen – monitor
untersuchen – examine
bestätigen – verify
inspizieren – inspect
lenken, steuern, im Griff halten – control

D Business Leaders | Ron Rosenhead

1 Reading

a. Complete the text below with the missing headings.

People | Change | Project roles | Closure | Defining the project | Planning

Your First Project? Hints and Tips

So, you have just been given your first project. You have been in the organisation about a year and really want to make a good impression. Here are some hints and tips that will help you to do that by delivering on time and to budget.

1 ....

We are often called upon to work with project teams who need to deliver a business specific project. One of the first things we do is ask the question "what are your objectives?" This needs to be your starting point. Discuss with your manager what is expected and turn these into realistic objectives. Discuss with key players what they want and write objectives down, and get agreement from them on what is written.

2 ....

You have been given the project to deliver, but what role do you play? Are you the project manager and if you are, what authority do you have in delivering the project? What role will your senior manager (and other senior managers) play in the project? Write down what each role holder should do. It will help everyone involved.

3 ....

You will need to ensure you take everyone involved along with you. Stakeholders include all those with an interest or who will be impacted by the project. Identify what their requirements are and what you need from them. You should also identify the perceived attitudes these groups and individuals will have to the project. Like risk analysis, you should continue this process regularly, checking who the stakeholders are and whether anything has changed.

4 ....

Ensure your project plan is credible. Identify all the activities you need to carry out, putting cost and time estimates against them. Plan the order in which the tasks will be done and produce a Gantt chart or milestone chart. How good are your estimates – cost and time? Research shows we suffer from optimistic planning bias, i.e. thinking we can deliver a task in a project within five days when it will actually take seven days.

5 ....

Ensure you have a system in place for dealing with any changes that occur. Identify the impact of the change before agreeing to it and ensure you are clear who can agree to any major changes, e.g. in budget or objectives. Any system you put in place will need to take account of your stakeholders and the project team.

6 ....

Stop project dribble. "The trouble is we never seem to finish projects here. They keep dribbling on and on ..." This was a quote from a course delegate on one of our project management courses. You need to plan to hold a closing meeting, putting it onto your Gantt chart to ensure it happens. Use a facilitator to ensure all the learning is shared among project team members and those in the organisation. Identify elements which need to be finished, and who will deliver them and close the project.

Ron Rosenhead, www.projectagency.co.uk 11 March 2007

Ron Rosenhead is a British project management expert and director of Project Agency, a consultancy that specialises in advising companies and individuals on how to deliver projects. He is a regular speaker at conferences, and has run many project events and workshops, and also hosts a popular project management blog and discussion site.

b. Work with a partner. Add more tips and hints of your own under the following headings.

Managing teams | Reporting on progress | Dealing with risk

c. Explain the expression 'project dribble'. In what sense(s) is the word 'dribble' normally used?

2 Killing off a project

Complete these Ron Rosenhead tips by matching the two halves of each sentence.

It's time to kill off a project when ...

1. ... it is obvious that the project will not
2. ... the project is so over budget
3. ... the project does not fit with
4. ... the risks are so high that
5. ... key stakeholders object

a. to the project and no longer support it.
b. the overall strategy of the company.
c. to continue would impact negatively on the company.
d. deliver what was required at the outset.
e. that you are simply pouring money into a hole.

E Business communication | Problem-solving meeting

1 The background

A project is in trouble. The project leader has been forced to step down, and now the CEO, Felix Barton, wants to find out the status of the project. Following an emergency meeting with the whole project team, he has asked four key members to update him by email. Read the emails and complete his notes below.

Problems identified (personal views):

1. Arlene Taylor: ....
2. Derek Mitchell: ....
3. Beate Ritzmann: ....
4. Tina Oswald: ....

Dear Mr Barton,

It was good to meet you last week, even though we were short of time and couldn't discuss very much. I'm sure I speak for the whole project team when I say how relieved I am that you are personally stepping in to sort out the situation.

I'm now in the process of preparing a review of the project's financial status, and I'll get that to you as soon as possible. But since you also asked for my own response to the situation, I think the main problem is communication, or rather the lack of it. It's been really difficult maintaining communication with the others as we always seem to be short of time, and there's no communication plan.

Everyone in the project is aware of the problem, so I'm not the only one saying this. It's frustrating for all of us to be so behind schedule. Let's hope things will pick up from now on!

All the best,
Arlene Taylor – Financial Controller

Dear Felix Barton

I'm sorry I wasn't able to attend the meeting last week, but I've received the minutes and I'm very encouraged by your positive approach to a difficult situation. As you know, our team is responsible for training the sales and after-sales staff, and we're doing our best to complete a very demanding schedule.

It's a great group of people and they're really keen to learn, but the product is new and there's a lot of complex technical stuff to take in. They'll need more hands-on training in giving practical demonstrations, as well as learning how to use the PowerPoint material.

We've tried asking Technical Support for help, but they're too busy. We're already two weeks overdue, so to make up time on this project we'll need to bring in at least two more trainers so that we can work with smaller groups for the practical sessions. I hope that this can be arranged.

Best
Derek Mitchell, Director of Training, HR Dept.

Dear Felix,

Following our meeting on Friday, I've prepared an outline of the marketing campaign to date, which you will find attached. I can send a more detailed report later as soon as I have the figures.

As you can see, the problem we face is lack of finance. The marketing budget was inadequate from the start, and the costs have increased sharply as we face tough competition in a difficult market. I've discussed this situation several times with Arlene Taylor from Finance, but it seems that no further funds are available – at least not for this project.

I believe we have a great opportunity to position this product successfully, but we need the resources to do so. I hope we can find a solution in the near future.

Best regards,
Beate Ritzmann – Marketing Manager

Dear Mr Barton,

As head of Technical Support, I am responsible for co-ordinating the project management software and providing technical advice. Everything was OK at first but now things are slowing down. I don't just mean the project is behind schedule, but the software is slow in responding to updates. It could be a virus, so we're installing a new anti-virus programme.

There's also a chance that it could be a fault in the software design, in which case the whole system will have to be shut down and tested and that will cause a hold-up!

I hope that this 'worst case scenario' won't happen, but I thought you should know. Some people have the idea that we have all the solutions and can sort out their problems at the drop of a hat, but they don't expect us to have problems too :-)

Yours sincerely,
Tina Oswold – IT and Technical Support

2 Analysing the situation

Set up a meeting. Felix Barton has hired you as a troubleshooting task force to come up with a rescue plan. Use the five-step framework to analyse the situation and decide on solutions.

Step 1 Define the problem → **Step 2** Explain the causes → **Step 3** Offer solutions → **Step 4** Weigh up the solutions → **Step 5** Decide on action

PHRASES

Problem-solving

Defining the problem
The problem is that there is no …
The real concern is the lack of …
The situation is now so bad that …

Explaining the causes
This arose because of …
The situation was caused by …
As far as we know, the cause is …

Offering solutions
Why don't we set up …?
How about contacting …?
I think they should start by …

Weighing up solutions
On the one hand, … On the other hand, …
That would be the last resort.
In the worst case scenario, …
If they …, they'll be able to … / perhaps they can …
If we don't … we won't be able to …
If you did that … you'd be able to …

Deciding action
Have we decided then?
Is that a decision?
So, we're going to …
OK, that's decided then.

3 Meeting preparations

Felix Barton is impressed by your solutions and has asked you to conduct a meeting with the people who reported to him by email. Carry out the following tasks:

- Create a communication plan for the team, based on the one below.
- Draw up the agenda for the meeting.

SKILLS

Effective agendas

- Include: title, subject, date, time, venue
- List the participants.
- Decide how many items can be discussed in the time allowed.
- List the items in a logical order and number them.
- Set a time limit for each item.
- Make sure the item headings are clear.
- Circulate the agenda before the meeting.

Communication Plan

- The people who should communicate with each other regularly are: …
- The following channels of communication should be used: …
- In email communication, the following people should be included in cc: …
- If the sender of an email doesn't get a confirmation or reply, they should: …
- ……………………………………………………
- ……………………………………………………

4 Simulation

Reshuffle the groups so that in each group there are four of you to take on the roles of Financial Controller, Marketing Manager, Director of Training and Manager of IT / Technical Support. There should also be a representative of the trouble-shooting task force to chair the meeting. Decide which agenda you will use: the one you prepared in your original group, or the 'best of the bunch' from all groups.

5 Writing

Write the minutes to send to the CEO. Attach a copy of the communication guidelines you have drawn up, explaining how you intend to implement them into the 'newly revived' project.

F Consulting | Creating a website

1 Preparation

This is a class project in which you create a website together. Read the scenario and do the tasks that follow.

Scenario

You have been asked to create a website called 'movers and shakers' showcasing the Top 20 most influential people in business at the moment. The website should be aimed at business students such as yourselves and be online by the start of next term.

Planning

1. Find out the meaning of 'movers and shakers'. Suggest a German translation and draw up a preliminary list of who could be included in the Top 20 Movers and Shakers in business.
2. Decide on a timescale that fits in with your Business English timetable and the demands of the project. This could be anything from an intensive week of regular meetings to a whole semester.
3. Read the role descriptions on the next page. Decide on the role you think would suit you best.
4. Hold a kick-off meeting in class, following the agenda on the right. Complete the missing details and if necessary add further items to 'Any Other Business' (AOB).

MOVERS AND SHAKERS PROJECT
Kick-off Meeting

Date:
Venue:
Participants:
Excused:
Agenda

- **Mission:** What do we want to achieve and why?
- **Objectives:** What are they? How can we make them SMART?
- **Teams and tasks:** Who will do what?
- **Timescale:** How much time do we have? What are the milestones or deadlines?
- **Website design:** Content and navigation – see handout 'Tips for website design'
- **Resources:** What do we need? Who can help us?
- **Communication:** How should we communicate?
- **Launch event:** Should we have one? Who could we invite?
- **AOB:**

Tips for website design

› The overall 'look' should reflect the tastes and interests of the target audience
› Develop a corporate identity with a consistent layout and design for all pages.
› Create a design that is 'easy on the eye'. The colour scheme should be simple, not too 'busy', and with just one font-type for the texts.
› Make the navigation straightforward and intuitive so that people can find their way around easily.
› Don't create long pages or text blocks. Some people never bother to scroll down, so put important content high on the page.
› Avoid pictures and animations that take too long to build.
› Consider having a choice of languages, depending on the people you want to attract to the site.
› Include content that is interesting and relevant for the target audience.
› ...?
› ...?

5. Once you have decided on your role or team, discuss what else you might need to do.

Role card: Project manager(s)

You have overall responsibility for the project. Make sure everyone understands their tasks and the importance of sticking to deadlines. If necessary, provide them with a project schedule and a communication plan. Coordinate the activities and liaise with the teams, monitor progress and troubleshoot if necessary.

Role card: Web designers

Your role is to plan and design the website, making sure that it fits in with the overall concept agreed by members of the project beforehand. Once you have designed the basic navigation of the website, you will receive the texts to upload. These texts will have been written by a team of authors and checked by the editors.

Role card: Resource team

You will be working closely with the project manager(s) on a range of tasks. You will need to help the team get the resources they need (material and financial), liaise with the institution's IT department, ensure that rules and regulations are met, and – if necessary – support other teams in their tasks in order to speed up progress.

Role card: Editors

You are responsible for planning the content of the website and editing the texts. You will be liaising closely with the project manager(s), web designers and authors. You may need to meet separately with the authors to decide who is going to write what and how long the texts should be. You will also need to edit the texts, so ask your teacher for help if needed.

Role card: Authors

As authors, you will be working closely with the editors. Once it has been decided who writes what, you will carry out research into the people you will be writing about. Make sure you stick to deadlines, but ask for help where necessary. Your texts will be edited, but careful proofreading will ensure that not too much is changed.

PHRASES

Monitoring progress
- So, how far have you got?
- Where have we got to so far?
- Have you contacted … about …?
- Have you decided what to do about …?
- It needs to be finished by … at the latest, otherwise …
- You're doing a great job. Keep it up!
- If you need any help, you know how to reach me.

2 Execution

Carry out the project, as planned. Note down any feedback you would like to give the project manager or the other teams on their performance. The project manager should monitor progress and give support where needed.

3 Debriefing and handover

a. When you have finished the project, hold a debriefing meeting. Discuss the questions below.

- Was the project a success? If not, what went wrong?
- What would you do differently next time?
- What lessons have you learned about project management?
- How useful was the experience for improving your English? Which teams used English the most?
- Will you continue working on the website, give it up, or pass it on to other students who may be interested in running the website?
- If you decided to pass it on, how will you manage the handover?

b. Write a handover report in which you describe the project and make recommendations for the students who will be taking over the website.

Unit 11
Quality

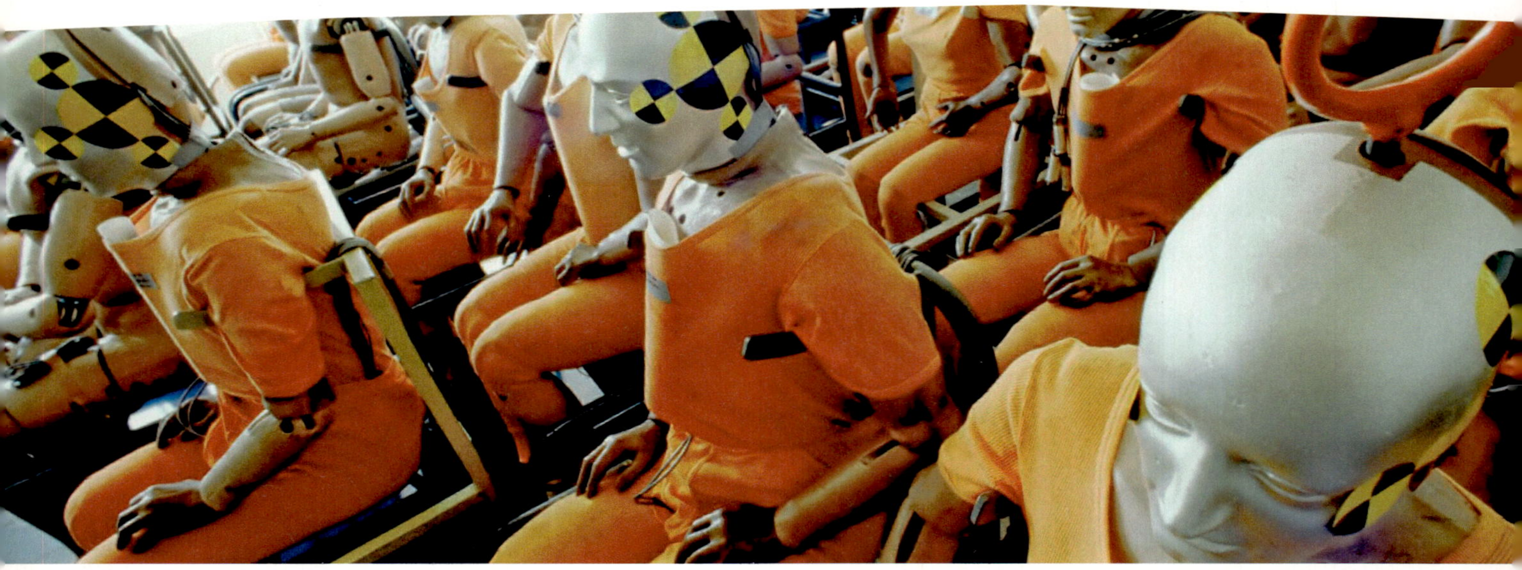

Online Link
800021-0011

A Introduction | Quality standards

1 Describing quality

a. Note down some examples of products or services that you have bought recently:

Food: ....
Clothing: ....
Gadgets: ....
Services: ....

b. On your own, answer questions about the products / services using the decision tree on the next page.

c. Using the same questions, interview people in your class to find out how they feel about the quality of their purchases, and how they respond when they are not satisfied.

d. Collect the answers to the questions 'Why?' 'Why not' and 'What did you do?' on the board. What conclusions do you draw about customer satisfaction?

2 Why complain?

a. Below are some excuses for not complaining. Choose the right word.

1. It's not worth the (attempt / trial / effort).
2. I don't want to (strike / kick / throw) up a fuss.
3. I wouldn't want to (pull / draw / drag) attention to myself.
4. I can't be (bothered / agitated).
5. I don't want to (make a theatre / create a scene).

PHRASES

Describing quality

Praising quality
- I was (quite) satisfied / impressed with / by the quality.
- It's a high / top quality product.
- It's (of) satisfactory / good / high quality.
- It's consistently high in quality.
- Quality has improved / gone up.
- The quality exceeded my expectations.
- The quality is outstanding / top-rate / first-class.

Criticising quality
- I was (a bit) disappointed with / by the quality.
- It's a low / poor quality product.
- It's (of) inferior / poor / shoddy quality.
- It varies in quality / It's uneven in quality.
- Quality has declined / suffered / gone down.
- The quality wasn't up to standard.
- The quality is appalling / shocking / rock-bottom.

b. Suggest ways of persuading someone to complain by completing the sentences.

1. Look at it this way. If you don't complain, then ....
2. It's always worth complaining because ....
3. If you complain, you might get a ....
4. Surely you don't really think ....
5. Come off it. It's not as if they're going to ....

c. Compare your own views about the value of complaining. Give examples from your experience.

LANGUAGE TIP

to be / *haben*
It is (of) excellent quality. (Es hat eine ausgezeichnete Qualität.)
It is a beautiful colour. (Es hat eine schöne Farbe.)
It is her birthday. (Sie hat Geburtstag)

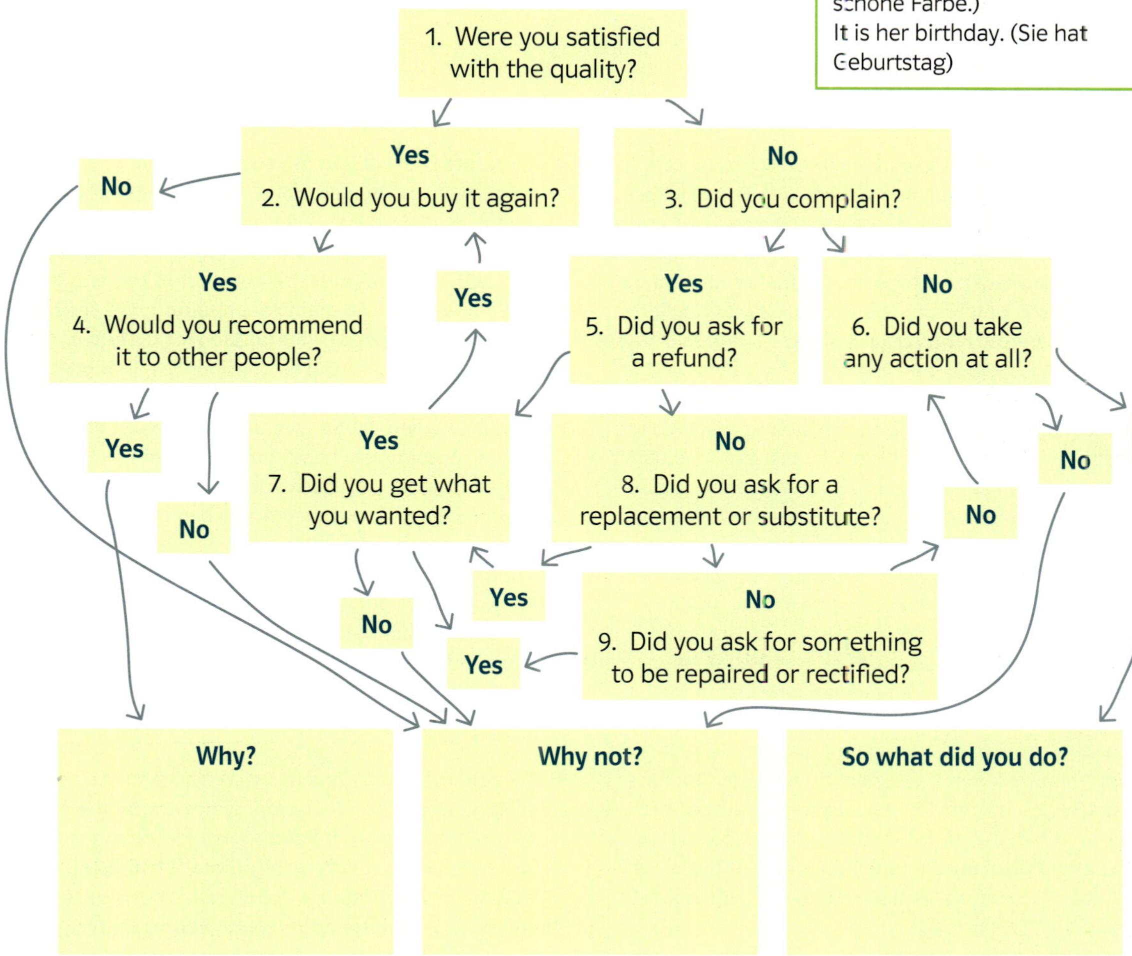

3 Standards

a. Insert vowels in the statements made by the International Standards Organisation (ISO) on its website.

1. The ISO is the world's largest **dvlpr** and **pblshr** of international standards.
2. Standards ensure **dsrbl** characteristics of **prdcts** and services such as quality, **nvrnmntl** friendliness, **sfty**, **rlblty**, **ffcncy** and interchangeability – and at an **cnmcl** cost.
3. When standards are absent, we **sn** notice.
4. Standards establishing an international consensus on **trmnlgy** make technology **trnsfr** easier and **sfr**.
5. Without the **stndrdztn** of telephone and banking cards, life would be more **cmplctd**.
6. **Stndrdzd** symbols provide danger **wrnngs** and information across linguistic **frntrs**.

b. How can national standards be misused as protectionist market restrictions? Check the web for examples, e.g. the German *Reinheitsgebot*, and the role played by international standard bodies in preventing such misuse.

WORD BANK

Collocations: to provide quality at reasonable prices | to have a reputation for quality | to show a lack of quality | to lack quality | to assess / evaluate / measure quality | to demand quality | to insist on quality | to keep up / maintain / preserve quality | to test / check / monitor quality | to neglect quality

B Business briefing | Quality management

1 Reading

a. Read the article and produce a word web of the main points, expressed as keywords.

b. Show your word web to another student. Explain the points and check that your partner is following you. Ask him / her to add any missing information.

PHRASES

Checking understanding

Offering clarification: Are you with me so far? | Are you following me? | Does this make sense? | Have I missed anything? | Do stop me if anything's unclear.

Asking for clarification: Sorry, I don't quite follow you. | Could you explain what you mean by …? | I didn't catch what you said about … | I'm afraid you've lost me there. | Could you go back to …?

Quality management

The word 'quality' usually carries connotations of excellence, and it seems that we all 'know' or 'feel' what quality is. However, the word can mean different things to different people. Is a gold-plated fountain pen superior in quality to a cheap disposable pen? Not necessarily, say the experts. The quality guru M. Juran defined quality as "fitness for use". A washing machine can be described as a quality product if it has no defects, works exactly as we expect and gives us the feeling of having received our money's worth. In the manufacturing sector, quality is typically expressed in terms of compliance with defined requirements. The same idea can be applied to services such as tourism, retailing or health care, where the concept of quality may be expressed as 'providing value for money', 'satisfying customers' or 'meeting patients' needs'. A product or service that fails to do these things may be judged as substandard or having poor quality. Quality is therefore a relative concept, where the degree of quality depends on expectations. Some organisations claim that they achieve quality by exceeding expectations. Others even attempt to satisfy customers' needs before the customers are themselves aware of them – a concept known as 'fitness to latent requirement'.

In an increasingly competitive environment, the survival of an organisation depends on quality in all areas of the organisation, from planning and production to customer service. But how does quality relate to profitability? Negligent or dishonest suppliers who sell shoddy products at high prices may achieve short-term profits, but they eventually go out of business. Their priority is immediate gain, not long-term, and so customers should follow the principle of caveat emptor, or 'let the buyer beware'. Organisations that provide consistent value for money, on the other hand, eventually gain a reputation for quality. This gives them an edge over their competitors and ensures their long-term survival and profitability.

If quality is crucial to the survival of an organisation, then so is the management of quality. There are a number of principles associated with the generic term 'quality management': First of all, top management must be committed to quality. At the same time, the main responsibility for quality lies with the people who do the work. Therefore, systems and procedures need to be established to enable the workers to control quality themselves, and they need training in the application of these procedures. Improving quality is seen as a continuous process, involving all levels of the organisation. These principles can be summed up in the concept of Total Quality Management (TQM), which is defined by the International Standards Organisation (ISO) as "a management approach for an organization, centred on quality, based on the participation of all its members and aiming at customer satisfaction, and benefits to all members of the organisation and society" (ISO 8412:1994).

Of course, quality has its price. Some of the costs of quality can be measured, for example the costs of quality control, in other words detecting defects (inspection) and correcting them. Then there are the costs of quality assurance. These include the costs of preventing defects from occurring, measuring performance against 'best practice' (benchmarking), and the costs of training, service, certification, new technology and so on. Some organisations invest heavily in concepts such as 'Six Sigma', a series of techniques or 'tools' for measuring and improving performance.

Quality managers will argue that any costs incurred will be recouped many times over by less waste, greater efficiency, better products and services, and higher profits. Some costs, however, are impossible to measure and impossible to justify. They include the potentially fatal costs of not having a quality management system at all.

gold-plated fountain pen vergoldeter Füller, **disposable pen** Einwegkugelschreiber, **crucial** wichtig, kritisch, **generic term** Oberbegriff, **to recoup** zurückzahlen

c. Find words or phrases in the first two paragraphs that fit the following definitions.

1. ideas or feelings connected with a word
2. can be thrown away
3. money well spent (two examples)
4. conformity to specifications
5. to be better than; to surpass
6. failure to take proper care in doing something
7. badly made
8. the customer buys at his / her own risk

d. Match the concepts of fitness with the statements below.

fitness to latent requirement | fitness to standard | fitness to cost | fitness for purpose / use

1. It has passed inspection. None of the parts are missing.
2. It is used as intended – showing the time.
3. It is cheap, but no less reliable than expensive brands.
4. It fulfils a new function – a collectible fashion item.

e. What do you use to tell the time? Describe the object in terms of functionality, reliability, durability, value for money, and any further aspects of quality that you consider important.

2 A quality problem

Read the problem below. As a quality consultant, what solution would you recommend?

A leading appliance company has received a large number of complaints from customers living in rural areas about a washing machine it launched two months ago. When the company sent its engineers to investigate, they found that the farmers were using the machines to wash the dirt off potatoes. The machines are not designed for dense loads, and so they keep breaking down.

3 Translation

a. Translate the definition of Six Sigma into English.

Six Sigma (6σ) ist ein statistisches Qualitätsziel und zugleich der Name einer Qualitätsmanagement-Methodik. Ihr Kernelement ist die Beschreibung, Messung, Analyse, Verbesserung und Überwachung von Geschäftsvorgängen mit statistischen Mitteln. Ziele orientieren sich an finanzwirtschaftlich wichtigen Kenngrößen des Unternehmens und an Kundenbedürfnissen.

b. Find out which company first introduced Six Sigma, and why.

INFO

Quality control vs. quality assurance
Quality control: testing and inspection of goods once they have been produced (focus on correction)
Quality assurance: managing every stage in the production of goods or the provision of services with the aim of ensuring customer satisfaction (focus on prevention and improvement)

4 Targets

"Project management systems which present their targets only in terms of cost and schedule can destroy a manager's natural instinct to produce work of which he can be proud. This is a very strong argument in favour of a quality system. It can provide a counterpoise to the two factors of cost and schedule."

John L. Ashford

counterpoise Gegengewicht

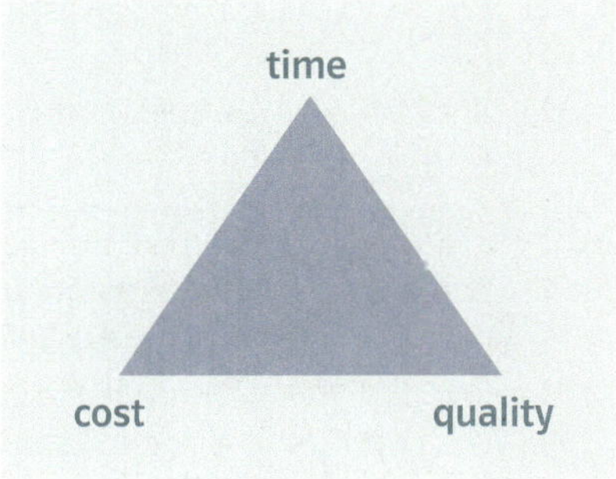

a. Explain why the targets of cost, schedule and quality may be seen as opposing forces.

b. Is the view of managers expressed here a positive or a negative one? Discuss whether it is closer to Theory X or Theory Y (Unit 9, page 119).

C Language | Getting things right

1 Mistakes

a. The same word is missing in each sentence. What is it, and how would you translate it in each case?

1. The event wasn't a success at all. In fact, it was a complete ....
2. There have been many business .... over the last few months.
3. The car crashed due to brake ....
4. An electricity .... caused all of our computers to crash.
5. In your country, is .... to appear in court a criminal offence?

"It's not a typo – everyone sits in the kitchen."

b. Match the words in bold with their German equivalents.

Fehlermeldung | Störfall | Tippfehler | Konstruktionsfehler | Rechtschreibfehler | menschliches Versagen | aus Versehen | Makel | Schuld | Versehen | Panne | ins Fettnäpfchen treten

1. Most plane crashes are due to **human error**.
2. I keep getting this **error message** that says 'File not found'.
3. I pressed the 'send' button **by mistake** before I finished writing the email.
4. Did you hear about that **incident** at the nuclear power plant?
5. Look, there's a slight **flaw** in this champagne glass.
6. It's not my **fault**. You're the one to blame!
7. Engineers have discovered a serious **defect in the design** of the machine.
8. You've really **put your foot in it** now. You'll have to apologise to her.
9. One of the most common **typos** is to write 'from' instead of 'form'.
10. A typical **spelling mistake** is to write 'accommodation' with only one 'c'
11. I'm sorry you didn't get an invitation. It was an **oversight** on my part.
12. I'm afraid we've had a bit of a **mishap** in the kitchen.

LANGUAGE TIP

Mistakes and failures
mistake: wrong action
error: more formal word for 'mistake'
failure: when something does not work, or does not work as well as it should
defect (adj. **defective**): problem that spoils something or causes it not to work correctly
fault (adj. **faulty**):
1. mistake for which you are responsible,
2. a broken part or weakness in a system

c. Discuss the questions.

1. What types of **mistakes** do you often make in English?
2. Have you ever had a **mishap** in the kitchen? Can you give an example?
3. How can you avoid making cultural **blunders** abroad?
5. What counts as a social **faux pas** in your culture?
4. Can you spot an object near you with a slight **blemish** or **imperfection**? What do you think caused it?

2 False friends

Replace the false friends (in italics) with better alternatives.

I *mean* that it was a good idea to hire a consultant to *proof* our quality management system and *berate* the *chef*. We learned that our *actual* system is inadequate. For example, it's not enough to *control* items after they have been produced. It's better to prevent *defect* products from occurring in the first place. In this way, we can reduce waste as well as the number of *reclamations* from customers and product *callbacks*. We've also decided to stop selling loss-making products and concentrate instead on the *rentable* ones. Investing in quality will *eventually* cost money, but on the other *side* we will be able to *spare* money in the long run.

3 Fine-tuning

Read the definitions of 'ensure', 'assure' or 'insure', then use them to complete the sentences below.

› ensure = to take steps to make sure something will happen ("Please ensure that…")
› insure = to arrange for financial compensation in the event of damage, loss, injury, etc.
› assure = reporting verb used in the sense of 'promise' or 'guarantee' ("I assure you that…")

1. The system is designed to .... that a good quality of service is maintained.
2 We can .... you that this will not happen again.
3. Did Fox Studio really .... Betty Grable's legs for $1,000,000?
4. Quality Managers need to .... that there is an adequate record-keeping system.
5. They .... me that the printer would be compatible with my computer.
6. Companies are required to .... their employees against accidents at work.
7. Please would you .... that there are no empty bottles lying around in the classroom.

4 Taking precautions

a. Explain why a company or an individual might decide to take out a particular form of insurance. Use 'in case', as in the example below.

health insurance | household insurance | car insurance | product liability insurance | marine insurance | accident insurance | insolvency insurance

Example:
People take out health insurance **in case** they fall ill and need expensive medical treatment.

b. Use 'in case' to describe precautions you take in your everyday life.

Example:
I always keep twenty euros in my wallet in case I need to take a taxi.

LANGUAGE TIP

Insurance
I took out insurance
(NOT: ~~an insurance~~)
Alliance is an insurance company.
(NOT: ~~Alliance is an insurance~~.)

5 Promises and threats

a. Combine the parts to make sentences that could be used at the end of a letter.

1. You may rest assured that this unfortunate
2. We will only be able to accept work of this
3. I will be contacting you in the very near
4. We trust that you will be able to settle the
5. This issue will need to be sorted out without
6. If you fail to rectify the matter within the given
7. We will hold you liable for any losses
8. We will do our best to ensure that every

a. future with a full explanation of what happened.
b. effort will be made to prevent this from recurring.
c. incident will not happen again.
d. incurred unless the matter is settled immediately.
e. matter within the next few days.
f. delay if our business relationship is to continue.
g. deadline, we will be obliged to take legal action.
h. quality if you grant us a 20% discount.

1. _______ 2. _______ 3. _______ 4. _______ 5. _______ 6. _______ 7. _______ 8. _______

b. Discuss the questions below.

1. Which are promises, and which are attempts to apply pressure or extract a concession?
2. What do you notice about the verb forms used?
3. Suggest further phrases using this verb form that a customer could use to end a letter of complaint:

› ....

› ....

› ....

6 A product recall

A 2.11 **a.** Anna is doing an internship at the Andover sales office of Magiplay Inc., a toy manufacturer. A colleague calls her from the Chicago HQ about a product recall. Listen and then write the product recall notice based on your notes.

Magiplay

PRODUCT RECALL NOTICE

Name of Product: SPEEEEEDY

Units sold: __________

Importer: __________

Hazard: __________

Incidents / Injuries: __________

Description: __________

Product No.: __________

Sold at: __________

Manufactured in: __________

Price: __________

Remedy: __________

Consumer contact: __________

b. Translate the following press release into English.

Deutschland, Österreich und Schweiz nicht vom Spielzeugrückruf von Magiplay betroffen

Das von der Rückrufaktion betroffene Produkt *Speeeeedy Tortoise* ist in Deutschland, Österreich und der Schweiz nicht erhältlich. Diese Länder sind daher von der heutigen Aktion nicht betroffen. Das vom Rückruf betroffene Produkt wurde im Rahmen einer Sonderfertigung innerhalb eines begrenzten Zeitraums hergestellt und ausschließlich in den USA, Großbritannien, Irland und Kanada verkauft.
Die Tatsache, dass Magiplay in der Lage war, ein einzelnes Produkt einer bestimmten Charge, das in nur vier Ländern verkauft wurde, zu identifizieren, zeigt, wie genau das Unternehmen seine Spielzeuge prüft und kontrolliert. Aus Magiplays Sicht hat sich das neue Prüfsystem bereits bewährt, und wir werden weiterhin alles unternehmen, um die Gesundheit der Kinder, die mit unseren Produkten spielen, nicht zu gefährden.
Weitere Informationen zur Rückrufaktion erhalten Sie auf der Firmenwebseite unter Service.magiplay.com.

LANGUAGE TIP

Word order

- *Das von der Rückrufaktion betroffene Produkt* = The product (that is) affected by the recall (NOT: ~~The by the recall affected product~~)
- *Weitere Information zur Rückrufaktion erhalten Sie* = You can find further information / Further information can be found (NOT: ~~Further information on the product recall you can find~~)

Charge batch, **begrenzter Zeitraum** limited timeframe, **sich bewähren** to prove to be effective

D Business leaders | Innovators in quality

1 Reading

a. Put in the headings in the right order.

› Western gurus who followed the Japanese industrial success
› Americans who took the message of quality to Japan
› Japanese who developed new concepts in response to the Americans

The original quality gurus

A guru, by definition, is a good person, a wise person, and a teacher. A quality guru should be all of these, plus have a concept and approach to quality within business that has made a major and lasting impact. There have been three phases of quality gurus over the last 60 years.

■ **Early 1950s:** ....

W. Edwards Deming made Japan's auto industry into the success it is today. He placed great importance and responsibility on management, believing it to be responsible for 94 % of quality problems. Deming is perhaps best known for the Plan, Do, Check, Act (PDCA) cycle which bears his name. The idea of PDCA is to constantly improve, and thereby reduce the difference between the requirements of the customer and the performance of the process.
Joseph M. Juran followed in Deming's footsteps and developed the quality trilogy – quality planning, quality control and quality improvement. He believed quality is associated with customer satisfaction and dissatisfaction with the product, and emphasised the necessity for ongoing quality improvement through a succession of small improvement projects done throughout the organisation.

■ **Late 1950s:** ....

Dr Kaoru Ishikawa made many contributions to the improvement of quality in Japan, and introduced many quality tools to support his total quality viewpoint and his emphasis on the human side of quality. His best-known problem-solving tool is the Ishikawa (or fishbone) diagram, which represents the causes behind a problem or effect.
Shigeo Shingo is strongly associated with Just-in-Time manufacturing and was the inventor of the Poka-Yoke (mistake proofing) system. In Poka-Yoke, defects are examined, the production system stopped and immediate feedback given so that the root causes of the problem can be identified and prevented from occurring again. Shingo distinguished between 'errors' which are inevitable, and 'defects' which result when an error reaches a customer, and the aim of Poka-Yoke is to stop errors becoming defects.

■ **1970s – 1980s:** ....

Philip B. Crosby is known for the concepts 'Quality is Free' and 'Zero Defects', and his quality improvement process is based on his four absolutes of quality:
1) Quality is conformance to requirements.
2) The system of quality is prevention.
3) The performance standard is zero defect.
4) The measurement of quality is the price of non-conformance.
Tom Peters identified leadership as being central to the quality improvement process, discarding the word 'management' for 'leadership'. The new role is one of facilitator, and the basis is 'Management by walking about' (MBWA), enabling the leader to keep in touch with customers, innovation and people, the three main areas in the pursuit of excellence. He believes that, as the effective leader walks, at least three major activities are happening: 1) Listening – suggests caring 2) Teaching – values are transmitted 3) Facilitating – able to give on-the-spot help.

Department of Trade and Industry: www.dti.gov.uk

b. Match the parts to make logical statements.

Deming	invented a system of	preventing defects through a process of immediate feedback.
Juran	argued in favour of	solving problems by examining causes and effects.
Ishikawa	emphasised the role of	the continuous improvement of quality in a four-step cycle.
Shingo	showed a visual way of	the concept of quality and customer satisfaction.
Crosby	stressed the link between	a facilitative approach to leadership.
Peters	developed a process for	prevention as a factor in quality improvement.

c. Discuss how the concepts and approaches outlined in the article could be applied to your own organisation / college.

E Business communication | Handling complaints

1 Discussion

a. What can a company do if a customer complains about faulty products?

b. In your opinion, what should a company always / never do when a customer complains?

c. When is it best to complain in a formal letter, rather than face-to-face or on the phone?

2 Writing a complaint

a. You work for the Customer Services Department of Light Fantastic, a company specialising in lighting systems. Complete the missing words in the letter below.

Customer Services Department
Light Fantastic Ltd
39 St George's St.
London W1S 2FW

22 Clarendon Square
Leamington Spa
CV31 1JZ
30th October 2009

Re: Faulty product Flamingo desk spotlight, reported 23rd October 2009

Dear Sir or Madam,
I am writing to c................ about a faulty desktop lighting unit that I p................ through your w................ two weeks ago. The lighting unit in q................ is a Flamingo desk spotlight, and I bought it after reading your c................ that it is the most flexible spotlight on the market, and built to the h................ quality standards.
When I set up the device in my office it worked p................ and produced a very good level of light, but it also gave off a lot of heat and after a few minutes I d................ a smell of burning. I i................ the bulb and n................ it was making contact with the reflector unit, which became so hot that I could not t................ it. I switched it off i................, to p................ a fire in my office. I was lucky not to be seriously b................ .
I telephoned your customer h................ last week and e................ the problem, but I did not receive a s................ response. I am therefore writing to ask what steps you are p................ to take in this m................ . As this is a serious h................ and safety issue, I expect you to take swift a................ .
The question of c................ must be discussed, but I do not want to contact a l................ at this stage as I have always found your products to be excellent. I am sure that this is a rare problem and that we can find a s................ without creating any u................ negative publicity for your company.

I look forward to a p................ reply from you in w................ .
Yours ....,

Dr. Julia Bradbury

b. Discuss whether the letter conforms to the suggestions on the right.

SKILLS

Making complaints in writing

The language and tone should be:
Concise | Authoritative | Factual | Constructive | Friendly

The following elements should be included:
- Subject line to help identify the product
- Relevant facts, dates and details
- The desired outcome (what the customer wants done)
- Request for prompt action
- Possible consequences if this action is not taken

3 Writing

Work with a partner. Discuss which of the phrases on the next page are suitable for a formal letter, and draft a reply to Dr. Bradbury. Then exchange letters with another pair and discuss the differences.

4 B2B – Dealing with a supplier

a. Read the scenario and make a note of the main points.

Weller Foods produces high quality ready-to-eat meals, and has one of the most prestigious brands in Europe. Their new *Gateway to Asia* range of authentic Thai and Indian cuisine has become a bestseller. However, a woman claims to have become ill after eating a *Gateway to Asia* curry. Weller has now received a letter from her lawyer threatening to sue them for failing to observe food safety regulations. To make matters worse, the consumer rights magazine *Public Eye* is preparing to use the story as part of an investigation into the hazards of ready-to-eat frozen meals.
Weller has always taken care to use good quality ingredients, and quality control in their factory is very strict. They suspect that the problem may originate with their supplier of meat and poultry products, Kiefer Fleischhandel GmbH, even though there have been very few problems in the past.
The CEO of Weller regards this as a matter of urgency, especially since there is a shareholders' meeting next week. The Quality Manager has been asked to deal with the situation.

b. Work in pairs and role-play the telephone conversation between the Quality Manager (Weller Foods) and the Customer Relations Manager (Kiefer GmbH). Make use of the phrases on the right.

Role card: Quality Manager

Call the supplier and explain the situation. You are under pressure from your CEO to find a solution, so try to get an assurance that they will deal with the matter as quickly as possible.

Role card: Customer Relations Manager

One of your major customers calls you with a complaint. Find out what the problem is and respond positively. Try to stall them, and ask them to send you the details of the problem in a letter or email.

c. Choose one of the following writing tasks:

- An email from the Quality Manager to the CEO, giving an update on the situation.
- An email from Kiefer GmbH to Weller, confirming the points discussed in the telephone call.
- A press release from Weller Foods to Public Eye magazine, presenting their view of the case and asking them to put the article on food safety on hold until all the facts are known.

PHRASES

Handling complaints

Asking for an explanation
- Perhaps you could explain how …
- How on earth did this come about?
- Please let us know how this happened.
- We look forward to receiving a full explanation in the near future.

Sorting out responsibility
- It seems that the fault is at your end.
- That's your responsibility, not ours.
- It's not our fault that …
- You can't blame it on us.
- You're just passing the buck.

Saying what you have done
- On receiving your letter, I immediately contacted …
- I have instructed our sales department to …

Offering solutions
- If you agree, we will replace the desk lamp.
- We would be pleased to offer you a €100 voucher towards the purchase of any of our products.

Showing understanding
- I'm sorry to hear this. If I understand you correctly, …
- So what you're saying is …
- I see what you mean / why you're concerned.
- I am very sorry that one of our products should have caused such distress.

Promising action
- We will investigate the matter straight away.
- It may take us a few days to trace the source of this problem.
- We'll get back to you as soon as we can.

Asking for action
- We may require some evidence to support this claim.
- Could you send us the details in writing?
- We trust that you will treat this as a matter of priority.
- This is an urgent matter, so …

Thanking and reassuring
- I am very grateful to you for raising this important issue.
- Thank you for bringing this matter to our attention. I was very concerned to hear about your alarming experience.
- We value you as a customer and hope that …

SKILLS

We/Us or I/me?
- **We** would like to offer you a $100 store credit. (*decision taken by more than one person*)
- **We** are doing our best to live up to your high expectations. (*the company as a whole*)
- **I** am very sorry for the trouble that you have had with this product. (*personal feeling*)
- **I** have also instructed the warehouse staff to notify you of any delays. (*personal action*)

F Consulting | Quality check

1 Scenario

You have an interview for an internship tomorrow and have heard through the grapevine that the Director of Quality Assurance is on the interview panel. You have just enough time to brush up on key areas of quality management in order to hold your own at the interview. The quiz below will point you in the right direction.

Start by answering as many of the questions as you can from your existing knowledge of the subject.
Then make use of the Internet to tackle the remaining questions. Keep your answers short, only using the space provided, and note down any websites or other useful sources.

1. Define the word 'stakeholder'.
2. In a nutshell, what is Total Quality Management?
3. What do you understand by the term 'benchmarking'?
4. What is the purpose of a quality audit?
5. What is the value of carrying out spot checks?
6. What is a quality circle?
7. How would you translate the Japanese word Kaizen into English? What about German?
8. In Six Sigma, what is a black belt? In what type of sport does this title originate?
9. What does the number 3.4 refer to in Six Sigma?
10. Which company pioneered the Six Sigma concept in the 1980s?
11. 'Shigeo Shingeo' is strongly associated with JIT manufacturing. What do you understand by JIT?
12. What is a DIN norm?
13. What do the following symbols stand for? What do they indicate on a product?

CE

14. Complete the 7-S Framework.

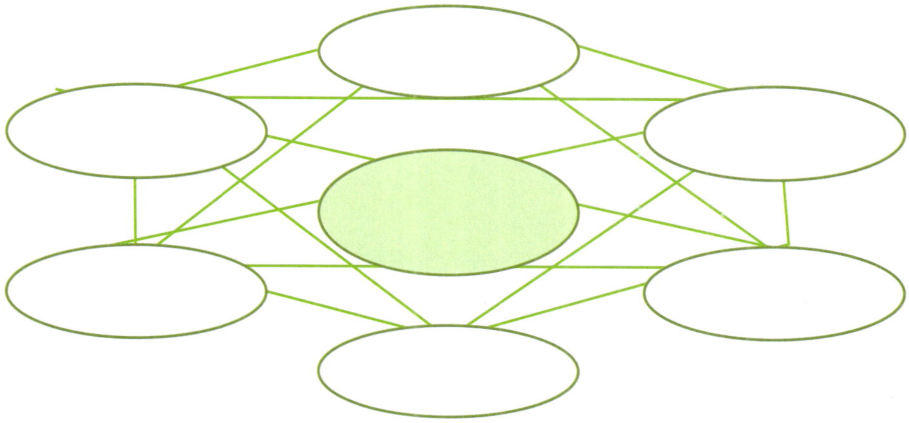

15. Give a brief description of the Framework here:

....

....

....

....

16. Which company is associated with the 7-S Framework?

....

17. Label the Ishikawa diagram (fishbone) with the missing words.

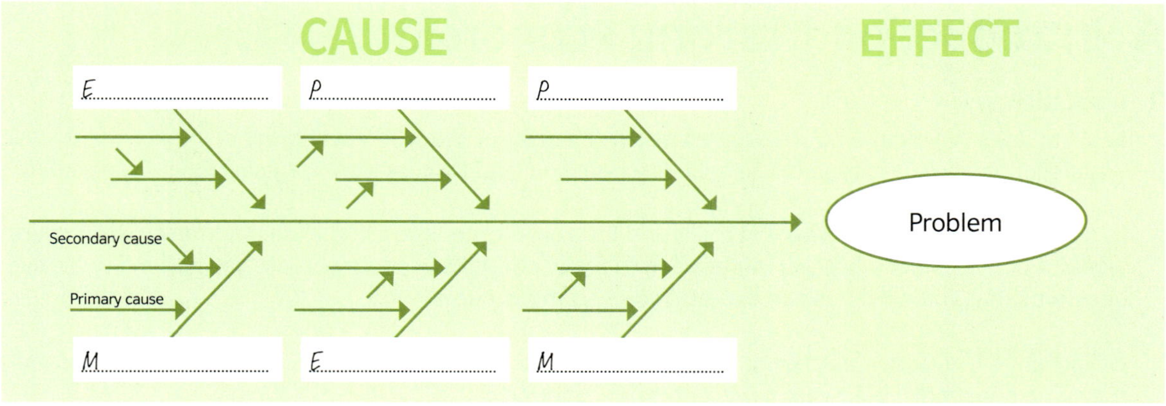

18. Complete the Deming cycle.

19. Make notes about the Deming cycle here.

....

....

....

....

2 Interview

Practise the interview with a partner. Take turns as interviewer (Director of Quality Assurance). When you are being interviewed, try to impress the interviewer with the depth and breadth of your knowledge.

Unit 12
Economics

Online Link
800021-0012

A Introduction | Talking economics

1 Discussion

a. What does the picture above suggest about the state of the world economy?
What economic issues are in the headlines where you live? Discuss how the government is handling them.

b. If you could choose anywhere in the world for a six-month internship or secondment, which country would it be? Consider what you might need to know about its economy before you go, and write five questions that you would ask an expert if you had the chance.

c. Exchange lists with a partner and try to answer your partner's questions. Then discuss how to answer the same questions about your own country's economy.

2 Business terms

What makes a country rich? Discuss possible criteria and suggest further terms to add to the word bank.

WORD BANK

Economic indicators
balance of payments (BOP) | balance of trade (BOT) | budget deficit / budget surplus | capital account balance | current account balance | consumer price index (CPI) | cost of living | disposable income | exchange rate | foreign direct investment (FDI) | gross domestic product (GDP) | gross national product (GNP) | hidden economy | infrastructure | inflation rate | property prices | purchasing power parity (PPP) | taxation | unemployment rate | visible trade balance / invisible trade balance

3 Listening

A 2.12 **a.** Jochen Köster has been offered the chance of a nine-month secondment in Dublin and needs advice. He calls his friend Daniela, an accountant. Listen and take notes on the following:

- Jochen's dilemma
- The economic situation in Ireland
- What Daniela likes / doesn't like about Dublin
- Daniela's advice to Jochen

b. Find out about the state of Dubai's economy. How does it compare with that of Ireland?

4 What is economics?

a. Read the definitions and the quote by Matthew Bishop below. Then discuss the questions that follow.

"Economics … should be understood as a way of thinking about the world – a way of thinking about it in terms of costs and benefits. Every decision has both an upside and a downside. I think that's the characteristic that marks out economics from the other sciences: it is the science of choices. We should look at it more in terms of smaller decisions and the choices people make, rather than whether the government can deliver miracles in the economy at large."

Matthew Bishop, Business Editor of The Economist

INFO

macroeconomics and microeconomics

Macroeconomics: the analysis of the economy in general, and phenomena such as growth, inflation and unemployment

Microeconomics: the study of the behaviour of individual markets, workers, households and firms

1. How would you translate 'microeconomics' and 'macroeconomics' into German?
2. What phrase sums up Bishop's definition of economics? Is this closer to macroeconomics or microeconomics?
3. Using Bishop's definition, give examples of other disciplines that might be of interest to economists.
4. Give an example of a decision you have made recently. What was the upside/downside of that decision?
5. In your view, what economic problems should/can governments try to solve? In what situations might their policies do more harm than good?

5 Fine-tuning

Read the language tip below. Then complete the sentences.

economy | economic | economical | economies | economise | economics | economists | economically

1. Exports account for three-quarters of our .... activity.
2. She's an expert on Keynesian ....
3. I always fly .... class, even when I'm travelling on business.
4. They blamed the drop in sales on the global .... downturn.
5. It isn't .... to sell these products in such small quantities.
6. We cancelled the project. It's not .... viable.
7. It might be more .... to lease business vehicles than buy them.
8. The bank's chief .... has reduced his forecast for growth to 0.5%.
9. If we increase our output, we might be able to achieve .... of scale.
10. You can .... on fuel by making sure your car tyres are pumped up.

LANGUAGE TIP

economical / economic / . . .

- It's an **economical** car. (good value, saves money)
- The **economic** outlook is good. (relating to the economy)
- The nation is facing a crisis, both socially and **economically**. (adverb)
- A cut in interest rates might boost the **economy**. (economic system)
- It's a **false economy** to buy cheap clothes. (a waste of money in the long run)
- She's got a degree in **economics / Economics**. (subject of study)
- **Economists** disagree about the BigMac index. (experts on the subject)
- In a recession people tend **to economise on** entertainment. (spend less money on)

B Business briefing | The business cycle

1 Defining 'business cycle'

a. Number the parts of the definition in the right order.

a. [ ] and bust (recession), with fluctuations in economic
b. [ ] and troughs, but none has ever completely solved the
c. [ ] The term business cycle refers to the tendency of
d. [ ] share or house prices, which inevitably burst.
e. [ ] growth occurring every five years or so. Governments
f. [ ] economies to move through periods of boom (growth)
g. [ ] problem. Economic expansions tend to create bubbles in
h. [ ] are in constant battle to even out the peaks

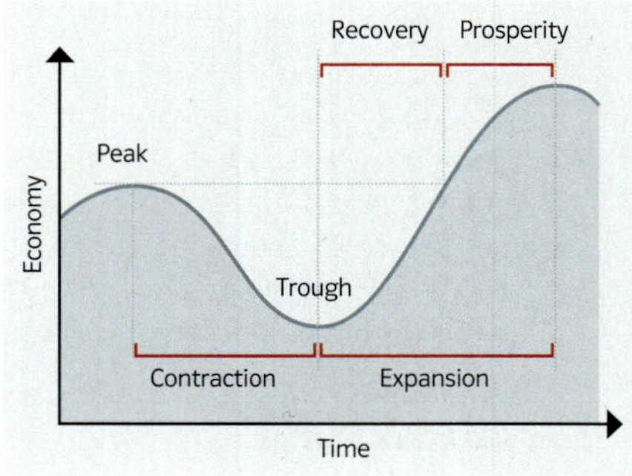

b. Who suffers most in a recession? Give examples of industries, interest groups, individuals, etc., and discuss why they are particularly vulnerable.

2 Reading

a. Scan the article for terms that have similar meanings to 'contraction' and 'trough'.

Clouds and silver linings

As the old joke goes: when your neighbour loses his job, it is called an economic slowdown. When you lose your job, it's a recession. When an economist loses his job, it's a depression. But does slower economic growth or even 'negative economic growth' always mean a doom and gloom scenario?

According to the textbooks, a depression is a sustained downturn in one or more economies. More extreme than a recession, a depression is characterised by abnormally high rates of unemployment, bankruptcies, volatile currency fluctuations, a restriction of credit, shrinking output and investment, and little economic activity. The Great Depression, beginning with the Wall Street Crash of 1929, affected most of the economies in the world throughout the 1930s. The spectre of such a disaster happening again still haunts governments, economists and business leaders.

The technical definition of a recession is a decline in a country's GDP for two or more successive quarters. The National Bureau of Economic research defines it more generally as "a significant decline in economic activity spread across the economy, lasting more than a few months". Recessions are usually considered to be a normal part of the business cycle. Employment falls, as well as investment spending, household incomes and business profits.

A recession is not bad news for everyone, however. According to Madsen Pirie, president of the Adam Smith Institute, "recession speeds up the process of evolution, forcing companies to become leaner. In good times, businesses get bloated. In a recession, they have to curb costs and learn new habits." And John van Reenen of the London School of Economics agrees: "It's an inevitable weeding-out process. For the good to flourish, the bad must go to the wall. It's happening all the time, but it's most intense in a recession." As well as resulting in leaner and meaner organisations, recessions offer opportunities for certain groups of people who are quick to spot that 'every cloud has a silver lining'.

With a stagnating economy and rising levels of debt, a recession is usually good news for pawnbrokers, for example. Although in the past they may have suffered from an image problem, they are now enjoying a revival and gaining respectability in the high street. Many people, especially younger customers, are attracted by the idea of raising quick cash by pawning a glitzy watch or piece of jewellery.

A recession also has positive knock-on effects for environmentalists. People are forced to consider how to cut energy costs, reduce waste and make savings by consuming less, for example by replacing their gas-guzzling automobile with a more economical model. A recession can also offer excellent opportunities to companies with 'green' products to market to anxious consumers who want to reduce their carbon footprint.

In 2007, when the most recent recession started, words like 'credit crunch' and 'sub-prime mortgages' were soon on everyone's lips, and on the front page of every newspaper. "Economics pundits love recessions," says the Guardian's economics editor, Larry Elliott. "Booms and busts are always good for us: we are treated like gods. Obviously we deeply regret the pain caused by a recession, but at the same time you can't help noticing that the only people walking round with big smiles on their faces during a recession are economists."

doom and gloom scenario Untergangsszenario, **sustained** anhaltend, **the spectre haunts** das Gespenst geht um, **bloated** aufgeblasen, **to weed out** ausmerzen, **Every cloud has a silver lining** Auf Regen folgt Sonnenschein, **glitzy** schick, **gas-guzzling** benzinfressend, **pundit** Experte, Expertin

b. Re-read the article for the main points. Note down useful vocabulary and discuss the questions below.

1. Explain the title and how it relates to the content of the article.
2. According to the article, who benefits from a recession, and why?

c. Find expressions with similar meanings:

1. business failures b……………………
2. likely to change suddenly v……………………
3. following one another s……………………
4. unavoidable i……………………
5. consequences k…………-on…e……………
6. property loan m……………………

d. Complete the expressions. Then match them to the definitions.

1. lean and m……………………
2. peaks and t……………………
3. boom and b……………………
4. doom and g……………………

a. pessimistic outlook
b. success followed by collapse
c extremely efficient
d. high points and low points

e. Explain the following expressions in your own words.

1. the bad must **go to the wall**
2. were soon **on everyone's lips**
3. who want to reduce their **carbon footprint**

3 Discussion

a. What exactly do pawnbrokers do, and who are their customers? Discuss what they could do to avoid their 'image problem'.

b. Even in the most difficult period of the Great Depression, certain groups of people prospered. Who were they, and what type of business activities did they find most lucrative?

c. What industries might be considered 'recession-proof'? Suggest further examples to add to the list below.

Recession-proof industries
› medicine and health care
› food staples
› cosmetics
› debt collection
› security / alarm services
› funerals
› tax advice
› career / job search
› energy (electricity, gas)
› defence
› tobacco and liquor
› education
› pornography
› …?
› …?

recession-proof konjunktursicher,
food staples Grundnahrungsmittel

C Language | Trends

1 Causes and effects

a. What do you understand by the saying below? Discuss whether it is valid.

"When the US sneezes, the rest of the world catches a cold."

b. Identify the main trends and findings mentioned in the article. Discuss the possible causes and effects of each one, as in the example below.

Demographic time bomb

People everywhere are living longer than they used to, and are having fewer children. With a shrinking workforce having to support more pensioners, the consequences of an ageing population are scary. According to the UN's latest population forecast, life expectancy at birth will go up in rich countries from 77 years to 83 by 2050. (These are averages for both sexes. Women generally live five or six years longer than men.) Epidemics such as swine flu can cause fluctuations in mortality rates, but the average potential life span has remained constant at 85.

The rich world is ageing fast, and the poor world is catching up. Fertility rates have plummeted in all OECD countries, from an average of 3.2 children per woman in 1960 to 1.6 now. Even in the poorer half of the world, fertility rates have come down spectacularly. In a few countries where fertility rates are already very low, such as Japan and South Korea, they are still falling. The population of Japan, currently about 127m, has started to dip. In China, which is already ageing rapidly, the population is expected to peak in 2030 and then decline gently.

Spending on pensions, health and long-term care in OECD countries has soared. Health care spending is growing considerably faster than their economies, and long-term care already accounts for 15 % of total health spending.

Labour forces are starting to contract and the number of pensioners is growing. In most countries, the ratio of people working to those of retirement age will deteriorate dramatically over the next few decades.

So what can governments do to defuse this demographic time bomb? One option is to rejuvenate the population by encouraging women to have more babies. Another is to put up the official retirement age in order to boost the number of old people in work. However, surveys find that when employers have a choice, they prefer to hire younger workers.

www.economist.com

mortality rate Sterberate, **life span** Lebensdauer, **to defuse** entschärfen, **to rejuvenate** verjüngen

Example: "It is said that women generally live longer than men. This could be because they take better care of their health. It also explains why most of the residents in old people's homes are women."

2 Trends and movements

a. Identify verbs and nouns in the text referring to trends and movements. Copy and complete the list below, adding corresponding verb / noun forms where possible.

UP	to increase (an increase), to climb (a climb), …
UP FAST	to increase (an increase), to climb (a climb), …
DOWN	to decrease, …
DOWN FAST	to plunge, to slump, to nosedive, …
UP AND DOWN	to be volatile (volatility), …
GOOD AND BAD	to improve (an improvement), …
HIGHS AND LOWS	to reach a high / low point, …
STATES	to be steady, to be down, to be up, …
SINGLE POINTS	to be at, to be below / above, …

LANGUAGE TIP

Causes and effects

Facts and interpretations
- According to the survey, …
- Surveys show / find that …
- The UN thinks that …
- It seems that … / it is said that …
- Current figures indicate / suggest that …

Personal response
- This figure is (hardly) surprising because …
- I wouldn't have expected …
- These figures are quite worrying.

Explaining causes
- One reason why … is that …
- This is largely due to … / because (of) …
- One (possible) reason for this …
- It might be a result of …
- This may be caused by …

Describing effects
- This may lead to … / could result in …
- This explains why …
- A possible (knock-on) effect will be …
- A (likely) result is that …

b. Think of a trend (short-term or long-term) that relates to you personally, e.g. fluctuations in your mood, your grades, your finances, your weight, the fortunes of your favourite football team, etc. Draw a graph and then – without showing it to your partner – describe it in detail. Your partner draws what you describe. Compare the two versions and discuss reasons for the fluctuations.

LANGUAGE TIP

Explaining a graph

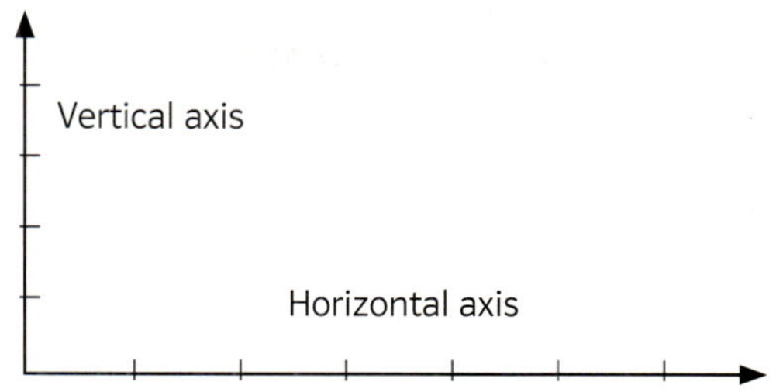

c. Discuss the questions below.

1. Should governments try to rejuvenate their populations? If so, what steps do you recommend?
2. Some countries have laws to prevent discrimination on age grounds, e.g. prohibiting references to age in advertisements, or imposing taxes on employers who sack older workers. Is this good for business?

3 Transitive and intransitive verbs

a. Choose the right form of the verb in brackets.

1. Four major companies have (raised / risen) petrol prices today by 5 cents a litre.
2. Oil prices have (raised / risen) to an eight-month high, despite a huge surplus in the US:
3. GDP is predicted to (fall / reduce) by more than 5% next year.
4. The retailer Laura Ashley has (declined / reduced) prices by up to 50%.
5. (Raising / Rising) the retirement age would not only (soar / boost) tax revenues but also (cut / decline) future pension costs.

LANGUAGE TIP

Raise and rise

- The verb **raise** is regular *(raise-raised-raised)*, and the verb **rise** is irregular *(rise-rose-risen)*.
- The verb **raise** is transitive, so it needs an object: *Banks are going to **raise** interest rates.*
- The verb **rise** is intransitive, so it is used without an object: *Interest rates are going to **rise**.*
- Other transitive verbs: *cut, reduce, lower, boost*
- Other intransitive verbs: *decline, fall, soar*
- Verbs used transitively or intransitively: *increase, decrease, drop, climb*
- Nouns: a pay **rise** (BE), a pay **raise** (AE), a **rise** in prices (BE/AE)

b. Suggest how to translate 'raise' in the examples below into German.

1. If you have a question, please **raise** your hand.
2. Do you think the official retirement age should be **raised** or lowered?
3. I'm glad you **raised** the subject of money.
4. He gave up his job in banking in order to **raise** chickens.
5. The aim of our campaign is to **raise** brand awareness.
6. It isn't easy to combine a career with **raising** young children.
7. We've managed to **raise** €3,000 to fund our project.
8. Recent indicators have **raised** hopes that economic recovery is around the corner.

4 Prepositions

Put in the prepositions.

Petrol prices have risen .... nearly 5p since mid-July to reach an average .... 122.66p a litre. This represents an increase .... 30% .... petrol prices .... the past six months. Fuel prices peaked .... 119.7p for unleaded and 133.3p for diesel in July last year, but then dropped .... 86.1p (unleaded) and 98.1p (diesel) in January. .... average, fuel tax accounts .... 70% of the price of petrol per litre in the UK, compared to 9% in the US.

LANGUAGE TIP

Prepositions

an increase **in** (+ subject)
an increase **of** (+ amount)
to increase **by** (+ amount)
to increase **from** (+ lower amount) **to** (+ higher amount)

5 Words in context

a. Complete the text with the missing words.

enforce | conducted | borders | fares | restricted | political | citizens | underground | immigrants | secretly | available | regulations | shown | earn | documents | booming

The .... economy, or black market, is a market where business is .... without regard for the law, taxation or .... Typically, the black market thrives in countries where legitimate economic activity is .... by corruption, monopolies or .... repression, but to a certain extent it exists everywhere. For example, in Europe the rise in the number of illegal .... entering EU states has led to an increase in activities such as smuggling people across ...., illegal housing and employment, and trading in forged .... In the street markets of Asia, where it is almost impossible to .... copyright law, the trade in cheap copies of DVDs, music and computer games is .... In the United States, studies have .... that in major cities many .... consider it more acceptable to travel in illegal taxis, where the .... are cheaper and the taxis more ...., than to use legally licensed companies. Of course, moonlighting goes on everywhere, too, with people who are doing second jobs .... without paying tax on the extra money they ....

b. Does the black economy exist in your country? Discuss the forms it takes, and the extent to which it is seen as a problem. For example, can moonlighting have any positive economic effects?

6 Figurative language

a. Descriptions of the economy often use figurative language drawn from agriculture and gardening. Match the examples on the left with the explanations of how they are used in a business context.

1. budding	a. radical or thorough
2. plough back	b. to reduce something by removing unnecessary or unwanted parts
3. green shoots	c. a large sum of money or good fortune received unexpectedly
4. root and branch	d. first signs of recovery
5. seed corn	e. doing something that will cause a particular result in the future
6. windfall	f. return on investment
7. to weed out	g. funds used to start something new or encourage growth
8. barren landscape	h. to remove unwanted elements
9. sowing the seeds	i. reinvest money
10. yield (n.)	j. just beginning and likely to succeed
11. to prune back	k. unproductive, offering no opportunities

b. Use the expressions to complete the sentences below.

1. Our cash flow situation means that we will have to .... our budget again this year.
2. There are signs of .... emerging, but the global economic crisis is not yet over.
3. We are expecting a good .... from our investment portfolio this quarter.
4. Some shareholders are hoping to receive .... when dividends are paid out.
5. The automotive sector is currently a .... for investors.
6. They plan to use their first year's profits as .... for future expansion.
7. We must take a .... approach to eliminating waste in our manufacturing process.
8. We think of 'investing in people' as .... of future prosperity.
9. The .... nanotechnology industry is looking very promising.
10. Our directors have decided to .... the profits into the company.
11. One way to save money is to .... the underperforming employees.

D Business leaders | John Maynard Keynes

1 Government policy

Combine phrases to create statements that express your views on how the government should manage the economy.

(un)employment | bail out | boost | competition | consumer spending | create | demand | firms in trouble | I believe that | In my view, | in order to | increase | the state ought to | inflation | public spending | reduce | stimulate | tackle | taxes | the budget deficit | cut | the government should | the money supply

2 Reading

Read the article and answer the questions below.

1. How might Keynes' background and personality have influenced his views?
2. What two related concepts sum up Keynesian economics? Discuss why they are controversial.
3. To what extent can your government be described as Keynesian? Give examples of how the government's economic policy is put into action, and whether it is effective.
4. Keynes also coined the terms 'animal spirits' and 'casino capitalism'. Find out what he was referring to, and how they might be relevant today.

JOHN MAYNARD KEYNES (1883–1946) was a Cambridge academic who became one of the most influential economists of the 20th century. Some of his ideas were revolutionary, and are still controversial, but 'Keynesian economics' has become the yardstick against which other economists are defined. His surname, which rhymes with 'canes', is often mispronounced.

THE LEGACY OF KEYNES

Born into an academic family and educated at Eton and Cambridge, John Maynard Keynes seemed destined to follow a traditional path in life. After graduating from university, he joined the civil service and later the Treasury. During this time, Keynes was chosen to be a delegate at the Paris Peace Conference of 1918, an experience that had a lasting effect on him. He resigned in protest at the way the Germans were treated in the aftermath of World War I, and wrote a critical account of the economic bungling that lay behind the Treaty of Versailles.

His outspoken opinions made him a celebrity. For the first time, economics (previously referred to as 'the dismal science') came to be seen as the driving force of social progress. As well as being a journalist and public speaker, Keynes was also an art-collector and member of the famously avant-garde Bloomsbury Group of writers, artists and intellectuals. In 1925 he caused a stir when he married the Russian ballet dancer Lydia Lopokova, giving rise to an unkind joke: "Oh what a marriage of beauty and brains: The fair Lopokova and John Maynard Keynes."

Keynes' really important idea was to be found in the book that he published in 1936, during the Great Depression. In his *General Theory of Employment, Interest and Money*, he proposed that governments should spend their way out of trouble during times of economic downturn. He argued that governments should stimulate demand and maintain full employment through large public spending programmes, and reduce taxation to encourage people to spend more This concept of 'deficit spending' met with initial opposition from those who thought government should always be based on a balanced budget, but the idea soon took hold. In the US, President Roosevelt successfully created the 'New Deal' programme by adopting Keynesian principles, putting people back to work by starting up major public works projects.

Constantly in and out of fashion, the ideas of Keynes have been endlessly revised, expanded and developed, and much of what is now known as Keynesian economics is the work of other economists. His original work is still a source of inspiration and controversy to economists today, particularly the idea that governments should 'pump-prime' their economies by spending borrowed money.

But his real legacy is that of a brilliant and radical thinker who was prepared to speak his mind, and a cultivated man with a wry sense of humour. He was impatient with economic theorists of his day who assumed that everything would work out in the long run, and reminded us that "In the long run we're all dead!"

to be destined bestimmt sein, **civil service** Staatsdienst, **Treasury** Finanzministerium, **aftermath** schwere Zeit (nach einem Ereignis), **bungling** Pfuscherei, **outspoken** freimütig, **celebrity** Berühmtheit, **to cause a stir** Aufsehen erregen, **to pump-prime** Ankurbelung der Wirtschaft durch Verschuldung, **public works** öffentliche Baumaßnahmen, **wry** trocken

E Business communication | Academic writing

1 Lecturer's comments

a. Identify the lecturer's comments as 'negative' (N), 'mixed' (M) and 'positive' (P).

[ ] A very weak effort indeed: Repetitive and no evidence of reading.
[ ] Confused in parts, but some relevant points.
[ ] Good introduction and well argued throughout.
[ ] Demonstrates application of critical thought and shows originality in handling arguments.
[ ] Disorganised. No structure, aims or conclusions, and referencing is absent.
[ ] Good background but weak on analysis.
[ ] Does not address the question and contains factual errors.
[ ] Excellent. Clearly structured and to the point.
[ ] Fails to demonstrate understanding of the subject.
[ ] Generally accurate but lacks focus.
[ ] Has clearly done some reading, but fails to mention the basics.
[ ] Good use of examples, but unfortunately only from lecture notes.
[ ] Has developed own ideas based on thorough understanding of the literature.
[ ] No attempt to define terms or give examples.
[ ] Outstanding. Persuasive argument and comprehensive answer to a complex question.

b. What other comments would you be pleased / not so pleased to find on your work?

c. Do you know the criteria on which your academic writing is assessed? If not, find out what they are.

2 Presentation guidelines

Your college probably has its own rules or guidelines for how academic papers should be presented. Discuss the checklist below with your business English teacher. Find out his / her preferences and compare them with other guidelines you know. Make notes on the following points:

- ☐ Handwritten or typed?
- ☐ Using one side or both?
- ☐ Page numbering at top or bottom of page? Centred or in left / right corner?
- ☐ Which font? (Ariel, Times New Roman, ...) Which size? (10, 12, ...) Should headings be bigger?
- ☐ Which numbering scheme? (Roman numerals – i, ii, iii, iv, Arabic numerals – 1, 2, 3, 4, letters – A, B, C, D)
- ☐ Should the lines be double-spaced?
- ☐ How wide should the left-hand / right-hand margins be?
- ☐ Name on each page?
- ☐ Title on each page?
- ☐ How personal? For example, do I refer to myself as 'I,' and the reader as 'you'?
- ☐ Should I use the passive or active voice? (Passive: A study was carried out. Active: I carried out a study.)
- ☐ Which method is to be used for references and / or bibliography? Any special layout? Footnotes required?
- ☐ Is there a word limit? What are the tolerances? Does this include words in tables?
- ☐ What should be included on the cover page? (e.g. name of college, department, title of report, name of student, name of tutor / supervisor, title of degree for which the work is being submitted, date submission)
- ☐ Is a list of abbreviations required? If so, where should it be placed?
- ☐ Am I allowed to submit my paper by email? If so, in what format? (e.g. PDF, rtf)
- ☐ Anything else I need to know? (Use of diagrams, charts, graphs, use of colour in diagrams)

double-spaced zweizeilig, **margin** Seitenrand, **submission** Einreichung, Abgabe

3 Titles

Re-word the instructions and questions below as titles.

Example:
"Discuss the extent to which consumer spending affects interest rates."

→ The Effect of Interest Rates on Consumer Spending

SKILLS

Titles and headings
- Avoid long, complex titles.
- Make sure the title relates to the content.
- Use capital letters for nouns, verbs and adjectives / adverbs.
- Check that the title is clear by asking a non-expert whether s / he understands it.
- Be careful when translating *'am Beispiel von'*, e.g. 'Crisis Management and Ypsilon AG', or 'Ypsilon AG's Approach to Crisis Management' (NOT: ~~Crisis Management with the Example of The Company Ypsilon~~)

1. "Outline how corporate culture might affect a firm's objectives."
2. "Describe what an organisation can do to avoid conflicts, and to solve conflicts if they arise."
3. "Explain how an advertiser might use statistical tools to measure advertising effectiveness."
4. "Why might a firm use benchmarking? What are the drawbacks of benchmarking?"
5. "Define TQM and evaluate its role with regard to the use of teams in an organisation."
6. "Summarise the methods that could be used to judge the effectiveness of a firm's HRM policies."

4 Paragraphs and punctuation

a. Explain the difference in meaning.

- Woman, without her man, is nothing.
- Woman: without her, man is nothing.

b. Draw symbols for these examples of punctuation.

1. full-stop / period / dot / point
2. comma
3. colon
4. semi-colon
5. question mark
6. hash
7. single quotation marks
8. double quotation marks
9. exclamation mark
10. paragraph symbol
11. back slash
12. forward slash (or stroke)
13. asterisk
14. plus (with numbers)
15. and (with words)
16. apostrophe
17. percentage
18. equals
19. brackets
20. dash
21. hyphen

c. How good are you at paragraphing and punctuation? Rewrite the following text, separating it into sentences and paragraphs, and punctuate where necessary.

SKILLS

Paragraphs
Paragraphs break up text into manageable proportions. They also organize meaning, helping your readers to think clearly about what you have written.

LUMP OF LABOUR FALLACY

this is based on the idea that there is a fixed amount of work to be done which can be described as a lump of labour so any increase in the amount each worker can produce reduces the number of available jobs this rather simple notion has been dismissed as a fallacy by economists indeed a famous example from the 1950's when workers believed that the introduction of automation would bring mass unemployment showed that such thinking is wrong yet the fallacy makes a comeback whenever there is an economic slowdown one popular element of the fallacy is the suggestion that reducing working hours will reduce unemployment as companies would need to hire more workers however this doesn't happen because in reality there is no fixed amount of work governments may decide to restrict the amount of work that is available and thus increase unemployment also companies would only consider creating more jobs if they could cut wages and the workers would not find that acceptable economists who oppose the lump of labour fallacy point to the fact that it costs more to hire two part time workers than one full time worker because the cost of recruiting and training staff which are after all fixed costs is substantial they argue that stimulating demand and thus increasing output is a better way of keeping unemployment figures down

fallacy Fehlschluss, Irrtum, **notion** Vorstellung, Idee, **hey presto** Schwupps!,

F Consulting | Making a documentary

1 Preparation

This is a class project in which you create a video documentary together. Read the scenario and do the tasks that follow.

Scenario

You are a creative consultancy and you have been commissioned to produce a documentary about economic changes in your country. This can be in the form of a single 45-minute documentary or a series of short documentaries of five minutes each.

Planning

1. Decide on a timescale that fits in with your Business English timetable and the demands of the project. This could be anything from an intensive week of regular meetings to a whole semester.
2. Watch the video 'Business trends in China' on the next page for inspiration.
3. Below is a list of some of the people typically involved in making documentaries. What exactly do they do, and what other roles can you add? Consider who else might be included in the list of credits.
   - Producer
   - Director
   - Film crew
   - Actors (for drama documentaries)
   - Production assistants
   - Reporter / journalist / interviewer
   - Voice over (heard, not seen)
   - …?
4. Conduct an initial meeting together, using the agenda.

Video documentary: Kick-off Meeting

Date:
Venue:
Participants:
Excused:

Agenda

Genre:	What type of documentary should it be? (Should it be serious, critical, tongue-in-cheek, promotional?)
Organisation:	Should we work together on a single 45-minute documentary, or a series of short and loosely connected documentaries?
Audience:	Who are the target viewers? What will they be interested in?
Message:	What information do we want to convey? What will the message be?
Teams and tasks:	What skills do we have? Who will do what?
Timescale:	How much time do we have? What are the milestones or deadlines?
Resources:	What do we need? Who can help us?
Communication:	How should we communicate?
Presentation:	What kind of event would be suitable for presenting the documentary? How else can it be shown to the public?
AOB	

tongue-in-cheek ironisch, augenzwinkernd

5. In your group, plan a narrative for your documentary. A starting point is to consider the 5 '**W**s': **W**ho, **W**hat, **W**hen, **W**here and **W**hy. You can present it in the form of a storyboard, as in the example below.

VIDEO STORYBOARD Page 1/of 1

Title of Documentary: Crisis? What Crisis?
Running time: 45 minutes
Intended production date: ASAP

VIDEO	DIAGRAM	AUDIO
Porsche zipping along motorway.		1975 music Kraftwerk: Autobahn
Cars on scrap heap		Kraftwerk music fades out. Fade in to bleak music.
Zoom into sign 'Otto Schrotthändler'		Voice over: The German automobile was once king of the jungle. But now it is fighting for survival.

SKILLS

Storyboard
A storyboard is a timeline that runs from top to bottom. The left column is for camera directions. The central column is for sketching diagrams that will help you visualise the scenes. The column on the right is for sounds, music and speech. Examples and templates of storyboards can be found on the internet.

PHRASES

Filming and directing
- The opening shot shows …
- The focus is on / should be on …
- The viewer should get an impression of …
- We need to convey an atmosphere of …
- In the foreground / background we see …
- At this point, the reporter talks directly to the camera.
- The camera takes a long shot of … / takes a close up of …
- The camera zooms in on / focuses on (an object).
- The camera pans / tracks / tilts / …
- The image fades out / dissolves / breaks up …
- Action!
- Cut!

2 Execution

Carry out the film project as planned. If possible, show early screenings to other students to get their comments on where cuts should be made or other improvements.

3 Writing

Write a report on your experience of making the documentary, or a review of a documentary made by one of the other groups.

Video lounge Business trends in China

BBC Motion Gallery

V 6 **a.** Before watching, discuss the questions below.

1. How much do you know about the Chinese political and economic system? Describe the changes that are happening and whether you think the outlook is positive or negative.
2. Based on the title of this documentary, what do you expect to learn from it?

b. Watch the video and make notes about changes that have affected the following:

- The young waitress
- Chinese workers in general
- Chinese restaurants
- Restaurant chefs
- Social equality

Revision 3
Units 9 – 12

Online Link
800021-0019

1 Listening

a. Listen and complete Frank Capper's notes.

A 3.3

SUNCYCLE SYSTEMS CALIFORNIA
TELEPHONE INTERVIEW – APPLICANT DETAILS

Call taken by: *Frank Capper, Head of Human Resources*
Time of call: ....
Name of applicant: ....
Country of residence: ....
Studying for degree in: ....
Major / Specialism: ....
Level: ■ Bachelor ■ Master ■ PhD ■ Other (...................)
Internship to take place: ■ during ■ after: .... semester / term
Status of internship: ■ voluntary ■ compulsory
Previous work experience: ....
Language skills: ....

Applicant's reasons for choosing SunCycle Systems: ....

Areas interested in: ■ Marketing ■ Human Resources ■ IT / software development ■ Project Management ■ Production ■ Finance
Further interests: ....
Personality: ....
Remuneration: ■ Paid internship ■ Unpaid internship
Action: ■ Candidate rejected ■ Further details requested (résumé) ■ Internship offered

b. Discussion: What is your overall impression of the candidate? Explain why.

....

....

c. Follow-up: Write the email that is sent to Frank Capper.

2 Issues faced by HR departments: Put in the missing letters, as in the example.

1. Stealing things of little value from the workplace *pilfering / pilferage*
2. Staying away from work, especially often and without good reason: a...................
3. The rate at which employees leave a company and are replaced: s................... t...................
4. When large numbers of employees have to be laid off: c................... r...................
5. Causes for complaint, e.g. about unfair treatment g...................
6. A policy of not recruiting any new staff, usually for cost reasons h................... f...................

3 Making suggestions: Complete the advice of a management consultant.

1. In order to reduce pilfering, I suggest ....
2. Before you announce more layoffs, I advise you to ....

4 Reference letter: Put in the missing words.

health | rights | position | asset | co-workers | patience | request | intern | deadlines | feet | skills | responsibility | directives | clerical | pressure | hesitation | researched | outgoing | part | attention | draft | valuable | maternity leave | short notice | adapt | stood in for | challenges | accurate | faithfully

TO WHOM IT MAY CONCERN

Reference for Ms Cheryl Kellermann

Ms Cheryl Kellermann worked as an .... at QuAD from 6 July to 4 September 2009, where she took .... in our 'High-flyer' internship program.

In her first week, she was asked to work at the reception at ...., demonstrating her ability to .... quickly to new .... and to think on her ....

At her own ...., she spent the main part of her internship in the Human Resources Department. During this time, she .... my assistant, who is currently on .... She performed routine .... tasks efficiently and with .... to detail, and carried out a range of duties that involve a high degree of .... and initiative. As well as this, she helped to .... job advertisements, and supported her .... in the planning and execution of training courses on .... and safety at work.

I was particularly impressed by a report she wrote on EU-.......... concerning social security and pension .... Her report was thoroughly ...., ... and well written.

In her dealings with other members of staff, she showed tact, ... and diplomacy, as well as an ability stay calm in difficult situations. She also demonstrated an .... personality, excellent communication ...., and an ability to meet ...., even when working under .... All these qualities make her a .... member of any team.

I am therefore confident that Ms Kellermann will be an .... to your organisation, and I have no .... in recommending her for a .... in Human Resources.

Yours ....,

Fernando Barriero

Director, Human Resources

5 Give the German translations.

1. References available on request. ....
2. He's handed in his notice. ....
3. I've been shortlisted for the vacancy. ....
4. The salary is negotiable. ....
5. I missed the closing date for applications. ....

6 Say it another way, using the clue in brackets. (Be careful with the tense.)

1. They're planning redundancies. (pipeline) *Redundancies are in the pipeline.*
2. They've shelved the project. (put / ice) *The project* ....
3. The project was abandoned. (pull / plug) *They* ....
4. We've got a sponsor for the project. (back) *Someone* ....
5. We can start once we get approval. (not / until) *We* ....

7 Put in the prepositions.

1. to be subject .... delays
2. to start .... the dot
3. to work flat .... to finish the job
4. to be held .... by problems
5. to account .... 20% of the profits
6. to put .... a meeting to a later date
7. to get a project back .... track
8. to do something .... your own risk

8 Counter the project leader's criticisms, using the expressions listed. Be careful with verb forms.

make up time | stick to | 100% commitment | be ahead of | success | on time | accomplish | stay within the budget

1. You've **failed to achieve** your objectives. — No, we haven't. We've .... them.
2. You've **fallen behind** schedule. — On the contrary! We're .... schedule.
3. You keep **missing** deadlines. — That's not true. We usually .... them.
4. Are you going to **be late** with the catalogue? — No, of course not. We'll complete it ....
5. You've **overrun your costs**. — But the figures show that we ....
6. Some people are **not pulling their weight**. — Nonsense. We're all showing ....
7. There's been too much **slippage**. — Actually, we've managed to ....
8. We don't want this project to be a **flop**. — Don't worry. It's bound to be a ....

9 Put in the words that match the definitions. Then complete the 16th clue.

1. estimation or prediction
2. meeting to start a project
3. chart showing the stages and progress of a project
4. important deadlines in a project
5. type of study that examines whether a project can be done
6. to check progress
7. money allocated to the project
8. meeting to discuss a completed project or task
9. academic project = study ...
10. the longest 'route' through a project, linking all tasks / events
11. made late
12. to put off to a later date
13 final stage in the project life cycle
14. WBS = 'work ... structure'
15. the backers of a project
16. Projects need them in case ....
....

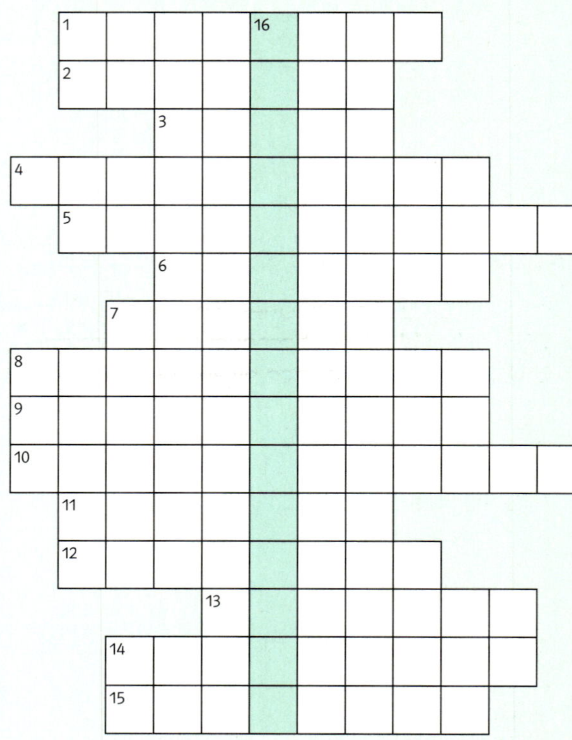

10 Complete the sentences with / without 'to', and the right form of the verbs listed.

shop | do | speak | eat out | be seen | stay | be paid | take | go | hear | work | buy | have | wait

MYSTERY SHOPPERS WANTED BY MARKET RESEARCH FIRM

Have you ever considered .... as a mystery shopper? It's certainly worth ...., especially if you enjoy .... shopping. Most us can't afford .... in fancy restaurants, ... designer handbags and .... in posh hotels every week, but imagine .... to dine at the Ritz, ... in Harrods and .... a luxury massage all in one day! It's hard work, of course. You have to get used .... notes on your experiences as a customer, and avoid .... while you take notes. You might be asked to report on how much time you had to spend .... before being served, or whether you managed .... to the manager. If you think you have what it takes to be a mystery shopper, we look forward .... from you!

11 Complete the extract from a book on quality management, using the full form of the words listed.

(1) MSR	(6) DCMNTTN	(11) RPLCMNT	(16) PYMNTS	(21) XCD
(2) PRV	(7) CRRSPNDNG	(12) CMPNNTS	(17) ATTMPTD	(22) PRVNT
(3) PRVNTN	(8) DFFCLT	(13) CRRD	(18) TRNVR	(23) PRPRTN
(4) SB-STNDRD	(9) SSSSMNT	(14) CMPLNTS	(19) CNVNTNL	(24) SVNGS
(5) SLRS	(10) DFCTV	(15) MRKTNG	(20) XTRM	(25) PRVD

The costs of quality

Very few organizations (1) .... the costs of poor quality. It is therefore exceedingly difficult to (2) .... that systems for the (3) .... of (4) .... work are cost-effective. Whereas the direct costs of a quality system can be quantified with some precision (the (5) .... of the system manager and his staff, the costs of (6) ...., expenditure on quality audits and so on) the (7) .... benefits are more (8) .... to assess. However, to counter the argument that quality systems cost more than they save, some (9) .... has to be made. Items contributing to the costs of poor quality include repair of (10) .... work, purchase of (11) .... materials and (12) ...., delay or disruption while repairs are (13) .... out, handling of customer (14) ...., after-sales remedial works, wastage of (15) .... effort, legal representation, court costs and compensation (16) ....

Companies that have seriously (17) .... to quantify these costs usually arrive at totals varying between 10 % and 40 % of (18) .... By comparison, the typical cost of a quality system for (19) .... construction work is likely to lie in fractions of 1 %. Even in (20) .... cases, such as offshore or nuclear construction, it is unlikely to (21) .... 5 %. So, even if the quality system can (22) .... only a small (23) .... of the costs of non-quality, the potential for (24) .... is enormous. But, how can this be (25) ....?

Adapted from The Management of Quality in Construction, J.L. Ashford

12 Put in if / in case / unless / even if.

1. .... your business supplies products to consumers, you need to make sure the products are safe.
2. You should take out product liability insurance .... you are sued for compensation by someone.
3. Anyone who is harmed by an unsafe product can sue, ... they didn't buy the product themselves.
4. Trading standards officers can order you to stop selling your products .... they think your products are unsafe.
5. Don't hire builders to work on your premises .... they have liability insurance.

13 Match the parts of the sentences.

1. Firms that are in trouble might expect to
2. Moonlighters usually want to
3. The aim of 'deficit spending' is to
4. Raising the retirement age could help to
5. People who buy economical cars might want to
6. Some wealthy philanthropists decide to

a. pump-prime the economy.
b. invest in budding entrepreneurs.
c. be bailed out by the government.
d. reduce their carbon footprint.
e. avoid paying tax.
f. boost the number of old people in work.

14 Give the full forms of the acronyms and the German equivalents.

	Long form	German
1. TQM		
2. GNP		
3. BOP		
4. PPP		
5. ROI		

Unit 13
International trade

Online Link
800021-0013

A Introduction | An export opportunity

1 Discussion

a. Look at the picture above and explain the connection to international trade.

b. Brainstorm products that you associate with each of the following countries. List them on the board, then discuss the questions below.

Switzerland | United States | Wales | France | Iran | Sweden | Russia | Costa Rica

1. Which of the products are (a) commodities, (b) agricultural produce, and (c) manufactured goods?
2. Which country has the longest list and which has the shortest? Suggest reasons for the differences.
3. Are there any products that appear in more than one list? Explain why this is so.
4. Are any of the items also brands? Which country or countries are they associated with?
5. Are there any countries that import the same product that they export? Why do they do both?
6. From this discussion, what general conclusions do you draw about international trade?

c. Comment on the statistics on the right. Which country had a trade deficit in 2008?

d. Find out who the current top exporters and importers are. Discuss reasons for any changes.

e. What makes international trade different from domestic trade? Is it just a question of cost, or are there fundamental differences?

› International trade differs from domestic trade in that …
› One could also argue that …

VALUE OF MERCHANDISE exports / imports 2008

World ranking 2008, Exports	
1 Germany	$1,530,000,000,000
2 China	$1,465,000,000,000
3 United States	$1,377,000,000,000

World ranking 2008, Imports	
1 United States	$2,190,000,000,000
2 Germany	$1,202,000,000,000
3 China	$1,156,000,000,000

The CIA World Factbook

2 Reading and listening

a. Claire Spencer is the owner of Cand-y-Craft Ltd, a Welsh company specialising in hand-made organic and novelty chocolates. Although the firm has only been in business for six months, sales are booming. Read the emails and say what advice you would give to Claire.

To: p.harvey@exportexpert.co.uk
From: c.spencer@candycraft.co.uk

Hi Phil,
I've just received a couple of enquiries from firms outside the UK (see attachments), and was wondering if I could ask for your advice. They'd give me a chance to enter the European market, but I don't know if I'm ready for export. Also, I've got enough red tape to battle with already! Could we meet for a drink so that I can pick your brains?
Claire

From: o.schneider@sueissli.ch
To: info@candycraft.co.uk

Dear Sir/Madam,
Sueissli is a fast-growing retailer of confectionery products, with stores located throughout Switzerland. The *Mint Condition* chocolate coins advertised on your website would be a welcome addition to our range.
Please send us your terms of payment and delivery for export, and also let us know what currencies are available. It is important, for example, that Swiss francs are included in the chocolate coins. We would also appreciate samples of the coins and a detailed list of ingredients.
If the coins meet our requirements and comply with Swiss legislation regarding imports of chocolate products, packaging and labelling, we would be willing to place regular orders with you.
Yours sincerely,
Oliver Schneider, Marketing Manager
Sueissli-Süsswaren

From: smendelsohn@gourmet.de
To: info@candycraft.co.uk

Dear Sir or Madam,
Gourmet GmbH is a distribution company based in Berlin that offers a wide range of specialty foods. We had the opportunity to sample your Madagascar Grand Cru Truffles during the Natural Trade Show in Brighton, and we believe this brand, with the Fair Trade label, has global potential.
To help you to break into new markets, we would be pleased to offer our services as a distributor. Attached you will find a list of our stockists in Europe and the US, who would be happy to give you any information you may require. Should you be interested in a distributorship agreement, please suggest a time when I may call to discuss terms.
Regards,
Svenja Mendelsohn
Managing Director, Gourmet GmbH

A 2.13 **b.** Listen to the advice that Phil gives to Claire and take notes about the following:

- How international trade differs from domestic trade
- General advice on exporting
- Pros and cons of Claire's options
- Phil's recommendations

c. Choose one of the enquiries above, and write Claire's response.

d. Find out the background to the 'Dijon de Cassis' case. What countries were involved? Do you agree with the verdict?

INFO

Switzerland and the EU
Switzerland is not a member of the EU, but it applies the 'Dijon de Cassis' principle of mutual recognition to imports from EU members. According to this principle, any product produced in the EU can be sold in another EU country without any restrictions concerning product standards.

B Business briefing | International marketing

1 Reading

a. Read the article, marking ten phrases giving advice to firms who want to break into foreign markets. Then compare to see whether other students have identified the same phrases as you.

Breaking into foreign markets

When a company is planning to expand internationally it will have to do a lot of detective work before proceeding. The key questions are the same as they are in the domestic market: What does your company have to offer, and who will want to buy it? Wherever in the world you plan to sell your products or services, good marketing and good segmentation are essential.

But a note of caution: moving out into overseas markets is notoriously risky, the road is a difficult one to navigate, and it is littered with the wrecks of those companies who have tried and failed. Even established names such as Marks & Spencer and Carrefour have flopped in overseas ventures. So, what steps should companies take to minimise risk when attempting to enter into foreign markets?

The effectiveness of market research, or lack of it, can make or break a foreign venture. The retail giant Tesco spent twenty years studying the US market before launching their highly successful Free & Easy supermarket chain on the west coast. Their research showed them, among other things, that while US consumers wanted better quality meat than UK consumers, they were less bothered by the selection of wines on offer. In contrast, their main UK rival Sainsbury's attempted to establish supermarket shopping in Egypt, where the concept was unknown, and was forced to pull out after just two years with losses of more than £100m.

Other major companies have likewise paid a heavy price for failing to take note of potentially important differences in consumer attitudes and behaviour. Sweden's IKEA, one of Europe's most successful home-improvement retailers, has experienced difficulties gaining acceptance in Asian countries. They found to their cost that the idea of having to assemble flat-packed furniture is not appreciated by customers who expect sales staff to deliver it to their homes.

Companies that hope to succeed in new and unfamiliar markets have to be prepared to immerse themselves in the local culture. Many companies fail in international business because they assume that what has worked well at home will work in the same way elsewhere. They have to realise that new consumers need time to get used to foreign brands, and may be reluctant to change from the products they know best. Adapting products to suit a completely different group of customers can avoid costly mistakes.

Even McDonald's, a company that is often regarded as one that has sought to impose its corporate culture across the world, has been careful to take local preferences into account. In India, for example, where cows are considered by many to be sacred animals, there is no beef on the McDonald's fast-food menu. In its place there are vegetarian products such as McAloo Tikki and Paneer Salsa McWrap.

In addition to this cultural diversity there is the challenge of dealing with very different business practices. Knowing the local rules, and being prepared to play by them, is as much a part of the preparation as profiling the market and the potential customers. What may be considered a normal way of doing things in some countries may be frowned upon in others, and lead to misunderstandings that can jeopardise success. For example, the use of bribes or 'sweeteners' to facilitate business deals is a common practice in some countries, but illegal in others. It is important to know when it is acceptable, or even permitted, to offer gifts or commission to foreign business contacts or intermediaries.

Local laws can be complex and mysterious. There is always the risky matter of late or defaulted payments, and in some cases copyright and patent laws are disregarded or non-existent. It is therefore vital to get expert advice from reliable lawyers in addition to building an infrastructure of trustworthy distributors, agencies and business partners. Without these strong relationships at local level, the chances of success are slim.

caution Vorsicht, **notoriously** altbekannt, **littered with wrecks** mit zugrunde gerichteten Geschäften übersät sein, **bothered by** (here) besorgt um, **flat-packed** im Flachgehäuse verpackt, **sought** (past form of 'seek') versucht, **to impose** aufdrängen, auferlegen **to immerse oneself in** sich hineinversetzen in, **sacred** heilig, **to jeopardise** aufs Spiel setzen, gefährden, **frowned on** nicht gerne gesehen, **'sweetener'** (coll.) Bestechung, **mysterious** schleierhaft, **disregarded** missachtet

b. List the companies that are referred to in the article. For each company, write a sentence suggesting what might have happened if it had / hadn't done market research.

Example: If Marks & Spencer and Carrefour had done market research, their overseas ventures might not have flopped.

2 Vocabulary

Complete the questions with words from the article. Then discuss possible answers to the questions.

1. In a s.................. study, what criteria can be used to divide potential customers into groups?
2. Is it a crime in your country to give a b.................. to a foreign public official? Is it i.................., or is it common p..................?
3. What happens in your country if a company is late in paying its invoices? How can companies m.................. the risk of d.................. payments?
4. McDonald's has t.................. note of local p.................. in India. Does this apply to your country, too?
5. Have you ever had to a.................. flat-packed f.................. yourself? Was it worth it?
6. What problems can occur if you export to a country where copyright and p.................. laws do not apply or are completely d..................?
7. In what situations might a firm decide to a.................. or modify a product to s.................. a different market?

3 Payment risk

A 2.14 **a. Phil Harvey is giving a talk on payment risks in international trade. Before you listen, decide where on the payment risk ladder you would put the four methods below. Then listen and check.**

letter of credit | open account | advance payment | bills for collection

Exporter:	Least secure	Less secure	More secure	Most secure
	....	....	....	....
Importer:	Most secure	More secure	Less secure	Least secure

A 2.14 **b. Listen again and complete the missing information from these notes taken during Phil's talk.**

Payment risks in international trade

Advance payment = the least .... for buyers.
Open account terms: Take out .... insurance in case the buyer goes bankrupt.

Bills for collection:

- Documents are sent .... the goods have been shipped.
- Some documents give title to the goods = the holder of documents .... the goods.
- Documents against payment (D/P): same as '.................. against documents'.
- Documents against .... (D/A): credit periods typically ...., ..., or .... days.
- Bill of exchange (B/E): Looks similar to a .... but functions more like an ....
- Importer confirms acceptance of B/E (i.e. promises to pay) by .... it.

Letter of credit:

- Shipping documents include: ....

Methods of payment:

- Avoid cheques because:
  - They might be dishonoured (i.e. they might '..................').
  - Cheques are inconvenient because:
    ....
    ....
    ....
- Better to use SWIFT (= ....).

C Language | Terms of trade

1 Expressions with 'trade'

a. Create compounds with 'trade'. Then use ten of them to fit the definitions below.

bilateral | multilateral | fair | free | visible | invisible | balance of | carousel | foreign	trade	agreement | surplus | deficit | mission | barrier | war | fair

1. ....: trade without restrictions or taxes on imports and exports
2. ....: a government restriction on trade
3. ....: a situation in which the value of a country's imports exceeds its exports
4. ....: trade that supports producers in developing countries
5. ....: a situation in which countries aggressively restrict each other's exports
6. ....: trade in services, capital and intellectual property
7. ....: difference between the value of exports and imports over a particular period
8. ....: arrangement between three or more countries to set special trading conditions
9. ....: complex form of VAT fraud involving traders in the EU
10. ....: a group of business people or officials who visit another country to promote trade

b. Write definitions for the remaining expressions.

2 Incoterms

Write the complete forms of the words where vowels are missing.

Incoterms – **I**nternational **C**ommercial **T**erms – are internationally RCGNSD *recognised* codes used in import and export TRNSCTNS .... They are used in QTNG .... prices to make clear who is RSPNSBL .... for the goods at each point of the TRNSPRT .... process. The Incoterms were first PBLSHD .... in 1936 by the NTRNTNL CHMBR .... of CMMRC .... (ICC) in Paris and have been RVSD .... several times. The CRRNT .... version, Incoterms 2000, CNSSTS .... of thirteen three-LTTR .... codes split into FR .... groups (Group E, Group F, Group C and Group D). The terms RNG .... from EXW, where the buyer has the most responsibility, to DDP, where the buyer has the LST .... responsibility.

› **Group E** has only one term: EXW (Ex Works). An Ex Works price carries the MXMM .... obligation for the buyer, who has to pay for the goods to be collected from the seller's premises, e.g. the FCTRY .... or WRHS ...., and who bears responsibility for any DMG .... after that.

› In **Group F**, the seller must deliver the goods to a carrier PPNTD .... by the buyer. FCA (Free Carrier) can be used with any MD .... of transport, but FAS (Free ALNGSD .... Ship) and FOB (Free on Board) are for maritime and inland WTRWY .... transport only. In the CS .... of FOB, the seller delivers the goods, cleared for XPRT ...., when they pass the ship's rail at the named port of SHPMNT ....

› **Group C** lists terms with the 'main CRRG .... paid'. A price quoted as $30,000 CIF Hamburg means that the seller delivers the goods on BRD .... a particular ship at the port of DPRTR ...., e.g. Cape Town, and pays the transport costs to the port of DSTNTN .... as well as the basic insurance WHL .... the goods are at sea. The buyer is responsible for transport and insurance after that. If a price is STTD .... CPT Heathrow, the seller can choose the carrier (in this case an ARLN ....), but has to send the goods to the carrier free of CHRG .... and pay the transport CSTS .... to the named DSTNTN .... However, the buyer is responsible for the goods once they have been DLVRD .... to the carrier.

› **Group D** terms refer to the RRVL .... of the goods. If a price is quoted $4,000 DDP Frankfurt Hbf, the seller is responsible for TRNSPRT .... costs and insurance until the goods RCH .... Frankfurt. The buyer pays to CLLCT .... the goods from the STTN .... and carries the risk of any DMGE .... after that.

Cand-y-Craft LTD.
10 Royal Arcade
Cardiff, CF10 1AE
Phone: #44 (0) 292 038 7438
www.candycraft.co.uk

Der Kleine Feine SchokoLaden
Stadtplatz 32
902 Klagenfurt Tamsweg
Austria

18 October ...

Your Order dated 16 October... for 300 boxes of 'Dandy Candy chocolate liqueurs'

Dear Mr Zehrer

Many thanks for your order, which arrived today. We are pleased to confirm the details as follows:

Article:	*300 boxes of 'Dandy Candy' hand-made chocolate liqueurs*
Payment terms:	*One third with order, one third on delivery and one third within 30 days of delivery, by bank transfer to our account at HSBC Bank, Cardiff*
Delivery terms:	*Within 14 days of receipt of order, DDP Vienna*
Mode of delivery:	*DHL/airfreight*
Packing:	*In special cardboard boxes, filled with polystyrene peanuts*
Unit price:	*20 euros per box, excluding VAT, postage and packing*
Total price:	*6300 euros DDP Vienna*

Please note that this order is subject to our General Conditions of Sale, a copy of which was sent to you with our offer dated 10 October 200... A pro forma invoice is enclosed with this order confirmation.

As stated in our offer, your order will be put in hand as soon as we receive confirmation of your first part-payment. The chocolates will be hand-made as specified, using high-quality organic chocolate and filled with Crème de Cassis from Dijon, France. We will do our best to ensure that the delivery is dispatched in time for the Christmas season.

We hope that the chocolates meet with your expectations and look forward to doing further business with you.

Yours sincerely,

David Beynon

Export Sales Department

Enclosure: Pro-forma invoice

3 Order confirmation

a. Put the events below into the right order, then read the letter above to check.

a. [ ] Der Kleine Feine SchokoLaden pays the first instalment (one third).
b. [ ] Der Kleine Feine Schokoladen pays the final instalment of 2100 euros.
c. [ ] Der Kleine Feine SchokoLaden sent an enquiry to Cand-y-Craft.
d. [ ] Cand-y-Craft sent an offer to Der Kleine Feine SchokoLaden.
e. [ ] Cand-y-Craft makes the chocolates and dispatches them to Austria.
f. [ ] Der Kleine Feine SchokoLaden receives the delivery and pays the next instalment.
g. [ ] Der Kleine Feine SchokoLaden placed an order with Cand-y-Craft.
h. [ ] Cand-y-Craft confirms the order and summarises the details.

b. Find phrases that can be substituted by the following:

1. which reached us
2. we would point out that
3. make every effort to
4. you are satisfied with our products
5. your order will be dealt with
6. are given notification of
7. as stipulated
8. we were delighted to receive

INFO

Order confirmations
If a supplier makes a **binding offer (firm offer)** and the customer accepts it, this amounts to a sales contract. If the supplier makes a **solicited offer** based on an **enquiry** and then sends an **order confirmation**, this is also a sales contract. In the case of an **order acknowledgement**, the supplier confirms receipt of the order, but not necessarily the terms. However, the terms confirmation and acknowledgement are often used interchangeably.

4 Contracts

a. Put in the key points that should be covered in a contract with an agent or distributor.

Marketing | Payment terms | Products | Territory | Confidentiality | Intellectual property | Commission | Pricing | Jurisdiction | Parties | Exclusivity | Period | After-sales care

The contract should cover:

- .... names and addresses of the businesses involved, and the nature of the relationship, e.g. agency or distributorship
- .... a description of your goods
- .... the geographic area within which the agent / distributor will sell your goods
- .... whether or not they have sole rights to sell your goods
- .... the price you will charge the distributor for your goods, or the price the agent will charge their customers
- .... the percentage of turnover the agent will receive
- .... when payments will be made, the currency, and the exchange rate
- .... how long the contract will be valid for (date when it comes into effect, termination date, and provisions for ending the agreement before that date)
- .... assurance that sensitive information about your business / products will be protected
- .... any rights the agent or distributor will have to use your business name, brand names, trademarks, etc.
- .... liability, insurance and warranties, and responsibility at each stage of the trading process
- .... promotional activities to support your products, and who will pay for them
- .... the country whose rules will apply to the contract

b. In response to a positive email (p. 165), Claire Spencer of Cand-y-Craft Ltd has started making notes for a phone call with Svenja Mendelsohn of Gourmet GmbH. In separate groups, prepare the phone call from either Claire's or Svenja's perspective, using the guide above to help you.

Parties:
Cand-y-Craft (manufacturer), Cardiff, Wales
Gourmet GmbH (distributor), Berlin, Germany

Goods:
Organic truffles (dark and milk chocolate), hand-made in UK, imported cocoa syrup, brand name 'Madagascar Grand Cru', Fair Trade label

c. Improvise the call between Claire and Svenja in which they discuss the terms of a possible distribution agreement. Make notes of any decisions.

d. Write the draft of a distribution agreement between Cand-y-Craft and Gourmet, based on your notes.

WORD BANK

International trade

Documentation: air waybill | bill of lading (B/L) | certificate of origin | commercial invoice | consignment note | consular invoice | customs declaration | export / import licence (AE license) | insurance policy / insurance certificate | packing list | 'red tape' | Single Administrative Document

Payment and delivery terms: bank guarantee | bill of exchange (B/E) | carriage paid to (CPT) | cash against documents | cash on delivery (COD) | cash with order (CWO) | cost, insurance and freight (CIF) | currency | customs duty | delivered ex ship / quay (DES/DEQ) | delivered, duty paid (DDP) | letter of credit | ex works (EXW) | exchange rate | free alongside ship (FAS) | free on board (FOB) | irrevocable and confirmed documentary letter of credit

Shipping: cargo | bonded warehouse | commodities | consignee | consignment | consignor | country of destination | port of destination | port of shipment | docks | forwarding agency | freight forwarder | haulier | merchandise | marine insurance | shipment | shipper

Trade issues: customs clearance | dumping | export ban / embargo | exchange controls | grey market | import restriction | non-tariff barrier (NTB) | parallel import | protectionism | trade barrier | quota | subsidy | tariff

D Business leaders | Harriet Lamb

1 Reading

a. Before you read: Discuss why people buy fair trade products.

b. Skim the article and explain how the title 'Banana Wars and other Battles' refers to the content.

c. Read the article in more detail and make notes under the following headings:

Harriet Lamb's background | her beliefs | her achievements | criticisms of fair trade

Harriet Lamb lived in India as a child and was later privately educated in the UK. After completing her university studies in political science and international development, she returned to India and helped poor farmers to form co-operatives to sell their produce. This experience, plus her work in other developing countries, led to the establishment of the Fairtrade Foundation. She has been Managing Director of the Foundation since 2001.

Banana Wars and other Battles

Harriet Lamb first became involved with the movement in 1997, when she was appointed to the oddly-named job of Banana Co-ordinator for the Fairtrade Labelling Organisation (FLO) in Bonn, the body that sets global Fairtrade standards and co-ordinates certification. This was just after she had visited Costa Rica, to find out about the lives of the workers who grew the bananas that were sold in British shops. As she later wrote in her book *Fighting the Banana Wars*, it was there that she met Maria, a woman whose husband worked on the banana plantations using the pesticide DBCP, a chemical considered so hazardous that its use had been banned in the USA. Maria had given birth to a baby with horrifying abnormalities as a result of contamination that her husband had absorbed, and it was later discovered that more than 3,500 Costa Rican children had suffered the same fate.

Harriet returned to the UK more than ever determined to fight for the cause of small producers facing lives of poverty because of the domination of the big multinational producers. She never forgot the plight of Maria and her severely deformed baby.

One of the steps that Fairtrade took was to call for a ban on the 'Dirty Dozen' – the twelve most harmful chemicals that were being used routinely in developing countries and creating health risks for workers and their families. The battle to provide growers with an alternative to doing business with big companies was long and hard, but gradually there has been a change in public opinion towards Fairtrade. Initially, only a few basic items were available, and only a few well-meaning people had heard of the scheme, but momentum has grown and now more than 3 000 products have received Fairtrade certification and are sold in 23 countries.

Producers are guaranteed a minimum price for their goods, plus a five per cent premium that allows them to invest in machinery, transport, education, and whatever else they need to improve their standard of living. According to Harriet Lamb, this results in progress, happiness, fewer economic refugees, and perhaps even fewer wars because people feel more settled and have more investment in the land. A recent success has been the certification of a coffee plantation in Rwanda, a country previously ravaged by civil war, which has led to a boost to the living standards of villagers – clean water, a transport system and primary schools.

Some critics of the scheme, especially those who promote purely organic produce, have pointed out that Fairtrade is less concerned with environmental issues than with social justice in developing countries. Harriet Lamb would agree on that point. She has often stated that her priority is poor and disempowered people. She has taken a firm stand against child labour, and has even likened Fairtrade to the campaign to abolish slavery.

There are other naysayers who point out that fair trade is anti free trade, creating artificially high prices and committing producers to low-tech 'peasant farming' that concentrates on cash crops. Lamb responds to this by pointing out that the much-vaunted claim that free trade creates a 'level playing field' is a distorted one, since rich countries such as the USA spend millions in supporting their own growers.

fate Schicksal, **plight** Misere, **to liken** vergleichen, **naysayer** Neinsager, **vaunted** gerühmt, **distorted** verzerrt

2 Discussion

What does Harriet Lamb say in response to her critics? Do you agree with her views?

3 Vocabulary

Explain what you understand by the terms 'economic refugee' and 'level playing field'.

E Business communication | Negotiating

1 Discussion

a. You are going to take part in an international sales negotiation. Decide where it should take place.

- on the exporter's premises
- on the importer's premises
- at a 'neutral' location, e.g. an airport hotel
- at a location suggested by the 'stronger' party

b. When you first meet, how much time should you allow for 'small talk' before the negotiations start?

- Less than five minutes
- Up to fifteen minutes
- More than fifteen minutes
- Depends on who is negotiating

2 Scenario

a. Read the following company profiles. Discuss what you think the negotiation will be about.

Ambiance Hotels Group GmbH

Ambiance Hotels Group GmbH runs a chain of small and exclusive 'wellness' hotels in beautiful and famous European locations such as Baden Baden, Lake Constance and the Austrian Tyrol. Each of the superior four-star hotels is managed with a very personal touch, inspired by a health and wellbeing philosophy that places the guests and their needs at the very centre. The most striking feature of the hotels is the individual wellness rooms, famous for their ingenious light effects and natural ambiance, complete with shower, treatment couch, massage bed and whirlpool. There is a wide range of treatment and therapy for the face and body, using international cosmetic brands. The **Ambiance** policy is to use only the purest organic cosmetics, sourced from their country of origin.

Rosella Bay Pty Ltd

Rosella Bay Pty Ltd is one of Australia's leading producers of premium-grade natural cosmetics. The company is located in the beautiful surroundings of the New England National Park in the mountains of New South Wales, an area rich in unique wildlife and plants. Rosella Bay is well known throughout Australia as a company that has promoted organic products and championed the rights of Aboriginal people. Their production processes combine advanced 'green' technology with the knowledge of local Aboriginal tribes who, throughout their long history in the region, have developed a wealth of traditional medicines and healing. The company is embarking on an international marketing strategy for their natural beauty products, aimed at breaking into the European 'wellness' industry.

b. Before you start the negotiation, study the phrases on the right. Decide which ones would be said by either the buyer of the seller.

c. Organise yourselves into groups of four. In each group, one pair represents Ambiance GmbH (buyers) and the other pair Rosella Bay Pty Ltd (sellers). Read the product descriptions on the next page and further information for your negotiation (Ambiance on page 222, Rosella Bay on page 223).

PHRASES

Negotiating a trade deal

- Do these products comply with international standards?
- Can you provide the necessary certification?
- All our products are subjected to a rigorous quality check.
- None of our products have been tested on animals.
- We'd like to look at some samples before committing ourselves.
- Can we talk about the packaging?
- Can you give us some idea of the price?
- What figure did you have in mind?
- I don't have detailed figures with me right now, but …
- Can we come on to the price in a minute?
- That seems rather more than we had in mind.
- Are you prepared to offer us a discount?
- How soon could we expect the first consignment?
- We will let you know as soon as the goods are dispatched.
- We need to talk about the packing.
- All the goods will be packed in bubble-wrap.
- How will the goods be transported?
- Who will carry the cost of the shipping?

Rosella Bay™ Tea Tree Oil
– natural beauty products from Australia

The leaves of the tea tree have traditionally been used by the Aborigine people of Eastern Australia as a source of natural healing powers. Long recognised for its medicinal properties, the pure essential oil of the tea tree is now available in a range of natural, organic cosmetics. All our Rosella Bay™ Tea Tree Oil products are produced to the required international standard (ISO 4730 – 2004) and are certified 100% organic.

Tea Tree Oil – Deep Soak Duo (33 oz)
Price: to be negotiated

The pre-blended tea tree oil formulation comes as a bath oil (Green) and as a massage oil (Blue) for a complete soothing experience. Add six drops of the bath oil into the bath once it has run. For the perfect treatment of tired muscles or feet, simply warm six drops of the massage oil in the palms of the hands and apply.

Tea Tree Oil – Superstar Shampoo (45 oz)
Price: to be negotiated

The unique, custom-made tea tree oil shampoo not only cleans the hair and adds lustre, but also protects the scalp and promotes healthy circulation. The power of tea tree oil gives your hair back its natural sheen and thickness and adds a refreshing fragrance. The shampoo comes in a polished aluminium pump dispenser.

Tea Tree Oil – Aromatic Balm (20 oz)
Price: to be negotiated

The delicious cool balm is a blend of tea tree oil with peppermint and jojoba oils that leaves your skin feeling fresh and tingling. Ideal for rashes and skin irritations, including dry skin and sunburn. Nature's gentle healing oils will give you a glowing skin and protect against bacterial infections.

essential oil ätherisches Öl, **soothing** lindernd, wohltuend, **palm** (of the hand) Handfläche, **scalp** Kopfhaut, **lustre** Glanz, **sheen** Glanz, **fragrance** Duft, **dispenser** Spender, **balm** Balsam, **tingling** angenehm prickelnd, **rash** Hautausschlag

d. Follow-up: Write a summary of the outcome of your meeting. Compare your results in class to see which was the toughest or most skilful negotiating team.

SKILLS

Feedback

When you do a simulation, it is useful to have another student present in the role of observer and consultant. Tell the observer beforehand what you would like feedback on. This could be general or specific. General feedback could focus on your overall communication skills, or whether the group has achieved its goals. Examples of specific feedback include your ability to deal with interruptions, show active listening or ask for clarification. Alternatively, you could ask the observer to look for three good points and three things that need improving.

F Consulting | Trade diplomacy

1 Quiz

Have you got what it takes to be a trade negotiator? Put yourself into the shoes of a diplomat in this quiz. Then check the solutions on the next page.

QUIZ Beat the world trade system

Scenario 1: You are ambassador to the World Trade Organization in Geneva. You represent the Republic of Bajaria, a small West African state which mainly exports cotton and cocoa. The rich and powerful Eurasian Union is putting Bajarian farmers out of work by its own agricultural subsidies and tariffs. Which of the following tactics should you try in order to create change?

QUESTION 1 Should you threaten to veto the current Doha Development Round if the Eurasian Union does not reduce its farm subsidies and tariffs?

A Yes B No

QUESTION 2 Should you create an alliance with other poor agricultural exporting countries and formulate a common negotiating position?

A Yes B No

QUESTION 3 Should you launch a case against the Eurasian Union through the WTO's Dispute Settlement Mechanism – its international court?

A Yes B No

QUESTION 4 Should you sign a bilateral free trade deal with the Eurasian Union?

A Yes B No

QUESTION 5 Should you put more money into training and staffing your Geneva operations?

A Yes B No

QUESTION 6 Should you launch a publicity campaign with Eurasian NGOs to highlight the unfairness of the situation?

A Yes B No

Scenario 2: You are ambassador to the World Trade Organization in Geneva. You represent the Eurasian Union, one of the most powerful economies on the planet. You want to gain access to developing world markets for your high-tech manufactured goods. But some pesky poor countries like the Republic of Bajaria are kicking up a fuss. How are you going to get what you want?

QUESTION 1 Should you invite the Bajarians to sign a bilateral free trade deal?

A Yes B No

QUESTION 2 Should you widen the discussion to issues of bilateral co-operation, especially development aid?

A Yes B No

QUESTION 3 Should you flood a ministerial meeting with your top negotiators?

A Yes B No

QUESTION 4 Should you quietly agree a memorandum of understanding with your chief rival, the rich United Regions of Neworldia?

A Yes B No

QUESTION 5 Should you get the president of Eurasia to call the Bajarian PM?

A Yes B No

QUESTION 6 Should you carefully distribute some "plants" – papers which apparently contain secret details of the Eurasian negotiating position?

A Yes B No

ambassador Botschafter(in), Repräsentant(in), **pesky** lästig, **to kick up a fuss** ein Theater machen, **memorandum of understanding** Vorvertrag, Absichtserklärung

Solutions

Scenario 1

1B Although every country at the WTO has veto power, exercising this right could turn your allies against you.

2A The WTO respects strength in numbers and if you can co-ordinate with countries with similar interests, it will be difficult for Eurasia to play divide and rule. The only countries that can go it alone with the WTO are those with huge markets which they can use as leverage in negotiations.

3B It would cost at least $500,000 to bring the case and could take a couple of years to conclusion. The only enforcement mechanism is retaliation – and how can you retaliate against the Eurasian market?

4B In any two-way negotiations, the Eurasions will have the upper hand. You'll just have to accept whatever terms are presented and those terms could be harder for you than WTO deals.

5A Many developing countries are outflanked at the WTO simply because they can't get to all the meetings and don't have the expertise to understand what's going on. More money spent here could pay off in the long term. Saving money could be a false economy.

6A If you can sway public opinion among ordinary Eurasian voters, this can act as a powerful counterweight to the Eurasian agricultural lobby. It will certainly keep their trade representatives on their toes.

Scenario 2

1A You can give the Bajarians the same pro-forma deal as you offer all the other developing countries. They'll have to take it or leave it. It will, of course, include clauses ensuring they slash tariffs on your manufactured goods. If not, you'll have to work through the WTO and that could mean facing up to powerful alliances of developing nations.

2A If you start hinting at cuts to aid, the Bajarians might get a fright and come into line. But make sure nothing gets to the press or to NGOs.

3A You can extend the negotiations around the clock, replacing each team of negotiators with another. The Bajarians and other poor countries won't be able to compete. They'll be so exhausted that in the end they'll sign anything.

4B Secret deals have gone out of fashion. It was exactly this kind of agreement that united the developing world in opposition at the Cancun meeting in 2003.

5A Few developing countries can resist pressure from the person at the top of your political tree. And the Bajarian PM is unlikely to imperil the whole bilateral relationship over just one issue.

6A Such papers are likely to be copied and read avidly by your opponents. They will think they know your bottom line – and they will be wrong.

to imperil gefährden, **to hint at** anspielen auf, andeuten, **avidly** begierig

2 Negotiating idioms

Complete the sentences with idioms from the quiz.

1. A large group is stronger than a small one. – There's ....
2. You can put pressure on them that way. – You can use that as ....
3. They're trying to weaken us by making us oppose each other. – They're playing ....
4. We've got the advantage over them. – We've got the ....
5. We got them into a position where we could defeat them. – We've managed to .... them.
6. What will you say to make people change their minds? How will you ....?
7. They won't be able to rest. – It'll keep them ....
8. That's the lowest we'll go in the negotiation. That's our ....

3 Research

Find out more about the WTO. What are the main issues that it deals with, and how effective do you think it has been?

Unit 14
Legislation

Online Link
800021-0014

A Introduction | The scope of company law

1 Listening

A 2.15–19 **a.** Listen to five phone messages for Gavin Mellor, head of the Legal Department at Port Vale Engineering Ltd. Four of the messages are from colleagues who work in other departments. For each caller, note down the legal issue that needs to be clarified.

Sally Beaumont | Justin Fisher | Ben Norris | Ahmed Dotani | Trudy Knight

b. Who is the caller from the Department for Environment, Food and Rural Affairs?

c. Suggest what departments Gavin's colleagues work for.

d. Write Gavin's 'to do' list, based on the phone messages.

2 Reading

a. Explain in your own words why Gavin Mellor wrote this email, and what he wants his colleagues to do.

Dear colleagues,
As you know, many aspects of business are becoming increasingly regulated, and non-compliance with the law can have serious consequences for Port Vale Engineering and for you personally.
You may not be aware that you are breaking a code or regulation, but ignorance of the law is no defence. Therefore it is vital that you understand the legal issues affecting your department and that you keep abreast of new legislation.
The Legal Department can support you in many ways, for example by answering your queries on a day-to-day basis. However, you also have a certain level of responsibility to ensure that you act within the law. Therefore we are holding a series of workshops to help you brush up on your knowledge of legal matters.
We strongly recommend that you attend these workshops, details of which are attached, and look forward to seeing you there.
Yours sincerely, Gavin Mellor

keep abreast of Schritt halten mit, der Entwicklung Rechnung tragen

FROM RED TAPE TO BLUE SKIES – WORKSHOPS FOR NON-LAWYERS

These workshops will be presented by experts in corporate legislation and are open to all members of staff.

Workshop A **Better Late Than Never** Monday, 21 July, 9:00–16:30

Late payment by customers is a perennial problem – so what can companies do to speed up the process? This workshop gives practical tips on how to ensure that customers pay on time, as well as providing an update on all matters concerning legislation on debt and insolvency. You will learn how to:

- Agree a credit period with customers, and put it in writing.
- Exercise discretion when sending reminders of late payment.
- Calculate interest on late payments, according to statutory rights.
- Take court action to recover debts.

Workshop B **Marketing and the Law** Tuesday, 22 July, 9:00–16:30

This workshop will help you to make sense of an evolving legal regulatory environment, so that you stay on the right side of the law and avoid making mistakes that could cost Port Vale Engineering millions! You will learn how to:

- Understand the common law aspects of the English legal system, such as contracts, copyrights and patents.
- Work within the laws on privacy and data protection.
- Understand the ASA codes and the rules that govern comparative advertising and misleading advertising.
- Identify applicable EU laws and understand what they mean to you.

Workshop C **Industrial Relations: Best practice** Wednesday, 23 July, 9:00–16:30

It is essential to maintain good working relations with staff and trade unions, and a thorough knowledge of the law can help to avoid industrial disputes. This workshop offers practical guidelines on legislation to all those involved in human resources management, with particular reference to employment law. You will learn how to:

- Draw up legally accurate job descriptions and written contracts.
- Manage the process of collective bargaining and wage claims.
- Deal openly and fairly with unfair dismissal claims brought by employees.
- Carry out redundancy consultation with employees and union representatives.

Workshop D **Consumer Rights and You** Thursday, 24 July, 9:00–16:30

This workshop will give you an overview of competition and consumer protection laws that affect your department. Using a case-study approach, we will look at the rules governing how you compete, how you treat your customers, and how you sell. You will learn how to:

- Understand competition law and anti-competitive behaviour.
- Work within laws and regulations that protect consumers from unfair commercial practices.
- Formulate contracts in plain English, and avoid 'legalese'.

All workshops will take place in Room 4 of the Training Zone, 'F' Block (first floor).
Please register by contacting Gavin Mellor at g.mellor@portvale.co.uk, stating your name and department.

b. Decide which workshops would be suitable for the staff members who left a message for Gavin.

c. For each of the topics listed under 'You will learn how to', indicate their relevance to you now or in the future. Then compare what you have noted and discuss any differences.

✔✔ (very important) ✔ (quite important)
✘ (not important / relevant) ? (not sure)

d. Create a mind map of company departments, with examples of legal issues that may affect them.

3 Translating

Find out the meaning of *'höhere Gewalt'* and the equivalent terms used in contracts that are written in English. Explain the differences in interpretation with reference to the legal systems involved.

INFO

Commercial codes

Many countries, especially in Europe, use a legal system based on **civil law** (sometimes called **Roman** or **code law**) in which laws are recorded in large written documents, for example the German *Handelsgesetzbuch* (HGB).
England has no commercial code. Its legal system is based on the **common law** system, where laws have been developed from customs and from decisions made by judges, not created by Parliament. Many laws are therefore 'unwritten'. The US legal system is based on common law, but the *Uniform Commercial Code* regulates business.

B Business Briefing | Litigation

1 Discussion

a. Describe the different methods used in shaving and their relative merits.

b. Suggest possible reasons why razor manufacturers might become involved in litigation.

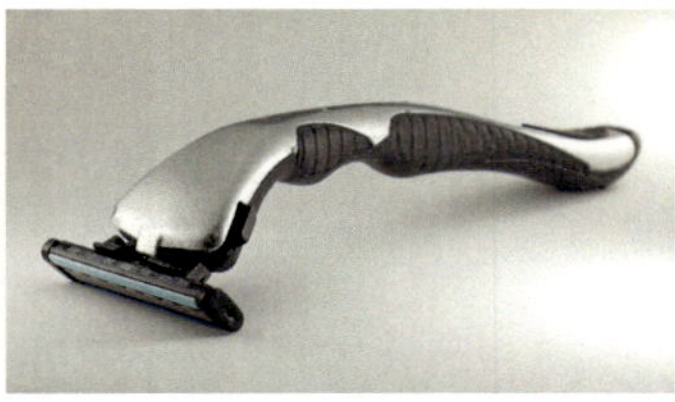

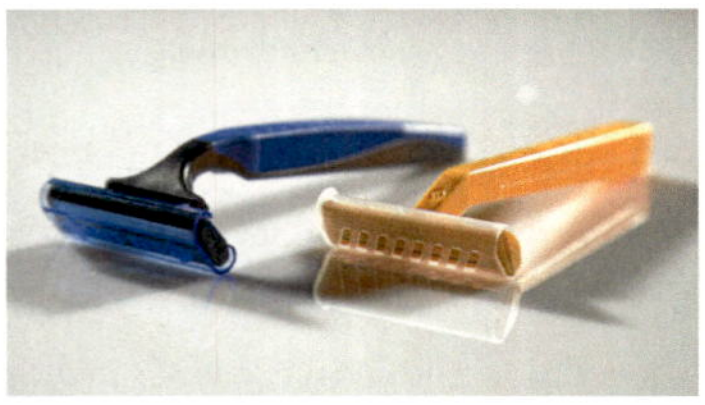

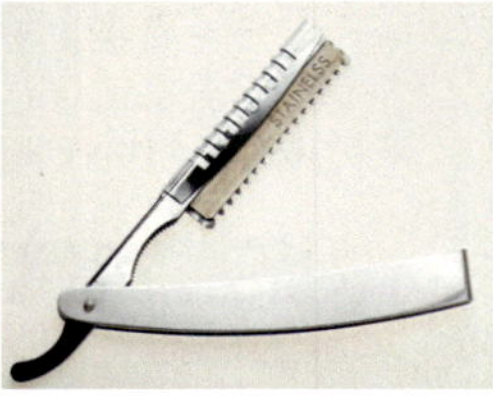

2 Reading

a. Collect expressions in the article that refer to conflict and litigation. List them under separate headings.

The Razor Wars

Gillette and Wilkinson Sword, the leaders of the global $6 billion wet-shaving equipment market, have a long history of fighting legal battles. The two brands currently enjoy a virtual duopoly of the market, although Gillette is now part of the Proctor & Gamble group, and Wilkinson Sword, sold under the Schick brand in the United States, is owned by the battery company Energizer Holdings. As in any business sector dominated by two big players, rivalry is strong.

The 'razor wars' began in earnest in 1989 when Gillette launched the *Sensor* range in 1989, the first razor with twin blades mounted on springs that 'continuously sense and automatically adjust to the face'. Wilkinson Sword hit back in 1992 with its 'intelligently designed' *Protector* razor. Gillette then unveiled the three-blade *Mach3*, but immediately faced competition from Wilkinson Sword's own innovative three-blade razor. With such cut-throat competition for market supremacy, they began to resort to litigation in an attempt to spoil each other's chances.

In August 2003 Wilkinson Sword announced plans to introduce the first four-bladed razor, *Quattro*. Just hours after the announcement, Gillette filed a patent infringement lawsuit against Energizer Holdings, charging that the *Quattro* razor illegally incorporated the blade technology of the three-bladed Gillette *Mach3* system. The court in Massachusetts rejected the charges, and when *Quattro* went on sale in September, it instantly gained market share.

It was not long before the two companies were doing battle in the European courts. In May 2004 Gillette released the battery-operated *M3Power* with an expensive advertising campaign featuring David Beckham. In November, the District Court of Hamburg granted a legal injunction against Gillette, in favour of Wilkinson Sword. In the *M3Power* advertising campaign, Gillette claimed that the new *M3Power* wet shaver used 'electrical micro-pulses' and guaranteed a closer shave than any other wet shaver. Wilkinson Sword presented test results showing there was 'no visible nor noticeable advantage' to the consumer. The court then ruled that Gillette's superiority claim was unsubstantiated and therefore misleading, and ordered Gillette to withdraw its advertising campaign.

In the same year, Wilkinson Sword went on to file a similar lawsuit in the Netherlands, whereupon Gillette responded with a countersuit attacking Wilkinson's Dutch ads for the *Quattro* shaver, which claimed that 'Independent tests and consumer research have shown that no other shaving system shaves smoother and softer than Quattro.' The judge decided to allow both ads to run, on the grounds that they would not necessarily be believed. He stated in his ruling that the buying public had become practically immune to claims of superiority used in advertising.

In December, in a massive €20 million patent dispute between Gillette and Wilkinson Sword, the District Court in Düsseldorf ruled that Gillette's European patents for the *Mach3* were not infringed by Wilkinson's four-bladed *Quattro* shaver. Gillette's lawyers argued that Gillette's three-blade patent also covers shavers with four blades, because the shaver makes use of the three-step solution patented by Gillette. Wilkinson contended that the Gillette patent was restricted to a three-blade shaver only, and proved that the fourth blade of the *Quattro* shaver uses a different technique than Gillette's *Mach3*. The judge agreed, and dismissed Gillette's claim for damages.

In September 2005, Gillette introduced the *Fusion* shaver, the first five-bladed wet shaver. However, the claim that 'the more blades on a razor, the smoother the shave' suffered a setback in Germany when Stiftung Warentest, an independent research institute, published findings that every additional blade increases the danger of skin injuries.

The duopoly is under threat from a newcomer, the UK's King of Shaves, which markets its *Azor* brand with the slogan 'Better because it bends'. It remains to be seen whether the giants will find an excuse to sue the King of Shaves, and what the verdict of the public will be.

blade Klinge, **to unveil** enthüllen, **to hand down a decision** ein Urteil sprechen, **to resort to** auf etwas zurückgreifen

b. Work with a partner. Using the words you listed as prompts, try to recount the 'razor wars' from memory. Then refer back to the article to check the details.

c. Answer the following questions.

1. Which of the two companies has won more battles?
2. What product claims were shown to be false or misleading, and what arguments were given in court?
3. What claim does King of Shaves make about *Azor*? How might it be challenged in court?
4. Which courts discussed Gillette's product claims? Why do you think different jurisdictions were involved?
5. Explain what is meant by the statement "the two brands enjoy a virtual duopoly".

d. Suggest different ways to complete the following statements.

1. Even though Wilkinson has only 20% of the world market, …
2. Smaller companies tend to be at a disadvantage in legal battles because …
3. Since razor blades are a popular target for shoplifters, many retailers have decided to …

e. Find words in the article that fit the following definitions:

1. l _ t _ _ _ _ _ _ n: the process of making or defending a claim in court
2. _ _ d _ _: public official appointed to decide cases in court
3. to _ _ _: to take legal action against someone or an organisation
4. i _ f _ _ _ g _ m _ _ t: the breaking of a law or rule
5. _ a w _ _ _ t: a complaint or claim made against sb. through the courts
6. v _ _ _ _ _ _: a decision or ruling made in a dispute
7. i n _ _ _ _ _ _ _ n: an official court order demanding that something must or must not be done
8. u n _ _ b _ _ _ _ _ _ _ a _ _ d: not supported by evidence

3 Lawsuits

a. Put the parts of the article in the right order.

The Stella Awards

[ ] A. increase as the recession drives people to more inventive moneymaking methods. California lawyer Jim Fedalen warned: "You'd be amazed at the companies who will shell out thousands, even when they

[ ] B. Washington lawyer who is suing the dry cleaners who lost his trousers for $65 million (£45m) on the basis of "mental suffering, inconvenience and discomfort" and the woman who threw her drink at her

[ ] C. suspect they're being conned, to avoid the adverse publicity of a court case. Juries tend to side with the plaintiffs, and damages they sometimes award are in the realms of the ridiculous."

[ ] D. The Stella awards take a light-hearted look at the civil litigation industry that now costs more than $247 billion (£172bn) a year – the equivalent of $825 (£574) per person in the US. They are named after

[ ] E. Stella Liebeck of Albuquerque, New Mexico, who successfully sued McDonald's for $2.86 million (£2m) in 1992 after burning herself on coffee that was "too hot". Among the cases featured in 2008 was the

[ ] F. boyfriend in a Philadelphia restaurant then slipped on the spilt liquid, broke her tailbone and successfully sued for $113,500 (£79,000). Lawyers are now warning that the number of frivolous lawsuits could even

From: *The Daily Telegraph*, February 2009

to shell out blechen, **discomfort** Unbehagen, **to con** betrügen, **tailbone** Steißbein, **frivolous** (hier) unbegründet, schickanös

b. What adjectives are used to describe the lawsuits? What other adjectives could you use?

c. What explanations are given for the rise in litigation, and the extent of damages awarded?

d. Compare the situation in the US with that of your own country.

e. Find out the winners of this year's Stella Awards.

C Language | Legal English

1 Contracts

a. What should you always do before you enter into a contract? List some 'dos and don'ts'.

b. Give an example of a contract you signed recently, e.g. to join a gym or to get a credit card.

c. Say which of the tips you did not follow before signing the contract, and explain why.

10 things to remember before you sign a contract
Once you enter into a contract, you are bound by its terms. Here are some things to bear in mind before putting your name on the dotted line.

1. Shop around: Find out what other companies offer in terms of price, duration of contract, etc.
2. Know who you're dealing with. Is the company trustworthy? Does it have a sound reputation?
3. Make sure you have read and understood every part of the contract, including the small print.
4. Pay attention to details: Go through the wording with a fine-tooth comb. Check any discrepancies.
5. Imagine worst case scenarios. Ask yourself 'What if?' questions and look for answers in the contract.
6. Delete elements you don't want to sign for, or ask the company to delete them.
7. Don't leave anything out. Fill in the blank or draw a line through it so that nobody else adds details later.
8. If the contract is written in legalese or gobbledegook, have a lawyer look through it for you.
9. Sleep on it, and remember that some terms are negotiable. If you have any reservations, don't sign.
10. Don't forget to keep a signed copy of the contract.

d. Find the English equivalents of the following expressions:

1. *beachten, berücksichtigen* ....
2. *sich umsehen und Angebote vergleichen* ....
3. *etwas genau unter die Lupe nehmen* ....
4. *Juristenjargon* ....
5. *Kauderwelsch* ....
6. *Bedenken* ....

e. What kind of contracts do people enter into on the Internet? Compare the process with signing a print contract, e.g. to rent property. Which process do you think is easier, and which carries greater risk?

f. Start your own word bank of language to do with contracts. Copy the grid below and add further examples as you go through this unit.

Making	Changing	Complying	Breaking	Ending
to sign to draw up to …	to revise to extend to …	to comply with to observe to …	to break (to be in breach of) to …	to end to …

LANGUAGE TIP

Legal English
Legal English comes in a variety of forms, depending on its different roles. It is used in legal documents such as contracts and insurance policies. It is also the rhetorical language of the courtroom, used by lawyers to defend their clients and by judges to give verdicts. Legal English that seems unnecessarily confusing is often described as 'legalese'. Standard legal English has certain features in common:

- a need to be clear and precise, in order to leave no room for misinterpretation
- a respect for tradition, e.g. in the use of phrases derived from Latin / French (*alibi, caveat emptor, decree nisi*)
- specific modal verbs that distinguish between obligation and discretion (*must, shall / will, may* …)
- specific modal substitutes (*be obliged to, to undertake to, to be entitled to, to be permitted to,* …)
- everyday words used in a special context (*to find someone guilty, to furnish proof*)
- words that help to avoid repetition, but are no longer used in standard English (*herein, thereof, hereinafter,* …)
- terms that may not be familiar to non-experts (*estoppel, rescission, irrevocable, waiver,* …)
- pairs of words with similar meanings (*will and testament, full and final, null and void, terms and conditions,* …)

2 Understanding the small print

a. JoyNup is a new social networking website. Read the terms below, looking up any new vocabulary. Highlight phrases referring to what members must or must not do. Explain them in your own words.

Terms and Conditions of Use

***JoyNup*.com** is a professional networking service that provides users with a platform on which to contact and share information with other users. By registering with **JoyNup**, you acknowledge that you have read and understood the following Terms and Conditions of Use Agreement (hereinafter the 'Agreement') and that you accept all provisions contained therein.

1. **Our rights:** By concluding this Agreement, you grant us a perpetual, unlimited, nonexclusive, irrevocable, worldwide and royalty-free right to us to copy, distribute, publish, improve, remove, retain, add, and commercialize anything that you submit to us, without any obligation on us to compensate you. You further agree to notify us in the event that any such information has changed since your registration with **JoyNup**, and, if appropriate, modify your profile accordingly. We have the right, but not the obligation, to remove content that we deem in our sole discretion to be unlawful, libellous, defamatory, obscene or otherwise objectionable or that violates the intellectual property of any third party. Under no circumstances shall **JoyNup** be held liable for any damages or claims resulting thereof.
2. **Your obligations:** When you register you will be required to choose a password. You are solely responsible for maintaining the confidentiality of your password, and are entirely responsible for the use of your password. **JoyNup** assumes no liability for identity theft.
3. **Privacy:** We value and respect your privacy. Information will only be collected in order to improve our services to you and the product offers of our third-party affiliates. We may disclose information provided by you to companies that work with us and assist us by providing services to you.
4. **Eligibility:** The services provided by **JoyNup** are intended solely for persons of legal age. By using the **JoyNup** services, you represent and warrant that you are 18 years old or older, that all the registration information you submit is accurate, and that you will maintain the accuracy of that information.
5. **Termination:** You are permitted to terminate your membership for any or no cause, at any time, with notice to **JoyNup**, effective upon **JoyNup** processing such notice. Notice of termination is to be given using the contact form available on the **JoyNup** website. We reserve the right to revoke your membership at any time in the event that you break any terms of this agreement. Upon termination, you lose access to all **JoyNup** services. The terms of this agreement shall survive any termination, with the exceptions of Sections 2 and 3.

☐ Yes, I have read the Agreement and agree to be bound by all of the above-mentioned provisions. I have saved and/or printed out a copy of the Agreement.

b. The text below is a 'plain English' draft of the agreement. Put in the modal verbs.

must | don't have to | may | mustn't | cannot

You .... read this Terms of Use agreement ('Agreement') before registering. If there is anything you don't understand or agree with, then you .... register.
We .... reproduce or sell any information you give us (your 'content') for as long as we like and wherever we like, but we .... prevent you from posting the same content elsewhere. If we sell your content, we .... pay you. If we think it is illegal or problematic in any way, we .... change or remove that content, but we ....
You .... be at least 18 to join. You .... give us a password, and you .... give it to anyone else. If someone gets hold of it and uses it in a way that harms you, or if someone sues you, we .... be held liable.
If you break this Agreement, we .... cancel your membership at any time. If you want to cancel your membership, you .... do so at any time. You .... give a reason. You .... let us know by using our contact form. Once your membership ends, you .... use our services. You .... always keep the information you give us accurate and up-to-date, even after your membership ends. You .... also keep a copy of the Agreement.
☐ Yes, I accept the Agreement and have kept a copy.

c. Would you agree to these terms? Discuss the risks involved, and whether they are worth taking.

d. Compare the agreements above with that of a social networking website popular in your country.

3 Plain English

a. Match the words on the left with the equivalents recommended by the Plain English Society. (Change the word form if necessary). Then complete the sentences below with the 'plain English' words.

complete | advise | prior to | ensure | forward | in excess of | commence | purchasing | particulars | additional | persons | should you wish | on request | terminate | per annum	make sure | details | if you want | tell | before | fill in | extra | a year | send | people | end | more than | start | buying | if you ask

1. We require ………………………… information from you.
2. We reserve the right to ………………………… the agreement.
3. A public inquiry is due to ………………………… on the 16th.
4. Please ………………………… us ………………………… to have a receipt.
5. Please ………………………… the attached form, listing the names of ………………………… who will be travelling with you.
6. His salary is ………………………… €300,000 ………………………… .
7. Please ………………………… that the ………………………… are accurate and up-to-date.
8. ………………………… to test the product ………………………… …………………………, samples can be ………………………… to you ………………………… .

b. What do you think of 'plain English'? Does it make English clearer or less clear for you?

4 Contingencies and precautions

a. Complete the EU leaflet with *unless, if, only if, or in the case / event of,* but not *in case* (see tip below).

AIR PASSENGER RIGHTS

LONG DELAYS

- You may request a refund of your ticket ……… the delay exceeds five hours, but ……… you decide not to travel.

ASSISTANCE BY AIRLINES

- ……… you are denied boarding or your flight is cancelled or delayed, you may be entitled to receive assistance.
- ……… a cancellation or a denied boarding, you may be offered the option of continuing your trip or a refund of your ticket.

CANCELLATION

- Financial compensation is due ……… you were informed 14 days before the flight, or you were rerouted close to your original times, or the airline can prove that the cancellation was caused by extraordinary circumstances.

PACKAGE HOLIDAYS

- Package tour operators must give accurate information on the holiday booked, comply with contractual obligations, and protect passengers ……… the organiser's insolvency.

This poster is for information purposes only. Any legal claim or action taken ……… a dispute should be based solely on the legal texts concerned.

www.cph.dk

b. How could a travel agent persuade people to take out travel insurance? Give reasons using 'in case'.

"You should take out travel insurance **in case** …"

LANGUAGE TIP

in case / in the case of / if

- Use *in case* to explain a precaution:
  An alarm system has been installed in case there's a break-in. (or: *because there might be a break-in*)
- Use *in the case of* (or: *in the event of*) in the sense of *if*:
  The police will be notified in the case of a break-in. (or: *if there is a break-in*)
- Use *if* in everyday English. It sounds more natural than *in the case of* or *in the event of.*
  in the case of an earthquake = *if there's an earthquake*
- Exception: *Break glass in case of fire* = short written form of *Break the glass in the case of a fire* (or: *if there is …*)

D Business leaders | Ralph Nader

1 Reading

a. Make notes on Nader's campaigns, methods and achievements.

RALPH NADER (born 1934) is a US lawyer, lecturer, writer and political activist. After graduating from Harvard Law School, he taught history before becoming a government advisor in Washington. He has also stood for election as US President. His main areas of concern are consumer protection, corporate responsibility, the environment, and fair and open government. He is best known for his consumer rights campaigns and for founding powerful lobby groups.

Ralph Nader – Consumer Rights Champion

Ralph Nader's first big campaign dealt with automobile safety. He wrote articles on the subject for a Harvard Law School publication and in 1965 he published his first book, *Unsafe at Any Speed*, which revealed that many American cars were unsafe. The book sparked controversy at the time, and General Motors tried to discredit Nader's research. However, it led to the 1966 National Traffic and Motor Vehicle Safety Act. This legislation introduced a series of important safety features for automobiles, beginning with seat belts and stronger windshields, marking a historic shift in responsibility for vehicle safety from the consumer to the manufacturer.

From that early success, Nader has devoted his lobbying career to regulating corporate responsibility and redefining consumer rights. Nader and his fellow lobbyists, the so-called 'Nader's Raiders', mobilised the American consumer activist movement by exposing the corporate and government powers behind business decisions. Everything from X-rays and airbags to prescription drugs and cigarettes were subject to the same scrutiny. Nader's Raiders serve as a successful example of 'grassroots' citizen lobbying. Hundreds of ordinary citizens sharing common beliefs came together and effected social change, without necessarily working as elected public officials. They helped to bring about legislative acts such as the Clean Air Act, the Occupational Safety and Health Act, and the Freedom of Information Act, and have promoted the concept of consumer rights far beyond the United States.

There have been few cases of abuse of corporate power in the US that have escaped Nader's gaze. His efforts were instrumental in bringing into force the 1977 Mine Health and Safety Act, which demanded two inspections a year of every surface coal mine and four at every underground coal mine in the US. The Act also provided workers' compensation for injured and disabled miners, and established criminal penalties for violations of health and safety standards. Needless to say, Nader's Raiders were not popular with the country's mine-owners.

A more recent Nader initiative has been the case of whistleblowers, in particular those people working for the government who report misconduct. The 1989 Whistleblower Protection Act guarantees protection from prosecution or punishment to any government employee who discloses information that he or she 'reasonably believes evidences a violation of a law, rule or regulation; gross mismanagement; gross waste of funds; an abuse of authority; or a substantial and specific danger to public health or safety'. This Act has had implications beyond the sphere of government, as individuals are increasingly encouraged to go public in cases of corporate malpractice.

Although Nader's efforts at getting elected have been unsuccessful – it has been said that he was more interested in raising controversial issues in the public eye than in getting a seat on Capitol Hill – his leadership and generous funding to consumer organisations has been inspirational. Public Citizen, the Nader-founded public interest organisation, continues to work on issues such as automobile safety, global trade, health research, government policy and energy legislation. Through such organisations, the spirit – and politics – of Nader's Raiders lives on.

to discredit in Verruf bringen, **raider** Angreifer, **prescription drugs** verschreibungspflichtige Arzneimittel, **subject to the same scrutiny** unter die gleiche Lupe genommen, **grassroots** Basis-, **to escape sb.'s gaze** von jmdm. übersehen werden

b. What has Nader founded, and what has he funded?

c. Discuss the obstacles that Nader's Raiders might have faced during their campaigns.

2 Vocabulary

a. Find four verbs meaning 'to make (previously unknown / secret) information available to others'.

b. Find four verbs meaning 'to cause something to happen'.

c. Explain in your own words the sentence starting 'There have been few cases …"

3 Research

a. *An Unreasonable Man* (2006) is a documentary about Nader that takes its title from a quote by the playwright George Bernard Shaw. Find the complete quote and discuss how it applies to Nader.

b. What areas are covered by your country's equivalent of the Occupational Safety and Health Act?

E Business communication | Debating

1 Why debate?

a. Before new legislation is passed, it is usual – at least in open societies – to debate the issue. Sometimes debates can get very heated. What rules can or should be put in place to prevent a debate from getting out of hand?

b. Read the info box below about the tradition of debating. Suggest where debating skills might come in useful in business.

INFO

Debating societies
Many British and American universities conduct formal debates as a team sport, where the art of debating is treated with as much respect as the topic. The rules are based on the British tradition of parliamentary debates, where opposing views are presented in short, formal speeches, and are followed by discussion, and then a vote. Debating societies are popular with students preparing for a career in law or politics, who want to develop their rhetorical skills. They are also popular with people who enjoy a good argument.

2 The debating process

Number the steps of a formal debate in the order in which they happen.

[ ] This is followed by a speech from the opposing speaker, who argues against the motion.
[ ] If there is an equal number of votes, the chair will have the casting vote.
[1] The chair announces the motion, introduced by the phrase "This House believes that …".
[ ] The chair opens the debate to the floor, so that everyone has a chance to express their views.
[ ] The 'proposer' makes the opening speech in favour of the motion.
[ ] The first and second speakers summarise their positions, reacting to arguments from the floor.
[ ] A third speaker adds further points in favour of the motion.
[ ] A fourth speaker adds further points against the motion.
[ ] The chair counts the votes: those in favour, those against, and the abstentions.
[ ] The motion is put to the vote. The chair asks for a show of hands.
[ ] The chair declares the result of the vote.

3 Collecting arguments

a. Work in groups, where one person takes notes. Brainstorm arguments in favour and against the motion below. The note-taker should note down the arguments and then prepare a summary.

"This House believes that EU subsidies to farmers should be abolished".

b. The note-takers present their summary in class. Compare your arguments with those of other groups.

LANGUAGE TIP

Debating terms
- The **House** represents the debating chamber, or the people who put forward the motion.
- The **motion** is the topic being debated.
- The **chair** is the person in charge of proceedings.
- The **floor** is the audience – the people who take part in the debate.
- A **show of hands** is when people vote by raising one arm.
- An **abstention** is a decision not to vote (verb: to abstain)
- **show of hands** Handzeichen

4 Tactics

a. Discuss the debating tactics below. Are there any that you disagree with?

- Try to anticipate possible objections to your arguments.
- Be prepared to concede a few points to your opponent.
- Show that you are an authority on the subject.
- Support your arguments with facts and figures.
- Patronise your opponent. (Give praise in a way that makes your opponent seem weaker.)
- Express scepticism or doubt.
- Mock your opponent. (Speak about your opponent in a scornful or contemptuous way.)

b. Decide which of the above tactics, excluding the first, these speakers are using:

1. "I think some of us may have enjoyed your opening speech, but …"
2. "Clearly, no one would argue with that point. However …"
3. "All we're hearing from my opponent are the same old clichés."
4. "It seems that my opponent has not done any homework on the subject."
5. "As you know, this is my area of expertise."
6. "The latest research on this subject clearly indicates that … "
7. "I'd like to congratulate my opponent on a good effort."
8. "Surely my opponent doesn't seriously expect us to believe that …"
9. "The figures cited by my opponent are highly questionable."
10. "I'm often asked this question by members of the public."
11. "Some of you may contend that diesel is cheaper, but in fact it's a false economy."

5 Preparation

a. Prepare to hold a debate. Choose one of the following motions, or a different one.

"The tourism industry benefits the world."
"Population growth should be limited."
"The internet should be regulated."
"Cash for clunkers' is a waste of taxpayers' money."

b. Decide who will take on the following roles:

- the chair
- two speakers to propose the motion (the main speaker in favour, and a second speaker)
- two speakers to oppose the motion (main speaker against, and a second speaker)

6 The debate

a. Hold the debate, making notes about the arguments and the presenters' skills.

b. Discuss the following questions, giving examples.

1. Why did the winning team win? Stronger arguments? Better tactics? …?
2. Where did the losing team go wrong? What advice could you give them?

c. Write an article about the debate starting with the sentence: "There was no shortage of viewpoints at today's debate. The motion was "This House believes "…".

PHRASES

Debating

Chairing the debate
This House proposes that …
The proposer of this motion is …
The opposer of the motion is …
I will now ask the proposer to speak …
The opposer will now answer …
I must ask you to keep to the agreed time limit.
The debate is now open to the floor.
I remind you all that the motion to be voted on is …
Those in favour please raise your hands.
All those against?
The motion is carried / defeated.

Proposing the motion
I'd like to start by explaining what is meant by …
You may be wondering what exactly is meant by …
I hope that I can convince you …
It is my intention to show that …
It has long been accepted that …
As I'm sure you all know …

Opposing the motion
I'd like to respond to the motion.
I'd like to present a very different picture.
In fact, the situation is very different.
Of course, there is another side to the story.
Let me start by looking at the facts.

Speaking from the floor
I'd like to address my question to …
I have a question for …
There's something I'm not clear about.
When you said …, did you mean …?
Could you tell us a little more about …?

Responding to questions from the floor
That's a very good question.
Yes, I think we can all agree with that.
I understand what you're saying, but …
No, that's not what I said at all.
Let me repeat what I said earlier.

F Consulting | A public hearing

1 Reading

You work for BW-Biogas GmbH in Döggingen, Baden-Württemberg. Your boss has forwarded an urgent email from the company's UK agent, Adam Harris. Read the email and the press cutting below, and make notes about the situation.

From: a.harris@energenics.co.uk
Subject: Public hearing in Somerset
To: walther.prost@BW-Biogas.de

Dear Walther,
I'm delighted to tell you that our plans to install three fully-operational biogas digester plants here in Somerset by the end of next year are making excellent progress. A date has now been set for the public hearing: Wednesday, August 19th at Safferton Town Hall at 8pm. This is sooner than I expected, but it's great that things are moving at last!
The local community are keen to know why a German company is constructing the plants, so I think it's essential that someone comes from Döggingen to attend the hearing. Ideally it will be you, but I realise that it's at such short notice and would understand if you decide to send a representative instead. Needless to say, this person should speak excellent English and be prepared for some tough questioning. Your company will have experience of public hearings in Germany, but I've put together some questions that people might ask here in Safferton. I'm also attaching an article from the local newspaper to give you an idea of the kind of publicity we're getting.
Please let me know whether you will be coming in person, or sending a representative, so that I can make arrangements for hotel accommodation and transport from Bristol Airport.
Hope to hear from you soon.

Best regards, Adam

biogas plant Biogasanlage, **digester plant** Kläranlage

NIMBYS BRACED FOR CLASH WITH GREENS

As the day of the public hearing in Safferton draws closer, a fierce debate is developing over whether the county's first biogas digester plants will get the go-ahead from the local council.

Many inhabitants strongly oppose the plan. Retired solicitor Alfred Daly, 68, is one of them: "Safferton is a rural community. They know we don't want development here, so why don't they take it somewhere else?"

Others hope the plants will bring environmental benefits. Green Party activist Alison Yeats, 34, argues that the future lies in alternative energy from renewable sources. "We welcome this innovative technology, especially if it reduces our carbon footprint."

Unemployed Matt Sadler, 23, supports the plans for different reasons. "As far as I'm concerned, anything that creates jobs in Safferton has to be good. I'm not one of those Nimbys. Most of them work in Bristol. They're just worried that their house prices might fall."

The local council are expecting a good turnout at the public hearing in Safferton Town Hall on 19 August. DEFRA official Ben Norris says that he is "looking forward to a frank and constructive exchange of views".

clash Konflikt, **Nimby** (**N**ot **I**n **M**y **B**ack **Y**ard) Nicht mit mir!, **braced** vorbereitet, **clash** (hier) Kampf, Auseinandersetzung, **fierce** hitzig, **good turnout** hohe Beteiligung, **frank exchange of views** offene Meinungstausch

2 Preparation

Your boss has chosen you to represent the company at the public hearing, so you need to make some preparations. Draw up a list of the various 'interested parties' who might be present, and decide which of them would be most likely to ask the questions below.

FAQs from the people of Safferton

1. What funding is available, and how do you apply for it?
2. What kinds of waste can be used in a digester?
3. How far from the village will they be? Will there be any smell or big lorries?
4. How much energy does a biogas plant produce? Is it cost effective?
5. What kind of red tape or legislation is involved in the application process?
6. How much land does a biogas plant need?
7. Is it possible to locate them underground, like in Asian countries?
8. Is there any environmental damage, due to waste products or effluence?
9. Is this an agricultural enterprise, or an industrial one?
10. What about danger to the public? Are these biogas plants safe?

3 Research

Find answers to the FAQs and any other questions you think might come up.

4 Writing

Create a flyer that you could distribute at the start of the hearing, based on information from your research. The flyer should present a positive image of BW-Biogas and explain the benefits of biogas plants, not only to investors and farmers, but also the local community.

INFO

Public hearings
A public hearing is an open meeting held by a committee in which members of the public, lobbyists, legislators, and representatives of other parties are given the opportunity to debate a proposal, and in some cases take a vote. Typically, public hearings are held on subjects that divide the public, for example planning permission for large-scale building projects.

5 Simulation

Carry out a simulation of the Safferton public hearing in which the proposal to build the plants is discussed. Organise yourselves into the five groups listed below, with one person acting as chair.
Prepare for the hearing with the instructions given in the appendix. See role cards on page 224.

- 'FOR' lobby group
- 'AGAINST' lobby group
- local media
- BW-Biogas representatives
- Local council / representatives of DEFRA

Decide on a time limit for the hearing. While it is in process, take notes that will help you in the follow-up tasks. At the end of the hearing, the chair should put the proposal to the vote.

6 Follow-up

Choose one of the following writing tasks, in which you report on the hearing and its outcome.

- Lobbyists: an open letter to the local (or national) press
- Media: a 'human interest' article
- BW-Biogas representatives: an email to your boss, Walther Prost
- Local council / DEFRA: a press release

Unit 15
Finance and investment

Online Link
800021-0015

A Introduction | Investment

1 Discussion

a. Choose the right words to complete the definition of 'bull market'. Then define the term 'bear market'.

"A bull market is one in which share prices are (rising / falling) and people are encouraged to (buy / sell)."

b. What groups of people might be interested in stock market trends, and why?

c. The origin of the terms 'bull market' and 'bear market' are uncertain.
What theories are there about these 'beasts of finance', and which do you think is the most convincing?

2 Listening

A 2.20 **a.** Lucy Snow, an investment advisor with SQQ Consulting, is talking to a prospective client.
Listen and take notes under the following headings.

Client | Investment amount | Source of investment | Investment goals | Bank deposits | Property | Shares and bonds | Asset growth | Debts and liabilities | Attitude to risk | Preliminary advice | Action

b. Explain the following idioms.

1. Don't put all your eggs into one basket.
2. It's important to put money by for a rainy day.
3. You've got to speculate to accumulate.
4. Does it come with strings attached?

c. What other forms of investment are mentioned, and what is the client's attitude towards them?

d. Discuss what an investment questionnaire might contain.

3 Options for saving and investment

a. Label the categories in the diagram with savings and investment options given in the list.

savings accounts | licences | wheat | paintings | venture capital | vintage cars | wine | diamonds | buy-to-rent | shares (AE stocks) | bonds | platinum | fixed-interest deposits | current accounts (AE checking accounts) | oil | currency trading | gold | corn | patents | sculpture | …

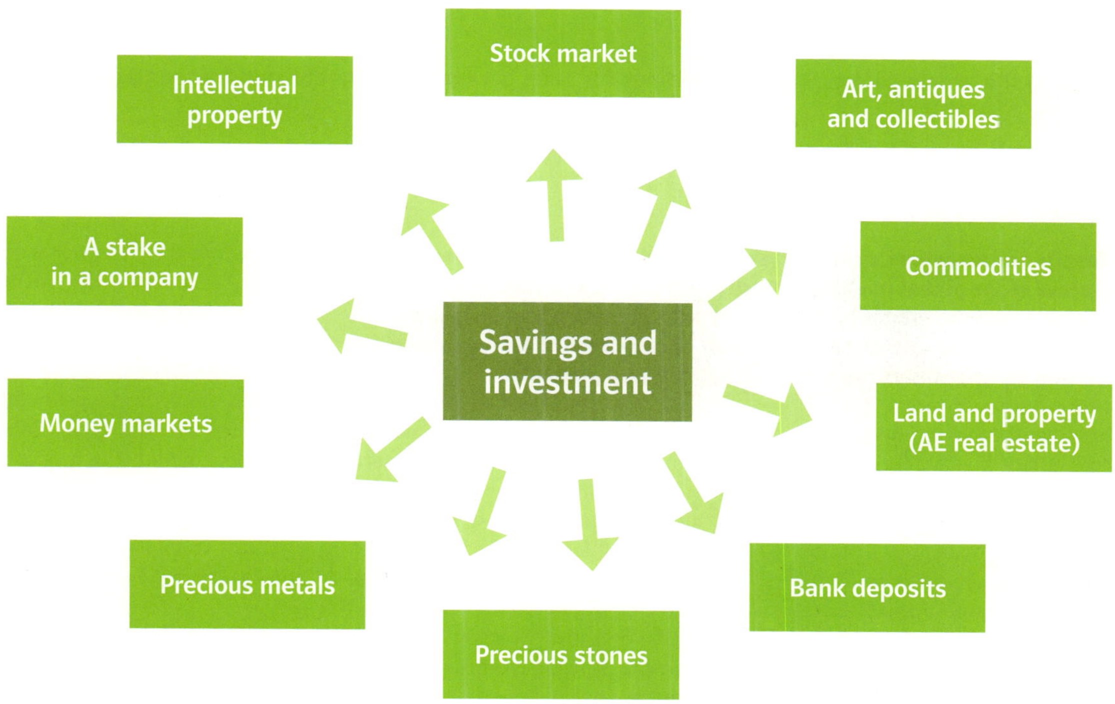

Example: Precious metals → gold, …

b. Develop the diagram by adding examples of your own.

c. Select three investment options that would appeal to the average investor. Prepare a sales pitch and try to 'sell' at least one of your options to the person next to you.

d. Crack the code to find the right words.

Shares (equity securities) Y4 dividends to the shareholders and give them part ownership of the company. Holders of ordinary shares (AE common stock) can V3 at the A5 G6 M6 (AGM). The dividend on ordinary shares is V7, depending on the P10 of the company. Holders of preference shares (AE preferred stock) E3 a fixed dividend, but do not normally have V5 rights.
Bonds (debt securities) Y4 interest. The holder of a company bond (debenture) is therefore a creditor to the company. Whereas shares can only be traded on the stock M5, bonds can be redeemed on maturity, which means that the creditor gets back the whole AM4 when the bond matures, plus any IN6 due. Bonds can also be S3 at a discount before maturity.
Holders of current accounts can withdraw their cash on D5. If you have cash-flow P7, a current account allows you to O7 your account up to a certain limit. It is better to have an authorised O8 than to have an unauthorised O8, which usually incurs a higher rate of IN6. If you N3 instant access to a large amount of cash, it is usually cheaper to T3 out a loan. You can service the loan (just pay IN6 on it), or pay off the loan (pay back the amount borrowed, which is C5 the 'principal') either in I10 or in one lump sum. The bank may ask you to provide S7 or collateral, but a secured loan is C6 than an unsecured one.
You can also keep your money in a S6 account in order to earn IN6. However, the IN6 rate is not necessarily index-linked (i.e. it may not keep up with the rate of I8). Also, these accounts usually require N5 of withdrawal, for example you may need to give two months' N5 if you want to withdraw a S2 exceeding, say €3,000. If you want to E3 a higher rate of IN6, you can buy a certificate of deposit (or fixed-IN6 deposit.) Here, you I5 your money for a fixed T3, e.g. three months. The longer the T3, the higher the rate of IN6, but your money is T3 up for that period.

B Business briefing | Islamic finance

1 Discussion

Discuss the following questions.

1. What services do banks offer to businesses?
2. Are there any businesses you would refuse to invest in? Explain why.

2 Reading

a. Read the article below. Suggest headings for each paragraph in the form of frequently asked questions (FAQs).

Islamic finance

Despite the recession, Islamic finance is one of the fastest growing sectors of the global banking industry, expanding at a rate of 15 % to 20 % a year. Financial products that comply with the principles of Islamic law (sharia) are also attracting the interest of non-Muslim investors who are looking for alternatives to conventional banking products.

Iran, Saudia Arabia and Malaysia are the top markets for Islamic finance. Britain is catching up fast, with an Islamic finance sector now bigger than Pakistan's. Britain's first stand-alone, sharia-compliant retail bank, the Islamic Bank of Britain, is planning to launch in Europe, and multinationals such as Deutsche Bank, Citigroup, HSBC and Lloyds TSB already offer sharia-compliant products.

The surge of interest in Islamic finance is also reflected in a mushrooming of academic degrees in the subject, especially in Britain. Stefan Szymanski, Professor of Economics at Cass Business School in London, recognises the potential for higher education. "You just have to measure how many billions of dollars Islamic finance handles in a year. If that grows over the years, it will become a universal part of every business school".

Islamic finance – the term is only a few decades old – started with the launch of Islamic banks in the Gulf during the oil boom in the 1970s, but it is based on the Sharia tenets laid out in the Qu'ran and the teachings of Muhammad 14 centuries ago. Sharia forbids usury (riba) and speculation (gharar). Banks are not allowed to pay or charge interest, and speculative investments such as hedging or trading in derivatives are forbidden. Sharia also prohibits investment in businesses linked to alcohol, pork, tobacco, armaments, gambling, pornography, and other activities thought to be morally or socially harmful. Also off-limits are companies with too much borrowing, in particular those with a debt-equity ratio of more than two thirds. Investing in 'toxic assets' such as subprime mortgages is definitely out of bounds.

Islamic banks therefore have to find ways of generating profits in forms other than interest. The finance model is based on sellers and buyers, not lenders and borrowers. Banks trade in sharia-compliant, asset-backed investments, and share the profits and losses with their customers. There are various alternatives to conventional interest-bearing mortgages. With an ijara (leasing) scheme, the bank buys the property and the customer pays rent to the bank. Ijara-wa-Iquitan (hire purchase) is a similar arrangement, except that the customer is able to buy the property at the end of the contract. The most common form of financing is murabaha (cost-plus financing). Here, the bank and the customer buy the property together. The customer then buys the bank's stake, paying for it in instalments and gradually acquiring ownership. The bank profits from the mark-up, which usually matches current interest rates on mortgages.

Islamic bankers argue that Sharia principles would have prevented the global banking crisis. At the same time, some Muslims worry that Sharia principles are being compromised, as Islamic banks introduce products and services that replicate those of the conventional banking system. There are also concerns about the lack of common rules. Sharia scholars disagree on the definition of usury, so a customer can buy a sukuk (a kind of bond) in liberal Malaysia, but not in orthodox Kuwait. Economists agree that the future of Islamic finance depends on standardisation. Only then will banks be able to create innovative products capable of competing in world markets.

stand-alone eigenständig, **surge** Welle, **to mushroom** wie Pilze aus dem Boden schießen, **tenet** Lehre, **off-limits** verboten, **armaments** Waffen, **toxic assets** von der Wertlosigkeit bedrohte Einlagen, **out of bounds** verboten, **to impede** verhindern

b. Identify suitable sections of the article where these quotes could be included.

"If you look at the development in the past few years, Islamic finance appears to be mimicking most of the products of conventional finance." Professor Habib Ahmed, expert on Islamic finance. (BBC News, 2009)

"We've got non-Muslim customers, including some really famous names, because they like the ethical standpoint we take." Stephen Amos, Head of Marketing at the Islamic Bank of Britain (The Times, 2008)

"Innovation will take place as long as the standards are set. But if you have an industry where even the basics are questioned, this will impede growth." Ozgur Tanrikulu, head of Islamic finance at McKinsey (Financial Times, 2009)

c. Compare Islamic and conventional banking with reference to the article. Give your own view as well.

d. Find words to match the definitions below.

1. debt as a percentage of overall financing (also known as 'gearing' or 'leveraging')
2. loans or debts that will probably never be repaid
3. property loans carrying a high risk of default (and therefore a high interest rate) because they are offered to people on low/unpredictable incomes or who have financial problems

e. It has been claimed that ***sharia*** principles could have prevented the credit crunch. Do you agree?

f. Is there an upper limit on the interest rate that can be charged on loans in your country? Discuss whether you think the limit is fair and reasonable.

3 Research

Choose one of the research topics below. Present your findings in class or in a report.

1. What are the criteria for ethical (or 'socially responsible') investments? How are they marketed, and what parallels are there – if any – with *sharia*-compliant investments?
2. What banks in your country offer *sharia*-compliant products? How are these products marketed, and who buys them?

INFO

Hedging and derivatives
Investors can protect themselves from losing money on their investments by **hedging** against the risk. Typically, they do this by buying or selling financial instruments such as **futures**, **options** or **swaps**, collectively known as **derivatives** because they 'derive' their value from other assets.

4 Transferring information

Read the explanation below. Write notes and draw pictures to help you to remember the explanation. Then show your pictures to another student and give an explanation in your own words.

Derivatives
For our example let's consider a commodities future. Supposing that the price of turkeys (the asset) is trading at €1,000/tonne today, but you are convinced that the price will rise because beef is going out of fashion and turkeys are becoming increasingly popular. You could buy up large quantities of turkeys, store them in your freezer until the price increases, and then reap the rewards. But this would mean putting a big sum upfront, and your freezer may not have enough space.
Alternatively, you could find someone who believes the price will go down. So you draw up a futures contract in which they agree to sell you 10,000 tonnes of turkeys, in three months time, at €1,000/tonne. No money changes hands at this point.
Three months later, the going rate for turkeys has rocketed to €1,500/tonne. Now your partner is obliged to sell you the 10,000 tonnes of turkeys at €1,000/tonne, in line with your original contract, but he has to pay his suppliers €1,500/tonne. He therefore loses €500 a tonne, or €500,000. You, in contrast, are in the money because you can sell the turkeys at a nice profit.
The risk of trading in derivatives is that large losses can accumulate on no initial outlay.
In practice, traders have to put up money to cover any accumulated losses as the contract progresses. On the other hand, they can 'cash out' early – either cutting their losses or going off with their winnings.
Options are very like futures, but are not so risky because any losses are limited to a fixed cash outlay. In the famous Barings Bank scandal of 1995, the rogue trader Nick Leeson brought down the bank by trading in derivatives.

to reap the rewards die Früchte ernten, **going rate** aktueller Preis, **to be in the money** in Geld schwimmen

C Language | Financial statements

1 Accounts

a. Insert the missing words in this text about the two most important financial statements.

surplus | funded | liabilities | expenditure | day | period | assets | performing | used

A balance sheet is a snapshot of the financial position of the organisation. It shows what an organisation owns or is owed (..............................) and what it owes (..............................) on a particular .... It is used to show how the organisation is being .... and how the funds are being ....

A profit and loss account (*AE* income statement) records an organisation's income and .... and shows the .... or shortfall over a given ...., usually 12 months. It is used to show how the organisation is ....

b. Who might be interested in these financial statements, and why?

c. What other accounts or information about a company's finances might they be interested in?

2 Income and expenditure

a. Read the excerpt from a budget airline's year-end accounts. Complete the grid with the marked words.

EXECUTIVE SUMMARY

Profit after **tax** decreased to € 125m compared to € 470.9m in the year ended March 31st, 2009. This was primarily due to a 57 % increase in **fuel** costs and other costs associated with the growth of the airline. The 3 % increase in total operating revenues to €2,824m was considerably slower than the 15 % growth in passenger volumes, because average **passenger fares** fell by 8 % to € 40. There was also a fall in revenue due to a drop in **baggage charges,** weaker euro / sterling exchange rates, and **aggressive fare promotions**. **Ancillary revenues** continued to outpace the growth of passenger volumes, rising by 25 % to €591m. This was a result of **onboard sales**, as well as **non-flight scheduled revenues** and other ancillary products.

Staff costs went up by 8 % to € 311.5m. This was due to a 21 % increase in average employee headcounts to 6,393. The majority of employee headcount was in cabin crew, who earn less than the average salary.

Gross **cash** increased by € 112m to € 2,294.5m. The company generated €410.5m of cash from operating activities, and € 316m from **sales of surplus aircraft** (16 Boeing 737-800s) which funded the higher fuel costs, a € 47m **share buy-back programme**, and capital expenditure incurred during the year. The capital expenditure largely consisted of **advance payments** for the **purchase of new aircraft**.

Maintenance costs increased by 20 % to € 67.5m, due to a 24 % increase in the number of **leased aircraft** from 30 to 39, and increased costs arising from activities at our new **maintenance bases**. **Marketing and distribution** costs fell by 28 %, mainly due to tight control on expenditure, and a focus on **Internet promotions**. However, **route charges** went up by 13 %, and **airport and handling charges** by 16 %.

Income	Expenditure

b. Answer the questions below:

1. Which of the increased costs are due to the growth of the airline?
2. Which are attributed to external factors?
3. How has the airline managed to cut costs?
4. What is the relationship between staff costs and 'average employee headcounts'? Suggest why the percentages differ.

c. Discuss further ways in which airlines can generate income and cut costs.

3 Understanding a balance sheet

a. Match the headings with the definitions.

fixed assets | current assets | current liabilities | long-term liabilities | capital and reserves

1. debts falling due after more than one year
2. money invested in the business, and amounts set aside that can be spent later
3. items of value that are held for a short time and can easily provide cash
4. debts that must be paid within one year
5. items of value intended to be used for several years

b. Label the balance sheet with the items below. (Many of them are synonyms.)

patents | bills receivable | brands | payables | equipment | receivables | copyrights | inventory | goodwill | work-in-progress | land | provisions | vehicles | accounts payable | dividends | buildings | mortgages | fixtures and fittings | bills payable | intellectual property | machinery | accounts receivable | owners' equity | taxes due within the year | semi-finished goods | plant | interest payments due

ACME Ltd.
Balance Sheet as at 31 September 2009

		£
Fixed assets		
Intangible assets		1,500
Tangible assets		25,000
Investments		500
		27,000
Current assets		
Stock		7,000
Debtors		
Trade debtors	7,500	
Prepayments and accrued income	500	
		8,000
Cash at bank and in hand		5,500
		20,500
Current liabilities		
Bank loans and overdrafts		(1,000)
Trade creditors		(3,000)
Other creditors including tax and social security		(1,000)
Accruals and deferred income		(500)
		(5,500)
Net current assets		15,000
Total assets less current liabilities		42,000
Long-term liabilities		
Bank loan		(2,000)
Net assets		**40,000**
Capital and reserves		
Called up share capital		35,000
Profit and loss account		5,000
Shareholders' funds		**40,000**

www.businesslink.gov.uk

INFO

Balance sheet

- There is no prescribed format for the balance sheet. It can be presented in two columns (assets on one side, liabilities and ownership capital on the other) or in one column.
- It is usual to present the items in order of liquidity, with the most / least liquid assets first.
- The International Accounting Standards Board (IASB) calls the balance sheet a 'statement of financial position'.
- Terminology can confuse even native speaker accountants. There are many synonyms (debtors = accounts / bills receivable = receivables), and many words with multiple meanings (investment, stock, provisions, dispose of).

4 Research

Compare the year-end accounts of two companies who published their accounts on the Internet, e.g. Lufthansa and British Airways. Which would you recommend as the better investment? Consider the price / earnings ratio, earnings per share and the debt / equity ratio (gearing / leverage).

5 Tax

a. Complete the text with expressions from the word bank on the right.

If you have lived and worked in Germany for more than 180 days, your worldwide income may be .... Germany has a .... with the UK, so you won't need to pay tax twice. However, if you want to minimise your ...., you should do some careful .... There is nothing illegal about ...., but if you deliberately conceal your assets, for example by putting your money in a .... such as the Cayman Islands, or working secretly without declaring your income (moonlighting), you could be charged with .... The same is true if you commit ...., i.e. lying on official documents. You will of course need to register with your local .... *(Finanzamt)*. A .... can help you with all the formalities to do with this, and advise you on any .... you may be entitled to. Remember to keep receipts of any income-related expenses, because these may be .... After you have filed your ...., you will receive a .... stating how much tax you have to pay and when. If you are lucky, you will get a ....

WORD BANK

Tax

Compounds and collocations: double-taxation agreement | tax advisor / consultant | tax allowance | tax break / tax relief | tax authority / authorities | tax avoidance | tax deductible | tax demand / tax bill / tax assessment notice | tax dodge | tax evasion | tax fraud | tax haven | tax hike | tax liability | tax planning | tax rebate / tax refund | tax return / tax declaration | value-added tax (VAT) (*AE* sales tax) | to be subject to tax | to levy a tax / to impose a tax (on something.)

Types of tax: capital gains tax | corporate tax | direct tax | excise tax | fuel tax | indirect tax | inheritance tax | income tax | payroll tax | trade tax | value-added tax (AE sales tax) | import tax

b. Read the questions and note down two further questions relating to tax.

1. Have you ever paid tax? If so, what type(s)?
2. What might happen if you are late in filing your taxes?
3. What good news might you find in a tax assessment notice?
4. Who is entitled to tax allowances or tax breaks in your country?
5. How do people try to avoid paying tax – legally or illegally?
6. ....
7. ....

c. With a partner, take turns asking and answering the questions. Use expressions in the word bank.

6 Translation

a. An English-speaking friend wants to start up her own business in Germany and has asked you for tips about writing a business plan. Translate this excerpt from a brochure published by the German Federal Employment Agency.

Finanzplanung und -Bedarf

Geld spielt bei der Existenzgründung eine große Rolle. Daher ist der Punkt zur Finanzierung sehr wichtig. Teil eins sind die geplanten Ausgaben: Welche Investitionen müssen Sie am Anfang und im Laufe der ersten Zeit tätigen? Listen Sie hier alle größeren Anschaffungen der nächsten drei bis fünf Jahre auf. Aus dieser Liste ergibt sich der Kapitalbedarf und die jährlichen Abschreibungen. Teil zwei ist der Liquiditätsplan: Er zeigt alle Ausgaben und Einnahmen, die Sie in den nächsten Jahren erwarten. Darüber hinaus erstellen Sie eine Gewinn- und Verlustrechnung über den voraussichtlichen Geschäftsverlauf samt Umsätzen, Ausgaben und Gewinnen. Eine Liquiditätsvorschau zeigt, welche Geldflüsse Sie in den nächsten Jahren erwarten. Anschließend ordnen Sie die Finanzierungsposten den Kapitalgebern zu: Wie viel Eigenkapital haben Sie, und wofür setzen Sie es ein? Und wie viel Unterstützung durch Banken oder andere Kreditgeber brauchen Sie für welche Posten? Vergessen Sie auch nicht eine Reserve für unvorhersehbare Ausgaben.

Existenzgründung 2009, S. 30, Bundesagentur für Arbeit

Abschreibung depreciation, **Posten** items, **zuordnen** to match, to allocate, **unvorhersehbare Ausgaben** contingencies

b. Suggest further tips for writing a business plan.

D Business leaders | Dragons

Dragons' Den is a popular BBC television series in which budding entrepreneurs pitch their ideas to multi-millionaire investors, the Dragons. If the Dragons are interested, they will put up the cash and offer business advice, but in return they negotiate for a share of the company.

Reading

a. Read the profiles of three Dragons. If you were an entrepreneur and each Dragon offered you the same deal, whose money would you accept? Explain why.

DEBORAH MEADEN had always wanted to run her own business. She started her first company at the age of 19, exporting glass and ceramics from Italy, and was soon supplying upmarket stores such as Harvey Nichols. Her next business venture was operating one of the first Stefanel clothing franchises in the UK. She went on to work in Butlins holiday camps before joining her family's holiday business, Weststar Holidays, eventually becoming Managing Director. In 1999 she acquired the majority shareholding in a management buyout, and later sold the company in a deal worth £33m. Famously grumpy, at least on TV, she is the only woman in the Dragons' Den.

THEO PAPHITIS is one of the UK's most popular entrepreneurs. He was born in Cyprus but grew up in the England. He started as a junior clerk with a Lloyds of London broker before switching to retail at the age of 18. He then moved into property and corporate finance, setting up his own company aged just 23. Today he commands a business empire that includes retail, property, and finance. Through his appearances on Dragons' Den, Theo has advised many young entrepreneurs and invested in several innovative businesses and brands. Since first appearing in 2005 has made investments in 28 businesses, totalling £1.8 million.

DUNCAN BANNATYNE started his career as an entrepreneur with an ice cream van that he bought for £450. He made such a success selling ice cream that he eventually sold the business for £28,000 and used the money to found a nursing home. In 1996 he sold his nursing home business for £46 million. During the last 10 years he has expanded into health clubs, and also owns bars, hotels and property. Bannatyne's is now the largest independent chain of health clubs in the UK. He was quoted on The Sunday Times 2009 Rich List as having a personal fortune of £320m. In Dragons' Den he is well known for his catchphrase: "I think the idea is ridiculous and so I won't be investing today"

grumpy mürrisch, **holiday camp** Ferienlager, **to command a business empire** ein Firmenimperium leiten, **nursing home** Pflegeheim

b. Match the parts of these quotes from the Dragons.

1. "There is absolutely no point in money unless …
2. "Being a millionaire is not a career. It's … something that happens because …
3. "A lack of cash is like a heart attack for a business. If you can't pay the rent, …
4. "It might seem blindingly obvious but business is all about …
5. "You must never underestimate the …
6. "If you're an entrepreneur and want to …
7. "You won't persuade other people to …
8. "Just because something is innovative or uses leading-edge …
9. "Making £100m is easy. Making …

a. you shut down, just like you would if your heart packed up. You're finished."
b. your first £1m is the difficult part."
c. you know what you want to do with it."
d. common sense. In fact, business is 90% common sense."
e. strength of the opposition."
f. believe in you if you don't believe in yourself."
g. technology it doesn't necessarily mean it's going to make pots of money."
h. start a business, start small."
i. you do something of value that enough people want to pay for."

c. On a slip of paper, write your own advice to budding entrepreneurs (one line only). One person in class should collect the quotes and read them out. Then vote for the best quote.

LANGUAGE TIP

hochpreisig, gehobene Preisklasse	upmarket (BE), upscale (AE)

E Business communication | Editing and proofreading

This section will help you to avoid some of the common mistakes that German-speakers make when writing formal texts.

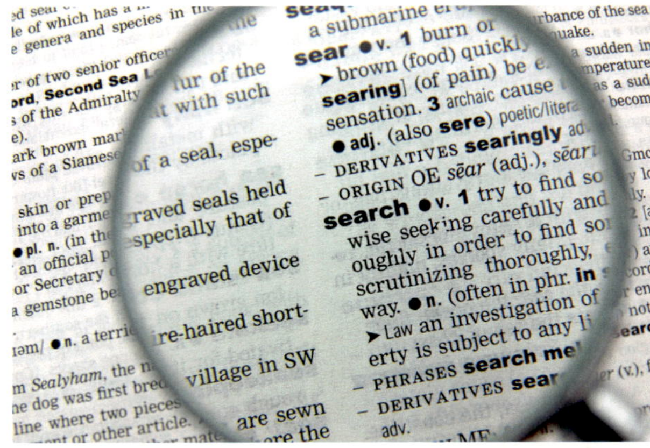

1 Discussion

a. Give examples of formal texts you have to write in English. Describe the process you go through when you write them, from the planning stage through to the final check.

b. Have you ever been asked to check someone else's text? What aspects did you comment on?

2 House style

Find examples of standard documents created by your organisation or college, such as brochures or letter templates. Look at the font type, the print size, the use of colour, etc. Does it create a professional impression, or are there any changes you would recommend?

3 Checking and improving

a. Work in groups. Check the text below and discuss ways to improve it. Refer to the checklist on the following page.

b. Suggest a suitable heading for the text.

The Goldring International Group delivered a satisfying financial performance this year, resulting in earnings of 26 billion EUR! A strong financial position means, that we were able to return 8 billion EUR to shareholders in dividends, while capital investment reached 38,4 billion EUR.
Especially in this highly volatile business environment is this an excellent result for Goldring International. We also are akquiring new „green“ companies to add to our portfolio, people pay a high prize for bio-products. So we expect a very rentable outcome. Only by diversifying we will have the possibility to generate higher revenue. In the last months we have overtaken 2 high-tech company's.
The first one is the company Sol-Dach, who are manufacturing and installing solar roof panels. Sol-Dach's headquarter is in Konstanz and they have a lot of experiences in marketing there panels in the EU. The second one is the company Windcatcher, they've been very successful due to the fact that they have developed highly innovative and state-of-the-art products with exciting cutting-edge technology in the wind-turbine market. Very important for our future success is to win market share form our main competitor Grossman AG. We're confident, that we can improve our market position. Because we have a very loyal costumer basis that is expanding. And we continue with our CRM program.
Last not least, we're going to open an other branch office in China. In case we succeed in the asian market, we can expect significant turnover respectively profits over the next years.

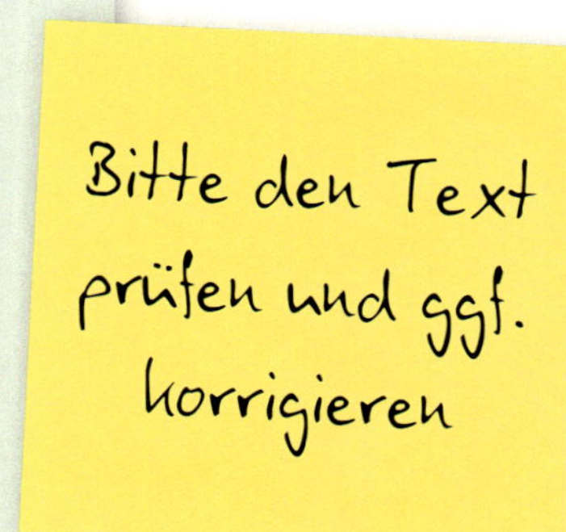

PROOFREADING CHECKLIST

BEFORE YOU START:

- **House style:** Find out whether the organisation you are writing for has any formatting requirements with regard to print size, font, line spacing, and so on.

- **Computer settings:** Decide on the type of English to use, e.g. British/American/Australian, etc. This affects not only spelling and grammar, but also punctuation, such as apostrophes and quotation marks. Also change the settings for splitting words at the end of lines, since the rules are different in English and can be controversial. It is best to avoid splitting words altogether.

AFTER DRAFTING:

- **Spelling:** Do a spell-check but also look for mistakes that the spell-check might not spot, such as customer/costumer, lose/loose and from/form.

- **Paragraphs:** Make sure the ideas are grouped into paragraphs, with a line space between each one.

- **Redundancy:** Use the KISS principle (Keep it Short and Simple). Look for words you can delete without affecting the meaning. You may also be able to shorten sentences by restructuring them.

- **Punctuation:** Make sure your punctuation helps, not hinders. Read the text aloud. Where you pause for a short breath, you will most likely need a comma. Where you need a big breath, you probably need a full stop. Do not use exclamation marks because they give the impression of shouting. Write numbers below 12 in full, but keep figures in statistical and scientific work, e.g. 32% and 14°.

- **Short forms:** Avoid contractions (use 'it is', not it's). When you first use an acronym, write the full form as well, e.g. International Financial Reporting Standards (IFRS).

- **Coherence:** Read the text to someone else. If it does not make sense consider your use of linking words. Also, some sentences may be too long or too short. Try varying the sentence length.

- **Headings:** Include headings if you want to flag up the main points or help readers find what they are looking for. Otherwise, leave them out.

- **Commas:** Avoid commas before 'that' and after verbs of reporting and perception (He explained why, NOT: ~~He explained, why~~). Use commas after introductory phrases (As far as I'm concerned, ...) and after subordinate clauses (If you want to start a business, start small.).

- **Translating '*beziehungsweise*':** Translate it as 'and', 'or', 'and/or', or 'or else', or to be more specific, depending on what you want to say. Only use 'respectively' if you want to clarify how two things relate to two other things, e.g. Jane and Mike worked in Japan and India respectively (Jane worked in Japan, Mike worked in India.)

- **In case/In the case of:** Do not confuse these two. Only use 'in case' when you refer to precautions.

- **Especially:** Avoid starting sentences with 'especially'. Either leave it out or restructure the sentence.

- **The following:** Remember the article, e.g. Please pay into *the* following account.

- **Company names:** Leave out the word 'company'. Just give the name (~~the company~~ Aesculap)

- **Tenses:** Use the present progressive to describe current trends, and the simple present to refer to facts, states and regular activities.

- **Grammar:** Use inversion when you start with 'only', 'never', 'rarely', and other negative adverbials (Only by cutting costs can we... (NOT: ~~we can~~)

F Consulting | Investment advice

1 What sort of investor are you?

You have received a windfall of €200,000 that you would like to invest. Your investment advisor has asked you to answer the questions on the right before meeting you.

2 Interview

Take turns in the role of investment advisor. Follow the steps below.

a. Interview the client, using the questionnaire and asking further questions that will help you to assess the client's needs, investment knowledge and attitude to risk. After the interview, swap roles.

b. Write a follow-up letter to the client, with an assessment of the client's investment needs and advice on suitable options. Use the structure below, or a similar one.

> **Risk assessment profile**
> Dear …
> Thank you for placing your trust in me as an investment advisor. I have drawn up a profile of your investment needs, based on your answers to the questionnaire and our interview today.
> I think you will agree that your attitude to risk is (…)
> Therefore I would recommend that you spread your risk as follows: (…)
> There are some exciting options available at the moment. In particular, you might be interested in (…)
> If you wish to know more about these options, please (…)
> I look forward to …

c. Read the letter your investment advisor has sent you. Write an email reply, commenting on the advice and saying what your next step will be.

WORD BANK

Risk and liquidity

Taking risks: to be ultra-conservative | to be (fairly) cautious | to play safe | to avoid risk | to be risk-averse | to cut your losses | to spread one's risk | to seize an opportunity | to take a (calculated) risk | to take a chance | to take a gamble (on sth.) | to be daring | to throw caution to the winds | to be reckless

Liquidity: to get at one's money | to access (money / funds) at short notice | to have instant access to money | to have money tied up (in) | to be cash-poor, asset-rich | to cash in an investment | to have liquidity / cash-flow problems | to run out of money | to be insolvent | to be broke (informal)

Please demonstrate your knowledge of investments by answering the following questions:

1 My knowledge of investments is …
- ☐ none
- ☐ limited
- ☐ good
- ☐ extensive

2 When do you plan to retire?
- ☐ I'm already retired.
- ☐ In the next 10 years
- ☐ more than 10 years
- ☐ not for a long time, 25 years at least

3 When will you need to access your money?
- ☐ I need it at a moment's notice
- ☐ Within the next five years
- ☐ In five to 10 years
- ☐ I have no specific plans for this cash – it's play money

4 Over the next 10 years and beyond, it is …
- ☐ Very important that my investment grows in value
- ☐ Somewhat important that my investment grows in value
- ☐ Important that my investment at least keeps its value
- ☐ Unimportant whether on not my investment grows in value

5 What growth rate do you expect?
- ☐ Less than 5%
- ☐ 5% to 7%
- ☐ About one year's income
- ☐ More than 10%

6 Which of the following investments are you interested in?
- ☐ Bonds
- ☐ Shares
- ☐ Alternative investments (e.g. art, toys, wine)
- ☐ Other (Please state):

7 During 2002 the stock market fell by 22.7%. What would have been your reaction if you had been a shareholder?
- ☐ Sell all my shares
- ☐ Sell some of my shares
- ☐ Keep all of my shares
- ☐ Buy more shares

8 If you could increase your chances of making even more money by taking even more of a gamble, would you be ...
- ☐ Not prepared to lose a penny
- ☐ Willing to take some very calculated risks
- ☐ Happy to take some risk – it is the only way to make money
- ☐ Prepared to do whatever it takes

9 If you were given €100 a month for the next 20 years on the condition that you did not touch it until you retired, what would you do with it?
- ☐ Put it in a bank or building society savings account
- ☐ Invest in a few different things, but keep some in a safer place such as a savings account
- ☐ Invest it in a tracker fund*
- ☐ Invest it all in some up-and-coming stock market trend. After all, it's extra money, so I can afford to take a chance

10 A month after you buy it, an investment falls 15% in a market correction. Assuming none of the other fundamentals have changed, do you
- ☐ Sell all and get out while you can
- ☐ Sell half
- ☐ Hold it and hope it recovers
- ☐ Buy even more – it is an opportunity

11 You are in the final round of a TV quiz show. Here are your choices ...
- ☐ Take €1,000 in cash
- ☐ Take a 50% chance of winning €4,000
- ☐ Take a 20% chance of winning €10,000
- ☐ Take a 5% chance of winning €100,000

12 You are given the option to invest in shares in the company you work for before it goes public. They tell you that it might make 10 or 20 times the investment when the company goes public, but that won't be for four years. Do you...
- ☐ Invest nothing
- ☐ Invest one month's salary
- ☐ Invest three month's salary
- ☐ Invest six month's salary

13 What is a unit trust?
- ☐ A pool of money from small savers that is used to buy shares, limiting the risk for the savers
- ☐ The relationship between a close-knit group of colleagues
- ☐ Cashing in one investment to pay for another
- ☐ An ethical investment

14 If the inflation rate is 5% and the interest rate on your savings is 3%, what will your money be worth in a year's time?
- ☐ The same
- ☐ Less than now
- ☐ More than now
- ☐ Don't know

15 If you borrowed €1,000 on a typical credit card with a minimum repayment of 2% a month, how long would it take to repay the debt if you stuck to the minimum repayment?
- ☐ About 10 years
- ☐ About 20 years
- ☐ About 30 years
- ☐ More than 50 years

16 You are planning a big summer break in the UK. What would be the best and cheapest way of handling money?
- ☐ Use travellers' cheques for everything
- ☐ Use credit cards for everything
- ☐ Use credit cards for purchases and a debit card for withdrawing cash
- ☐ Change money at the airport and take a wallet-full of sterling

17 How often is it recommended that you review your bank statements?
- ☐ Once a month
- ☐ Once a quarter
- ☐ Sometimes
- ☐ Never

**Thank you for your co-operation.
Your investment advisor will be happy to answer any questions you may have.**

* Tracker fund: Rather than paying for the expertise of a particular manager, you pay a lower fee for a computer to run a fund that mirrors the performance of a stock market index, up or down, for as long as you remain invested. Charges are relatively low – between 0.3% and 1.5% of the total value of funds invested annually but there may also be an up-front entry fee.

The Guardian, 2 April 2007

Unit 16
Corporate strategy

Online Link
800021-0016

A Introduction | Mission statements

1 Discussion

a. Why do companies have mission statements?
Where are you most likely to find them?

b. Say what you think is the core business of the following companies. Then match them with the mission statements below.

Ford | Mattel Inc | Google | Adidas Group | Chevron | Wal-Mart | ebay

INFO

Mission statements
A **mission statement** is an official statement that describes the aims and philosophy of an organisation. Similar to this is a **vision statement**, which describes how the organisation would like to be in the future.

1. .... makes a difference in the global community by effectively serving children in need.
2. ....'s mission is to help people save money so that they can live better.
3. ....'s mission is to organise the world's information and make it universally accessible.
4. The .... strives to be the global leader in the sporting goods industry.
5. At the heart of the .... Way is our vision … to be the energy company most admired for its people, partnership and performance.
6. .... to provide a global trading platform where practically anyone can trade practically anything.
7. ....: To become the world's leading consumer company for automotive products and services.

c. Which companies used to have the following mission statements? Find out what their mission statements are today, and discuss whether you think they are useful or not.

To make people happy | Beat Coke | Crush Reebok | We will crush, squash and slaughter Yamaha | Become the company most known for changing the worldwide poor-quality image of Japanese products.

d. Develop a 'mission statement generator'. Add further expressions that frequently appear in mission statements.

Our mission is to We strive to …	provide become …	the most a …	cost-effective high-quality …	solutions service …	to every customer at all times …	throughout the world. in tomorrow's world. in the (…) industry. …
We are dedicated to We are committed to …	satisfying exceeding …		customer stakeholder …	needs expectations …		

2 Culture clash

a. DeCartaret Spas, a chain of health clubs, has merged with a sportswear manufacturer to form DeCartaret Sports and Leisure PLC. As part of the restructuring process, the two PR departments have been combined. Read the email and explain what the new Communications Department needs to do.

Dear team,
Thanks once again for agreeing to collaborate on writing the new mission statement. I feel confident that the synergies created by your joint efforts will result in a mission statement that reflects the vitality, values and vision of our newly merged corporation.
I'm attaching a summary of the ideas that came up in yesterday's brainstorming session. Of course, speed is of the essence, so I hope to receive your draft tomorrow if possible.
Best ,
Victor Magnus
CEO, DeCartaret Sports & Leisure PLC

Ideas for mission statement

- healthy sporting lifestyle
- striving to be the global leader
- passion for sport
- sponsoring the best
- innovation, inspiration and quality
- partnership and performance
- commitment to people
- constantly ahead
- value to shareholders

b. Work in teams to draft a mission statement using ideas from the brainstorming session and your mission statement generator. Then compare statements and vote for the best one.

3 A leaked email

An email from a DeCartaret employee to a friend has been leaked. It can now be read by anybody on the Internet. Read the email and answer the questions that follow.

Hi Pete,
Have you seen the photo of our new CEO in the local press? LOL – What a clown. He's posing in a ridiculous golf outfit with our new corporate logo splashed all over it, but he couldn't play golf to save his life.
I expect you've heard about the merger by now. The staff only found out about it through the media. The internal communication here is a joke – either that or the management were trying to keep things under wraps so we don't leave like rats deserting a sinking ship. Obviously, we're worried now because jobs are bound to go. Nobody knows yet where the axe will fall, but my whole department could disappear! Of course, the guys at the top will keep their jobs. Turkeys don't vote for Christmas.
Anyway, they can't keep us out of the loop for much longer. They've started to integrate the computer systems and the databases, so it's chaos (as we expected). But it also brings to light some VERY interesting details about salaries and expense accounts.
Hope you don't mind me getting things off my chest like this. Things are looking pretty bleak here. Maybe we could meet up for a beer – I could let you in on some of the latest juicy gossip ;o)
Cheers, Barry

1. In what ways does Barry's description of the company differ from Victor's?
2. How might the staff and management of DeCartaret react to seeing the email on the Internet?
3. What action do you think Victor himself should take, and why?
4. What is meant by the expression 'Turkeys don't vote for Christmas'?

B Business briefing | Mergers and acquisitions

1 Preparing for a lecture

You are going to listen to a lecture on mergers and acquisitions. Prepare in groups. Discuss what you know about the subject already and take notes in the grid below.

Merger	Definition:
	Types:
Acquisition	Definition:
	Types:
Processes (how they happen)	
Failure rate	
Why they happen: Potential benefits	
Why they fail: Risks / reasons for failure	
Examples of recent M&A activity	

2 Listening

A 2.21 **a.** Listen to the lecture and take notes. (You may need to listen more than once.)

b. Work in groups. Compare the notes you took during the lecture with the notes you made in the grid, and discuss the following questions.

1. What information was new, difficult or interesting to you?
2. What points would you like the lecturer to clarify? How would you express your request?
3. When would you ask the questions – during the lecture or after, and why?
4. Are there any points you disagree with? How would you express this?
5. Are there any important areas that the lecturer did not cover? Give examples.

PHRASES

Contributing to lectures

- You referred to / mentioned … Would you mind explaining that again?
- You raised an interesting point about … Could you tell us a bit more about it, please?
- You used the expression … What exactly do you mean by that?
- I didn't quite understand the point about …
- I'd just like to add the point that …
- Wouldn't it be more accurate to say that …?
- I've always thought the opposite was true. That is, …
- Could you suggest some further reading?
- Could I take up some of those points with you later?

WORD BANK

Integration and alliances

Types of merger: horizontal merger | vertical (forward / backward) merger | reverse merger | conglomerate merger | to combine as equals / by mutual agreement | cross-border merger | value chain

Types of acquisition / takeover: hostile / contested takeover | friendly takeover | target acquisition / company

Processes: leveraged buyout (LBO) | management buyout (MBO) | management buy-in (MBI) | takeover bid / attempt | dawn raid | to win over shareholders | insider (share) dealing | poison pill | to gain a controlling interest | to acquire a majority stake | due diligence | white knight | to pool resources | demerger

Regulation: regulators / regulatory body | antitrust legislation (AE) | law against monopolies (BE)

Alliances: joint venture | consortium | affiliated group

3 Summary

a. Work out what the words are in bold. (You will find many of them in the word bank).

MGRS ND NTGRTNS

CMPNS wishing to expand can do so by **PLGHNG** back the **PRFTS** into the business. This type of **RGNC GRWTH** tends to be slow. A faster but riskier way to grow is through **MRGRS** and **CQSTNS**. In the case of a **MRGR**, two companies **CMBN** as **QLS** and by **MTL GRMNT**. The companies lose their **SPRT** identities and form a completely new company. **NWDYS** the term refers to any **CMBNTN** where one company is completely **BSRBD** by another.

There are different types of **NTGRTN**, depending on where the companies are in the **DSTRBTN CHN**.

- **HRZNTL NTGRTN**: **MRGNG** of businesses at the same stage of production, e.g. two supermarkets
- **LTRL NTGRTN**: **MRGNG** of related but different businesses
- **VRTCL NTGRTN**: **MRGNG** of businesses at different stages of production. In **FRWRD NTGRTN**, a supplier acquires a customer. In **BKWRD NTGRTN**, a customer acquires a supplier
- **CNGLMRT NTGRTN**: **MRGNG** of organisations that operate in different industries or lines of business.
- **RVRS MRGR**: a **PRVT** company becomes a **PBLC** company by being **BSRBD** into a dormant 'shell company', to **vd** the time and **XPNS** of an IPO

In an **CQSTN** (or **TKVR**) one company buys more than 50% of the **SHRS** in another from its existing **SHRHLDRS** and thereby **GNS** a **CNTRLLNG NTRST**. This may be an agreed **BD** or it may be a **HSTL TKVR**, involving the company buying the **MJRTY** of the **SHRS** in its **TRGT CQSTN**. **SHRHLDRS** can accept or **RJCT** the **BD**, and the target company can also protect itself with a **PSN PLL** – a tactic intended to make a **HSTL TKVR** prohibitively **XPNSV**. The **TRGT** company can also be rescued from a **HSTL TKVR** by a **WHT KNGHT**, a 'friendly' **PRSN** or company that buys the firm.

In a **DWN RD**, a firm buys a substantial **MNT** of **SHRS** in the **TRGT CQSTN** first thing in the morning when the **STCK MRKT** opens. This is **CHPR** than if it made a formal **TKVR BD**.

In a **LVRGD BY-T** (LBO), a company is bought using a loan borrowed against its **SSTS**. A **MNGMNT BY-T** (MBO) happens when a company's top **XCTVS** buy a company they work for. If they buy into the ownership of another company, this is known as a **MNGMNT BY-N** (MBI).

An **LLNC** is simply an **GRMNT** between two companies to work together. If they have **NVSTD** together, this is known as a **JNT VNTR**.

MRGRS can result in one company **DMNTNG** the market. Laws against **MNPLS**, (in the US known as **NT-TRST LGSLTN**) restrict activity that would inhibit **CMPTTN**.

b. Work with a partner to test each other's vocabulary for mergers and acquisitions. One person reads out the text to the other, leaving out particular words. Pause for a few seconds so that your partner can supply the word. Then swap roles. Every time you swap, leave out more words.

c. Put in the numbers corresponding to the diagram. Add examples, e.g. 'farm' for raw materials.

[ ] conglomerate
[ ] lateral
[3] backward vertical
[ ] forward vertical
[ ] reverse merger
[ ] horizontal

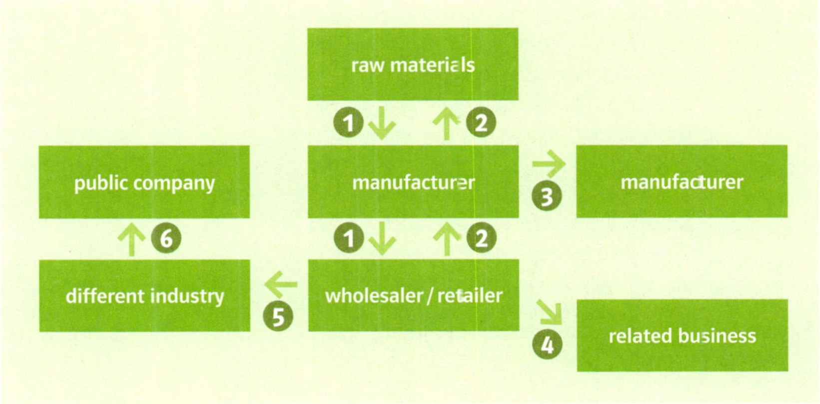

C Language | Strategy and goals

1 Compound nouns

a. Find pairs that form 13 compound nouns. Discuss what they mean.

profit | cash | corporate | due | asset | product | competitive | cost | feasibility | marketing | bargaining | customer | niche	+	stripping | cow | mix | cutting | study | focus | power | advantage | market | governance | diligence | maximisation | differentiation

b. Use 10 of the compounds in the sentences below.

1. Easy access to cheap energy gives Synysys Inc. a huge .... over other firms.
2. After the company was bought, everything was sold off – a classic example of ....-............ .
3. Every firm longs for a .... product, a money spinner to produce a reliable profit.
4. Good .... requires a set of guidelines for decision-making at board level.
5. Brokers were criticised for not doing enough .... on investment funds.
6. We're doing a .... on building a desalination plant in Australia.
7. What are the four Ps of the ....?
8. Some businesses trade for community benefit rather than the desire for ....
9. If you offer to pay in cash, you'll have far greater .... in the negotiation.
10. Our marketing strategy is less sales-oriented. Now we have a stronger ....-............ .

c. Write example sentences with the remaining compounds.

1. ....
2. ....
3. ....

2 Hyphens

a. Explain the differences.

1. a black-cab driver / a black cab-driver
2. a little-used car / a little used-car
3. a high school-girl / a high-school girl

b. Study the texts in this book to find examples of usage corresponding to the tips below.

LANGUAGE TIP

Hyphens

- Hyphens (-) connect (or separate) words: *mass-produced*
- Dashes (–) connect – or separate – phrases and sentences. They function in a similar way to brackets.
- Hyphens are normally used in the following cases:
  - Compound adjectives: *a well-known company* (BUT: *the company is well known*)
  - Compound nouns that function as adjectives: *public-sector employees, air-traffic control*
  - Fractions: *two-thirds, four-fifths*
  - After certain prefixes: *non-smoking, neo-conservative, anti-war, pro-American, an ex-army general*
  - In some titles: *vice-president* (BUT: *deputy director*)
  - To avoid ambiguities: *a fine-tooth comb* (NOT: ~~a fine tooth-comb~~)
  - Some writers use hyphens to separate identical letters. (*coordinate* → *co-ordinate*)
- In the case of compound nouns, there are no hard-and-fast rules. They are normally written as two words, but this can be a matter of taste: *think tank (BBC), think-tank (The Economist), thinktank (The Guardian)*
- Some collocations and phrasal verbs have evolved into compounds:
  - *to break one's fast* → *to breakfast* → *breakfast*
  - *to score with a card* → *a score card* → *a scorecard*
  - *to lay someone off* → *a lay-off* → *a layoff*
- The trend is to avoid hyphens as they clutter up text. If you are not sure, write compound nouns separately.

hyphen Bindestrich, **dash** Gedankenstrich, **brackets** Klammern, **to clutter up** überladen, vollstopfen

3 Analysis

a. Mark the syllable where the stress falls. (The first has been done for you.)

analyse | analysis | analyses | analytical | analysts | analysing

b. Complete the text with the words above. Then read it aloud to practise your fluency.

Business academics take an .... approach to strategic management. There are a variety of ...., suggested by different .... and business schools, to help a firm with its marketing strategy. One way of .... markets and product positions is through product portfolio .... There are a number of different ways in which a firm can .... the range of products (its portfolio) that it offers and therefore make decisions about what sort of marketing mix is needed.

4 Strategy

a. There is one word missing in every line. Decide on a suitable word and insert it in the right place.

Marketing Strategy

The **Boston Matrix**, also known the growth share matrix, is a framework that groups the parts of a company's business into four categories according market share and market growth.

- **Stars** have a high market share in fast-growing market. They may need high marketing expenditure to keep them competitive as new entrants come the market.
- **Question marks**, also known as 'problem children' or 'wild cats', a comparatively small market share but growth prospects.
- **Cash cows** have a market share but low growth prospects; they are often established product lines in mature markets and they generate cash that can used to support other products.
- **Dogs** are products with a small market share low growth prospects.

The framework can help companies decide whether keep or lose each product (hold or divest), and how to use the cash that is generated by successful products to maximise potential of the others. Typically, the company will decide to sell off the dogs and 'milk the cows', i.e. use the they generate to turn the stars into cows and turn the marks into stars.

SWOT analysis looks at the factors that might affect the or failure of an organisation. It is formed from the initial of 'strengths', 'weaknesses', 'opportunities' and 'threats'. The first two are regarded as internal factors, where could include the firm's reputation or a currently valuable patent. Weaknesses could include high staff turnover. The opportunities and threats are external that the company has no control over. New methods production or new materials present an opportunity, whereas new entrants on the market or new government legislation may pose a.

b. Complete the diagrams using information from the text.

Boston matrix

	High market share	Low market share
High market growth		
Low market growth		

SWOT analysis

	Strengths	Weaknesses
Internal		
	Opportunities	Threats
External		

5 Your personal strategy

a. Think of a goal that is important to you. It could be a personal goal, a financial goal, an academic goal or a career goal. Specify your goal in one short statement.

My goal is to ....

....

b. Complete the questionnaire (note-form only).

QUESTIONNAIRE

1. Is the goal short-term, long-term or medium-term? ....
2. Did you set the goal yourself? (If not, who else was involved?) ....
3. Is there a deadline or time scale? (If so, what is it?) ....
4. Does (or would) a deadline help you to achieve the goal? ....
5. Have you started working towards the goal yet? ....
6. If you haven't, what has prevented you? ....
7. How close are you to reaching your goal? ....
8. Is your progress measurable? ....
9. Does your personality obstruct you in your efforts to achieve your goal? ....
....
10. Are you willing and / or able to deal with this personality trait? ....
11. Do external circumstances hinder you in any way? ....
....
12. Are you willing and / or able to overcome these circumstances? ....
13. Is luck (good or bad) likely to affect your chances of attaining your goal? ....
....
14. Is the goal (un)realistic, (un) attainable, or (un)challenging? ....

to obstruct behindern, verhindern, **personality trait** Persönlichkeitsmerkmal, Charakterzug

c. Work with a partner and use the questionnaire to interview each other. If the answer is 'yes' or 'no', ask probing questions to find out more. Afterwards, give each other feedback.

PHRASES

Giving personal feedback
You strike me as … | I get the impression that you are … | I'd say you were … | You come across as … | My feeling is that you are …

+

PHRASES

Personal characteristics
an over-achiever | a bit starry-eyed | a bit of a drifter | a very goal-oriented kind of person | unrealistic as far as goals are concerned | a driven personality | someone who's got their feet firmly on the ground | somewhat optimistic.

d. List collocations with the word 'goal'.

Adjective + noun: *short-term goal,* ....
Verb + Noun: *to work towards a goal,* ....

e. Discuss the questions below.

1. Is it always good to be goal-oriented?
2. Briefly explain the concepts, models and frameworks listed below (all of which feature in this book). Which of them could be applied to personal strategy?

Covey's Time Management Matrix | Handy's 4 Cultures | Ansoff Matrix | 4Ps / 7Ps | STEP / PEST Analysis | Theory X / Theory Y | Critical Path Analysis | Gantt chart | SMART | Six Sigma | Deming cycle (PDCA) | Zero Defects | MBWA | Just-in-time | 7-S Framework | Ishikawa diagram | Boom-bust cycle | Boston matrix | SWOT Analysis

D Business leaders | Michael E. Porter

A Competitive Force

Michael Porter has become a 'living legend' in the world of management thinking. However, he considers himself to be an academic first and foremost and does not take his guru status too seriously. He never allows his books to be published in paperback, for example, and his lectures are always serious and devoid of publicity gimmicks. As *The Economist* wrote: 'Porter's work is academic to a fault. He is about as likely to produce a blockbuster full of anecdotes and boosterish catchphrases as he is to deliver a lecture dressed in bra and stockings.' Nevertheless, he has been highly influential and his book *Competitive Strategy*, first published in 1980, is still regarded as the 'bible of choice' by business managers wishing to brush up on their strategic thinking.

At the heart of Porter's ideas is the belief that the underlying purpose of every business is to gain competitive advantage. He suggests that to achieve this there are only three 'generic' strategies that can be followed. The first is to make things as cheaply as possible, therefore undercutting competitors and becoming the lowest cost producer in the market. The second is to become a specialist producer, offering something better and different, and therefore able to command a premium price. The third strategy is to dominate a niche market, and close out the competitors.

In order to choose the correct generic strategy, it is important to identify what type of industry you are in – is it emerging, or mature, or declining? Is it fragmented? Is it a global industry? Another set of factors to be considered is what Porter calls the 'five forces of competition', namely the state of rivalry between existing companies, the threat of new entrants to the market, the prospect of substitute products or services, the bargaining power of suppliers, and the bargaining power of consumers. Porter's way of presenting his ideas in simple lists became a hit with managers.

Following the successful uptake of his ideas on competitive strategy, Porter moved his gaze wider to consider the strategy of nations, and why some states were wealthy and others were not. In the *Competitive Advantage of Nations* (1990), he presented a model based on a four-sided diamond in which the components were traditional economic resources, domestic rivalry, infrastructure (including the education level of citizens) and the 'cluster phenomenon' – the tendency of similar businesses and their suppliers to group in the same geographical area. Porter observed that location was still a source of competitive advantage, despite high-speed communications and globalisation.

Most recently, Porter has started to write about health care and corporate social responsibility, applying his theories and models of strategy and competitiveness to current social issues.

Michael E. Porter (b. 1947, Michigan, USA) is an authority on competitive strategy and possibly the world's most famous business academic. He trained as an engineer at Princeton University before studying business. He now holds an MBA and a PhD in Business Economics from Harvard University, where he leads the Institute for Strategy and Competitiveness. As well as being a best selling author, he also set up a consulting firm, Monitor.

devoid of publicity gimmicks ohne Werbungsschnickschnack, **academic to a fault** extrem wissenschaftlich, **boosterish** (etwa) ermunternd, **bra and stockings** BH und Strümpfe, **to move one's gaze** seinen Blick abwenden, **cluster** Gruppierung

1 Reading

a. Write six questions or instructions based on the article that a business lecturer might use in an exam.

To what extent…? | Explain… | Outline… | Summarise… | Critically evaluate… | Comment on…

b. Work in groups. Compare your questions and discuss possible answers.

2 Vocabulary

Describe another remarkable person using the same structure as in the ***Economist*** quote..

"(*Name*) is (*adjective*) to a fault. S/he is as likely to (*example of unlikely behaviour)* as s/he is to (*example of highly improbable behaviour*)."

3 Balloon debate

You are flying in a hot-air balloon that is overloaded and quickly losing height. Half of the passengers must be thrown out, otherwise the balloon will crash and everyone will die. The passengers are business leaders featured in this book. Decide which one you will represent, and present a case arguing why you should stay in the balloon.

E Business communication | Negotiating a takeover

1 Discussion

1. When is it better to negotiate in a team than to negotiate alone?
2. What are the pitfalls of negotiating in teams? How can they be avoided?

2 Scenario

You are going to conduct a negotiation in teams. Read the company profiles and say which company is most likely to be the target of a takeover.

PRO-SEKT GMBH

Pro-Sekt GmbH started life as a cooperative of idealistic vineyard owners producing organic wines in the Kaiserstuhl region of southern Germany. It has developed a highly successful range of sparkling wines, known in the German-speaking world as *Sekt*. It also has a best-selling *Weißherbst* wine in its portfolio.

The Pro-Sekt brand is becoming well known throughout Europe, and is marketed through fine food outlets. The company is also associated with 'eco-food' and other environmental lobbies.

Kearson Inc

Kearson Inc. is a US-based multinational with an extensive foods and beverages portfolio that ranges from ice cream to powdered soup, and includes a number of major brewing and distilling brands.

A market leader in an increasingly competitive food sector, Kearson Inc. is currently diversifying into niche markets. They are keen to extend their portfolio to specialist organic foods and beverages that appeal to discerning customers who are willing to pay a premium for fine foods with green credentials.

pitfall, Falle, Tücke, **fine food(s)** Feinkost, **brewing** Bierbrauen, **organic** Bio-, **green credentials** Beitrag zum Umweltschutz

3 Background research

Discuss the questions below. If you do not know the answers, carry out research.

1. What are the best-selling wines in your region / in Europe / worldwide?
2. What are the differences between sekt, prosecco, cava and champagne (all types of sparkling wine)? What are the risks in classifying sparkling wine as champagne?
3. What exactly is organic wine?
4. What are the market trends for organic wine?
5. Which are the leading food and beverage companies? Which of them have famous drinks brands?

4 Preparation

a. Decide who will represent Pro-Sekt GmbH and who will represent Kearson Inc. Read your instructions (Pro-Sekt and Kearson on page 225), and the phrases below.

b. Try to anticipate what the other team wants – the information they are likely to ask for and the demands they might make. Decide what information you are prepared to give, and what you might need to conceal, and co-ordinate your response to any likely demands.

c. Assign roles so that you can play to your strengths and tactical advantages.

5 The negotiation

a. Decide on a date and venue for the negotiation, and note any further points you would like to discuss on the agenda below.

PRO-SEKT GMBH

– Adding Sparkle to Your Life

Date: ....
Venue: ....
Participants: ....
Excused: ....

Agenda: Proposed merger with Kearson Inc

1. Potential synergies
....
2. Brand image
....
2. Human resources
....
3. Management structure
....
4. Production
....
5. Price
....
6. AOB
....
....
....

PHRASES

Preparing a negotiation

Agreeing on aims
› We have to maintain a strong position.
› We need to be very clear about our terms.
› We must keep up a good relationship.

Deciding on roles
› So, how are we going to organise this?
› Would you like to start things off?
› Can you deal with the financial aspects?

Anticipating reactions
› They're bound to ask us about …
› We can expect them to …
› They won't like that!

Deciding what to reveal
› We need to set out our position.
› We should make it very clear that …
› Should we tell them about …?

Deciding what to conceal
› I don't think we should mention …
› Don't say anything about …
› Let's try to keep off that topic.

Predicting the outcome
› I feel pretty confident.
› I think we can do a deal.
› We may have to make concessions.

b. Meet to carry out the negotiation. Remember to set a time limit. (See the information in the box below.)

6 Follow-up

a. Debriefing: Discuss how the negotiation went. Which side got the best deal, and why?

b. Writing: Write a press release publicising the outcome and presenting your company in the best possible light.

SKILLS

Team negotiations
Team negotiations require careful co-ordination. It is important that everyone is clear about their role, the aims of the negotiation, and any concessions they may make. Roles can be assigned according to strengths of particular members, e.g. chief negotiator (carries overall responsibility), number cruncher (financial expert), facilitator (builds relationships, manages conflict). Roles can also be tactical, e.g. one negotiator (the 'good cop') adopts a conciliatory role in order to soften up members of the opposing team. They are then more likely to give in to the demands made by a much tougher negotiator (the 'bad cop').

F Consulting | Starting an airline

1 Scenario

Timo works for a management consultancy that specialises in start-ups and corporate branding. He received these emails from his boss just before he fell ill, and is now off work for three weeks. You have been asked to stand in for Timo. Read the emails and note down the tasks that you need to do.

From: kuegler.s@highfly.biz
Subject: Fwd.: Nicoli Enterprises
To: buchwald.t@highfly.biz

Hi Timo,

I'm forwarding this email to you – it's an exciting project and I'd like you to be the one to carry out the feasibility study. I'm confident that you'll do a fantastic job and – who knows – maybe you'll be able to apply some of that management strategy theory you picked up at business school.
Before you get cracking, please reply to Ms Lefevre thanking her for choosing us and promising to send the report within the next few days. Suggest some possible dates when we can fly to Lugano to present the pitch.
Btw, I'd like to have the draft of your report by Friday if possible. Let me know if there's a problem.

Best,
Simone Kügler
CEO Highfly Consultancy

>>

Dear Sir or Madam,

I am writing to you on behalf of my client, the celebrated Formula One racing driver and three-time world champion Fabio Nicoli, who is keen to invest his considerable personal capital in an exciting new project. As a trained pilot with many flying hours' experience, Fabio Nicoli would like to launch his own European-based airline as a way of extending his personal brand into the travel and leisure sectors.
We are currently seeking a consultancy to advise us on the best way to proceed, and we are approaching you as a leading authority in the airline business. In particular, we would like your recommendations on how to develop a successful and competitive business strategy for an exceptional new airline.
Should you be interested in this unique opportunity, we would like you to present your recommendations, based on a feasibility study, to Fabio Nicoli in person at our headquarters in Lugano. This study should be carried out in strict confidence. If you agree to undertake it, the timescale for delivering the report would be two weeks after we have given the go-ahead.
In anticipation of a positive response, I very much look forward to hearing from you.

With best regards,
Carola Lefevre
Personal Business Manager
Fabio Nicoli (Enterprises)

2 Writing

Write the email to Carola Lefevre as requested.

NEW AIRLINE – Fabio Nicoli – Feasibility study – Points to consider

- Target market: Celebrities? Business executives? Tourists? …?
- Competition/market saturation: Porter's 5 forces??? Benchmarking? (Research similar ventures that have failed – why did they fail?)
- Positioning
  - Budget airline, cut-price fares, cost-conscious travellers
  - Mainstream airline, scheduled/charter flights, all passengers
  - Corporate jet (charter?) for top managers
  - Exclusive airline for jet-set celebs (funky? classy?)
  - …?
- Brand
  - Strategy – promote personality and reputation of Fabio Nicoli
  - Name of airline
  - Slogan? Mission statement?
  - Corporate design (overall 'look', livery, cabin interior, uniforms, logo, etc.)
    --> commission a designer (Philippe Starck? Terence Conran? …?)
  - …?
- Finance
  - "Considerable personal capital" :o) = The sky's the limit???????
    --> Ask for more info, e.g. more investment needed?
  - Pricing model – low fares/mixed pricing, special offers, etc.
  - Get quotes from jet fuel suppliers, e.g. World Fuel Services?
  - Fleet: Buy, charter or lease aircraft? Which ones (Airbus? Lear Jet, Fokker,…?)
  - Costs – insurance, fuel, …
  - …?
- Timescale
  - Draft report by Friday (!!!)
  - Pitch?
  - Bureaucracy: airline certification, flight plan paperwork, …
  - Launch date?
  - …
- Routes
  - Short-haul only? …? Which airports? Also to lesser-known ones?
  - Regional? Global?
  - …
- USPs + extras
  - In-flight perks?
  - Published customer standards (e.g. JetBlue's Customer Bill of Rights)
  - E-ticketing? Online booking?
  - **V. IMPORTANT:** The 'WOW factor'? What will make this airline a WINNER?
- Exit strategy
  - What if it all goes pear-shaped? How can Fabio exit the venture 'gracefully'?

celebrities Prominenz, **livery** (hier) Beschriftung, **funky** flippig, cool, **The sky's the limit** Alles ist möglich, **in-flight perks** Flugkomfort, **to go pear-shaped** völlig danebengehen, **to exit gracefully** sich einen guten Abgang verschaffen

3 Research

Above are some notes you discovered on Timo's desk. Add further points and carry out the feasibility study. Then draft a report with recommendations that can also be presented in a pitch to Fabio Nicoli.

4 Presentation

Present your pitch in class. Compare the strengths and weaknesses of each one and choose the best.

Practice exam

A Listening

A 3.4 The managing director of Wetbacks Ltd, an outdoor clothing manufacturer, is speaking at a board meeting.

1 Complete the SWOT analysis, using no more than three words in each gap. (16 points)

STRENGTHS › Established firm with over .... years' experience in the UK, ... and continental Europe. › Strong brand image owing to: › Reputation for .... and durability of products › Successful .... centres in UK	**OPPORTUNITIES** › Growing interest in outdoor activities because: › Consumers are more .... › They also have more .... & .... › New export markets due to › EU expansion in .... › EU promotion of .... industry
WEAKNESSES › .... product range inhibits potential for sales growth › Our clothing is perceived by some people as too	**THREATS** › Competition from manufacturers in the .... (esp. .... & ....) whose products are › ...., › ...., › and more varied in design

2 Delete the four strategies that the MD does not recommend. (4 points)

- › Consolidate the current market position
- › Apply for EU grants and subsidies
- › Promote export sales in Eastern Europe.
- › Modernise Wetback's image
- › Create a new range of lightweight raincoats for rural customers.
- › Show commitment to fair trade and the environment
- › Manufacture clothing made from locally-grown fibres
- › Raise finance through bank loans
- › Go public

B Language

1 Complete the missing words. (5 points)

1. US equivalent of 'profit and loss account'	i..............................	s..............................
2. 'unfriendly' takeover attempt	h..............................	b..............................
3. period of falling share prices and weak trading	b..............................	m..............................
4. price at which one currency is traded for another	e..............................	r..............................
5. situation when exports exceed imports	t..............................	s..............................
6. informal expression for 'accountant'	n..............................	c..............................

2 Give the full forms of these abbreviations. (2 points)

1. DDP (Incoterm) ....
2. D/P (payment term) ....

3 Underline the correct option. (Only one is possible in each case.) (8 points)

1. Shares yield dividends *(whereas / however / even though)* bonds yield *(interest / interests)*.
2. If you need *(advise / advice / advices)*, I suggest *(you to contact / that you contact)* a lawyer.
3. Do you think the government's *(economy / economic / economical)* policies *(lead/led)* us into recession?
4. I'm considering *(to buy / that I buy / buying)* vintage wine, because I hear that it is *(a quite / quite a)* lucrative investment.
5. The CED *(denied completely / completely denied)* the allegation, *(whereas / however / even though)* there was some truth in it.
6. You *(mustn't / don't need to / have not to)* tip the waiter, but he'd appreciate *(if you do / it if you did)*.
7. Some banks have *(raised / risen)* their charges without *(declining / reducing)* management bonuses.
8. If you want to prevent *(that people use / people from using)* your credit card, keep your PIN *(save / safe)*.

4 Complete the sentences with suitable expressions chosen from the list. (5 points)

security | securities | turnover | fluctuation | credit | loan | rent | pension | immaterial | intangible | ensure | assure | commission | provision | lawsuits | processes | damage | damages | incur | occur

1. We always give our agents a 10% .... on sales.
2. Patents and copyrights are examples of .... assets.
3. Let me .... you that this problem will not .... again.
4. He finds it difficult to live on his state ....
5. If you want to take out a ...., the bank will ask for ....
6. With an out-of-court settlement we can avoid expensive .... and .... to our reputation.
7. We could reduce staff .... by improving pay and working conditions.

5 Translate, or give the English equivalents. (4 points)

1. Wettbewerbsvorteil ....
2. Umlaufvermögen ....
3. Skaleneffekte ....
4. Steuerhinterziehung ....

6 Give the noun forms of the verbs (1–4), and the adjective forms of the nouns (5–8). (4 points)

1. subsidise ....
2. withdraw ....
3. dismiss ....
4. prove ....
5. insolvency ....
6. deduction ....
7. litigation ....
8. analysis ....

7 Complete the text with the missing prepositions (6 points)

Brown PLC, which supplies the automotive industry .... machine tools, went .... the red last year and nearly had to be wound .... In the end it was bailed .... by the government. In 2007, the firm outsourced production .... Poland, causing labour costs to fall .... *(um)* almost a quarter. However, its reputation .... quality has suffered. Even though a slight rise .... profits has been reported for this quarter, it is not a good time to buy shares .... Brown PLC. Demand .... their products is sluggish. If you want a better return .... investment, you should invest .... pharmaceuticals.

8 Give a verb with a similar meaning. (6 points)

1. to **infringe** the law — to **v**..................................
2. to **comply with** the law — to **o**..................................
3. to **amend** a contract — to **m**..................................
4. to **reveal** information — to **d**..................................
5. to **cancel** membership — to **r**..................................
6. to **end** the agreement — to **t**..................................

EXAM TIP

Strategy
Answer all the questions. Do the 'easy' ones first. This will help you to manage your time. If you are not sure of an answer, just guess. You may be lucky.
In multiple-choice tasks, never mark more than one option if only one is asked for. Even if one of the options is correct, you will not get any points.

C Reading

You work for Gottlieb GmbH, a family-owned company in Dresden that manufactures kitchens. There are rumours of a takeover by a US multinational, Spurway Inc. and your boss has asked you to do some research. You have found their website on the Internet. Read the text and do the tasks that follow.

1 Find the English equivalents in the text: (2 points)

1. nachhaltig, tragfähig ....
2. Gewinnspanne ....
3. unternehmerisch ....
4. Rentabilität ....

2 Translate into German (2 points)

1. shareholders ....
2. maintenance ....
3. market share ....
4. chain retailers ....

Spurway Inc.

Home | Corporate information | Investor relations | Our companies | Our products

Profile
Spurway Corporation is one of the world's largest manufacturers of kitchenware and white goods, with a portfolio of leading brands and a worldwide network of installation and service companies. Our kitchen products include sink units, ovens and hobs, freezers, dishwashers and microwaves.
Spurway's headquarters are in Cleveland, Ohio. Manufacturing facilities for our products are located throughout the United States, and international operations are located primarily in Europe. Today, Spurway has approximately 7,200 shareholders and 67,000 employees.

Growth strategy
Acquisitions are key to Spurway's growth strategy. We have had significant successes in acquiring companies in both the US and abroad. These include companies with products and services that fit within our three core divisions:
- Complete kitchen units and related products
- Sinks, dishwashers and plumbing products
- Installation and maintenance services (non-manufacturing)

Acquisition criteria
Spurway currently seeks to acquire companies that design and manufacture complete kitchens to customers' requirements. Candidates for acquisition are companies which:
- Have a proven record of profitability, with profit margins in the mid-teens or better
- Offer the prospect of sustainable, above average growth and profitability
- Are leaders in their particular market or technology
- Are dedicated to enhancing the personal growth and development of their employees.
- Are entrepreneurial

Proven history of success
Asset stripping is not one of our objectives. Generally, companies that join Spurway Inc. experience growth for a number of reasons:
- Added resources (which include capital) as well as support from corporate staff in areas related to environmental matters, human resources, marketing, information systems, research and development, and legal advice
- Extensive synergies with our consumer products businesses to collectively gain market share
- Expanded distribution opportunities
- Participating in our corporate programs that target leading chain retailers and large manufacturers

This has allowed Spurway to achieve significant annual increases in sales, profits and market share for its many products and services.

For more information, please contact: Robin Larsen, Tel. 303-343-2400

Spurway Inc.

3 Answer your boss's questions by marking the answers below. (10 points)

		Yes	No
1.	It's important that we keep our brand name. Will this be possible?		
2.	Are our products compatible with their product range?		
3.	Do they only acquire companies that make products like ours?		
4.	Will we be the first of their acquisitions outside the US?		
5.	We may need help in legal matters. Do they offer this?		
6.	Do they take over unprofitable companies ('turnarounds')?		
7.	Would they provide us with capital?		
8.	Would an acquisition offer us a wider distribution network?		
9.	Do they specify a minimum shareholding?		
10.	Do they claim in any way that they are committed to the environment?		

4 Find words with the same meaning (2 points)

1. main office ....
2. mainly ....
3. roughly (not exactly) ....
4. situated ....

5 Choose the right option. (2 points)

1. If Spurway Inc. acquires Gottlieb, what type of merger would it NOT be?
   a. horizontal b. vertical c. cross-border
2. Which of the following is NOT an appliance?
   a. sink unit b. freezer c. dishwasher

6 Explain the meaning of 'asset stripping' in your own words. (2 points)

D Writing (40 points)

You work for the German subsidiary of Kick-Start, an international management consultancy. Your boss has asked you to reply to this email in the form of a letter, signed by you. Give the advice and information requested, and suggest a meeting to discuss the details.

EXAM TIP

Writing

Ask your teacher how points are awarded for the writing section. Criteria typically include:
- Language accuracy (grammar, spelling, etc.)
- Range of business vocabulary
- Appropriate style and register
- Task fulfilment

From: John Coverdale <coverdale@mac.com>
Subject: Enquiry about company start-up
To: Kathrin Becker
Date: 20.06.2010 at 13:07:44 CEST

Dear Sir/Madam,

My wife and I are moving to Germany next month and we plan to set up a language school in your town providing in-company Business English courses to management consultants. We would be grateful if you could tell us what you think of our business idea.

Any other tips and suggestions you could give us would also be welcome, e.g. sources of finance in addition to our own capital, the type of company we should register as, and so on.

As we are looking for a management consultancy to work with on a regular basis, we would also be interested in what services you could offer us.

A prompt reply would be appreciated.

Regards,

John Coverdale

25 Chippenham Close, Malmesbury, Wiltshire SN16 9TA, United Kingdom

Appendix

UNIT 1 E 5 | Page 17

Dictating information over the phone

❶

Meeting
Tomorrow, 10.00am – 11.30 am
Marketing Dept.
Room 130
Subject: New Packaging

❷

Plane arriving 13.50
Frankfurt airport
Flight number BA 253
Terminal 3
Meet Mr Hamish Mullen

❸

Restaurant booking
'Chiang Mai' Thai Restaurant
Burkstraße 56
Table for six people
7.30 pm

❹

Invoice number: 2304/566D
Total to pay: €354.56
Please pay by: 30 April 2009
Pay to: account no. 0206677
Bank: Deutsche Bank, Bonn

Telephoning role card: A (caller)

❶ You've left your diary in **B**'s office after a meeting. You're calling from Frankfurt airport and your plane leaves in 20 minutes. Ring up to explain.

❷ It's 2.45 pm. You realise you had an appointment with **B** at 2.30 pm. Ring up and apologise.

❸ You are a supplier. The distribution company that you use are on strike. Phone your customer (**B**) and explain that there will be a problem with deliveries.

Telephoning role card: B (receiver)

❶ **A** calls you with a problem. Try to help – you will need to ask for precise information.

❷ **A** was supposed to come to your office at 2.30 pm. It's now 2.45 pm and he/she phones to apologise. Arrange a new appointment.

❸ You are waiting for an urgent delivery from a supplier (**A**). He/she phones to say that he/she has a problem. Try to find a solution.

UNIT 3 E 7 | Page 42

Role card A: Student borrower

You are meeting with your bank manager to discuss a bank loan. You need €5000 in order to finance a study semester in the USA. You would like to know if it is possible to borrow the money and pay it back when your university course finishes in two years time. You also need to know what interest you have to pay (if you borrowed the money from your parents you wouldn't have to pay any interest) and what security you would need to offer on the loan.

Role card B: Bank lender

You are meeting a customer of your bank who would like to discuss a loan. Find out the reason for the loan, the amount required, and the required duration of the loan. Before the discussion, decide what the bank's policy is on:

- interest rate
- repayment schedule
- security required on the loan

Be flexible, but remember that your bonus depends on getting a good deal.

duration [djuːˈreɪʃn] Dauer, Laufzeit

UNIT 5 F Exercise b. | Page 71

They're not so grrr-eat!

Kellogg's responded by stressing that Frosties did have a part to play in forming part of a healthy balanced diet and they were well known for encouraging and supporting sporting activities. They produced tables of information comparing the levels of sugar, fat and calorie content found in a typical serving of Frosties with other well known cereal brands. They also illustrated how Frosties and a selection of breakfast cereals compared with other 'typical' breakfast foods such as grilled bacon, sausages, fried eggs and toast with jam in terms of the sugar, fat and calorie content. Finally they highlighted how many children and teenagers replaced breakfast with confectionary items and used a table to show the number of calories and grams of sugar and fat found in a selection of snack foods. The advertisers also pointed out that a 30g serving of Frosties without milk provided a high percentage of the recommended daily intake of several essential vitamins and minerals. Furthermore they indicated that they were going to put information on balanced diets and exercise on the backs of their packets. The ASA noted the advertisers encouraged children to participate in sport and that they were going to provide information on balanced diets on their packets. The Authority was concerned however that despite the advertiser arguing Frosties had a role to play as part of a balanced diet they had not actually referred to this in the commercial. Rather, the claim "... eat right ..." referred to Frosties. When looking at the evidence sent by the advertisers the ASA saw that Frosties bore similar comparison to some other cereals in terms of fat, calorie and sugar content. Overall though, Frosties contained more sugar than an apple, fruit juice or plain yoghurt. Nor did the comparison with a selection of confectionery and snack foods demonstrate that Frosties were a healthy product. Notably the table provided by the advertiser showed that Frosties with 125ml of milk contained more sugar than a jam doughnut, a custard tart or a flap jack. The Authority believed the underlying message of the commercial which showed children playing football with the claim "eat right" implied that the product was healthy. Because of the high sugar content of Frosties the Authority believed the claim was misleading. Because it was found to be in breach of the code the advertisers were told not to repeat the claim "eat right" in future advertisements for Frosties. As the food industry comes under the public spotlight amid growing concerns about advertising to children, this case provided serious food for thought not only for Kelloggs but for all food industry advertisers about the claims they can and can't make about their product.

Is it clear that this is an advertisement?

The Committee of Advertising Practice (CAP) Code says that ads should be designed so that it clear that they are marketing material. The ASA agreed with the complainants' assertions that it was not clear that the first mailing sent by Jaguar was marketing material, especially as it arrived in a typewritten envelope that carried a first class stamp. We also agreed that the mailing was irresponsible as its sexually suggestive tone could cause distress and offence to recipients. Jaguar issued a public apology and sent personal letters of apology to those that had contacted them directly.

The stuff of nightmares?

In defending its decision not to place a scheduling restriction on the ad the body responsible for pre-clearing the commercial, the BACC, pointed out that the horror depicted was very mild and clearly comical. No one was hurt, the blob didn't attack anyone and some people even dived into it with smiles on their faces. They believed that the fact people were positively attracted to the blob and were shown emerging from it unharmed and happy emphasized the message that the blob was not a thing of terror. Responding to the complaints, the advertiser said it would liaise with the BACC and revise the broadcast schedule so that the ads did not appear around children's programmes or on children's channels. However, they said they wanted to avoid the imposition of a formal ex-kids scheduling restriction. This restriction would mean their ad could not be shown around programmes made for or specifically targeted at children. Because only very young children had been scared by the ad they believed this would limit the opportunity of the ad to reach a general audience. Concluding its investigation, the ASA acknowledged that it was difficult to anticipate the effect the ad was going to have on young children. The ASA agreed with the advertiser's decision not to broadcast in or around children's programming but decided to impose a formal ex-kids restriction as the best way to reduce the likelihood of young children seeing the ad.

Source: asa.org.uk

UNIT 9 C 5 Exercise a. | Page 118

Sample internship application

Zur Zolltafel 74
78052 Weilersbach
Germany

13th October 2009

Erica Harmer
Human Resources Department
Shell UK Ltd
Shell Centre
London SE1 7NA

Re: Application for internship in July 2010

Dear Ms Harmer

I am a second-semester business student studying on an international bachelor degree programme in Germany. This programme is taught in both German and English, and in their third semester all students are encouraged to seek internships of up to six months in international companies abroad in order to further their business experience.

As you will see from the enclosed curriculum vitae, I already have work experience in companies here in Germany. I am particularly interested in human resources management and international corporate relations, and studying on an international business degree programme has been invaluable in broadening my experience of the issues involved in intercultural communication.

I decided to contact your company regarding the possibility of an internship because of the outstanding reputation that Shell enjoys within the international business community as a leader in the field of communication and human resources management. I was very encouraged to read on your website that you welcome enquiries from prospective internees who wish to spend some time working with the company. I am especially motivated to work in the UK, where I feel that I could further improve my communication skills in English.

If you think that I might fit into your organisation for an internship, I would very much look forward to hearing from you.

Yours sincerely

Anne Schneider

Encl: CV, certificates and grade reports

UNIT 9 C 5 Exercise a. | Page 118

Sample job application

Zur Zolltafel 74
78052 Weilersbach
Germany

14th October 2009

Erica Harmer
Human Resources Department
Shell UK Ltd
Shell Centre
London SE1 7NA

Re: Advertisement for International Sales Manager, *Economist* 12.10.2009

Dear Ms Harmer,

With reference to your advertisement in the appointments page of this week's *Economist*, I would like to submit my application as I consider that I have the necessary qualifications and experience for such a challenging and interesting position within a leading multinational organisation.

As you will see from the enclosed curriculum vitae, I have a background in both the petrochemical and pharmaceutical sectors. I also have a wide range of knowledge of international markets and have been involved in major deals with well-known multinational companies.

You will also note that I am currently working on a short-term contract for Sanofi-Synthelabo AG, as part of a team that has been actively and successfully promoting the company's products and services in the Middle East and North Africa. This contract is due to terminate at the end of the year.

You will further note that I am single and am currently based in the Black Forest region of southern Germany. I enjoy travelling and experiencing new cultures, and I am quite used to living abroad. I therefore consider myself to be highly mobile and flexible where international postings are concerned.

If you feel that my professional profile matches that of the person you are looking for, I would very much look forward to hearing from you.

Yours sincerely,

Anne Schneider

Encl: CV, professional reference, personal reference, copies of certificates

UNIT 9 C 6 Exercise b. | Page 118

Sample CV

Jan-Peter Ulrich

Friedrich-Ebert-Straße 30
78054 Schwenningen
Germany

Tel. +49 7720 39060
Mobile: +49 163 3423432
Email: jandu@t-online.de

OBJECTIVE

To obtain an internship in which I can improve my language skills and acquire experience of working in another culture

EDUCATION AND TRAINING

2009 – present	**Hochschule Furtwangen University**, Germany International study programme (IBM) taught in English, leading to a Bachelor of Arts degree in International Business Management; expected graduation 2012 Major: International Business (Asian region)
1999 – 2008	**Wirtschaftsgymnasium am Hoptbühl**, Villingen, Germany (business college) Qualification: Abitur (advanced school-leaving certificate)
1999 – 2008	**Realschule Bickenberg**, Villingen, Germany (secondary school) Qualification: Mittlere Reife: Grade 2,0 (standard school-leaving certificate)

EMPLOYMENT

May 2008 – May 2009	**Neurologische Klinik Schweizer**, Königsfeld (psychiatric clinic) Civilian service: operated the post, advised patients and visitors, distributed the post, sold newspapers at the hospital kiosk, developed software for the computer system
June – July 2008	**Mediamarkt GmbH**, Bad Dürrheim (retailer in consumer electronics) Sales assistant (summer job): handled payments, advised customers, dealt with telephone enquiries, assisted in the stock room

LANGUAGE SKILLS

German	Native language (L1)
English	Fluent in speaking and writing (C1 level/proficient user)
Spanish	Fluent in speaking and writing (B2 level/independent user)
Mandarin	Intermediate level (approx. 1200 words speaking/writing)

FURTHER SKILLS

IT/computer: SAP EBP, MS Office, Linux/Solaris, Photoshop
Graphic design and website development

POSITIONS OF RESPONSIBILITY

Student representative and course speaker at the Hochschule Furtwangen University
Member of DLRG (German Search and Rescue Life Saving Association)
Elected to serve on Jugendrat (Youth Council of Freiburg): Involved in event management including financial planning, fundraising and team leadership
Clean German/EU driving licence

INTERESTS

Handball, cross-country running
Theatre and music events
Science fiction

References available on request

UNIT 13 E 2 Exercise c. | Page 172

Role card: Ambiance Hotels Group GmbH

Your company, Ambiance Hotels Group GmbH, runs a chain of small and exclusive 'wellness' hotels in beautiful and famous European locations such as Baden Baden, Lake Constance and the Austrian Tyrol. Your hotels cater for discerning customers and they are especially popular with celebrities who appreciate the high level of service and the discreet and secure environment in which to relax.

Your up-market concept has proved highly successful. However, you are operating in an increasingly competitive environment and you are constantly striving to stay ahead of the field. Your latest marketing drive will combine top-end quality with the idea of 'green lifestyle and beauty', so you are now concentrating on building a range of products that are 100% pure, natural, and organic, and sourced from the country of origin.

You are meeting today with representatives of Rosella Bay Pty Ltd, a company that your research has shown may be able to supply you with high quality tea tree oil products.

Plan ahead and decide on your goals. During the negotiation, find out whether Rosella are able to supply what you need, and try to negotiate a deal.

Points to discuss:

The product

- Specifications – special requirements for wellness market?
- Safety issues – is the tea tree oil correctly diluted with other oils?
- Customised bottles and jars? Produced with the Ambiance logo?

The order

- Sample bottles, or a regular order?
- Quantity

Payment

- Price and discounts
- Method and terms of payment

Delivery

- Time / date
- Transportation
- Packing details

AOB

UNIT 13 E 2 Exercise c. | Page 172

Role card: Rosella Bay Pty Ltd

Your company, Rosella Bay Pty Ltd, manufactures a range of specialist organic cosmetics products. You are the leading producer of 'green lifestyle' natural cosmetics in Australia and have become famous with your Zero Carbon Footprint campaign, featuring native Australians in your TV spots. Now you are hoping to expand your sales worldwide, focusing on the highly lucrative European market where the fashion for wellness hotels cultivates a philosophy of natural beauty, anti-ageing and healing.

Today you are meeting with representatives of Ambiance Hotels Group GmbH, a highly successful and up-market 'wellness' hotel chain that boasts many high profile media and sports personalities among its clientele. The company has expressed interest in your current range of tea tree oil products.

Your information is that they are keen to present their philosophy of green lifestyle and beauty with a range of cosmetics and healing products that are 100 % pure, natural, and organic, and sourced from the country of origin.

Plan ahead and decide on your goals. Then meet to negotiate a deal with them.

Points to discuss:

Product description
- Specifications – purity, organic, custom-blended …
- USPs

The order
- Sample bottles, or regular order?
- Quantity

Payment
- Price and discounts
- Method and terms of payment

Delivery
- Time / date
- Transportation
- Packing details

AOB

UNIT 14 F 5 | Page 187

Role card: The 'FOR' lobby group

Prepare arguments in favour of the biogas plant, e.g. alternative technology, renewable energy, new opportunities for farmers, jobs for local people, cheap electricity, using up waste, supporting rural communities, reducing carbon emissions.

Role card: The 'AGAINST' lobby group

Prepare arguments opposing the biogas plant, e.g. industrial eyesore in rural area, smell, noise and disturbance, big lorries on small country roads, danger to people, too close to village, risk of disease, polluting waste in water system.

Role card: The local media (print media / TV)

Prepare questions for BW and local council, e.g. why is a German company involved instead of a British company, who is putting up the money, will taxpayers' money be used, who benefits from the energy, is there a need for this technology, who is making money from the scheme.

Role card: The local council / DEFRA representatives

Use the hearing to show that government is committed to alternative energy and new technology. Emphasise the benefits of EU co-operation and German innovation, and government commitment to rural development in a farming area with high unemployment. The biogas scheme will mean more jobs, cheaper energy, less waste.

Role card: The BW-Biogas representatives

Use the flyer you have prepared with the FAQs. Emphasise the benefits of green solutions, new opportunities for farmers, natural energy, cheaper electricity, possibility of local employment, better than wind farms or nuclear power stations.

UNIT 16 E 4 Exercise a. | Page 209

Role card: Kearson Inc.

You have been searching for new companies to extend your multinational food and beverages portfolio, and a golden opportunity has now presented itself in the form of Pro-Sekt GmbH, a German company producing high quality organic wines.

Your consultants think that the company has excellent potential for growth in a very lucrative market. They have learned that the owners are willing to sell a substantial part of the business, which would result in Kearson taking a controlling interest.

The advice is to move quickly, as according to the M&A grapevine there is considerable interest in this highly successful young business. A meeting has been arranged today with directors of Pro-Sekt.

Kearson: future ideas for Pro-Sekt

- Overhaul the brand image ('family values' is not the Kearson style)
- Reduce labour costs (e.g. part-time rather than full-time employees)
- Headhunt top managers by attracting them with competitive salaries and perks
- Introduce bulk handling and automation to reduce material costs
- Charge premium prices, marketing wine as a specialist niche product

You are meeting with them today to negotiate a deal. You are hoping to pay a price of about €120m (your upper limit is €160m).

During the negotiation try to find out more about what has made their business so successful, and try to persuade them to agree to measures that would increase profitability.

golden opportunity einmalige Gelegenheit, **grapevine** Flurfunk, Gerüchte

Role card: Pro-Sekt GmbH

You are the directors of Pro-Sekt GmbH. You have been highly successful in growing the organic wine business, and as 'serial entrepreneurs' you are now eager to pursue further 'eco-business' activities. In order to raise working capital you would like to sell off 70% of the company.

However, you would like to ensure that the integrity of the Pro-Sekt 'fine and natural' concept is maintained. You are therefore inviting a friendly takeover that would allow the existing management to continue with the day-to-day running of the business.

Several companies have expressed interest in a deal, and today a meeting has been arranged with representatives of the global food and beverages giant, Kearson Inc.

Pro-Sekt: the USPs

- cooperative image – small traditional producers with family values
- secure, long-term working relationship with trusted employees
- flat hierarchy, with low salary differentials3
- finest raw materials, highest organic standards and purity certificatior
- affordable prices, in line with wholesome natural image

You would only agree to a takeover if you were satisfied that the core values and hard-won reputation of the Pro-Sekt brand were not going to be jeopardised.
You estimate that a 70% stake of the business is worth about €150m (your bottom line is €110m). You are keen to sell, but you are not prepared to 'sell out'.

core values Kernwerte, **wholesome** gesund, gesundheitsfördernd, **to jeopardise** gefährden, aufs Spiel setzen, **to sell out** Verrat begehen

Transcripts

CD1

A 1.1 **Unit 1** A1 Exercise a.

Tanja: Good morning, David. You're here early today. It's not even eight o'clock and you're already working!

David: Morning, Tanja. Yeah, I got a lift into town because the weather's so bad. I didn't feel like standing at the bus stop getting wet.

Tanja Hey, I thought you English were used to rainy weather.

David: Ha ha ha.

Tanja: Anyway, the weather forecast says it's going to be better tomorrow.

David: Thank goodness for that. So, did you have a nice weekend, Tanja?

Tanja: Yes, I went to Freiburg with a friend. We were lucky because it was the last day of the warm sunshine. You won't believe it, but we had lunch outside. Anyway, what about your weekend?

David: Well, we spent most of the time getting Luke ready for his first day at kindergarten.

Tanja: Oh, is it his first day today? How did he feel about it?

David: I thought he'd be nervous, but he was really excited. I don't know how long that'll last, but it'll be great if he settles in and makes some friends.

Tanja: I'm sure he will. Hey, I see you've got yet another photo of Luke on your desk! Oh, he's so cute! By the way, something else seems different in here. Has someone moved the furniture?

David: Yes, it was me, actually. I decided to turn my computer around so I can face the window.

Tanja: Oh, David, you can't do that. It's bad for your eyes and anyway it's against the regulations.

David: What regulations?

Tanja: The health and safety regulations. Didn't you know? Our offices have to be ergonomic1!

David: No one tells me anything around here. Anyway, I enjoy looking out of the window.

Tanja: Okay, but don't be surprised if they come and tell you to turn it back to where it was.

David: Well, thanks for warning me, Tanja! I'm amazed. You've only been at the company for two months and you already know everything!

Tanja: I was told that when you're a trainee, you need to keep your ears and eyes open all the time.

David: Good advice, I guess.

Tanja: Hey, David, look at your pot plants! I think they need water. Look how dry they are.

David: Oh, yeah, thanks – I'll water them now. Are there regulations against pot plants, too?

Tanja: I don't think so … But you know what, with our new management, anything can change. They seem to have lots of new ideas.

David: Yes, having all internal communication in English was a good move, in my opinion. After all, we are a global corporation. But apart from that, I expect it'll be business as usual.

Tanja: Well, not exactly, David. There may be some bigger changes than you think.

David: Oh?

Tanja: I've just heard a few rumours, that's all. From people who are worried about their jobs. Probably nothing in it, of course. But since the takeover everything has gone quiet. Too quiet some people think. But you're probably right. And anyway, for us it'll be business as usual. In fact, I can see a load of paper-work waiting for me already.

David: At least you're getting interesting tasks to do – not just photocopying all day.

Tanja: I guess so. A friend of mine – she's a trainee in another company – she has to make coffee for her boss. I'd refuse to do that!

David: So would I. Oh, Tanja, there are some phone messages for you …

Tanja: Okay, I'll listen to them while I have my breakfast. I picked up a couple of butterpretzels from the bakery on the way here. Can I offer you one?

David: No, thanks, Tanja, not while I'm working. I don't want butter and crumbs all over my keyboard. By the way, er, Tanja, if you're getting yourself a coffee, could you bring me one, too?

Tanja: Sure, I'll do it for you David, since you're not my boss! Capuccino with milk and sugar?

David: Yes, please. The usual!

A 1.2 **Unit 1** A2 Exercise a.

Voiceover: You have three new messages. Please enter your code.

Message 1

Recorded voice: Friday, the twenty-fourth of October, 2.45pm

Man: Hi this is Mick from Outback Training, calling with a message for Tanja Fisher. It's about the training course in January. It's great that twelve people have signed up – and thanks for sending me the list so quickly. It means I can go ahead and sort out accommodation at the Schwarzwald Treeline Centre. As you know, they're all going to be climbing trees, so what I need from you is information about the size of each person who's signed up. In that way, I can organise safety equipment that fits correctly. So, Tanja, can you measure each person and send me the details as soon as you can. Oh, and if anyone else registers, let me know by Tuesday. Thanks Tanja, and have a nice day.

A 1.3 Message 2

Recorded voice: Friday, the twenty-fourth of October, 13.23pm

Woman: Hi Tanja, it's Penny here. Tanja I can't find my office keys anywhere, and I was wondering whether I may have left them in your office this morning. That's where I saw them last, anyway. I remember they were lying on top of my file, and it's possible that when I picked up the file the keys slipped off. If they're not on the desk, they might be under the desk. So would you mind checking, just in case? And maybe ask David if he's seen them. If you find them, you can reach me at home – I decided to go home early today because I'm absolutely lost without my office keys! Oh, and the key ring's got a fluffy pink pig mascot, and the pig's wearing a kilt. Anyway, Tanja, thanks, and hope to hear from you soon!

A 1.4 Message 3

Recorded voice: Friday, the twenty-fourth of October, 4.22pm

Woman: Guten Tag Frau Fischer. Hier ist Nicola Stahl von EazyPrinz. Zuerst einmal vielen Dank für die Bestellung von 500 Plakaten. Leider brauchen wir doch noch eine Angabe von Ihnen: Soll das Papier matt oder glänzend sein? Könnten Sie uns sobald wie möglich Bescheid geben? Andernfalls werden wir die Lieferfrist nicht einhalten können. Ich bin nächste Woche nicht im Büro, aber meine Kollegin, Frau Schweizer, wird Ihnen weiter helfen. Sie können Frau Schweizer unter dieser Telefon-Nummer erreichen: 07721- 3404, Durchwahl 112. Ihre E-Mail-Adresse lautet schweizer@eazyprinz.de, das ist s-c-h-w-e-i-z-e-r at e-a-z-y-p-r-i-n-z-punkt de. Auf Wiederhören!

A 1.5 **Unit 1** E2 Exercises a. and b.

Call 1

Markus: Guten Tag, Bahu Interiors.

Bob: Oh, good morning, this is Bob Holder from Graphic Solutions. Could I speak to Markus Burger, please?

Markus: Yes, speaking. How can I help you, Mr Holder?

Bob: I'm calling about the new graphics software. I got an email from Anita Schmelz saying that it was ready and that I should contact you.

Markus: Ah, yes, that's right. I'm standing in for her this week. Anyway, we've got the complete package now, and I've prepared a short demonstration for you. You'll like it – it's very user-friendly.

Bob: Great. Then shall I come over and pick it up? I could come tomorrow or on Friday.

Markus: Tomorrow would be fine. Just a moment, I'll just check my diary. Yes, how about ten o'clock?

Bob: Ten o'clock? Yes, that suits me. Where shall we meet?

Markus: Um, if you just report at the reception, I'll come down and meet you there. It's easier than trying to find my office!

Bob: OK, so I look forward to seeing you then. Bye for now,

Markus: Goodbye.

◎ A 1.6 Call 2

Markus: Guten Tag, Bahu Interiors, Markus Burger.
Dennis: Oh, er, do you speak English?
Markus: Yes, no problem. What can I do for you?
Dennis: I'd like to speak to a Mr Peter Cooper.
Markus: Oh, he's on a different extension, but I can put you through to him. Can I have your name please?
Dennis: It's Dennis Wiseman.
Markus: Thank you, Mr Weissmann. If you hold, I'll just connect you.
Dennis: Thank you.
Markus: Okay, well, I'm afraid Mr Cooper is not picking up the phone – he may be out of the office. Can I get him to call you back?
Dennis: Yes, please. It is rather urgent that I speak to him today.
Markus: Well, if I take your contact details, I'll make sure he returns your call as soon as possible. May I have your telephone number, please?
Dennis: Mr Cooper knows my number, but let me give it to you anyway. It's oh seven seven one three five double seven extension nine one one.
Markus: I'll read that back to you. Oh seven seven one three five double seven extension nine one one.
Dennis: That's right.
Markus: And it's Mr Weißmann. Weiß as in … um … Edelweiß?
Dennis: No, it's Dennis Wiseman. That's W-I-S-E-M-A-N.
Markus: Mr Wiseman - my apologies. I'll get him to call you back.
Dennis: Thank you very much for your help. Goodbye.
Markus: Goodbye.

◎ A 1.7 **Unit 1** E 3

Fabian: So, when should we meet?
Jim: How about Friday morning?
Fabian: I'm afraid I'll be busy then. The afternoon would suit me better.
Jim: Hmm, that might be tricky. What's your schedule like for next week?
Fabian: Well, I can't make Monday or Tuesday, and I'll be out of the office all morning on Wednesday. But I'd be free any time in the afternoon.
Jim: That sounds fine. I haven't got anything on then either. So what time would you prefer?
Fabian: Oh, any time would suit. Shall we go for 3pm, and have the meeting in your office?
Jim: I just need to check with Anita, since we share the office. Can I call you back to confirm it?
Fabian: I'll be in my office until lunchtime. If I don't hear from you by then, I'll assume it's OK.

◎ A 1.8 **Unit 1** E 4

1. **When's the next meeting?**
   February 13th.
2. **And what time does it start?**
   Half past ten.
3. **Could I have your phone number, please?**
   It's oh seven seven two oh, six five three double seven
4. **Could you give me your credit card number?**
   Three four oh seven, double oh nine seven, four two oh one, nine triple eight.
5. **And what's the expiry date?**
   March two thousand and twelve.
6. **How big is your flat?**
   About two hundred and thirty square metres2.
7. **And how much rent do you pay?**
   Six hundred and thirty euros a month.
8. **Could you give me your address please? I've got a pen.**
   OK. It's S-H-S bracket U-K close bracket P-L-C, new line, twenty five slash twenty eight Curran Square, Curran that's C-U-R-R-A-N Square, new line, Slough spelt S-L-O-U-G-H, and the postcode is S-L three, five Q-A. Then next line, U-K.
9. **Have you got an email address?**
   It's foster dot j at spaceholder dot com. That's F-O-S-T-E-R dot J at spaceholder, all one word dot com.
10. **And who is the contact person?**
    Mr Philippe Crespeau. That's P-H-I-L-I-P-P-E, then C-R-E-S-P-E-A-U

A 1.9 **Unit 2** C 3 Exercises b. and c.

Part 1

Organisation is essential for any business, whether it is a sole trader or a multinational giant. Without some sort of organisation the business would be unable to function. However, there are many different ways in which an organisation can be structured, and this depends on the size of the company, the type of business, the aims and objectives, and so on.
Typically, small businesses have less formal structures, because communication is easier and everyone is clear about their role and responsibilities. These informal structures cannot be shown on an organisation chart. But larger organisations require more formal structures which show who does what, who is in authority, and how information is communicated. These formal structures can take different forms, which can be shown as diagrams.

A 1.10 Part 2

A tree diagram shows each level of the organisation, and also the connections to other levels. It is set out like a family tree diagram, and as well as showing the hierarchy of the organisation it can also show the name and job title of all the people in the organisation.
The organisation can also be shown as a pyramid, with a small number of people at the top with greater authority, and more people at the bottom with less authority. Some pyramids are tall and thin, indicating that there are many levels of responsibility. Other pyramids, showing organisations that have fewer layers, are wide and flat. The flatter the pyramid, the more authority is spread across each level of the organisation.
An organisation may also be shown as a circle diagram, with the levels as rings spreading out from the centre. So for example, the CEO will be at the centre, and then the directors in the first ring, followed by managers, and then the workers outside that. Although there is still a hierarchy in the organisation, the circle diagram does not show it as vertical, with a top and a bottom.
An organisation can also be shown as a matrix, in which the relationship between parts of the organisation are shown in a non-hierarchical way. So the matrix diagram could show the various functions carried out in different departments, and how they are connected. The matrix is sometimes called a cat's cradle structure.

A 1.11 **Unit 2** C 4

1. SU-PER-VISE
2. SU-PER-VI-SOR-Y
3. EX-E-CU-TIVE
4. EX-E-CUTE
5. AD-MIN-IS-TRA-TIVE
6. AD-MIN-IS-TRA-TION
7. REP-RE-SENT-A-TION
8. REP-RE-SENT-A-TIVE
9. OB-LI-GA-TION
10. OB-LI-GA-TOR-Y
11. PAR-TI-CI-PATE
12. PAR-TI-CI-PA-TION

A 1.12 **Unit 2** E 2 Exercises a., b. and d.

Part 1

Presenter: Good morning, everyone. Are we ready to begin? I'd like to introduce myself. My name is Peter Haas and I'm a partner in the Weindler-Haas Design Consultancy. Today I'm going to talk about a success story that has grown and grown in only a few years. I'm going to speak for about ten minutes, and I've divided my presentation into three parts: firstly, some key facts about the partnership, secondly, a couple of outstanding achievements for this year, and finally some reasons why we think that we should be considered for the Company of the Year Award. If you have any questions I'll be pleased to deal with them at the end of my presentation.

So, let's start with who we are. Here on the slide you'll see our partnership logo and three key milestones in our development. Martin Weindler and I studied together at college, and after we left in 2003 we started to work on several design projects. They proved very successful, so we formed a partnership and opened our office in Munich. Then, in 2005, we set up the Weindler-Haas Interactive Studio, which allows customers to work with us directly online to create designs for packaging and brands. Then, in 2007 we extended our activities outside Germany and opened offices in London and Paris.

Now let's look at our recent achievements. This year has been a remarkable one for us, and I'd like to focus on two particular projects in particular. The first was to design a range of packaging for a food retailer that would look like plastic but which could be composted after use. This 'Green Genie' concept has been successfully tested and is now being used in many supermarket chains. The second project, also a first in design, is the 'Jet Pak' cosmetic aerosol spray, which is also 100% recyclable. We'll show you some samples after the presentation, so you can see what they look like and how they work.

So why do we think we should be considered for the Company of the Year Award? Well, first of all, we believe we have an excellent record for innovative packaging. We have a strong commitment to the environment, so our packaging is also environmentally-friendly. I'm sure you'll agree that this is a major breakthrough in design and technology. Secondly, we are ideally located to expand into the lucrative European market. And finally, there can be no doubt that we are well on the way to becoming a leader in packaging and brand design. This is reflected in our healthy profit margin.

Thank you for your attention. And now, if you have any questions, I'll be happy to answer them.

A 1.13 Part 2

Woman 1: I have a question. You said your company started as a partnership of two people. But now you have opened offices in London and Paris. So how many people work for you now?
Presenter: Thank you for the question. In fact, we now have a staff of fifteen. But the company is still run by the two original partners, Martin Weindler and myself.

Man : You mentioned that you recently designed packaging for a food retailer. Don't you think there is too much packaging in the food industry?
Presenter: That's a very good question. I'm sure we all agree that packaging on food items should be reduced, and that is why we've worked so hard on the 'Green Genie' solution which is consumer-friendly as well as helping the environment.

Woman 2: I'd like to follow up on the green aspect. There has been a lot of negative publicity about aerosol sprays damaging the environment, and yet you're designing them for the cosmetics industry. How do you explain that?
Presenter: I think the issue about aerosol sprays is an important one, you're right. What we've done is completely revolutionize the design of the spray can. If you'd like more information on this, you'll find the technical details on our website.

A 1.14 **Unit 3** B 2 Exercise b.

Presenter: Good morning, and welcome to this week's edition of Money Minders. Today we'll be looking at cash flow, and here in our studio to discuss the subject is Dr Malcolm Norris, Professor of Finance from Dumbarton Business School. Dr Norris, thank you for coming all the way from Dumbarton to talk to us!
Norris: Good morning! And thank you for inviting me.
Presenter: Dr Norris, I'd like to start by asking a basic question. How important is cash for business?
Norris: Absolutely vital. A business can survive for a while without sales or profits, but without cash, it'll die. It's like oxygen. And that's why it's important to manage the inflow and outflow of cash very carefully.
Presenter: Is the aim to have more money flowing in than flowing out?
Norris: Ideally, yes. You want your income to be higher than your expenditure. But the difficulty is that inflows usually lag behind the outflows, for example when customers pay late. It becomes a big problem when they don't pay at all, or when demand falls and you don't get as many orders as you'd expected. Basically, effective cash management is all about speeding up the inflows and slowing down the outflows.
Presenter: So what can a business do to improve everyday cash flow?
Norris: I would say that the key is customer management. You need to manage your customers so that they pay sooner rather than later, and that means setting clear payment terms that your customer understands. Then you need to issue your invoices quickly, but check them before you send them. Just one small mistake in an invoice can cost time and money.
Presenter: Yes, you don't want to give your customers an excuse to pay late! So what else can a company do to prevent late payment?
Norris: As I said, a lot depends on the terms and conditions you set. For example, you could ask your

customer to pay in advance, either in part or in full. If it's a big contract, you could negotiate staged payments.

Presenter: Staged payments?

Norris: Yes, for example, a third of the payment with the order, a third on delivery, and a third after delivery. By asking your customers to pay in stages, or in instalments, you keep the money flowing in. You could also offer discounts for paying by a certain date or for paying within, say, seven days of the invoice date. At any rate, you should always set a credit period. If you don't, the law sets a standard period of thirty days.

Presenter: Thirty days … from when?

Norris: Ah – good question. It's either from when the goods are delivered, or from when the customer receives the bill. Whichever is the later date.

Presenter: Something we haven't talked about yet is creditworthiness. Don't you need to check how creditworthy your customer is?

Norris: Yes, I was just coming to credit risks. It's extremely important to do a credit check, especially when you're dealing with new or potential customers.

Presenter: How do you do that, exactly?

Norris: Ask them for references – or get them to complete a form that authorises you to get references from a bank or credit agency. Remember that if you don't know their credit history, you risk being paid late or not at all.

Presenter: Right, so it's clear that there are ways of ensuring that customers pay on time. But you may find that some still pay late – despite your best efforts. What are your options then?

Norris: Again, you need a strategy. You can telephone the customer to remind them that payment is overdue. Or send reminder letters. And if you think your calls and letters are being ignored, send emails or faxes. And don't forget to set a clear deadline for payment. It's not enough to just say 'as soon as possible'.

Presenter: Dr Norris, you haven't mentioned lawyers yet …

Norris: Yes, threatening legal action can be very effective.

Presenter: After all, companies have legal rights, don't they?

Norris: Yes, you can charge interest for late payments, for example, or even claim compensation for debt recovery costs. But you should only take legal action if it's really necessary. It depends very much on your relationship with the customer.

Presenter: Dr Norris, we've talked about customer management, but what about the suppliers? On the one hand, you're waiting for your money, but on the other hand the suppliers are waiting for theirs! Isn't this the basic problem in cash flow management?

Norris: Absolutely, and it's important to pay your suppliers on time. If necessary, you can ask your suppliers for an extension of credit, in other words you can ask them for more time to pay. Indeed, this is what normally happens in business. However, the problem is that …

A 1.15 **Unit 3** E 2 Exercises a. and b.

Conversation 1

Journalist: Ah, hello. I wonder if you might be able to iron this for me?

Assistant: We can do that for you, no problem.

Journalist: And, uh, how much will it cost?

Assistant: £2.50.

Journalist: Ah, OK. And would you have, er, any flexibility with that price?

Assistant: Sorry?

Journalist: Well, what I mean is … can you knock 10 % off?

Assistant: You want to haggle over the price of your dry-cleaning?

Journalist: Well actually I don't want the shirt dry-cleaned. I just want it ironed. So come on! How about two quid?

Assistant: Just a moment, I'll get the manager to speak to you.

Manager: Good morning. Are you the gentleman looking for a discount?

Journalist: That's right. I'm asking for a 20 % reduction.

Manager: Well, I can't really do you anything on the one shirt but if it's a bulk order then maybe we could work something out.

Journalist: OK, so how about 20 % off ten shirts?

Manager: Well, I could do you 10 %.

Journalist: 15 % - and that's my final offer.

Manager: All right, bring the shirts in and we'll talk.

Journalist: I'd like to try to get a better deal, but I'll take your card anyway. Thanks.

A 1.16 Conversation 2

Journalist: Hello, do you have two tickets for the evening's performance?
Assistant: Yes we do. There are some very good seats still available for £55.
Journalist: That's just too much for me. Can you reduce them at all? Since it's for tonight's show.
Assistant: Hmm, we might be able to something. How does £25 sound?
Journalist: Still too much, I'm afraid. Would you accept £20?
Assistant: Sorry, I can't … If you came back before the performance, then maybe.
Journalist: You'll sell them at twenty quid?
Assistant: Well, I might . Make sure you come back to this window.
Journalist: Ah, all right then. I'll see you this evening.

A 1.17 Conversation 3

Journalist: How much would a haircut be?
Assistant: A cut for men starts at £24, and they go up to £52. Depends on which stylist you want.
Journalist: What! Fifty quid? But I only want a normal haircut, nothing fancy. Can't we find some middle ground here?
Assistant: Well, if you're ready to get it done right now, our top stylist is free and you can have a stand-by appointment for £15.
Journalist: And that would usually be £52?
Assistant: Yes, Stand-by appointments are not advertised and available only to those who ask. If a stylist is free, we'd rather they were working. And we will always put clients with the best stylist available because we see it as good for sales. If they like the cut, they'll come back again.

A 1.18 Conversation 4

Journalist: How much to press a shirt, please?
Assistant: Two pounds.
Journalist: Can you do it for any less than that?
Assistant: Nope.
Journalist: You can't even move on that figure by, say, 5%?
Assistant: You want 10p off?
Journalist: Yes, just 10p. That's all I'm after.
Assistant: No, I said two pounds.
Journalist: Is that your final offer?
Assistant: It's not an offer, it's the price!
Journalist: OK then, here's two pounds.

A 1.19 **UNIT 4** A 5 Exercise b.

Sarah: As you know, Pedro, the Smoothie face cream has been a real hit with the teen market. Now we're thinking of extending the brand to target a slightly older age group.
Pedro: You what? Wait a minute … I thought the big idea behind Smoothie is that it appeals to young people, you know, teenagers with acne. That's why we added the antiseptic.
Sarah: Sure, but what we'd like to do now is offer Smoothie to the more … mature consumer.
Pedro: Mature consumers with acne?
Sarah: No, Pedro, to anyone who wants smooth and youthful skin! Listen, in terms of European sales, we already have over 30% of the market share for women in the under-25 range and nearly 50% for men in the same age group. That's a fantastic performance!
Pedro: You're telling me!
Sarah: Of course, there's still some growth possible in those markets, but we now want to target men and women in the 25–50 age range.
Pedro: Fine, but then surely you'll have to come up with a totally new concept, a totally new cream, and a totally new brand.
Sarah: Well, it doesn't need to be totally new. We want to keep the brand name because consumers have come to associate it with youth. Smoothie is … a young brand!
Pedro: So we just take out the antiseptic, right? Well, that's easy! But do you really believe older people will go for cheap products like Smoothie? I'd have thought they'd like something more sophisticated, something more upmarket, something that …
Sarah: Exactly. What we want to do is build on our success by attracting older, wealthier customers to the brand. They expect to pay more for cosmetics and, as you say, they want something designed for them, with the promise of smooth and young-looking skin.

Pedro: Okay, I get it, so you do want a new product. Fine. You want an anti-aging cream, right? Well, everyone wants an anti-aging cream. We've been working on that for years! Is that what you want?

Sarah: No, actually. That's what I wanted to talk to you about, Pedro. What we want to do is re-position the brand as a natural product that is environmentally friendly. Our research shows that older consumers are becoming more concerned about green issues, and are attracted to natural cosmetics. So we're planning a marketing campaign that will focus on Smoothie as a globally sensitive product … and with no carbon footprint!

Pedro: But most people know Smoothie from the Party Animal campaign. That had nothing to do with saving the planet! And what about the shiny packaging? You know how long it took us to create that glitter effect! We even took out a patent on it!

Sarah: Yeah, you did a great job. But for the new market we'd like to change the packaging materials to make it look less glossy, more recycled, more like a fair trade product. We'll keep the Smoothie logo, of course, but on the new range it'll be green, not red.

Pedro: But Sarah, what about the product itself? Where does R&D come in here?

Sarah: Okay, well, we're really excited about the idea of fragrances based on fruit and nuts. It could be the theme for our fall promotion. And of course there should be no additives at all, no animal products, and no testing on animals.

Pedro: We can't guarantee that, Sarah, you know we can't! And as for smelling of fruit and nuts, we'll need more time for research – and a bigger budget. When are you planning to launch?

Sarah: We're hoping you can send us the first samples in a month.

Pedro A month? Are you kidding? No way! Why so fast, Sarah?

Sarah: It's important that we have the green Smoothie range on the market by Christmas. We're all going to be working very hard on this project.

Pedro: Listen, we need more time and more money. We should talk to the Product Manager.

Sarah: Good idea. I'll email him and tell him what I want… I mean, what we discussed.

Pedro: Well, keep me in the picture, Sarah, okay?

Sarah: Don't worry, Pedro. I won't step on your toes. I'll cc you any emails I send.

A 1.20 Unit 4 E 3

Alan: Good morning, everyone. Thank you all for being here on time. Are we waiting for anyone?

Tanja: No, I don't think so. Peter won't be coming, as he's still in Munich.

Alan: Yes, I know. Thank you Tanja. I'll be speaking to him by phone later, I'll update him on what decisions we take. OK, are we ready to begin? Has everyone got a copy of the agenda?

All: Yes … yes, thank you …

Alan: Good. Well as you can see, the purpose of today's meeting is to make a decision about whether to go ahead with our new wireless laser-jet printer. It's a very complex product, and we've had some delays with the development stage, so it is essential that we come to some agreement today about the feasibility of the project. Agreed?

All: Well, yes … of course …

Alan: Right. You'll see that there are six items on the agenda, I'll run through them quickly. Firstly, identifying our target market, that's obviously a key point. Then technical description, I'll ask Martin to do that, and on to item three which deals with the problems to be overcome. After that we'll discuss some ideas about the marketing approach, and then item five is the timescale, which will have to be reorganised. Finally, we'll decide on who will do what, as you can see I've called item six allocation of tasks. OK?

All: Yes … fine …

Alan: So, a quick check on the time, we have an hour for this and six points to get through, so I'll try to limit each point to ten minutes. Oh, and could somebody take the minutes, please?

Tanja: I'll do it.

Alan: Thanks Tanja. Right then, let's get started. Item one on today's agenda, the target market … who is going to buy the product? Simon, you've been busy with market research so let me come to you first …

A 1.21 **Unit 5** A 4 Exercises b. and c.

Part 1

Alan: Today we're talking to Jackie Parsons, who has come into our Brighton studio to talk about her online shopping business, Gifted in Design. Jackie, welcome to the programme, and can I start off by asking you how you came up with the name of your company.

Jackie: Thank you for the question! Basically, I set out to sell jewellery and hand-crafted gifts that all had a unique design element, so I decided to deal directly with artists and craftsmen who wanted an outlet for their work.

Alan: And why did you want to set up your own company and become an entrepreneur?

Jackie: I was working as an advertising executive for a radio station and did a marketing diploma at college in my spare time to gain new skills and improve my knowledge. I loved the idea of eventually working for myself and the course gave me the confidence to look at different business ideas and ways of using my marketing expertise.

Alan: Well I'd like to ask you about that. You mentioned that you studied marketing at college, and I wonder whether what you learned there has been of value since then. What were the really useful things that you learned on the course?

Jackie: Oh, lots of things. For me, what was really invaluable was what I learned about business planning and market research, how to analyse a market and deal with all the statistics, to make sense of all the numbers and get really accurate information. That's vitally important if you're going to have any success breaking into a market.

Alan: So, when you started your online business back in 2004 there was quite a lot of risk involved. Weren't you worried that you might not sell anything at all, and be left with a huge pile of stock. I mean, that's the classic scenario, running a business from home and ending up with a garage full of stock!

Jackie: You've been watching too much Mr Bean! The reality is not quite like that. One of the benefits of being an online business is that you can keep your overheads low because you don't carry much stock. People come and browse on the website where there are hundreds of items to choose from, and when they order from me, I send an order out to the relevant supplier. I also did a lot of market research in the early days. I would take items to craft fairs & local markets to get customer's reactions so I knew which ones would sell and I could buy stock with confidence.

Alan: The business has grown a lot since those early days, but can you remember the first thing you ever sold?

Jackie: Oh definitely. I had some little ceramic clocks, they were in the shape of lucky pigs and they were very popular. The only problem was that they were very fragile, so I had to spend ages wrapping them so that they didn't break in the post. Now I try to deal in more robust products, like the personalised silver picture-frame, that's my top selling item at the moment.

Alan: So when you get an order, and you have to get the item very quickly from your supplier, the artist if you like, that can be a problem, surely. How can you ensure that you don't have a hold-up with supply?

Jackie: Well it isn't a problem with most of my artists. I've been working with the same people for some time now, and we've built up a really good system. As many of my products are personalised, there is a 10 day timescale which usually covers any potential stock problems. The real problem is with the postal system when orders go missing or get delayed in transit.

Alan: And as a small business, operating in a niche market, do you ever worry that a change in the economic situation could put you out of business?

Jackie: I don't think so. My gifts are very affordable and whatever the state of the economy, people are always going to want to buy presents, if only to cheer someone up when the things are looking bad.

A 1.22 Part 2

Alan: OK, let me turn to a question that will interest our listeners. You've obviously been very successful with your online business, so what advice can you offer for someone thinking of going into on-the-web retailing?

Jackie: Make sure you've done your research and preparation before spending any money on a website! One thing is knowing who and where your customers are. Defining your customer is as important as defining your products or naming your business. But then, yes, you have to know your products too, make sure you know which ones are performing, where and why? If some aren't working, replace them with others that might perform better.

Alan: What about competition? How do you keep ahead of them?

Jackie: Good question! Understanding your competition can help your business in so many ways. Find out what they're doing, scour their websites. Are their offers more innovative than yours? Higher quality than yours? And you keep ahead by spotting opportunities that no one has yet captured. I also attend art fairs and gift exhibitions to see what's out there. You need to be first if you're going to seize the market!

Alan: So you're looking at your competitors' websites, but they are also getting a lot of ideas from what you're doing, surely?

Jackie: Yes, this is really important when you're doing business on the web. You have to keep finding ways to improve your online marketing. People are going to check out your site, but then visit competitor sites as well and then make comparisons. So it is especially important that your website outshines the competition.

Alan: Well, Jackie, it's been great talking to you, and we hope your business goes from strength to strength.

Jackie: Thank you.

A 1.23 Unit 5 C 4

Expert: It's not only companies who are big slogan spenders, but also councils. In 2005, the City of Leeds spent one hundred and fifty thousand pounds on rebranding itself with the slogan "Live it, love it". This caused problems, partly because it wasn't effective, but also because it emerged that it wasn't even original. Hong Kong had already been using "Live it, love it" for two years. Another council that generated an unpopular and expensive slogan was Nottingham. Their slogan consisted of just one letter, "N". This was seen as particularly uninspiring. And Wales created the slogan "Big Country", which is strangely contradictory since Wales is actually quite a small country. Some campaigns turn out to be highly controversial, especially when public money is spent. The new campaign from the Local Government Association featured posters of drunk women vomiting in the street, accompanied by the catchphrase "My council clears up my mess".

A 1.24 Unit 5 E 1 Exercise a.

Max: Julia Hobday is Marketing Director of Red Reef Lifestyles, the New Age fashion chain that has created some of the most memorable marketing campaigns of the last few years. We're very pleased to have her in the studio this morning to talk us through some of the basics of successful marketing.

Julia: Thank you for inviting me along to Talking Business.

Max: I'd like to start, if I may, by asking about the market research that you do. How do you gather the data that you need in order to spot new opportunities and target the right people?

Julia: Well, firstly we have access to a lot of published market information, where we can get useful quantitative data on general market and economic trends, and buying behaviour.

Max: By quantitative data you mean statistics, right?

Julia: Yes, that's right. We use what we call desk research to get data that already exists, for example company records or findings from market research that is published in journals or on the Internet. Another important thing we do is benchmarking, where we look at what our competitors are doing, their market share, their new products, pricing strategy, and so on.

Max: So that would also be part of your desk research?

Julia: Absolutely, because we can do it from our desks! Of course, we also get out and do field research, because we also need to get a good idea about the attitudes of our customers – not only our existing customers but also the potential ones.

Max: So field research means going out and collecting information. Are you talking about market surveys?

Julia: Yes, surveys are one very important aspect of field research. There are a lot of different ways of conducting them, but with the spread of the Internet I guess email and online surveys have become the most popular methods.

Max: Sounds like desk research to me.

Julia: True, we could argue about the definitions. But anyway, it's a useful method, and also very cost effective. Having said that, I believe that the other more traditional ways are still valuable, depending on how you do them. You can send people questionnaires, but the problem there is that response rates are unreliable.

Max: How about telephone interviews? You know, cold calls.

Julia: Telephone interviews can work in some sectors, but they require a lot of skill on the part of the interviewer. People don't like cold calling, they feel they're being pestered, or think someone is calling to sell something. Also, the response rates aren't good. People hang up. That's why we still prefer face-to-face interviews, where there is human contact. Of course the way you conduct your survey depends on a number of factors including time, resources, money and target market.

Max: And what other types of field research do you carry out?

Julia: As I said, we have to do the quantitative research, to get statistics about numbers of customers, and incomes and so on. But we also need qualitative research, which is about people's feelings and attitudes towards our products, and what motivates them. So we might run focus groups with small groups of customers, where we ask them to give their opinions about a particular subject. Or we could observe customer behaviour, for example by watching shoppers in a supermarket. Tastings are also useful in supermarkets.

Max: You mean when you give people samples?

Julia: Yes, but not for the purpose of promotion, but in order to get their feedback. Here it's especially important that they do blind tastings, in other words you don't tell them the name of the product. But tastings are useful because people like doing them. They like the idea of getting something free.

Max: And what tips would you give for successful field research?

Julia: That's a tricky one to answer. But I would say … prepare well, so you're asking the right questions. Talk to the right people, the ones you want to connect to your product. Talk to enough people, so that you get the complete picture. And try not to lead people to the answer you want, try to be impartial. It's not easy to stay objective, but it's important not to show bias. And a final point, make sure you interpret the results you get very carefully. Market research is only of any value if you draw the right conclusions and act accordingly.

A 1.25 Unit 6 A 4

Interviewer: More and more artists are distributing their music online rather than going through record stores. So what are the benefits of online distribution? And how do you actually go about it?

Greg: Well, basically there are two options. One is to sell through a website where people can pay to download whole tracks or albums as MP3s. The other is to use a website that lets them download sample MP3s, which are just short clips of your tracks, and if people like them, they can order your CD.

Interviewer: So which option is better? MP3 downloads only, or sample MP3s as a way of promoting CDs?

Greg: Depends. I'll come back to that later. But whichever option you choose, the advantage is that you have 100% creative control over the music you make. You don't have to sign deals with distributors, where you give away your rights. And another huge benefit of going online is that it gives you a worldwide audience. Anyone can get access to your music, anytime, wherever they are on the planet, and you get most of the cash. Bonus!

Interviewer: Sounds great!

Greg: And in this way you can find out who's buying your music, and where. So let's say you find that a lot of the people who are buying your music come from Southern Germany, for example. Then you can think about including the region in your European tour plans.

Interviewer: Another question: Payment. How do you take payment when you distribute online?

Greg: There are various ways, but whatever you do, you need to make sure the payment method is secure. Otherwise people won't want to part with their money. Some Internet service providers like PayPal and WorldPay offer secure payment systems. They do the credit card processing for you and then transfer the money to your account. Of course, they charge a fee for this.

Interviewer: What about people who don't have access to credit and debit cards. The under-18s fans, for example.

Greg: Yeah, that's a problem. You just have to make sure that they have other options, such as money transfers. The important thing is to open up the site to as many users as you can.

Interviewer: To be honest, if you're an unsigned artist, without a distributor or a promoter, are you likely to make much money selling CDs online?

Greg: Maybe, maybe not. The good news is that you can determine the profit margins since you control the distribution process. To give you an example, I know one artist who charges 50p to download an MP3 and £3.50 for the CD. He sells more MP3s than CDs, simply because they're so easy to download. The customer has instant access to the MP3 and can then purchase a CD afterwards.

Interviewer: So you'd say that MP3s could be quite lucrative …

Greg: If you sell enough, yeah. The problem with CDs is the cost of production and distribution. You have to pay for pressing the CDs, then there's the packaging and postage. If you send them abroad then the postage will be more. But if someone buys an MP3 file you don't need to worry about that stuff. It's the most direct way of getting your music to the ears of listeners.

Interviewer: Is there any advantage in having your own website?

Greg. It depends. If you like the idea of running a website, and if you're an enterprising person, then the answer is yes. You don't only have to sell music on a website. You can also sell merchandise such as T-Shirts, photos, stickers and so on. I know a band that offers a deal where for £30 you get their album, some stickers, a t-shirt and a promo CD of new stuff. If you have total control of your site, you can do exactly what you like. It's all a matter of being creative!

Interviewer: So ... it looks as if the Internet offers great potential to musicians.

Greg: Yeah, my advice is to work with it rather than against it.

A 1.26 **Unit 6** B 1 Exercises a. and c.

Lecturer: Good morning. Can everyone hear me at the back?

Students: No! Louder!

Lecturer: Thank you. Right, well, you will remember that last week we looked at aspects of marketing strategy, focusing on the marketing mix. Today I'd like to talk about channels of distribution. Now, as you know, there are many definitions of distribution. But for the purposes of this lecture, I shall define it simply as the way that suppliers get their goods and services to customers at the right place at the right time.
If you take a look at this slide, you'll see that the simplest method for the producer would be to sell directly to the final customer. An example of this direct selling method is a factory outlet, where customers can buy designer goods directly from the producer. In this way, no intermediaries or middlemen are involved. Can anyone suggest any other examples? ... Yes?

Student 1: Farmers who sell their produce at the market.

Lecturer: Exactly. A market stall is a good example of a direct marketing outlet. The farmer can keep all the profits himself.

Student 2: Or herself!

Lecturer: Or herself, of course. So, are intermediaries a bad thing? Although they take a cut of the profits, there are certain advantages to be gained from using them in the distribution process. They can play an important part in promoting and selling the product. For example, an agent may have expert knowledge about local markets and competition, and good networking links to customers. At this point, it is important to draw a distinction between agents, representatives and distributors. Often the terms are used interchangeably, so it can all be a bit confusing. But a way to understand the difference is to look at the types of contract that exist between the various parties in the supply chain. As you can see, agents work on a commission basis. There is an agency contract between the agent and the producer, who is referred to in the contract as the principal. The commission that the agent gets is calculated as a percentage of sales, and the agent can also claim for any expenses incurred. Some agents may also receive a small fee, known as a retainer, to keep their services and maintain an ongoing professional relationship. Representatives, or sales reps, on the other hand, are employees of the producer. So they receive a basic salary as well as commission. They also sell goods and bring in orders for the company they represent. But unlike the agent they are bound by an employment contract. Some representatives receive incentives such as a bonus or a prize for reaching or exceeding sales targets. Is everything clear so far?

Students: Yes.

Lecturer: Let's move on to another type of intermediary: distributors. They trade on their own account, buying and selling, rather than on a commission basis. In a typical distribution chain, a distributor or wholesaler buys goods in bulk from the producer and stores them in a warehouse before selling them on to the retailer in smaller amounts. This is known as breaking bulk. The retailer in turn reduces the goods further into individually priced items that are offered for sale to the final customer. As you know, there are many different types of retail outlet. Basically, a retail outlet is really any place where goods are sold to the final customer. This could be a supermarket, or a car showroom, a small corner shop or even a vending machine. So a factory outlet is just one type of outlet. Retailers are also referred to as resellers. Of course, they may receive goods directly from the producer, or from distributors or wholesalers. The chain is of course much more complex than the way it is shown on the slides. Ah, I can see someone has a question. Yes?

Student 3: May I just ask something here?

Lecturer: Of course, go ahead!

Student 3: You said that agents work on a commission basis, whereas distributors work on their own account. Is that right?

Lecturer: That's the basic difference, yes.

Student 3: But in the music business, isn't it the other way round? The music distributors get commission. They don't buy and sell records as such.

Lecturer: Ah! Good point. You're absolutely right, of course. In the music business, the distributor acts more like an agent! To repeat a point I made earlier, the terms can be used in confusing ways. And this is why when we look at distribution channels we need to understand the contractual relationships between the parties involved. So, to move on, one of the more recent forms of distribution has been franchising. This is where a trader, called the franchisee, buys the right to sell the goods or services of a producer or service provider, called the franchisor, in a particular area. Customers will recognise well-known brands, and standardised products or services. Typical examples of franchises can be found in the areas of fast food, car rentals, and clothing. Can anyone give an example of a franchise?

Student 1: Subway?

Lecturer: Yes.

Student 2: Avis.

Lecturer: Exactly. And what are the advantages of franchising for the franchisee. Any ideas?

Unit 6 E 2 Exercise a.

A 1.27 **Message 1**

Jim: This is Jim here. I'm at the Dover ferry terminal, but there's no way I'm going to get a crossing this afternoon. The weather in the Channel is rough, and there is an expected delay of at least five hours. I've got a load of aluminium sheets for Kränzle in Troisdorf, but they won't get their delivery today. I've tried calling them on the mobile but I'm not getting connected. Can you please call them, and explain the delay. The number is 00-49 77 23 27 721. Thanks.

A 1.28 **Message 2**

Stella: Ah yes, is that McKellars? I got your company details from the 'Moving to Europe' website. It said that you specialise in removals over any distance. We'd like a quote please, for a house move from here in Glasgow to Alicante in Spain. The total distance is 1,968 kilometres. Could you include in the quote all packing and handling charges, and removal boxes. My name is Stella McKeenen, and my number is 0 14 15 52 27 39. I'll be at home today, so I'd appreciate it if you could call me back. Bye.

A 1.29 **Messge 3**

Ranza: Oh hello, this is Ranza Patel calling from Pride of India Foods. We've just received a bulk delivery of powdered milk here at our production plant in Basingstoke but there is a problem. It seems that the delivery has been contaminated by a leak of diesel oil, and it is now unfit for consumption. Our Goods Inward department have told your driver that they won't unload the truck. This is an urgent matter as we're waiting to start a production run, so we need a quick response, please!

A 1.30 **Unit 7** A 3

Interview 1

Teen 1: Excuse me, may we ask you some questions? We're doing a pro …

Armin: Moment mal! Ich schalte es ab! Wie bitte?

Teen 1: Er, do you speak English?

Armin: Well, yes, a little.

Teen 1: We'd just like to ask you some questions about your job. Do you have a minute?

Armin: Yes, no problem.

Teen 1: We're interviewing people who work in manufacturing. We were told you're a maintenance engineer.

Armin: That's right.

Teen 1: And your name's Armin, right?

Armin: Yes, it's Armin Schmidt.

Teen 1: How do you spell that?

Armin: S-C-H-M-I-D-T.

Teen 1. Thanks. And could you tell us something about your job, and what you do as a maintenance engineer?

Armin: Well, I've been working at the Alustahl plant for three years now, on and off. I'm responsible for the maintenance of all the mechanical systems that operate here. It's my job to make sure that everything runs smoothly on the assembly line, and that we keep downtime to a minimum.

Teen 1: Downtime? Like, is that when you guys take a break and, like, chill?

Armin: No, not exactly. It's when production has to stop, for example when we need to repair a machine.

When there's a major breakdown, we don't have time to relax! People start to panic! That doesn't happen too often, touch wood.

Teen 1: So do you like your job?

Armin: Yeah. It can be hectic sometimes, but I like it. I'm a subcontractor, which means that I make routine visits to do checks on all the machines, but I'm also on call 24-hours-a day in case there's an emergency. That suits me. It gives me a lot of flexibility.

Teen 1: Well, thanks, Armin. We'll let you get back to your work!

Armin: Sure, no problem.

A 1.31 Interview 2

Teen 2: Excuse me, are you Jörg Burger?

Jörg: Er, yes. It's Jörg, actually.

Teen 2: Oh, OK. Jörg, do you mind if we ask you a few questions? We heard that you speak English!

Jörg: Did you? Well, I can try. Anyway, hello and welcome to Alustahl.

Teen 2: Thanks! Jörg, we're interviewing people about their jobs. Could you tell us something about what you do?

Jörg: Well, as you can see, this is the packing department, and I'm a packer. I do shift work. At the moment it's from six o'clock in the morning to two o'clock in the afternoon. My night shift is from ten o'clock in the evening until six in the morning.

Teen 2: Hey, we're lucky we're here on your day shift!

Jörg: Yes.

Teen 2: So, Jörg, what's it like doing night shift? Don't you get, like, tired?

Jörg: No, not really. I'm used to working at night. The money is better on the night shift, and it gives me time to do another job during the day.

Teen 2: And what are you doing at the moment?

Jörg: You mean in my other job? I'm a …

Teen 2: No, what are you doing right now, with these bits of metal here?

Jörg: Ah, these are finished parts that are going to Norway. I'm putting them onto these pallets. After that I'm going to wrap the pallets in … what do you call this Plastikfolie in English?

Teen 2: Plastic, I guess.

Teen 3: I'd call it polythene film.

Jörg: Polythene. Thanks. And then when I've done that, I'll barcode the pallets before they go to the … Versand? Over there.

Teen 3: The dispatch area?

Jörg 1: Ah, yes, the dispatch area. Oh, my English! I forget so many words!

Teen 3: It's great, you're doing fine!

Teen 1: One more question, Jörg. Is Alustahl a good company to work for?

Jörg: Well, it's a bit boring but, as I said, night work suits me. I've worked for worse companies, at least there's a good atmosphere here. I get on well with the other packers – we have a lot of fun. I'd like longer coffee breaks though.

A 1.32 Interview 3

Marion: Herein!

Teen 3: Hi, my name's Sam. We're on a visit from the States, and the guy who organised the tour said we could interview you. It's Marion Weiß, right?

Marion: Oh, hello, yes, I was expecting you. Welcome to Alustahl! Yes, my name is Marion Weiß and I'm Head of Purchasing here at Alustahl.

Teen 3: So you're in charge of the department.

Marion. Yes, I'm responsible for a team of buyers who deal directly with the suppliers.

Teen 3: So what kind of things do you buy? Raw materials?

Marion. Yes, we buy raw materials from all over the world, but we also buy finished goods like machinery for the production, office equipment, packaging systems and so on.

Teen 3: What do you like about your job?

Marion: Oh, it's a great job, and I've been doing it for nearly two years. I was a buyer before that, so I know the job very well and I have a really great team to work with. We're under a lot of pressure because keeping costs down has become so important, but I like that because I'm a very competitive person. We sometimes have very tough negotiations with our suppliers!

A 1.33 **Unit 7** C4 Exercise a.

1. a. We only sell fresh produce.
   b. Bees produce honey.

2. a. Did you record it?
   b. I don't have a record of it.
3. a. We convert raw materials into useful items.
   b. He's a recent convert to the church.
4. a. I'll have to reject it.
   b. It's a reject.
5. a. How are you going to transport it?
   b. What form of transport are you going to use?
6. a. There has been an increase in productivity
   b. We need to increase productivity.
7. a. Can you present us with a better offer?
   b. It was given to me as a present.
8. a. We only hire graduates.
   b. He graduates in September.

A 1.34 **Unit 7** C 4 Exercise b.

1. a. Only add a minute amount of chilli.
   b. Could you hold on a minute?
2. a. Your passport is invalid.
   b. He quit his job because he became an invalid.
3. a. I've had some awful rows with my boss.
   b. Seats are arranged in rows in lecture halls.
4. a. It was located in the desert.
   b. Please don't desert me.
5. a. I need to put a bandage on my wound.
   b. The company had to be wound up.
6. a. Petrol that contains lead is dangerous to health.
   b. He has no idea of how to lead a team.

A 1.35 **Unit 7** C 4 Exercise c.

1. a. You need a hard head.
   b. You need a hard hat.
2. a. I'd like a white desk.
   b. I'd like a wide desk.
3. a. It's the wrong batch.
   b. It's the wrong badge.
4. a. Four tickets.
   b. Forty kids.
5. a. No access
   b. No excess
6. a. It's a vast machine.
   b. It's a fast machine.
7. a. I always walk there.
   b. I always work there.
8. a. the gross rate
   b. the growth rate
9. a. a tiny fairy
   b. a tiny ferry

CD2

A 2.1 **Unit 7** C 6 Exercises d. and e.

A: Good morning everyone, we're now outside the Class-One Assembly Hall. This is the area where the microprocessors are made, and it's a clean-room environment, so before we continue I'd like to give you some information about the procedure we all have to follow each time we enter a clean-room. Can everyone hear me OK?

All: Yes, fine, thank you.

A: So, this may be the first time you'll be entering a clean-room. I'd like to start with a few facts and figures. Each of the microprocessors we produce contains millions of microscopic transistors, and the tiniest speck of dust landing on it could damage it and cause it to be defective. So the clean-room has to be completely free of dust and particles, in fact clean-rooms are 10,000 times cleaner than a hospital operating room. It takes a lot of technology to achieve and maintain such cleanliness. Air filtration systems completely change the air in clean-rooms about 10 times per minute. And yet it is still very difficult and costly keeping the level of contamination low. So, where does this contamination come from?

B: Uh, people in the room? And … people coming in and out?

A: Exactly right. And that is why we have a special process, called suiting up, and that's what you'll be doing here today. All the people who work in our clean-rooms, whether they are assemblers, maintenance staff or supervisors, have to wear clean-room clothing from top to bottom. This includes a cap over the hair, a gown and special shoes, and it's called a bunny-suit.

A: No, this is nothing to do with Playboy bunny costumes, as you'll find out very soon. It's a uniform made of anti-static material that ensures that nothing, not even a single hair, gets onto the work in the clean-room. The suiting up process takes some time, and in a few moments you will be going through this door into the dressing room. I have to wait for the green light to come on before I can open the door, because all personnel have to get changed in an airlock before being inspected and then allowed to continue into the clean-room.

C: It's a bit like going into outer space.

A: It is, and a lot of the techniques were developed by NASA, as well as the atomic energy industry. The aim is to protect you, and the special dust-free environment, and the tiny products that we make. When you go in, you'll be measured and given the correct size of bunny-suit. But before we do that, here are some basic guidelines. It is forbidden to suck sweets or chew gum in the clean-room, and you must make sure that any beard or other facial hair is covered by a mask. You will also be asked to remove any make-up, to prevent oils and particles from coming into contact with the clean environment. Oh, and everyone is required to wear an ID badge at all times, you'll be issued with one of those. Yes … do you have a question?

D: What about our normal clothes? Must we take them off?

A: No, there's no need to remove your clothes, the bunny-suit is worn over the top of them. You'll only have to change your shoes. Ah, the green light is on, so we can go in now. Remember to move slowly and carefully, and …

A 2.2 **Unit 7** E 1 Exercise a.

Supervisor: OK, now I'd like to run through the process with you, and as I do, I'll show you the sequence of actions here in the assembly workshop. You can watch how other workers carry out the tasks, and then we'll arrange for you to have some hands-on training.

Worker: Great. I've already been given handouts with the step-by-step instructions, but it's always better to get practical experience.

Supervisor. Exactly. Well, as you'll see, the task itself is simple. Basically, you are bonding two components together. The parts are very delicate though, so the work must be done with precision and careful handling.

Worker: What kind of parts are they?

Supervisor: They're the basic platform for the DVD disk-drive assemblies that are installed in our laptop computers. You will get to see how the completed disk drive is installed in the computer when we follow the assembly line into the main assembly hall. Now, let's look at the equipment you'll be using. At each workstation, there is a gun containing the ceramic bonding liquid …

Worker: Bonding liquid?

Supervisor: Yes. Let's call it the glue for now. There is also an oven for hardening the glue, and two boxes of parts called BASE A1 and BODY A2.

Worker: Hang on, I'll need to remember this. Or is it all in the instructions?

Supervisor: Don't worry, you'll find that all the boxes of parts are clearly labelled and colour-coded as part of our Kanban system. Right, let's move over to this workstation … and we can observe the first procedure. See that gun? It automatically places a drop of glue on the part BASE A1, and then the BODY A2 is pressed firmly onto the base and you can hear it snap together. Just like a plastic toy brick. Then the joined component goes into the oven and the door is closed. It's switched on, and the curing process will take exactly 10 seconds. In a few moments we'll hear a buzzer, which means that the door can be opened and …

Worker: Can I ask something? Is that thing hot, coming out of the oven?

Supervisor: No, not at all. I'll come to that in a minute. The second procedure – now, as the part comes out of the oven, it's being checked to ensure that the bond is hard … you see, a quick twisting movement. You'll be shown how to do that later. Also there's another check to make sure that no glue has squeezed out of the joint. Any defects must be reported – they'll be put in a tray marked 'REWORKING'. All finished parts are put in a tray marked 'PROGRESS'. Now then, you had a question about hot materials.

Worker: Well, my question is about general safety, really.

Supervisor: The procedure's completely safe, providing the instructions are correctly followed. The oven produces no heat, it looks like a small microwave but the process is not baking the component, it's called curing. The glue hardens very quickly when it's exposed to ultra-violet light. Notice that all the workers are provided with safety glasses, a white laboratory coat, and also special gloves for handling the parts. The glue is harmless, by the way, but try not to get it on yourself. If there's anything else you'd like to know about safety, you can ask your workstation leader. Now, are you ready to turn this theory into practice?

Worker: Yeah. I'd like to have a go!

A 2.3 **Unit 8** C 1 Exercise c.

Diana: Can you help me with this, George, since we've got ten minutes before the taxi gets here?

George: What is it? One of those customer feedback things? Oh, alright then.

Diana: "Please take a moment to rate our services." OK, let's start with the first one, which is 'service on arrival and check-in'. What do you think?

George: They were very efficient, handling the luggage and dealing with the paperwork, no complaints there. I suppose the only problem was that the receptionist was difficult to understand. It was her English that let her down. And the man who brought our bags up wasn't much better.

Diana: So, language problems with staff. Well, some staff. There isn't a category for language in this list, but I'll make a note at the bottom where it says 'comments'. I'll suggest that they select staff with better English, or maybe they could send staff on a training course.

George: They were all very friendly, to be fair.

Diana: OK, I'll put 'good' for the first one, and the second one is 'staff hospitality' so I'll put 'good' for that one too. Now, the next one is 'in-house services' which includes laundry, concierge and babysitting.

George: We didn't use any of those services.

Diana: No, so I can put 'not applicable' for that one. Let's move on. 'Décor of room' is the next category, and here I would say it was really special. It's not just a very high standard, but they have made an extra effort with small details that give it a touch of luxury. D'you agree, George?

George: Oh yes, the room is certainly 'good'. Very nice indeed.

Diana: No, I'm going to put 'excellent'. I don't do that very often, but this room is really lovely and very well-decorated. And what about 'cleanliness'? Also good?

George: Yes, nothing wrong with it. Put 'good'. Is that it then? They do want a lot of information – we only stayed two nights!

Diana: Just a few more. 'Facilities in room' which means TV, mini-bar and internet access. Any comments?

George: The TV wasn't much use. I know this is Switzerland but it seemed that every channel was in a different language! And I don't like the way hotels charge you nowadays for watching films. You could easily add a lot onto your bill without realising it. Same with the mini-bar. And internet access is no big deal these days, all hotels should have it as standard. So I'd say 'average'.

Diana: Hmmm … OK. And 'temperature in room'? I didn't really notice the temperature, so they must have got it right. It certainly feels comfortable, so I'll put 'good'. But now we come to bathroom, which we will have to mark down. What do you think?

George: It wasn't impressive, I didn't like the towels for one thing. The quality wasn't really what you expect. And some of the shower fittings were difficult to operate – you want things to be easy when you're staying in a hotel.

Diana: Well what it has written here is 'bathroom amenities package' which means all those little soaps and shampoo bottles. They were just about OK, but on overall satisfaction the bathroom was not satisfactory so I'll put 'poor' for that, and I can add a comment at the bottom. I'll say that for a luxury hotel, and a luxury double-room, the bathroom is inadequately furnished. And that's it, apart from a question about room service but that's not applicable in our case so I'll mark it N/A.

George: So generally OK, but some negative points on the small details.

Diana: It also asks if we're likely to stay here again. Would we? I think so.

George: It's not cheap, but the main advantage is location. It's very convenient for the city centre and the business area, good for shopping and going out in the evening. And it is a friendly, professional atmosphere. So put yes for that one. Now leave it on the desk, we need to get down to the lobby or someone else will get our taxi!

◎ A 2.4 **Unit 8** C 2 Exercise a.

Mark: I think you will like this place, Stefan. The Xi Garden is one of Shanghai's most popular restaurants. We were lucky to get a table.

Stefan: It's very nice. I like the atmosphere in here, it's very traditional. And the food smells good. I would say it is definitely gemütlich.

Mark: It is! And look, here comes the waiter with the menus. Would you like a beer while we choose our food? You can have a German beer if you want, made in Shanghai. It's a Bavarian brand I think, they brew it under licence.

Stefan: No, a normal Chinese beer will be fine. And I'm interested in trying some real Chinese food, too. The problem is that this menu is not very easy to understand, you'll have to help me.

Mark: Of course. It isn't easy for visitors to understand a Chinese menu. Sometimes the dishes are translated into English, but in a confusing way that is not very helpful. Let's see, what would you like for a starter – a soup? Let me recommend this one. It's a soup containing little dumplings stuffed with meat.

Stefan: Dumplings?

Mark: Well, Chinese dumplings are a bit like ravioli, but the skin is very thin.

Stefan: That sounds good to me. In fact it sounds a bit like Maultaschensuppe.

Mark: Hmmm … this one is quite a spicy soup, I hope you like spicy things. The dumplings are made by hand, and then boiled before being added to the soup. If it is a pork dumpling it is in the shape of a pig, and if it is a chicken dumpling it is in the shape of a hen, and so on. We can order one pork soup, and one chicken soup, if you like.

Stefan: I'm OK with spicy food, so yes, I'll try it. But now what about the main course? There seem to be hundreds of things to choose from. I always have a problem making my mind up, even when I'm in a German restaurant.

Mark: Well here in Shanghai the seafood is very good, including shellfish such as crab and lobster. Or another dish you could try is duck, there are many lovely ways of cooking duck. This one, for example, is a local speciality called Steamed-and-Fried Duck. One of my favourite dishes!

Stefan: I might try that. How can it be steamed and fried?

Mark: First it's marinated in rice wine and spices and then steamed in a basket. When it is partly cooked, the meat is shredded and mixed with finely chopped vegetables, and wrapped in the duck skin and fried to make a crispy ball. Of course it comes with other side dishes, and there are various types of rice.

Stefan: I'm definitely going to have that. Are you going to have the same?

Mark: No, I think I'll have the Lion's Head Meatball. That's another of the chef's special dishes.

Stefan: It's not made from a real lion, surely?

Mark: No, it's a type of stew, cooked in a clay pot. Let's see … it's made of minced pork, with black mushrooms and a bright green vegetable called Peking cabbage, which is similar to spinach when it's boiled. The pork is made into the shape of a lion's head, and when it is served it rises up out of the vegetables to create a symbol of strength.

Stefan: That's interesting, there seems to be a lot of creativity in the dishes. For example, can you tell me what the people at the next table are having? Is it some kind of jelly?

Mark: Yes, it's called Crystal Fish Jelly. It has small pieces of fish and crab in it, and then the jelly is made into the shape of a fish and frozen. You could have that as a starter if you like.

Stefan: Oh, I thought it was a dessert, because it was bright red. No, I won't try that, I'll have the soup.

Mark: Well, you can always have a dessert later, if you are still hungry. But look, here is our beer. I remembered what to say in German: Zum Wohl!

◎ A 2.5 **Unit 8** E 2 Exercises a. and b.

Part 1

The best conference venue, I think, is a hotel that provides everything – accommodation, facilities, the meals, and so on. From a networking point of view, it's a lot more convenient if everyone is staying at the same hotel. So the first thing I do when I arrive is check in at the reception desk - a fairly logical step for anyone staying at a hotel. But if you're attending a conference, you need to pick up information from the moment you walk in. Often the receptionist will give me a visitor's pack, which contains basic information such as a map of the hotel and the conference area.

As soon as I've checked in I go straight to my room, as this will be my base during my stay. Before I unpack, I always have a good look at the room to check that it has the facilities I need. Wi-Fi connectivity is a must, for example, because I need Internet access in my room. If it doesn't have it, I ask to change the room. It's also important that there's a safe for valuables – money, passport, and other documents. There's usually a TV and a mini-bar, but I'm usually too tired for television after a hard day of conferencing! Also, my expense account doesn't cover drinks for the mini-bar!

After I've unpacked, I might go and look for the conference organiser. Even if I've received the programme in advance, there may be some further information that I can get by talking to the organiser and making myself known. The programme is important because it tells you who the key speakers are, and anyone else who may be of interest.
I usually attend conferences as a delegate, but even if I'm giving a talk or holding a workshop, it's useful to attend as many other sessions as you can. Some are a waste of time, of course, so I avoid those. Sometimes there are pre-conference events such as round-table discussions. They also offer good networking opportunities.
I like to arrive early if I can, so that I have time to look around. As well as the conference rooms, I like to check the other places where people meet informally, such as bars and restaurants, lounge areas and corridors. There may be a gym or a spa, but these aren't ideal places for networking. A room with Internet access and office services is much more interesting, because this is where business people gather. As I said, bars are good, and of course there are usually organised events to get people mingling, such as cocktail receptions. If there are going to be stands or exhibitions at the conference, these will be set up in advance, so they are worth visiting early.

A 2.6 **Part 2**

Then it's back to my room to prepare myself for the conference and make myself presentable for the more formal types of meeting and greeting. Personal appearance is important for making an immediate impression, so a business suit is a must. It is better to be over-dressed than too casual, in my opinion. The only exception might be if an outside event has been organised, such as a sightseeing trip or some kind of entertainment. It's good to have lots of pockets, too, so I'll often wear a three-piece suit. That way I don't have to carry too much stuff about. If I do take a small shoulder bag, it's for things that I pick up during the day such as brochures and handouts.
Into the pockets go my business cards, in a small leather wallet, some company brochures with our latest products, and some photos of the company headquarters in Zurich. I always carry my Blackberry of course, some spare paper and a good supply of company pens. Oh and my mobile phone, in case I want to show more photos or even take some. Of course I switch it off when meeting people face-to-face, taking calls at an awkward moment would definitely give the wrong impression. Finally, I check my ID badge to make sure the details are correct before clipping it onto my jacket. It's unbelievable how many times the conference organisers get my name wrong. I want people to be absolutely sure who they're talking to!

A 2.7 **Unit 9** A 3 Exercises b. and c.

Part 1

Cheryl: Good morning, Cheryl Kellermann speaking.
Nick: Hi Cheryl, it's Nick. I just thought I'd give you a call to see how it's going.
Cheryl: Nick, hi! I'm fine! I've got my own office now. It's great.
Nick: Hey, lucky you.
Cheryl: Well, things didn't get off to a good start. I was a bit disappointed at first because I was hoping to have something interesting and challenging to do. I didn't want them to give me all the boring jobs like photocopying and filing, so in my application letter I said I'd like to work on a project with a very dynamic team and be involved with tasks that required creative problem-solving.
Nick: That's a tall order. But what did they give you?
Cheryl: Well, the first thing I found out is that in a busy company like this an intern often has to stand in for someone else. When I started, one of the secretaries was ill, and the person who worked at reception had to take over her job. That meant they needed someone to work at reception, so they asked me! That was my first day, and I was thinking: 'Great!' Answering the phone all day, connecting calls, giving visitors directions. Not exactly what I'd had in mind, as a stepping-stone to an international business career!
Nick: That doesn't sound fair. Did you say anything?
Cheryl: Oh no, I didn't want to start off on the wrong foot. Besides, I was told it would only be a temporary situation. I wasn't very motivated but I did my best to be cheerful and positive, since I was representing the company. And then, after a few days, I began to realise that it was a better job than I thought. For one thing, I had to think on my feet, because you never know who's going to call. There's a constant flow of people coming through reception, and lots of calls to deal with. It helped me get to know who's who in the company, and who the customers and suppliers are. And we get a lot of calls from abroad, and that taught me to speak much more clearly and slowly.
Nick: So where are you now?
Cheryl: Well, I was on the reception desk until last Friday. Now I'm in the Human Resources department. This time I'm standing in for someone who has just left to have a baby, and she'll be on maternity leave for at least six months!

Nick: Well, I guess it'll be more interesting than working in reception …
Cheryl: I hope so, and now I feel I've got a foot in the door, because this is really what I want to do.
Nick: Well good luck, and if you need any advice, just give me a call.
Cheryl: Thanks, Nick. I'd better hang up. I can hear the boss coming! Bye.
Nick: Bye.

A 2.8 Part Two

Nick: Nick Paget speaking.
Cheryl: It's me, Cheryl. Sorry to bother you, Nick, but have you got a moment? I've got a problem.
Nick: Sure. I hope it's not the job.
Cheryl: Well, not the job exactly, but I've got a real mess to sort out. Remember I told you that I'm standing in for someone?
Nick: Someone on maternity leave?
Cheryl: Yes, she was the personal assistant to the Human Resources Director and there was some problem with her replacement at the last minute, so they've asked me to take over.
Nick: Ah, so they've thrown you in at the deep end.
Cheryl: Oh, I don't mind in principle, because it's a great chance for me to learn the ropes. But you won't believe what's happened …
Nick: Go on.
Cheryl: Well, there's been a mix-up with some job applications. Peter went through the roof when he found out.
Nick: Peter?
Cheryl. Oh, he's my boss, the Human Resources Director. Anyway, what happened was that they've advertised a job and last week they sorted through the applications and drew up a short list of five people to interview. The assistant – the one who's gone off on maternity leave – was asked to write letters to the candidates inviting them to an interview, and send rejection letters to the rest. She put all the applications from the shortlisted candidates in one pile, and the ones from the people who had been rejected in another. And, being efficient, she had made lists of all the names and addresses for each pile. But then for some reason, maybe because it was her last day and she had her mind on other things …
Nick: Don't tell me – let me guess. The two lists got mixed up!
Cheryl: Exactly! She sent the shortlisted applicants a rejection letter, and the unsuccessful candidates an invitation to an interview.
Nick: Oh no! How embarrassing! Do they know about the mistake?
Cheryl: No! That's the problem, and my first task is to sort out the mess. The interviews are in two weeks.
Nick: But surely Peter should do it himself. He can't dump on you like that! After all, he's the boss. It's his responsibility!
Cheryl: Well, actually, I offered to sort it out. When he told me what had happened I found myself saying: 'Don't worry, I'll deal with it straight away!'
Nick: Oh, Cheryl!
Cheryl: I guess I was trying to make a good impression. But now I'm left alone with two lists of candidates and a lot of explaining to do!
Nick: Well, it's not often you get such a golden opportunity to get into the boss's good books.
Cheryl: That's why I need your advice. You're the expert at this sort of thing. What would you do?
Nick: Cheryl, I'm really sorry to cut you short here, but someone has just come into my office. Can I call you back in ten minutes?
Cheryl: Please!

A 2.9 **Unit 10** A 3 Exercise a.

Ruth: So, Leo, how do you feel about the project?
Leo: I'm excited. I've never worked on one quite as big as this. It's going to be a great opportunity to learn on the job.
Ruth: Well yes, but it's also an opportunity to show what you can already do.
Leo: True …
Ruth: In other projects I've worked on, I only played a very small part, but with this one I'm a lot more motivated. I'll have the chance to get some real responsibility and put my ideas into practice.
Leo: Yeah, but don't forget that working in a project is all about being a team player. We'll all have to work closely together. What was it that Sharon said? 'There's no "I" in team"!
Ruth: Oh, I know that. And I'm looking forward to working with new people. It looks like Sharon has chosen the right people, with the right attitude and a wide range of skills and expertise. But it's

not just a matter of learning on the job. You have to push yourself forward and contribute your own know-how. Otherwise people think you aren't pulling your weight.

Leo: That's true. Nobody likes a hanger-on. But I thought the kick-off meeting was good. Sharon made it clear what our roles are and what's expected of us.

Ruth. Yeah, Sharon will be good as project leader – she explained the breakdown of tasks and our roles very clearly. And I'm pleased that she carried out a feasibility study. It made me feel a bit more confident about the project, and also about her.

Leo: So what are your feelings about the project?

Ruth: Well, it's obviously a very complex one, with lots of sub-projects and overlapping phases. Sometimes we'll be working on three different tasks at the same time! I think Sharon has done a great job with the planning, and since we've got a strong sponsor, resources won't be a problem. But I'm worried about the timescale. I just don't think it's realistic. The deadlines are really tight, and I noticed from Sharon's breakdown of tasks she hasn't built in any time buffers.

Leo: Yeah, I noticed that, too. I'm worried that if I fall behind on my part of the project, I'll be letting down the other members. I always see a project like climbing a mountain, where you're all roped together. If anyone slips or makes a mistake, that holds back the project.

Ruth: Well, don't make any mistakes then!

Leo: And what if someone drops out altogether?

Ruth: I'm sure Sharon has made some contingency plans, but you can't avoid all risks. No, seriously, remember that we've been picked for the project because we've shown we can deliver. There'll be a lot of pressure, of course, but you have to have the confidence to show that you can not only perform to the highest expectations, but also exceed them.

Leo: And if everyone supports each other, we'll all reach the summit together, right on time.

Ruth: I agree up to a point, but I think it's vital that we concentrate on our own tasks, not other people's tasks. Otherwise we lose sight of our objectives.

Leo: I guess so. But hey, the company really pushed the boat out today. That buffet lunch was fantastic.

Ruth: Yeah, it was a feast. But I would have preferred a sit-down meal, actually. I hate standing in line.

Leo: Oh, I thought it was an excellent idea. Buffets are much better for networking than sit-down meals. I managed to talk to loads of people. It's a really international team, isn't it?

Ruth: Yeah. I must admit that I was a bit worried that language might be a problem, with so many different nationalities, but …

Leo: I thought their English was amazing! I don't think language will be a problem. And I think we'll work well together as a team.

Ruth: Yeah, there's certainly a high level of commitment in the team.

A 2.10 **Unit 10** C 1 Exercise c

Manager: OK, it's now the end of September and we're well into the second phase of the project. As you can see from the chart, we should be ready to build the prototype. But according to the latest status report, we're not there yet. Jens, you're supposed to have the product design details ready by now. What's going on?

Jens: Well, we've got a great team working on this and the preliminary product designs were finished on schedule. The problem is that we're being held up by the design of the manufacturing process, which keeps changing. We won't be able to complete our final product design until the problems with the manufacturing process get sorted out.

Manager: Just a second … are you telling me that you're still waiting for that? The manufacturing process was supposed to be ready by the end of July, before work on the final product design started. Carola, you're responsible for the manufacturing process, you were supposed to start at the beginning of June. What's taking so long?

Carola: It isn't our fault. As you know, there is a lot of new automation in this process, and our main supplier has let us down. They guaranteed to deliver all the parts that we needed for the production line by July at the latest, but we didn't get them until August. And then some of them had to be sent back because they didn't conform to our specifications, and then …

Manager: All right, all right, we can go into the details later. Look, we have a deadline for launching the product – the beginning of February – and everything else has to work around that. As you know, the launch date was originally set for the beginning of the year, so it's already been put off once. We can't risk another delay. Besides, the marketing campaign is now well under way, and there will be a lot of interest in the product already. We can't afford to be late to market, or our competitors will get in ahead of us.

Jens: I don't understand why the marketing campaign starts before we've even created the product. They don't even have the final design details yet.

Manager: It's essential to get our product information out into the market as early as possible. This was agreed right back at the kick-off meeting. The marketing people are doing a fantastic job and it's up to us to make sure we deliver the product on time. So we need solutions, it's no use blaming other people because we're falling behind schedule. Carola, you haven't just missed your deadline, you're now two months overdue. I'd like you to arrange a meeting with the suppliers and their technical people, I want to be there and I think you should be there too, Jens.

Carola: OK, when shall I arrange it for?

Manager: This week. OK Jens?

Jens: Sure.

Manager: And meanwhile, let's figure out how we're going to reschedule things. The problem, as I see it, is that we didn't put any time buffers into the original plan. We can't postpone the launch date any more. That's out. So we'll have to start the first production run by the beginning of the year or we won't have a product. So those two deadlines are fixed. We'll have to find some flexibility between now and the end of the year.

Carola: If we can get the parts delivered, we'll only need a couple of weeks to complete our process design. I'm absolutely sure we can do it.

Manager: We'll have to count on that. So let's say you have until the middle of October. That means that the product design team would have to complete their work by the end of the month, so that the prototype stage could begin in November. Is that OK with you, Jens?

Jens: Yes, I suppose so, if we work flat out. But then it means handing over the design to the prototype engineers a month late, so how will that work out?

Manager: Well, we'll just have to bring in other resources. I'll explain the problem to the senior management and tell them that we need to bring in more people to build and test the prototype, and we'll need more funding if we're going to make up time. They won't be happy about pouring even more money into the project. But you can leave that to me. The important thing is to get over this problem with the suppliers. Carola, can you get onto that straight away, and let me know when you have the meeting fixed? As soon as possible, tomorrow would be great.

Carola: I'll do my best.

Manager: Good. It's time we got this project back on track!

A 2.11 **Unit 11** C 6 Exercise a

Paul: Hi, Anna. Did get my email?

Anna: Hello, Paul. Um, which email was that?

Paul: The one about the product recall.

Anna: Product recall?

Paul: Yes, it's to do with Speeeeedy.

Anna: Sorry, Paul, but I don't think I got an email from you about a recall. Maybe I missed it. Just a moment, let me check my emails.

Paul: Listen, Anna. I think it'll be faster to do this by phone, OK? We need to issue a product recall notice, and we need to do it today, like now. I was told you'd be doing the recalls, so is it OK if I give you the details right now?

Anna: Sure, if you've got the details with you. I've brought the template up on my screen, but I'm not going to be able to type and hold the receiver at the same time. I'll just have to note things down. OK, go ahead.

Paul: Right, well as I said, the name is Speeeeedy, with five 'e's.

Anna: Ah, yes, the five 'e's. How this helps children to spell I don't know. How many have been sold?

Paul: I can tell you that. It's 28,000 in the United States. Not exactly 28,000, of course, but about 28,000, nationwide.

Anna: And Magiplay is the importer, obviously.

Paul: Yeah, but you'll need to include the town and the state.

Anna: Andover, Illinois?

Paul: No, The headquarters. Chicago, Illinois.

Anna: And what was the hazard? Hey, let me guess. Was it the wheels falling off?

Paul: No, it was the paint. The levels of lead are too high.

Anna: The levels of lead in the paint? Oh, that's bad.

Paul: Yeah, the levels are excessive. You can add that the federal standards prohibit lead paint on children's toys, so it's a violation of the law.

Anna: That's been a big problem with toys from China, right? Is that where they're from?

Paul: Yeah, the manufacturer is based in Shanghai.

Anna: And have any kids been harmed by the lead paint?

Paul: Well, we haven't actually had any reports of kids being harmed. Not yet.
Anna: None at all? So why is there a product recall?
Paul: Anna, it's a voluntary recall. We need to protect ourselves …
Anna: … and the kids…
Paul: … from any injuries or incidents.
Anna: Of course we do. So how should I describe Speeeeedy? Isn't Speeeeedy that tortoise car that is driven by a hare?
Paul: Yeah, but the description needs to sound … a bit more technical.
Anna: What would you say?
Paul: 'The toy is a green and brown vehicle'… No, not 'vehicle', write 'automobile'.
Anna: Automobile? I would call it a car.
Paul: OK, call it a car. Thank you. Write 'The toy is a green and brown car in the shape of a tortoise, with a hare at the steering wheel'.
Anna: Steering wheel? Hmm … What about 'with a hare in the driving seat'?
Paul: Yeah, Anna, write that. Oh, and you'll need to include the Magiplay product number. That's T1709.
Anna: I'll read that back. T1709.
Paul: Correct.
Anna: OK. And what retail stores were they sold at? And when?
Paul: Retail stores across the nation, and … hang on, I just need to check the dates, … June 2007 through October 2009.
Anna: And the price?
Paul: Around twenty dollars.
Anna: Twenty dollars – that's not cheap! Anyway, what should the customers do now?
Paul: Take the recalled toy away from their children immediately, and contact us in order to receive a free replacement toy.
Anna: Do they also need to return Speeeeedy?
Paul: Oh, yeah. I nearly forgot. Yes, they need to return Speeeeedy to Magiplay. And you also need to include all the contact details.
Anna: I can fill out the rest myself. For additional information contact Magiplay at eight eight eight, two double-nine, oh five nine seven.
Paul: No! That's the old number.
Anna: Old number? Nobody told me!
Paul: Didn't they? Well, it's changed. It's still triple eight two double-nine, but then it's oh-seven-two-four.
Anna: Hey, it's a good thing I talked to you! I wouldn't have known! But the website is the same, right? It's www dot service dot magiplay dot com.
Paul: Yeah, no change there.
Anna: OK, I'll go ahead and write the recall notice. Do you want me to send it to you to check?
Paul: Please.
Anna: You'll have it in ten minutes. Really speeeeedy.

A 2.12 **Unit 12** A3 Exercise a

Jochen: Hi, is that Daniela?
Daniela: Jochen? Great to hear from you! How are things?
Jochen: Really good. In fact, I may be coming to Dublin.
Daniela: You're coming to Dublin? Fantastic. Is it business or pleasure?
Jochen: Both, I hope! My company has a policy of sending new employees on overseas secondments, so we get some international experience.
Daniela: Hey! It sounds like you've found a great employer!
Jochen: Yes, I can choose between a nine-month assignment in Dublin and a six-month assignment in Dubai. I can't decide, so I thought I'd call you. Do you have a few minutes?
Daniela: Sure, no problem! I don't know much about Dubai, but I've lived in Dublin for ten years now, and it feels like home.
Jochen: Do you miss Rome at all?
Daniela: Of course I do, especially my family. But I visit whenever I can. You can get really cheap flights to Rome from here.
Jochen: I hear that Dublin's quite a cosmopolitan city
Daniela: It is, but it still has a lot of charm. The people are so friendly and I love the Irish lifestyle. Very easy-going, and a great nightlife!
Jochen: So it's a bit like Rome, then?
Daniela: Except for the weather. Don't forget to bring your umbrella – it rains a lot!

Jochen: And what about driving? I was thinking of bringing my car from Germany. You know, driving to England and then taking a car-ferry to Dublin.
Daniela: No! Don't bring a car. The traffic in Dublin is terrible!
Jochen: Really?
Daniela: Yes, when Ireland had its boom, the sale of cars shot up. Now the traffic is nearly as bad as in Rome. With the recession, sales have fallen, but the traffic is still a nightmare. It's better to use public transport. They have quite a good system here.
Jochen: What about the cost of living? I've heard that Ireland is a relatively cheap place to live.
Daniela: Not any more, I'm afraid. That used to be the case, but during the economic boom prices shot up, as you'd expect. And even though we've had a recession, things like food are still quite pricey.
Jochen: What about rent? If I come for nine months, I'd like to find somewhere nice that's quite central. I was thinking maybe a penthouse flat with a view across the river.
Daniela: That would cost a fortune! But generally, the housing situation is good for people who want to buy or rent. Property prices are really low and there are so many unsold houses everywhere. I'm sure you'll find some good offers.
Jochen: Well, that sounds positive. But I'm surprised at what you say about the Irish economy. Since Ireland is so strong on exporting, I would expect the economy to be in good shape.
Daniela: Actually, some people here think that the boom years are over. Don't forget, a lot of the exporting companies are in sectors like technology, chemicals, finance, and they're foreign-owned. They helped the Irish economy by bringing in capital and know-how. In fact, I think it's because of them that Ireland has such a big trade surplus. But now they're leaving. Ireland already has a budget deficit and if exports fall, it will get even bigger.
Jochen: The accountancy firm you work for is American-owned, isn't it?
Daniela: Yes, but they're staying here, so I think my job is quite safe. The construction industry has been hit most, but unemployment is rising in all sectors. It would be even higher if it weren't for the fact that so many immigrants are returning home.
Jochen: You're not planning to go back to Rome, are you?
Daniela: Oh, no. As I told you, I feel really at home here. And besides, business is really good for accountants at the moment. A lot of firms are going bankrupt, and they need us to sort out their tax matters. People always need accountants, in good times and bad!
Jochen: Daniela, since you mention tax, is it true that if I come on a secondment I won't have to pay tax?
Daniela: That depends on how long you stay. You said nine months, right?
Jochen: Yes, either nine months in Dublin or six months in Dubai.
Daniela: If you stay longer than 180 days, you'll be liable for tax. From that point of view, Dubai might be better for you! But, please don't be put off Dublin. You'll have a great time here if you decide to come. We can meet up for a Guinness. You know, there are some great bars …

A 2.13 **Unit 13** A2 Exercise b

Claire: Phil, it's really good of you to meet me at such short notice.
Phil: No problem, Claire, I'm always happy to help. Anyway, cheers!
Claire: Cheers!
Phil: So, from what I read in the emails you sent me, business is looking up.
Claire: Yes, and it's all been a bit sudden. The thing is, I don't know if I'm ready to go into exporting.
Phil: Well, in any business, you need to take opportunities that come along. If you don't, you might kick yourself later. So I think you should consider the options carefully, and weigh up the pros and cons.
Claire: I'm worried about all the extra paperwork – I've got enough on my hands already. And also I don't know if my company has the capacity to expand, especially into unknown territory.
Phil: That's understandable. Exporting goods is a lot more complex than selling in your domestic market. For one thing, more parties are involved.
Claire: More parties?
Phil: Parties as in customs and government authorities, banks, insurance companies, export service providers, international carriers, and so on …
Claire: Yeah, I know what you mean … It's not just the customer and me. I guess the whole process of selling is more complex, what with the distances involved, the different cultures, languages, business practices, and so on. That's what puts me off.
Phil: OK, let's take one step at a time. Have you thought of drawing up an export plan?
Claire: You mean like a business plan?
Phil: Yes, sort of. You define your export goals and then say how you're going to reach them, listing things like market research, staff training, costs and price, production capacity. And then you have to consider things like the language you'll use to invoice customers, and the currency you'll quote in. And of course there's the issue of VAT.

Claire: But Phil, do I really need an export plan at this stage? I'm not sure whether export is worth the hassle.
Phil: I'm coming on to that point. Let's consider the two enquiries you've had. The Swiss company are obviously keen on your Mint Condition coins. Great name, by the way.
Claire: Thanks.
Phil: And the idea of selling chocolate in Switzerland of all places could be good publicity for you. But obviously there are strings attached.
Claire: I know – I'd have to get my head round all those rules and regulations. Sending them a list of ingredients shouldn't be a problem, though.
Phil: They might ask for a German translation.
Claire: Oh.
Phil: And you might have to modify the ingredients. Switzerland is outside the EU, and they might have special requirements regarding chocolate products. On the other hand, I've heard they now apply the Cassis de Dijon principle.
Claire: The Cassis de what?
Phil: Oh, Cassis de Dijon. It's a trading principle that says that any product made in the EU can be sold in another EU country without restrictions. I think the Swiss have adopted it, but I'm not sure it applies to all products.
Claire: In the email it says that the company is a fast-growing retailer, so they should know their market.
Phil: You should check them out, just as you would with any customer. Have a look at their website and do a bit of research. But remember that you'll have the added problem of packaging and labelling.
Claire: You mean it would need to be redesigned?
Phil: Yeah, so that it's labelled the way they want it. And I think it has to be in at least two of Switzerland's main languages, French, German and Italian.
Claire: Hmmm … it sounds even more complicated than I thought.
Phil: Not necessarily. If they're keen on your product, they might be willing to give you advice. Why don't you write a positive response to their email, and ask for a bit more clarification on those points? You can't lose and your brand could be a winner. Having said that, I'd be more interested in the other company, the specialty foods distributor in Berlin.
Claire: Gourmet. As I understand it, they're offering to act as distributor and would like to take on the Madagascar truffles because it's a fair trade product.
Phil: Exactly. It's got a lot going for it. For one thing, it's based in Germany, which means you'd be dealing with a distributor in the EU single market. In that sense it's hardly even export. At the same time they'd help you break into markets outside the EU, for example the USA. If that's what you want.
Claire: Well, as you said, I might kick myself if I don't follow this up.
Phil: Again, I'd send a positive response to their email. There's no harm in discussing terms.
Claire: They'd want a cut of the profits, of course.
Phil: True. But your retailers in the UK also take a cut. I tell you what, Claire. Why don't I send you some links about dealing with distributors, because you'd also need to check their creditworthiness. If you like, I could also write a list of questions you could ask during your discussion.
Claire: Oh, Phil, you've been so much help! Can I get you another drink?
Phil: No, this one's on me! Same again?
Claire: Er … no, actually, maybe I'll try a Cassis de Dijon, if they have it.

A 2.14 **Unit 13** B 3 Exercises a. and b.

Phil: Right, has anyone here ever had problems with getting customers to pay? Hands up! … Aha! Most of you, I see. Me, too … Right, and how many of you have paid for something without actually getting what you wanted? … Just about everyone in the room! So, as you can see, payment issues can arise for both the seller and the buyer. In international trade, payment is an even riskier and more complex process, and the types of risk involved will of course depend on whether you're an exporter or an importer.
As you can see on this payment risk ladder, the lower the risk for the importer, the higher it is for the exporter. Now, the least secure method of trading for the exporter is open account terms. Here, the seller sends the goods directly to the buyer, who pays at some later date. Obviously, this is the most advantageous method for the buyer, both in terms of cash flow and costs. So my advice to exporters is: Only offer open account terms if you're confident you'll get paid. Now that's a big 'if', of course. And don't forget - your customer might even go bankrupt! So if you think there's a risk of buyer insolvency, take out some form of export credit insurance. Or better still – don't do business with that customer at all.

At the other end of the scale we have advance payment. This is where the exporter gets paid before shipping the goods. As you can see, it's the most secure method of trading for exporters. Of course, this option is the least advantageous to buyers.

In international trade, the choice tends to be between these two extremes. And this is where banking products come in, such as bills for collection and letters of credit. From the exporter's point of view, bills for collection offer a more secure option than open account terms. These bills involve documents that the exporter sends to the buyer's bank after the goods have been shipped. They contain specific instructions, and if the buyer doesn't comply with them, the exporter can retain title to the goods. Having title means the same as owning, so in other words the goods still belong to the exporter.

Now, there are two types of bill for collection. The first is documents against payment, which is usually written as D/P. This means that the importer has to pay for the goods before getting the documents. Ah – does someone have a question at the back?

Member of audience: Yes, is 'documents against payment' the same as 'cash against documents'?

Phil: Well, it's the same process, yes. Good question. Right, the other type of bill for collection is known as documents against acceptance, abbreviated as D/A. In this case, the buyer is allowed more time to pay, typically with credit periods of 30, 60 or 90 days. The documents are usually accompanied by a kind of invoice called a bill of exchange, which the importer has to sign. The bill of exchange looks a bit like a cheque, but it functions more like an invoice. The importer accepts the bill of exchange by signing it, and then the bank releases the documents.

Finally, we have letters of credit, also known as documentary credits. Basically, a letter of credit is a letter that one bank sends to another bank asking them to pay money to the exporter. The first bank, the bank of the importer, guarantees to pay the importer's supplier, once certain conditions have been fulfilled. For example, the importer can stipulate which documents the exporter has to provide, for example the commercial invoice and various shipping documents such as the insurance certificate, bill of lading, packing list, and so on. The bank passes these documents on to the importer when he pays or accepts a bill of exchange. In this way, the importer can pay the exporter before getting the goods, and be reasonably sure that the goods are on their way and are insured. Any questions so far?

Member of audience: Yes, I have a question. If I'm an importer, can I pay by cheque?

Phil: No, I'd definitely advise against cheques. First of all, it carries the risk of dishonour, in other words, if the buyer doesn't have enough money in his account, the cheque will bounce. And secondly, cheques are really inconvenient. If you get a cheque, you have to send it to your bank, and it may take weeks or even months to clear. Also, it may be written in the currency of the buyer, which means that it takes even longer to clear, and it's you who has to pay the additional bank charges. Of course, there's also the very real danger of the cheque being lost in the post!

Member of audience: So what do you recommend?

Phil: Well, has any one heard of SWIFT? … And does anyone know what SWIFT stands for?

Member of audience: Society for Worldwide International Financial Transactions?

Member of audience: No, it's Financial Transfers.

Phil: Almost. It's the Society for Worldwide Interbank Financial Telecommunication. This is now standard practice in the major trading nations. If you're an importer, all you have to do is instruct your bank to transfer payment to the bank account that has been specified by the exporter. So if you're an exporter, it's good practice to include your account details on your correspondence and invoices.

A 2.15 **Unit 14** A1 Exercise a

Message 1

Trudy: Hi, Gavin, it's Trudy. I was hoping to catch you in your office. Could you give me a call as soon as you get in? We've had another letter from the Advertising Standards Authority. This time it's about our print ad for the BTX power drill. There've been some complaints - someone is accusing us of making false or misleading claims. Gavin, this TV ad has cost us an absolute fortune. It'd be a disaster if we had to withdraw it. Anyway, hope to talk to you soon!

A 2.16 Message 2

Sally: Good morning, Gavin. Sally Beaumont here. Sorry to bother you again, but the union reps have asked for an emergency meeting, and I need your advice. As you know, we've drawn up a table of redundancy payments for everyone who's being laid off, based on the length of their employment with us. It seems that some of them have heard through the grapevine that the redundancies will be on a last in, first out basis, and that anyone who's worked for us for less than two years won't qualify for payments. I've also been told that they're getting legal advice from a trade union lawyer.

Gavin, we need a watertight legal case, and I'm not sure I'm up to speed on all the rules and regulations about redundancy plans. So could you call me when you get in? I'll be here until five.

A 2.17 **Message 3**

Justin: Hello, Justin, here, Justin Fisher. You may remember me calling you the other day about the defective sensors. Fortunately, it's not a safety hazard, but we're going to do as you suggested anyway and send out a product recall notice and also a press release. The thing is, we'd like to offer customers the choice of either a refund or returning the product to us for repair, but I just wanted to check with you first that both options are possible. Um ... if you like, I could send you both the recall notice and the press release. They're just drafts, but it might be good if you could look over them first. Anyway, maybe you could call me back. Or send an email. Thanks, bye.

A 2.18 **Message 4**

Ahmed: Oh, hello, this is Ahmed Dotani with a call for Gavin Mellor. I have a question regarding a billing. It's to do with a customer who hasn't responded to any of our reminders, and now he's querying our late payment charge. He claims he didn't receive our reminders and he says the late payment charge is illegal. I'd be grateful if you could take up this matter, because we've had problems with this bloke before. We suspect that he's playing for time because he's about to go bankrupt. Er, Gavin, I'll put all of this in an email, and send you copies of the correspondence. But could you give me a call anyway? I'm on extension 137. Bye for now.

A 2.19 **Message 5**

Ben: Good morning, this is Ben Norris from DEFRA, returning a call for Gavin Mellor. You left a message earlier about the Environmental Damage Regulations ... er, you wanted to know how environmental damage is defined in the Regulations, and what it means to say that the polluter has to pay. You'll find some information about this legislation on the DEFRA website. That's www.defra.gov.uk. Click on environmental liability, and that'll take you to the relevant European Directive. That's European Directive number 2004/35/EC. The way they define environmental damage is very specific; it covers only the most serious cases, so perhaps it doesn't affect you. If you want to know who to contact in your region, I suggest you call the DEFRA helpline, which is 08459 33 66 77. Hope that answers your questions, Mr Mellor. Goodbye.

A 2.20 **Unit 15** A2 Exercise a

Lucy: Ah, do come in. Nice to meet you! It's Mr Hopcroft, isn't it?
Peter: That's right. Peter Hopcroft – but do call me Peter. And you must be ...
Lucy: ... Lucy, Lucy Snow. Do have a seat, Peter!
Peter: Thank you.
Lucy: I understand you had a phone call with my colleague. He probably explained that I'm a partner here at SQQ Consulting.
Peter: That's right.
Lucy: He passed your enquiry on to me, since I deal with all matters to do with personal finance.
Peter: Yes, it's very good of you to see me at such short notice.
Lucy: I'm happy to, Peter. Now, I hear you need some advice on investments, so ...
Peter: Well, I don't have much experience in this field, so before going any further I thought I should at least find out what's involved
Lucy: Well, you're doing the right thing, Peter. It's good to get as much information as you can before you make any decisions about money.
Peter: It feels like quite a big step to take.
Lucy: I can imagine. But you've come to the right place! So what I need to do, before we start talking about figures, is to get some background details about you. Now, you say you're looking for investment advice. Can I take it that you don't currently have a financial portfolio?
Peter: Er ... that's right. I don't currently have a ... What exactly is a portfolio?
Lucy: Right, well, basically it's a collection of investments. You could call it a mixed bag. The idea is rather like the old saying 'don't put all your eggs into one basket'. If you have a range of assets that are properly managed, you can reduce certain risks. We can talk about the different types of investment later. But first we need to work out what you can afford, what your financial goals are, and what kind of risk you're prepared to take on in order to achieve those goals.
Peter: I don't actually want to take any risks! At least, I don't want to gamble with my money.
Lucy: I see. So ...?
Peter: Well, I've always been very careful up to now, and only done business with my bank. I've got a current account, a joint account with my wife, and a savings account. That's it, basically.

Lucy: That sounds like a fairly standard setup. And do you have any loans, or other arrangements with your bank?
Peter: No, I've never been keen on borrowing money. Well, apart from the mortgage on the house, but that's mostly paid off now. And I always pay off my credit card at the end of every month.
Lucy: So the only interest you get is from your savings account.
Peter: That's right. It's not much interest, but it's something.
Lucy: In other words, your assets are not growing. In fact, you're barely keeping up with inflation.
Peter: Well, I've never been into stocks and shares and the like. Some people say you've got to speculate to accumulate, but I don't agree. There are too many bankrupt speculators!
Lucy: Well, it's good to be cautious. But, really, there's a degree of risk in any investment. The key thing is to understand the risks involved and manage them, ideally with professional help.
Peter: Yes …
Lucy: So what is it you're saving for, Peter?
Peter: For my retirement, mostly, as a nest egg to boost my pension. And I think it's important to put something by for a rainy day. Just in case something unexpected happens …
Lucy: Yes, you never know what life's going to throw at you. So why exactly have you come to us for advice?
Peter: Well, I've had a bit of a windfall, actually. I've just inherited half a million!
Lucy: Ah, I see. And you're wondering just what to do next.
Peter: Yes, It was a legacy that came to me when my uncle died. He owned a shipping company and made a lot of money, but then he fell out with his family and changed his will to spite them. When he died, all the money came to me!
Lucy: Did this inheritance come with strings attached? Or are you free to do whatever you like with it?
Peter: According to the will, I can do what I like. But I know that my uncle would want me to invest it wisely. I'm looking for something safe, so that the money will be put to work and earn interest gradually without me having to worry about ups and downs.
Lucy: That's a good way to think, Peter. You want your money to grow without getting caught up in too many fluctuations. What we need to discuss is how to spread your risk. And that depends on how much of the five hundred thousand pounds you want to be able to access at short notice.
Peter: Well, I'm not sure. I mean, if something happens like … you know … um, for example if my wife has to … or if I can't … I think I'd like to have at least twenty-five thousand pounds readily available.
Lucy: So about five per cent of your investment should be available on demand, and the rest in other forms of investment with a higher yield. And there are a lot of interesting options …
Peter: I know. I've got friends who invest in things like fine art, or even classic cars, but it's confusing and I'm sure there are lots of sharks waiting to take advantage of people like me.
Lucy: That's true. You hear horror stories in the media every day about people who've lost everything through dodgy schemes. That's why it's important to shop around, get advice and study all the options. Our policy here at SQQ is to create a profile of our client, and then match that personal information to suitable investment options. In other words, we build a portfolio that fits your individual needs.
Peter: That sounds good to me. So, what's the first step?
Lucy: Well, before I ask a new client to sign anything, I give them some homework to do. It's a questionnaire that I'd like you to fill in and send back to me. It provides me with some idea of the sort of investor that you think you are, and what you are expecting from your investments. We'll then look around for the right kind of eggs for your basket! How does that sound?
Peter: Fine, yes! I'd be interested to know what ideas you come up with.
Lucy: Great! I'll just go and print out a copy for you. Would you like a coffee, by the way?
Peter: Thanks, I'd love one.

A 2.21 **Unit 16** B2 Exercise a.

Lecturer: Good morning everyone. So, shall we start? Thank you. And has everyone got a handout?
Students: Yeah.
Lecturer: Good. Well, as you know, our subject today is mergers and acquisitions. Here, we'll be focusing on three questions: What are they? Why do they happen? And what are the risks involved? So, let's start with some definitions. Now, the terms 'merger' and 'acquisition' are often used together under the acronym 'M & A', as though they were synonymous. But it's important to draw a distinction.
Strictly speaking, a merger is the act of combining two companies, often about the same size. They combine as equals, and by mutual agreement, and new shares are issued in place of the

old shares. An acquisition, on the other hand, is when one company acquires or takes over another company, establishing itself as the new owner. So, basically, an acquisition is a takeover. Typically, the acquiring company is able to buy more than 50% of the shares of the target company, and thereby gain a controlling interest. From a legal point of view, the target company ceases to exist, and the buyer 'swallows up' the business.

In practice, 'mergers of equals' don't happen very often. Usually, one company buys another. In fact, a lot of the time the word 'merger' is used when it's technically an acquisition. Any ideas why? ... Yes?

Student 1: Could it be that if the deal is described as a merger, then the people affected are more likely to accept it? The word 'takeover' doesn't sound as good.

Lecturer: Exactly. Being bought out often carries negative connotations. Basically, whether a purchase is considered a merger or an acquisition really depends on whether the purchase is friendly or hostile, and how it is announced. In other words, the real difference lies in how the purchase is communicated to the target company's board of directors, employees and shareholders – and how it is perceived by them. So, moving on, why do companies merge with – or acquire - other companies? Any ideas?

Student 2: To get bigger, and to increase their market share.

Lecturer: Yes. It's a way to achieve a more dominant market position, especially if the takeover target is a competitor. And they can get access to new markets. Anything else?

Student 3: Synergy?

Lecturer: Good! Yes, that magic word, synergy. By working together, each company gains in a way that they wouldn't if they worked alone. There are economies of scale, and cost savings that accrue from staff reductions, for example. Companies that merge also improve their purchasing power. When they place larger orders, they're in a stronger position in price negotiations with their suppliers. A merger can also improve a company's standing in the investment community: bigger firms often have an easier time raising capital than smaller ones. And companies can also acquire new expertise and technology by buying other companies. Ah - is that a question at the back?

Student 1: Yes. Isn't it the case that what's good for the acquiring company isn't necessarily good for the target company?

Lecturer: Good point. Yes, a benefit for one company may be a risk or a drawback for the other. And of course the risks for both are considerable. It's no secret that a lot of mergers simply don't work. Two out of every three mergers fail, and there are a number of reasons for this.

Firstly, a merger may have more to do with prestige than sound corporate strategy. The executive ego is boosted by buying the competition, and this can be a major force when combined with the influences from the bankers, lawyers and various other advisers who can earn big fees from clients engaged in mergers.

Secondly, coping with a merger can cause top managers to spread their time too thinly and neglect their core business, and this can spell trouble – especially if the merger hasn't been prepared carefully enough.

And a third important factor is culture clash – the chances for success may be seriously hampered if the national or corporate cultures of the companies are very different. When a company is acquired, the decision is typically based on product or market synergies, but cultural differences are often ignored. It's a mistake to assume that personnel issues can be easily overcome.

There's a study by the consulting group McKinsey that shows how companies often focus too much on cutting costs. Their revenues, and ultimately profits, suffer. Another study carried out by KPMG of seven hundred mergers found that only seventeen per cent created real value, and that more than half of them destroyed value. Indeed merging companies can focus on cost-cutting so much that they neglect their day-to-day business – and their most important asset - their customers. And if customers get nervous, they go elsewhere. Of course, this doesn't please the shareholders. Ah – is that another question?

Student 1: Actually, I'd just like to add another point ...

CD3

A 3.1 **Revision 1** Units 1 – 4

Presenter: So, here we have the latest version of the Baby Beam. It's the smallest projector of its kind on the market, only ten centimetres by eight centimetres, and it's also very thin - only five centimetres. It weighs just under a kilogram. As you can see, it's small enough to fit in your pocket, so it's

easily portable. The outer casing is now available in two colours, polished aluminum or white. I think you'll agree that it's very stylish, but it's also robust.
At the same time, it's packed with state-of-the-art technology. The LED projector is easy-to-use and it's also reliable. As far as technology is concerned, the most important feature is the LED lamp. This reaches full power after a few seconds, without producing any heat. And since no heat is produced, there's no risk of expensive bulb damage – and it's quiet! There's no need for a fan to cool down the bulb. Oh, and there's a two year guarantee on all the interior parts.
As you'd expect with a top-end projector like this, the Baby Beam comes with a full range of accessories, including USB hub connector, an extension cable, and a spare lamp. It also comes with this attractive nylon shoulder bag, which has special anti-shock padding in case it's dropped. Also included are cleaning materials and a comprehensive instruction book in six languages.
Now, even though the Baby Beam is a highly sophisticated product, it's very competitively priced. It retails at only 150 euros which represents excellent value for money. So, whether for private or corporate use, this slim and elegant projector makes real sense to users who want advanced technology that is affordable and convenient.

A 3.2 **Revision 2** Units 5 – 8

Interviewer: Hello, This is Jenny Swallow and you're listening to 'Business Breakfast'. Today we're very pleased to have as our guest in the studio Professor Ian Champion from the Bartlebooth Consulting Group. Welcome!

Professor: Hello. And thank you for inviting me.

Interviewer: This morning we're turning our attention to the current state of British manufacturing. A report published this week shows that our manufacturing sector has declined by six point five per cent in the last three months, and car production in particular has been hit hard, with a fall of fifty per cent in the last year.

Professor: Yes, the figures make depressing reading. But we need to look at this current situation in a historical perspective. The heyday of British manufacturing was already over during the boom years of the nineteen eighties. Between 1980 and 2008, manufacturing cut four million jobs, and went from thirty one per cent of GDP to just thirteen per cent.

Interviewer: So is it true to say that Britain is no longer a manufacturing nation?

Professor: No, on the contrary! Thanks to increased efficiency among the industries that have survived, Britain's manufacturing output, at least until the recent recession, was better than ever. OK, services now make up seventy five per cent of the British economy – this is a trend that has affected most developed countries. But manufacturing still employs three million people and provides more than half of our exports. And it's one and a half times the size of our financial services sector.

Interviewer: That might surprise some people. So, what do we actually make?

Professor: Well, Britain is a leading producer of chemicals, green technologies, electrical and optical equipment, and it's home to two of the world's largest pharmaceutical groups, GlaxoSmithKline and AstraZeneca. The UK aerospace industry is the largest in the world outside the US. It employs a hundred and twenty five thousand people. The problem, though, is that these firms are high-tech, and relatively few British companies make globally branded consumer goods. This means that we tend to overlook them.

Interviewer: What about how we compare internationally? Is British manufacturing still competitive?

Professor: Oh yes, very much so. We're still the sixth largest manufacturing nation in the world, obviously well behind countries like Germany and Japan, but ahead of France. But the downside of having such a high-tech, export-oriented manufacturing sector is that it's very vulnerable in a recession. The collapse in world trade has hit Britain's manufacturers hard. A lot of companies have become leaner and more efficient, but some won't be able to shrink any further.

Interviewer: Can anything be done about it? Do you have a positive message for manufacturers out there?

Professor: Ha! Well unlike many people commentating on the current situation, I'm an optimist. I think that the downturn in the economy could have a positive side, destroying weaker manufacturers and stimulating innovation. OK, so only the strong will survive, but that's always the case in business and it can be a healthy thing. The big problem is cash. That's why industry is turning to government to set up a rescue fund, to help them through the crisis.

Interviewer: And do you think the state should help manufacturing to play a bigger role in the economy?

Professor: This is a tricky question for an economist. You could argue that we've been relying too much on our financial services sector, and manufacturing is a more solid way of restoring the economy. Stimulating the manufacturing sector will help to create a more balanced economy and create more jobs. But on the other hand, since Britain exports most of what it produces, and exports have been hit hardest of all, an expensive 'stimulation package' by the state might actually make matters worse. It's not an easy question to answer, I'm afraid.

Interviewer: Well on that note, we'll have to end our discussion. Professor Champion, as always, it's been a pleasure to have you on our programme. Thank you.

Professor: Thank you, Jenny.

A 3.3 Revision 3 Units 9 – 12

Receptionist: Good morning, SunCycle Systems.

Sonja: Oh, good morning. Could you put me through to Frank Capper in Human Resources, please?

Receptionist: Sure. Who shall I say is calling?

Sonja: It's Sonja Gerhardt.

Receptionist: OK, thank you, hold the line please.

Frank: Hello, this is Frank Capper speaking. How may I help you?

Sonja: Ah yes, hello, Mr Capper ... my name is Sonja Gerhardt ... and I'm speaking to you from Germany. I found your contact details on the SunCycle website. I'm calling because I'm very interested in your company.

Frank: I see. And what exactly is your business, Ms Gerhardt?

Sonja: Well, actually I'm a student, and at the moment I'm studying for a Bachelor degree in International business at a Business School in southern Germany. My specialist subject is finance.

Frank: Uh huh ... so you're studying finance in Germany. That's good to hear. And why are you interested in SunCycle Systems, exactly?

Sonja: I contacted you because your company is one of the leaders in business software systems. I have to do an internship abroad during my fourth semester, and I'd really like to get some practical experience with a top US company like SunCycle Systems.

Frank: Hmmm. I can understand that, but apart from your current studies do you have any hands-on experience in business? I mean, the normal way to apply for an internship with us is to send us a résumé and cover letter so that we get some idea of your qualifications and background.

Sonja: Yes, I know. But I thought it might be better to contact you directly, that's why I'm calling now. It's ten past six in the evening here in Germany, so I thought it would be the best time to reach you in your office in San Francisco, at ten past nine in the morning. But in answer to your question about practical experience, I've already done a four-month internship here in Germany, with a financial consulting firm in Frankfurt. I really learned a lot there. Now I want to extend my knowledge by working with an international company in an English-speaking country.

Frank: OK, well I must say your English is good. What about other languages?

Sonja: Apart from German and English, I've been studying Spanish as one of my elective courses, and I now have quite a high standard. I think this would be a very useful language for doing business in California. And I know that SunCycle Systems does a lot of business in Latin America.

Frank: Aha, I can tell you've done your research. But you know, we get applications from business students all the time, people wanting internships with our company. What do you have to offer that makes you so special?

Sonja: Well, I think I have a lot to contribute. I'm mainly interested in project management, and ways in which software tools can be developed to make projects run efficiently. But I'm also interested in working with people, especially people from other cultures, and I'd like to play a leading role in an international team. In that way I could match my people skills with my knowledge of finance.

Frank: And what exactly do you think you have to offer in the way of people skills, Ms Gerhardt?

Sonja: My biggest strength is that I'm a team player. Whoever I'm working with, and whatever my role, I'm reliable and supportive. But I also realise it's important to stick to deadlines, so I can be motivated by a tight schedule to get things delivered on time. That means being well-organised, and very focused.

Frank: Well, if you can combine being a great team player with meeting deadlines, that's excellent. We could certainly use a few people like that around here! You realise that our internships are unpaid, don't you?

Sonja: Yes, I'm aware of that. It wouldn't be a problem at all, Mr Capper.

Frank: Listen, Sonja, it's been good talking to you – why don't you email your résumé to the Human Resources department and we might be able to fit you onto our intern program. OK?

Sonja: That would be great, Mr Capper. Only ... could I send it to you personally, now that we've had this conversation?

Frank: Uh, yes, OK, go ahead. Send it to me and I'll see what I can do for you.
Sonja: Great! I'll send my details to you right away! Thank you! Bye.

A 3.4 **Practice Exam** Units 1 – 16

MD: As you know, ladies and gentlemen, Wetbacks Ltd. is a well-known name in upmarket waterproof clothing, not only in the UK and Ireland, but throughout much of Europe. Our waxed cotton jackets and storm-proof overcoats are popular with farmers and fishermen as well as outdoor people who love walking, climbing and camping.

Today, I would like to present a SWOT analysis of the companyTranscripts s strengths and weaknesses, and also the threats and opportunities. I will then outline my vision for the companyTranscripts s future strategy. I have listed the points for you here on the slide.

As far as our strengths are concerned, we are an established company with more than 50 years of experience. We also have a strong brand image. This is partly due to the reputation for quality and long life of our products. It is also a result of the success of the after-sales centres that we have set up across the UK.

However, there are also some weaknesses we should be aware of. Our product range is limited, and although the brand is popular and our clothing is robust and reliable, our products are seen by some people as old-fashioned, using out-of-date designs. We must admit, ladies and gentlemen, that our clothing is heavy and traditional. Of course, we should feel pleased that our sales are excellent at the moment, but our limited product range makes it hard for us to grow.

This is why we need to be aware of our opportunities. It is important to note that the market for our products is changing in a number of ways. First of all, the interest in outdoor activities is increasing again. After years of indoor hobbies and watching TV, people are becoming more health-conscious and want to get out and enjoy nature, whatever the weather! Consumers have more free time and also more money to spend on hobbies such as bird-watching, climbing and hiking. Another opportunity for us is the expansion of the European Union. The addition of member states in Eastern Europe has created a new export market for us. These countries are developing new consumer markets and the leisure industry is being promoted with the help of EU grants and subsidies.

Of course, such changes present a danger to established companies that are not flexible in responding to new trends. The market for waterproof outdoor clothing will become highly competitive, as new products from China and India are launched onto the market. As you know, producers in the Far East are already posing a serious threat to Wetbacks Ltd. Although their products are not of the same quality as ours, it must be said that theyTranscripts re lighter and cheaper and come in a greater variety of designs.

This SWOT analysis sets out to show you WetbacksTranscripts potential. Now let me move on to the second part of my presentation, which is my vision for the future of the company.

So moving on to strategy, I believe that Wetbacks should take steps to consolidate its existing market position and increase its share of this growing and lucrative market.

Firstly, we need to reposition the company and we can do this by developing a range of newly-designed lightweight raincoats, which will appeal to fashionable urban consumers as well as traditional country-loving customers.

Secondly, we should invest in new R & D projects, in particular to create and test new materials made from organically-grown, fair-trade fibres. This would modernise our image and show our commitment to the environment, as well as growers in the developing world.

Thirdly, we should encourage export sales in Eastern Europe, because our outdoor clothing is ideal for their wide range of weather conditions. Of course, this is a fast-growing and competitive market, but I believe we can compete with manufacturers in the Far East, especially on quality and after-sales service.

This brings me to my final point, ladies and gentlemen. All of this will require investment, of course, but we are not in a position to increase our bank loans. We already have enough debt. Therefore I recommend that we go public. Yes, I realise that this is a big step for us, but by selling shares on the stock exchange as Wetbacks PLC, we will be able to achieve our vision of …

Topic vocabulary

Overview

Communication

- Written communication
- Spoken communication
- Collocations relating to communication
- Social skills and body language
- On the phone
- Events in the workpace
- Information and communcation technology

Company Organisation

- Types of company and company structures
- Departments and functions
- Jobs and responsibilities
- Places at work

Corporate Strategy

- Mergers and acquistions
- Corporate strategy
- Image and values

Products, Brands And Marketing

- Describing products
- Marketing and promotion

Sales And Distribution

- Distribution channels
- Terms of payment and delivery
- Transport and shipping
- Packing and labelling

Manufacturing

- Places, equipment and materials
- Describing a process

Business Travel

- Preparation and booking
- Flying and the airline industry
- Hiring a car
- Staying in a hotel
- Rail travel
- Wining and dining
- Conferences, trade fairs and exhibitions

Human Resources

- Hiring and firing
- Issues
- Wages and salaries
- Training and assessment

Project Management

- Types of project
- Project life cycle
- Planning
- Execution
- Controlling and monitoring
- Managing time
- Money
- People

Quality

- Expressions with the word 'quality'
- Standards
- Measures and approaches

Economics

- Business sectors
- Cycles and trends
- Government policy
- Economic and financial indicators

International Trade

- Issues and policy
- Documentation
- Payment and delivery

Legislation

- Legal issues affecting businesses
- Policy and compliance
- Collocations with 'legal'
- Litigation

Finance

- Payment, credit control, banking
- Finance and investment
- Taxation and auditing
- Some acronyms and international organisations

Communication

Written communication
agenda Tagesordnung
application Bewerbung, Antrag
attach, to anhängen
attachment Anhang
brochure Broschüre, Prospekt
catalogue (AE catalog) Katalog
documents Unterlagen
draft Entwurf
itinerary Reiseroute
leaflet Flugblatt, Infoblatt, Prospekt
letter Brief
message Nachricht
minutes Protokoll
notice Aushang
paperwork Verwaltungsarbeit, Schreibarbeit
post-it note Haftnotiz, Klebezettel
report Bericht
sales literature Verkaufsliteratur
schedule ≈ itinerary, timetable Zeitplan, Fahrplan, Stundenplan
subject (in a letter/email) Betreff
bullletin Bulletin, Bekanntmachungsblatt
memo (short for: memorandum) interne Notiz, Vermerk
paragraph Absatz, Paragraph
contract Vertrag
enclosure Anlage (Brief)
attachment Anhang (E-Mail)
enquiry (AE inquiry) Anfrage
offer Angebot
order Auftrag, Bestellung
reminder (Zahlungs-)Erinnerung, Mahnung

Spoken communication
advise, to beraten
advice Rat, Ratschlag
announce, to ankündigen, bekannt geben, ansagen
announcement (to make an announcement) Ankündigung, Bekanntgabe, Durchsage
apologise for sth., to sich für etwas entschuldigen
apology Entschuldigung
available erhältlich, erreichbar, verfügbar
chat, to plaudern, schwätzen
controversy Kontroverse, Auseinandersetzung
debriefing Nachbesprechung
demonstration (to give/do a demonstration) Vorführung, Demonstration
dispute Streit
gossip Klatsch, Gerede
gossip 'around the water cooler' Kaffeeküchenklatsch
gossip, to schwätzen, plaudern
grapevine ("I heard it on the grapevine.") inoffizielle Weitergabe von Nachrichten; Mundpropaganda; „Mir ist es zu Ohren gekommen."
interview (to hold/give an interview) Interview, Vorstellungsgespräch
lecture (to hold/give a lecture) Vortrag, Vorlesung
negotiate, to verhandeln
negotiation Verhandlung
phone call (= telephone conversation) Telefongespräch
presentation (to give/do a presentation) Präsentation, Vortrag, Referat
rumour Gerücht
sales pitch (to make a pitch) Verkaufsargument
speech (to hold/give a speech) Rede
thank sb. for sth. sich bei jmdm. für etwas bedanken

Collocations relating to communication
circulate the agenda, to die Tagesordnung verteilen
clarify a matter, to eine Angelegenheit klären
co-ordinate an event, to eine Veranstaltung koordinieren/ organisieren
confirm an agreement, to eine Vereinbarung bestätigen
have an objection to sth., to (= to object to sth.) Einwand gegen etwas erheben, etwas beanstanden
liaise with colleagues/business partners, etc., to zusammenarbeiten mit …, in Verbinding stehen mit …
make a complaint about sth., to (= to complain) etwas reklamieren, sich über etwas beschweren
make an appointment, to einen Termin vereinbaren
make an enquiry, to (= to enquire about sth.) eine Anfrage machen
make an offer, to ein Angebot machen
make arrangements, to Vorkehrungen treffen
notify sb. of sth., to jmdn. über etwas informieren, Bescheid geben
place an order, to (with a firm, for a product) einen Auftrag erteilen
postpone an appointment, to einen Termin verschieben
solve a problem, to ein Problem lösen
take the minutes, to das Protokoll führen
update information, to Daten/Informationen aktualisieren
write up the minutes, to das Protokoll schreiben

Social skills and body language
appeal to, to ansprechen
appearance Aussehen, Auftreten, Erscheinungsbild
awareness Bewusstsein
balanced ausgeglichen
bear hug ungestüme Umarmung
casual leger, zwanglos, informell
confidence Vertrauen, Selbstsicherheit
courteous höflich
diplomacy Diplomatie
disloyal abtrünnig
dress (= attire, clothing) Kleidung
dress code Kleiderordnung, Kleidervorschrift
embarrassing peinlich
embrace, to umarmen
encourage, to ermutigen, fördern
etiquette (≠ Etikett) Verhaltensregel, 'Knigge'
facial expression Gesichtsausdruck, Mimik, Mienenspiel
gesture Geste
give/slap a high five, to abklatschen
high five Abklatschen zur Begrüßung oder Gratulation
passion Leidenschaft
posture (Körper-)Haltung
put one's foot in it, to ins Fettnäpfchen treten
semiotics Semiotik
sensitivity Feingefühl, Fingerspitzengefühl, Takt
show off, to angeben
shrug, to die Achseln zucken
silence Schweigen
social skills Sozialkompetenz
treat, to behandeln

On the phone
'I'll put you through.' ‚Ich stelle Sie durch.'
'Speaking' ‚Am Apparat'
'The line is busy.'/ 'The line is engaged.' ‚Die Leitung ist besetzt.'
answerphone, answering machine Anrufbeantworter
bad line schlechte Verbindung
dial the wrong number, to sich verwählen
dial, to wählen

extension Durchwahl
hang up, to auflegen
hold the line, to am Apparat bleiben
landline phone Festnetztelefon
leave a message, to eine Nachricht hinterlassen
mobile phone (AE cell phone) Mobiltelefon, Handy
put through, to durchstellen, verbinden
receiver Hörer
return a call, to zurückrufen

Events in the workplace
anniversary Jubiläum
annual general meeting (AGM) Jahreshauptversammlung
conference Sitzung, Tagung, Konferenz
get-together Zusammentreff
knees-up (BE, coll.) (to have a knees-up) Feier
meeting (to hold a meeting) Sitzung, Konferenz
trade fair Messe, Handelsmesse
works meeting, meeting of the workforce Betriebsversammlung

Information and communications technology (ICT)
cursor Cursor, Positionsmarke
click on sth., to anklicken auf etwas
digital projector Beamer
keyboard Tastatur
landline phone Festnetztelefon
mobile phone (AE cell phone) Handy
screen Bildschirm
text message SMS

Company organisation

Types of company and structure
affiliate Schwestergesellschaft, Schwesterfirma
agency Agentur, Vertretung
board of directors Geschäftsleitung, Vorstand und Aufsichtsrat
branch Filiale, Niederlassung, Zweigstelle
company Firma, Gesellschaft
conglomerate Firmengruppe
consultancy Beratungsfirma
cooperative Genossenschaft
core business Hauptgeschäft, Kerngeschäft
cost centre Kostenstelle
executive board Vorstand
firm Firma
float shares, to Aktien emittieren
franchise Franchise
franchisee Franchisenehmer
franchisor Franchisegeber
go public, to an die Börse gehen
group Konzern
headquarters Hauptsitz, Firmenzentrale, Hauptgeschäftsstelle
holding company Holdinggesellschaft, Dachgesellschaft
Inc. (incorporated) Abkürzung für amerikanische Kapitalgesellschaft
IPO (= initial public offering) Börsengang
joint stock company (US: stock corporation) Kapitalgesellschaft
limited liability beschränkte Haftung
limited partnership Kommanditgesellschaft
listing of shares Aktienemission, Notierung der Aktienwerte
Ltd. (= limited company) etwa: GmbH
mail order business Versandhandel
multinational company (MNC) multinationales Unternehmen
offshoring das Auslagern ganzer Geschäftsprozesse ins Ausland
outsourcing Produktionsverlagerung, z. B. ins Ausland
parent company Muttergesellschaft
partnership Personengesellschaft, etwa: OHG
PLC (= public limited company) (UK) britische Aktiengesellschaft
private limited company britische Gesellschaft mit beschränkter Haftung
retail outlet Verkaufsstelle
retailer Einzelhändler
self-employed selbständig
service provider Dienstleister
share flotation Aktienemission
shell company Mantelfirma
sleeping partner stiller Teilhaber
sole trader (US: sole proprietorship) Einzelunternehmer
stakeholder Interessenvertreter, Mitglied einer Interessengruppe
subcontractor Sub-Unternehmer
subsidiary Tochtergesellschaft, Tochterfirma
supervisory board Aufsichtsrat
supplier Lieferant, Zulieferer
wholesaler Großhändler

Departments and functions
accounts, accountancy Finanzbuchhaltung, Finanzabteilung
advertising Werbung
after-sales service Kundendienst
board of directors Direktion, Geschäftsleitung
customer service Kundendienst, Kundenbetreuung
department (dept.) Abteilung
distribution Vertrieb
executive board Vorstand
finance Finanz-
human resources/personnel Personal
legal department (= lawyers) Rechtsabteilung
logistics Logistik
maintenance Wartung
marketing Marketing
organisation chart Organigramm
payroll Lohn- und Gehaltsabrechnung
PR (public relations) Öffentlichkeitsarbeit
production Produktion
purchasing (≈ procurement) Einkauf, Beschaffung
quality assurance Qualitätssicherung
recruitment Personalbeschaffung
research and development (R & D) Forschung und Entwicklung
sales Verkauf
security Sicherheit
supervisory board Aufsichtsrat

Jobs and reponsibilties
accountant Bilanzbuchhalter(in)
administration Verwaltung
agent Vetreter(in) (auf Provisionsbasis)
apprentice Lehrling, Auszubildende(r), Praktikant(in)
automated teller machine (ATM) Geldautomat
billing clerk Sachbearbeiter(in) Rechnungswesen
blue-collar workers Arbeiter (in der Produktion)
board (of directors) Geschäftsleitung, Vorstand
boss Chef(in)

caretaker (AE janitor) Hausmeister(in)
Chief Executive Officer (CEO) Vorstandsvorsitzende(r), Hauptbeschäftsführer(in)
Chief Financial Officer Leiter(in) der Finanzabteilung
clerical staff (= clerk) Büroangestellte
co-worker (AE) Mitarbeiter(in)
colleague Kollege/Kollegin
consultant Berater(in)
craftsman Kunsthandwerker
department head Abteilungsleiter(in)
director Mitglied des Vorstands/ des Aufsichtsrats
employee Arbeitnehmer(in), Mitarbeiter(in)
employer Arbeitgeber(in)
executive leitende(r) Angestellte(r)
executive board Vorstand
facility/facilities manager Gebäudemanager(in)
factory workers Fabrikarbeiter
foreman Vorarbeiter
founder Gründer(in)
franchisee Franchisenehmer(in)
freelancer Freiberufler(in), freie(r) Mitarbeiter(in)
head of department / department
head Abteilungsleiter(in)
health and safety officer Arbeitsschutzbeauftragte(r)
internee Praktikant(in)
machine operator Maschinist(in)
maintenance engineer Wartungstechniker(in)
maintenance Wartung und Instandhaltung
management Geschäftsleitung
management assistant (industrial business) etwa: Industriekaufmann/frau
managing director (MD) Geschäftsführer(in)
owner Eigentümer(in), Besitzer(in)
PA (= personal assistant) etwa: Chefsektretär(in)
person responsible Verantwortliche(r)
predecessor Vorgänger(in)
procurement (purchasing) Beschaffung (Einkauf)
project manager Projektleiter(in), Projektmanager(in)
research and development (R&D) Forschung und Entwicklung
sales representative Außendienstmitarbeiter(in), Vertriebsmitarbeiter(in)
semi-skilled angelernt
skilled worker Facharbeiter(in),
staff (= personnel) Personal
subordinate Untergebene(r)
successor Nachfolger(in)
supervisor Vorgesetzte(r), Betreuer(in), Aufseher(in), Kontrolleur(in)
supervisory board Aufsichtsrat
team leader Teamleiter(in)
technical support Technischer Dienst
temp (= temporary staff) Aushilfe, Zeitarbeiter(in)
trainee Praktikant(in)
trainer Ausbilder(in), Trainer(in)
unskilled ungelernt
welder Schweißer(in)
white-collar staff Büroangestellte
workforce Arbeiterschaft, Belegschaft

Places at work

assembly line (= production line) Fließband
body shop Karosseriewerkstatt, Autolackiererei
canteen (= cafeteria) Kantine, Mensa
clean-room Reinraum
conference room Konferenzraum, Sitzungszimmer
conference venue Konferenzort, Tagungsort
desk Schreibtisch
environment Umwelt
factory Fabrik
headquarters Firmensitz, Hauptsitz, Zentrale
infrastructure Infrastruktur
lift (AE elevator) Aufzug
located, to be (≈ situated) sich befinden
location Ort
locker room Umkleideraum
mill Mühle, Walzwerk, Walzanlage
on the outskirts am Rande von (einer Stadt)
open-plan office Großraumbüro
paint shop Abteilung für Mal- und Spritzarbeit, Lackiererei
plant Anlage
premises Räumlichkeiten, Firmengelände, Geschäftsräume
reception Empfang
relocation Standortwechsel, Umzug
shop floor (= production area) Produktionsbereich, Fertigungsbereich
stockroom Lager, Lagerraum
venue Veranstaltungsort
warehouse Lager, Lagerhalle
work station Arbeitsplatz, Arbeitsstation
workshop Werkstatt

Corporate strategy

Company integration - mergers, acquisitions and alliances

acquire, to (= take over) erwerben, übernehmen
acquisition (= takeover) Erwerb, Übernahme, Akquisition
affiliated group Konzern
alliance Allianz, Bündnis
anti-trust legislation/law (AE) Kartellgesetzgebung, Kartellrecht
bid Angebot (Auktion, Firmenübernahme)
bid, to anbieten (Auktion, Firmenübernahme)
bidder Bieter(in), Bietende(r), Anbietende(r)
collaborate, to zusammenwirken, mitarbeiten, zusammenarbeiten, kollaborieren
collaboration Zusammenarbeit, Mitwirkung
compatibility Kompatibilität, Vereinbarkeit
compatible kompatibel, vereinbar
conglomerate, conglomerate merger Mischkonzern, konglomerater Zusammenschluss
consortium (pl. consortia, consortiums) Konsortium, Syndikat
controlling interest (= majority stake) Mehrheitsbeteiligung
core business (= core activity) Kerngeschäft
corporate raider "Heuschrecke", "Unternehmensplünderer"
cross-border merger grenzüberschreitender (internationaler) Zusammenschluss
cross-cultural misunderstandings interkulturelle Missverständnisse
culture clash Aufeinanderprallen von Kulturen, interkulturelle Konflikte
dawn raid plötzlicher Aufkauf von Aktien (bei Übernahme)
demerger Entfusionierung
due diligence Unternehmensbewertung, gebührende Sorgfalt, sorgfältige Prüfung, detaillierte Untersuchung
friendly bid/takeover Strategie der Unternehmensakquisition, bei der dem Management des Zielunternehmens ein Zusammenschluss der beteiligten Unternehmen angeboten wird.
golden parachute „Goldener Fallschirm"; Kompensationszahlung eines Unternehmens an die eigenen Top-Manager im Falle einer Unternehmensübernahme.

goodwill (ideeller) Firmenwert
group (of companies) Unternehmensgruppe, Konzern
have a (minority/majority) stake in, to Eine Minderheits-/Mehrheitsbeteiligung haben
horizontal merger (≈ horizontal integration) horizontaler Zusammenschluss
hostile takeover (= contested takeover) feindliche Übernahme, Übernahme einer Aktienmehrheit gegen den Willen des Managements
insider share-dealing (= insider trading) Insiderhandel
joint venture Joint Venture, gemeinsames Unternehmen, Gemeinschaftsprojekt
legislation against monopolies (AE anti-trust law) Kartellgesetzgebung
leveraged buyout (LBO) Fremdfinanzierte Übernahme eines Unternehmens durch eigenes Management
majority stake (= controlling interest) Mehrheitsbeteiligung
management buyout (MBO) Aufkauf einer Kapitalgesellschaft durch eigenes Management
market value Verkehrswert, Marktwert
merge, to fusionieren
merger Fusion, Unternehmenszusammenschluss
mergers and acquisitions (M&A) Fusionen und Übernahmen
monopolies law (AE anti-trust law) Kartellrecht, Kartellgesetz
monopoly Monopol, Monopolstellung
pay a premium, to eine Prämie zahlen, über Nennwert zahlen
poison pill „Giftpille"; Übernahme einer Firma verhindernde Maßnahmen
pool resources, to Ressourcen zusammenlegen
predator Raubtier, Räuber
predatory rücksichtslos, aggressiv
prey Beute, Übernahmekandidat
regulator (= regulatory authority) Regler, Überwachungsbehörde, Kontrollbehörde
reverse merger Transaktion, bei der ein nicht börsennotiertes Unternehmen ohne Börsengang zu einem börsennotierten Unternehmen wird
shareholders Aktieninhaber
stake Beteiligung, Anteil
synergy Synergie, Ergebnispotenzierung
take over, to übernehmen, erwerben
takeover (= acquisition) Übernahme, Erwerb
takeover attempt/bid Übernahmeversuch
takeover target Ziel eines Übernahmeangebots
tender offer Übernahmeangebot, Ausschreibung
valuation Bewertung
value chain Wertschöpfungskette
vertical integration vertikale Integration, vertikale Fusion
white knight Weißer Ritter, Retter vor Übernahmen

Strategy and goals

analysis (pl. analyses) Analyse
annual report Jahresbericht
asset-stripping Zerschlagung durch Verkauf von Teilbereichen
backer (≈ sponsor) Geldgeber
bail out, to finanziell retten
bargaining power (= negotiating strength) Verhandlungsmacht
break up a corporation, to ein Unternehmen auflösen
business forecast (Umsatz)Voraussage/Prognose
business unit Geschäftsbereich
cash cow (= moneyspinner) hohe Gewinne abwerfender Bereich eines Unternehmens
centralisation (↔ decentralisation) Zentralisierung
competitive advantage Wettbewerbsvorteil
competitive strategy Wettbewerbsstrategie
consolidate, to festigen, konsolidieren
consolidation Festigung, Konsolidierung
corporate governance Unternehmensführung (im weitesten Sinne)
cost-cutting Kostensenkung
customer-focused (= customer-oriented) kundenorientiert
dispose of, to (= to sell off) veräußern
diversification Diversifizierung, Risikostreuung
diversify, to diversifizieren
divestment Veräußerung
downsizing Stellenabbau
economies of scale (EOS) Betriebsgrößenersparnisse, Skaleneffekte, Kostenersparnis durch Massenproduktion
exit strategy Ausstiegsstrategie
feasibility study Machbarkeits-/Durchführbarkeitsstudie
focus on core activities, to sich auf die Kernkompetenzen konzentrieren
go public, to an die Börse gehen
goal-oriented zielorientiert
implement, to umsetzen
implementation Umsetzung
industrial espionage Firmenspionage
Initial Public Offering (IPO) (= flotation) Börsengang, öffentliche Erstemission
integrate, to integrieren
issue shares (AE stocks), to Aktien ausgeben
long-term objective Fernziel, langfristiges Ziel
long-term viability Langzeitrentabilität
market dominance marktbeherrschende Stellung, Marktdominanz
market penetration Marktdurchdringung
marketing mix Marketingmix
measurable objective messbares Ziel
plough back profits, to Gewinn reinvestieren
pool resources, to Ressourcen zusammenlegen, sich zusammentun
portfolio analysis Portfolioanalyse
product differentiation Produktdifferenzierung
productivity Produktivität
profit maximisation Gewinnmaximierung, Profitmaximierung
profit motive Gewinnmotiv
redundancy (= layoff) Entlassung, Rationalisierungsmaßnahme
repositioning Umpositionierung
restructuring Konzernumbau, Restrukturierung
return on assets Rendite im Bezug auf das Vermögen
return on investment (ROI) Rentabilität
risk analysis Risikoanalyse
risk averse risikoscheu
seasonal demand saisonbedingte Nachfrage
sell off (a part of the business), to eine Beteiligung abgeben, ausverkaufen
setting a new strategic direction (eine) strategische Weichenstellung (vornehmen)
short-term goal kurzfristiges Ziel
strategic management strategisches Management
strategic planning strategische Planung
SWOT analysis (strengths, weaknesses, opportunities, and threats analysis SWOT-Analyse (Stärken-Schwächen- und Chancen-Risiko-Analyse)
target Planziel, Soll, Plansoll
target, to zum Ziel setzen

undercut, to unterbieten
wind up a company, to eine Firma auflösen/liquidieren

Image and values

brand-building Markenentwicklung
business ethics Wirtschaftsethik
code of conduct/ethics Verhaltensregel
conflict of interest Interessenskonflikt
corporate accountability Rechenschaftspflicht eines Unternehmens
corporate culture Firmenkultur, Unternehmenskultur
corporate design Firmenbild, Firmenerscheinungsbild
corporate identity Unternehmensidentität
corporate image Firmendarstellung, Firmenimage
corporate social responsibility (CSR) soziale Verantwortung des Unternehmens
corporate vision Unternehmensziel(e)
customer focus Kundenorientierung
customer relationship management (CRM) Kundenbeziehungsmanagement
diversity Mannigfaltigkeit, Verschiedenheit
entrepreneurial spirit Unternehmergeist
ethical stance, to take an ethical stance on sth. ethischer Standpunkt; einen ethischen Standpunkt vertreten
goodwill Firmenwert
green image Öko-Image
hierarchical hierarchisch
misconduct Fehlverhalten, Straftat
mission statement Leitbild, Firmenphilosophie
moral Moral, Lehre
morale (Arbeits-)Moral
paternalistic bevormundend, paternalistisch
public relations Öffentlichkeitsarbeit
reputation (= standing) Ruf
tarnish a reputation, to einen Ruf schädigen

Products, brands and marketing

Describing products

additives Zusatzstoffe
affordable bezahlbar, erschwinglich
approximately (approx.) ungefähr, zirca (ca.)
brand image Markenimage
brand loyalty Markentreue
brand name Markenname
brand stretching Markendehnung
commodity Handelsware, Handelsgut, Gebrauchsgut
common-or-garden (run-of-the-mill, bog standard) 'nullachtfünfzehn', ganz gewöhnlich
consumer durables langlebige Konsumgüter
consumer non-durables kurzlebige Konsumgüter, Verbrauchsgüter
convenience Bequemlichkeit
convenient praktisch, gelegen, bequem
convert (conversion), to umrechnen, konvertieren (Umrechnung)
device Gerät, Mittel
economical sparsam, effizient, wirtschaftlich
environmentally-friendly umweltfreundlich
equipment Gerät, Ausrüstung, Ausstattung
fabric Stoff
fast-moving consumer goods (FMCG) kurzlebige Konsumgüter
faulty defekt, fehlerhaft
feature Eigenschaft, Merkmal
fuel capacity Benzinverbrauch
gadget Gerät, Apparat
gorgeous prachtvoll. großartig. wunderschön
handy praktisch, nützlich
have a good reputation for s.th., to einen guten Ruf in Bezug auf etwas haben
high (height) hoch (Höhe)
impractical (impracticality) unpraktisch (Unbrauchbarkeit)
inconvenient (inconvenience) unpraktisch, ungelegen (Unannehmlichkeit)
industrial goods Industriegüter, Investitionsgüter, Produktionsgüter
ingredient Zutat
label Label, Marke
long (length) lang (Länge)
manufacturer's brand Herstellermarke
measure (measurement), to messen (Maß)
merchandise Ware, Handelsware, Handelsgüter
no-frills ohne Schnickschnack
obsolete überholt, veraltet
on average im Durchschnitt
option (Auswahl-)Möglichkeit
optional extras Extras auf Wunsch
own brand Eigenmarke, Hausmarke
practical (practicality) praktisch (Nutzbarkeit)
product line Produktlinie
product range Produktpalette, Produktsortiment
prototype Prototyp
range Sortiment, Auswahl
recognisable erkennbar
reliability Zuverlässigkeit
reliable zuverlässig
sell well, to sich gut verkaufen (lassen)
semi-finished halbfertig
sophisticated anspruchsvoll, hoch entwickelt
speed Geschwindigkeit
standard version Standardausführung
state-of-the-art auf dem neuesten Stand der Technik
sturdy robust
stylish (to have style) stilvoll (Stil haben)
synthetic künstlich, aus Kunststoff
tool Werkzeug
trademark Markenzeichen, Schutzmarke, Warenzeichen
unreliable (unreliability) unzuverlässig (Unzuverlässigkeit)
up-to-date modern, aktuell
user-friendly benutzerfreundlich, anwenderfreundlich
USP (unique selling proposition) Alleinstellungsmerkmal, Hauptverkaufsargument
versatile (versatility) vielseitig (Vielseitigkeit)
weigh (weight), to wiegen (Gewicht)
well-built gut gebaut
well-designed gut gestaltet, gut konzipiert
wide (width) breit, weit (Breite)
widget Produkt(teil), Dingsbums, Gerät, Vorrichtung

Marketing and promotion

account manager (≠ accounts manager) Kundenbetreuer (≠ Finanzmanager)
advertise, to werben
advertisement Werbung, Annonce, Reklame
advertising Werbung (als Tätigkeit)
advertising agency Werbeagentur
advertising executive Werbeakquisiteur(in), Werbemanager(in), Werbefachmann/frau
advertising copy Werbetext
advertising strategy Werbestrategie
after-sales Kundendienst

appeal Anziehungskraft, Reiz
appeal to s.b., to (⟷ put s.b. off, to) jmdn. ansprechen, auf jmdn. wirken
associate sth. with s.th., to eine Sache mit etwas in Verbindung bringen
attract, to anziehen
banner ad Bannerwerbung
benchmarking test Vergleichstest
benefit Nutzen, Vorteil
bias Voreingenommenheit, Einseitigkeit
black market schwarzer Markt, illegaler Warenhandel
buy s.th. on impulse, to einen Impulskauf tätigen
break into a market, to in einen neuen Markt einbrechen
buzz marketing etwa: Werbung durch Mundpropaganda
catchphrase Schlagwort, Werbespruch
catchy (a catchy jingle/slogan) eingängig, einprägsam
claim (to make a claim) Anspruch, Behauptung, Werbeversprechen
claim, to (to claim a benefit) in Anspruch nehmen, beantragen
cold call, cold calling Kaltakquisition, Kaltanruf, unangemeldeter Anruf
commercial Werbespot
compete with, to konkurrieren mit
competition Konkurrenz, Wettbewerb, Preisausschreiben
competitive konkurrenzfähig, wettbewerbsfähig
competitively priced zu einem konkurrenzfähigen Preis
competitor Konkurrent
consumer Verbraucher, Konsument
consumption Verbrauch
copywriter (≠ copyright) Werbetexter(in)
cross-selling Querverkauf, Angebot und Verkauf von Zusatzprodukten
dealer mark-up Händleraufschlag
demand (for) Nachfrage (nach)
demonstrate, to vorführen
demonstration Vorführung
desk research Schreibtischforschung, Sekundärforschung
disposable income (≈ purchasing power) verfügbares Einkommen, (Kaufkraft)
diversification Diversifikation, Ausweitung des Produktprogramms
downmarket (to go downmarket) 'billig', (Gegenteil siehe "upmarket")
encourage, to ermutigen, fördern
encouragement Ermutigung
end user Endverbraucher
endorse, to unterstützen, werben für
endorsement Werbung mit prominenten Persönlichkeiten
enter a market, to einen neuen Markt erschließen
event Veranstaltung
face to face (F2F) interview persönliches Interview/ Gespräch
feature (≈ characteristic) Eigenschaft, Merkmal
field research Feldforschung, primäre Erhebung
flop (= failure, ⟷ success) Misserfolg
focus group (≠ target group) Fokusgruppe, Gesprächsgruppe
gap in the market (≠ niche market) Marktlücke
gimmick Werbegag, ausgefallene Idee
giveaway (= freebie) Werbegeschenk
guerrilla marketing Guerilla-Marketing (mit unkonventionellen und sehr begrenzten Mitteln möglichst viel Wirkung erzielen)
hype (v. to hype) Publicity, Hype, Werberummel, übertriebene Werbung
impartial unparteiisch, objektiv, unvoreingenommen
industrial goods Investitionsgüter
jingle Werbemelodie
launch a product on(to) the market, to ein Produkt auf den Markt bringen/einführen
margin Gewinnmarge, Handelsspanne
market research Marktforschung
market share Marktanteil
marketing campaign Marketingkampagne
market penetration Marktdurchdringung
marketing mix Marketing-Mix
mass-market Massenmarkt
maturity Reife
media Medien
mid-market am Massenmarkt orientiert
niche market Marktniche, Nischenmarkt
offer, to (offer) anbieten, (Angebot)
packaging Verkaufsverpackung
persuade, to (persuasion, persuasive) überzeugen, überreden
phase out a product, to ein Produkt (langsam) auslaufen lassen
press screening Filmvorführung
press release Pressemitteilung
price war Preiskrieg
product development Produktentwicklung
product placement Produktplatzierung, Schleichwerbung im Film/Fernsehen
promote, to fördern
promotion Verkaufsförderung
promotional item Werbegeschenk
prospective customer (prospect) Kaufinteressent(in)
public relations Öffentlichkeitsarbeit
purchasing power Kaukraft
questionnaire Fragebogen
quote/quotation Preisangebot, Zitat
response rate Rücklaufquote
repositioning Umpositionierung
sales Absatz, Verkauf, Schlussverkauf
sales force/team Verkaufsstab
sales pitch Verkaufsargument, Geschäftsvorschlag
sample Muster, Probe, Kostprobe
sample, to kosten, probieren
saturated (a saturated market) gesättigt
saturation Sättigung
segment (≠ sector) Segment
segment, to segmentieren
segmentation Segmentierung
slogan (≈ strapline, tag) Werbespruch
special offer Sonderangebot
strapline (≈ slogan, tag) Werbeslogan
subject to availability (= while stocks last) solange der Vorrat reicht
survey (to carry out/conduct a survey) Umfrage
take a cut of the profit, to am Gewinn teilhaben
target market/group Zielmarkt, angestrebter Markt
target, to als Zielgruppe nehmen
tastings (≠ testing, tests) Verkostungen
trade fair Handelsmesse
upmarket (to go upmarket) exklusiv, (Gegenteil siehe "downmarket")
vox pop öffentliche Meinung, Stimme des Volkes
withdraw a product from the market, to ein Produkt aus dem Markt nehmen, oder nicht mehr anbieten
word-of-mouth advertising Mundpropaganda

Sales and distribution

Distribution channels

agency contract Händlervertrag
agent Handelsvertreter(in) (auf Provisionsbasis)
break bulk, to größere Mengen teilen und weiterkaufen
brick and mortar store Ladengeschäft (nicht virtuell)
broker Makler(in)
bulk delivery Großlieferung
buy in bulk, to in großen Mengen einkaufen
chain Kette, Ladenkette
commission Provision
contractual relationship Vertragsverhältnis
corner shop (AE: mom 'n pop store) Tante-Emma-Laden
department store Kaufhaus
discount store Billigladen
distribution channels Vertriebswege
distributor Lieferant, Händler, Vertragshändler, Vertreiber
distribution chain Absatzkette, Verteilerkette
end user (≈ final customer) Endverbraucher
expenses, to incur Auslagen/Kosten übernehmen
factory outlet Direktverkauf, Fabrikverkauf
franchising (Vertriebsform) Franchising
grey market (AE: gray market) grauer Markt
intermediary (= middleman) Zwischenhändler
mail order Versandhaus
mall (AE), shopping centre (BE) Einkaufszentrum
middlemen Zwischenhändler
outlet Verkaufsstelle
on one's own account auf eigene Rechnung
parallel import 'grauer Markt', Fluss von Gütern über Vertriebswege, die nicht vom Hersteller autorisiert sind
principal (in an agency contract) Auftraggeber
pyramid selling Schneeballverkaufssystem
representative Vertreter(in), Außendienstmitarbeiter(in)
retail outlet Einzelhandelsgeschäft, Einzelhandelsverkaufsstelle
retailer Einzelhändler
retailing, retail Einzelhandel
retainer Vorschusshonorar
sales rep (representative) Vetreter(in), Außendienstmitarbeiter(in)
sell on one's own account, to auf eigene Rechnung verkaufen
sole distributer Alleinvertrieb
specialty store (AE), speciality shop (BE) Fachgeschäft
supply chain Lieferkette
telesales/telemarketing Telefonmarketing
trader (= dealer) Händler
vending machine Warenautomat
vendor Verkäufer, Anbieter, Lieferant
wholesale, wholesaling Großhandel
wholesaler Großhändler

Terms of payment and delivery

at your expense auf Ihre Kosten
cash discount (= early-payment discount) Skonto
cash on delivery (= payment on delivery) Zahlung bei Lieferung
DDP (delivered, duty paid) frei Haus, verzollt geliefert
ex works ab Werk
guarantee, to garantieren
handling charges Abladegebühren, Bearbeitungsgebühren
loyalty rebate Treuerabatt
make an offer, to ein Angebot machen
place an order, to einen Auftrag erteilen, eine Bestellung aufgeben
purchase, to kaufen
quantity discount (= bulk-purchase discount) Mengenrabatt
sales contract Kaufvertrag
to your premises an Ihre Firma/auf Ihr Firmengelände
trade discount Handelsrabatt
trial order Probeauftrag
warranty (= guarantee) Garantie

Transport and shipping

aircraft Flugzeug (Sammelbegriff)
barge Kahn
batch Bündel, Stapel, Charge, Los
bonded warehouse Zolllager, Freilager
bulk goods Massen-, Schüttgüter
bulky goods sperrige Waren
cargo Fracht, Ladung
carrier Frachtführer
commodities Handelswaren, Rohstoffe
consignee Empfänger (einer Warensendung)
consignment Warensendung, Lieferung
consignor Versender (einer Warensendung)
consolidated shipment Sammelladung, Sammeltransport
consulate Konsulat
country of destination Bestimmungsland
country of origin Ursprungsland, Herkunftsland
customs clearance Zollabfertigung
damage Beschädigung, Schaden
delayed verspätet
deliver, to liefern
delivery Lieferung
delivery van Lieferwagen
depot Lager, Warendepot
destination Ziel, Bestimmungsort
dispatch, to versenden
dispatch/despatch Versand
distance Entfernung
docks Hafen
embassy Botschaft
EU single market EU-Binnenmarkt
exporter Exporteur
forwarder/forwarding agent Spedition/Spediteur
forwarding agency, freight forwarder Spedition/Spediteur
freight Fracht
freight train Güterzug
haulier, haulage company Lkw-Unternehmer, Lkw-Spediteur
Goods Inwards / Goods Outwards Wareneingang / Warenausgang
helicopter Hubschrauber
importer Importeur
in stock, to have am Lager führen, vorrätig haben
in time rechtzeitig
in transit auf dem Transportweg
inland waterway Binnengewässer, Wasserstraße
merchandise Waren
modes of transport Transportmittel
on time pünktlich
paperwork Formalitäten, Dokumentation
port of destination Bestimmungshafen
port of shipment Verschiffungshafen
receipt of delivery Empfangsbeleg, Wareneingang
road train (langer) Sattelzug, Lastwagenzug
sea transport Seetransport
ship goods, to Waren versenden
shipment Warensendung, Lieferung
shipper Versender

shipping (= delivery) Verschiffung, Versand
shipping documents Versanddokumente
stock Lagerbestand, Vorrat
truck (BE: lorry) Lastwagen
vehicle Fahrzeug
vessel (≈ ship) Schiff, Wasserfahrzeug
warehouse Lager (≠ Warenhaus)
warehousing Lagerung

Packing and labelling
aerosol can Spraydose, Sprühdose
bar-code Strichcode, Balkencode, Barcode
barrel Fass
bubble wrap Blisterfolie, Luftpolsterfolie (Verpackungsmaterial)
cardboard box Pappkarton
crate Lattenkiste
drum Trommel
fragile zerbrechlich
hazardous gefährlich
inflammable entzündbar, brennbar, feuergefährlich
label Etikett, Bezeichnung
labelled beschriftet, gekennzeichnet, etikettiert, bezeichnet
markings Markierungen
packing (≠ packaging) Versandverpackung
packing list Packliste
padding Füllung
pallet Palette
perishable (leicht) verderblich, vergänglich
polystyrene peanuts Schaum-Erdnüsse
protection Schutz
seaworthy packing seefeste Verpackung
sell-by-date Haltbarkeitsdatum
shrink wrap Schrumpffolie
sturdy robust
toxic giftig, schädlich
toxic waste Giftmüll

Manufacturing

Places, equipment and materials
assembly Fertigung, Montage
assembly line Fließband, Fabrikationsstraße
automation Automatisierung
batch Stapel, Posten, Ladung
body shop Karosseriewerkstatt, Fertigungsbereich
bottleneck Engpass
breakdown Betriebsstörung, Betriebsausfall, Panne
capacity Kapazität
clean-room Reinraum
component Teil
cottage industry Heimindustrie
craft (production) Handwerk
contamination Verunreinigung, Verseuchung, Kontaminierung
customisation kundenspezifische Anpassung, individueller Zuschnitt
defect (n.) Mangel, Schaden, Defekt
defective defekt
detect, to entdecken, feststellen, aufspüren
dispatch/dispatch Versand
downtime Ausfallzeit, Stillstandzeit
ear defenders Gehörschutz
energy efficient kraftsparend, energiesparend
factory equipment Betriebseinrichtung, Maschinenausstattung
finished goods Fertigfabrikate, Fertigerzeugnisse
fire extinguisher Feuerlöscher
flow-rate Durchfluss, Durchsatz
fluorescent jacket Signalweste/-jacke
forklift (truck) Gabelstapler
fuel Brennstoff, Treibstoff
goggles Schutzbrille
hard hat Schutzhelm
hazard warning sign Gefahrenhinweis, Warnzeichen
identity badge (AE: button) Namensschild
industrial relations Beziehung zwischen Arbeitgeber und Arbeitnehmern
inventory Vorrat, Lagerbestand, Inventur
just-in-time production (JIT) bedarfsorientierte Produktion
label Etikett, Aufkleber
lead time (Fabrikations-)Durchlaufzeit, Produktionszeit, Vorbereitungszeit, Vorlaufzeit
lean production schlanke Produktion
machine-tools Werkzeugmaschinen
machinery Ausrüstung, Maschinen
manufacturing Fertigung, Herstellung
mask Gesichtsmaske
mass-produced in großen Mengen hergestellt
mass production Massenfertigung, Massenproduktion
order processing Auftragsbearbeitung
output (= turnout) produzierte Menge, Ausstoß, Produktonsleistung
overalls Schutzanzug
paint shop Abteilung für Mal- und Spritzarbeit, Lackiererei
pallet Palette
printing press Druckerpresse
process Arbeitsgang, Prozess, Verfahren, Vorgang
produce (n.) Erzeugnisse
production line (= assembly line) Fertigungsband, Fließband
productivity Produktivität, Leistungsfähigkeit
ramp up, to (e.g. production aufstocken, erhöhen, steigern
raw materials Rohstoffe
resources Ressourcen, Betriebsmittel
retooling Umrüstung
rolling machine Drehmaschine, Walzmaschine
scheduling Vorbereitung
semi-finished goods Halbfertigfabrikate
set-up time Rüstzeit
shop floor Produktionsbereich, Fertigungsbereich
stockroom Lagerraum
stockpile Vorrat, Lagerhalde
throughput Durchsatz, Ausstoß, Verarbeitungsmenge
time clock Stechuhr, Stempeluhr
time-and-motion study Arbeitsablaufstudie, Zeit- und Bewegungsstudie
time-to-market Produkteinführungszeit
tool Werkzeug
turn out products, to (Produkte) produzieren
warehouse Lagerhalle
waste Verschwendung, Abfall
waterproof suit wasserdichter Anzug

Describing a process
adjust, to einstellen, anpassen
apply s.th. to s.th. (application), to etwas anwenden auf etwas, auftragen
approve, to genehmigen
cool down, to abkühlen
correct (correction), to berichtigen (Berichtigung)
enter data, to Daten eingeben

gear up, to die Maschinen für die Produktion vorbereiten
out of order außer Betrieb
plug in, to einstecken
press a button, to einen Knopf drücken
print (print, printer, printing), to drucken (Druck, Drucker, Drucken)
process (process), to bearbeiten, verarbeiten (Bearbeitung, Verarbeitung)
prototype Prototyp
release, to freigeben, entlassen
remove, to entfernen, wegnehmen
Research and Development Forschung und Entwicklung
select, to wählen, aussuchen, auslesen
set, to einstellen
store/save, to speichern, aufbewahren
turn off/ to switch off, to ausschalten
turn on/ to switch on, to anschalten
warm up, to aufwärmen

Business travel

Preparation and booking

appointment (≠ date), to book/make an appointment Termin, Verabredung, einen Termin vereinbaren
arrangements, to make arrangements Vorkehrungen
arrival Ankunft
cancel, to stornieren
cancellation Stornierung
change (trains, buses), to umsteigen
confirm, to bestätigen
confirmation Bestätigung
connection Anschlussflug, Anschlusszug
delay Verspätung
departure Abfahrt, Abflug
due: to be due to do sth. fällig; (planmäßig) etwas tun werden
fare Fahrpreis, Flugpreis
injections (≈ vaccinations, jabs) Impfungen
itinerary (≈ travel schedule) Reiseplan/-route
miss a connection, to einen Anschluss verpassen
phrase book Sprachführer
return ticket (AE: round-trip ticket) Rückfahrkarte, Hin- und Rückreise
stopover Zwischenstopp
take out insurance, to eine Versicherung abschließen
travel agent Reisebüro
travel expenses Reisekosten, Spesen
travel insurance Reiseversicherung
traveller's cheque (AE traveler's check) Reisescheck
upgrade, to aufwerten, z. B. eine bessere Klasse bekommen (Zug, Flugzeug)

Flying and the airline industry

air miles Flugmeilen
aircraft Flugzeug, Maschine
airline Fluggesellschaft
aisle seat Sitzplatz am Gang
baggage/luggage Reisegepäck
baggage/luggage hall Gepäckhalle
baggage/luggage trolley (AE: luggage cart) Gepäckwagen
belt (AE: carousel) Gepäckband
board a flight, to an Bord eines Flugzeugs gehen
boarding pass/card Bordkarte
bumpy flight turbulenter Flug
carrier Fluglinie (Gesellschaft)
declare sth. etwas zollamtlich melden
emergency exit Notausgang
fasten one's seatbelt, to sich anschnallen
hand luggage (AE: carry on luggage) Handgepäck
interfere with, to stören, manipulieren
long-haul flight Langstreckenflug
no-frills airline Billigfluggesellschaft
overhead compartment (AE: bin) Gepäckfach
runway Laufbahn
security Sicherheitskontrolle
short-haul flight Kurzstreckenflug
smooth flight reibungsloser Flug
take off, to starten
taxes and charges Steuern und Gebühren
turnaround time Abfertigungszeit, Umschlagszeit
upright senkrecht
What's the nature of your business? Welcher Art von Geschäften gehen Sie nach?
window seat Sitzplatz am Fenster
X-ray screened mit Röntgenstrahlen durchleuchtet

Hiring a car

A-Z of London berühmter Stadtplan von London
bonnet (AE: hood) Motorhaube
boot (AE: trunk) Kofferraum
car hire desk (AE: car rental desk) Mietwagenschalter
car hire/rental Autovermietung
driving licence (AE driver's license) Führerschein
excess (AE: deductible) Selbstbehalt, Eigenanteil
fully comprehensive insurance Vollkaskoversicherung
gear Gang
hatchback Hecktürmodel, Heckklappe
hire/rental car Mietwagen
inspection form Abnahmeformular
left-/right-hand drive Linkssteuerung/Rechtssteuerung
mileage Kilometerstand, Kilometer(leistung)
petrol (AE: gas) Benzin
pick up the car, to das Auto abholen
rear-view mirror Rückspiegel
saloon car (AE: sedan) Limousine
SatNav (satellite navigator) Satellitennavigation (Navi)
spare wheel Ersatzrad
take out insurance, to eine Versicherung abschließen
third-party (insurance) Haftpflichtversicherung
unleaded bleifrei
upgrade, to eine höhere Autoklasse bekommen
vehicle Fahrzeug
wing mirror Außenspiegel

Staying in a hotel

breakfast buffet Frühstücksbuffett
complimentary gratis, kostenlos
corporate rates (special prices for companies) Firmentarife
double room with shower Doppelzimmer mit Dusche
hair dryer Fön, Haartrockner
ironing board Bügelbrett
lift (AE: elevator) Fahrstuhl, Aufzug
porter Portier
reception Empfang
registration form Anmeldeformular
room service Zimmerservice
service (a room), to (ein Zimmer) herrichten
single room Einzelzimmer
spa Wellness-Einrichtung, Kurort
tea-and-coffee-making facilities Möglichkeiten zum Tee- und Kaffeekochen

trouser press Hosenpresse, -bügler
turndown service Wohlfühl-Service
twin room Zweibettzimmer
Wi-Fi connectivity kabellose Netzwerkverbindung

Rail travel

buffet car Speisewagen
carriage (AE: car) Wagen
communication cord Notbremse
connection Anschlusszug
forward- / rear-facing seat Sitz in Fahrtrichtung/in entgegengesetzter Fahrtrichtung
late-running train verspäteter Zug
luggage rack Gepäcknetz, -fach
off-peak in der Nebenverkehrszeit
platform Gleis, Bahnsteig
season ticket Saisonticket, Zeitkarte
taken besetzt
ticket inspector Fahrkartenkontrolleur(in)
trolley (AE: cart) Servierwagen, Gepäckwagen
waiting room Wartezimmer

Wining and dining

chef Koch
corked wine korkiger Wein
dish of the day Tagesgericht
doggy bag Tüte für Essensreste (im Restaurant), Vespertüte
draught beer Fassbier
put a bill down to expenses, to auf die (Spesen-)Rechnung setzen
main course Hauptgang
pick up the bill, to die Rechnung bezahlen
pudding Nachtisch
rare, medium, well-done (of steak) englisch (blutig), medium, durch
reserve at table, to einen Tisch reservieren
slap-up meal, to have a Feudal essen
sparkling water (= carbonated, fizzy) Mineralwasser mit Sprudel
split the bill, to die Rechnung teilen
starter Vorspeise
still water Wasser ohne Kohlensäure
tap water Leitungswasser
tip Trinkgeld
tip, to Trinkgeld geben
waiter/waitress Kellner/in

Conferences, trade fairs and exhibitions

badge, button Namensetikett
booth Messestand
business card (≠ visiting card) Visitenkarte
convention centre Kongresszentrum
courtesy bus kostenfreier Bus
delegate Messebesucher
demonstration Vorführung
display Anzeigetafel
event Veranstaltung
exhibition Ausstellung, Messe
exhibition hall, exhibit hall Messehalle
exhibitor Aussteller(in)
freebies (= giveaways) Werbegeschenke
guide (Messe-) Führer
hospitality Bewirtung, Gastfreundlichkeit
host Gastgeber(in)
prospective customer Interessent(in)
purchaser (= buyer) Einkäufer(in)
register, to sich anmelden
registration Anmeldung
sales literature Verkaufsliteratur
sales rep Außendienstmitarbeiter(in)
salesperson Standdienst, Vertriebsmitarbeiter
sample Muster, Probe
showcase, to etwas ausstellen
site map Ortsplan, Übersichtsplan
speaker (= presenter) Referent(in)
stand (≈ booth) Messestand, Ausstellungsstand
tasting Kostprobe
trade fair (= trade show; expo) (Handels)Messe
venue Veranstaltungsort
virtual tradeshow selbstablaufende Verkaufspräsentation

Building relationships

business card Visitenkarte
business etiquette Umgangsformen (im Geschäftsleben (≠ Etikett)
buy someone lunch, to jmdn. zum Mittagessen einladen
catch up on sth, to sich über den neuesten Stand von etw. informieren
chit-chat Geplauder
circulate, to herumgehen, um viele Leute kennenzulernen
cultivate a relationship, to eine Beziehung pflegen
establish rapport, to ein gutes Verhältnis aufbauen
face-to-face persönlich
forge a relationship, to eine Beziehung herstellen
get in touch with someone, to sich bei jmdm. melden
get to know someone jmdn. kennenlenren
hobnob with someone, to mit jmdm. freundschaftlich verkehren
host, to bewirten, veranstalten
make contacts, to Kontakte herstellen
mingle, to (to circulate) sich unter (die Gäste) mischen
movers and shakers führende Köpfe
nice talking to you nett, mit Ihnen zu sprechen
rapport harmonisches Verhältnis
strike up a conversation, to ein Gespräch anbahnen

Human resources

Hiring and firing

applicant Bewerber(in)
application form Bewerbungsformular
application letter Bewerbungsschreiben
apply for a job/a post, to sich bewerben
aptitude test Eignungstest
candidate Kandidat(in)
closing date for applications Bewerbungsschluss
covering letter (US: cover letter) Begleitbrief
CV – curriculum vitae (US: résumé) Lebenslauf
degree Hochschulabschluss
dismiss, to entlassen
draw up a short-list, to eine Liste der aussichtsreichsten Bewerber/innen anfertigen
early retirement Frührente
entry requirments Zugangsvoraussetzungen
equal opportunities Chancengleichheit
fire (s.o), to feuern, entlassen
give (s.o.) notice, to kündigen
hand in one's notice, to die Kündigung einreichen, kündigen
hire (s.o), to einstellen
hiring freeze Einstellungssperre

interview Vorstellungsgespräch
job advertisement Stellenanzeige, Stellenausschreibung
job description Stellenbeschreibung
job vacancy offene Stelle
lay (s.o.) off, to (jmdn.) entlassen
make (s.o.) redundant, to (jmdn.) entlassen, freisetzen, überflüssig machen
period of notice Kündigungsfrist
recruit, to einstellen, anwerben, rekrutieren
recruitment Personalbeschaffung
reference (AE testimonial) Referenzschreiben, Zeugnis
rejection letter Absagebrief
replacement Vertretung, Nachfolger(in)
take (s.o.) on, to jmd. einstellen
vacancy offene Stelle (Arbeit)
without notice fristlos

Issues

absenteeism Arbeitsausfall, Fehlzeiten, häufiges Nichterscheinen
be off sick, to krankgeschrieben sein
bully, to mobben
collective bargaining Tarifverhandlungen mit Gewerkschaften
compulsory vepflichtend, Pflicht-
discriminate (against sb.), to jmdn. diskriminieren
employ, to beschäftigen
employee Arbeitnehmer
employer Arbeitgeber
employment law Arbeitsrecht
employment tribunal Arbeitsgericht
equal opportunities Chancengleichheit
flexitime Gleitzeit
freelancer Freiberufler(in), freie(r) Mitarbeiter(in)
full-time job Vollzeitstelle
go on strike, to streiken
grievance procedure Beschwerdeverfahren
harass, to belästigen
Human Resources (HR) Personalwesen
induct (s.o.), to (jmdn.) in die Arbeit einführen
Industrial relations Arbeitgeber-Arbeitnehmer Beziehungen
industrial dispute Streit zwischen Arbeiter und Geschäftsleitung
internship Praktikum
maternity leave Mutterschaftsurlaub
occupational accident Betriebsunfall
on leave auf Sonderurlaub
on secondment, to auf (vorübergende) Versetzung, Auslandseinsatz
overtime Überstunden
parental leave Erziehungsurlaub
part-time job Teilzeitjob
paternity leave Vaterschaftsurlaub
pay negotiations Tarifverhandlungen
personnel Personal
pilferage (v. to pilfer) Kleindiebstahl (im Betrieb)
positive discrimination (= affirmative action) Fördermaßnahme zugunsten benachteiligter Gruppen
probationary period Probezeit
promotion Beförderung
qualifications Qualifikationen
retire, to in den Ruhestand gehen
shop steward Gewerkschaftsvertreter im Betrieb
staff Personal, Arbeitnehmer, Mitarbeiter
staff turnover Personalfluktuation, Mitarbeiterfluktuation
stand in (for s.o.), to (jmdn.) vertreten
supervise, to überwachen, betreuen, beaufsichtigen
supervisor Vorgesetzter(in)
take a day off, to einen Tag frei nehmen
temp (temporary staff) Aushilfskraft, Zeitarbeiter, Leiharbeiter
trade union Gewerkschaft
voluntary freiwillig
work permit Arbeitserlaubnis
work-to-rule Dienst nach Vorschrift
workforce Arbeitskraft
working conditions Arbeitsbedingungen
works council Betriebsrat

Wages and salaries

annual salary Jahresgehalt
benefits Zusatzleistungen, Sozialleistungen
bonus Gratifikation
commission Provision
expenses Auslagen
expenses claim form Reisekostenabrechnungsformular
fee (for a service) Honorar
golden handshake hohe Abfindung
holiday pay Urlaubsgeld
hourly rate Stundensatz
incentive Anreiz
lump sum payment Pauschalbetrag
minimum wage Mindestlohn
payment by seniority Zahlung nach Betriebszugehörigkeit
pay rise (US: raise) Gehaltserhöhung
pension Rente, Pension
performance-related pay leistungsorientierte Bezahlung
perks (= fringe benefits) Zusatzleistungen des Arbeitgebers (außer Gehalt/Lohn)
redundancy pay (US: severance pay) Abfindung
reimburse, to (rück)erstatten
remunerate, to vergüten
remuneration Vergütung
salary Gehalt
unemployment benefit Arbeitslosengeld
wage Lohn
weekly wage Wochenlohn

Training and assessment

360° appraisal 360°-Beurteilung
appraisal Bewertung
apprentice Auszubildende(r)
apprenticeship Ausbildung, Lehre
assess, to bewerten, evaluieren
assessment Bewertung, Evaluierung
assessment centre (US: center) Assessmentcentre
carrot and stick Zuckerbrot und Peitsche
evaluate, to bewerten, evaluieren
induct, to einweisen, einführen
job satisfaction Zufriedenheit am Arbeitsplatz
peer pressure Gruppendruck
performance appraisal (= performance evaluation) Leistungsbeurteilung, Leistungsbewertung
promote, to befördern
promotion Beförderung
skills Fertigkeiten, Fähigkeiten, Kompetenzen
track record Erfolgsbilanz, (gute) Leistungen am Arbeitsplatz
trainee Auszubildende(r), Praktikant(in), Lehrling
training course Ausbildung
vocational training Berufliche Aus-/Weiterbildung Berufsausbildung

Project management

Types of project
aerospace project Raumfahrtprojekt
construction project Bauprojekt, Baumaßnahme
development project Entwicklungsprojekt
housing project Siedlungsprojekt
large-scale project Großprojekt
long-term project Langzeitprojekt
pilot project Pilotversuch
research project Forschungsprojekt
sub-project Teilprojekt, Unterprojekt
turnkey project Gesamtprojekt, schlüsselfertiges Projekt/Objekt
viable project lebensfähiges od. realisierbares Projekt

Project life cycle
acceptance Abnahme, Absegnung
approval Genehmigung, Freigabe
at each stage/at each step bei jedem Schritt/jeder Stufe
at the planning stage in der Planung befindlich
bid for a project, to (= to tender for) ein Projekt anbieten
closure Projektabschluss
controlling Überwachung, Steuerung
execution Ausführung
feasibility study Machbarkeitsstudie
in the pipeline in Vorbereitung, in der Planung
initiation Initiierung
kick-off meeting Eröffnungssitzung für ein neues Projekt
planning Planung
project handover Projektübergabe
project tracking (= project follow-up) Projektverfolgung
pull the plug on sth. etwas beenden, mit etwas Schluss machen
scrap a project, to (= to reject a project) ein Projekt verwerfen
shelve a project, to (= to spike a project) ein Projekt einstellen
sign-off Abzeichnung, Genehmigung
tender for a project, to ein Projekt anbieten

Planning
forecast, to vorhersagen
back a project, to (= support a project) ein Projekt befürworten, unterstützen
breakdown of tasks Projektstruktur
business requirements Geschäftserfordernisse
constraint Beschränkung, Grenze
consultation Beratung
contingency Risikozuschlag, Eventualität, unvorhergesehenes Ereignis
contingency plan Ausweichplan, Alternativplan
contractual requirements vertragliche Bestimmungen
critical-path analysis Analyse des kritischen Wegs, Methode des kritischen Pfades
customer requirements Kundenbedürfnisse, Bedürfnisse der Auftraggeber
deliverables zu erledigende Aufgaben, Projektergebnisse
estimate (v. to estimate) schätzen, Schätzung
fast-tracking Überlappen von Vorgängen, Beschleunigen von Vorgängen
feasible durchführbar, machbar, umsetzbar
Gantt chart Gantt-Diagramm
interface Schnittstelle
mission Auftrag
objective Ziel(setzung), (Projekt)Vorgabe
overlap Überschneidung
outcome Ergebnis
precautions (to take precautions) Vorsichtsmaßnahmen (ergreifen)
procurement plan Beschaffungsplan
project charter Projektauftrag
project manual Projekthandbuch
resource planning Einsatzmittelbedarfsplanung
risk analysis Risikoanalyse, Risikomanagementplanung
risk avoidance Risikovermeidung
safety margin Sicherheitspuffer
scope Umfang
sign off, to abzeichnen
SMART (= specific, measurable, attainable, relevant, time-bound) = konkret/deutlich, messbar, erreichbar, zuständig, zeitlich definiert
work breakdown structure (WBS) Projektstrukturplan (PSP)

Execution
abandon, to (n. abandonment) abbrechen
carry out, to ausführen, durchführen
complete a task, to eine Aufgabe erfüllen
delegate, to delegieren
deliver, to etw. erfüllen, abgeben, liefern
execute sth., to etw. ausführen
get sth. back on track etw. wieder auf Kurs bringen
implement, to umsetzen
procedure Vorgehensweise
process Verfahren
status report Statusbericht

Controlling and monitoring
control, to (≠ kontrollieren) steuern, lenken
amendment (v. amend) Korrekturmaßnahme
check, to kontrollieren, prüfen
conform to expectations, to Erwartungen erfüllen
corrective action Abhilfemaßnahmen, Korrekturmaßnahmen
debriefing (v. to debrief) Nachbesprechung
exceed the target, to das Ziel übertreffen
meet a target, to ein Ziel erreichen
miscalculation (v. miscalculate) Fehlkalkulation
monitor, to (laufend) überwachen
on target, to be unter Beobachtung
overestimation (v. overestimate) Überschätzung
reporting Berichtswesen
revise, to ändern, anpassen
scope creep schleichende Umfangserweiterung
supervise, to überwachen
underestimation (v. to underestimate) Unterschätzung
user acceptance Benutzerakzeptanz

Managing time
ahead of schedule dem Zeitplan voraus
catch up, to nachholen
deadline Abgabefrist
delay Verspätung
delayed verspätet, im Verzug sein
duration Dauer, Laufzeit
fall behind schedule, to in Verzug geraten, in Rückstand sein
finish date Endzeitpunkt
forecast Prognose
in time (= not delayed) rechtzeitig
lag Rückstand
lead Vorlaufzeit
lifetime of a project Projektlaufzeit
make up time, to die Zeit aufholen
meet a deadline, to (= stick to a deadline) eine Frist einhalten

milestone Meilenstein, bedeutendster Projektabschnitt
miss a deadline, to eine Frist verpassen
observe a deadline, to eine Frist einhalten
on schedule, to be im Plan sein
on time (= punctual) fristgerecht, pünktlich
overdue überfällig
phase (= stage) Phase
schedule Terminplan, Zeitplan, Ablaufplan
scheduled to do sth., to be etwas nach Plan tun sollen
scheduling Zeitplanung
slippage Zeitverlust
timescale zeitlicher Rahmen, Zeitachse
time buffer Zeitpuffer

Managing money

budget busting Etatausweitung
budget constraints Etatgrenzen
budgeted cost of work completed (BCWC) Budgetkosten der erledigten Arbeit
budgeted cost of work scheduled (BCWS) Budgetkosten der geplanten Arbeit
budgeting Etatplanung, Budgetierung
calculate, to berechnen, (ein)kalkulieren
calculation Kalkulation, Berechnung
cost-benefit ratio Kosten-/Nutzenverhältnis
finance a project, to (= to fund a project) Mittel für ein Projekt bereitstellen
funds Finanzmittel
money to spare Geld übrig haben, verfügbares Geld
over budget Etatausweitung
overrun (costs, a budget), to überschreiten
pour money into a project, to Geld in ein Projekt stecken
pricing Preispolitik
stay within budget, to im Rahmen des Budgets bleiben
within budget (AE on budget) ohne Kostenüberschreitung

Managing people

able to work in a team teamfähig
authority Befugnis
commitment (≠ engagement) Verpflichtung, Engagement
liaise with so., to zusammenarbeiten mit
project champion Projektbeste(r)
project leader (= project manager) Projektleiter(in)
project team Projektbeteiligte, Management
pull one's weight, to seinen Beitrag leisten
put together a good team, to ein starkes Team auf die Beine stellen
report to so., to jmdm. unterstellt sein
stakeholder Anspruchsberechtigte(r), am Projekt Beteiligte(r)
steering group/committee Lenkungsausschuss/-gruppe

Quality

Expressions with the word 'quality'

We provide quality at reasonable prices. Wir bieten Qualität zu einem vernünftigen Preis.
We have a reputation for quality. Wir sind bekannt für Qualität.
... is of (a) good/high/top quality ... ist von hervorragender Qualität
... is of (a) low/poor/varying quality ... ist von niedriger/minderwertiger Qualität
a lack of quality mangelnde Qualität
Quality has declined. Die Qualität hat abgenommen.
Quality has improved. Die Qualität hat sich verbessert.
Quality is suffering. Die Qualität leidet.
She has leadership qualities. Sie hat Führungsqualitäten.
We specialise in quality products. Wir haben uns auf Qualitätsprodukte (Güteprodukte) spezialisiert.
quality assurance Qualitätssicherung, QM-Darlegung
quality control Qualitätskontrolle, Qualitätssteuerung
quality circle Qualitätssicherungsgruppe, Qualitäszirkel
Total Quality Management (TQM) umfassendes Qualitätsmanagement

Standards

below standard, to be unter dem Standard sein
compliance (with) Einhaltung, Übereinstimmung (mit),
comply with, to einhalten
conforming to specifications /requirements genau nach den technischen Vorgaben; den Vorschriften entsprechend
conformity (⟷ nonconformity) Übereinstimmung
contaminated verseucht
cracked gesprungen, rissig
customer satisfaction Kundenzufriedenheit
decline in quality, to in der Qualität sinken
defect Defekt
defective defekt
detect flaws, to Mängel entdecken
durable haltbar, robust
ensure compliance, to Gewährleistung erfüllen
error Irrtum, Fehler
exacting/tight specifications genaue/strenge Vorgaben
exceed expectations, to die Erwartungen übertreffen
excellent exzellent
failure Versagen, Misserfolg,
fall short of expectations, to hinter den Erwartungen zurückliegen
fit for purpose, to be für eine besondere Verwendung geeignet sein
fitness for use Gebrauchstauglichkeit, einsatzgerechte Eignung
flaw Makel
flawed defekt
flawless makellos
flimsy schwach, dünn, nicht sehr stabil
fragile zerbrechlich
fulfil a requirement, to (= to meet a need) eine Voraussetzung/Bedingung erfüllen
heavy-duty strapazierfähig
immaculate perfekt, makellos, vollkommen
imperfection Fehlerstelle, Mangel, Unvollkommenheit
improve (in quality), to (sich) verbessern
in compliance with entsprechend, gemäß, in Übereinstimmung mit
International Standards Organisation (ISO) ISO (Internationale Organisation für Normung)
latent defect verdeckter Mangel, verborgener Fehler
maintain standards, to Standards einhalten
non-compliance Nichteinhaltung
of (a) high/good/top quality, to be von hervorragender Güte (Spitzenqualität) sein
of (a) low/poor/varying quality, to be von minderwertiger Güte/Qualität sein
of a high standard, to be hohen Standard erfüllen
of a low standard, to be von niedrigem Standard sein
out of service außer Betrieb
pass inspection, to eine Kontrollprüfung überstehen
perfect einwandfrei
poorly-designed schlecht konstruiert sein
satisfy customers, to Kunden zufriedenstellen

scratched zerkratzt
set high standards, to hohe Anforderungen stellen
shoddy goods/quality minderwertiger Artikel, schäbige Ware, schlampige Qualität
show a lack of quality, to zeigt Qualitätsmängel
substandard unzulänglich, minderwertig, unter den Norm liegend,
tough, rigorous, exacting streng
up to standard, to be den Anforderungen entsprechen
value for money Preis-Leistungs-Verhältnis
waste Verschwendung

Measures and approaches
benchmarking Benchmarking, Vergleichstest
best practice optimaler Geschäftsablauf, bestes Verfahren
carry out checks, to Kontrollmaßnahmen durchführen, kontrollieren
certification Zerfifizierung, Abnahme
continuous/continual improvement (Kaizan) kontinuierlicher Verbesserungsprozess
corrective and preventive action Korrektur- und Vorbeugemaßnahme
customer feedback Kundenbewertung
investigate, to untersuchen, ermitteln
inspection Besichtigung, Prüfung, Kontrolle
external audit außerbetriebliche Revision/Prüfung
internal audit betriebseigeine Revision/Prüfung
Just-in-time (JIT) bedarfsorientierte Produktion
measurable objective messbares Ziel
peer review Begutachtung, geregelte Kollegenkontrolle
performance appraisal Leistungsbeurteilung
procedure Verfahren
quality audit Qualitätsaudit, Qualitätsmanagement
quality control Qualitätskontrolle
questionnaire Umfrage
random sample Stichprobe, Zufallsauswahl
right first time (RFT) Verpflichtung gegenüber Kunden, keine Fehler zu machen (TQM)
spot check Stichprobe
verify, to auf Richtigkeit prüfen, kontrolliern
validation Gültigkeitsprüfung, Bewertung, Bestätigung
verification Nachweis, Nachprüfung, Feststellung der Richtigkeit,

Business and the economy

Business sectors
aerospace Luft- und Raumfahrt
agriculture Landwirtschaft
automotive Automobil-
biotechnology Biotechnologie, Biotechnik
chemicals Chemikalien
fashion Mode
civil engineering Hoch- und Tiefbau
construction Bauwesen, Konstruktion
consumer electronics Unterhaltungselektronik
cosmetics Kosmetik
energy Energie, Strom
engineering Maschinenbau, Technik
financial services Finanzdienstleistungen
fisheries Fischereien
food and beverages Lebensmittel
furniture and furnishings Möbel und Ausstattung
healthcare Gesundheitsversorgung
household goods Haushaltswaren
insurance Versicherung
manufacturing Herstellung, Produktion, Fertigung
media and publishing Medien- und Verlagsbuchhandel
mining Förderung, Bergbau
pharmaceuticals Pharmaindustrie, Arzneimittelindustrie
restaurant and catering Gastronomie
retail Einzelhandel
telecommunications Telekommunikationsbranche
textiles Textilien
tobacco Tabak
tourism and leisure Touristik
transport and logistics Transport und Logistik
utilities Versorgungsunternehmen
waste and recycling Wiederverwertung
wholesale Großhandel

Cycles and trends
accelerate, to beschleunigen
appreciate (in value), to im Wert steigern, aufwerten
appreciation Wertzuwachs, Aufwertung
average, to durchschnittlich betragen
boom Hochkonjunktur
boom-bust cycle Boom-Bust-Zyklus
boom, to florieren, boomen, haussieren
business cycle Konjunktur, Konjunkturzyklus
bust Abschwung
climb, to steigern, klettern
contraction Schrumpfung, Rückgang
credit crunch Finanzkrise
cycle (Konjunktur-)Zyklus
decline, to sinken, fallen
decrease, to sinken, fallen
depreciate (in value), to Im Wert fallen
depreciation Wertverlust, Wertfall, Abschreibung
depression langanhaltende Rezession
deteriorate, to verschlechtern
dip, to (sich) senken, abfallen
downturn Abschwung
downward spiral Abwärtstrend
fluctuate, to (n. fluctuation) schwanken
economic cycle Konjunkturzyklus
economic situation Wirtschaftslage
economic slowdown/lull Konjunkturabschwung, Konjunkturflaute
go up, to steigern
growth (= expansion) Wachstum
hit a low/a high einen Tiefpunkt/ einen Höhepunkt erreichen
improve, to (sich) verbessern
improvement Verbesserung
increase, to steigern
nosedive Sturzflug
on average im Durchschnitt
plummet, to abstürzen
plunge, to abstürzen, drastisch sinken
reach a peak, to einen Höchststand erreichen
recession Rezession, Tiefkonjunktur
recover, to sich erholen
recovery Wirtschaftsaufschwung
rise Anstieg
rise, to ansteigen
rocket, to hochschießen
shoot up, to hochschießen
shrink, to schrumpfen
slowdown (in the economy) Abschwung, Konjunkturrückgang
slump Absturz
slump, to plötzlich fallen, abstürzen

soar, to hochschießen, schnell aufsteigen
stagflation (high interest + high unemployment) Stagnation bei steigenden Preisen
stand at , to stehen bei, liegen bei
steady gleichbleibend, stabil
tailspin, to be in a im Sturzflug sein
tank, to abstürzen (Aktienpreise)
trough Talsohle der Rezession, Konjunkturtief
tumble, to abstürzen (Aktienpreise)
volatile stark schwankend
volatility Volatilität, Schwankungsanfälligkeit
weaken, to abschwächen

Government policy

bail (a company) out, to finanziell retten
bail-out Rettungsmaßnahme, Rettungspaket
base rate / prime rate / minimum lending rate (AE: discount rate) Diskontsatz
borrowing Verschuldung
business cycle Konjunktur
currency Währung
debt default Nichtzahlung von Schulden
debt relief Schuldenerlass
default on one's debts, to die Schulden nicht zahlen
deficit spending öffentliche Verschuldung durch Geldaufnahme
deregulation Zahlungsbilanz
devalue, to abwerten
domestic demand Binnennachfrage
economic wirtschafts-, wirtschaftlich, volkswirtschaftlich
economic recovery plans/packages Konjunkturprogramme, Rettungspakete
economic system Wirtschaftssystem
economical wirtschaftlich (i.S.v. sparsam)
economist Wirtschaftswissenschaftler(in)
economy Wirtschaft
exchange rate Wechselkurs
expenditure on Ausgaben für
fiscal policy Steuerpolitik, Finanzpolitik
fiscal-stimulus packages Konjunkturprogramme, Rettungspakete
globalisation Globalisierung
government policy Regierungspolitik, Politik
impose, to auferlegen, einführen
infrastructure Infrastruktur
inward investment Investition aus dem Ausland
laissez-faire (French) freie Kraft des Marktes
legislation Gesetzgebung
macroeconomic policies volkswirtschaftliche Politik
macroeconomics Makroökonomie, (allgemeine) Volkswirtschaftslehre
microeconomics Betriebswirtschaftslehre
monetary policy Geldpolitik
pension and health-care costs Renten- und Gesundheitskosten
public debt Staatsverschuldung
public opinion öffentliche Meinung
public spending offentliche Ausgaben, Staatsausgaben
quota (≈ limit on imports) Mengenbeschränkung
red tape (unnötige) Formalitäten, Amtsschimmel
regulators Regulierungsbehörde
revaluation (of a currency) Aufwertung (einer Währung)
shorter working hours Arbeitszeitverkürzung
subsidise, to subventionieren
subsidy Subvention
tariff (≈ tax on imports) Einfuhrzoll
taxation Besteuerung
think tank Expertenkommission
trade barriers Handelsbeschränkungen
write off a debt, to Schulden abschreiben

Economic and financial indicators

balance of payments (BOP) Zahlungsbilanz
balance of payments deficit negative Zahlungsbilanz, Zahlungsbilanzdefizit
balance of payments surplus positive Zahlungsbilanz
balance of trade (BOT) Handelsbilanz
bilateral trade bilateraler Handel
budget deficit Haushaltsdefizit
budget surplus Haushaltsüberschuss
capital account balance Kapitalbilanz
capital flight Kapitalflucht
consumer durables langlebige Gebrauchsgüter
consumer price index (CPI) Lebenshaltungspreisindex, Verbraucherpreisindex
cost of living Lebenshaltungskosten
currency reserves Devisenreserven
current account balance Leistungsbilanz
deficit Defizit
economies of scale Skaleneffekt, Ersparnisse der Massenproduktion
emerging economy/nation/market Schwellenland
exchange rate fluctuations Kursschwankungen
fair trade fairer Handel
foreign direct investment (FDI) ausländische Direktinvestition(en)
foreign exchange Devisen-
free trade freier Handel
global economy Weltwirtschaft
gross domestic product (GDP) Bruttoinlandsprodukt (BIP)
gross national product (GNP) Bruttosozialprodukt
hidden economy Schattenwirtschaft
hyperinflation Hyperinflation
inflation ⟷ deflation Inflation
inflation rate Inflationsrate
infrastructure Infrastruktur
intangible resources immateriell, nicht greifbar
interest rate Zinssatz
invisible trade balance Diensleistungsbilanz
market forces Kräfte des Markts
mature economy (= advanced economy) entwickelte (reife) Volkswirtschaft
money supply Geldmenge, Geldumlauf
multilateral trade multilateraler Handel
national debt Staatsverschuldung
natural resources Bodenschätze
non-renewable (finite) resources nicht-erneuerbare Energien (Ressourcen)
non-tariff barriers (NTB) nichttarifäre Handelschranken
output Produktionsleistung
per capita pro Kopf
producer price index (PPI) Erzeugerpreisindex
property prices Immobilienpreise
protectionism Schutzzollpolitik, Protektionismus
purchasing power Kaufkraft
quota Mengenbeschränkung
stagflation (high inflation + high unemployment) hohe Inflation mit hoher Arbeitslosigkeit
staples, staple foods Grundnahrungsmittel
supply and demand Angebot und Nachfrage
surplus Überschuss
sustainable resources erneuerbare Energien (Ressourcen)
taxation Steuer, Besteuerung, Steuerbemessung
trade barriers Handelsschranken

trade deficit Handelsdefizit
trade figures Handelsbilanzzahlen
trade surplus positive Handelsbilanz
trading conditions Geschäftsklima
unemployment rate Arbeitslosenquote
utilities Versorgungsunternehmen
visible trade balance (Waren-)handelsbilanz

International trade

Issues and policy

apply for a licence, to eine Lizenz beantragen
arrange insurance, to eine Versicherung abschließen
balance of trade (= trade balance) Handelsbilanz
bilateral trade bilateraler Handel
carousel trade Karussellgeschäfte
claim a customs refund, to eine Zollerstattung beantragen
customs clearance Zollabfertigung
deal with customs formalities, to Zollformalitäten bearbeiten
domestic trade Binnenhandel, inländischer Handel
dumping unter Preis anbieten
exchange controls Devisenkontrolle
export ban, embargo Ausfuhrsperre, Embargo
export credit guarantee Exportkreditbürgschaft
fair trade fairer Handel
foreign trade Außenhandel
free trade Freihandel
free-trade agreement Freihandelsabkommen
grey market grauer Markt
import restriction Einfuhrbeschränkung
international trade Welthandel, Außenhandel, internationaler Handel
invisible trade unsichtbarer Handel
multilateral trade multilateraler Handel
negotiate terms of payment and delivery Zahlungs- und Lieferbedingungen verhandeln
non-tariff barrier (NTB) nichttarifäre Hürde od. Handelsbeschränkung
notify the exporter that the goods have arrived, to den Lieferanten über den Empfang der Waren informieren
open an L/C in favour of the supplier, to ein Akkreditiv eröffnen zugunsten des Lieferanten
protectionism Protektionismus, Schutzzollpolitik
quota Kontingent, Quote
sign the sales contract, to den Kaufvertrag unterschreiben
subsidy Subvention
tariff (Einfuhr)Zoll
trade barrier Handelshemmnis, - schranke
trade deficit/surplus Außendhandelsdefizit/- überschuss
trade term Handelsklausel
trade war Handelskrieg
transfer the invoice amount, to den Rechnungsbetrag überweisen
translate documents, to Unterlagen übersetzen
visible trade Warenhandel

Documentation

air waybill Luftfrachtbrief
bill of lading (B/L) Konossement, Frachtbrief, Ladeschein
certificate of origin Ursprungszeugnis
commercial invoice Handelsrechnung
consignment note Frachtbrief, Ladeschein
consular invoice Konsulatsfaktura
customs declaration Zollerklärung
customs invoice Zollfaktura, Zollrechnung
dispatch advice Versandanzeige
export declaration Ausfuhrerklärung/-anmeldung
export/import licence (AE license) Export-/Importlizenz
import licence (AmE: license) Einfuhrgenehmigung, Importlizenz
in duplicate/ in triplicate In zweifacher/ dreifacher Ausfertigung
insurance policy/certificate Versicherungspolice/ Versicherungsschein
insurance policy/certificate Versicherungspolice/-schein
marine insurance Seeversicherung
packing list Packliste
packing list Packliste, Versandliste
pro-forma invoice Proforma Rechnung
red tape (unnötige) Bürokratie, Papierkrieg, Amtsschimmel
shipping documents Versanddokumente
Single Administrative Document (SAD) Einheitspapier

Payment and delivery

advance payment Vorauszahlung, Vorkasse, Vorschusszahlung, Anzahlung
bank guarantee Bankbürgschaft
bill of exchange (B/E) Wechsel
carriage paid to (CPT) frachtfrei, fracht bezahlt
cash against documents (Bar)Zahlung gegen Dokumente
cash on delivery (COD) Lieferung gegen Nachnahme
cash with order (CWO) Zahlung bei Auftragserteilung
cost, insurance and freight (CIF) Kosten, Versicherung, Fracht
currency Währung
customs duty Zoll
delivered ex ship/quay (DES/DEQ) Lieferung ab Schiff/Kai
delivered, duty paid (DDP) verzollt, geliefert
documentary letter of credit (L/C) (Dokumenten)Akkreditiv
documents against acceptance (D/A) Dokumente gegen Akzept
documents against payment (D/P) Dokumente gegen Zahlung
ex works ab Werk
exchange rate Wechselkurs
free alongside ship (FAS) frei Längsseite Schiff
free on board (FOB) frei an Bord
irrevocable and confirmed letter of credit unwiderrufliches, bestätigtes Akkreditiv
letter of credit Akkreditiv, Bankbürgschaft
open account offenes Konto, (Kredit im) laufende Rechnung
payment and delivery terms Zahlungs- und Lieferbedingungen

Legislation

Legal issues affecting businesses

act of God / force majeure höhere Gewalt
collective bargaining Tarifverhandlungen
company law Gesellschaftsrecht
comparative advertising Vergleichende Werbung
competition law Kartellrecht, Wettbewerbsrecht
consumer protection Verbraucherschutz
data protection Datenschutz
employee rights Arbeitsrecht
fraud Betrug
intellectual property (patents, copyrights) geistiges Eigentum

international laws internationales Recht
medicines Arzneimittel
mercantile law (law dealing with commerce) Handelsrecht, Wirtschaftsrecht
misleading advertising irreführende Werbung
occupational health and safety Arbeitsschutz, Sicherheit und Gesundheit am Arbeitsplatz
pricing claims Preisbehauptungen
product descriptions Produktbeschreibungen
product liability Produkthaftung
sales contracts Verkaufsverträge
unfair commercial practices unlautere Geschäftspraktiken
white-collar crime Wirtschaftskriminalität

Policy and compliance

abide by the law, to (= adhere to the law) sich an das Gesetz halten
abolish, to abschaffen
act Gesetz
act within the law, to das Gesetz befolgen od. einhalten
amendment (to a law) Änderung, Ergänzung, Zusatzartikel (zur Verfassung)
apply, to anwenden
article (= section) Paragraph
be bound by the terms of a contract vertraglich verpflichtet sein
bill Gesetzesvorlage, Gesetzenentwurf
break the law, to das Gesetz brechen, gegen das Gesetz verstoßen
bring in legislation, to (= to introduce) einführen
cancel, to aufheben
circumvent a law, to ein Gesetz umgehen
clause Satz , Klausel
close a loophole in the law, to eine Gesetzeslücke schließen
come into effect/come into force, to in Kraft treten
commit a crime, to ein Verbrechen begehen
comply with the regulations, to den Vorschriften nachkommen
conclude an agreement eine Vereinbarung schließen, einen Vertrag abschließen
enforce, to (= to uphold) durchsetzen, vollstrecken
EU Directive EU-Richtlinie
extend, to (≈ prolong) verlängern
fall foul of a law, to mit dem Gesetz in Konflikt geraten
I won't enter into a contract with them. einen Vertrag abschließen/eingehen
Ignorance is no defence. (AE: defense) Unkenntnis schütz vor Strafe nicht.
make something illegal, to etwas gesetzlich verbieten
obey the law, to (= observe/respect the law) das Gesetz beachten
onus Beweislast, Verpflichtung
pass a law/ a bill, to ein Gesetz verabschieden
permit, to (= allow) erlauben, erstatten
prohibit, to (= forbid) verbieten, untersagen
put the onus on sb. to do sth., to verpflichten
require/oblige sb. to do sth., to verpflichen
revise, to überarbeiten, ändern
revoke, to widerrufen
stipulate, to (= require) fordern, festsetzen, vorschreiben
terminate, to beenden
They tried to bend the rules. Sie haben versucht die Vorschriften zu umgehen.
violate the law, to gegen ein Gesetz verstoßen
We're in legal hot water. Wir haben Schwierigkeiten mit dem Gesetz.
You might find yourself behind bars. Sie könnten hinter Gittern landen.

Collocations with 'legal'

legal action Rechtsweg, gerichtliches Vorgehen
legal advice, to seek sich rechtlich beraten lassen
legal assistance (= legal redress) Rechtshilfe
legal battle (= legal dispute) Rechtsstreit
legal claim Rechtsanspruch
legal constraint (= legal restriction) Gesetzlicher Zwang
legal costs Prozesskosten
legal entity Rechtsperson
legal expenses Gerichtskosten, Anwaltskosten
legal expert Jurist
legal implications gesetzliche Auswirkungen
legal proceedings Gerichtsverfahren, Prozess
legal provisions (legal requirements) Rechtsvorschriften
legal rights juristische Rechte
legal steps, to take gerichtliche Schritte eingehen
legal terminology Rechtssprache
legally binding rechtsverbindlich
legally liable gesetzlich verpflichtet

Litigation

accuse sb. of sth. (accusation) jmdm. etwas vorwerfen, jmdn. beschuldigen
advocate Anwalt, Anwältin
allege, to (allegation) behaupten
arbitration court Schiedsgericht
attorney (AE) Rechtsanwalt, Rechtsanwältin
bail Kaution
barrister Rechtsanwalt (bei oberen Gerichten)
blame so. for sth., to jmdm. die Schuld geben
bring/lodge a claim, to eine Klage erheben od. vorbringen
charge sb. with a crime, to jmdn. eines Verbrechens beschuldigen
claimant (= plaintiff) Kläger(in)
commit a crime, to ein Verbrechen begehen
conviction Verurteilung, Überführung, Schuldigsprechung
countersuit Gegenklage
court Gericht
court order Anordnung, Gerichtsbeschluss, gerichtliche Mahnung
court proceedings Gerichtsprozess
defence Verteidigung
defendant Angeklagte(r)
deny, to abstreiten
dismiss a claim, to eine Klage abweisen
face a heavy/severe fine/penalty, to eine hohe Strafe zu erwarten haben
file a lawsuit, to eine Klage einreichen
guilty of sth., to be sich einer Sache schuldig machen
harsh sentence harte Bestrafung
infringement Rechtsverletzung, Verstoß gegen das Recht
injunction, to grant/award an eine einstweilige Verfügung erlassen
innocent of sth., to be unschuldig sein
judge Richter(in)
judgement Gerichtsurteil, Spruch
jurisdiction Rechtssprechung, Gerichsbarkeit
jury (jurors) Jury, Gruppe der Geschworenen
lawsuit Prozess, Gerichtsverhandlung
lawyer Rechtsanwalt, Rechtsanwältin
legislate, to Gesetze geben/verabschieden
legislation Gesetzgebung
legislative Legislative, gesetzgebend, durch den Gesetzgeber

legislator Gesetzgeber
litigant Prozessführer(in), Prozesspartei
litigate, to anfechten, bestreiten, prozessieren
litigation Rechtsstreit, Prozess, Gerichtsverfahren, Streitsache
litigious prozessfreudig, streitsüchtig
magistrate Richter(in)
malpractice Berufsvergehen, Amtsvergehen, Untat
negligence Fahrlässigkeit
negligent fahrlässig
offence Straftat
on trial, to put den Prozess machen
out-of-court settlement außergerichtliche Einigung, außergerichtlicher Vergleich
penalty Strafe
plaintiff Kläger(in)
plea bargain Verständigung im Strafverfahren
plead guilty/innocent, to sich schuldig/unschuldig bekennen
prosecution Anklage, Staatsanwaltschaft
public hearing öffentliche Anhörung
reject a charge, to eine Klage zurückweisen
ruling Entscheidung, Urteil
sentence Strafurteil, Richterspruch
settle out of court, to sich außergerichtlich einigen
solicitor Jurist(in), Rechtsanwalt, Rechtsanwältin (nicht vor höheren Gerichten)
sue sb. for damages/compensation, to jmdn. auf Schadenersatz verklagen
to take court action / legal action rechtliche Schritte einleiten, gerichtlich vorgehen
tribunal Strafgericht, Tribunal
unsubstantiated claim unbegründete Klage
verdict Urteil, Urteilsspruch
witness Zeuge, Zeugin

Finance

Payment, credit control, banking

access, to Zugang (haben)
account Konto
affluent wohlhabend, reich
afford, to sich leisten können
affordable erschwinglich, bezahlbar
allocate, to zuteilen, zuordnen
assets Vermögen
ATM (= automated teller machine) Bankautomat
bad debt uneinbringliche Forderung
balance Kontostand, Saldo, Bilanz
bank account Bankkonto
bank balance (= account balance) Kontostand, Saldo
bank details Bankverbindung, Kontoverbindung
bank loan Bankkredit, Darlehen
bank statement Kontoauszug
bankrupt bankrott
bargain (to strike a bargain) Schnäppchen
bargain, to handeln (um Preise)
barter Tauschhandel, Bartergeschäft
bill (AE) Banknote, Geldschein, Rechnung
bill (s.o.), to berechnen, Rechnung senden
borrow, to (sich) ausleihen, borgen
broke pleite
budget Budget, Haushalt
budgeting Budgetierung, Haushaltsplanung
bursary (= scholarship) Stipendium
cash Bar, Bargeld
cash flow Cashflow
cash in, to einlösen
cashless payment bargeldlose Zahlung
charge (s.o.), to berechnen, belasten, in Rechnung stellen
charity Wohltätigkeit, Wohltätigkeitszweck
cheque (AE check) Scheck
clear a cheque, to einen Scheck verrechnen
coin Münze, Geldstück
collateral (dingliche) Sicherheit
come to some agreement, to sich einigen
compensation Entschädigung, Schadensersatz
concession Entgegenkommen
cost a fortune, to ein Vermögen kosten
credit card Kreditkarte
credit limit Dispolimit
credit period Kreditlaufzeit Zahlungsziel
credit risk Kreditrisiko
credit transfer Überweisung
creditworthiness Bonität, Kreditwürdigkeit, Zahlungsfähigkeit
creditworthy kreditwürdig
current account Girokonto
deadlock gesperrtes Konto
debit card Kundenkarte, EC-Karte
debt Schuld
debt recovery Inkasso
deduct, to abziehen
defraud, to betrügen, hintergehen
deposit Einlage, Pfand, Anzahlung
deposit, to einzahlen
direct debit Lastschrift, Bankeinzug, Einzugsermächtigung
discount Rabatt, Skonto
do a deal, to ein Geschäft machen
donate, to spenden
donation Spende
due fällig
earn, to verdienen
earnings Einkommen, Einkünfte
exchange rate Wechselkurs
expenditure Ausgaben
expense Kosten, Aufwand
expensive (= costly) teuer
extension of credit Verlängerung des Kredits od. Zahlungsziel
fare Fahrpreis
fee Gebühr
fine Geldstrafe
fraud Betrug, Hinterziehung
get into debt, to sich verschulden
grant Zuschuss
haggle, to feilschen, handeln
handling fee Bearbeitungsgebühr
hole-in-the-wall (= ATM, cashpoint) Bankautomat
identity theft Identitätsdiebstahl
in advance im Voraus
in return als Gegenleistung
in the black schwarze Zahlen schreiben
in the red rote Zahlen schreiben
income Einkommen, Einkünfte
inherit erben
inheritance Erbe
instalment Rate
interest Zins(en)
interest rate Zinssatz
invest, to (Geld) anlegen
investments Geldanlagen

invoice Rechnung
invoice (s.o.), to Rechnung senden, berechen
issue, to ausstellen
late payment Zinsverzug
lease, to pachten, leasen, mieten
lend, to ausleihen
letter of credit Akkreditiv
liquidity Liquidität
loan Darlehen, Kredit
loss Verlust
lump sum payment Pauschalbetrag
margin Gewinnspanne, Gewinnmarge
markup (Preis)Aufschlag, Einzelhandelsmarge
meet halfway, to ein Kompromiss machen
mortgage Hypothek
net price Nettopreis
note (AE bill) Geldschein
outgoings Ausgaben
overdraft Kontoüberziehung
overdrawn überzogen
overdue überfällig
overhead(s) Gemeinkosten, Fixkosten, fixe Kosten
pay off a loan, to ein Darlehen tilgen
pay off the balance, to den Restbetrag bezahlen
payment terms Zahlungsbedingungen
postage and packing Porto und Verpackung
prepaid card Prepaid Karte
profit(s) Gewinn
purchase, to kaufen
query Rückfrage
quid (BE) pl. quid Pfund (Währung)
reasonable price Vernünftiger Preis
rebate Rückerstattung (fall zu viel bezahlt worden ist)
receipt Beleg, Quittung
reduction Preisnachlass
refund Rückerstattung
refund, to rückerstatten, vergüten
reminder Zahlungserinnerung, Mahnung
rent Miete
revenue Einkommen, Einkünfte
royalties Tantiemen, Absatzhonorar
savings account Sparkonto
settle a debt/an invoice, to Schulden/eine Rechnung begleichen
spend, to (Geld) ausgben
squander, to Geld verschwenden
stage(d) payments (= payment in instalments) Zahlungen in Raten
standing order Dauerauftrag
subtotal Zwischensumme
subtract, to abziehen
terms and conditions Allgemeine Geschäftsbedingungen (AGB)
tip, to Trinkgeld geben
transfer, to überweisen
traveller's cheque (AE traveler's check) Reisescheck
unemployment benefit Arbeitslosengeld
unit price Stückpreis, Einzelpreis
Value-for-money Preislestungsverhältnish
VAT (= value added tax) Mehrwertssteuere
wealth Wohlstand
welfare Wohlfahrt
well-to-do (= well-off, prosperous)) wohlhabend
withdraw, to (Geld) abheben
withdrawal Abhebung

Finance and investment

backer Geldgeber, Investor, Sponsor
backing, to give finanzielle Unterstützung geben
bail out (a business), to (eine Firma) finanziell retten
bailout Rettungsmaßnahme
bankrupt (to go bankrupt) in Konkurs gehen
bankruptcy Konkurs, Insolvenz, Zahlungsfähigkeit
bear market Baissemarkt, Markt mit stetig fallenden Kursen
blue chip company führende Gesellschaft mit erstklassiger Bonität, erstrangiges Großunternehmen
blue chip investment erstklassige Anlage, Aktie mit hohe Marktkapitalisierung
bond Anleihe, Obligation, Schuldverschreibung
break even, to die Gewinnschwelle erreichen; die Kosten decken
breakeven point Gewinnschwelle; Kostendeckungspunkt
bull market Hausse-Markt
business angel Investor, der auch Beratung geben
business plan Unternehmenskonzept
cash in, to (to cash in an investment) einlösen
certificate of deposit von Banken emittiertes handelbares Geldmarktzertifikat
collateral (≈ security) (dingliche) Kreditsicherheit
controlling interest Kontrollpaket; Mehrheitsbeteiligung
cost-cutting Kostensenkung, Kostenreduktion
cut down on, to (= to reduce spending or consumption) reduzieren (ausgaben, Verbrauch)
debenture (BE) Firmenanleihe, Schuldverschreibung, Obligation
debt equity ratio (= gearing) Verschuldungsgrad, Verhältnis von Eigenkapital und Fremdkapital, Eigenkapitalüberdeckung
debt securities (e.g. bonds) Schuldobligationen (Wertpapiere)
debt, to be in debt Schuld, verschuldet sein
derivative Derivat
divestment Veräußerung
early-stage (or start-up) finance Investition in der Frühphase
equity Eigenkapital
equity securities (e.g. shares) Aktienkapital, Eigenkapital
factoring Ankauf/Verkauf von Forderungen
fees (= charges) Gebühren
financial instrument Handelspapier, Finanzinstrument
fixed-interest security (= certificate of deposit) festverzinsliche Wertpapier, Festgeld
float a company an die Börse gehen
flotation Börsengang
foreign currency Devisen
futures Terminwaren, - papiere
gearing (= debt-equity ratio) Verschuldungsgrad, Verhältnis von Eigenkapital und Fremdkapital, Eigenkapitalüberdeckung
get a business off the ground, (a company that is doing business effectively)
get a business up and running, to ein Unternehmen (erfolgreich) aufbauen
gilts (= gilt-edged securities) Staatsanleihe, Schatzbriefe
go bust, to (informal) Pleite gehen
go into liquidation, to in Konkurs gehen
go public, to an die Börse gehen
going concern laufendes Unternehmen, gut gehendes Geschäft
grant Zuschuss
hedge (against a risk), to sich gegen ein Risiko absichern
hedging Sicherung
Initial Public Offering (IPO) Börsengang
insolvency Zahlungsunfähigkeit
insolvent zahlungsunfähig
interest-bearing verzinslich

invest money in sth., to Geld anlegen
invest, to (to invest in a business) investieren, (Geld) anlegen
investment bank Anlagebank
investor Investor, Kapitalanleger, Geldgeber
issue shares, to Aktien emittieren
launch, to starten, gründen
leveraged fremdfinanziert
loan Kredit, Darlehen
loan shark Kredithai
maturity (to reach maturity) Fälligkeit
merchant bank Handelsbank
micro-finance (= micro-credit) Mikrofinanz
minority stake (to have a minority stake) in (eine) Minderheitsbeteiligung (haben)
money market Geldmarkt
mortgage-backed securities Pfandbriefe
mutual fund (BE unit trust) Investmentfond
no longer a going concern nicht mehr aktiv
nominal value (= face value) Nennwert
non-profit organisation gemeinnütziges Unternehmen
ordinary shares (AE common stock) Stammaktien
outside investors fremde Anleger
over-the-counter (OTC) market Freiverkehrsmarkt für nichtbörsenzugelassene Wertpapiere
overdraft (for day-to-day borrowings) Überziehungskredit, Kontokorrentkredit
pension fund Rentenfond
plough back profits, to Gewinn reinvestieren
preference shares (AE preferred stock) Vorzugsaktie
premium, to pay a Eine Prämie zahlen, über Nennwert zahlen
price-earnings ratio Kurs-Gewinn Verhältnis
put up capital, to Kapital bereitstellen
raise capital, to Kapital beschaffen
reckless leichtsinnig
redeem (e.g. a loan), to einlösen
return Rendite
return on investment (ROI) Gewinn bei Veräußerung, Gesamtkapitalrentabilität
risk-averse risikoscheu
savings Ersparnisse
secured loan gesichertes Darlehen od. Kredit
securities (pl.) Sicherheiten, Wertpapiere
seed capital Startkapital, Finanzierung der Ausreifung einer Idee
set up a business, to (= to start up) eine Firma gründen
shareholder (AE stockholder) Aktionär
shares (AE stocks) Aktien
spread one's risk, to das Risiko verteilen
stake (to have a stake in a company) Beteiligung
stock exchange Börse
stockbroker Börsenmakler
subsidise, to subventionieren
subsidy Subvention
treasury bonds (AE) Staatsanleihe, Schatzbriefe
unit trust (AE mutual find) offener Investmentfond
unsecured loan ungesichertes Darlehen od. Kredit
venture capital = risk capital Risikokapital, Wagniskapital
venture capitalists (= private equity firms) Risikokapitalgeber, Wagniskapitalgeber
viable lebensfähig
volatility (Wert-)Schwankungen
voting rights Stimmrechte
wind up a business, to eine Firma auflösen od. liquidieren
windfall Geldsegen

Taxation and auditing

account for, to betragen, ausmachen
accountant Bilanzbuchhalter/in
accounts payable (= creditors, payables) Verbindlichkeiten, Kreditoren
accounts receivable (= debtors, receivables) Forderungen, Kundenforderungen, Debitoren
accrued income and deferred expenses aktive Rechnungsabgrenzung, Rückstellungen
allocate, to zuteilen, zuordnen
assess, to (n. assessment) bewerten, beurteilen, einschätzen
assets Vermögen, Aktiva
assets and liabilities Aktiva und Passiva
audit Wirtschaftsprüfung, Revision
audit, to prüfen, kontrollieren
auditing Prüfungswesen, Rechnungsprüfung, Revision
auditor Wirtschaftsprüfer
bad debt dubiose, uneinbringliche Schuld
bad debt losses Forderungsausfälle
balance sheet Bilanz
bank balance Kontostand
bank statement Kontoauszug
bean counter (informal expression for accountant) Erbsenzähler
bookkeeping Buchhaltung, Buchführung
borrowed capital Fremdkapital
called up share capital (= paid up capital) einbezahltes Kapital
capital gains tax Kapitalertragssteuer, Steuern auf Veräußerungsgewinn
cash in hand or at the bank Bargeld, Bankkonten
Chartered Accountant (UK), Certified Public Accountant (US) entspricht etwa Steuerberater/in od. amtlich zugelassener Wirtschaftsprüfer
comply with (rules and regulations), to (Vorschriften) einhalten
compound interest Zinseszins
consistency Kohärenz, Übereinstimmung
cook the books, to (= to falsify the accounts) Bücher 'frisieren', fälschen
corporate tax (= corporation tax) Körperschaftssteuer
corporate tax rate Körperschaftsteuersatz
creative accounting Bilanzkosmetik
credit Guthaben, Gutschrift, Zahlungsziel
credit (an account) with (an amount), to (ein Konto) gutschreiben
creditors (= accounts payable) Verbindlichkeiten, Kreditoren
currency Währung
current account (AE checking account) Girokonto
current assets Umlaufvermögen
current liabilities (= short-term liabilities) kurzfristige Verbindlichkeiten
debit, to abbuchen
debtors (= receivables, accounts receivable) Forderungen, Debitoren
deduct, to abziehen, absetzen
deductible absetzbar
deduction Abzug
default (on debt repayments), to Zahlung einstellen oder nicht erfüllen
deferred income and accrued expenses passive Rechnungsabgrenzung
defraud, to betrügen, unterschlagen, übervorteilen
depreciate (an asset), to abschreiben
depreciate (in value), to Wert verlieren, im Wert sinken
depreciation (AE amortization) Abschreibung

depreciation (in value) Wertverlust
deviation Abweichung
direct debit Einzugsermächtigung, Lastschriftverfahren
disclose, to offen legen, bekannt machen, veröffentlichen
disclose, to offen legen, veröffentlichen
disclosure Offenlegung
dispose of, to verfügen über
dividend(s) Dividende
do the books/accounts/bookkeeping Buchhaltung machen
dodgy (a dodgy deal, a dodgy business) fragwürdig, nicht ganz legal, anrüchig
donation Spende
double-entry bookkeeping Doppelte Buchführung
due fällig
due diligence Sorgfaltspflicht, detaillierte Untersuchung, Kaufprüfung, Unternehmensbewertung
earnings Einkommen
economical wirtschaftlich (i.S.v. sparsam)
economise, to Sparen
embezzle, to Unterschlagen
embezzlement Veruntreuung, Unterschlagung
exchange rate Wechselkurs
excise tax Verbrauchssteuer
exempt from, to be befreit sein von
expenditure Ausgaben
expenses Auslagen, Spesen
fiddle the expenses, to (to cook the books) Bücher frisieren
financial statement(s) Finanzaufstellung, Finanzbericht, Jahresabschluss
fixed assets Anlagevermögen
fixtures and fittings (furnishings) Betriebs- und Geschäftsausstattung
fraud Betrug
fraudster (= conman) Schwindler, Hochstapler
fraudulent betrügerisch
fuel tax Benzinsteuer, Mineralölsteuer
gearing (= borrowing as a percentage of overall financing) Verschuldungsgrad
generally accepted accounting principles (GAAP) allgemein annerkannte Prinzipien der Buchhaltung, Grundsätze ordnungsmäßiger Buchführung (GoB)
going concern principle Grundsatz der Unternehmensfortführung
goodwill Firmenwert
import tax Einfuhrsteuer, Importsteuer
income Einkommen
income tax Einkommensteuer
income tax return/declaration Einkommensteuererklärung
incur (losses, expenses, costs, etc.), to geraten in, sich zuziehen, etw. auf sich laden
independent oversight body Überwachungsbehörde
inheritance tax Erbschaftssteuer
insider share-trading/insider dealing Insiderhandel
intangible assets immaterielle Vermögenswerte
intellectual property geistiges Eigentum
interest (to earn interest on an investment) Zinsen
interest rate Zinssatz
internal audit interne Revision
Internal Revenue Service (IRS) US Bundesfinanzamt
International Financial Reporting Standards (IFRS) internationale Rechnungslegungsvorschriften
inventory (BE stock levels) Lager, Lagerbestand, Vorräte
law on financial reporting compliance Bilanzkontrollgesetz
levy a tax, to (= impose a tax) eine Steuer erheben
liabilities Verbindlichkeiten, Passiva
long-term investments langfristige Anlagen
long-term liabilities langfristige Verbindlichkeiten
loss Verlust
lump sum Pauschale, Pauschbetrag, fixe Summe
misconduct Fehlverhalten, Straftat
monthly VAT return Umsatzsteuervoranmeldung
mortgage Hypothek
National Insurance UK Sozialversicherung
notes to the accounts Anhang zur Bilanz
number crunching (informal expression for accounting) Zahlenverarbeitung
offset, to (to offset a loss against a profit) ausgleichen, wettmachen, gegenrechnen
one-off processing fee (= up-front administrative charge) Bearbeitungsgebühr (einmalig)
overdraft limit/facility Dispolimit
overdraw, to überziehen
overheads Gemeinkosten
owe, to (to owe money to someone) Schulden
Pay As You Earn (PAYE) Einbehaltung der Lohnsteuer, Lohnsteuerabzug
pay off, to (to pay off a debt/a loan) tilgen, einen Kredit od. Schuld zurückzahlen
payroll accounting Lohn- und Geschäftsabrechnung
payroll tax Lohnsteuer
penalty for late filing Säumniszuschlag
performance Leistung
plant Anlage, Fabrik
principal Tilgung
profit Gewinn
profit and loss account (AE income statement) Gewinn- und Verlustkonto
profitability Rentabilität
profitable rentabel
property (AE real estate) Immobilien
proprietors capital (BE ownership capital) Eigenkapital
provisions Rückstellungen, Vorräte
receipts Belege
reserves Rücklagen
retained profits einbehaltener Gewinn
running expenses laufende Kosten
sales Absatz
sales tax (AE) Umsatzsteuer, Mehrwertsteuer
savings account Sparkonto, Sparbuch
semi-finished goods halbfertige Waren, Halbfertigfabrikate
service a loan, to Zinsen zahlen (auf ein Darlehen)
short-term investments kurzfristige Einlagen
short-term liabilities (= current liablities) kurzfristige Verbindlichkeiten
solvency Zahlungsfähigkeit
solvent zahlungsfähig
standing order Dauerauftrag
stock (AE inventory) Lager, Lagerbestand, Vorräte
subject to tax, to be steuerpflichtig sein, der Steuer unterliegen
suppliers Lieferanten
tangible assets Sachanlagen, Sachvermögen
tax Steuer
tax advisor (= tax consultant) Steuerberater(in)
tax allowance Steuerfreibetrag, Absetzbetrag, Steuerermäßigung, Steuernachlass
tax avoidance (legale) Steuervermeidung, Steuersparmodelle, Steueroptimierung
tax break Steuervergünstigung, Steuererleichterung
tax consultant/advisor Steuerberater(in)
tax deductible steuerabzugsfähig, steuerlich absetzbar
tax demand (= tax bill, tax assessment) Steuerbescheid
tax demand (= tax bill, tax assessment) Steuerbescheid

tax dodge Steuertrick
tax evasion Steuerhinterziehung
tax fraud Steuerbetrug
tax haven Steuerparadies, Steueroase
tax hike Steuererhöhung
tax liability Steuerpflicht, Steuerschuld
tax rebate (= tax refund) Steuerrückerstattung
tax relief Steuerentlastung, Steuervergünstigung
tax return (= tax declaration) Steuererklärung
taxes due fällige Steuerzahlungen
term (of a loan) Laufzeit
trade tax Gewerbesteuer
transfer Überweisung
true and fair view of the company's affairs den tatsächlichen Verhältnissen entsprechendes Bild der Vermögens-, Finanz- und Ertragslage der Gesellschaft
turnover Umsatz
value added tax (BE) Umsatzsteuer, Mehrwertsteuer
VAT (Value Added Tax) Mehrwertsteuer, Umsatzsteuer
white-collar crime Wirtschaftskriminalität, Wirtschaftsverbrechen
window dressing (= creative accounting) Bilanzkosmetik
work-in-progress (= semi-finished goods) halbfertige Waren
worth Wert
write off, to abschreiben
yield Ertrag
yield, to bringen, ertragen

Acronyms and International organisations

(OPEC) Organisation of the Petroleum Exporting Countries Organisation Erdöl Exportierender Länder (OPEC)
(SWIFT) Society for Worldwide Interbank Financial Telecommunication System des gegenseitigen, internationalen, direkten Datenaustauschs im Auslandszahlungsverkehrs (SWIFT)
BRIC (Brazil, Russia, India, China) BRIC-Staaten
CPI (consumer price index) Verbraucherpreisindex
ECB (European Central Bank) Europäische Zentralbank (EZB)
FDI (Foreign Direct Investment) ausländische Direktinvestition(en)
G-20
GDP (gross domestic product) Bruttoinlandsprodukt (BIP)
GNP (gross national product) Bruttosozialprodukt (BSP)
ICC (International Chamber of Commerce) Internationale Handelskammer (ICC)
ICC (International Chamber of Commerce) Internationale Handelskammer
IMF (International Monetary Fund) Internationaler Währungsfond (IWF)
NGO (Non-governmental organisation) Nichtregierungsorganisation (NGO)
NGO (non-governmental organisation) Nichtregierungsorganisation (NGO)
NIC (newly industrialised countries) Schwellenland
NTB (non-tariff barrier) nicht-tarifäre Handesbeschränkung
OECD (Organisation for Economic Cooperation and Development) Organisation für wirtschaftliche Zusammenarbeit und Entwicklung (OECD)
PPP (purchasing power parity) Kaufkraftparität
WTO (World Trade Organisation) Welthandelsorganisation (WTO)

Notes

Vocabulary

A

to abolish [əˈbɒlɪʃ] abschaffen 184
absenteeism [ˌæbsənˈtiːɪzm] Arbeitsausfall, Fehlzeiten, häufiges Nichterscheinen 119
to abstain [æbˈsteɪn] sich der Stimme enthalten 184
abstention [æbˈstenʃn] Enthaltung, Stimmenthaltung 52
abuse [əˈbjuːs] Missbrauch 183
academic [ˌækəˈdemɪk] Akademiker(in), Hochschuldozent(in) 155
acceptance [əkˈseptəns] Abnahme, Absegnung, Akzeptanz 125
access [ˈækses] Zugang 35
to access [ˈækses] etw. abrufen, auf etw. zugreifen, eingelassen werden 72
accessories [əkˈsesərɪz] Zubehör 42
accident insurance [ˈæksɪdənt ɪnˌʃɔːrəns] Unfallversicherung, Unfallschutz 141
accommodation [əˌkɒməˈdeɪʃn] Unterbringung, Unterkunft 9
to accomplish [əˈkʌmplɪʃ] vollbringen, erreichen 125
accountancy [əˈkaʊntənsɪ] Finanzbuchhaltung, Rechnungswesen, Bilanzbuchhaltung 21
accountant [əˈkaʊntənt] Bilanzbuchhalter(in); Buchhalter(in); Steuerberater(in) 112
to account for [əˈkaʊnt fɔː] betragen, ergeben, ausmachen, verantwortlich sein für 32
account management [əˈkaʊnt ˌmænɪdʒmənt] Kundenbetreuung 60
accounts department [əˈkaʊnts dɪˌpɑːtmənt] Buchhaltung, Finanzabteilung 14
accounts payable [əˌkaʊnts ˈpeɪəbl] Verbindlichkeiten, Kreditoren 193
accounts receivable [əˌkaʊnts rɪˈsiːvəbl] Forderungen, Kundenforderungen, Debitoren 193
accruals and deferred income [əˌkruːəlz ənd‿dɪˌfɜːd ˈɪnkʌm] Rechnungsabgrenzungsposten 193
to accrue [əˈkruː] anfallen (z. B. Zinsen), entstehen 202
accrued income [əˌkruːd ˈɪnkʌm] aktive Rechnungsabgrenzung 193
to accrue from [əˈkruː frɒm] sich ergeben aus 202
accuracy [ˈækjʊrəsɪ] Genauigkeit, Richtigkeit, Sorgfalt 114
accusation [ˌækjʊˈzeɪʃn] Vorwurf, Anschuldigung, Anklage 103
to accuse [əˈkjuːz] anklagen, beschuldigen, anlasten 176
to achieve [əˈtʃiːv] erreichen 27
achievement [əˈtʃiːvmənt] Errungenschaft, Leistung 12
to acknowledge [əkˈnɒlɪdʒ] anerkennen, bestätigen, zustimmen, einräumen 181
to acquire [əˈkwaɪə] erwerben, übernehmen 203
acquisition [ˌækwɪˈzɪʃn] Erwerb, Übernahme, Akquisition, Ankauf 202
to act within the law [ˌækt wɪˌðɪn ðə ˈlɔː] das Gesetz befolgen, das Gesetz einhalten 176
a cut of the profits [ə ˌkʌt əv‿ðə ˈprɒfɪts] ein Anteil am Gewinn 167
to adapt [əˈdæpt] sich anpassen, sich einstellen auf 10
ad campaign [ˈæd kæmˌpeɪn] Werbekampagne 52
additives [ˈædɪtɪvz] Zusatzstoffe 54
to adjourn a meeting [əˌdʒɜːn ə ˈmiːtɪŋ] eine Sitzung vertagen od. unterbrechen 51
to administer [ədˈmɪnɪstə] verwalten, ausführen, organisieren, erteilen 68
administrative [ədˈmɪnɪstrətɪv] Verwaltungs- 27
advancement [ədˈvɑːnsmənt] Beförderung, Weiterentwicklung 116
advance payment [ədˌvɑːns ˈpeɪmənt] Vorauszahlung, Vorkasse, Vorschusszahlung 167
advert [ˈædvɜːt] Anzeige 42
to advertise [ˈædvətaɪz] werben 42
advertising [ˈædvətaɪzɪŋ] Werbung 24
advertising agency [ˈædvətaɪʒɪŋ ˌeɪdʒənsɪ] Werbeagentur 60
advertising campaign [ˈædvətaɪzɪŋ‿kæmˌpeɪn] Werbekampagne 64
advertising copy [ˈædvətaɪzɪŋ ˌkɒpɪ] Werbetext 65
advertising executive [ˈædvətaɪzɪŋ ɪgˌzekjətɪv] Werbeakquisiteur(in), Werbemanager(in), Werbefachmann / frau 68
advertising strategy [ˈædvətaɪzɪŋ ˌstrætədʒɪ] Werbestrategie 64
aerosol can [ˈeərəʊsɒl ˌkæn] Spraydose, Sprühdose 78
aerosol spray [ˈeərəsɒl ˌspreɪ] Sprühdose, Aerosol 29
aerospace [ˈeərəʊspeɪs] Raumfahrt 125
affiliate [əˈfɪlɪət] Geschäftspartner(in) 181
affiliated group [əˌfɪlɪeɪtɪd ˈgruːp] Konzern, Unternehmensgruppe 202
affluent [ˈæflʊənt] wohlhabend, reich 39
to afford [əˈfɔːd] sich leisten 98
affordable [əˈfɔːdəbl] bezahlbar, erschwinglich 48
after-sales [ˌɑːftəˈseɪlz] Kundendienst, Kundenbetreuung 61
agenda [əˈdʒendə] Tagesordnung 11
ahead of schedule [əˌhed‿əv ˈʃedjuːl] dem Zeitplan voraus 127
airfreight [ˈeəfreɪt] Luftfracht 169
air waybill [ˈeə ˌweɪbɪl] Luftfrachtbrief 170
alliance [əˈlaɪəns] Allianz, Bündnis 202
to allocate [ˈæləʊkeɪt] zuteilen 35
ambiguous [æmˈbɪgjʊəs] mehrdeutig, zweideutig, doppelsinnig, missverständlich 69
amount [əˈmaʊnt] Betrag, Menge, Summe 36
analyst [ˈænəlɪst] Analytiker(in) 205
analytical [ˌænəˈlɪtɪkl] analytisch, rechnerisch 205
ancillary [ænˈsɪlərɪ] Zusatz-, zusätzlich 192
to announce [əˈnaʊns] ankündigen, bekannt geben, ansagen 12
announcement [əˈnaʊnsmənt] Ankündigung, Bekanntgabe, Durchsage 12
annual general meeting (AGM) [ˌænjʊəl ˌdʒenrəl ˈmiːtɪŋ, ˌeɪdʒiːˈem] Jahreshauptversammlung 11
to anticipate [ænˈtɪsɪpeɪt] vorwegnehmen, vorausahnen, zuvorkommen 69
anti-competitive [ˌæntɪkəmˈpetətɪv] wettbewerbshemmend, wettbewerbswidrig 177
antitrust legislation [ˌæntɪˈtrʌst ledʒɪˌsleɪʃn] Kartellgesetzgebung, Kartellrecht 202
AOB [ˌeɪəʊˈbiː] Sonstiges 53
apology [əˈpɒlədʒɪ] Entschuldigung 16
appealing [əˈpiːlɪŋ] ansprechend, verlockend, einladend 63
to appeal to [əˈpiːl tuː] ansprechen, zielen auf, auf jmdn. einwirken 69
appendix (pl. appendices) [əˈpendɪks, əˈpendɪsiːz] Anhang 187
appliance [əˈplaɪəns] Elektrogerät, Haushaltsgerät 21
applicant [ˈæplɪkənt] Bewerber(in) 113
application [ˌæplɪˈkeɪʃn] Antrag 43
application letter [ˌæplɪˈkeɪʃn ˌletə] Bewerbungsschreiben 118
application process [ˌæplɪˈkeɪʃn ˌprəʊses] Anmeldeverfahren, Antragsverfahren 187
to apply sth (to) [əˈplaɪ] etw. anwenden (auf) 71
to apply for [əˈplaɪ fɔː] sich bewerben um 11

to apply to [ə'plaɪ tu:] gelten für, betreffen 20
to appoint [ə'pɔɪnt] ernennen 22
appointment [ə'pɔɪntmənt] Ernennung, Termin, Verabredung 22
to appreciate [ə'pri:ʃieɪt] schätzen, begrüßen 43
apprentice [ə'prentɪs] Auszubildende(r) 112
apprenticeship [ə'prentɪʃɪp] Ausbildung, Lehre 112
appropriate [ə'prəʊprɪət] angemessen 52
approval [ə'pru:vl] Genehmigung, Freigabe 125
to approve of sth. [ə'pru:v əv ˌsʌmθɪŋ] mit etw. einverstanden sein, einer Sache zustimmen 20
approximately [ə'prɒksɪmətlɪ] ungefähr, etwa 21
aptitude test ['æptɪtju:d‿test] Eignungstest 113
arrangements [ə'reɪndʒmənts] Vorkehrungen, Vorbereitungen 8
arrival [ə'raɪvl] Ankunft 9
ASA (Advertising Standards Authority) [ˌeɪes'eɪ, ˌædvətaɪzɪŋ 'stændədz ɔ:ˌθɒrətɪ] britische Werbeaufsichtsbehörde 177
as agreed [əz‿ə'gri:d] wie vereinbart 80
asap [əz‿su:n əz 'pɒsəbl] (as soon as possible) sobald wie möglich 8
as requested [əz rɪ'kwestɪd] wunschgemäß, wie verlangt 80
to assemble [ə'sembl] zusammenbauen, montieren, zusammenstellen 166
assembly [ə'semblɪ] Fertigung, Montage 86
assembly line [ə'semblɪ ˌlaɪn] Fließband, Fabrikationsstraße 85
assertive [ə'sɜ:tɪv] durchsetzungsfähig 10
to assess [ə'ses] bewerten, evaluieren, abschätzen, beurteilen 120
asset ['æset] Vermögen, Vermögensgegenstand 34
asset-backed [ˌæset‿'bækt] durch Aktiva gesichert 190
asset stripping ['æset ˌstrɪpɪŋ] Zerschlagung durch Verkauf von Teilbereichen, Ausschlachtung von Anlagen 204
to assign a task to sb. [ə'saɪn] jmdm. eine Aufgabe übertragen / zuweisen 123
assignment [ə'saɪnmənt] Einsatz, Auftrag, Auslandsentsendung 148
as stipulated [əz‿'stɪpjəleɪtɪd] wie vereinbart, wie gefordert 169
to assume no liability [əˌsju:m ˌnəʊ laɪə'bɪlətɪ] keine Haftung übernehmen 181
assurance [ə'ʃʊərəns] Versprechen, Zusage, Zusicherung, Versicherung 145
at a discount [ət ə 'dɪskaʊnt] unter pari, unter Nennwert, mit Preisnachlass 189
at grassroots level [ət ˌgrɑ:sru:ts 'levl] an der Basis, unten (in der Hierarchie) 18
at one's own risk [ət wʌnz ˌəʊn 'rɪsk] auf eigene Gefahr, auf eigenes Risiko 139
ATM (Automated Teller Machine) [ˌeɪti:'em, ˌɔ:təmeɪtɪd‿'telə məˌʃi:n] Geldautomat 36
at such short notice [ət sʌtʃ‿ˌʃɔ:t 'nəʊtɪs] so kurzfristig 186
to attach [ə'tætʃ] anhängen, anbringen, beiheften 176
attention to detail [əˌtenʃn tə 'di:teɪl] Detailgenauigkeit, Beachtung von Einzelheiten 114
Attn. (for the attention of) [fə ðɪ‿ə'tenʃn əv] zu Händen 80
attorney [ə'tɜ:nɪ] Rechtsanwalt, Rechtsanwältin 91
at your earliest convenience [ət‿jɔ:r‿ɜ:lɪɪst kən'vi:nɪəns] sobald es Ihnen möglich ist, umgehend 12
to audit ['ɔ:dɪt] auditieren, prüfen, kontrollieren 118
authority [ɔ:'θɒrətɪ] Genehmigung, Berechtigung, Vollmacht 43
authority [ɔ:'θɒrətɪ] maßgebende Persönlichkeit, Experte/Expertin 207
Automated Teller Machine [ˌɔ:təmeɪtɪd‿'telə məˌʃi:n] Geldautomat 36
automotive [ˌɔ:tə'məʊtɪv] Automobil- 20
available [ə'veɪləbl] verfügbar, erhältlich 40
available on demand [əˌveɪləbl ɒn dɪ'mɑ:nd] jederzeit verfügbar, erhältlich ohne Kündigungsfrist 188
average ['ævrɪdʒ] Durchschnitt 94
award [ə'wɔ:d] Preis, Auszeichnung 8
award ceremony [ə'wɔ:d ˌserɪmənɪ] Preisverleihungszeremonie 12

B

to back [bæk] (finanziell) unterstützen, befürworten 125
backer ['bækə] Geldgeber 125
badge [bædʒ] Plakette, Ausweis 105
to bail sb. out [beɪl ˌsʌmwʌn 'aʊt] jmdm. (finanziell) aus der Klemme helfen 155
balance ['bæləns] Kontostand, Bilanz, Saldo 35
balance due [ˌbæləns 'dju:] fälliger Betrag 37
balance of payments [ˌbæləns‿əv 'peɪmənts] Zahlungsbilanz 148
balance of trade [ˌbæləns‿əv 'treɪd] Handelsbilanz 148
balance sheet ['bæləns‿ˌʃi:t] Bilanz 192
to ban [bæn] verbieten 65
ban [bæn] Verbot 18
bank account [ˌbæŋk ə'kaʊnt] Bankkonto 35
bank details ['bæŋk ˌdi:teɪlz] Bankverbindung, Kontoverbindung 43
bank guarantee [ˌbæŋk‿gærən'ti:] Bankbürgschaft 170
bankrupt ['bæŋkrʌpt] bankrott, pleite, insolvent 148
bankruptcy ['bæŋkrʌpsɪ] Insolvenz, Konkurs, Bankrott 150
bank teller ['bæŋk ˌtelə] Kassierer(in), Bankangestellte(r) 62
bank transfer ['bæŋk ˌtrænsfɜ:] Banküberweisung 169
banner ad ['bænə ˌæd] Bannerwerbung 67
bar-code ['bɑ:ˌkəʊd] Strichcode, Streifencode, Balkencode 80
bargain ['bɑ:gɪn] Schnäppchen 36
to bargain ['bɑ:gɪn] handeln, feilschen, verhandeln 27
bargaining power ['bɑ:gənɪŋ ˌpaʊə] Verhandlungsmacht, Verhandlungsstärke 204
barge [bɑ:dʒ] Kahn 76
barrel ['bærl] Fass 73
barter ['bɑ:tə] Tauschhandel, Bartergeschäft 32
batch [bætʃ] Bündel, Stapel, Charge, Los 80
to be accountable to s.b. [bɪ‿ə'kaʊntəbl tə ˌsʌmbədɪ] jmdm. gegenüber verantwortlich sein 25
bear hug ['beə ˌhʌg] ungestüme Umarmung 11
bear market ['beə ˌmɑ:kɪt] Baissemarkt, Markt mit stetig fallenden Kursen 183
to bear with s.o. [beə 'wɪð ˌsʌmwʌn] Geduld haben mit jmdm. 16
to hold liable [ˌhəʊld 'laɪəbl] jmdn. haftbar machen 181
to be in debt [bɪ‿ɪn det] verschuldet sein 63
to be liable for [bɪ 'laɪəbl fɔ:] haftbar sein für, haften für 23
benchmarking ['bentʃˌmɑ:kɪŋ] Benchmarking, Vergleichstest 138
benefit ['benəfɪt] Nutzen, Vorteil 15
benefits ['benəfɪts] Sozialleistungen, Vergünstigungen 114
to be off work [bɪ‿ɒf 'wɜ:k] krankgeschrieben sein 210
to be on the payroll [bɪ‿ɒn ðə 'peɪrəʊl] angestellt sein 127
best practice [ˌbest 'præktɪs] optimaler Geschäftsablauf, bestes Verfahren 138
bestseller [ˌbest'selə] Verkaufsschlager 145
to be subject to [bɪ 'sʌbdʒekt‿tu:] unterliegen, unterworfen sein, für etwas anfällig sein, abhängen von 126
to be subject to tax [bɪ ˌsʌbjekt‿tʊ 'tæks] steuerpflichtig sein, der Steuer unterliegen 194
beverage ['bevərɪdʒ] Getränk 20

bias ['baɪəs] Neigung, Tendenz, Voreingenommenheit, Einseitigkeit 68
to bid (for) ['bɪd fɔ:] anbieten 125
bidder ['bɪdə] Bieter(in), Submittent 126
bilingual secretary [ˌbaɪlɪŋgwəl 'sekrətrɪ] Fremdsprachensekretär(in) 113
bill [bɪl] Banknote, Geldschein (AE), Rechnung 32
billboard ['bɪlbɔ:d] Plakatwand, Werbetafel, Plakatwerbung 67
bill of exchange (B/E) [ˌbɪl‿əv ɪks'tʃeɪndʒ] Wechsel 167
bill of lading (B/L) [ˌbɪl‿əv 'leɪdɪŋ] Konnossement, Frachtbrief, Ladeschein 170
bills for collection [ˌbɪlz fə kə'lekʃn] Inkassowechsel 167
bills payable [ˌbɪlz 'peɪəbl] Verbindlichkeiten, Kreditoren 193
bills receivable [ˌbɪlz rɪ'si:vəbl] Forderungen, Außenstände, Debitoren 193
binding offer [ˌbaɪndɪŋ 'ɒfə] festes Angebot, verbindliches Angebot 169
black market [ˌblæk 'mɑ:kɪt] schwarzer Markt, Schwarzhandel, illegaler Warenhandel 154
blister pack ['blɪstə ˌpæk] Blisterverpackung 78
blue-chip company [ˌblu:tʃɪp 'kʌmpənɪ] erstrangiges Großunternehmen, Unternehmen mit hoher Marktkapitalisierung 67
board [bɔ:d] Geschäftsleitung, Vorstand 15
board of directors [ˌbɔ:d‿əv daɪ'rektəz] Direktion, Aufsichtsrat 24
body shop ['bɒdɪ ˌʃɒp] Karosseriewerkstatt, Autolackiererei 85
bonded warehouse [ˌbɒndɪd 'weəhaʊs] Zolllager, Lagerhaus für unverzollte Waren 170
bonus ['bəʊnəs] Zulage, Gratifikation, Prämie, Sondervergütung 116
boom [bu:m] Hochkonjunktur 150
BOP (balance of payments) [ˌbi:əʊ'pi:] Zahlungsbilanz 148
to borrow ['bɒrəʊ] (sich) ausleihen, borgen 33
BOT (balance of trade) [ˌbi:əʊ'ti:] Handelsbilanz 148
bottom line [ˌbɒtəm 'laɪn] Nettoprofit 127
to be bound by (the terms of) a contract [bɪ ˌbaʊnd‿baɪ‿ə 'kɒntrækt] vertraglich verpflichtet sein 180
branch office [ˌbrɑ:ntʃ 'ɒfɪs] Niederlassung, Zweigstelle 196
brand [brænd] Marke, Markenname 21
brand awareness [ˌbrænd ə'weənəs] Markenbewusstsein, Markenbekanntheit 45
brand conscious [ˌbrænd 'kɒnʃəs] markenbewusst 45
brand equity [ˌbrænd 'ekwɪtɪ] Markenwert 75
brand extension [ˌbrænd ɪk'stenʃn] Markendehnung 45
brand image [ˌbrænd 'ɪmɪdʒ] Markenimage 45
brand loyalty [ˌbrænd 'lɔɪəltɪ] Markentreue 45
brand stretching [ˌbrænd 'stretʃɪŋ] Markendehnung 45
breakdown ['breɪkdaʊn] Betriebsstörung, Betriebsausfall, Panne 95
to break bulk [ˌbreɪk 'bʌlk] in kleineren Mengen verkaufen 72
to break into a market [breɪk ˌɪntʊ‿ə 'mɑ:kɪt] in einem neuen Markt Fuß fassen, in einen neuen Markt einbrechen 68
breakthrough ['breɪkθru:] Durchbruch 29
bribe [braɪb] Bestechung, Bestechungsgeld, Schmiergeld 166
brick and mortar store [ˌbrɪk‿ən‿'mɔ:tə ˌstɔ:] konventionelles Geschäft (Gegenstück zum Internetshop) 79
brief [bri:f] Kurzanweisung 69
briefing ['bri:fɪŋ] Beratung, Einsatzbesprechung, Einweisung 54
brochure ['brəʊʃə] Broschüre 11
brought-in capital [ˌbrɔ:tɪn 'kæpɪtl] Kapitaleinlage, einbezahltes Kapital 193
to brush up on [ˌbrʌʃ 'ʌp ɒn] etwas wieder auffrischen 146
bubble wrap ['bʌbl ˌræp] Blisterfolie, Luftpolsterfolie (Verpackungsmaterial) 78
budding ['bʌdɪŋ] angehend 195
budget deficit [ˌbʌdʒɪt‿'defɪsɪt] Haushaltsdefizit 148
budgeting ['bʌdʒɪtɪŋ] Budgetierung, Haushaltsplanung 35
budget surplus [ˌbʌdʒɪt 'sɜ:pləs] Haushaltsüberschuss 148
building society ['bɪldɪŋ səˌsaɪətɪ] Bausparkasse 199
bulk delivery [ˌbʌlk dɪ'lɪvərɪ] Großlieferung 72
bulk order [ˌbʌlk 'ɔ:də] Großbestellung 40
bulky ['bʌlkɪ] sperrig 76
bullet point ['bʊlɪt‿ˌpɔɪnt] Aufzählungszeichen 74
bull market ['bʊl ˌmɑ:kɪt] Haussemarkt, Markt mit stetig steigenden Kursen 188
bureaucracy [bjʊə'rɒkrəsɪ] Bürokratie, Bürokratismus 27
bursary ['bɜ:sərɪ] Stipendium 35
business card ['bɪznɪs ˌkɑ:d] Visitenkarte 106
business cycle ['bɪznɪs‿ˌsaɪkl] Konjunktur, Konjunkturzyklus 150
business plan ['bɪznɪs ˌplæn] Business-Plan, Geschäftsplan, Existenzgründungsvorhaben, Rentabilitätsvorschau 194
business studies ['bɪznɪs‿ˌstʌdɪz] Betriebswirtschaftslehre 114
business trip ['bɪznɪs ˌtrɪp] Geschäftsreise 14
bust [bʌst] Tiefkonjunktur 150

C

cancellation [ˌkænsə'leɪʃn] Stornierung, Streichung, Annullierung, Ausfall 182
candidate ['kændɪdət] Kandidat(in), Bewerber(in) 116
canteen [kæn'ti:n] Kantine 9
capital account balance [ˌkæpɪtl ə'kaʊnt‿ˌbæləns] Kapitalbilanz 148
capital expenditure [ˌkæpɪtl ɪk'spendɪtʃə] Investition, Kapitalaufwand 192
capital gains tax [ˌkæpɪtl 'geɪnz ˌtæks] Kapitalertragssteuer, Steuer auf Veräußerungsgewinn 194
carbon footprint [ˌkɑ:bn 'fʊtprɪnt] CO2-Bilanz 87
cardboard box [ˌkɑ:dbɔ:d 'bɒks] Pappkarton 78
cargo ['kɑ:gəʊ] Fracht, Ladung 170
car insurance ['kɑ:r‿ɪnˌʃɔ:rəns] Autoversicherung, Kraftfahrzeugversicherung 141
car mechanics ['kɑ: məˌkænɪks] Automechanik 112
carpentry trade ['kɑ:pəntrɪ ˌtreɪd] Zimmerergewerbe 112
car rental ['kɑ: ˌrentl] Autovermietung 72
carriage paid to (CPT) [ˌkærɪdʒ 'peɪd‿tʊ] frachtfrei 170
carrier ['kærɪə] Spediteur, Frachtführer 77
to carry a motion [ˌkærɪ‿ə 'məʊʃn] einen Antrag annehmen 185
car showroom [ˌkɑ: 'ʃəʊru:m] Autosalon 72
cash [kæʃ] Bar, Barzahlung, bar 32
cash against documents [ˌkæʃ‿əˌgenst‿'dɒkjəmənts] (Bar) Zahlung gegen Dokumente 170
cash at bank and in hand [ˌkæʃ ət 'bæŋk ənd ˌɪn 'hænd] Bargeld, Bankkonten 193
cash cow ['kæʃ ˌkaʊ] hohe Gewinne abwerfender Bereich eines Unternehmens, umsatzstarkes Produkt, Melkkuh, Cash Cow 204
cash crops ['kæʃ ˌkrɒps] für den Verkauf bestimmte Anbaufrucht, Marktfruchtbau 171
cash for clunkers [ˌkæʃ fə 'klʌŋkəz] Abwrackprämie 185
to cash in [kæʃ 'ɪn] einlösen, auszahlen 198
cash on delivery (COD) [ˌkæʃ ɒn dɪ'lɪvərɪ, ˌsi:əʊ'di:] Zahlung per Nachnahme, zahlbar bei Lieferung 77
to cash out [kæʃ 'aʊt] auszahlen 191

cashpoint ['kæʃpɔɪnt] Geldautomat 35
cash-strapped [ˌkæʃ'stræpt] knapp bei Kasse 116
cash with order (CWO) [ˌkæʃ wɪð 'ɔːdə] Zahlung bei Auftragserteilung 77
casting vote [ˌkɑːstɪŋ 'vəʊt] entscheidende Stimme, ausschlaggebende Stimme 184
catalogue ['kætəlɒg] Katalog 11
catchphrase ['kætʃfreɪz] Schlagwort 65
catchy ['kætʃɪ] eingängig 52
catering ['keɪtərɪŋ] Gastronomie, Versorgung mit Speisen und Getränken 20
cat's cradle [ˌkæts 'kreɪdl] Abnehmspiel, Fadenspiel 26
caveat emptor (Latin) [ˌkævɪæt 'emptɔː] Ausschluss der Gewährleistung, Gewährleistungsausschluss 138
Chief Executive Officer (CEO) [ˌtʃiːf ɪgˌzekjʊtɪv 'ɒfɪsə, ˌsiːiː'əʊ] Vorstandsvorsitzende(r), Geschäftsführer(in) 8
certificate of deposit [səˌtɪfɪkət‿əv dɪ'pɒzɪt] festverzinsliches Wertpapier, Einlagenzertifikat, Festgeld 189
certificate of origin [səˌtɪfɪkət‿əv 'ɒrɪdʒɪn] Ursprungszeugnis 170
certification [ˌsɜːtɪfɪ'keɪʃn] Zertifizierung, Abnahme 138
CFO (Chief Financial Officer) [ˌsiːef'əʊ, ˌtʃiːf‿faɪˌnænʃl 'ɒfɪsə] Leiter(in) der Finanzabteilung 9
chain of command [ˌtʃeɪn‿əv kə'mɑːnd] Befehlskette, Befehlsweg 25
to chair [tʃeə] eine Diskussion leiten, den Vorsitz führen 51
chairman, pl. chairmen ['tʃeəmən] Vorsitzender, Diskussionsleiter 51
chairperson ['tʃeəˌpɜːsn] Vorsitzende(r), Diskussionsleiter(in) 51
to chair a meeting [ˌtʃeər‿ə 'miːtɪŋ] den Vorsitz führen, ein Meeting leiten 75
challenge ['tʃælɪndʒ] Herausforderung 10
charge [tʃɑːdʒ] Gebühr 37
to charge up [ˌtʃɑːdʒ 'ʌp] berechnen, verlangen 72
to charge [tʃɑːdʒ] berechnen, belasten, in Rechnung stellen 34
to charge (sb. with sth.) ['tʃɑːdʒ ˌsʌmbədɪ wɪð ˌsʌmθɪŋ] Anklage gegen jmdn. erheben, jmdm. etwas anlasten, jmdn. wegen etwas anklagen 178
charity ['tʃærɪtɪ] Wohltätigkeit, Wohltätigkeitszweck 33
checking account ['tʃekɪŋ əˌkaʊnt] Girokonto (AE) 189
chemicals ['kemɪklz] Chemikalien 20
chequebook ['tʃekbʊk] (BE) Scheckbuch, Scheckheft 33
to circulate ['sɜːkjəleɪt] verteilen 51
civil service [ˌsɪvl 'sɜːvɪs] öffentlicher Dienst, Beamtentum 27
claim [kleɪm] Behauptung, Anspruch 45
to claim [kleɪm] fordern, beanspruchen, verlangen, Anspruch erheben auf 72
to clarify ['klærɪfaɪ] klären 17
clean-room ['kliːnruːm] Reinraum 84
to clear a cheque [ˌklɪər‿ə 'tʃek] einen Scheck verrechnen 33
clerical ['klerɪkl] Büro-, Schreib-, (auf die Büroarbeit bezogen) 114
clerk [klɑːk] Angestellte(r), Sachbearbeiter(in) 26
closing date for applications ['kləʊzɪŋ ˌdeɪt fə ˌæplɪ'keɪʃnz] Bewerbungsschluss 117
closure ['kləʊʒə] Schließung, Geschäftsaufgabe, Betriebsstilllegung 22
closure ['kləʊʒə] Projektabschluss 125
co-founder [ˌkəʊ'faʊndə] Mitbegründer(in) 15
coin [kɔɪn] Münze 32
cold call ['kəʊld ˌkɔːl] Kaltanruf, unangemeldeter Anruf 68
to collaborate [kə'læbəreɪt] zusammenwirken, mitarbeiten, zusammenarbeiten, kollaborieren 201
collateral [kə'lætərəl] (dingliche) Sicherheit, Pfand 189
colleague ['kɒliːg] Kollege, Kollegin 9
collective bargaining [kəˌlektɪv 'bɑːgənɪŋ] Tarifverhandlungen 177
to command a price [kəˌmɑːnd ə 'praɪs] den Kurs bestimmen, einen Preis verlangen 207
commercial [kə'mɜːʃl] Werbespot 64
commercial invoice [kəˌmɜːʃl 'ɪnvɔɪs] Handelsrechnung 170
commission [kə'mɪʃn] Provision 37
to commission sb. [kə'mɪʃn ˌsʌmbədɪ] jmdn. beauftragen 123
commitment [kə'mɪtmənt] Verpflichtung 63
commodity [kə'mɒdətɪ] Handelsware, Handelsgut, Gebrauchsgut 45
common law [ˌkɒmən 'lɔː] Rechtssystem basierend auf dem Gewohnheitsrecht 177
common stock [ˌkɒmən 'stɒk] Stammaktie(n) (AE) 189
company law [ˌkʌmpənɪ 'lɔː] Gesellschaftsrecht 176
comparative advertising [kəmˌpærətɪv 'ædvətaɪzɪŋ] vergleichende Werbung 177
to compensate ['kɒmpənseɪt] entschädigen, erstatten, vergüten, ausgleichen 181
compensation [ˌkɒmpən'seɪʃn] Entschädigung, Schadenersatz 35
competition [ˌkɒmpə'tɪʃn] Wettbewerb, Konkurrenz 45
competition law [ˌkɒmpə'tɪʃn ˌlɔː] Kartellrecht, Wettbewerbsrecht 177
competitive [kəm'petɪtɪv] konkurrenzfähig, wettbewerbsfähig 95
competitive advantage [kəmˌpetɪtɪv əd'vɑːntɪdʒ] Wettbewerbsvorteil 207
competitive edge [kəmˌpetətɪv 'edʒ] Wettbewerbsvorteil 86
competitive environment [kəmˌpetətɪv ɪn'vaɪərənmənt] Wettbewerbsumfeld 138
competitively-priced [kəmˌpetətɪvlɪ'praɪst] zu einem konkurrenzfähigen Preis 48
competitive strategy [kəmˌpetɪtɪv 'strætədʒɪ] Wettbewerbsstrategie 207
competitor [kəm'petɪtə] Konkurrent(in), Wettbewerbsteilnehmer(in) 22
to complain (about) [kəm'pleɪn] sich beschweren (über), etwas beanstanden, reklamieren, klagen 136
complaint [kəm'pleɪnt] Beschwerde, Reklamation 71
compliance [kəm'plaɪəns] Einhaltung, Konformität, Erfüllung, Übereinstimmung 138
complimentary [ˌkɒmplɪ'mentrɪ] gratis, kostenlos 100
to comply with [kəm'plaɪ wɪð] einhalten, erfüllen, übereinstimmen mit 38
component [kəm'pəʊnənt] Komponent, Bestandteil, Bauteil 24
to conceal [kən'siːl] verheimlichen, wegstecken, nicht bekannt geben 194
to concede [kən'siːd] abgeben (Punkte), einräumen, erlauben 185
concession [kən'seʃn] Entgegenkommen 41
concise [kən'saɪs] kurz und bündig, präzise 144
to conclude an agreement [kənˌkluːd ən ə'griːmənt] eine Vereinbarung schließen, einen Vertrag abschließen 181
conclusion [kən'kluːʒn] Schlussfolgerung 68
to conduct ['kɒndʌkt] durchführen 54
confidence ['kɒnfɪdəns] Selbstvertrauen, Vertrauen 16
confident ['kɒnfɪdənt] selbstsicher 10
confidentiality [ˌkɒnfɪdenʃɪ'ælətɪ] Vertraulichkeit 170
to confirm [kən'fɜːm] bestätigen 9
conformity to specifications [kənˌfɔːmətɪ tʊ ˌspesɪfɪ'keɪʃnz] Anfertigung nach genauen technischen Angaben 139
conglomerate merger [kənˌglɒmərət 'mɜːdʒə] Mischkonzern, konglomerater Zusammenschluss 202

consensus [kən'sensəs] Übereinstimmung, allgemeine Meinung 52
consignee [ˌkɒnsaɪ'niː] Empfänger (einer Warensendung) 170
consignment [kən'saɪnmənt] Lieferung, (Waren)Sendung, Versendung 80
consignment note [kən'saɪnmənt ˌnəʊt] Frachtbrief, Ladeschein 170
consignor [kən'saɪnə] Versender (einer Warensendung) 170
consistent [kən'sɪstənt] einheitlich, durchgängig, übereinstimmend, konsequent 134
consolidated shipment [kənˌsɒlɪdeɪtɪd 'ʃɪpmənt] Sammelladung, Sammeltransport 77
consortium [kən'sɔːtɪəm] Unternehmensgruppe, Syndikat, Konsortium 202
constraint [kən'streɪnt] Beschränkung, Grenze 125
construction project [kən'strʌkʃn ˌprɒdʒekt] Bauprojekt, Baumaßnahme 125
consular invoice [ˌkɒnsjələr‿'ɪnvɔɪs] Konsulatsfaktura 170
consultation [ˌkɒnsəl'teɪʃn] Beratung, Beratungssitzung 177
consulting [kən'sʌltɪŋ] Unternehmensberatung 21
consumer [kən'sjuːmə] Verbraucher(in), Konsument(in) 20
consumer durables [kənˌsjuːmə 'djʊərəblz] dauerhafte Konsumgüter, langlebige Konsumgüter 45
consumer electronics [kənˌsjuːmər‿ɪlek'trɒnɪks] Unterhaltungselektronik 20
consumer habits [kənˌsjuːmə 'hæbɪts] Verbrauchergewohnheiten 95
consumer price index (CPI) [kəmˌsjuːmə 'praɪs ˌɪndeks, ˌsiːpiː'aɪ] Lebenshaltungskostenindex 148
consumer protection law [kənˌsjuːmə prə'tekʃn ˌlɔː] Verbraucherschutzgesetz 177
consumer rights [kənˌsjuːmə 'raɪts] Verbraucherrechte 145
consumption [kən'sʌmpʃn] Verbrauch 49
to contaminate [kən'tæmɪneɪt] kontaminieren, verseuchen 72
contamination [kənˌtæmɪ'neɪʃn] Verunreinigung, Verseuchung, Kontaminierung 90
to contend [kən'tend] vortragen (im Gerichtsverfahren), argumentieren 178
contingency [kən'tɪndʒənsɪ] Notfall, Eventualität 182
contingency plan [kən'tɪndʒənsɪ ˌplæn] Notfallplan 125
to contract [kən'trækt] schrumpfen, schwinden 152
contraction [kən'trækʃn] Schrumpfung, Rückgang (Konjunktur) 150
contractual [kən'træktʃʊəl] vertraglich, Vertrags- 27
contractual obligation [kənˌtræktʃʊəl ˌɒblɪ'geɪʃn] Vertragspflicht, vertragliche Verpflichtung 182
contractual relationship [kənˌtræktʃʊəl rɪ'leɪʃnʃɪp] Vertragsverhältnis 72
contractual requirements [kənˌtræktjʊəl rɪ'kwaɪəmənts] vertragliche Bestimmungen 125
contribution [ˌkɒntrɪ'bjuːʃn] Beitrag 35
controlling [kən'trəʊlɪŋ] Überwachung, Steuerung 125
controlling interest [kəmˌtrəʊlɪŋ 'ɪntrest] Mehrheitsbeteiligung 202
controversy ['kɒntrəvɜːsɪ] Kontroverse, Auseinandersetzung 18
convenience [kənˌvɪːnɪəns] Bequemlichkeit, Annehmlichkeit, Komfort 33
convenience store [kən'viːnɪəns‿ˌstɔː] Nachbarschaftsladen, Mini-Markt 21
convention centre [kən'venʃn ˌsentə] Konferenzzentrum 96
conventions [kən'venʃnz] Konventionen, Gepflogenheiten 12
conversion rate [kən'vɜːʃn ˌreɪt] Wechselkurs, Umrechnungskurs 37
to convert ['kɒnvɜːt] umbauen, umwandeln, umrechnen 89
cooperative [kəʊ'ɒprətɪv] Genossenschaft 23
copyright law ['kɒpɪraɪt ˌlɔː] Urheberrecht 154
copywriter ['kɒpɪˌraɪtə] Werbetexter(in) 60
core business [ˌkɔː 'bɪznɪs] Kerngeschäft 200
corporate client [ˌkɔːpərət 'klaɪənt] Firmenkunde/ -kundin 62
corporate culture [ˌkɔːpərət 'kʌltʃə] Unternehmenskultur 18
corporate social responsibility [ˌkɔːpərət ˌsəʊʃl rɪˌspɒnsə'bɪlɪtɪ] soziale Verantwortung des Unternehmens 207
corporate tax ['kɔːpərət‿ˌtæks] Körperschaftssteuer 194
corporation [ˌkɔːpər'eɪʃn] großes Unternehmen 39
to correspond to [ˌkɒrɪ'spɒnd‿tuː] entsprechen, zu etwas passen 70
to cost a fortune [ˌkɒst ə 'fɔːtʃuːn] ein Vermögen kosten 148
cost-conscious [ˌkɒst'kɒnʃəs] kostenbewusst 211
cost-cutting ['kɒstˌkʌtɪŋ] Kostensenkungen, Kosteneinsparung, Einsparungsmaßnahme 202
cost, insurance and freight (CIF) [ˌkɒst ɪnˌʃɔːrəns‿ən 'freɪt, ˌsiːaɪ'ef] Kosten, Versicherung, Fracht 170
cost of living [ˌkɒst‿əv 'lɪvɪŋ] Lebenshaltungskosten 148
cost-plus [ˌkɒst'plʌs] mit Kostenaufschlag 190
cottage industry [ˌkɒtɪdʒ 'ɪndəstrɪ] Heimindustrie 85
council ['kaʊnsəl] Gemeinderat 66
to counsel ['kaʊnsəl] beraten, Rat erteilen 114
counter ['kaʊntə] Theke 33
counterfeit ['kaʊntəfɪt] gefälscht, nachgemacht 75
countersuit ['kaʊntəsuːt] Gegenklage 178
country of destination [ˌkʌntrɪ‿əv ˌdestɪ'neɪʃn] Bestimmungsland 170
courier ['kʊrɪə] Kurier, Eilbote, Kurierdienst 77
court case ['kɔːt ˌkeɪs] Gerichtsfall, Prozess 91
courteous ['kɜːtɪəs] höflich 12
court order [ˌkɔːt 'ɔːdə] Anordnung, Gerichtsbeschluss, gerichtliche Mahnung 179
covering letter ['kʌvərɪŋ ˌletə] Begleitschreiben, Bewerbungsschreiben 117
craft [krɑːft] Handwerk 85
to craft [krɑːft] (von Hand) fertigen, (kunsthandwerklich) gestalten 21
craftsman, pl. craftsmen ['krɑːftsmən] Handwerker 68
crate [kreɪt] Lattenkiste 78
to create an alliance [krɪˌeɪt ən ə'laɪəns] ein Bündnis schmieden, sich mit jmdm. verbünden 174
credit crunch ['kredɪt ˌkrʌntʃ] Finanzkrise 96
creditor ['kredɪtə] Gläubiger(in), Kreditgeber(in), Kreditor(in) 189
creditors ['kredɪtəz] Verbindlichkeiten, Kreditoren, Gläubiger 193
credit period ['kredɪt‿ˌpɪərɪəd] Kreditlaufzeit, Zahlungsziel 42
credit transfer ['kredɪt‿ˌtrænsfɜː] Überweisung 32
creditworthiness ['kredɪtˌwɜːðɪnəs] Kreditwürdigkeit, Bonität, Zahlungsfähigkeit 35
creditworthy ['kredɪtˌwɜːðɪ] kreditwürdig 35
critical path [ˌkrɪtɪkl 'pɑːθ] kritischer Pfad 126
cross-border merger [ˌkrɒsbɔːdə 'mɜːdʒə] grenzüberschreitender (internationaler) Zusammenschluss 202
crude oil [ˌkruːd 'ɔɪl] Erdöl, Rohöl 48
culture clash ['kʌltʃə ˌklæʃ] Aufeinanderprallen der Kulturen, interkulturelle Konflikte 202
to curb [kɜːb] reduzieren (z. B. Kosten) 150
currency ['kʌrənsɪ] Währung 36
currency exchange [ˌkʌrənsɪ‿ɪks'tʃeɪndʒ] Geldumtausch 100
currency trading ['kʌrənsɪ ˌtreɪdɪŋ] Devisenhandel 189
current account balance [ˌkʌrənt ə'kaʊnt‿ˌbæləns] Leistungsbilanz 148
current account [ˌkʌrənt ə'kaʊnt] (BE) Girokonto 35

current assets [ˌkʌrənt 'æsets] Umlaufvermögen 193
current liabilities [ˌkʌrənt ˌlaɪə'bɪlətɪz] kurzfristige Verbindlichkeiten 193
customer focus [ˌkʌstəmə 'fəʊkəs] Kundenorientierung 204
customer relations [ˌkʌstəmə rɪ'leɪʃnz] Kundendienst 24
customer requirements [ˌkʌstəmə rɪ'kwaɪəmənts] Kundenanforderungen 86
customer satisfaction [ˌkʌstəmə ˌsætɪs'fækʃn] Kundenzufriedenheit, Zufriedenstellung der Kunden 136
customs clearance [ˌkʌstəmz 'klɪərəns] Zollabfertigung 170
customs declaration ['kʌstəmz dekləˌreɪʃn] Zollerklärung 170
customs duty ['kʌstəmz ˌdju:tɪ] Zoll 170
to cut one's losses [ˌkʌt wʌnz 'lɒsɪz] seinen Schaden/seine Verluste begrenzen 191
cut-price [ˌkʌt‿'praɪs] Billig- 211
curriculum vitae [kəˌrɪkjələm'vi:taɪ] Lebenslauf 118
CV (Curriculum Vitae) [ˌsi:'vi:, kəˌrɪkjələm'vi:taɪ] Lebenslauf 30
CWO (cash with order) [ˌsi:ˌdʌblju:'əʊ, ˌkæʃ wɪð 'ɔ:də] Zahlung bei Auftragserteilung 77

D

damages ['dæmɪdʒɪz] Schadenersatz 178
database ['deɪtəbeɪs] Datenbank 86
data protection [ˌdeɪtə prə'tekʃn] Datenschutz 177
dawn raid [ˌdɔ:n 'reɪd] plötzlicher Aufkauf von Aktien (bei Übernahme), aggressives Überraschungsmanöver 202
day-to-day business [ˌdeɪtədeɪ 'bɪznɪs] Tagesgeschäft, laufender Geschäftsverkehr 202
DDP (delivered, duty paid) [ˌdi:di:'pi:, dɪˌlɪvəd‿dju:tɪ 'peɪd] frei Haus, verzollt geliefert 80
deadline ['dedlaɪn] Termin, Frist 60
to meet a deadline [ˌmi:t ə 'dedlaɪn] eine Frist/einen Termin einhalten 13
deadlock ['dedlɒk] völliger Stillstand, Sackgasse 41
deal [dɪəl] Geschäft; Handel 41
debenture [dɪ'bentʃə] Firmenanleihe, Schuldverschreibung, Obligation 189
debit card ['debɪt‿kɑ:d] Kundenkarte, EC-Karte 32
debriefing [ˌdi:'bri:fɪŋ] Nachbesprechung, Besprechung nach dem Einsatz 135
debt [det] Schuld, Schulden 23
debt-equity ratio [ˌdet'ekwɪtɪ ˌreɪʃɪəʊ] Verschuldungsgrad, Verhältnis von Eigenkapital und Fremdkapital, Eigenkapitalüberdeckung 190
debtor ['detə] Forderung, Debitor, Schuldner 193
debt recovery [ˌdet rɪ'kʌvərɪ] Inkasso 35
debt securities ['det sɪˌkjʊərətɪz] Schuldobligationen, Darlehenssicherheiten (Wertpapiere) 189
decade ['dekeɪd] Jahrzehnt 21
decision tree [dɪ'sɪʒn ˌtri:] Entscheidungsbaum 136
decline [dɪ'klaɪn] Rückgang, Abnahme 150
to decline [dɪ'klaɪn] sinken, zurückgehen, fallen 152
to deduct [dɪ'dʌkt] abziehen 83
to deem [di:m] halten für, erachten als/für 181
defamatory [dɪ'fæmətərɪ] verleumderisch, übel nachredend 181
defaulted [dɪ'fɒltɪd] notleidend 166
to defeat a motion [dɪˌfi:t ə 'məʊʃn] einen Antrag ablehnen 185
defect ['di:fekt] Defekt, Fehler, Mangel 86
deficit spending [ˌdefɪsɪt 'spendɪŋ] öffentliche Verschuldung durch Geldaufnahme 155
to defraud [dɪ'frɔ:d] betrügen, hintergehen 33
degree [dɪ'gri:] Hochschulabschluss 114
delay in delivery [dɪˌleɪ ɪn dɪ'lɪvərɪ] Lieferverzug 81
delegate ['delɪgət] Konferenzteilnehmer(in), Abgeordnete(r), Abgesandte(r) 105
to delete [dɪ'li:t] löschen (Text), durchstreichen 180
to deliver [dɪ'lɪvə] liefern 9
deliverables [dɪ'lɪvrəblz] zu erledigende Aufgaben, Projektergebnisse 125
delivered, duty paid (DDP) [dɪˌlɪvəd‿dju:tɪ 'peɪd, ˌdi:di:'pi:] verzollt, geliefert 170
delivered ex ship/quay (DES/DEQ) [dɪˌlɪvəd ˌeks‿'ʃɪp/ˌeks 'ki:, ˌdi:i:'es/ˌdi:i:'kju:] Lieferung ab Schiff/Kai 170
delivery [dɪ'lɪvrɪ] Lieferung 38
delivery service [dɪ'lɪvərɪ ˌsɜ:vɪs] Lieferdienst, Zustelldienst 21
demand [dɪ'mɑ:nd] Nachfrage, Bedarf,Forderung, Anforderung, Anspruch, Verlangen 35
demanding [dɪ'mɑ:ndɪŋ] anspruchsvoll, wählerisch 45
demerger [ˌdi:'mɜ:dʒə] Entfusionierung, Spaltung (von Unternehmen) 202
demonstration [ˌdemən'streɪʃn] Vorführung, Demonstration 16
department [dɪ'pɑ:tmənt] Abteilung 14
departure [dɪ'pɑ:tʃə] Abflug 9
deposit [dɪ'pɒzɪt] Anzahlung 41
to deposit [dɪ'pɒzɪt] (Geld) einzahlen 36
depreciation [dɪˌpri:ʃɪ'eɪʃn] Abschreibung, Wertverlust 194
depression [dɪ'preʃn] lang anhaltende Rezession 150
derivative [dɪ'rɪvɪtɪv] Derivat, sekundäres Wertpapier 190
desalination plant [ˌdi:sælɪ'neɪʃn ˌplɑ:nt] Wasserentsalzungsanlage 204
desk research ['desk ˌri:sɜ:tʃ] Schreibtischforschung, Sekundärforschung 63
destination [ˌdestɪ'neɪʃn] Ziel, Bestimmungsort 77
to deteriorate [dɪ'tɪərɪəreɪt] sich verschlechtern 152
development aid [dɪ'veləpmənt ˌeɪd] Entwicklungshilfe 174
device [dɪ'vaɪs] Gerät 15
digital projector [ˌdɪdʒɪtl prə'dʒektə] Beamer 11
to dip [dɪp] (sich) senken, abfallen 152
direct debit [daɪˌrekt‿'debɪt] Lastschrift, Bankeinzug, Einzugsermächtigung 32
directive [daɪ'rektɪv, dɪ'rektɪv] (EU-) Richtlinie 115
director [daɪ'rektə] Geschäftsführer(in) 43
disability allowance [ˌdɪsə'bɪlətɪ‿əˌlaʊəns] Beihilfe für Erwerbsunfähige 35
disabled [dɪ'seɪbld] behindert 183
disciplinary procedure [ˌdɪsɪplɪnərɪ prə'si:dʒə] Disziplinarverfahren 114
to disclose [dɪs'kləʊz] offenlegen, veröffentlichen, (Information) weitergeben 181
discount ['dɪskaʊnt] Rabatt, Skonto, Preisnachlass 79
discount price ['dɪskaʊnt ˌpraɪs] Rabattpreis 21
discrepancy [dɪ'skrepənsɪ] Unstimmigkeit, Abweichung, Diskrepanz, Widersprüchlichkeit 180
discretion [dɪ'skreʃn] Ermessen 181
to dishonour [dɪ'sɒnə] nicht einlösen (Wechsel), platzen lassen (Scheck) 167
dishwasher ['dɪʃˌwɒʃə] Spülmaschine 21
to dismiss [dɪ'smɪs] entlassen 116
to dismiss a claim [dɪˌsmɪs ə 'kleɪm] eine Klage abweisen 178
dispatch [dɪ'spætʃ] Versand 80
to dispatch [dɪ'spætʃ] versenden, verschicken 169
disposable [dɪ'spəʊzəbl] Einweg- 138
disposable income [dɪˌspəʊzəbl 'ɪnkʌm] verfügbares Einkommen 148
to dispose of [dɪ'spəʊz ɒv] entsorgen, veräußern, verkaufen, loswerden, über etwas verfügen 193
dispute ['dɪspju:t] Streit, Streitfall, Auseinandersetzung, Disput 75

dispute settlement [ˈdɪspjuːt ˌsetlmənt] Streitschlichtung, Beilegung eines Streits 174
to distribute [dɪˈstrɪbjuːt] verteilen, austeilen 187
distribution [ˌdɪstrɪˈbjuːʃn] Vertrieb, Verteilung 24
distribution chain [ˌdɪstrɪˈbjuːʃn ˌtʃeɪn] Absatzkette, Verteilerkette 74
distribution channel [ˌdɪstrɪˈbjuːʃn ˌtʃænl] Vertriebskanal, Absatzweg 61
distributor [dɪˈstrɪbjətə] Lieferant, Händler, Vertragshändler, Vertreiber 75
distributorship agreement [dɪˈstrɪbjətəʃɪp əˌgriːmənt] Vertriebsvertrag, Alleinvertriebsvertrag 165
diversification [daɪˌvɜːsɪfɪˈkeɪʃn] Diversifizierung, Erweiterung der Produktpalette, Ausweitung des Sortiments 47
to diversify [daɪˈvɜːsɪfaɪ] diversifizieren, verschiedenartig gestalten 45
dividend [ˈdɪvɪdend] Dividende, Gewinnanteil 189
division [dɪˈvɪʒn] Geschäftsbereich, Abteilung 24
division of labour [dɪˌvɪʒn‿əv ˈleɪbə] Arbeitsteilung 119
docks [dɒks] Hafen 170
documents against acceptance (D/A) [ˌdɒkjəmənts əˌgenst ækˈseptəns] Dokumente gegen Akzept 167
documents against payment (D/P) [ˌdɒkjəmənts əˌgenst ˈpeɪmənt] Dokumente gegen Zahlung, Zahlung gegen Dokumente, Kasse gegen Dokumente 167
dodgy [ˈdɒdʒɪ] heikel, riskant, windig, unzuverlässig 188
domestic [dəˈmestɪk] Binnen- 95
domestic trade [dəˌmestɪk ˈtreɪd] Binnenhandel, inländischer Handel 164
to donate [dəʊˈneɪt] spenden 33
donation [dəʊˈneɪʃn] Spende 39
door-to-door salesman [ˌdɔːtədɔː ˈseɪlzmən] Vertreter(in) 11
dormant [ˈdɔːmənt] nicht aktiv 203
double-taxation agreement [ˌdʌbltækˈseɪʃn əˌgriːmənt] Doppelbesteuerungsabkommen 194
downtime [ˈdaʊntaɪm] Ausfallzeit, Produktionsunterbrechung 88
downturn [ˈdaʊntɜːn] Abschwung 94
draft [drɑːft] Entwurf 8
to draft [drɑːft] entwerfen, erstellen 75
drawback [ˈdrɔːbæk] Nachteil 202
to draw up [ˌdrɔː ˈʌp] entwerfen, zusammenstellen 51
to draw up a shortlist [ˌdrɔː‿ʌp ə ˈʃɔːtlɪst] eine engere Auswahl treffen 31
dress code [ˈdres ˌkəʊd] Kleiderordnung, Kleidervorschrift 18
drum [drʌm] Trommel 78
due [djuː] fällig 189
due diligence [ˌdjuː ˈdɪlɪdʒəns] Unternehmensbewertung, Kaufprüfung, Sorgfaltspflicht, gebührende Sorgfalt, detaillierte Untersuchung 202
duopoly [dʒʊˈɒpəlɪ] Duopol 178
durability [ˌdjʊərəˈbɪlətɪ] Haltbarkeit, Langlebigkeit, Lebensdauer 139
duration [djʊəˈreɪʃn] Dauer, Laufzeit 42

E

to earn [ɜːn] verdienen 34
earnings [ˈɜːnɪŋz] Einkommen, Einkünfte 33
earnings per share [ˌɜːnɪŋz pə ˈʃeə] Gewinn pro Aktie, Ergebnis je Aktie 193
economic [ˌiːkəˈnɒmɪk] wirtschaftlich, volkswirtschaftlich, ökonomisch 148
economical [ˌiːkəˈnɒmɪkl] sparsam, wirtschaftlich, ökonomisch, billig, sparsam im Verbrauch 48
economic output [ˌiːkənɒmɪk ˈaʊtpʊt] wirtschaftliche Ausbeute 94
economic situation [ˌiːkənɒmɪk sɪtjʊˈeɪʃn] Wirtschaftslage 95
economic slowdown [ˌiːkənɒmɪk ˈsləʊdaʊn] Konjunkturabschwung, Konjunkturflaute 150
economies [ɪˈkɒnəmɪz] Ersparnisse 149
economies of scale [ɪˌkɒnəmɪz‿əv ˈskeɪl] Betriebsgrößenersparnisse, Kostenersparnis durch Massenproduktion, Skaleneffekte, Größenvorteile 202
to economise (on) [ɪˈkɒnəmaɪz] einsparen (bei) 149
economist [ɪˈkɒnəmɪst] Wirtschaftswissenschaftler(in) 149
economy [ɪˈkɒnəmɪ] Wirtschaft 94
edge [edʒ] Vorsprung 138
edge over one's competitors [ˈedʒ ˌəʊvə wʌnz kəmˈpetɪtəz] Wettbewerbsvorteil 138
to edit [ˈedɪt] (redaktionell) bearbeiten, überarbeiten, editieren 135
effective upon [ɪˈfektɪv əˌpɒn] gültig ab, mit Wirkung ab 181
effluence [ˈeflʊəns] Ausfluss 187
eligibility [ˌelɪdʒəˈbɪlətɪ] Teilnahmeberechtigung 181
to embark on a strategy [ɪmˌbɑːk ɒn‿ə ˈstrætədʒɪ] eine Strategie verfolgen 172
emergency meeting [ɪˌmɜːdʒənsɪ ˈmiːtɪŋ] Notsitzung 176
emerging market [ɪˌmɜːdʒɪŋ ˈmɑːkɪt] Schwellenmarkt 22
to employ [ɪmˈplɔɪ] beschäftigen, einstellen 21
employee [ɪmˈplɔɪiː] Angestellte(r), Arbeitnehmer(in) 32
employer [ɪmˈplɔɪə] Arbeitgeber(in) 114
employment contract [ɪmˈplɔɪmənt ˌkɒntrækt] Arbeitsvertrag 72
employment law [ɪmˈplɔɪmənt ˌlɔː] Arbeitsrecht 114
employment tribunal [ɪmˈplɔɪmənt‿traɪˌbjuːnl] Arbeitsgericht 120
to empower [ɪmˈpaʊə] bevollmächtigen, berechtigen 18
Enc. [ɪnˈkləʊʒə, ɪnˈkləʊzd] Anlage 12
to enclose [ɪnˈkləʊz] beifügen, beilegen 12
enclosed [ɪnˈkləʊzd] anbei, beigefügt, in der Anlage 80
to encourage [ɪnˈkʌrɪdʒ] fördern, ermutigen 10
endorsement [ɪnˈdɔːsmənt] Empfehlung, Werbung 64
energy efficient [ˌenədʒɪ‿ɪˈfɪʃənt] kraftsparend, energiesparend 87
enforcement [ɪnˈfɔːsmənt] Durchsetzung, Durchführung 18
engineering [ˌendʒɪˈnɪərɪŋ] Maschinenbau, Technik 20
enquiry [ɪnˈkwaɪərɪ] Anfrage 11
to ensure [ɪnˈʃɔː] gewährleisten, sicherstellen, garantieren, sichergehen, (ver)sichern 60
to enter into a contract [ˌentə ˌɪntʊ‿ə ˈkɒntrækt] einen Vertrag abschließen 180
enterprise [ˈentəpraɪz] Unternehmen, Unternehmung, Vorhaben 39
to enter a market [ˌentə ə ˈmɑːkɪt] einen neuen Markt erschließen 47
entitled [ɪnˈtaɪtld] berechtigt 182
entitlement [ɪnˈtaɪtlmənt] Anspruch, Berechtigung 35
entrants [ˈentrənts] Bewerber, Einsteiger 205
entrepreneur [ˌɒntrəprəˈnɜː] Unternehmer(in), Existenzgründer(in) 21
entrepreneurial [ˌɒntrəprəˈnɜːrɪəl] unternehmerisch 27
entry requirements [ˈentrɪ rɪˌkwaɪəmənts] Zugangsvoraussetzungen 114
environment [ɪnˈvaɪərənmənt] Umwelt, Umfeld 10
environmental damage [ɪnˌvaɪərənmentl ˈdæmɪdʒ] Umweltschäden 187
environmental liability [ɪnˌvaɪərənmentl‿laɪəˈbɪlətɪ] Umwelthaftung 176
environmentally-friendly [ɪnˌvaɪərənˌmentəlɪ ˈfrendlɪ] umweltfreundlich 29
equal opportunities [ˌiːkwəl ɒpəˈtjuːnətɪz] Chancengleichheit 114
equation [ɪˈkweɪʒn] Gleichung, Ausgleich 35

equipment [ɪ'kwɪpmənt] Ausrüstung, Ausstattung 9
equity ['ekwɪtɪ] Eigenkapital 193
equity securities ['ekwɪtɪ sɪˌkjʊərətɪz] Aktienkapital 189
ergonomic [ˌɜ:gə'nɒmɪk] ergonomisch 8
to establish [ɪ'stæblɪʃ] gründen, feststellen, etablieren 22
establishment [ɪ'stæblɪʃmənt] Einrichtung, Gründung 22
etiquette ['etɪket] Benimmregeln, Umgangsformen im Geschäftsleben 106
to evaluate [ɪ'væljʊeɪt] evaluieren, bewerten 68
eventually [ɪ'ventʃʊəlɪ] schließlich 10
evidence ['evɪdəns] Beweis, Nachweis, Beleg 95
to exceed [ɪk'si:d] überschreiten, übertreffen, größer sein als 102
exchange [ɪks'tʃeɪndʒ] Umtausch, Austausch 79
exchange controls [ɪks'tʃeɪndʒ kənˌtrəʊlz] Devisenbestimmungen 170
exchange rate [ɪks'tʃeɪndʒ ˌreɪt] Wechselkurs, Umrechnungskurs, Kurs 36
excise tax ['eksaɪz ˌtæks] Verbrauchssteuer 194
exclusivity [ˌeksklu:'sɪvətɪ] Ausschließlichkeit, Ausschließlichkeitsklausel (im Vertrag) 170
exclusivity deal [ˌeksklu:'sɪvətɪ ˌdɪəl] Alleinvertriebsklausel 75
to execute ['eksɪkju:t] ausführen, durchführen 118
execution [ˌeksɪ'kju:ʃn] Durchführung, Ausführung, Umsetzung 135
executive board [ɪg'zekjətɪv ˌbɔ:d] Vorstand 24
exhibition [ˌeksɪ'bɪʃn] Ausstellung 104
exit strategy ['egzɪt ˌstrætədʒɪ] Ausstiegsstrategie 211
expenditure [ɪk'spendɪtʃə] (Kosten)Aufwand, Ausgaben 34
expense [ɪk'spens] Kosten, Aufwand 35
expense account [ɪk'spens əˌkaʊnt] Spesenkonto 201
expenses [ɪk'spensɪz] Auslagen, Ausgaben, (Reise)Kosten, Spesen 96
to incur expenses [ɪnˌkɜ:‿ɪk'spensɪz] Auslagen machen 72
expertise [ˌekspɜ:'ti:z] Fachkenntnisse, Fachwissen 68
to exploit [ɪk'splɔɪt] Kapital schlagen aus, ausbeuten, ausnutzen 73
export ban ['ekspɔ:t‿bæn] Ausfuhrsperre, Embargo 170
export credit insurance [ˌekspɔ:t 'kredɪt ɪnˌʃɔ:rəns] Exportkreditversicherung 167
to extend [ɪk'stend] verlängern 180
extension [ɪk'stenʃn] Durchwahl 16
extension of credit [ɪkˌstenʃn‿əv 'kredɪt] Verlängerung des Kredits 35
extraction [ɪk'strækʃn] Gewinnung, Förderung 20
extraordinary circumstances [ɪkˌstrɔ:dənrɪ 'sɜ:kəmstænsɪz] außergewöhnliche Umstände 182
ex works (EXW) [ˌeks 'wɜ:ks] ab Werk 170

F

face-to-face contact [ˌfeɪstəfeɪs 'kɒntækt] persönlicher Kontakt 20
facial expression [ˌfeɪʃl ɪk'spreʃn] Gesichtsausdruck 11
facilitator [fə'sɪlɪteɪtə] Moderator(in), Prozessbegleiter(in) 131
facilities [fə'sɪlətɪz] Einrichtungen, Ausstattung, technische Hilfsmittel 61
factory ['fæktrɪ] Fabrik 50
factory outlet [ˌfæktrɪ‿'aʊtlet] Direktverkauf, Fabrikverkauf 72
factual ['fæktʃʊəl] Sach-, sachlich 144
failure ['feɪljə] Versagen, Misserfolg, Unterlassung 50
failure rate ['feɪljə ˌreɪt] Durchfallquote, Abbruchquote 202
fair [feə] (Handels)Messe, Markt 68
fair trade [ˌfeə 'treɪd] fairer Handel, Freihandel, lauterer Wettbewerb 55
to fall behind schedule [ˌfɔ:l bɪˌhaɪnd 'ʃedju:l] in Verzug geraten, im Rückstand sein 128
to fall due [fɔ:l 'dju:] fällig werden 193
false economy [ˌfɒls ɪ'kɒnəmɪ] das Sparen am falschen Platz 97
family status [ˌfæmɪlɪ 'steɪtəs] Familienstand 68
fare [feə] Fahrpreis, Fahrgeld 37
fast-moving consumer goods [ˌfa:stmu:vɪŋ kənˌsju:mə 'gʊdz] kurzlebige Verbrauchsgüter 45
fast-tracking [ˌfa:st‿'trækɪŋ] Überlappen von Vorgängen 125
faulty ['fɒltɪ, 'fɔ:ltɪ] fehlerhaft, defekt 140
feasibility [ˌfi:zə'bɪlətɪ] Durchführbarkeit, Machbarkeit 55
feasibility study [ˌfi:zə'bɪlətɪ ˌstʌdɪ] Durchführbarkeitsstudie, Machbarkeitsstudie 125
feasible ['fi:zəbl] durchführbar, machbar, praktikabel 125
feature ['fi:tʃə] Eigenschaft, Merkmal, Besonderheit 15
to feature ['fi:tʃə] aufweisen, sich auszeichnen durch, etw. groß herausbringen 71
federal ['fedərəl] Bundes- 142
fee [fi:] Gebühr 37
ferry ['ferɪ] Fähre 76
field research ['fi:ld ˌri:sɜ:tʃ] Feldforschung, primäre Erhebung 68
to file a lawsuit [ˌfaɪl ə 'lɔ:su:t] eine Klage einreichen 178
to file a tax return [ˌfaɪl ə 'tæks rɪˌtɜ:n] die Steuererklärung einreichen/abgeben 194
to file a complaint [ˌfaɪl ə kəm'pleɪnt] eine Beschwerde einreichen 79
file-sharing ['faɪlˌʃeərɪŋ] gemeinsamer Dateizugriff, Datentausch 72
to finalise ['faɪnəlaɪz] erledigen, beenden 8
findings ['faɪndɪŋz] Ergebnisse, Befunde 54
finished products [ˌfɪnɪʃt 'prɒdʌkts] Fertigwaren 87
fisheries ['fɪʃərɪz] Fischerei 20
fitness for purpose [ˌfɪtnəs fə 'pɜ:pəs] Eignung für eine besondere Verwendung 139
fitness for use [ˌfɪtnəs fə 'ju:s] Gebrauchstauglichkeit, einsatzgerechte Eignung 138
fittings ['fɪtɪŋz] Beschläge, Armaturen, Montagen 53
fixed assets [ˌfɪkst 'æsets] Anlagevermögen 193
fixed-interest deposit [ˌfɪkstˌɪntrəst‿dɪ'pɒzɪt] festverzinsliches Wertpapier, Festgeld 189
flotation [fləʊ'teɪʃn] Börsengang, Emission 23
to flourish ['flʌrɪʃ] blühen, florieren, großen Erfolg haben 22
fluctuation [ˌflʌktʃʊ'eɪʃn] Schwankung 150
fluency ['flu:ənsɪ] Sprachgewandtheit 16
flyer ['flaɪə] Flugblatt, Handzettel 187
FMCG [ˌefemsi:'dʒi:] kurzlebige Konsumgüter 45
focus group ['fəʊkəs ˌgru:p] Fokusgruppe, Gesprächsgruppe 68
font [fɒnt] Schriftart 96
forecast ['fɔ:ka:st] Vorhersage, Prognose 126
to forecast ['fɔ:ka:st] prognostizieren, vorhersagen, schätzen, voraussagen 125
foreign direct investment (FDI) [ˌfɒrən daɪˌrekt ɪn'vestmənt ˌefdi:'aɪ] ausländische Direktinvestition(en) 148
foreman ['fɔ:mən] Vorarbeiter 85
to forge [fɔ:dʒ] fälschen 154
forklift ['fɔ:klɪft] Gabelstapler 84
formula, pl. formulae ['fɔ:mjələ, 'fɔ:mjəlaɪ] Formel 10
fortune ['fɔ:tʃu:n] Vermögen 39
to forward ['fɔ:wəd] weiterleiten 186
forwarding agency ['fɔ:wədɪŋ ˌeɪdʒənsɪ] Spedition 170
to found [faʊnd] gründen 183
foundation [faʊn'deɪʃn] Stiftung 39
founder ['faʊndə] Gründer(in) 61

fragile ['frædʒaɪl] zerbrechlich, bruchanfällig 68
franchisee [ˌfræntʃaɪ'zi:] Franchisenehmer, Konzessionsnehmer 21
franchising company ['fræntʃaɪzɪŋ ˌkʌmpənɪ] Franchisegeber 21
fraud [frɔ:d] Betrug 33
free alongside ship (FAS) [ˌfri:‿əˌlɒŋsaɪd 'ʃɪp, ˌefeɪ'es] frei Längsseite Schiff 170
freebie ['fri:bɪ] Werbegeschenk 97
freelancer ['fri:lɑ:nsə] Freiberufler(in), freie(r) Mitarbeiter(in) 21
free on board (FOB) [ˌfri:‿ɒn 'bɔ:d, ˌefəʊ'bi:] frei an Bord 170
free trade deal [ˌfri: 'treɪd‿di:l] Freihandelsabkommen 174
freezer ['fri:zə] Tiefkühlschrank, Tiefkühltruhe 21
freight forwarder [ˌfreɪt 'fɔ:wədə] Spedition 170
freight train ['freɪt‿treɪn] Güterzug 76
friendly takeover [ˌfrendlɪ 'teɪkˌəʊvə] freundliche Übernahme 202
fuel [fjʊəl] Treibstoff, Brennstoff, Kraftstoff, Benzin 49
fuel tax ['fjʊəl ˌtæks] Benzinsteuer, Mineralölsteuer 194
functionality [ˌfʌŋkʃn'ælətɪ] Funktionalität, Zweckmäßigkeit 139
furnishings ['fɜ:nɪʃɪŋz] Einrichtungen, Mobiliar, Ausstattung 20
futures ['fju:tʃəz] Termingeschäfte, Terminpapiere 191

G

gadget ['gædʒɪt] Gerät, technische Spielerei, technische Vorrichtung 96
gadgetry ['gædʒɪtrɪ] Geräte, Schnickschnack 15
to gamble ['gæmbl] (Glücksspiele) spielen 188
gambling ['gæmblɪŋ] Spekulation, Spielen 190
Gantt chart ['gænt‿tʃɑ:t] Gantt-Diagramm 126
gearing ['gɪərɪŋ] Verschuldungsgrad, Verhältnis von Eigenkapital und Fremdkapital 191
generic [dʒə'nerɪk] generisch, allgemein, exemplarisch 207
generous ['dʒenərəs] großzügig 53
genuine ['dʒenjʊɪn] echt 41
to be/get delayed [bɪ/get‿dɪ'leɪd] sich verspäten, sich verzögern 68
to get into debt [get ˌɪntʊ 'det] sich verschulden 35
to get sth. back on track [get ˌsʌmθɪŋ ˌbæk ɒn 'træk] etw. wieder auf Kurs bringen 128
gimmick ['gɪmɪk] Aufhänger, Gag, ausgefallene Idee, technischer Schnickschnack 69
to give a 'high five' [gɪv ə ˌhaɪ'faɪv] abklatschen 11
to give someone (his/her) notice [gɪv ˌsʌmwʌn (ˌhɪz/ˌhɜ:) 'nəʊtɪs] jmdm. die Kündigung aussprechen, kündigen 116
to give the go-ahead (for sth.) [ˌgɪv ðə 'gəʊəhed] das grüne Licht geben (für etwas), freie Fahrt geben 210
goal-oriented [ˌgəʊl'ɔ:rɪentɪd] zielorientiert 206
to go bankrupt ['bæŋkrʌpt] Bankrott gehen, in Konkurs gehen, Pleite gehen 148
going rate [ˌgəʊɪŋ 'reɪt] aktueller Preis 191
Goods Inwards [ˌgʊdz 'ɪnwədz] Wareneingang 72
goodwill [gʊd'wɪl] Firmenwert, immaterieller Firmenwert, Goodwill 193
to go on sale [ˌgəʊ‿ɒn 'seɪl] in den Handel kommen, in den Verkauf kommen 178
to go out of business [ˌgəʊ‿aʊt əv 'bɪznɪs] das Geschäft aufgeben, Betrieb einstellen 138
to go public [gəʊ 'pʌblɪk] an die Börse gehen 199
gossip 'around the water cooler' [ˌgɒsɪp əˌraʊnd‿ðə 'wɔ:tə ˌku:lə] Kaffeeküchenklatsch 11
graduate ['grædʒʊət] Hochschulabsolvent(in) 10
to graduate ['grædʒʊeɪt] den Schul- oder Hochschulabschluss machen 89
grain [greɪn] Getreide 48
grant [grɑ:nt] Stipendium, Zuschuss 35
to grant [grɑ:nt] gewähren, erteilen, einräumen 181
grapevine ['greɪpvaɪn] Flurfunk, Mundpropaganda 11
green shoots [ˌgri:n 'ʃu:ts] erste Anzeichen einer Erholung 154
grievance procedure [ˌgri:vəns prə'si:dʒə] Beschwerdeverfahren 114
grocery ['grəʊsərɪ] Lebensmittelgeschäft 21
grocery store ['grəʊsərɪ ˌstɔ:] Lebensmittelgeschäft 22
gross [grəʊs] Grob- 183
gross domestic product (GDP) [ˌgrəʊs dəˌmestɪk 'prɒdʌkt ˌdʒi:di:'pi:] Bruttoinlandsprodukt 148
gross margin [ˌgrəʊs 'mɑ:dʒɪn] Bruttohandelsspanne, Bruttogewinnspanne, Deckungsbeitrag 83
gross national product (GNP) [ˌgrəʊs ˌnæʃənl 'prɒdʌkt ˌdʒi:en'pi:] Bruttosozialprodukt 148
group [gru:p] Konzern 178
group financial report [ˌgru:p faɪˌnænʃl rɪ'pɔ:t] Finanzbericht des Konzerns 9
guarantee [ˌgærən'ti:] Garantie, Gewährleistung 79
guideline ['gaɪdlaɪn] Richtlinie 95

H

to haggle ['hægl] feilschen, handeln 40
to hand in one's notice [ˌhænd ɪn wʌnz 'nəʊtɪs] die Kündigung einreichen, kündigen 116
handling charges ['hændlɪŋ ˌtʃɑ:dʒɪz] Abladegebühren, Bearbeitungsgebühren 72
handling fee ['hændlɪŋ ˌfi:] Bearbeitungsgebühr 35
to hang on [hæŋ‿'ɒn] warten, am Apparat bleiben 142
to hang up [hæŋ‿'ʌp] den Telefonhörer auflegen 123
harbour ['hɑ:bə] Hafen 76
haulage company ['hɔ:lɪdʒ ˌkʌmpənɪ] Logistikunternehmen 77
haulier ['hɔ:lɪə] Transportunternehmer, Spediteur 77
hazard ['hæzəd] Gefahr, Risiko 142
hazardous ['hæzədəs] gefährlich 76
hazard warning sign [ˌhæzəd 'wɔ:nɪŋ ˌsaɪn] Warnzeichen 90
headhunter ['hedˌhʌntə] Personalabwerber, 'Kopfjäger' 116
head office [ˌhed 'ɒfɪs] Hauptbüro, Hauptgeschäftstellen, Hauptsitz, Firmenzentrale 127
headquarters [ˌhed'kwɔ:təz] Hauptgeschäftsstelle, Firmenzentrale 9
head of department [ˌhed‿əv dɪ'pɑ:tmənt] Abteilungsleiter(in) 9
health and safety officer [ˌhelθən'seɪftɪ‿ɒfɪsə] Arbeitsschutzbeauftragte(r) 85
health and safety regulations [ˌhelθ‿ən 'seɪftɪ ˌregjə'leɪʃnz] Arbeitsschutzvorschriften 8
healthcare ['helθkeə] Gesundheitsversorgung, Gesundheitswesen 20
health insurance ['helθ ɪnˌʃɔ:rəns] Krankenversicherung 141
hedging ['hedʒɪŋ] Absicherung mit Deckungsgeschäften, Hedging 190
hidden economy [ˌhɪdn ɪ'kɒnəmɪ] Schattenwirtschaft 148
hierarchical [ˌhaɪə'rɑ:kɪkl] hierarchisch 26
hierarchy ['haɪərɑ:kɪ] Hierarchie 19
to hire [haɪə] einstellen 10
hire car [ˌhaɪə 'kɑ:] Mietwagen 9
hire purchase [ˌhaɪə 'pɜ:tʃɪs] Mietkauf, Ratenkauf 190
hiring freeze ['haɪərɪŋ ˌfri:z] Einstellungssperre 116
to hold [həʊld] am Apparat bleiben 16
to hold a meeting [ˌhəʊld ə 'mi:tɪŋ] eine Konferenz/Sitzung abhalten, tagen 52
holding company ['həʊldɪŋ ˌkʌmpənɪ] Holdinggesellschaft, Dachgesellschaft, Unternehmensbeteiligungsgesellschaft 23
hold-up ['həʊldʌp] Engpass, Verzögerung 68

to hold one's own [ˌhəʊld wʌnz ˈəʊn] sich behaupten, standhalten 146

horizontal merger [ˌhɒrɪzɒntəl ˈmɜːdʒə] horizontaler Zusammenschluss 202

hostile takeover [ˌhɒstaɪl ˈteɪkˌəʊvə] feindliche Übernahme 202

household appliance [ˌhaʊshəʊld əˈplaɪəns] Haushaltsgerät 21

household goods [ˌhaʊshəʊld‿ˈgʊdz] Hausrat, Haushaltswaren 20

household insurance [ˈhaʊshəʊld ɪnˌʃɔːrəns] Hausratversicherung 141

HR (Human Resources) manager [ˌeɪtʃˈɑː (ˌhjuːmən ˈriːsɔːsɪz) ˌmænɪdʒə] Personalmanager(in), Personalleiter(in) 113

Human Resources [ˌhjuːmən ˈriːsɔːsɪz] Personalabteilung 12

I

ignorance of the law is no defence [ˌɪgnərəns əv‿ðə ˈlɔː‿ɪz ˌnəʊ dɪˈfens] Unwissenheit schützt vor Strafe nicht 176

impact [ˈɪmpækt] Auswirkung, Effekt 131

to impact (on) [ɪmˈpækt] einwirken auf, sich auswirken auf 131

impartial [ɪmˈpɑːʃl] unparteiisch, objektiv, unvoreingenommen 69

to implement [ˈɪmplɪment] umsetzen, einführen 115

import tax [ˈɪmpɔːt‿ˌtæks] Einfuhrzoll, Importsteuer 194

impulse buy [ˈɪmpʌls ˌbaɪ] Spontankauf 83

in advance [ɪn‿ədˈvɑːns] im Voraus 35

in breach of contract [ɪn ˌbriːtʃ‿əv ˈkɒntrækt] vertragswidrig, vertragsbrüchig 180

in bulk [ɪn ˈbʌlk] in großen Mengen 76

incentive [ɪnˈsentɪv] Anreiz 35

in charge of [ɪn ˈtʃɑːdʒ‿əv] verantwortlich für, zuständig für 24

incident [ˈɪnsɪdənt] Vorfall, Ereignis, Zwischenfall, Störfall 142

income [ˈɪnkʌm] Einkommen 35

income-related expenses [ˌɪnkʌmrɪˌleɪtɪd ɪkˈspensɪz] Werbungskosten (steuerlich absetzbar) 194

income statement [ˈɪnkʌm ˌsteɪtmənt] Gewinn- und Verlustkonto (AE) 192

income tax [ˈɪnkʌm ˌtæks] Einkommenssteuer 194

inconvenience [ˌɪnkənˈviːnɪəns] Unannehmlichkeiten, unnötige Mühen 54

inconvenient [ˌɪnkənˈviːnɪənt] unpraktisch, umständlich, ungünstig, unangenehm 167

to incorporate [ɪnˈkɔːpəreɪt] beinhalten, umfassen, einbauen, integrieren 21

index-linked [ˌɪndeksˈlɪŋkt] inflationsangepasst, indexgebunden 189

to induct [ɪnˈdʌkt] einweisen, einführen 116

industrial dispute [ɪnˌdʌstrɪəl ˈdɪspjuːt] Arbeitskonflikt, Arbeitskampf, Arbeitsstreit 177

industrial goods [ɪnˌdʌstrɪəl ˈgʊdz] Industriegüter, Investitionsgüter, Produktionsgüter 45

industrial management [ɪnˌdʌstrɪəl ˈmænɪdʒmənt] Betriebsführung, Industriewirtschaft 119

industrial relations [ɪnˌdʌstrɪəl rɪˈleɪʃnz] Beziehungen zwischen Arbeitnehmer und Arbeitgeber 95

inevitable [ɪˈnevɪtəbl] unvermeidlich 143

inferior [ɪnˈfɪərɪə] minderwertig, mangelhaft 136

inflammable [ɪnˈflæməbl] entzündbar, brennbar, feuergefährlich 76

inflation rate [ɪnˈfleɪʃn ˌreɪt] Inflationsrate 148

to infringe [ɪnˈfrɪndʒ] verletzen, gegen etwas verstoßen 178

infringement [ɪnˈfrɪndʒmənt] Rechtsverletzung, Verstoß gegen ein Recht, Ordnungswidrigkeit 178

ingredient [ɪnˈgriːdɪənt] Zutat, Inhaltsstoff 165

to inherit [ɪnˈherɪt] erben 39

inheritance [ɪnˈherɪtəns] Erbe, Erbschaft 63

inheritance tax [ɪnˈherɪtəns ˌtæks] Erbschaftssteuer 194

Initial Public Offering (IPO) [ɪˌnɪʃl ˌpʌblɪk ˈɒfərɪŋ ˌaɪpiːˈəʊ] Börsengang, öffentliche Erstemission 23

initiation [ɪˌnɪʃɪˈeɪʃn] Initiierung (Projektmanagementphase), Aufnahme, Einführung, Start 125

injunction [ɪnˈdʒʌŋkʃn] einstweilige Verfügung 178

inland waterway [ˌɪnlənd ˈwɔːtəweɪ] Binnengewässer, Wasserstrasse 76

in return [ɪn rɪˈtɜːn] als Gegenleistung 41

insolvency [ɪnˈsɒlvənsɪ] Insolvenz, Zahlungsunfähigkeit, Konkurs 177

insolvency insurance [ɪnˈsɒlvənsɪ‿ɪnˌʃɔːrəns] Insolvenzsicherung 141

instalment [ɪnˈstɔːlmənt] Rate, Teilzahlung 169

instant access [ˌɪnstənt ˈækses] sofortiger Zugang 189

in strict confidence [ɪn strɪkt ˈkɒnfɪdəns] streng vertraulich 210

insurance [ɪnˈʃɔːrəns] Versicherung 20

insurance certificate [ɪnˈʃɔːrəns‿səˌtɪfɪkət] Versicherungsschein 170

insurance policy [ɪnˈʃɔːrəns ˌpɒləsɪ] Versicherungspolice, Versicherungsvertrag 170

intangible assets [ɪnˌtændʒɪbl ˈæsets] immaterielle Vermögenswerte 193

intellectual property [ˌɪntəlˈektjʊəl ˈprɒpətɪ] geistiges Eigentum 168

intellectual property rights [ɪntəlˌektjʊəl ˈprɒpətɪ ˌraɪts] Schutz- und Urheberrechte, geistige Eigentumsrechte 95

intention [ɪnˈtenʃn] Absicht 185

interest (sing. only) [ˈɪntrəst] Zins(en) 34

interest-bearing [ˈɪntrəst‿ˌbeərɪŋ] zinstragend 190

interest rate [ˈɪntrəst ˌreɪt] Zinssatz 95

intermediary [ˌɪntəˈmiːdɪərɪ] Zwischenhändler 75

intern [ˈɪntɜːn] Praktikant(in) 60

international trade [ɪntəˌnæʃənl ˈtreɪd] internationaler Handel, Außenhandel, Welthandel 164

internship [ˈɪntɜːnʃɪp] Praktikum 8

interview [ˈɪntəvjuː] Interview, Vorstellungsgespräch 113

in the event that [ˌɪn ðɪ‿ɪˈvent‿ðət] im Falle, dass 181

in the pipeline [ˌɪn ðə ˈpaɪplaɪn] in Vorbereitung, in der Planung 125

in the region of [ɪn ðə ˈriːdʒən əv] ungefähr, so um die 114

in transit [ɪn ˈtrænsɪt] unterwegs, auf dem Transportweg, im Transit 68

invalid [ɪnˈvælɪd] ungültig 89

invention [ɪnˈvenʃn] Erfindung 86

inventor [ɪnˈventə] Erfinder(in) 143

inventory [ˈɪnvəntrɪ] Lager, Lagerbestand, Vorräte 193

to invest [ɪnˈvest] investieren, anlegen 22

to investigate [ɪnˈvestɪgeɪt] erforschen, untersuchen, ermitteln, recherchieren 71

investigation [ɪnˌvestɪˈgeɪʃn] Untersuchung, Ermittlung, Nachforschung 145

investment [ɪnˈvestmənt] Anlage, Investition 39

investment adviser/advisor [ɪnˈvestmənt ədˌvaɪzə] Anlageberater(in) 62

investment bank [ɪnˈvestmənt‿ˌbæŋk] Investmentbank, Anlagebank 27

investments [ɪnˈvestmənts] Kapitalanlagen 193

invisible trade balance [ɪnˌvɪzɪbl ˈtreɪd‿ˌbæləns] Dienstleistungsbilanz 148

invoice [ˈɪnvɔɪs] Rechnung 34

to invoice [ˈɪnvɔɪs] in Rechnung stellen, berechnen 38

IPO (Initial Public Offering) [ˌaɪpiːˈəʊ, ɪˌnɪʃl ˌpʌblɪk ˈɒfərɪŋ] Börsengang, öffentliche Erstemission 203

iron ore [ˈaɪən͜ɔː] Eisenerz 48
irrevocable [ɪˈrevəkəbl] unwiderruflich 181
irrevocable and confirmed documentary letter of credit [ɪrɪˌvəʊkəbl͜ən kənˈfɜːmd ˌletər͜əv ˈkredɪt] unwiderrufliches, bestätigtes Akkreditiv 170
to issue [ˈɪʃuː] ausstellen 34
item [ˈaɪtəm] Gegenstand, Punkt, Tagesordnungspunkt 51
itinerary [aɪˈtɪnərərɪ] Reiseplan, Tagesordnung 11

J

jingle [ˈdʒɪŋgl] Werbesong, Werbelied 65
JIT (just-in-time) [ˌdʒeɪaɪˈtiː, ˌdʒʌstɪnˈtaɪm] bedarfsorientierte Produktion 146
job advertisement [ˈdʒɒb ədˌvɜːtɪsmənt / ædvɜːˌtaɪzmənt] Stellenanzeige, Stellenausschreibung 116
job description [ˈdʒɒb dɪˌskrɪpʃn] Stellenbeschreibung, Tätigkeitsbeschreibung 116
job title [ˈdʒɒb ˌtaɪtl] Berufsbezeichnung, Stellenbezeichnung 20
joint account [ˌdʒɔɪnt əˈkaʊnt] Gemeinschaftskonto, gemeinsames Konto 188
joint-stock company [ˌdʒɔɪntˌstɒk͜ˈkʌmpənɪ] Kapitalgesellschaft 23
joint venture [ˌdʒɔɪnt ˈventʃə] Gemeinschaftsunternehmen, Gemeinschaftsprojekt, gemeinsames Unternehmen, Joint Venture 202
judge [dʒʌdʒ] Richter(in) 177
junior clerk [ˌdʒuːnɪə ˈklɑːk] Bürogehilfe, Bürogehilfin 195
jurisdiction [ˌdʒʊərɪsˈdɪkʃn] Rechtssprechung, Gerichtsbarkeit 170
to justify [ˈdʒʌstɪfaɪd] rechtfertigen 71
just-in-time production [ˌdʒʌstɪntaɪm prəˈdʌkʃn] bedarfsorientierte Produktion 85

K

to keep track of [ˌkiːp ˈtræk ɒv] nachverfolgen, (den Kosten) nachgehen, den Überblick behalten über 35
keyboard [ˈkiːbɔːd] Tastatur 8
to key in [kiː͜ˈɪn] eingeben, eintippen 36
kickoff meeting [ˈkɪkɒf ˌmiːtɪŋ] Eröffnungssitzung für ein neues Projekt 125
knock-on effect [ˌnɒkˈɒn ɪˌfekt] Kettenreaktion 150

L

label [ˈleɪbl] Label, Marke 45
labelled [ˈleɪbld] beschriftet, gekennzeichnet, etikettiert, bezeichnet 80
labelling [ˈleɪblɪŋ] Warenauszeichnung, Beschriftung, Etikettierung 47
labour [ˈleɪbə] Arbeit, Arbeitskräfte 126
labour force [ˈleɪbə ˌfɔːs] Arbeitskraft 27
labour law [ˈleɪbə ˌlɔː] Arbeitsrecht 19
labour market [ˈleɪbə ˌmɑːkɪt] Arbeitsmarkt 94
to lag behind [ˌlæg bɪˈhaɪnd] zurückliegen, hinterherhinken 35
landline phone [ˈlændlaɪn ˌfəʊn] Festnetztelefon 11
landlord [ˈlændlɔːd] Vermieter, Wirt 32
large-scale project [ˌlɑːdʒskeɪl ˈprɒdʒekt] Großprojekt 125
last in, first out [lɑːst͜ˌɪn fɜːst͜ˈaʊt] zuletzt herein, zuerst hinaus; in umgekehrter Reihenfolge 176
latent [ˈleɪtənt] verborgen, versteckt 139
late payment [ˌleɪt ˈpeɪmənt] Zahlungsverzug 34
late payment charge [ˌleɪt͜ˈpeɪmənt͜ˌtʃɑːdʒ] Säumniszuschlag 176
launch [lɔːntʃ] (Markt)Einführung 79
to launch [lɔːntʃ] auf den Markt bringen, (Produkt) einführen 178
law against monopolies [ˌlɔː əˌgenst məˈnɒpəlɪz] Kartellgesetzgebung, Kartellrecht 202
lawsuit [ˈlɔːsjuːt] Klage, Rechtsstreit, Gerichtsverfahren, Prozess 122
lawyer [ˈlɔɪə] Rechtsanwalt, -anwältin 27
to lay off [leɪ͜ˈɒf] entlassen 116
LBO (leveraged buyout) [ˌelbiːˈəʊ, ˌliːvərɪdʒd͜ˈbaɪaʊt] fremdfinanzierte Übernahme eines Unternehmens durch eigenes Management 202
to lead [liːd, led, led] führen, leiten 10
leadership [ˈliːdəʃɪp] Führung, Leitung 10
leading [ˈliːdɪŋ] führend 139
leading-edge [ˌliːdɪŋˈedʒ] Spitzen- 195
lead time [ˈliːd͜ˌtaɪm] (Fabrikations-)Durchlaufzeit, Produktionszeit, Vorbereitungszeit, Vorlaufzeit 86
leaflet [ˈliːflət] Prospekt, Flugblatt, Broschüre 11
lean production [ˌliːn prəˈdʌkʃn] schlanke Produktion 85
lecture [ˈlektʃə] Vorlesung, Vortrag 28
lecturer [ˈlektʃərə] Dozent(in) 119
lecture theatre [ˈlektʃə ˌθɪətə] Hörsaal 10
legal action [ˌliːgl ˈækʃn] gerichtliche Schritte, Gerichtsverfahren, Klage vor Gericht 34
legal advice [ˌliːgl ədˈvaɪs] Rechtsberatung 176
legal battle [ˌligl ˈbætl] Rechtsstreit 75
legal claim [ˌliːgl ˈkleɪm] Rechtsanspruch, gesetzlicher Anspruch 182
legal department [ˈliːgl dɪˌpɑːtmənt] Rechtsabteilung 24
legalese [ˌliːgəlˈiːz] Juristensprache, Juristenjargon 177
legal issue [ˌliːgl ˈɪʃuː] Rechtsangelegenheit 176
legal matter [ˌlɪgl ˈmætə] Rechtsangelegenheit, Rechtsstreit 176
legislation [ˌledʒɪˈsleɪʃn] Gesetzgebung, Gesetze 95
legislator [ˈledʒɪsleɪtə] Gesetzgeber 187
to lend (to) [lend] leihen 33
length of employment [ˌleŋkθ͜əv ɪmˈplɔɪmənt] Beschäftigungsdauer, Dauer der Beschäftigung 176
letterhead [ˈletəhed] Briefkopf 12
letter of credit [ˌletər͜əv ˈkredɪt] Akkreditiv, Bankbürgschaft 167
level playing field [ˌlevl ˈpleɪɪŋ ˌfiːld] Chancengleichheit 171
leverage [ˈliːvərɪdʒ] Einfluss (in einer Verhandlung) 175
leveraged buyout [ˌliːvərɪdʒd ˈbaɪaʊt] fremdfinanzierte Übernahme eines Unternehmens durch eigenes Management 202
leveraging [ˈliːvərɪdʒɪŋ] Verschuldungsgrad, Verhältnis von Eigenkapital und Fremdkapital 191
to levy [ˈlevɪ] erheben (z. B. eine Steuer) 194
liability [ˌlaɪəˈbɪlətɪ] Haftung 23
to liaise with [lɪˈeɪz wɪð] mit jmdm. in Kontakt sein, eng zusammenarbeiten mit 26
libellous [ˈlaɪbələs] beleidigend, verleumderisch 181
life insurance [ˈlaɪf ɪnˌʃɔ.rəns] Lebensversicherung 27
limited liability [ˌlɪmɪtɪd ˌlaɪəˈbɪlətɪ] beschränkte Haftung 23
limited partnership [ˌlɪmɪtɪd ˈpɑːtnəʃɪp] entspricht etwa Kommanditgesellschaft 23
line manager [ˈlaɪn ˌmænɪdʒə] Linienmanager(in) 25
line of inquiry [ˌlaɪn͜əv ɪnˈkwaɪərɪ] Befragungsgebiet 70
listing of shares [ˌlɪstɪŋ͜əv ˈʃeəz] Aktienemission, Notierung der Aktienwerte 22
litigation [ˌlɪtɪˈgeɪʃn] Rechtsstreit, Prozess, Gerichtsverfahren, Streitsache 178
to live up to expectations [lɪv ˌʌp tʊ͜ˌekspekˈteɪʃnz] den Erwartungen gerecht werden 145
loan [ləʊn] Darlehen, Kredit 35
local council [ˌləʊkl ˈkaʊnsl] Gemeinderat 186
location [ləʊˈkeɪʃn] Standort, Ort 30
logistics [ləˈdʒɪstɪks] Logistik 20

long-term [ˌlɒŋ'tɜ:m] langfristig 206
long-term liabilities [ˌlɒŋtɜ:m ˌlaɪə'bɪlətɪz] langfristige Verbindlichkeiten 193
long-term project [ˌlɒŋtɜ:m 'prɒdʒekt] Langzeitprojekt 125
to lose track [lu:z 'træk] den Überblick verlieren 35
loss [lɒs] Verlust 47
low-maintenance [ˌləʊ'meɪntənəns] wartungsarm, pflegeleicht 48
lump sum [ˌlʌmp 'sʌm] Pauschalsumme, Pauschalbetrag 35

M

machine operator [mə'ʃi:n ɒpəˌreɪtə] Maschinist(in) 85
machinery [mə'ʃi:nərɪ] Maschinen 24
macroeconomics [ˌmækrəʊˌi:kə'nɒmɪks] Makroökonomie, allgemeine Volkswirtschaftslehre 149
mailing ['meɪlɪŋ] Briefwerbung, Wurfsending 71
mail-order business ['meɪlɔ:də ˌbɪznɪs] Versandhandel 21
mainland Europe [ˌmeɪnlænd 'jʊərəp] europäisches Festland 21
to maintain [meɪn'teɪn] aufrechterhalten, erhalten 95
maintenance ['meɪntənəns] Wartung und Instandhaltung, Instandsetzung 24
maintenance engineer ['meɪntənəns endʒɪˌnɪə] Wartungstechniker(in) 85
major ['meɪdʒə] Haupt- 21
majority shareholding [məˌdʒɒrətɪ 'ʃeəˌhəʊldɪŋ] Mehrheitsbeteiligung 195
majority stake [məˌdʒɒrətɪ 'steɪk] Mehrheitsbeteiligung 202
to make every effort to [meɪk ˌevrɪ‿'efət‿tʊ] sich alle Mühe geben 169
to make it ['meɪk‿ɪt] es schaffen 8
to make redundant [ˌmeɪk rɪ'dʌndənt] entlassen, freisetzen, überflüssig machen 116
malpractice [ˌmæl'præktɪs] Berufsvergehen, Untat, Kunstfehler, gewissensloses Handeln, Delikt, Missbrauch 183
management ['mænɪdʒmənt] Geschäftsleitung 8
management board ['mænɪdʒmənt‿bɔ:d] Vorstand 24
management buyout [ˌmænɪdʒmənt‿'baɪaʊt] Übernahme durch die vorhandene Geschäftsleitung, Management-Buyout 195
to manufacture [ˌmænjə'fæktʃə] fertigen, produzieren, herstellen 50
manufacturer's brand [mænjəˌfæktʃərəz 'brænd] Herstellermarke 45
manufacturing [ˌmænjə'fæktʃərɪŋ] Herstellung, Produktion, Fertigung 20
margin ['mɑ:dʒɪn] Gewinnspanne, Gewinnmarge 83
marine insurance [mə'ri:n ɪnˌʃɔ:rəns] Seetransportversicherung 141
marital status [ˌmærɪtl 'steɪtəs] Familienstand 118
market growth [ˌmɑ:kɪt 'grəʊθ] Marktwachstum 205
marketing mix ['mɑ:kɪtɪŋ ˌmɪks] Marketingmix, Mischstrategie für das Marketing 60
market penetration [ˌmɑ:kɪt ˌpenɪ'treɪʃn] Marktdurchdringung 47
market research [ˌmɑ:kɪt 'ri:sɜ:tʃ] Marktforschung 60
market share [ˌmɑ:kɪt 'ʃeə] Marktanteil 47
markup ['mɑ:kʌp] (Preis)Aufschlag, Einzelhandelsmarge 72
mass market [ˌmæs 'mɑ:kɪt] Massenmarkt 69
mass-produced [ˌmæsprə'dju:st] in großen Mengen hergestellt 93
mass production [ˌmæs prə'dʌkʃn] Massenfertigung, Massenproduktion 85
maternity leave [mə'tɜ:nətɪ ˌli:v] Mutterschaftsurlaub, Erziehungsurlaub 123
maternity rights [mə'tɜ:nətɪ ˌraɪts] Mutterschutz 115
to mature [mə'tjʊə] fällig werden 189
mature [mə'tjʊə] reif 45
maturity [mə'tjʊərətɪ] Fälligkeit 189
MBO [ˌembi:'əʊ] Aufkauf einer Kapitalgesellschaft durch eigenes Management 202
measurable ['meʒərəbl] messbar 206
measure ['meʒə] Maßnahme 60
media ['mi:dɪə] Medien, Werbeträger 20
medium-term [ˌmi:dɪəm'tɜ:m] mittelfristig 206
merchandise ['mɜ:tʃəndaɪs] Werbeartikel 73
merchandising ['mɜ:tʃəndaɪzɪŋ] Merchandising, Vermarktung, Werbeartikel 72
merchant ['mɜ:tʃənt] Händler(in) 79
merchant account [ˌmɜ:tʃənt ə'kaʊnt] Firmenkonto 43
to merge [mɜ:dʒ] fusionieren, zusammenlegen 18
merger ['mɜ:dʒə] Fusion, Unternehmenszusammenschluss 201
merit ['merɪt] Verdienst, Vorzug 11
microeconomics [ˌmaɪkrəʊi:kə'nɒmɪks] Mikroökonomie, Betriebswirtschaftslehre 149
middlemen ['mɪdlmen] Zwischenhändler 72
milestone ['maɪlstəʊn] Meilenstein 128
mill [mɪl] Mühle, Walzwerk, Walzanlage 85
mining ['maɪnɪŋ] Förderung, Bergbau 20
minutes ['mɪnɪts] Protokoll 11
miscalculation [ˌmɪskælkjʊ'leɪʃn] Fehlberechnung, Fehlkalkulation, Fehlrechnung 126
misleading advertising [mɪsˌli:dɪŋ 'ædvətaɪzɪŋ] irreführende Werbung 177
mission statement ['mɪʃn ˌsteɪtmənt] Leitbild, Firmenphilosophie 200
mobile phone [ˌməʊbaɪl 'fəʊn] Handy 11
to modify ['mɒdɪfaɪ] ändern, abändern, verändern, modifizieren, umrüsten 167
money market ['mʌnɪ ˌmɑ:kɪt] Geldmarkt 62
money spinner ['mʌnɪ ˌspɪnə] Kassenschlager, Renner 204
money supply ['mʌnɪ səˌplaɪ] Geldmenge, Geldumlauf 155
money transfer ['mʌnɪ ˌtrænsfɜ:] Geldüberweisung 72
to monitor ['mɒnɪtərɪŋ] überwachen 18
moonlighting ['mu:nlaɪtɪŋ] Schwarzarbeit 154
mortgage ['mɔ:gɪdʒ] Hypothek 33
motion ['məʊʃn] Antrag, Gegenstand einer Debatte 184
multinational company (MNC) [ˌmʌltɪnæʃənl 'kʌmpənɪ, ˌemen'si:] multinationales Unternehmen 21
mutual agreement [ˌmju:tʃʊəl ə'gri:mənt] gegenseitiges Einvernehmen, beiderseitige Zustimmung 202
mutual recognition [ˌmju:tʃʊəl ˌrekəg'nɪʃn] gegenseitige Anerkennung 165

N

to neglect [nɪ'glekt] vernachlässigen 202
negligent ['neglɪdʒənt] fahrlässig, unachtsam 138
negligible ['neglɪdʒəbl] unbedeutend, geringfügig, unerheblich 32
negotiable [nɪ'gəʊʃəbl] verhandelbar, Verhandlungssache 117
negotiation [nɪˌgəʊʃɪ'eɪʃn] Verhandlung 11
net margin [ˌnet 'mɑ:dʒɪn] Nettogewinn, Nettogewinnmarge 83
NGO (non-governmental organisation) [ˌendʒi:'əʊ, 'nɒngʌvənˌmentl ˌɔ:gənaɪ'zeɪʃn] Nichtregierungsorganisation 175
niche market ['ni:ʃ ˌmɑ:kɪt] Nischenmarkt, Marktnische 68
no-frills [ˌnəʊ'frɪlz] ohne Extras, ohne Schnickschack, Billig- 46
non-compliance [ˌnɒnkəm'plaɪəns] Nichteinhaltung, Nichtübereinstimmung, Nichterfüllung 176
non-tariff barrier (NTB) [ˌnɒnˌtærɪf 'bærɪə, ˌenti:'bi:] nichttarifäre Handelsbeschränkung 170

not applicable [ˌnɒt əˈplɪkəbl] nicht zutreffend 104
note [nəʊt] (BE) Banknote, Geldschein 32
notice [ˈnəʊtɪs] Kündigung 181
notice of termination [ˌnəʊtɪs‿əv ˌtɜːmɪˈneɪʃn] Kündigung, Aufkündigung 181
notification [ˌnəʊtɪfɪˈkeɪʃn] Bescheid, Ankündigung, Bekanntgabe, Benachrichtigung 169
to notify [ˈnəʊtɪfaɪ] benachrichtigen 80
number cruncher [ˈnʌmbə ˌkrʌntʃə] Zahlenakrobat, Erbsenzähler 209

O

objective [əbˈdʒektɪv] Ziel, Zielvorgabe, Ansatz 124
obligation [ˌɒblɪˈgeɪʃn] Verpflichtung, Pflicht 181
to observe (a contract) [əbˌsɜːv ə ˈkɒntrækt] sich an einen Vertrag halten 180
to observe (a regulation, a law) [əbˈzɜːv] beachten, einhalten 145
obsolete [ˌɒbsəlˈiːt] überholt, veraltet, außer Gebrauch 45
occupational accident [ɒkjəˌpeɪʃənl ˈæksɪdənt] Arbeitsunfall 112
occupational safety and health [ɒkjʊˌpeɪʃənl ˌseɪftɪ‿ənd ˈhelθ] Arbeitsschutz, Sicherheit und Gesundheitsschutz am Arbeitsplatz 183
offer [ˈɒfə] Angebot 11
office equipment [ˌɒfɪs ɪˈkwɪpmənt] Büroeinrichtung, Büroausstattung 95
on behalf of [ɒn bɪˈhɑːf‿əv] im Namen (von), im Auftrag von 12
on demand [ɒn dɪˈmɑːnd] auf Abruf, bei Bedarf 188
on schedule [ɒn ˈʃedjuːl] termingerecht, pünktlich, nach Plan 60
on one's own account [ɒn wʌnz ˌəʊn əˈkaʊnt] auf eigene Rechnung 72
on track [ɒn ˈtræk] auf Kurs 128
open account [ˌəʊpn əˈkaʊnt] offenes Konto, (Kredit) in laufender Rechnung 167
open account terms [ˌəʊpn əˌkaʊnt‿ˈtɜːmz] Verkauf auf offene Rechnung 167
to operate [ˈɒpəreɪt] betreiben, bedienen 21
to oppose [əˈpəʊz] ablehnen, dagegen sein 23
option [ˈɒpʃn] Auswahlmöglichkeit 31
order [ˈɔːdə] Bestellung, Auftrag 11
order acknowledgement [ˌɔːdər‿əkˈnɒlɪdʒmənt] Auftragsbestätigung 169
order confirmation [ˌɔːdə kɒnfəˈmeɪʃn] Auftragsbestätigung 169
order processing [ˌɔːdə ˈprəʊsesɪŋ] Auftragsbearbeitung 86
ordinary share [ˌɔːdɪnrɪ ˈʃeə] Stammaktie 189
organic [ɔːˈgænɪk] biologisch angebaut, Bio- 173
organisation chart [ˌɔːgənaɪˈzeɪʃn ˌtʃɑːt] Organigramm 24
to originate [əˈrɪdʒəneɪt] entstammen, abstammen, seinen Ursprung in etwas haben 145
outcome [ˈaʊtkʌm] Ergebnis, Auswirkung, Folge, Resultat 125
outgoings [ˈaʊtˌgəʊɪŋz] Ausgaben 35
outlay [ˈaʊtleɪ] Aufwand, Auslagen, Vorleistung 191
outlet [ˈaʊtlet] Verkaufsstelle, Vertriebsstelle, Outlet 21
outstanding [aʊtˈstændɪŋ] hervorragend 12
over budget [ˌəʊvə ˈbʌdʒɪt] Etatausweitung, mit Kostenüberschreitung 126
to overcharge [ˌəʊvəˈtʃɑːdʒ] zu viel berechnen 38
overdraft [ˈəʊvədrɑːft] Kontoüberziehung 35
overdue [ˌəʊvəˈdjuː] überfällig, ausbleibend 34
overhead(s) [ˈəʊvəhed] Gemeinkosten, Fixkosten, fixe Kosten 68
to overrun [ˌəʊvəˈrʌn] überschreiten 126
to oversee [ˌəʊvəˈsiː] beaufsichtigen, überwachen 26
oversight [ˈəʊvəsaɪt] Versehen 38
overstocks [ˈəʊvəstɒks] zu hohe Bestandsgrößen, 'Ladenhüter' 79
overtime [ˈəʊvətaɪm] Überstunden 88
to own [əʊn] besitzen 21
own brand [ˌəʊn ˈbrænd] Eigenmarke, Hausmarke 45

P

package holiday [ˌpækɪdʒ ˈhɒlɪdeɪ] Pauschalreise, Pauschalurlaub 182
packaging [ˈpækɪdʒɪŋ] Verkaufsverpackung, Verpackungsmaterial 28
packing list [ˈpækɪŋ ˌlɪst] Packliste 170
paint shop [ˈpeɪntʃɒp] Abteilung für Mal- und Spritzarbeit, Lackiererei 85
pallet [pælɪt] Palette 78
paperwork [ˈpeɪpəwɜːk] Formalitäten, Dokumentation 77
paragraph [ˈpærəgrɑːf] Absatz, Paragraph 12
parental leave [pəˌrentl‿ˈliːv] Erziehungsurlaub, Elternzeit 115
parent company [ˈpeərənt ˌkʌmpənɪ] Muttergesellschaft 23
partnership [ˈpɑːtnəʃɪp] Personengesellschaft, offene Handelsgesellschaft, Teilhaberschaft 21
part-payment [ˌpɑːtˈpeɪmənt] Teilzahlung, Abschlagszahlung 80
temporary worker [ˌtempərərɪ ˈwɜːkə] Aushilfskraft 27
part-time (P/T) [ˌpɑːtˈtaɪm] Teilzeit- 27
to pass inspection [ˌpɑːs ɪnˈspekʃn] eine Kontrollprüfung überstehen 139
to pass the buck [ˌpɑːs ðə ˈbʌk] den Schwarzen Peter weitergeben, die Verantwortung für etwas abschieben 145
to pass sth. on [pɑːs‿ˌsʌmθɪŋ ˈɒn] etwas weitersagen, weiterleiten 9
to patronise [ˈpætrənaɪz] jmdn. gönnerhaft/herablassend behandeln 185
to pawn [pɔːn] verpfänden 150
pawnbroker [ˈpɔːnˌbrəʊkə] Pfandleiher 150
payables [ˈpeɪəblz] Verbindlichkeiten, Kreditoren 193
payment terms [ˈpeɪmənt‿ˌtɜːmz] Zahlungsbedingungen 43
to pay off the balance [peɪ‿ɒf ðə ˈbæləns] den Restbetrag bezahlen 33
payroll [ˈpeɪrəʊl] Lohn- und Gehaltsabrechnung 26
payroll tax [ˈpeɪrəʊl ˌtæks] Lohnsteuer 194
peak [piːk] Höhepunkt, höchster Punkt, Spitze 150
to peak [piːk] den Höhepunkt/Höchststand erreichen 152
penalty [ˈpenəltɪ] Strafe 183
penalty for late payment [ˌpenəltɪ fə ˌleɪt‿ˈpeɪmənt] Säumniszuschlag 37
pension [ˈpenʃn] Pension, Rente 22
pensioner [ˈpenʃənə] Rentner(in) 85
pension rights [ˈpenʃn ˌraɪts] Rentenansprüche 115
percentage [pəˈsentɪdʒ] Prozentsatz, Prozent, prozentualer Anteil 32
perception [pəˈsepʃn] Wahrnehmung 65
performance [pəˈfɔːməns] Aufführung, Auftritt, Leistung 15
performance appraisal [pəˈfɔːməns əˌpreɪzl] Leistungsbeurteilung, Leistungsbewertung 112
perishable [ˈperɪʃəbl] (leicht) verderblich, vergänglich 76
perishables [ˈperɪʃəblz] leicht verderbliche Waren, kurzlebige Verbrauchsgüter 83
perks [pɜːks] Nebenleistungen 60
permission [pəˈmɪʃn] Erlaubnis 69
personnel [ˌpɜːsənˈel] Personal 61
person responsible [ˌpɜːsn rɪˈspɒnsɪbl] Verantwortliche(r) 53
to persuade [pəˈsweɪd] überreden 27

persuasive [pə'sweɪsɪv] überredend, überzeugend 65
pharmaceuticals [ˌfɑ:mə'su:tɪklz] Arzneimittel, Pharmazeutika 20
philanthropist [fɪ'lænθrəpɪst] Wohltäter, Philanthrop 39
pilot project [ˌpaɪlət 'prɒdʒekt] Pilotversuch, Pilotprojekt 125
pitch [pɪtʃ] Werbepräsentation, Verkaufsgespräch 60
to pitch [pɪtʃ] anpreisen 195
to place an order [ˌpleɪs‿ən 'ɔ:də] einen Auftrag erteilen, eine Bestellung aufgeben 86
plain English [ˌpleɪn 'ɪŋglɪʃ] bürgernahes Englisch, klares und deutliches Englisch 177
plaintiff ['pleɪntɪf] Kläger(in) 179
planning permission ['plænɪŋ pəˌmɪʃn] Baugenehmigung, Planfeststellungsbeschluss 187
plc (public limited company) [ˌpi:el'si:, ˌpʌblɪk ˌlɪmɪtɪd 'kʌmpənɪ] britische Aktiengesellschaft 21
to plough back [plaʊ 'bæk] (Gewinn) reinvestieren 154
to plummet ['plʌmɪt] abstürzen, drastisch sinken 152
to plunge [plʌndʒ] stürzen, drastisch sinken 98
to point out [pɔɪnt‿'aʊt] hinweisen auf 169
poison pill [ˌpɔɪzən 'pɪl] Übernahme einer Firma verhindernde Maßnahme, eine Klausel, die (durch ihren unattraktiven Inhalt) das Unternehmen davor schützen soll, von anderen übernommen zu werden, 'Killerklausel' 202
policy ['pɒləsɪ] Grundsatz, Politik, politische Linie, Richtlinie 8
polystyrene peanuts [pɒlɪˌstaɪəri:n 'pi:nʌts] Schaum-Erdnüsse 78
port [pɔ:t] Hafen 76
port of destination [ˌpɔ:t əv ˌdestɪ'neɪʃn] Bestimmungshafen 170
port of shipment [ˌpɔ:t əv 'ʃɪpmənt] Verschiffungshafen 170
postage and packing [ˌpəʊstɪdʒ‿ən 'pækɪŋ] Porto und Verpackung 83
to postpone [pəʊs'pəʊn] verschieben 51
posture ['pɒstʃə] Körperhaltung 11
power drill ['paʊə ˌdrɪl] elektrische Bohrmaschine 176
PR (Public Relations) [pi:'ɑ:, ˌpʌblɪk rɪ'leɪʃnz] Öffentlichkeitsarbeit 122
practice ['præktɪs] Kanzlei 27
precaution [prɪ'kɔ:ʃn] Vorsichtsmaßnahme 125
precedent ['presɪdənt] Präzedenzfall 75
precious metals [ˌpreʃəs 'metlz] Edelmetalle 189
preference ['prefrəns] Vorliebe 166
preference share ['prefrəns‿ˌʃeə] Vorzugsaktie 189
preferred stock [prɪˌfɜ:d 'stɒk] Vorzugsaktie(n) (AE) 189
preliminary [prɪ'lɪmɪnrɪ] vorläufig, vorausgehend 128
premises ['premɪsɪz] Räumlichkeiten, Firmengelände, Geschäftsräume 22
press releases ['pres rɪˌli:sɪz] Pressemitteilung 60
press screening ['pres‿ˌskri:nɪŋ] Filmvorführung 60
prestigious [pres'tɪdʒəs] renommiert, namhaft, angesehen 145
price/earnings ratio (PER) [ˌpraɪs'ɜ:nɪŋz ˌreɪʃɪəʊ, ˌpi:i:'ɑ:] Kurs-Gewinn-Verhältnis 193
principal ['prɪnsɪpl] Darlehensbetrag, Kapital(summe) 189
print size ['prɪnt ˌsaɪz] Schriftgröße 197
private label [ˌpraɪvət 'leɪbl] Eigenmarke, Hausmarke 45
private limited company [ˌpraɪvət ˌlɪmɪtɪd 'kʌmpənɪ] britische Gesellschaft mit beschränkter Haftung 22
procedures [prə'si:dʒə] Verfahren, Vorgehensweise, Vorschrift 23
to process ['prəʊses] verarbeiten, bearbeiten 88
processing ['prəʊsesɪŋ] Verarbeitung, Bearbeitung, Abwicklung (eines Vorgangs) 20
procurement [prə'kjʊəmənt] Beschaffung, Einkauf 85
produce ['prɒdju:s] landwirtschaftliches) Erzeugnis 88
product differentiation [ˌprɒdʌkt‿ˌdɪfərenʃɪ'eɪʃn] Produktdifferenzierung 204
Production Dept. (Department) [prə'dʌkʃn dɪˌpɑ:tmənt] Produktionsabteilung 9
production line [prə'dʌkʃn ˌlaɪn] Fertigungsband, Fließband 84
productivity [ˌprɒdʌk'tɪvətɪ] Produktivität, Leistungsfähigkeit 86
product launch ['prɒdʌkt ˌlɔ:ntʃ] Produkteinführung 15
product liability [ˌprɒdʌkt ˌlaɪə'bɪlətɪ] Produkthaftung 141
product liability insurance [ˌprɒdʌkt ˌlaɪə'bɪlətɪ‿ɪnˌʃɔ:rəns] Produkthaftpflichtversicherung 141
product placement [ˌprɒdʌkt 'pleɪsmənt] Produktplatzierung, Schleichwerbung in Film/Fernsehen 67
product recall [ˌprɒdʌkt rɪ'kɔ:l] Rückrufaktion 142
profitability [ˌprɒfɪtə'bɪlətɪ] Rentabilität 138
profitable ['prɒfɪtəbl] rentabel, gewinnbringend, lukrativ, einträglich 98
profit after tax [ˌprɒfɪt ˌɑ:ftə 'tæks] Gewinn nach Abzug der Steuern 192
profit and loss account [ˌprɒfɪt ənd 'lɒs əˌkaʊnt] Gewinn- und Verlustkonto 192
profit margin ['prɒfɪt ˌmɑ:dʒɪn] Gewinnmarge, Gewinnspanne 29
profit maximisation [ˌprɒfɪt ˌmæksɪmaɪ'zeɪʃn] Gewinnmaximierung 204
pro forma invoice [prəʊˌfɔ:mə 'ɪnvɔɪs] Proformarechnung 169
to prohibit [prə'hɪbɪt] untersagen, verbieten 142
project leader ['prɒdʒekt ˌli:də] Projektleiter(in), Projektmanager(in) 124
to promote [prə'məʊt] fördern, begünstigen, befördern, vorantreiben 22
promotion [prə'məʊʃn] Verkaufsförderung, Werbung 61
promotional item [prəˌməʊʃənl 'aɪtəm] Werbegeschenk, Werbeartikel 60
proof [pru:f] Beweis 180
proofreading ['pru:fˌri:dɪŋ] Korrekturlesen, Lektorat 135
property prices ['prɒpətɪ ˌpraɪsɪz] Immobilienpreise 148
proposal [prə'pəʊzl] Vorschlag, Antrag, Vorhaben, Angebot 187
prosecution [ˌprɒsɪ'kju:ʃn] Strafverfolgung, strafrechtliche Verfolgung 183
to prosper ['prɒspə] erfolgreich sein 99
prosperity [prɒs'perətɪ] Wohlstand, Erfolg, Reichtum 39
prosperous ['prɒspərəs] wohlhabend, reich 39
prototype ['prəʊtətaɪp] Prototyp, Muster, Vorläufer 50
to prove [pru:v] beweisen 178
provision [prə'vɪʒn] Versorgung, Bereitstellung 20
provisions [prə'vɪʒnz] Bestimmungen, Rückstellungen, Vorräte 181
Pty Ltd (proprietory limited company) [prəˌpraɪətrɪ ˌlɪmɪtɪd 'kʌmpənɪ] entspricht GmbH (Australien) 172
public hearing [ˌpʌblɪk 'hɪərɪŋ] öffentliche Anhörung 186
public inquiry [ˌpʌblɪk ɪn'kwaɪərɪ] öffentliche Untersuchung 182
public limited company [ˌpʌblɪk ˌlɪmɪtɪd 'kʌmpənɪ] britische Aktiengesellschaft 22
public official [ˌpʌblɪk ə'fɪʃl] Beamter/Beamtin, Angestellte(r) im öffentlichen Dienst 167
public-sector employee [ˌpʌblɪkˌsektər‿ɪm'plɔɪi:] Angestellte(r) im öffentlichen Dienst 204
public spending [ˌpʌblɪk 'spendɪŋ] öffentliche Ausgaben, Staatsausgaben 155
to publish ['pʌblɪʃ] veröffentlichen 71
publishing ['pʌblɪʃɪŋ] Verlagswesen, Veröffentlichung 20
to pull the plug on sth. [ˌpʊl ðə 'plʌg ɒn ˌsʌmθɪŋ] mit etwas Schluss machen, etwas verwerfen 125

purchase ['pɜ:tʃəs] Kauf, Einkauf 35
to purchase ['pɜ:tʃəs] kaufen 72
purchasing ['pɜ:tʃəsɪŋ] Einkauf, Beschaffung 24
purchasing power ['pɜ:tʃəsɪŋ ˌpaʊə] Kaufkraft 148
purchasing power parity (PPP) [ˌpɜ:tʃəsɪŋ ˌpaʊə 'pærətɪ, ˌpi:pi:'pi:] Kaufkraftparität 148
to put sb. out of business [pʊt ˌsʌmbədɪ‿aʊt‿əv 'bɪznɪs] jmdn. aus dem Markt drängen 68
to put s.o. through [pʊt ˌsʌmwʌn 'θru:] jmdn. verbinden, durchstellen 16

Q

to qualify for ['kwɒlɪfaɪ fɔ:] Anspruch haben auf, berechtigt sein, in Frage kommen (für) 176
quality assurance [ˌkwɒlətɪ‿ə'ʃʊərəns] Qualitätssicherung 24
quality assurance [ˌkwɒlətɪ‿ə'ʃʊərəns] Qualitätssicherung 85
quality audit [ˌkwɒlətɪ‿'ɔ:dɪt] Qualitätsaudit 146
quality control [ˌkwɒlətɪ kən'trəʊl] Qualitätskontrolle 138
query ['kwɪərɪ] Rückfrage, Suchanfrage 176
to query ['kwɪərɪ] beanstanden, in Frage stellen, mit einem Fragezeichen versehen 176
questionnaire [ˌkwestʃə'neə] Fragebogen, Umfrage 30
quid, pl. quid [kwɪd] (BE) Pfund (Währung) 40
quota ['kwəʊtə] Kontingent, Quote, Mengenbeschränkung 170
quote [kwəʊt] Preisangebot, Kostenvoranschlag 72
to quote (a price) [kwəʊt] einen Preis angeben 168

R

to raise capital [reɪz 'kæpɪtl] Kapital aufbringen, Kapital beschaffen 22
range [reɪndʒ] Auswahl, Sortiment, (Produkt)Palette 23
to range from ... to ... [reɪndʒ] reichen von ... bis ... 21
rapport [ræ'pɔ:, rə'pɔ:] harmonisches Verhältnis 105
rationale [ˌræʃə'nɑ:l] Begründung 70
raw materials [ˌrɔ: mə'tɪərɪəlz] Rohstoffe 20
Research and Development (R&D) [ˌri:sɜ:tʃ‿ən‿dɪ'veləpməmt, ˌɑ:rən'di:] Forschung und Entwicklung 9
to reach deadlock [ˌri:tʃ 'dedlɒk] stecken bleiben 75
readily available [ˌredɪlɪ‿ə'veɪləbl] sofort verfügbar 188
real estate ['rɪəl‿ɪˌsteɪt] (AE) Immobilien, Grundstücks- und Hausbesitz, Grundbesitz, Liegenschaft 33
recall [rɪ'kɔ:l] Rückrufaktion 142
to recall [rɪ'kɔ:l] (ein Produkt) zurückrufen 142
receipt [rɪ'si:t] Erhalt, Quittung, Beleg 36
receipt of order [rɪˌsi:t‿əv 'ɔ:də] Auftragseingang 169
receivables [rɪ'si:vəblz] Forderungen, Debitoren 193
to receive/get/have one's money's worth [rɪsi:v/ˌget/ˌhæv wʌnz 'mʌnɪz ˌwɜ:θ] etwas für sein Geld bekommen, auf seine Kosten kommen 138
receiver [rɪ'si:və] Telefonhörer 142
reception [rɪ'sepʃn] Empfang 19
recession [rɪ'seʃn] Rezession, Konjunkturrückgang, Konjunkturabschwung 148
recipient [rɪ'sɪpɪənt] Empfänger(in) 71
recommendation [ˌrekəmen'deɪʃn] Empfehlung 31
record ['rekɔ:d] Ruf, Ansehen 29
recorded message [rɪˌkɔ:dɪd 'mesɪdʒɪz] automatische Ansage 81
to recover debts [rɪˌkʌvə 'dets] Schulden eintreiben 177
recovery [rɪ'kʌvərɪ] Wirtschaftsaufschwung 95
to recruit [rɪ'kru:t] einstellen, anwerben, rekrutieren 114
to redeem [rɪ'di:m] einlösen, auszahlen 189
red tape [ˌred‿'teɪp] (übertriebene) Bürokratie, Papierkrieg 165
reduction [rɪ'dʌkʃn] Preisnachlass, Reduzierung 41
redundancy [rɪ'dʌndənsɪ] Entlassung, Freisetzung von Arbeitnehmern, Rationalisierungsmaßnahme 115
redundancy payment [rɪ'dʌndənsɪ ˌpeɪmənt] Abfindungszahlung (bei Entlassung) 176
redundancy plan [rɪ'dʌndənsɪ ˌplæn] Entlassungsplan, Sozialplan 176
redundancy programme [rɪ'dʌndənsɪ ˌprəʊgræm] Sozialplan (für Arbeitnehmer, die entlassen werden) (BE) 114
ref ['refrəns, ref] Zeichen 12
reference ['refrəns] Referenz, Zeugnis 121
refrigerated transport [rɪˌfrɪdʒəreɪtɪd‿'trænspɔ:t] Kühltransport 77
refrigerator [rɪ'frɪdʒəreɪtə] Kühlschrank 21
refund ['ri:fʌnd] Rückerstattung 38
to refund [ˌri:'fʌnd] rückerstatten 33
registration form [ˌredʒɪ'streɪʃn ˌfɔ:m] Anmeldeformular 105
regulatory body [ˌregjələtrɪ 'bɒdɪ] Aufsichtsbehörde 202
reimburse [ˌri:ɪm'bɜ:s] (rück)erstatten 113
to reject a charge [rɪˌdʒekt ə 'tʃɑ:dʒ] eine Klage zurückweisen 178
rejection letter [rɪ'dʒekʃn ˌletə] Absagebrief 123
reliability [rɪˌlaɪə'bɪlətɪ] Zuverlässigkeit 139
reliable [rɪ'laɪəbl] zuverlässig 48
relocation [ˌri:ləʊ'keɪʃn] Standortwechsel, Umzug 22
remaining sum [rɪˌmeɪnɪŋ 'sʌm] Restbetrag 80
remedy ['remədɪ] Lösung, Mittel, Abhilfe 142
reminder [rɪ'maɪndə] Mahnung, Zahlungserinnerung 34
removal [rɪ'mu:vl] Umzug 72
renewable resources [rɪˌnju:əbl 'ri:sɔ:sɪz] nachwachsende Rohstoffe, erneuerbare Ressourcen 87
rent [rent] Miete 35
rep (representative) [rep] Vertreter(in) 176
replacement [rɪ'pleɪsmənt] Vertretung, Nachfolger(in), Ersatzteil 123
to report [rɪ'pɔ:t] sich melden, melden, berichten 16
to report directly to [rɪˌpɔ:t‿daɪ'rektlɪ tu:] jmdm. direkt unterstellt sein 117
to reposition [ˌri:pə'zɪʃn] neu positionieren 45
repositioning [ˌri:pə'zɪʃənɪŋ] Repositioning 45
to reposition [ˌri:pə'zɪʃn] repositionieren 69
to represent [ˌreprɪ'zent] darstellen, ausmachen 54
reputation [ˌrepjʊ'teɪʃn] Ruf 42
request [rɪ'kwest] Bitte, Aufforderung 9
to request [rɪ'kwest] (um etwas) bitten, wünschen 9
requirement [rɪ'kwaɪəmənt] Bedürfnis, Anforderung 31
researcher [rɪ'sɜ:tʃə] Forscher(in) 44
reservation [ˌrezə'veɪʃn] Bedenken 180
reserves [rɪ'zɜ:vz] Rücklagen 193
to reserve the right to [rɪˌzɜ:v ðə 'raɪt‿tu:] das Recht vorbehalten zu 181
to resign [rɪ'zaɪn] zurücktreten, ausscheiden, (ein Amt) aufgeben 15
response rate [rɪ'spɒns ˌreɪt] Rücklaufquote 68
responsible for [rɪ'spɒnsəbl fɔ:] zuständig für, verantwortlich für 24
restructuring [ˌri:'strʌktʃərɪŋ] Konzernumbau, Restrukturierung 201
résumé ['rezju:meɪ] Lebenslauf 118
retail ['ri:teɪl] Einzelhandels-, Einzelhandel 20
retailer ['ri:teɪlə] Einzelhändler(in) 21
retailing ['ri:teɪlɪŋ] Einzelhandel 22
retail outlet [ˌri:teɪl 'aʊtlet] Einzelhandelsgeschäft, Einzelhandelsverkaufsstelle 72
retail price [ˌri:teɪl 'praɪs] Einzelhandelspreis, Ladenpreis, Verkaufspreis 83
retainer [rɪ'teɪnə] Vorschuss, Honorarpauschale 72
to retaliate [rɪ'tælɪeɪt] sich rächen, Vergeltung üben 175

retaliation [rɪˌtælɪ'eɪʃn] Gegenschlag 175
retirement [rɪ'taɪəmənt] Ruhestand, Pensionierung 152
to retire [rɪ'taɪə] in Rente gehen, in den Ruhestand gehen 88
retooling [ˌriː'tuːlɪŋ] Umrüstung 86
return on investment (ROI) [rɪˌtɜːn ɒn ɪn'vestmənt, ˌɑːrəʊ'aɪ] Gewinn bei Veräußerung, Kapitalrendite, Gesamtkapitalrentabilität 154
to return a call [rɪˌtɜːn ə 'kɔːl] zurückrufen 16
to reveal [rɪ'viːl] enthüllen, erkennen lassen, offenlegen 69
revenue ['revənjuː] Erlös, Einkommen, Einkünfte, Ertrag 72
to revise [rɪ'vaɪz] abändern, überarbeiten 180
to revoke [rɪ'vəʊk] widerrufen 181
reward [rɪ'wɔːd] Belohnung 27
risk-averse [ˌrɪskə'vɜːs] risikoscheu 198
risk of default [ˌrɪsk‿əv dɪ'fɒlt] Kreditausfallrisiko 191
rivalry ['raɪvəlrɪ] Konkurrenz, Rivalität 207
road train ['rəʊd‿ˌtreɪn] Lastwagenzug 76
rock-bottom prices [ˌrɒkbɒtəm 'praɪsɪz] Tiefstpreise, Billigpreise 22
to rocket ['rɒkɪt] in die Höhe schießen 191
round-table discussion [ˌraʊndˌteɪbl dɪ'skʌʃn] Diskussion am runden Tisch 104
royalties ['rɔɪəltɪz] Tantiemen, Absatzhonorar 83
to rule [ruːl] entscheiden 178
ruling ['ruːlɪŋ] Entscheidung, Spruch 178
rumour ['ruːmə] Gerücht 11
to run [rʌn] führen 21
to run smoothly [rʌn 'smuːðlɪ] reibungslos verlaufen 95

S

to sack [sæk] feuern, entlassen 116
safety features ['seɪftɪ ˌfiːtʃəz] sicherheitstechnische Einrichtungen 183
safety hazard ['seɪftɪ ˌhæzəd] Gefahrenquelle, Sicherheitsrisiko 176
sales [seɪlz] Absatz, Schlussverkauf, Ausverkauf, Vertrieb 21
sales contract ['seɪlz ˌkɒntrækt] Kaufvertrag 169
sales director ['seɪlz daɪˌrektə] Verkaufsleiter(in) 21
sales literature ['seɪlz ˌlɪtrətʃə] Verkaufsliteratur, Werbematerial 11
sales meeting ['seɪlz ˌmiːtɪŋ] Verkaufsbesprechung, Verkaufstagung 11
sales pitch ['seɪlz ˌpɪtʃ] Verkaufsmasche 28
sales rep ['seɪlz ˌrep] Vertreter(in), Außendienstmitarbeiter(in) 72
sales target ['seɪlz ˌtɑːgɪt] Absatzziel, Umsatzziel 72
sales tax ['seɪlz ˌtæks] Umsatzsteuer, Mehrwertsteuer 194
sales team ['seɪlz ˌtiːm] Verkaufsmannschaft 127
salutation [ˌsæljə'teɪʃn] Anrede (im Brief) 12
sample ['sɑːmpl] Muster, Probe 165
sample ['sɑːmpl] Muster, Musterprobe, Kostprobe 29
to sample ['sɑːmpl] kosten, probieren 165
satisfactory [ˌsætɪs'fæktərɪ] zufriedenstellend, ausreichend 136
satisfied ['sætɪsfaɪd] zufrieden 136
to satisfy ['sætɪsfaɪ] zufriedenstellen 61
saving ['seɪvɪŋ] Sparen 34
schedule ['ʃedjuːl, 'skedjuːl] Terminplan, Zeitplan, Ablaufplan 125
science [saɪəns] Naturwissenschaft(en), Wissenschaft 11
scope [skəʊp] Umfang 125
to scrap sth. ['skræp ˌsʌmθɪŋ] etwas verwerfen 125
seasonal worker [ˌsiːʒənl 'wɜːkə] Saisonarbeiter(in) 27
secondment [sɪ'kɒndmənt] (vorübergehende) Versetzung 101
secured loan [sɪˌkjʊəd 'ləʊn] gesichertes Darlehen 189
segmentation [ˌsegmen'teɪʃn] Segmentierung, Marktsegmentierung 62
to seize a market [ˌsiːz ə 'mɑːkɪt] einen Markt erobern 68
selection committee [sə'lekʃn kəˌmɪtɪ] Auswahlausschuss 12
self-employed [ˌselfɪm'plɔɪd] selbstständig 23
self-sufficient [ˌselfsə'fɪʃnt] unabhängig, autark, autonom 127
sell-by date ['selbaɪ ˌdeɪt] Haltbarkeitsdatum, Mindesthaltbarkeitsdatum 83
semi-finished [ˌsemɪ'fɪnɪʃt] halbfertig 48
semi-finished goods [ˌsemɪˌfɪnɪʃt 'gʊdz] halbfertige Erzeugnisse, unfertige Waren, Halbfertigfabrikate 193
to service a loan [ˌsɜːvɪs ə 'ləʊn] Zinsen zahlen (auf ein Darlehen) 189
setup ['setʌp] Einrichtung, Konstellation 188
set-up time ['setʌp ˌtaɪm] Rüstzeit 86
share [ʃeə] Aktie 22
shareholder ['ʃeəˌhəʊldə] Aktionär(in), Aktieninhaber(in) 22
shell company ['ʃel ˌkʌmpənɪ] Mantelgesellschaft, Firmenmantel, Strohgesellschaft 203
to shelve a project ['ʃelv ə ˌprɒdʒekt] ein Projekt einstellen 125
shift [ʃɪft] Schicht 91
to ship [ʃɪp] verschicken, versenden 77
shipment ['ʃɪpmənt] Lieferung, Warensendung 37
shipper ['ʃɪpə] Versender 170
shipping ['ʃɪpɪŋ] Versand 24
shipping documents ['ʃɪpɪŋ ˌdɒkjʊmənts] Versandpapiere, Verschiffungsdokumente 77
shoddy ['ʃɒdɪ] minderwertig, schlampig 136
shop floor [ˌʃɒp 'flɔː] Produktionsbereich, Fertigungsbereich 85
shoplifting ['ʃɒplɪftɪŋ] Ladendiebstahl 83
shorter working hours [ˌʃɔːtə 'wɜːkɪŋ ˌaʊəz] Arbeitszeitverkürzung 94
shortfall ['ʃɔːtfɔːl] Fehlbetrag, Defizit, Deckungslücke 192
short-haul ['ʃɔːthɔːl] Kurzstrecke 211
to shortlist ['ʃɔːtlɪst] jmdn./etwas in die engere Wahl nehmen/ziehen 116
short-term [ˌʃɔː't'tɜːm] kurzfristig 206
to shrink [ʃrɪŋk] schrumpfen 150
shrink wrap ['ʃrɪŋk ˌræp] Schrumpffolie 78
to sign [saɪn] unterschreiben 42
to sign up [saɪn 'ʌp] sich anmelden 9
skilled worker [ˌskɪld 'wɜːkə] Facharbeiter(in) 85
skimming [skɪmɪŋ] Auslesen von Daten auf Zahlkarten 33
sleeping partner [ˌsliːpɪŋ 'pɑːtnə] stiller Gesellschafter, stiller Teilhaber 23
slide [slaɪd] Folie, Dia 74
slightly ['slaɪtlɪ] wenig, gering 32
slippage ['slɪpɪdʒ] Zeitverlust, Pufferzeitverzehr 128
slogan ['sləʊgən] Slogan, Werbespruch 52
slump [slʌmp] (starker) Rückgang, Einbruch 94
to slump [slʌmp] stark zurückgehen 94
small and medium-sized firms [ˌsmɔːl ənd ˌmiːdɪəmsaɪzd 'fɜːmz] kleine und mittelständische Unternehmen 94
small print ['smɔːl prɪnt] Kleingedrucktes 180
to soar [sɔː] schnell aufsteigen, hochschießen 152
social security [ˌsəʊʃl sɪ'kjʊərɪtɪ] Sozialhilfe (BE), Sozialversicherung, soziale Sicherheit 115
soft skills [ˌsɒft 'skɪlz] Sozialkompetenz 10
solely ['səʊllɪ] allein, ausschließlich 181
sole proprietorship [ˌsəʊl prə'praɪətəʃɪp] Einzelunternehmen 23
sole trader [ˌsəʊl 'treɪdə] Einzelunternehmer 22

solicited offer [sə,lɪsɪtɪd 'ɒfə] angefordertes Angebot 169
sophisticated [sə'fɪstɪkeɪtɪd] anspruchsvoll, ausgeklügelt, raffiniert, komplex 45
source [sɔ:s] Quelle 146
spa [spɑ:] Wellness-Einrichtung, Kurort 104
to spare [tə 'speə] übrig haben 127
to spearhead ['spɪəhed] anführen 118
speculation [,spekjə'leɪʃn] Spekulation, Gewinnerwartung 190
to spend [spend] (Geld) ausgeben, (Zeit) verbringen 35
spender ['spendə] jmd., bei dem das Geld locker sitzt 33
spending power ['spendɪŋ ,paʊə] Kaufkraft 75
sponsorship deal ['spɒnsəʃɪp ,dɪəl] Sponsorenvertrag 72
spot check [,spɒt‿'tʃek] Stichprobe, unangemeldete Prüfung 146
to spread one's risk [,spred wʌnz 'rɪsk] sein Risiko verteilen 198
square metre [,skweə 'mi:tə] Quadratmeter 17
staff [stɑ:f] Personal, Belegschaft 8
staff turnover [,stɑ:f 'tɜ:n,əʊvə] Personalfluktuation, Mitarbeiterfluktuation 119
staged payments [,steɪdʒd 'peɪmənts] Zahlungen in Raten 35
stagnating [stæg'neɪtɪŋ] stagnierend 150
stake [steɪk] Anteil, Beteiligung 190
stakeholders ['steɪk,həʊldəz] Interessensvertreter, Mitglieder eines am Unternehmen interessierten Kreises 87
to stall sb. ['stɔ:l ,sʌmbədɪ] jmdn. hinhalten, auf Zeit spielen 145
stand [stænd] Messestand 104
to stand in (for sb.) [stænd 'ɪn (fə ,sʌmbədɪ)] die Vertretung (für jmdn.) übernehmen/haben, für jmdn. einspringen 116
standing ['stændɪŋ] Ansehen, Stellung, Ruf (z. B. einer Firma) 202
standing order [,stændɪŋ 'ɔ:də] Dauerauftrag 32
start-up ['stɑ:tʌp] neugegründetes Unternehmen 43
statement ['steɪtmənt] (Konto)auszug 33
statement of financial position [,steɪtmənt‿əv‿faɪ,nænʃl pə'zɪʃn] Bilanz 193
state-of-the-art [,steɪtəvðɪ'ɑ:t] auf dem neuesten Stand der Technik, topmodern 42
state of the economy [,steɪt‿əv ðɪ‿ɪ'kɒnəmɪ] Wirtschaftslage 68
stationery ['steɪʃənrɪ] Schreibwaren 53
statutory ['stætjʊtərɪ] gesetzlich festgelegt. Rechts- 177
stay [steɪ] Aufenthalt 13
stock [stɒk] Lager, Lagerbestand, Vorräte 193
to stock [stɒk] am Lager führen, vorrätig haben 75
stock corporation [,stɒk‿kɔ:pə'reɪʃn] Kapitalgesellschaft 23
stock exchange ['stɒk ɪks,tʃeɪndʒ] Aktienbörse, Börse 22
stockist ['stɒkɪst] Fachhändler 165
stock market ['stɒk ,mɑ:kɪt] Aktienmarkt, Börse 199
stockpile ['stɒkpaɪl] Vorrat, Lagerhalde 86
stockroom ['stɒkru:m] Lagerraum 85
stocks [stɒks] Aktien (AE) 189
stocks and shares [,stɒks‿ən 'ʃeəz] Wertpapiere, Effekten 188
store credit ['stɔ: ,kredɪt] Gutschein, Gutschrift 145
strapline ['stræplaɪn] Werbeslogan 64
student union [,stju:dənt 'ju:nɪən] Studentenwerk 35
studies ['stʌdɪz] Studium 34
sturdy ['stɜ:dɪ] stabil, rubust (Material), kräftig 48
subcontractor [,sʌbkən'træktə] Subunternehmen, Zulieferer 95
subject line ['sʌbdʒekt ,laɪn] Betreffzeile 12
to submit [səb'mɪt] einreichen, unterbreiten, liefern, vorlegen, abgeben 181
subordinate [sə'bɔ:dɪnət] Untergebene(r) 25
sub-prime mortgage [,sʌbpraɪm‿'mɔ:gɪdʒ] zweitklassige Hypothek (bei mangelhafter Kreditwürdigkeit) 150
sub-project [,sʌb'prɒdʒekt] Teilprojekt, Unterprojekt 125
subsidiary [səb'sɪdɪərɪ] Tochtergesellschaft 8
subsidy ['sʌbsədɪ] Subvention, Zuschuss 94
subsidy ['sʌbsədɪ] Subvention 170
substandard [sʌb'stændəd] minderwertig, unzulänglich 138
substitute product [,sʌbstɪtju:t 'prɒdʌkt] Ersatzprodukt 207
to succeed (in + noun or gerund) [sək'si:d] Erfolg haben (in, bei) 27
success [sək'ses] Erfolg 10
succession [sək'seʃn] Reihe, Aufeinanderfolge 143
to sue (for damages) [,su: fə 'dæmɪdʒɪz] auf Schadenersatz klagen, gerichtlich vorgehen 178
to sue sb. for sth. [su:] jmdn. wegen etwas verklagen 47
suggestion [sə'dʒestʃn] Vorschlag 8
summary minutes ['sʌmərɪ ,mɪnɪts] Ergebnisprotokoll 53
to supervise ['su:pəvaɪz] beaufsichtigen, betreuen, überwachen 112
supervision [,su:pə'vɪʒn] Überwachung, Betreuung 87
supervisor ['su:pəvaɪzə] Aufseher(in), Kontrolleur(in), Aufsichtsperson, Leiter(in) 85
supervisory board [,su:pə'vaɪzərɪ ,bɔ:d] Aufsichtsrat 24
to supplement ['sʌplɪment] aufbessern, ergänzen 35
supplier [sə'plaɪə] Lieferant, Zulieferer 19
supply [sə'plaɪ] Versorgung, Bereitstellung 68
to supply [sə'plaɪ] beliefern 21
supply chain [sə'plaɪ ,tʃeɪn] Lieferkette, Versorgungskette 72
to surge [sɜ:dʒ] (stark) ansteigen 94
surplus ['sɜ:pləs] Überschuss, Mehrbetrag, Überhang, überschüssig, überzählig 192
survey ['sɜ:veɪ] Umfrage, Studie, Überblick 51
SWIFT (Society for Worldwide Interbank Financial Telecommunication) [swɪft] 167
SWOT analysis (Strengths, Weaknesses, Opportunities, Threats) ['swɒt ə,næləsɪs] SWOT Analyse (Stärken-Schwächen- und Chancen-Risiko-Analyse) 205
synergy ['sɪnədʒɪ] Synergie, Ergebnispotenzierung 201
synthetic [sɪn'θetɪk] künstlich, synthetisch 48

T

to tackle ['tækl] angehen, anpacken, beantworten 146
tag cloud ['tæg ,klaʊd] Schlagwortwolke 96
to take a cut [,teɪk ə 'kʌt] einen Teil des Gewinns für sich nehmen 72
to take a gamble (on sth.) [,teɪk ə 'gæmbl] ein Risiko (bei etwas) eingehen 198
to take court action [teɪk‿,kɔ:t 'ækʃn] rechtliche Schritte einleiten, Klage erheben 177
to take over [teɪk 'əʊvə] übernehmen, erwerben 8
takeover ['teɪk,əʊvə] Übernahme 8
takeover bid ['teɪkəʊvə ,bɪd] Übernahmeangebot 202
to take precautions [,teɪk prɪ'kɔ:ʃnz] Vorsichtsmaßnahmen ergreifen 125
to take the minutes [,teɪk ðə 'mɪnɪts] das Protokoll führen 51
tangible assets [,tændʒɪbl 'æsets] Sachanlagen, Sachvermögen 193
to target sb. ['tɑ:gɪt] sich jmdn. zur Zielgruppe nehmen 55
target market [,tɑ:gɪt 'mɑ:kɪt] Zielmarkt, angestrebter Markt 47
tariff ['tærɪf] (Einführ)Zoll 170
to assign tasks [ə,saɪn 'tɑ:sks] Aufgaben verteilen/zuteilen 82
tasting ['teɪstɪŋ] Verkostung 68
tax [tæks] Steuer 33

tax allowance ['tæks əˌlaʊəns] Steuerfreibetrag, Steuerermäßigung, Steuernachlass 194
tax assessment notice [ˌtæks ə'sesmənt ˌnəʊtɪs] Steuerbescheid 194
taxation [tæk'seɪʃn] Besteuerung, Steuer, Steuerveranschlagung 148
tax authority ['tæks ɔ:ˌθɒrətɪ] Finanzamt 194
tax avoidance ['tæks əˌvɔɪdəns] Steueroptimierung, (legale) Steuervermeidung, Steuersparmodelle 194
tax bill ['tæks ˌbɪl] Steuerbescheid 194
tax break ['tæks ˌbreɪk] Steuervergünstigung, Steuererleichterung 194
tax consultant ['tæks kənˌsʌltənt] Steuerberater(in) 103
tax declaration ['tæks dekləˌreɪʃn] Steuererklärung 194
tax deductible [ˌtæksdɪ'dʌktəbl] steuerlich absetzbar 194
tax demand ['tæks dɪˌmɑ:nd] Steuerbescheid 194
tax dodge ['tæks ˌdɒdʒ] Steuertrick 194
tax evasion ['tæks ɪˌveɪʒn] Steuerhinterziehung 194
tax fraud ['tæks ˌfrɔ:d] Steuerbetrug 194
tax haven ['tæks ˌheɪvən] Steuerparadies 194
tax hike ['tæks ˌhaɪk] Steuererhöhung 194
tax liability ['tæks laɪəˌbɪlətɪ] Steuerpflicht, Steuerschuld 194
tax rebate ['tæks ˌri:beɪt] Steuerrückerstattung 194
tax refund ['tæks ˌri:fʌnd] Steuerrückerstattung 194
tax relief ['tæks rɪˌli:f] Steuerentlastung, Steuervergünstigung 194
tax return ['tæks rɪˌtɜ:n] Steuererklärung 194
template ['templeɪt] Vorlage 31
tenant ['tenənt] Mieter(in) 35
to tender (for) ['tendə fɔ:] anbieten (z. B. ein Projekt) 125
tenure ['tenjə] Festanstellung 27
to terminate ['tɜ:mɪneɪt] beenden, kündigen 181
termination [ˌtɜ:mɪ'neɪʃn] Kündigung 181
terms and conditions [ˌtɜ:mz‿ənd kən'dɪʃnz] Allgemeine Geschäftsbedingungen (AGB) 43
terms of payment and delivery [ˌtɜ:mz‿əv ˌpeɪmənt ənd‿dɪ'lɪvərɪ] Zahlungs- und Lieferbedingungen 165
territory ['terɪtrɪ] Gebiet 170
text message ['tekst ˌmesɪdʒ] SMS 11
theft [θeft] Diebstahl 76
think tank ['θɪŋktæŋk] Expertenkommission, Denkfabrik 204
third party [ˌθɜ:d 'pɑ:tɪ] Dritte(r), dritte Person 181
threat [θret] Bedrohung, Risiko, Gefährdung 205
to threaten ['θretn] (be)drohen 34
throughput ['θru:pʊt] Durchsatz, Ausstoß, Verarbeitungsmenge 86
tied up [ˌtaɪd'ʌp] fest angelegt (Geld) 198
till [tɪl] Kasse 83
timber ['tɪmbə] (Bau-)Holz 48
time-and-motion study [ˌtaɪmən'məʊʃn ˌstʌdɪ] Arbeitsablaufstudie, Zeit- und Bewegungsstudie 88
time buffer ['taɪm ˌbʌfə] Zeitpuffer 125
time clock ['taɪm ˌklɒk] Stechuhr, Stempeluhr 88
timescale ['taɪmskeɪl] Zeitraum, Zeitplan 68
time-to-market [ˌtaɪmtə'mɑ:kɪt] Produkteinführungszeit 88
title ['taɪtl] Eigentumsrecht 167
tool [tu:l] Werkzeug, (Hilfs)Mittel, Gerät 50
tour operator ['tʊər‿ɒpəreɪtə] Reiseveranstalter 182
toxic ['tɒksɪk] giftig, schädlich 76
toxic waste [ˌtɒksɪk 'weɪst] Giftmüll 76
to trace the source of sth. [ˌtreɪs ðə 'sɔ:s] etw. bis zum Ursprung zurückverfolgen, etw. aufspüren 145
tracker fund ['trækə ˌfʌnd] Indexfonds 199
track record ['træk ˌrekɔ:d] Erfolgsgeschichte, Erfolgsbilanz 117
trade [treɪd] Gewerbe, Handwerk, Handel 112

T

to trade [treɪd] Handel treiben, handeln (mit) 75
trade barrier [ˌtreɪd‿'bærɪə] Handelshemmnis, Handelsschranke 170
trade fair ['treɪd ˌfeə] (Handels)Messe 14
trademark ['treɪdmɑ:k] Markenzeichen, Schutzmarke, Warenzeichen 45
trader ['treɪdə] Händler(in) 62
trade tax ['treɪd‿ˌtæks] Gewerbesteuer 194
trade union [ˌtreɪd 'ju:njən] Gewerkschaft 177
trainee [ˌtreɪ'ni:] Praktikant(in), Auszubildende(r), Lehrling 112
trainer ['treɪnə] Ausbilder(in), Trainer(in) 85
to transfer [træns'fɜ:] überweisen 36
traveller's cheque ['trævləz ˌtʃek] Reisescheck 32
troubleshooting ['trʌblˌʃu:tɪŋ] Fehlersuche, Störungssuche, Fehlerbehebung 133
trough [trɒf] Konjunkturtief, Talsohle der Rezession, Tiefstpunkt 150
tuition fees [tju:'ɪʃn ˌfi:z] Studiengebühren 36
turnaround time ['tɜ:nəraʊnd‿ˌtaɪm] Abfertigungszeit, Umschlagszeit 103
turnkey project [ˌtɜ:nki: 'prɒdʒekt] Gesamtprojekt, schlüsselfertiges Projekt 125
to turn out [tɜ:n 'aʊt] produzieren, fertigen 91
turnover ['tɜ:nˌəʊvə] Personalfluktuation 205
typo ['taɪpəʊ] Tippfehler, Druckfehler 79

U

unconditional [ˌʌnkən'dɪʃənl] uneingeschränkt 79
to undercut [ˌʌndə'kʌt] unterbieten 207
under no circumstances [ʌndə ˌnəʊ 'sɜ.kəmstænsɪz] unter keinen Umständen, auf keinen Fall 181
uneconomical [ʌnˌi:kə'nɒmɪkl] unrentabel 77
unemployment rate [ˌʌnɪm'plɔɪmənt ˌreɪt] Arbeitslosenquote 95
uneven [ʌn'i:vn] ungleichmäßig, unbeständig, uneinheitlich, ungerade, uneben 136
unfair commercial practices [ˌʌnfeə kəˌmɜ:ʃl 'præktɪsɪz] unlautere Geschäftspraktiken 177
unfair dismissal [ˌʌnfeə dɪ'smɪsəl] unberechtigte Entlassung, ungerechtfertigte Entlassung 177
unfit for consumption [ʌnˌfɪt fə kən'sʌmpʃn] ungenießbar 72
union representative [ˌju:njən ˌreprɪ'zentətɪv] Gewerkschaftsvertreter(in) im Betrieb 177
unique [ju:'ni:k] einmalig, einzig, einzigartig 60
Unique Selling Proposition [jʊˌni:k 'selɪŋ prɒpəˌzɪʃn] Alleinstellungsmerkmal, einzigartiger Wettbewerbsvorteil 61
unit labour costs [ˌju:nɪt 'leɪbə ˌkɒsts] Lohnstückkosten 94
unit trust [ˌju:nɪt‿'trʌst] offener Investmentfond 199
unprofitable [ʌn'prɒfɪtəbl] unrentabel, nicht gewinnbringend 22
to update [ʌp'deɪt] aktualisieren 8
up front [ˌʌp 'frʌnt] im Voraus (Anzahlung) 42
up-front entry fee [ˌʌpfrʌnt 'entrɪ ˌfi:] einmalige Bearbeitungs- oder Eintrittsgebühr 199
upfront sum [ˌʌpfrʌnt 'sʌm] Vorauszahlung 191
upmarket [ˌʌp'mɑ:kɪt] exklusiv, vornehm 21
to be up to speed [ˌʌp tə 'spi:d] auf dem Laufenden sein, auf dem neuesten Stand sein 176
to be up to standard [ˌʌp tə 'stændəd] den Anforderungen entsprechen 136
urgency ['ɜ:dʒənsɪ] Dringlichkeit, Eile 145
urgent ['ɜ:dʒənt] dringend 42
user-friendly [ˌju:zə'frendlɪ] benutzerfreundlich 15

USP (Unique Selling Proposition) [ˌju:es'pi:, jʊˌni:k 'selɪŋ prɒpəˌzɪʃn] Alleinstellungsmerkmal 61
usury ['ju:zjʊrɪ] Wucher 190
utilities [ju:'tɪlɪtɪz] Versorgungsunternehmen, Leistungen der öffentlichen Versorgungsbetriebe 20
utility [ju:'tɪlɪtɪ] Versorgungsbetrieb, Versorgungsunternehmen 94

V

vacancy ['veɪkənsɪ] offene Stelle (Arbeit) 116
valid ['vælɪd] gültig 170
valuable ['væljʊəbl] wertvoll 76
valuables ['væljʊəblz] Wertsachen 104
to value ['vælju:] (den Wert) schätzen, bewerten 22
value chain ['vælju: ˌtʃeɪn] Wertschöpfungskette 202
value-for-money [ˌvælju:fə'mʌnɪ] Preis-Leistungs-Verhältnis, Kosteneffektivität 48
to vary in quality [ˌveərɪ‿ɪn 'kwɒlɪtɪ] in der Qualität variieren 136
vat [væt] Fass, Behältnis, Bottich 89
VAT (value added tax) [ˌvi:eɪ'ti: ˌvalju:‿ˌædɪd‿'tæks] Mehrwertsteuer 37
vehicle ['vɪəkl] Fahrzeug 76
vending machine ['vendɪŋ məˌʃi:n] Warenautomat 72
vendor ['vendə] Verkäufer, Anbieter, Lieferant 72
venture ['ventʃə] Projekt, unternehmerisches Vorhaben, Unternehmung 166
venture capital [ˌventʃə 'kæpɪtl] Risikokapital, Wagniskapital 189
venue ['venju:] Veranstaltungsort 51
verdict ['vɜ:dɪkt] Urteil, Urteilsspruch, Gerichtsurteil 165
versatile ['vɜ:sətaɪl] vielseitig 48
vertical merger [ˌvɜ:tɪkl 'mɜ:dʒə] vertikaler Zusammenschluss 202
to veto ['vi:təʊ] Veto einlegen gegen 174
viable ['vaɪəbl] lebensfähig, realisierbar, durchführbar, funktionsfähig 125
violation [ˌvaɪə'leɪʃn] Verstoß, Verletzung, Missachtung, Nichteinhaltung 183
visible trade balance [ˌvɪzɪbl 'treɪd‿ˌbæləns] Warenhandelsbilanz 148
vocational training [vəʊˌkeɪʃənl 'treɪnɪŋ] berufliche Aus-/ Weiterbildung, Berufsausbildung 112
volatile ['vɒlətaɪl] labil, unbeständig, schwankungsanfällig 22
volatility [ˌvɒlə'tɪlətɪ] Schwankungsanfälligkeit, Volatilität, Unbeständigkeit 152
voluntary ['vɒləntrɪ] freiwillig 142
voucher ['vaʊtʃə] Gutschein, Bon, Beleg, Coupon 12
vox pop [ˌvɒks 'pɒp] öffentliche Meinung, Stimme des Volkes 69

W

wage(s) claim ['weɪdʒ ˌkleɪm] Lohnforderung 177
wages ['weɪdʒɪz] Lohn, Löhne 33
waiver ['weɪvə] Verzichterklärung, Außerkraftsetzung, Befreiung (von Pflichten usw.) 180
warehouse ['weəhaʊs] Lager, Lagerhalle 85
warehousing ['weəhaʊzɪŋ] Lagerhaltung, Lagerung 77
to warrant ['wɒrənt] garantieren, zusichern, gewähren, befugen, 181
warranty ['wɒrəntɪ] Garantie, Gewährleistung, Gewähr 170
waste [weɪst] Abfall, Abfallprodukt(e) 187
to waste [weɪst] verschwenden 36
waste of (public) funds [ˌweɪst‿əv‿'fʌndz] Verschwendung (öffentlicher) Gelder/Mittel 183
wealth [welθ] Wohlstand 39
to weigh up [weɪ‿'ʌp] abwägen, einschätzen 20
welder ['weldə] Schweißer(in) 85
welfare benefits ['welfeə ˌbenəfɪts] Sozialleistungen 35
well-off [ˌwel'ɒf] wohlhabend 39
well-to-do [ˌweltə'du:] wohlhabend, reich 39
whistleblower ['wɪslˌbləʊə] Informant(in), Hinweisgeber(in) 183
white knight [ˌwaɪt 'naɪt] 'Weißer Ritter', Retter vor Übernahmen 202
wholesale ['həʊlseɪl] Großhandel-, Großhandel 20
wholesaler ['həʊlˌseɪlə] Großhändler 72
widget ['wɪdʒɪt] Produkt(teil), Dingsbums, Gerät, Vorrichtung, Kniff 48
Wi-Fi connectivity [ˌwaɪfaɪ ˌkɒnek'tɪvətɪ] kabellose Netzwerkverbindung 104
windfall ['wɪndfɔ:l] Geldsegen, überraschender Gewinn, unerwarteter Gewinn 154
to withdraw [wɪð'drɔ:] (Geld) abheben 36
to withdraw (a product) from the market [ˌwɪðˌdrɔ:‿ə ˌprɒdʌkt frəm ðə 'mɑ:kɪt] (ein Produkt) aus dem Markt ziehen 47
withdrawal [wɪð'drɔ:əl] Abhebung 189
within budget [wɪˌðɪn 'bʌdʒɪt] im Rahmen des Budgets 60
without notice [wɪˌðaʊt 'nəʊtɪs] fristlos 116
with strings attached [wɪð 'strɪŋz əˌtætʃt] mit Bedingungen, mit Auflagen 188
work breakdown structure (WBS) [ˌwɜ:k 'breɪkdaʊn ˌstrʌktʃə, ˌdʌblju:bi:'es] Projektstrukturplanung (PSP) 125
worker participation [ˌwɜ:kə pɑ:tɪsɪ'peɪʃn] Mitbestimmung 24
working conditions ['wɜ:kɪŋ kənˌdɪʃnz] Arbeitsbedingungen, Arbeitsverhältnisse 115
work-in-progress [ˌwɜ:kɪn'prəʊgres] halbfertige Waren, unfertige Erzeugnisse, in Ausführung befindliche Arbeit 193
work permit ['wɜ:k ˌpɜ:mɪt] Arbeitsgenehmigung, Arbeitserlaubnis 113
work placement ['wɜ:k ˌpleɪsmənt] Praktikum 30
workshop ['wɜ:kʃɒp] Werkstatt, Workshop 85
worst case scenario [ˌwɜ:st‿keɪs‿sɪ'nɑ:rɪəʊ] schlimmster Fall 180
to wind up a company [waɪnd ˌʌp ə 'kʌmpənɪ] eine Firma auflösen 89
to write (up) the minutes [ˌraɪt ʌp ðə 'mɪnɪts] das Protokoll niederschreiben 51

Y

yacht [jɒt] Yacht 76
yardstick ['jɑ:dstɪk] Maßstab 155
yield [ji:ld] Ertrag, Ergebnis, Rendite, Gewinn 154
Yours faithfully [ˌjɔ:z 'feɪθfəlɪ] Mit freundlichen Grüßen (very formal and rarely used today) 12
Yours sincerely [ˌjɔ:z‿sɪn'sɪəlɪ] Mit freundlichen Grüßen 12

Acronyms and abbreviations

Abbreviation: shortened form of a word.
Acronym: abbreviation formed from the first letters of each word in a term.

Short form Full form *German*

a.m. anno meridian *morgens/vormittags (24 Uhr–12 Uhr)*
AGM annual general meeting *Jahreshauptversammlung*
AIDA attention, interest, desire, action *AIDA Aufmerksamkeit, Interesse, Verlangen, Aktion*
AOB any other business *Sonstiges*
approx. approximately *ungefähr*
ASA Advertising Standards Authority *britische Werbeaufsichtsbehörde*
asap as soon as possible *so schnell wie möglich*
ATM automated teller machine *Geldautomat*
Attn. for the attention of *zu Händen (von)*
B/E bill of exchange *Wechsel*
B/L bill of lading *Konnossement, Frachtbrief*
B2B business to business *Business-to-Business*
B2C business to consumer *Business-to-Consumer*
BCWC budgeted cost of work completed *Budjetkosten der erledigten Arbeit*
BCWS budgeted cost of work scheduled *Budgetkosten der geplanten Arbeit*
BIC bank identifier code *Internationaler Bank-Code*
BOP balance of payments *Zahlungsbilanz*
BOT balance of trade *Handelsbilanz*
BRIC Brazil, Russia, India, China *Brasilien, Russland, Indien, China*
cc carbon copy, copy circulated, cubic centimetres *(Kohlepapier-)Durchschlag, Verteiler, Kubikzentimeter*
CEO Chief Executive Officer *etwa: (Haupt-) Geschäftsführer(in), Firmenchef(in), Vorstandsvorsitzende(r)*
CFO Chief Financial Officer *Finanzleiter(in)*
CIF cost, insurance and freight (Incoterm) *Kosten, Versicherung und Fracht*
COD cash on delivery *Lieferung per Nachnahme*
CPI consumer price index *Verbraucherpreisindex*
CPT carriage paid to (Incoterm) *frachtfrei, Fracht bezahlt*
CRM customer relationship management *Kundendienst, Kundenbetreuung*
CV curriculum vitae *Lebenslauf*
CWO cash with order *Zahlung bei Auftragserteilung*
D/A documents against acceptance *Dokumente gegen Akzept*
D/P documents against payment *Kasse gegen Dokumente*
DDP delivered, duty paid (Incoterm) *frei Haus, verzollt geliefert*
dept. Department *Abteilung*
DES/DEQ Delivered ex ship/quay (Incoterm) *Lieferung ab Schiff/Kai*
e.g. exempli gratia = for example *zum Beispiel (z.B.)*
ECB European Central Bank *Europäische Zentralbank (EZB)*
encl. enclosed *beiliegend, in der Anlage*
etc. etcetera *und so weiter (usw.)*
EU European Union *Europäische Union (EU)*
ex works (Incoterm) *ab Werk*
FAO for the attention of *zu Händen von*
FAQ frequently asked question *häufig gestellte Fragen*
FAS free alongside ship (Incoterm) *frei Längsseite Schiff*
FDI foreign direct investment *ausländische Direktinvestitionen*
FMCG fast-moving consumer goods *kurzlebige Konsumgüter*
FOB free on board (Incoterm) *frei an Bord*
GAAP Generally Accepted Accounting Principles *Grundsätze ordnungsgemäßer Buchführung*
GDP gross domestic product *Bruttoinlandsprodukt (BIP)*
GMT Greenwich Mean Time *Greenwich-Zeit*
GNP gross national product *Bruttosozialprodukt (BSP)*
HQ headquarters *Hauptsitz, Zentrale*
HR human resources *Personalabteilung, -wesen*
HS horsepower *Pferdestärke*
i.e. id est (Latin) = that is *das heißt (d.h.)*
IBAN International Bank Account Number *Internationale Kontonummer*
ICC International Chamber of Commerce *Internationale Industrie- und Handelskammer (ICC)*
IFRS International Financial Reporting Standards *Internationale Rechnungslegungsvorschriften*
IMF International Monetary Fund *Internationaler Währungsfond*
Inc.; inc incorporated (US) *Aktiengesellschaft*
IPO Initial Public Offering *Börsengang, öffentliche Erstemission*
ISO International Standards Organisation *ISO (Norm)*
JIT just-in-time *bedarfsorientierte Produktion (gerade rechtzeitig)*
L/C letter of credit *Akkreditiv*
LBO leveraged buyout *fremdfinanzierte Übernahme*
lbs pounds *Pfunde (Gewicht)*
Ltd. limited *mit beschränkter Haftung*
M&A mergers and acquisitions *Fusionen und Übernahmen*
MBA Master of Business Administration *höherer Hochschulabschluss in Betriebswirtschaftslehre (BWL)*
MBO management buyout *Aufkauf einer Kapitalgesellschaft durch eigenes Management*
MD Managing Director *Geschäftsführer(in)*
MNC Multinational company *multinationales Unternehmen*
mpg miles per gallon *Kraftstoffverbrauch (Meilen/Gallone)*
mph miles per hour *Meilen pro Stunde (Geschwindigkeit)*

NGO non-governmental organisation *Nichtregierungsorganisation*
NIC newly industrialised county *Schwellenland*
no. number *Nummer (Nr.)*
NTB non-tariff barrier *nichttarifäre Handelsbeschränkung*
NVC non-verbal communication *nichtverbale Kommunikation*
o.n.o. or nearest offer *etwa: auf Verhandlungsbasis*
OECD Organisation for Economic Cooperation and Development *Organisation für wirtschaftliche Zusammenarbeit und Entwicklung*
OPEC Organisation of the Petroleum Exporting Countries *Organisation erdölexportierender Länder (OPEC)*
OTC over-the-counter (market) *außerbörslicher Verhandlungsmarkt*
P&L Profit and Loss *Gewinn und Verlust*
p.a. per annum *jährlich, pro Jahr*
p.m. post meridian *nachmittags / abends (12 Uhr – 24 Uhr)*
PAYE pay as you earn (BE) *Lohnsteuerabzug*
PER price/earnings ratio *Preis-Ertrags-Verhältnis*
PIN Personal Identification Number *PIN (Erkennungsnummer)*
plc; PLC public limited company *etwa: AG*
pp paginae = pages *Seiten*
pp/ppa per procurationem = on behalf of *im Auftrag von, per Prokura*
PPI producer price index *Erzeugerpreisindex*
PPP purchasing power parity *Kaufkraftparität*
PR public relations *Öffentlichkeitsarbeit*
Pty Ltd proprietary limited company *entspricht: GmbH (Australien)*
R&D research and development *Forschung und Entwicklung*
Re. regarding *bezüglich*
Re. reply (email) *Antwort*
Ref. reference *Aktenzeichen*
ROI return on investment *Rentabilität, Kapitalertrag*
SME BE: small and medium (-sized) enterprise; AE: small to mid-sized enterprise *Mittelstand; kleines und mittelständisches Unternehmen (KMU)*
Sq. square *Quadrat (Maß), Platz (Ort))*
SWIFT Society for Worldwide Interbank Financial Communication *SWIFT (Telekommunikationsnetz der Geldinstitute)*
SWOT Strengths, Weaknesses, Opportunities, Threats *Stärken, Schwächen, Möglichkeiten, Gefahren/Risiken*
TQM Total Quality Management *umfassendes Qualitätsmanagement*
USP unique selling proposition *Alleinstellungsmerkmal, einzigartiger Wettbewerbsvorteil*
VAT value added tax (UK) *Mehrwertsteuer/ Umsatzsteuer*
WBS work breakdown structure *Projektstrukturplan (PSP)*
WIFM What's in it for me? *Was für Vorteile habe ich?*
WTO World Trade Organisation *Welthandelsorganisation*

False friends

German	=	English	≠	English	=	German
aktuell	=	current, latest	≠	actual	=	tatsächlich
beraten	=	advise	≠	berate	=	ausschimpfen, schelten
Brief	=	letter	≠	brief	=	kurz
Chef	=	boss	≠	chef / chief	=	Koch / Häuptling
defekt	=	defective	≠	defect (n.)	=	Mangel, Fehler, Defekt
dezent	=	subtle, discreet	≠	decent	=	anständig
Direktion	=	management	≠	direction	=	Richtung
engagiert	=	hard-working, committed	≠	engaged	=	verlobt
Etikett	=	label	≠	etiquette	=	Protokoll, Umgangsform
Expertise	=	expert's report	≠	expertise	=	Fachkenntnisse
Fabrik	=	factory, manufacturing plant	≠	fabric	=	Gewebe, Stoff
familiär	=	personal, friendly	≠	familiar	=	vertraut, bekannt
Fonds	=	(investment) fund	≠	fond	=	liebevoll, zärtlich
Formular	=	form	≠	formula	=	Formel (mathem.)
Gang	=	corridor, aisle (planes, trains)	≠	gang	=	Bande
Gift	=	poison	≠	gift	=	Geschenk
Gymnasium	=	grammar school, academic high school (AE / BE)	≠	gymnasium	=	Sporthalle
Handy	=	mobile (phone), cell phone (AE)	≠	handy	=	nützlich; praktisch
Haus (Firma)	=	building, premises	≠	house	=	Einfamilienhaus, Wohnung
Hochschule	=	university, college	≠	high school	=	etwa: Realschule, Gymnasium

German	=	English	≠	English	=	German
Interessent	=	prospective customer	≠	interests	=	Interessen
irritieren	=	confuse	≠	irritate	=	verärgern, nerven
jmdm. etw. borgen	=	lend sth. to so.	≠	borrow	=	ausleihen
Kasse	=	cash desk, checkout	≠	cash	=	Bargeld
Kaution	=	(safety) deposit	≠	caution	=	Vorsicht, Warnung
konkurrieren	=	compete	≠	concur	=	zustimmen
konservieren	=	preserve	≠	conserve	=	sparen
kontrollieren	=	check	≠	control (v.)	=	lenken, steuern
Kostüm	=	outfit, (skirt) suit	≠	costume	=	Verkleidung
Kredit	=	loan	≠	credit	=	Gutschrift, Guthaben
Kritik	=	criticism	≠	critic	=	Kritiker(in)
Labor	=	Laboratory	≠	labor / labour	=	Arbeit
Mappe	=	briefcase / file	≠	map	=	Karte, Stadtplan
Maschine (Flug)	=	plane	≠	machine	=	Gerät, Anlage, Motor
meinen	=	think, feel		mean	=	sagen wollen, bedeuten
Meinung	=	opinion	≠	meaning	=	Bedeutung
Menü	=	set meal / menu	≠	menu	=	Speisekarte
Mist	=	dung, fertilizer	≠	mist	=	leichter Nebel
nobel	=	posh, elegant, upscale	≠	noble	=	edelmutig, adelig
Note (Leistung)	=	mark, grade	≠	note	=	Notiz, Musiknote
Paragraf	=	section	≠	paragraph	=	Abschnitt, Absatz
Personal	=	personnel	≠	personal	=	persönlich
Police	=	insurance policy	≠	police	=	Polizei
Probe	=	sample	≠	probe	=	Untersuchung, Sonde
Promotion	=	doctorate, PhD	≠	promotion	=	Beförderung, Verkaufsförderung
Prospekt	=	brochure, leaflet	≠	prospect	=	Aussicht, Chance
Protokoll	=	minutes	≠	protocol	=	Benimmregel
Provision	=	commission	≠	provision	=	Vorrat, Versorgung
Prozess	=	lawsuit, trial	≠	process	=	Vorgang, Arbeitsablauf
Quote	=	quota	≠	quote	=	Kostenvoranschlag, Zitat
Rate	=	instalment	≠	rate	=	Satz, Kurs
rationell	=	efficient	≠	rational	=	logisch, vernünftig
Reformhaus	=	health-food store	≠	reform house	=	Besserungsanstalt
Reklamation	=	complaint	≠	reclamation	=	Rückforderung
rentabel	=	profitable	≠	rentable	=	vermietbar (Wohnung)
Rente	=	retirement pay, pension	≠	rent	=	Miete
Rezept (vom Arzt)	=	prescription	≠	recipe receipt	=	Kochrezept Quittung
scharf	=	spicy, hot	≠	sharp	=	spitz, scharf (Gegenstand)
schwarzes Brett	=	bulletin board, notice board	≠	blackboard	=	Tafel (im Klassenzimmer)
sensibel	=	sensitive	≠	sensible	=	vernünftig
sparen	=	save	≠	spare	=	Zusatz- / zusätzlich
spenden	=	donate	≠	spend	=	(Geld) ausgeben
Stadium	=	stage, level	≠	stadium	=	Stadion
starten	=	leave, depart, take off	≠	start	=	anfangen, anspringen (Auto)
sympatisch	=	likeable, friendly	≠	sympathetic	=	mitfühlend
Tarif	=	rate (of pay)	≠	tariff	=	Zolltarif, Gebührensatz
terminieren	=	schedule, fix	≠	terminate	=	beenden
übersehen	=	overlook	≠	oversee	=	beaufsichtigen
Übersicht	=	overview	≠	oversight	=	Versehen
Unternehmer	=	entrepreneur, company owner	≠	undertaker	=	Leichenbestatter
Warenhaus	=	department store	≠	warehouse	=	Lager(halle)

Picture credits

8 Corbis, Düsseldorf; **15** Corbis (Bernard Bisson/Sygma), Düsseldorf; **15** iStockphoto (Tom Nulens), Calgary, Alberta; **16** Avenue Images GmbH RF (Imgram Publishing), Hamburg; **19** A1PIX, Taufkirchen; **20** iStockphoto (Stefan Klein), Calgary, Alberta; **21** iStockphoto (Dmitry Ejov), Calgary, Alberta; **21** iStockphoto (hypergon), Calgary, Alberta; **22** Yahoo! Deutschland GmbH, München; **27** Elizabeth Handy, London; **29** Fotosearch Stock Photography, Waukesha, WI; **31** iStockphoto (Warwick Lister-Kaye), Calgary, Alberta; **32** shutterstock (MaGutosh), New York, NY; **33** Corbis (Contographer), Düsseldorf; **33** Picture-Alliance (Photoshot), Frankfurt; **33** Getty Images (Gareth Davies), München; **33** Ullstein Bild GmbH (Lebrecht Music & Arts Photo Library), Berlin; **34** BBC Information and archives, London; **39** Wikimedia Foundation Inc. (PD), St. Petersburg FL; **39** laif (Bettina Flitner), Köln; **39** laif (Timothy Fadek/Polaris), Köln; **40** iStockphoto (1001nights), Calgary, Alberta; **41** iStockphoto (Liz Leyden), Calgary, Alberta; **42** iStockphoto (Sandy Jones), Calgary, Alberta; **44** Corbis (Jose Fuste Raga), Düsseldorf; **45** shutterstock (photomak), New York, NY; **45** Avenue Images GmbH RF (Stockbyte), Hamburg; **45** Fotolia LLC (Aleksandr Ugorenkov), New York; **45** MEV Verlag GmbH, Augsburg; **46** Imago Stock & People, Berlin; **47** Getty Images (David Levenson), München; **48** MEV Verlag GmbH, Augsburg; **48** iStockphoto (RF/Ingvald kaldhussæter), Calgary, Alberta; **48** Fotolia LLC, New York; **48** Dreamstime LLC (Ifocus), Brentwood, TN; **49** iStockphoto, Calgary, Alberta; **49** Dreamstime LLC, Brentwood, TN; **49** iStockphoto (Alexander Hafemann), Calgary, Alberta; **49** Toyota Deutschland GmbH Köln; **50** Picture Press (Mark Fairhurst/Camera Press), Hamburg; **51** JupiterImages photos.com (RF/Photos.com), Tucson, AZ; **53** shutterstock (Yuri Arcurs), New York, NY; **55** BBC Information and archives, London; **60** Corbis (Paul Hardy), Düsseldorf; **60** iStockphoto (Platinus), Calgary, Alberta; **61** iStockphoto (kutay tanir), Calgary, Alberta; **64** iStockphoto (Heiko Grossmann), Calgary, Alberta; **65** Fotolia LLC (Torsten Schon), New York; **67** Picture-Alliance (Photoshot), Frankfurt; **69** iStockphoto (Paula Connelly), Calgary, Alberta; **70** BBC Information and archives, London; **72** Corbis (Jim Craigmyle), Düsseldorf; **73** Corbis (Krista Kennell), Düsseldorf; **73** The Associated Press GmbH (Ronald Zak), Frankfurt am Main; **76** iStockphoto (Linda & Colin McKie), Calgary, Alberta; **76** shutterstock (mundoview), New York, NY; **78** Fotolia LLC (Carsten Reisinger), New York; **78** shutterstock (Kathy Burns-Millyard), New York, NY; **78** Fotolia LLC (ZTS), New York; **78** Fotolia LLC (PANORAMO.de), New York; **78** Fotolia LLC (Gudellaphoto), New York; **78** iStockphoto (Claudio Arnese), Calgary, Alberta; **78** iStockphoto (rocksunderwater), Calgary, Alberta; **79** Logo, Stuttgart; **82** shutterstock (Kenneth V. Pilon), New York, NY; **86** Corbis (Bettmann), Düsseldorf; **90** shutterstock (Perrush), New York, NY; **91** Ullstein Bild GmbH (Granger Collection), Berlin; **93** Tchibo GmbH, Hamburg; **93** BBC Information and archives, London; **96** Corbis (Heide Benser), Düsseldorf; **98** Alamy Images (David Bleeker Photography.com), Abingdon, Oxon; **101** shutterstock (reihe13), New York, NY; **103** Corbis (Thierry Tronnel), Düsseldorf; **105** Fotolia LLC (Stefano Viola), New York; **106** Fotolia LLC (Yuri Arcurs), New York; **112** shutterstock (Tyler Olson), New York, NY; **115** www.cartoonstock.com (Deckmyn, Dominique), Bath; **116** iStockphoto (YinYang), Calgary, Alberta; **119** Wikimedia Foundation Inc. (PD), St. Petersburg FL; **119** The Associated Press GmbH, Frankfurt am Main; **119** Corbis (Bettmann), Düsseldorf; **121** iStockphoto (vm), Calgary, Alberta; **121** BBC Information and archives, London; **124** Getty Images (RABIH MOGHRABI/AFP), München; **126** www.cartoonstock.com (Baldwin, Mike), Bath; **127** Corbis (Adam Gault/Science Photo Library), Düsseldorf; **130** iStockphoto (Michael Fernahl), Calgary, Alberta; **131** Project Agency Limited (www.ronrosenhead.co.uk), London; **136** Corbis (Peter Ginter/Science Faction), Düsseldorf; **140** www.cartoonstock.com (Baldwin, Mike), Bath; **143** Corbis (Catherine Karnow), Düsseldorf; **146** Logo, Stuttgart; **146** iStockphoto (Henry Chaplin), Calgary, Alberta; **148** Corbis, Düsseldorf; **149** www.cartoonstock.com (Schwadron, Harley), Bath; **151** Corbis, Düsseldorf; **152** The Associated Press GmbH (Alex Brandon), Frankfurt am Main; **155** Corbis (Bettmann), Düsseldorf; **159** BBC Information and archives, London; **164** Corbis (Anders Ryman), Düsseldorf; **171** Fairtrade Foundation; **173** Fotolia LLC (womue), New York; **173** Fotolia LLC (Edyta Anna Grabowska), New York; **173** Fotolia LLC (EuToch), New York; **173** iStockphoto (MARIA TOUTOUDAKI), Calgary, Alberta; **176** Ullstein Bild GmbH (Nowosti), Berlin; **178** shutterstock (Cristian Cortes), New York, NY; **178** Fotolia LLC (Andreas Hilger), New York; **178** Fotolia LLC (Nick Holtz), New York; **178** BigStockPhoto.com (MichelleAnnB), Davis, CA; **183** Corbis (Rick Friedman), Düsseldorf; **184** iStockphoto (Anja Hild), Calgary, Alberta; **186** Fotolia LLC (Springfield Gallery), New York; **188** Imago Stock & People, Berlin; **190** Corbis (Georgina Bowater), Düsseldorf; **192** shutterstock (iNNOCENt), New York, NY; **195** Getty Images (Gareth Cattermole), München; **195** Getty Images (Mike Marsland/WireImage), München; **195** Getty Images (Jon Furniss/WireImage), München; **196** Fotolia LLC (Norman Chan), New York; **200** iStockphoto (Emrah Turudu), Calgary, Alberta; **207** Picture-Alliance (ZB), Frankfurt; **208** shutterstock (Roman Sigaev), New York, NY; **208** iStockphoto (Joe Gough), Calgary, Alberta; **210** iStockphoto (Dane Wirtzfeld), Calgary, Alberta; **214** iStockphoto (Brad Wieland), Calgary, Alberta; **COVER** Alamy Images RF (Stockbyte), Abingdon, Oxon; **Softwareaufgabe** Corel Corporation Deutschland, Unterschleissheim; iStockphoto (Cynthia Baldauf), Calgary, Alberta; Fotolia LLC (Torsten Schon), New York; Fotolia LLC (iofoto), New York; Avenue Images GmbH RF (StockDisc), Hamburg; Fotosearch Stock Photography, Waukesha, WI; shutterstock (Jlqf), New York, NY; MEV Verlag GmbH, Augsburg; Renault Deutschland AG, Brühl; Klett-Archiv (Hoke), Stuttgart; shutterstock (Alessio Ponti), New York, NY; shutterstock (designalldone), New York, NY; shutterstock (tkemot), New York, NY; BigStockPhoto.com Davis, CA; shutterstock (Zlatko Guzmic), New York, NY; Fotolia LLC (LaCatrina), New York; Klett-Archiv (KomaAmok), Stuttgart; URW, Hamburg; Getty Images RF (PhotoDisc), München; Dreamstime LLC (Alon-o), Brentwood, TN; shutterstock (silver-john), New York, NY; iStockphoto (Zoran Jovanovic), Calgary, Alberta; iStockphoto (Elena Aliaga), Calgary, Alberta; shutterstock (Ocean Image Photography), New York, NY; Fotolia LLC (Tony Baggett), New York; shutterstock (visi.stock), New York, NY; Fotosearch Stock Photography (Corel), Waukesha, WI; MEV Verlag GmbH, Augsburg; Klett-Archiv (A. Raftaki), Stuttgart; Klett-Archiv (Meyle + Müller/Harter), Stuttgart; Klett-Archiv (Meyle + Müller/Harter), Stuttgart; Klett-Archiv (Zachris), Stuttgart; Klett-Archiv (Meyle + Müller/Harter), Stuttgart; Klett-Archiv (Erik Nöldeke), Stuttgart; Klett-Archiv (Meyle + Müller/Harter), Stuttgart; Klett-Archiv (Frau Hacker), Stuttgart; Klett-Archiv (A. Raftaki), Stuttgart; Klett-Archiv (Dr. Thomas Hoffmann, Lauf), Stuttgart; Klett-Archiv (Henry Zeidler), Stuttgart; Klett-Archiv (A. Raftaki), Stuttgart; Klett-Archiv (A. Raftaki), Stuttgart; Klett-Archiv (Frau Hacker), Stuttgart; Fotolia LLC (Jan Prchal), New York; Klett-Archiv (Meyle + Müller/Harter), Stuttgart; Klett-Archiv (A. Raftaki), Stuttgart; Klett-Archiv (A. Raftaki), Stuttgart; Klett-Archiv (Meyle + Müller/Harter), Stuttgart; Klett-Archiv (Meyle + Müller/Harter), Stuttgart; Klett-Archiv (Meyle + Müller), Stuttgart; Klett-Archiv (Mel Smith), Stuttgart; Fotolia LLC (Ralf Siemieniec), New York; Klett-Archiv (A. Raftaki), Stuttgart; Klett-Archiv (A. Raftaki), Stuttgart; Klett-Archiv (Hermann Summer, Hohenpeißenberg), Stuttgart; Getty Images RF (Photo Disc), München; Geoatlas, Hendaye

Nicht in allen Fällen war es uns möglich, den Rechteinhaber der Abbildungen ausfindig zu machen. Berechtigte Ansprüche werden selbstverständlich im Rahmen der üblichen Vereinbarungen abgegolten.